THE MARSHALL COLLECTION OF WORCESTER PORCELAIN IN THE ASHMOLEAN MUSEUM, OXFORD

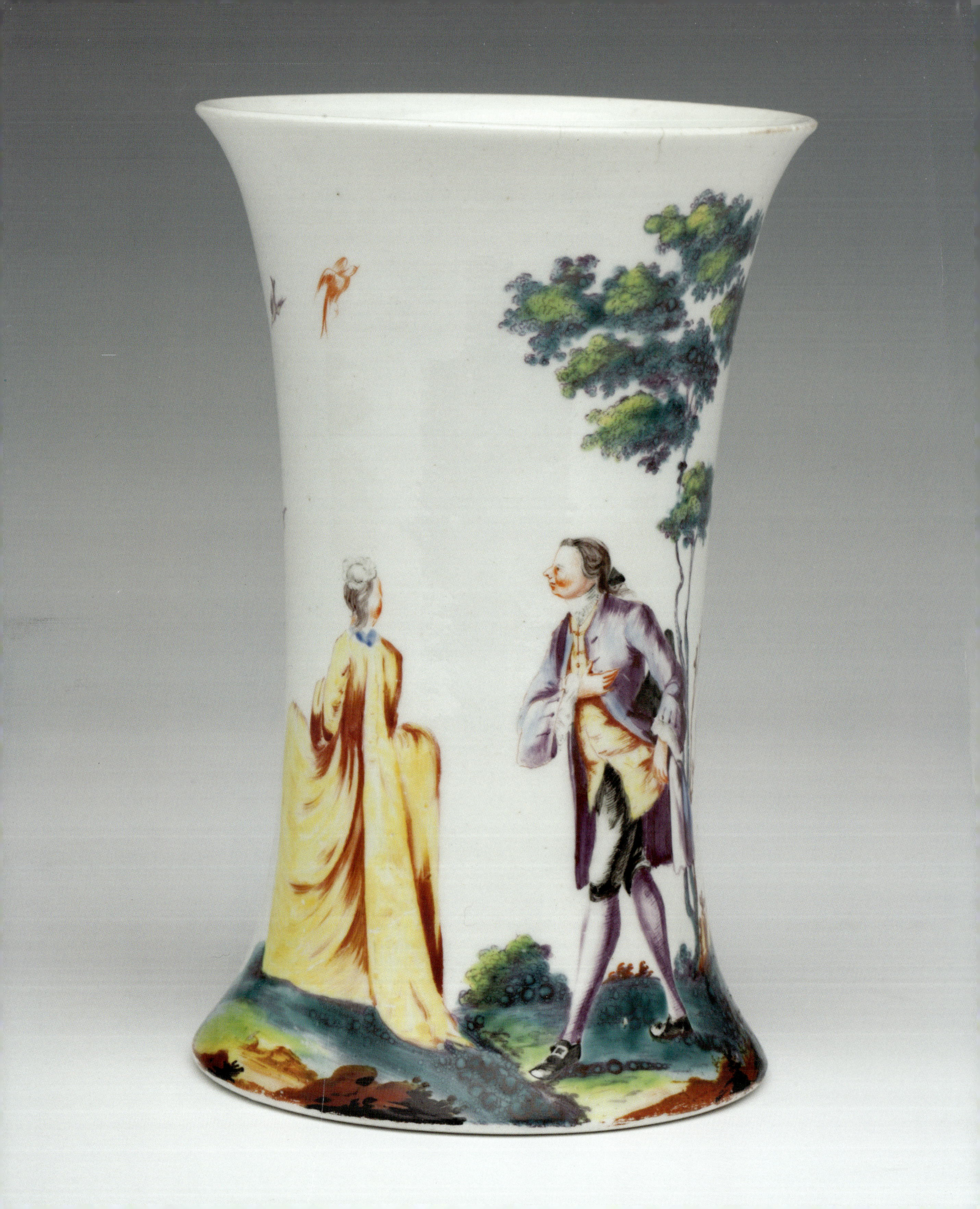

THE MARSHALL COLLECTION OF WORCESTER PORCELAIN

IN THE ASHMOLEAN MUSEUM, OXFORD

Rosalind Sword

with contributions by

Dinah Reynolds, Stephen Hanscombe,
Kelly Domoney and Joanna Dunster

VOLUME ONE

ASHMOLEAN
MUSEUM OF ART AND ARCHAEOLOGY UNIVERSITY OF OXFORD

First published in the United Kingdom by the Ashmolean Museum,
Publications Department, Beaumont Street, Oxford OX1 2PH

ISBN 978-1-910807-05-7

British Library Cataloguing in Publication Data
A catalogue record for this book is available
from the British Library

Edited by Johanna Stephenson
Designed by Stephen Hebron

Typeset in Albertina
Printed and bound in the UK by Short Run Press Ltd.

For further details about the Ashmolean Museum's publications please visit:
www.ashmolean.org/shop

Frontispiece: cat. 221, vase, 1756–8

ASHMOLEAN
MUSEUM OF ART AND ARCHAEOLOGY UNIVERSITY OF OXFORD

UNIVERSITY OF OXFORD

Contents

Preface

THIS CATALOGUE DESCRIBES what is probably the most encyclopaedic collection of early coloured Worcester porcelain in existence. The Marshall Collection was given to the University of Oxford in 1956, through the National Art-Collections Fund (now the Art Fund) in memory of William Somerville Marshall, Mr and Mrs Marshall's only son, who had been killed on active service in the Second World War.

Mr Marshall, who assembled the collection between the two World Wars and in the years following, sought to represent as comprehensive a range of patterns as possible, with minimal duplication, so that his collection would become a true reference work in itself. Every piece seems to have been acquired with a reason, many of them either to further his knowledge or because they were very rare. He was also one of a small group of ceramic collectors who sought in collecting to document sources and influences, in this case specifically the Oriental and other prototypes used by the decorators of Worcester porcelain.

It was therefore a logical consequence of the special nature of the collection for Mr Marshall to make it a condition of the gift that the Ashmolean show the collection in its entirety. It is difficult to imagine any museum nowadays accepting such a condition, without a limitation in time, but it is the nature and tradition of the Ashmolean to keep faith with promises once made to donors and the collection is still shown as a whole, now in the centre of the Museum's main gallery of European ceramics. The more than a thousand pieces do, in some people's eyes, occupy a disproportionate amount of space in a gallery that seeks to cover many types of European ceramics from fifteenth-century Spain through to Hans Coper; but such eccentricities are part of the particular personality of the Museum's collections. The porcelain not only makes a spectacular concentrated display but provides an unparalleled source of reference for collectors and other interested visitors.

This catalogue, like the collection itself, seeks to present early Worcester porcelain to collectors and a wider public in a systematic way. It describes, classifies, and reproduces every item in the Marshall Collection. It does not seek to present detailed new research, but to record the state of knowledge about the subject at the time of writing.

The great bulk of the work of putting together this catalogue has been heroically assumed by Rosalind Sword, a long-standing volunteer in the Department of Western Art who is herself a Worcester collector and shares Mr Marshall's passion for the subject. She has built on the work of an even longer-serving volunteer, Dinah Reynolds, who has for many years acted effectively as curator of the European porcelain in the Museum and wrote an *Ashmolean Handbook* on Worcester porcelain, first published in 1988. The Ashmolean has long owed much to skilled and committed volunteers, but few can match the dedicated contribution over so many years of Mrs Sword and Mrs Reynolds.

We are glad also to be able to include an essay by one of the country's prime specialists on eighteenth-century porcelain-painting, the late and much-missed Stephen Hanscombe, and an essay summarising results of technological analysis of some of the pigments, carried out by our valued collaborators from Cranfield University, Kelly Domoney and Joanna Dunster.

The need for a complete published catalogue of this collection was something long felt inside the Museum and beyond. The impetus to the present volume came from Mrs Alexandra Taylor, who, encouraged by the then Chairman of the Visitors of the Museum, Nicholas Barber, approached the Keeper of Western Art, Timothy Wilson, with a proposal to support a programme of photography, so that a new catalogue of the Marshall Collection might be fully illustrated in colour. Without her generosity, enthusiasm and inspiration, this work would not have happened. Similarly, generous and critical support for the publication has been provided by the Ceramica-Stiftung of Basel, the Friends of the Ashmolean and the Oxford Ceramics Group and we thank them all.

Mrs Sword also wishes to thank, for all their wisdom and advice: the late William Buck, Paul Crane, Aileen Dawson, Helen Espir, Anton Gabszewicz, Brian and Anna Haughton, Maurice and Lynn Hillis, Charlotte Jacob-Hanson, John Mallet, Errol Manners, Jill McNeile, Thomas Michie, Andrew Renton, Robyn Robb, John Sandon, Simon Spero, Sir Richard Baker Wilbraham and Colin Wyman. Especial thanks go to Felicity Marno and Antonia Agnew of Stockspring Antiques, who provided constant advice and encouragement. The English Ceramic Circle and the porcelain collections at the Victoria and Albert Museum, British Museum, Fitzwilliam Museum, Museum of Royal Worcester Porcelain, DeWitt Wallace Decorative Arts Museum, Williamsburg and the Museum of Fine Arts, Boston, have provided her with inspiration and advice over many years. This publication would not have been possible without the expert help of the photographers, John Griffin and David Gowers; the editor, Johanna Stephenson; the designer, Stephen Hebron; and the staff at the Ashmolean. The book has been seen though production with his customary energy and ability by the Ashmolean's Head of Publications, Declan McCarthy.

We hope, therefore, that this catalogue will serve a purpose of which Mr Marshall would have approved, to present the Marshall Collection to interested publics in attractive and usable form, with the intention of encouraging further research and interest in Worcester porcelain.

Dr Alexander Sturgis
Director, The Ashmolean Museum

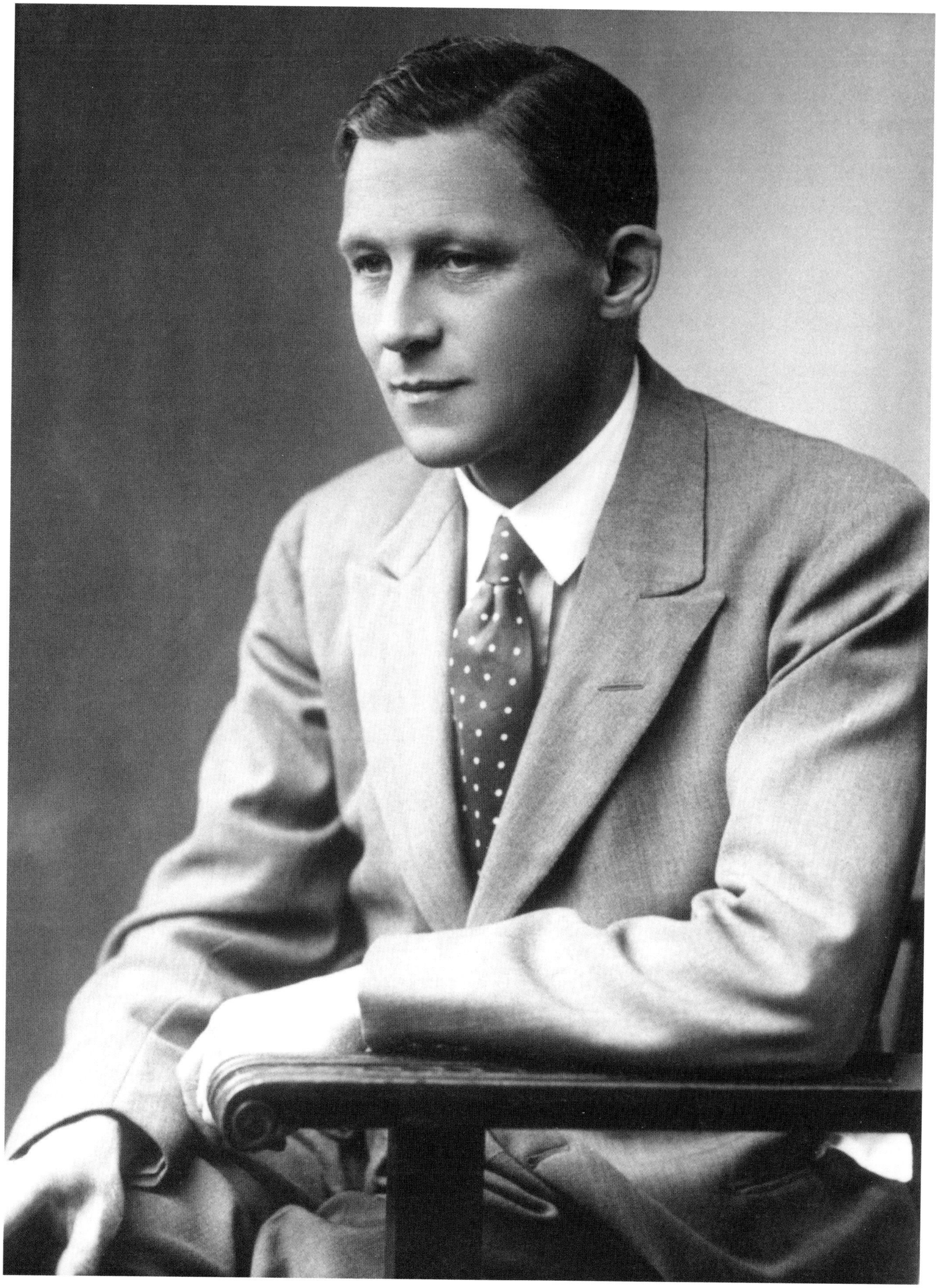

Fig. 1 Henry Rissik Marshall. © Ashmolean Museum, University of Oxford

Henry Rissik Marshall (1891–1959)

Dinah Reynolds

HENRY RISSIK MARSHALL (fig. 1) was born in South Africa in 1891. His family background, and the source of much of the wealth which enabled him to form the collection that is the subject of this catalogue, is linked to the exciting early days of Johannesburg.

In 1876 his maternal grandfather, Dr Gerrit Rissik of Utrecht in the Netherlands, had moved with his family to South Africa and settled in Pretoria. In 1885 his daughter Anna married Henry Brown Marshall, who had arrived in South Africa from Glenhove, Lanarkshire, in 1878. H.B. Marshall ran a transport business, which later had the mail contract.

In the 1880s gold was found where Johannesburg now stands. H.B. Marshall sold his transport firm and became managing director of three gold mines. After the abortive British incursion led by L.S. Jameson in December 1895, Marshall was suspected of conspiracy and imprisoned by the Transvaal Government. He was released on payment of a fine, but the family left South Africa and came back to Britain almost immediately.

The following year they bought an estate at Rachan, in the Scottish Borders, where they brought up their family of three boys and four girls. Harry, as he was often called, was their third child and second son; he was educated at Marlborough and at Trinity College, Oxford. After university he studied accountancy in Edinburgh for two years and, as he was already a keen Territorial, was mobilised with his regiment, the Lancashire Yeomanry, in August 1914; he saw service in Gallipoli and Palestine.

In August 1918 Harry married Monica, the daughter of William Somerville (1860–1932), Oxford's Sibthorpian Professor of Rural Economy, with whom two of his Rissik cousins had lodged while they were at Trinity. In her obituary of Harry in 1960, Monica wrote that she and her husband:

> … soon began to take an interest in antiques and to study and collect them, but by 1922 First Period Worcester Porcelain became the main preoccupation. Marshall, keen and thorough in all he undertook, tackled his hobby from every aspect. He applied himself to reading books on ceramics, visited leading salerooms and dealers, and haunted museums, where he was soon on friendly terms with curators of those days, including R.L. Hobson, Bernard Rackham, W.B. Honey and W.A.H. King. From them he learnt much as he did from two great collectors of Worcester, C.W. Dyson Perrins and H.W. Hughes, and he owed a great deal too to his membership of the English Ceramic Circle, of which he eventually became President.
>
> Prices between the wars were reasonable, and at the beginning of the last war were low, so the collection grew without the difficulties which are experienced today and became well-known and readily available to all those with ceramic interests. Marshall was never happier than when showing his treasures to

fellow enthusiasts and discussing problems with them and he was particularly pleased if he could attract the young disciples, for he felt that they would reap a lifetime of benefit from such a hobby. Marshall gradually became convinced that his collection ought to be kept intact, for he knew that it would be hard to get together again such a representative collection of coloured First Period Worcester and its prototypes, though for reasons of space, he had had to forgo the pleasure of collecting blue and white specimens or monochrome transfer.

Two unusual aspects of the collection are his interests in armorial subjects and in the influences on Worcester from other countries and factories. Regarding the former, in 1942 he wrote to a leading heraldic expert, Sir Algernon Tudor-Craig (1873–1943), that he, Marshall, was trying to draw up as comprehensive a list as possible of coloured armorial specimens of Dr Wall Worcester. Sir Algernon died in 1943 but Marshall continued to correspond with his son, James Tudor-Craig (d. 1969), on armorial matters until 1953, and also with A.J. Toppin (1881–1969) of the College of Arms. In November 1943 Marshall gave a lecture to the English Ceramic Circle on 'Armorial Worcester Porcelain of the Dr Wall Period 1751–83' (see p. 558). Many of the armorial items in his collection were displayed at the Tea Centre, London, in June and July 1953.

Marshall collected many prototypes. In the Ashmolean Museum these are displayed beside the Worcester version, which allows the visitor to see how the factory adopted, and in some instances adapted, the designs to create something that was essentially Worcester. In January 1956 Marshall gave a paper to the English Ceramics circle on 'Notes on the Origins of Worcester Decoration', in which he used over fifty examples to illustrate 'Some Prototypes of, and Replacements by, Worcester of the Products of Other Factories'.[1] He had been inspired by Robert Drane (1833–1914), an antiquarian and pharmacist from Cardiff, whose collection had been exhibited in London by Albert Amor in May 1922, and by H.W. Hughes (1862–1937) of Dudley, Worcestershire, from whose collection Marshall bought many prototypes.

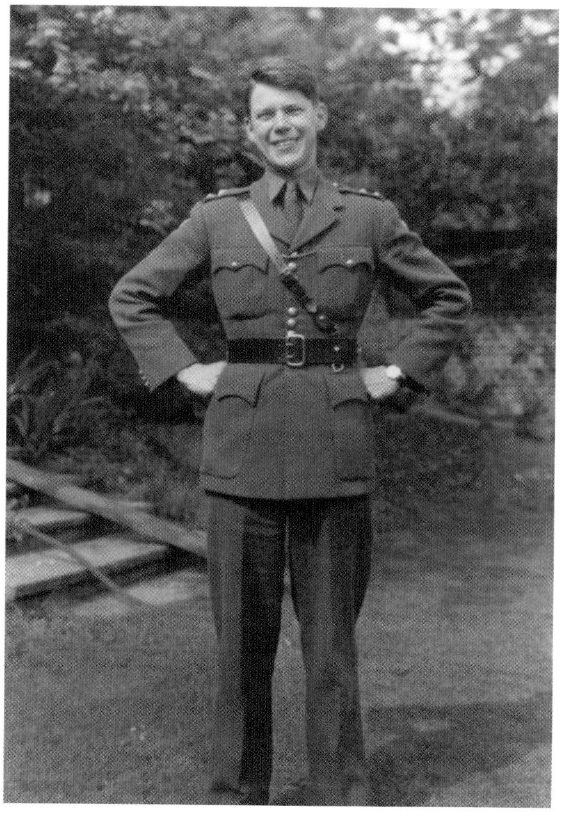
Fig. 2 William Somerville Marshall. © Ashmolean Museum, University of Oxford

Another aspect of porcelain decoration that interested Marshall was that of the so-called named services. These are patterns that have been associated with a particular person, such as Sir Joshua Reynolds (1723–1792) or Lady Mary Wortley Montague (1689–1762), although often the association is erroneous. Marshall gave a lecture on this subject at Messrs Filkins Galleries, South Kensington, at the end of January 1943; the chairman was Dr Severne Mackenna, to whom he had sent the text of the lecture beforehand. In his reply to Marshall, Dr Mackenna wrote: 'I am sure that it will prove to be a most interesting and instructive lecture and should do much to dispel the fatuous illusions of many complacent collectors!' Marshall subsequently wrote two articles, published in *Apollo*, in March and August 1945, in which he listed twenty-three named patterns.[2]

The Marshalls had one son (a daughter died as a baby), William Somerville (fig. 2), who was born in 1923 and educated at Winchester College then at Trinity College, Oxford in 1941–2. He joined the Scots Guards and was killed in the Netherlands in November 1944, leaving a young widow but no children. His wife, Sylvia, was the only child of Edward Hasell of Dalemain in Cumbria, where Marshall had envisaged his collection being displayed on one of the upper floors. As Mrs Marshall says in her obituary of her husband,

Marshall turned to his collection for distraction and solace, and the idea came to him that there could no fitter memorial to a boy who himself was a collector of promise, than the gift of the Worcester porcelain to some museum. He knew that many museums contained choice examples of Worcester, but when he learnt that the Ashmolean possessed no English porcelain, he felt that he had found the perfect setting, for Oxford had meant so much in the lives of himself, his wife and his son.

So in July 1951 he wrote to the Vice-Chancellor of Oxford University, Dean Lowe of Christ Church, stating that he possessed one of the finest collections, and certainly the most representative, of coloured First Period Worcester Porcelain in England. The letter continued with the statement that he and his wife were prepared either to give or to leave this collection to the University. He also stated that he would 'within limits be prepared to endow the housing and maintenance of the collection'. His letter ended with a postscript: 'any expert would tell you that the collection could be sold in America for about a hundred thousand pounds'. The Vice-Chancellor replied by return, and on 13 July the Keeper of the Ashmolean, K.T. Parker, told Dean Lowe that the 'collection should be accepted by the University on its intrinsic merit'. Then on 17 July the Warden of New College and Chairman of the Visitors of the Ashmolean, A.H. Smith, wrote: 'I have talked now to all the members of the Standing Committee and also to the Vice-Chancellor about Mr. Rissik Marshall's proposed gift. We all feel strongly that this magnificent gift should be accepted forthwith.'

The Marshalls were not able to visit the Museum to see the proposed gallery for the collection until May 1952, due to Harry's illness following a fall, and there was a further delay before the Keeper was able to go to Hampstead to see the collection in February 1953. Monica Marshall had by then also offered the Museum her collections of glass and wine labels. On 12 February 1953 Marshall wrote to the dealer Leonard Crow:

> My sale on the 27th of January (Sothebys) was on the whole successful. The china fetched about £3,400 while the expenses came to about £400, leaving in round figures £3,000 nett. I estimate that the china I sold actually cost me about £1,800, so that I had a profit of about £1,200. Prices were very odd, sometimes things went extremely high and at other times really quite low. This was especially true of the armorial patterns from which it appears that I am really the only serious buyer of first period Worcester Armorial, and that I have, in fact, been making a market in it against myself, so that I shall have to be more careful in future.

This sale was mainly of duplicates.

Marshall had been involved in the organisation of the major exhibition held in London for the 200th anniversary of the foundation of the Worcester Porcelain Company, following which he produced his book, *Coloured Worcester Porcelain of the First Period* (fig. 3), published at the end of 1954, with chapters entitled 'James Giles, Enameller', 'Jefferyes Hammett O'Neale', 'Worcester Figures', 'The Ground Colours' and 'Borders', and 'Figure and Landscape Painting' showing other important areas of interest. This book is

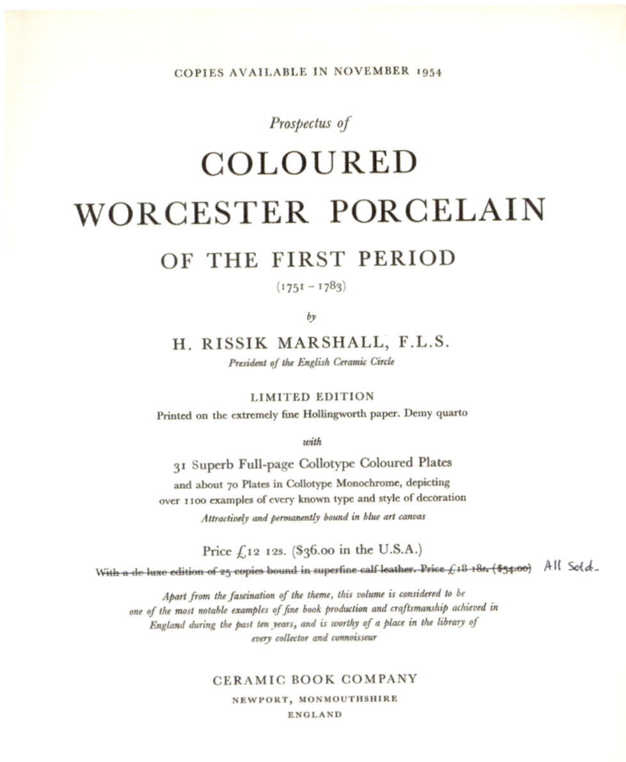
COPIES AVAILABLE IN NOVEMBER 1954

Prospectus of

COLOURED
WORCESTER PORCELAIN
OF THE FIRST PERIOD
(1751 – 1783)

by

H. RISSIK MARSHALL, F.L.S.
President of the English Ceramic Circle

LIMITED EDITION
Printed on the extremely fine Hollingworth paper. Demy quarto

with

31 Superb Full-page Collotype Coloured Plates
and about 70 Plates in Collotype Monochrome, depicting
over 1100 examples of every known type and style of decoration
Attractively and permanently bound in blue art canvas

Price £12 12s. ($36.00 in the U.S.A.)
~~With a de luxe edition of 25 copies bound in superfine calf leather. Price £18 18s. ($54.00)~~ All Sold.

Apart from the fascination of the theme, this volume is considered to be one of the most notable examples of fine book production and craftsmanship achieved in England during the past ten years, and is worthy of a place in the library of every collector and connoisseur

CERAMIC BOOK COMPANY
NEWPORT, MONMOUTHSHIRE
ENGLAND

Fig. 3 Prospectus for H.R. Marshall, *Coloured Worcester Porcelain of the First Period*, London 1954. © Ashmolean Museum, University of Oxford

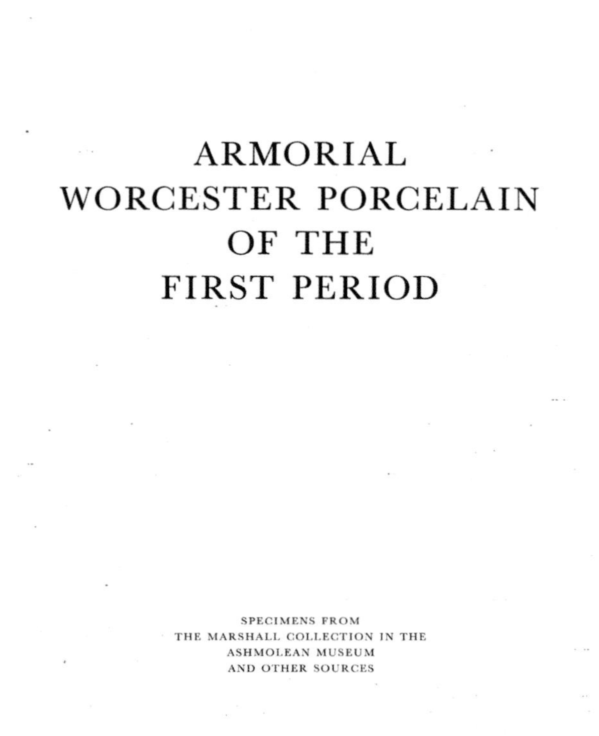

ARMORIAL
WORCESTER PORCELAIN
OF THE
FIRST PERIOD

SPECIMENS FROM
THE MARSHALL COLLECTION IN THE
ASHMOLEAN MUSEUM
AND OTHER SOURCES

Fig. 4 Title-page of H.R. Marshall, *Armorial Worcester Porcelain of the First Period*, privately published, 1954. © Ashmolean Museum, University of Oxford

illustrated with photographs taken at the exhibition, including many pieces loaned by other collectors. A letter to Marshall from Dr Severne MacKenna of 13 January 1955 reveals that the publication was well received: 'You must feel a very satisfying glow of complacency and contentment at this brilliant outcome of your immense work and outlay'.

At this time Marshall contemplated a further book, *Armorial Worcester Porcelain of the First Period*, so he had twenty-four additional colour plates made from some original armorial paintings by H. Norman Eastaugh that were in his possession. These arms were mainly copied from pieces in his own collection, but six were from the Victoria and Albert Museum, two from the Dyson Perrins Museum (now the Museum of Royal Worcester Porcelain) and one from a private collection. Marshall had the intention of reproducing every known armorial used by Worcester but sadly became too ill to do so. However, after his death a booklet with Eastaugh's illustrations was printed (figs 4 and 5).

In 1954 it was decided that the Marshall porcelain collection should be allocated the room that had been used for temporary exhibitions. The new Vice-Chancellor, A.H. Smith, Warden of New College, invited the Marshalls to lunch in the Warden's Lodgings at New College. Marshall wrote to him afterwards to say that he and his wife were 'content' with the room but that they would need to find a small house in the vicinity of Oxford in which to live, and that this, with other complications, would mean a delay of three or four years before the collection could come to the Museum.

On 8 March 1956 Congregation, the University of Oxford's parliament, accepted the Marshall collections of Worcester porcelain, glass and wine labels by decree. By this date it had been decided that the collections would be given through the National Art-Collections Fund (now The Art Fund). Marshall had imposed three conditions: that the collection should always be shown in its entirety; that the Museum could dispose of an item if a finer version was acquired but that nothing made later than 1783 could be added to the collection; and that the Museum could lend pieces from the collection for exhibition elsewhere. The gift was in memory of his son, William Somerville Marshall, which was stated on a marble wall plaque at the entrance to the collection while the collection was displayed on its own. The fact that it has always been shown in its entirety has been appreciated by collectors, who know that if a piece is in the Marshall Collection it can be seen easily.

In August 1956 Monica Marshall informed the Museum that she and her husband had bought a house in Kidlington, just north of Oxford, and that they hoped to move there the following April, which meant that the collection should arrive at the Museum in March. Work was already being carried out at the Museum to install the appropriate showcases, to which the Marshalls contributed financially. In September Harry was diagnosed as having tuberculosis, for which he had an operation, and was still convalescent when the porcelain arrived at the Museum in March 1957. In July he was well enough to begin to arrange it himself. The collection remained essentially as he arranged it, with a few minor alterations, until it was moved to the new Ceramic Gallery in 2009, where it is displayed surrounded by other English and Continental ceramics.

In June 1958 the Marshall Room was officially opened to the public, with the bound catalogues that Marshall had prepared despite having had another spell in hospital. He continued to acquire items for the collection and bring them to the Museum himself. In December 1958 *The Antique Collector* published a review of the collection in its new

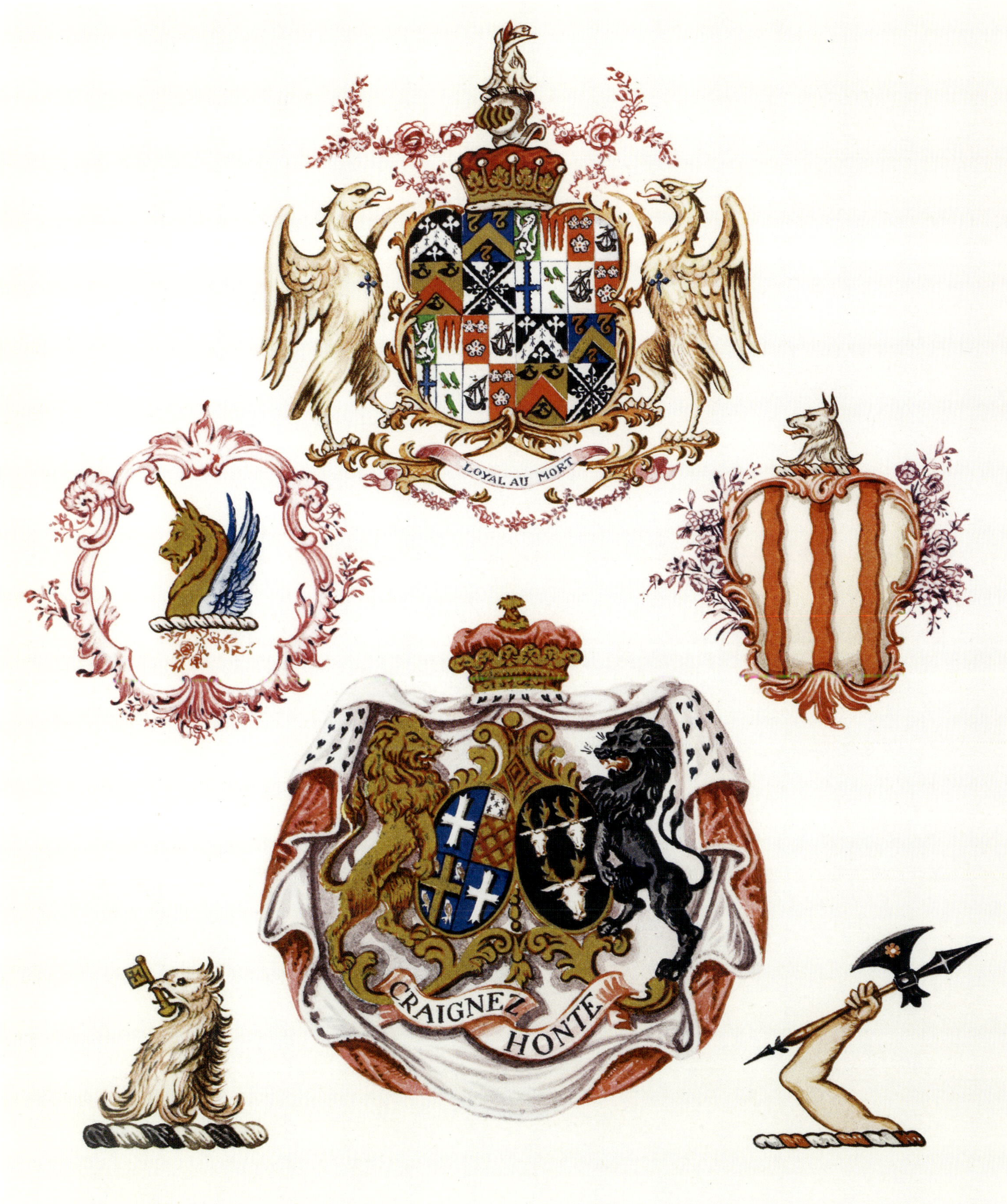

Fig. 5 H. Norman Easthaugh, armorial watercolour paintings. © Ashmolean Museum, University of Oxford

home written by Frank Tilley, a well-known dealer from and through whom Marshall bought many items. In his article Tilley remarks that as Marshall was in a nursing home at that time, he persuaded Sotheby's to send the rare cabaret service (nos. 450–455) 'into the country for Mr. Marshall to see. This method, I was assured by Mrs. Marshall, was the only means of preventing her husband from leaving his bed and coming to town as soon as he saw the catalogue'. The article ends: 'here is assembled … the crystallised history of a great English contribution to ceramic art … exhibited here in the apotheosis of scholarly classification.'

Marshall had a long association with the English Ceramic Circle (ECC): he was a member for over twenty-five years and served on the committee from November 1934. He was Treasurer from 1949 to December 1953, when he was succeeded by his wife, and President from November 1953 until January 1957, when ill health forced him to resign. In 1948 he loaned more than thirty items to an exhibition at the Victoria and Albert Museum celebrating twenty-one years of the ECC. Several times the Marshalls invited members of the ECC to see the collection at their home, 60 Redington Road, Hampstead, and in October 1951 the Circle inspected the Worcester Bicentenary Exhibition organised by Marshall at Worcester House, Curzon Street, London. In Marshall's obituary in the ECC *Transactions*, Aubrey Toppin described him as a driving force in the activities of the Circle, which suffered a grievous loss by his death:

> Harry Marshall was a born collector, and a serious student of English Ceramics – particularly Worcester Porcelain, his knowledge of which was profound and the collection of it that he 'amassed' was the largest and most complete ever assembled.
>
> Son of H.B. Marshall of Rachan, he was educated at Marlborough and Trinity College, Oxford and had important family interests in South Africa. But his main 'interest' for the last 30 years of his life, was his beloved Worcester Porcelain.
>
> By his generous gift to the Ashmolean Museum, Oxford, his unique collection has been preserved there for posterity. His collection consisted of over one thousand patterns of coloured Worcester porcelain of the first period. It was particularly rich in armorial pieces and included four pairs of figures, a Worcester version of 'La Nourice' and a great many other rarities…
>
> He contributed many well-written papers to our Transactions, and arranged and catalogued the extensive collection of Worcester Porcelain exhibited at Worcester House, Curzon Street (the home of the Royal Worcester Company), in 1951 – commemorating the bicentenary of the Worcester China Factory, 1751–1951. Most of the exhibits there were from his own collection. This was followed by his magnum opus, 'Coloured Worcester Porcelain of the First Period', published in 1954, with a wealth of illustrations, many of which were faithfully reproduced in colour.
>
> The Circle were guests of the Marshalls on many happy occasions at their delightful house at Hampstead. And our visit to the Ashmolean on June 3rd, 1959, was a memorable occasion. There we saw the famous Worcester Collection, beautifully housed and arranged. The meeting must have been an ordeal for Harry Marshall;, as he was then frail and obviously ill, but the old enthusiasm was still there and we were greeted with his usual friendly smile. It was a moving experience.[3]

On Boxing Day 1959 Monica Marshall wrote that her husband was seriously ill with a virus infection, so he was unable bring to the Museum two rare Worcester pieces that he had acquired for the collection. He died the following day. In his will Marshall stipulated that he should be cremated and the ashes put in one of the Worcester vases decorated with ruins: his widow commented that what 'Harry in his dry witty way said was so appropriate'. She never lost interest in the Ashmolean and the collections that she and her husband had given, and continued to write to the curators until her death on 15 May 1969.

1 This lecture was published in *English Ceramic Circle Transactions*, vol. 4, no. 3 (1957), pp. 24–5.

2 'Named Services of Dr Wall Worcester', part I, *Apollo*, vol. XLI, no. 241 (March 1945), pp. 58–60, and part II, *Apollo*, vol. XLII, no. 246 (August 1945), pp. 188–91.

3 *English Ceramic Circle Transactions*, vol. 5, part 1 (1960), pp. 65–6.

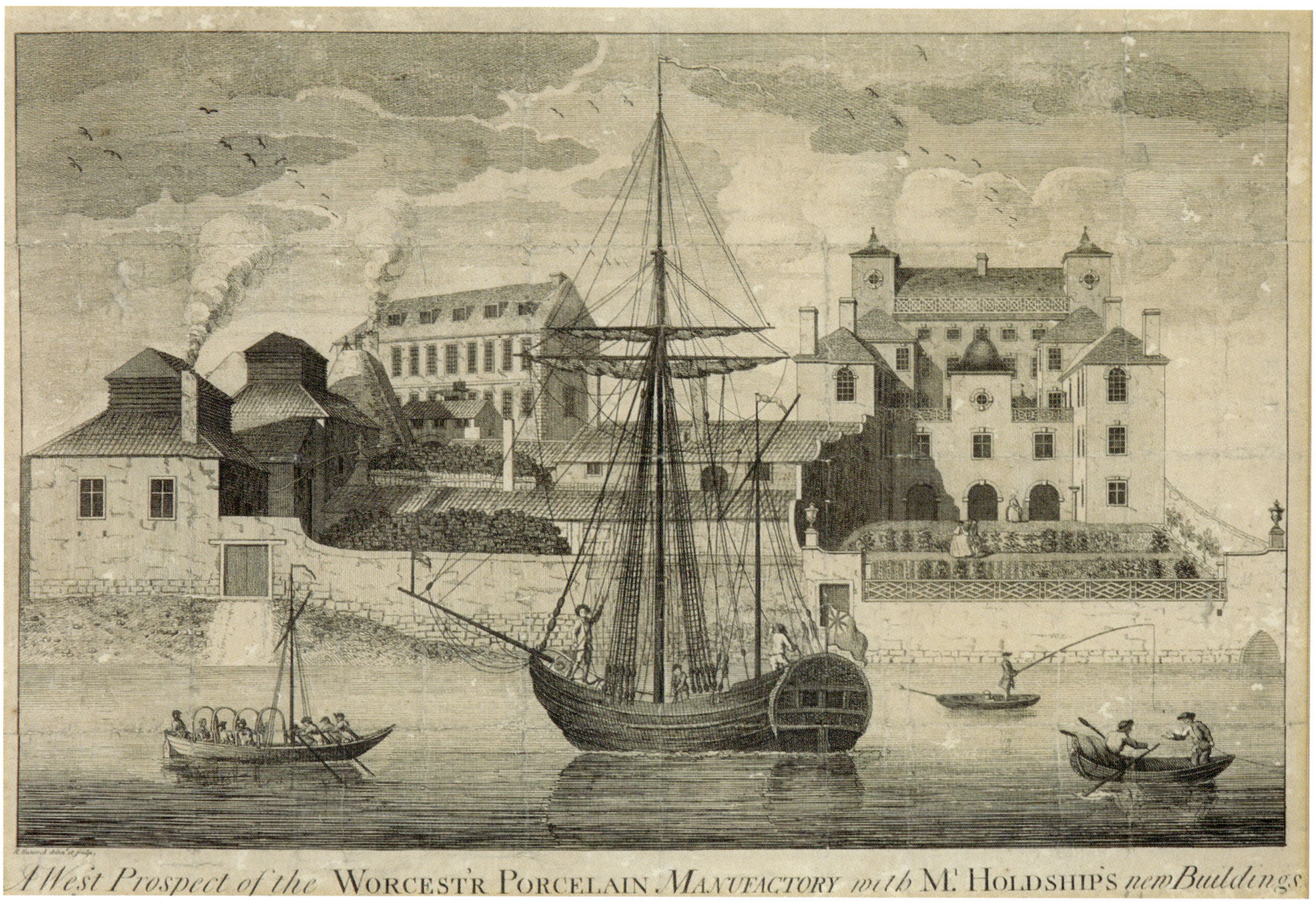

Fig. 6 Robert Hancock, *The Worcester Porcelain Manufactory from the River Severn*, engraving, 1757. © Museum of Royal Worcester Porcelain

A Short History of Worcester Porcelain in the Eighteenth Century

THE 'WORCESTER TONQUIN MANUFACTURE' was founded by a deed of partnership (fig. 7) signed on 4 June 1751. Among the original fifteen partners, subscribing a total of £4,500, were Dr John Wall (1708–1776), who was elected a fellow of Merton College, Oxford, in 1734 (fig. 8); William Davis (1710–1791), an apothecary; and brothers Josiah (1712–1783) and Richard Holdship (1709–1785), a maltster and a glover respectively. The partners all lived in Worcestershire, with the exception of Edward Cave (1691–1754), a London printer and publisher of *The Gentleman's Magazine*. A twenty-one-year lease had previously been taken out on Warmstry House on the banks of the river Severn on 16 May 1751 by Richard Holdship on behalf of the subscribers.

The partnership agreement describes John Wall and William Davis as the inventors of the 'new Manufacture of Earthenware … under the denomination of Worcester Porcelain'. Prior to attracting investment, it is thought that some experiments had been carried out, probably in Davis's shop in Broad Street, Worcester, and a method of making a porcelain-type material had been discovered. Excavations carried out in 1977–9 on the lowest levels of the factory site uncovered remains of a high proportion of poor-quality items, indicating evidence of a period of experimentation.[1]

On 21 February 1752 Richard Holdship purchased for the company the rival business of Benjamin Lund (1692–1768) in Bristol. According to traveller and travel writer Dr Richard Pococke (1704–1765), in a letter to his mother of 2 November 1750, the

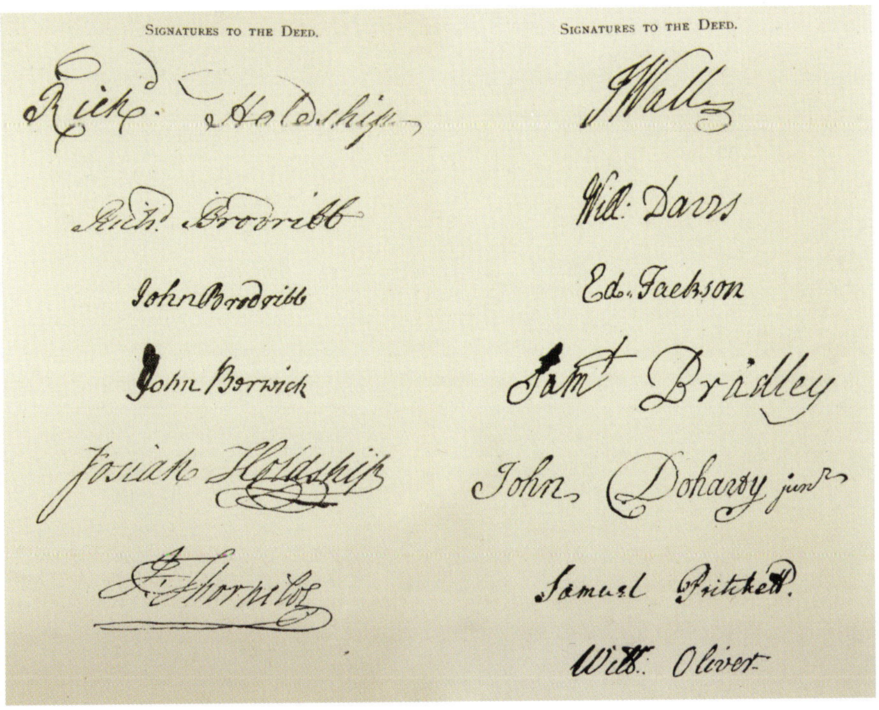

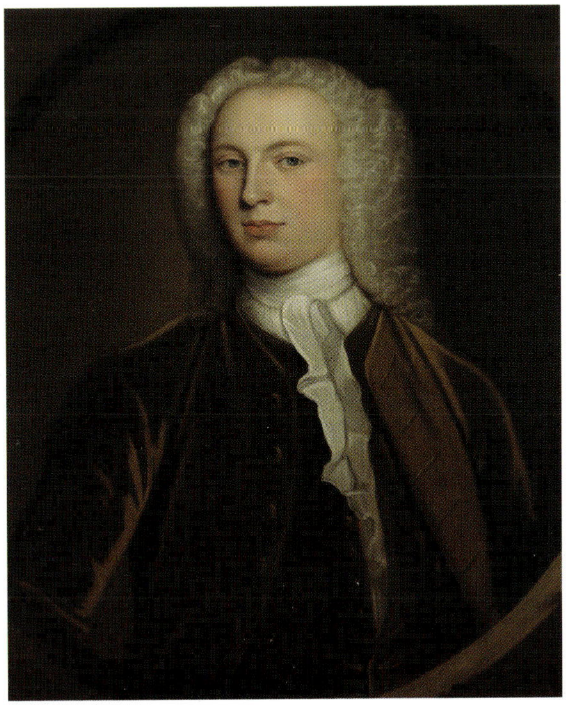

Fig. 7 Signatures to the Deed of Partnership, 4 June 1751. © Museum of Royal Worcester Porcelain

Fig. 8 Unknown artist, *Portrait of Dr John Wall*, oil on canvas, *c.*1745–50. © Museum of Royal Worcester Porcelain

company had been founded in 1749 by 'one of the principal manufacturers at Limehouse which failed'. The Limehouse porcelain factory in east London, *c.*1746–8, was possibly the first factory to specialise in underglaze blue decoration. Holdship personally acquired the lease of the soaprock (steatite) mines near the Lizard in Cornwall, Worcester agreeing to buy 20 tons of soaprock a year for twenty years. A naturally occurring mixture of china clay and magnesium silicate, soaprock provided a malleable clay that could produce a body that was thin, white and translucent; that could be crisply moulded; and that had the additional quality of withstanding hot liquids without cracking. Commenting on English china in the *Annual Register* for the year 1763, it was said that 'except the Worcester, they all wear brown, and are subject to crack, especially the glazing, by boiling water: the Worcester has a good body, scarce inferior to that of Eastern China, it is equally tough, and its glazing never cracks or scales off'.[2] This gave Worcester a commercial advantage over other porcelain manufacturers. The penalty for disclosing the secret formula, the property of the subscribers, was £4,000, although it was never invoked. Some Bristol workmen, including Lund, are thought to have moved to Worcester, and modellers, potters and painters may also have come from Staffordshire. In 1764 Valentine Green wrote: 'This work is the employ and subsistence of a great number of people'; six years later, on 13 July 1770, after a visit to the factory, Lady Shelburne wrote: 'They told us the China employ'd 600 people', although this may be exaggerated.[3] On 28 August 1771 Mrs Philip Lybbe Powys (1738–1817) gave a more reliable account: 'They employ 160 persons, a vast number of them very little boys'.[4]

The first sale of Worcester porcelain took place at the annual Worcester Music Meeting on 20 September 1752. It was also sold in Samuel Bradley's goldsmith's shop at 33 High Street. Much of the early output was also sold by auction in London. In order to handle the wares, in 1754 the company opened a warehouse, London House

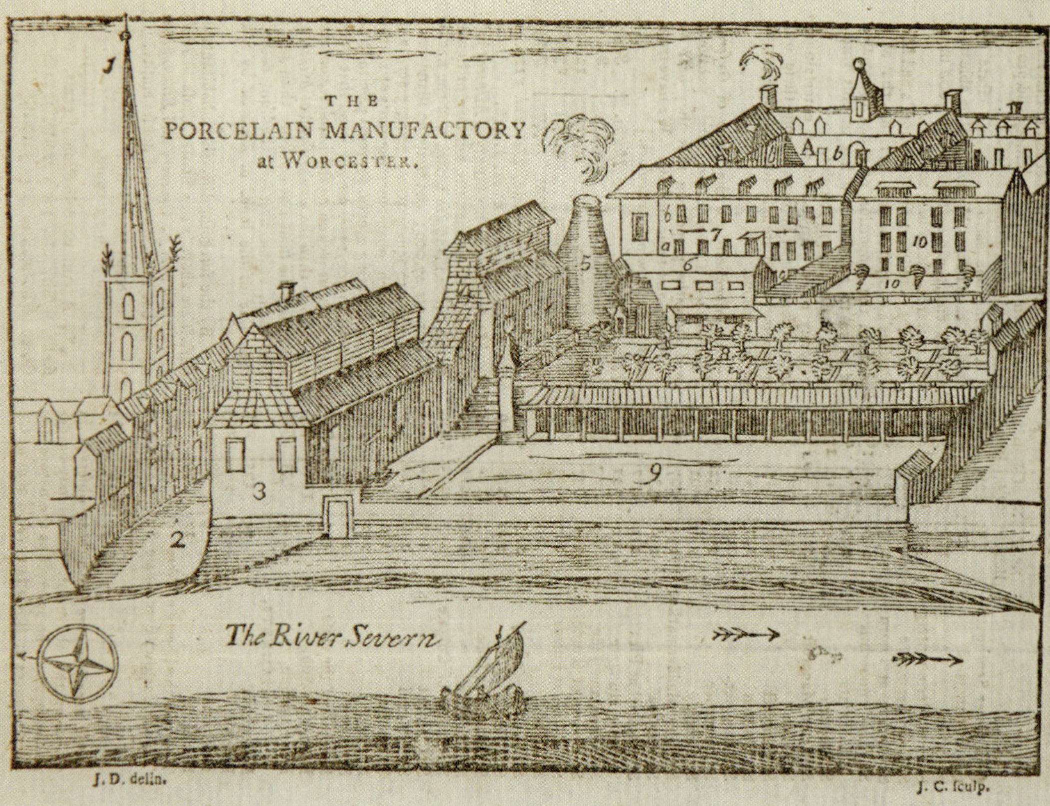

EXPLANATION. 348

1 St Andrews. 2 Warmfley flip. 3 Bifcuit kilns. 4 Glafing kilns. 5 Great kiln for fegurs. 6 Preffing and modelling gallery.— 7 Rooms for throwing, turning, and ftove drying the ware on the firft floor *a*, of the chamber floors. 8 The garden. 9 The yard for coals. 10 Mr Evett's houfe and garden, landlord of the premifes. *b* The eight windows in two large chambers, in which the ware is placed on ftallions, on the Eaft and North, where are the painters rooms.——All the beginning of the procefs is carried on under the quadrangular building ground floor, mark'd A; in its N. W. angle is the great rowl and ring; in the N. E. the horfes turn the fame, and the levigators near to the rowl. The next (on the ground floor) is the flip and treading rooms, behind Number 4 is the glafing room, behind 5 is the fecret room on the ground floor.

N. B. A fale of this manufacture will begin at the *Worcefter* mufic meeting, on *Sept.* 20, with great variety of ware, and, 'tis faid, at a moderate price.

Fig. 9 The layout of the factory at Warmstry House, from *The Gentleman's Magazine*, August 1752. © Museum of Royal Worcester Porcelain

in Aldersgate Street, from which a single, undated price list survives in the Museum of Royal Worcester Porcelain. On 15 March 1754 about forty thousand pieces of Worcester porcelain were sold at the Royal Exchange Coffee House in Threadneedle Street.

It seems that no account books, letters or pattern books from the First Period of Worcester porcelain have survived. However, the production process is illustrated in an engraving of the Worcester factory in *The Gentleman's Magazine* of August 1752 (fig. 9). Further information can be gleaned from contemporary accounts, such as that by Valentine Green (1738–1813), who trained as an engraver with Robert Hancock, in *A Survey of the City of Worcester* (Worcester 1764). Mrs Philip Lybbe Powys wrote about the layout of the factory and stages of production the day after her visit in August 1771.[5] Two important auctions held in 1769, one in May by Mr Burnsall and one in December by Mr Christie, provide details about the shapes and decoration used.

From the beginning the factory concentrated on functional pieces, particularly those that could not be obtained from China, such as silver-inspired sauceboats, cream-boats and pickle leaves. Initially the factory decorated its porcelain in close imitation of the Oriental style, in blue and white, *famille verte* and *famille rose*, often interpreting the designs as chinoiserie. However, it developed its own palette and style during the 1750s and by the middle of the decade began to draw on Meissen for inspiration, with pieces painted with European figures in landscapes or harbour scenes and superb flower painting. Richard Holdship's 1761 bankruptcy papers refer to Worcester as a 'porcelain manufactory in imitation of Dresden ware'.

Printing on porcelain from engraved copper plates was probably introduced by Richard Holdship and his brother Josiah and developed by the engraver Robert Hancock (1730–1817), who arrived in Worcester in about 1756. The introduction of underglaze printing in blue in Worcester was extremely important in the development of the ceramics industry, both at home and abroad.

In the 1760s coloured grounds, especially underglaze blue, were introduced, emulating Meissen, Sèvres and Chelsea. In 1768 Worcester's London manager claimed that the factory had engaged 'the best Painters from Chelsea & c.', who may have included John Donaldson (1737–1801) and Jefferyes Hamett O' Neale (1734–1801). Associated with the arrival of the modeller John Toulouse (d. 1807), who had worked at Bow and Chelsea, a greater range of moulded designs and some figures, many incorporating applied flowers, was produced.

By 1767 an agreement is thought to have been drawn up with James Giles (1718–1780), a London decorator, who advertised that he could decorate in the styles of Meissen and Sèvres. The agreement was formally terminated in 1771. Large quantities of Worcester porcelain were decorated in Giles's London studio in Berwick Street, Soho, to be sold at his warehouse in Cockspur Street, as can be seen from the Christies' sale of part of his stock in March 1774.

The Worcester Porcelain Company was sold on 2 January 1772, when the original twenty-one-year lease expired, to a consortium of previous shareholders, including John Wall, William Davis (father and son) and Robert Hancock. Dr Wall retired in 1774 and, before his death in 1776, sold his shares to William Davis senior. This brought to an end the so-called Dr Wall Period. From December 1776 the company traded as William Davis & Co. and the factory closed its London warehouse. Robert Hancock had been bought out in 1774, possibly due to a disagreement over his involvement with Thomas Turner (b. 1749), who was developing the Caughley porcelain factory in Shropshire. This was established by 1775 and later joined by Hancock.

A change of direction took place with a greater French influence seen in teawares with vertical flutes, often decorated with patterns copied from Sèvres porcelain. In the

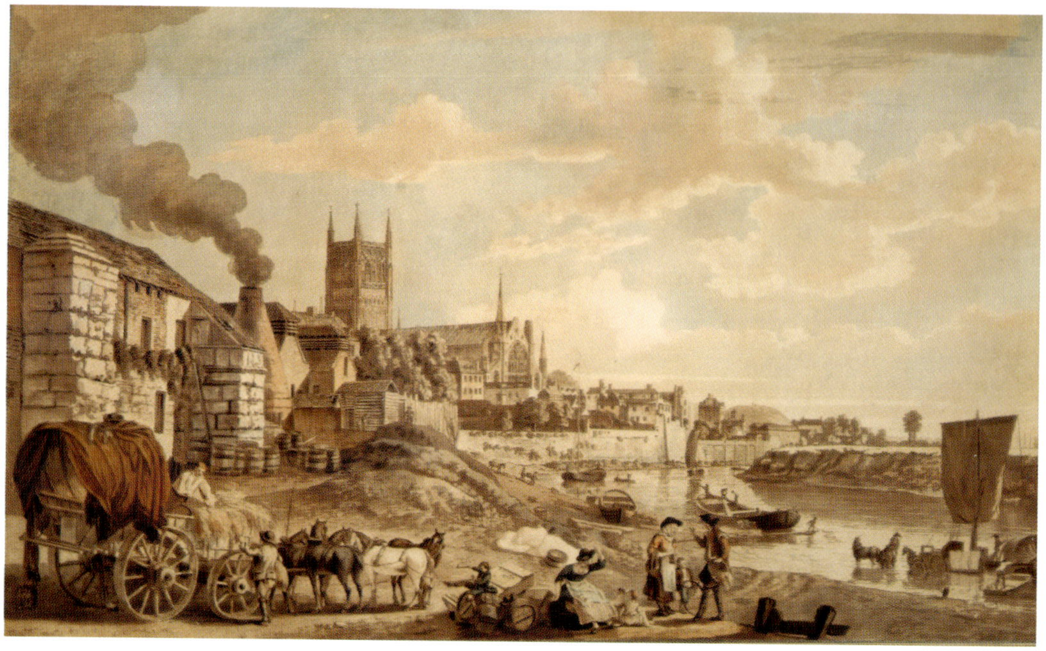

Fig. 10 Paul Sandby, *View of the Worcester Porcelain Manufactory*, aquatint with watercolour wash, 1778. © Museum of Royal Worcester Porcelain

1780s, copying Derby, Worcester introduced deep blue underglaze borders, the new fashion in London.

The First Period of Worcester porcelain came to an end in April 1783, when the company was purchased by Thomas Flight (1726–1800), its London agent, for his sons, Joseph (1762–1838) and John (about 1766–1791), for a mere £3,000. The head of the decorating department at that time was Robert Chamberlain (1736–1798), who had worked there as a decorator since the early 1750s. Chamberlain and his son left the company to set up on their own, taking most of the Worcester decorators and gilders with them. According to John Flight's diary, in 1789 his sons brought in Charlotte Hampton from London to run the decorating department. Mercury was introduced as a medium for gilding, replacing honey, to give a brighter, harder, smoother appearance after burnishing. Following the visit of George III in 1789, important orders came from the Duke of Clarence, his third son, acceding later as William IV, and a royal warrant was issued.

After the death of his son John in 1791, Thomas Flight lost interest in the business. His elder son, Joseph, joined with Martin Barr (about 1757–1813) and by June 1792 was trading as Flight & Barr. Thus a new era at the Worcester Porcelain Company began. A new, harder body and glaze were developed, together with new shapes and a totally new style of decoration; blue and white was abandoned and prosperity gradually returned (fig. 10).

1 Sandon 1981, p. 2.
2 *The Annual Register, or a View of the History, Politics, and Literature for the Year 1763*, 7th edn, London 1796, p. 102.
3 Mallet 1982, p. 109.
4 *Passages from the Diary of Mrs Philip Lybbe Powys of Hardwick House, Oxon, AD 1756 to 1808*, ed. E.J. Climenson (London 1899), p. 125.
5 Ibid., pp. 125–6.

CATALOGUE

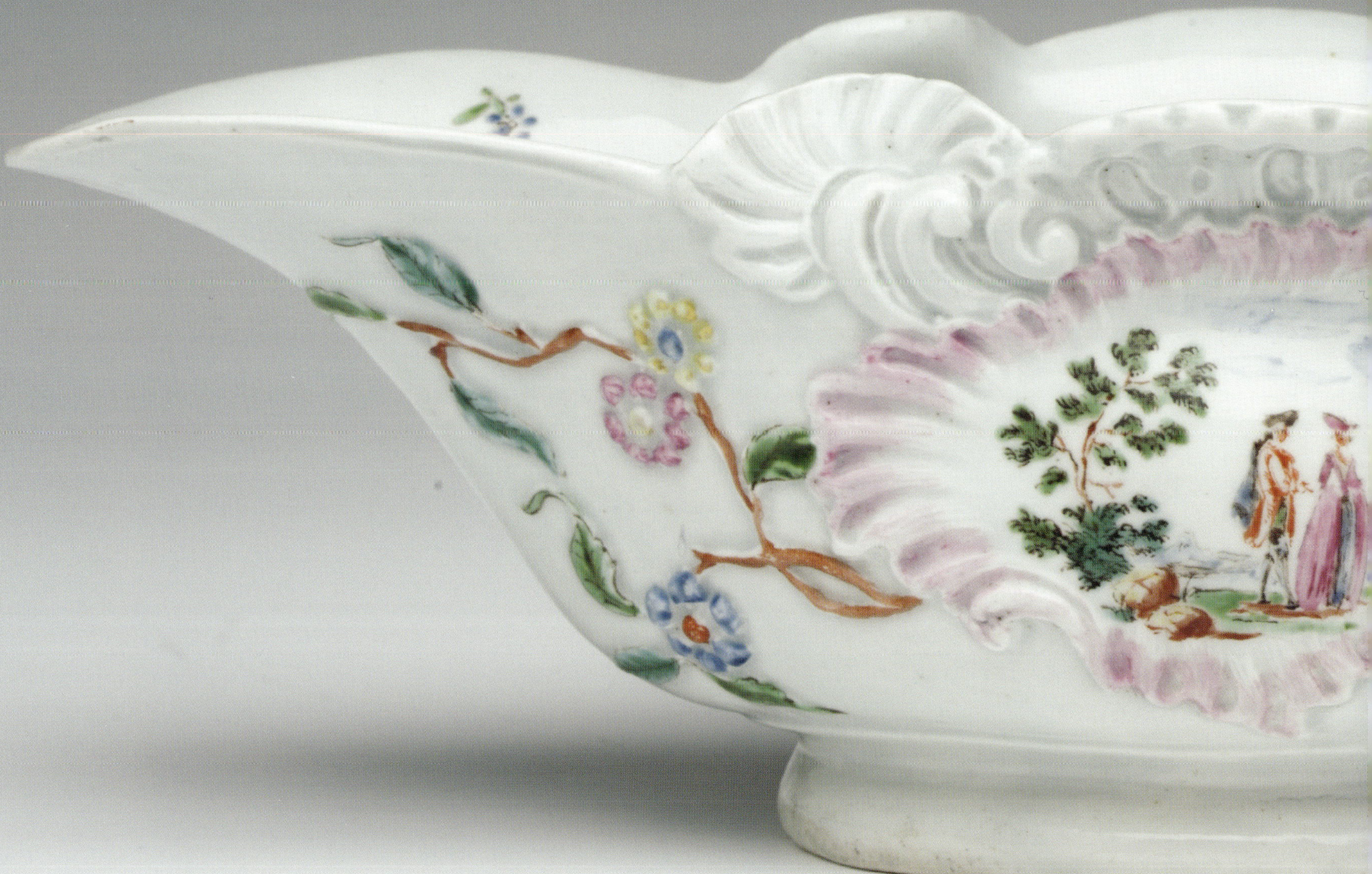

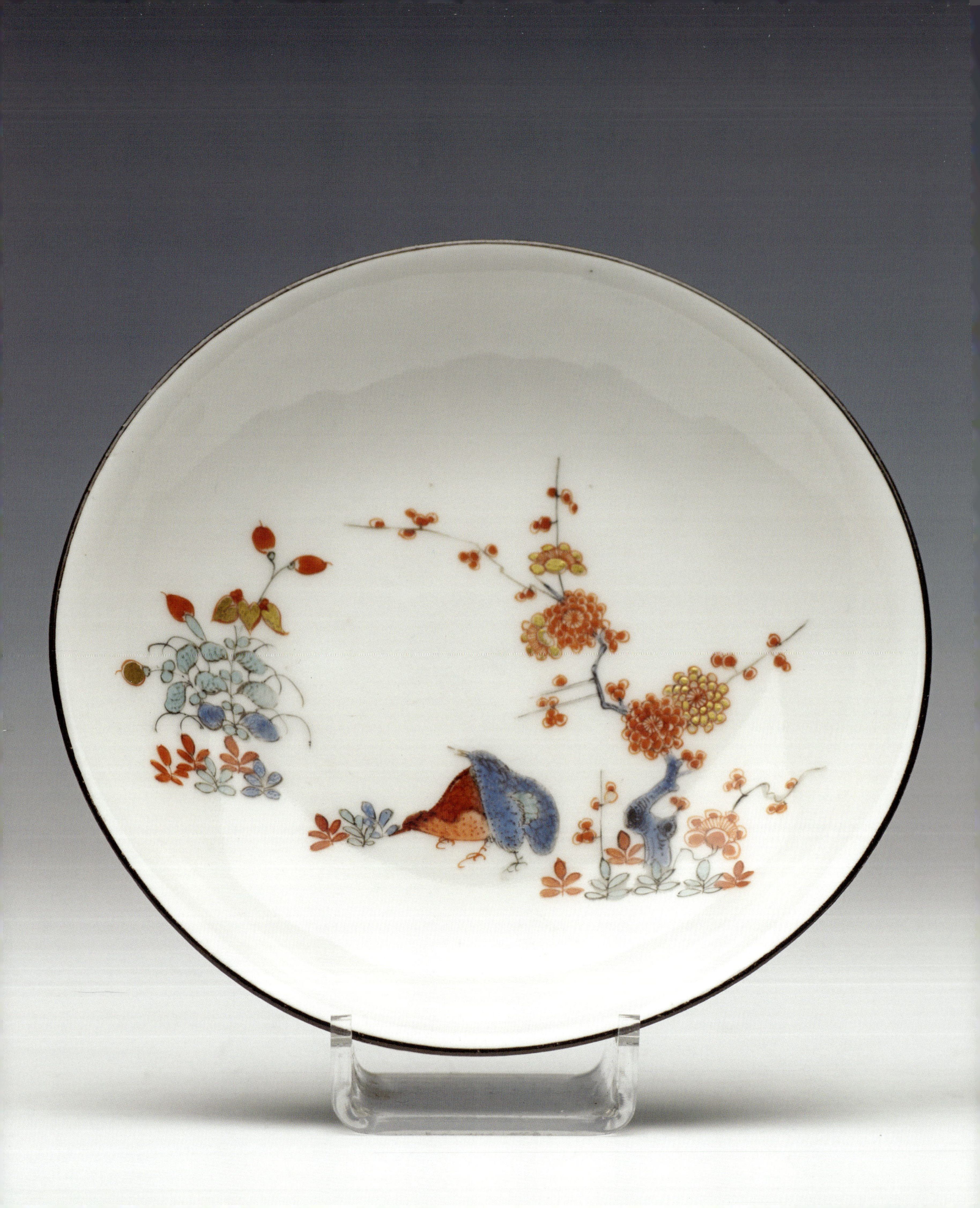

1
Prototypes and Replacements

Henry Marshall was interested in collecting items of Worcester porcelain together with their prototypes from other factories and countries. Although these items were not eligible for inclusion in the 1954 edition of *Coloured Worcester Porcelain of the First Period*, in his paper 'Notes on the Origins of Worcester Decoration', to the English Ceramics Circle on 21 January 1956, he showed fifty-six different patterns with their prototypes, many of them illustrated from his own collection. Of these, thirty-two were Chinese designs, ten Japanese, four Meissen, four Chelsea, two Sèvres and one Derby. In some instances the immediate influence was a European version of an Eastern original.

Marshall was inspired by the collection of 'link' specimens belonging to the late Robert Drane (1833–1914), exhibited by Albert Amor Ltd in May 1922 and later dispersed. Drane, a pharmacist in Cardiff, was also a naturalist and antiquarian with wide interests. He was involved with the foundation of the National Museum of Wales and a Fellow of the Linnaean Society. In an appreciation of his collection in the Amor exhibition catalogue, Frederick Litchfield wrote that Drane 'would trace the motive of some particular kind of decoration to the parent factory where this class of design was first in use, and he would then purchase, as opportunity offered, a representative example of the factory from which the Worcester artist had adopted his design'. These words could equally apply to Henry Marshall, who said of Robert Drane (in a letter to Leonard Crow, a leading dealer, on 9 January 1953): 'If he was not, as I think he was, the origin of comparative collecting, he was certainly the greatest exponent of it.'

In letters Marshall refers to sharing his enthusiasm with a fellow collector, H.W. Hughes (1862–1937). Writing to the latter's son, Ronald Hughes, in January 1944, he says:

> Out of the 1138 pieces listed in the inventory [of the Hughes Collection], I see that some 250 are of factories other than Dr Wall Worcester, many being, I assume, prototypes of the Dr Wall pieces, which seem to have interested your father almost as much as they do me. But we, in the company of old Robert Drane, seem to be the only Worcester collectors interested in these products of sundry other factories. I feel certain that at auction or if privately bid for by a dealer, these to your Father and me most interesting pieces, would fetch practically nothing. If I can arrange to see them I might make a bulk bid to take them off your hands.

Marshall purchased a significant number of items from the Hughes Collection, including items displayed in the 1939 Albert Amor exhibition.

During the eighteenth century there was no embargo on the importation of ceramics from China, although a tax was levied, varying from 12½ per cent at the beginning of the century to about 33 per cent in the 1760s and 50 per cent by 1790. The earliest English porcelain factories were founded in response to the large quantities of imports, and much porcelain of the 1750s and 1760s closely imitated or was inspired by the Chinese prototypes.

Japanese porcelain, particularly Kakiemon and Imari from the first twenty years of the eighteenth century, was more highly valued than Chinese because of its relative rarity, and fetched higher prices. By the 1740s almost all exports from Japan had ceased. Kakiemon was copied at Meissen, St Cloud and Chantilly from the 1720s but it is likely that English factories directly copied Japanese pieces as well as their Continental imitations.

Until 1775 legislation governed the importation of Continental porcelain for sale. However, as it could be legally imported for private use, this was easily circumvented. By 1753 Meissen was readily available in England, although from 1756 supplies were cut off with the outbreak of the Seven Years' War. French porcelain was similarly restricted by heavy duties and legislation, and also by conflicts between England and France. After 1775 it could be legally imported but with a 150 per cent duty, reducing to 12 per cent after 1786. However, enough was available in England to have an influence on the large range of coloured grounds, reserves painted with exotic birds, figure subjects after Jean-Antoine Watteau (1684–1721) and François Boucher (1703–1770), 'Hop Trellis' patterns and rich gilding, sometimes elaborately tooled, produced by English manufacturers.

English factories copied imported wares both as inspiration and as substitutes or replacements. Marshall attempted to distinguish these items by suggesting that an item was a design prototype if it became a standard Worcester pattern and, if it was a very close copy, it was more likely to be a replacement. Certainly imports from China, Japan, Germany and France set the standards to be matched by English factories. This was further complicated by inter-factory copying in England.

Following the Restoration the Huguenots had an enormous influence on the decorative arts of England. Anthony Supply (d. about 1750), associated with Chelsea, Charles Gouyn (1737–1785) of the St James's factory and the Duvivier family of decorators, as well as artists such as Simon François Ravenet (1706–1774) and Hubert-François Gravelot (1699–1773), were all of Huguenot extraction. Nicholas Sprimont (1716–1771), the founder of the Chelsea factory, although not a Huguenot, was born in Liège and arrived in England in 1740 as a fully trained goldsmith. These artists and craftsmen maintained links with the Continent and thus contributed to the styles being introduced into England. There is little evidence to suggest that English factories tried to employ craftsmen from the Continent, with the exception of Derby, which employed the modellers Pierre Stephan (fl. 1770–1819), Nicholas-François Gauron (b. 1736) and Jean-Jacques Spängler (fl. 1790–92).

Virtually no Chinese or Japanese and very few German practitioners are recorded in the English porcelain trade. The Seven Years' War, the presence of experienced Staffordshire potters and the different paste requiring different technology may have been factors affecting the apparent lack of Continental potters in England. Another may have been the existence of the Anti-Gallican Association, an informal group set up in about 1745, the year of a French-supported Jacobite invasion, to oppose the influx of French goods then coming into England and the pervasive cultural influence of France. Two of the three partners of the Battersea enamel factory are known to have been members of the Association.

Very little is known about copying between English factories. Until the Garrard Act of 1798 there was no copyright law protecting sculptural works of art and no system of registering patterns or designs until 1842. It would appear that very little value was put on originality in design and decoration in the eighteenth century. Plagiarism and imitation of imports were prevalent, not only in England but also on the Continent. Worcester copied Chelsea freely, particularly after 1768, and Worcester's own shapes, patterns and marks were widely copied in turn by other factories. Decorators also travelled between factories, which led to further similarities. However, no factories or decorators marketed their wares as direct imitations, with the exception of the London china and glass painter James Giles (1718–1780).

Worcester made replacement pieces for Oriental porcelain services, although the shapes differ slightly, as do the body and glaze. The company also made additional items, such as coffee cups, which were not always supplied with the original service. Other factories, in particular Derby, also made exact copies of Oriental porcelain. A description of Worcester porcelain for the tea table in the *Annual Register* for 1763 states that '… some of it is so well enamelled as to resemble the finest foreign china so that costly sets which are broken it makes up without a palpable difference'. In his *Survey of the City of Worcester* of 1764 Valentine Green (1739–1813) describes Worcester porcelain thus:

> the finer sort which is enamelled, so nearly resembles in every particular the finest oriental pieces, whether of China or Japan, that when it has been made in imitation of these, as has been often the case, in order to match and make up setts that have been broken, the difference is scarcely discernible even to judges themselves.

Early collectors gave the name 'Jesuit' to a distinctive style of decoration on Chinese porcelain, with figure subjects in black only or with some pink washes and gilding. This reflects the influence of Jesuit missionaries in China in the eighteenth century. The term was originally restricted to subjects taken from engravings in illustrated bibles, but subsequently used to describe any European subject drawn in black enamel. Worcester porcelain items decorated in this manner are usually considered to be replacement pieces for Chinese services.

Many questions remain to be answered. Marshall was justified in observing that 'The whole question of whether a pattern is originally Japanese, true Chinese or a Chinese copy of a Japanese pattern or even a painting by the Dutch on Chinese porcelain is very complicated'. There are also many other pieces in his collection that derive from Oriental or Continental designs but for which there is no accompanying prototype.

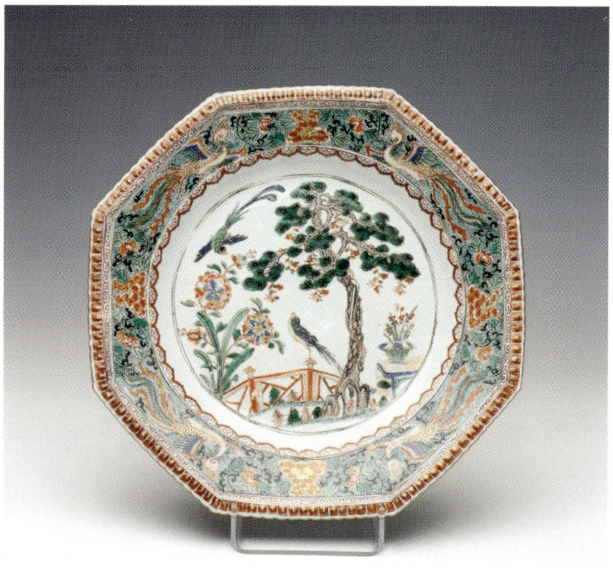

1

1

Chinese dish

1700–25
Diam. 34.7 cm
1957.24.1.157

Based on a European silver shape with gadrooned edge, painted in *famille verte* palette, red border with green stippling and four phoenixes; in centre two birds with acacia tree, fence and flower sprays.

PROVENANCE
H.R. Hancock & Sons, St James's, London, 12 June 1957, £70.

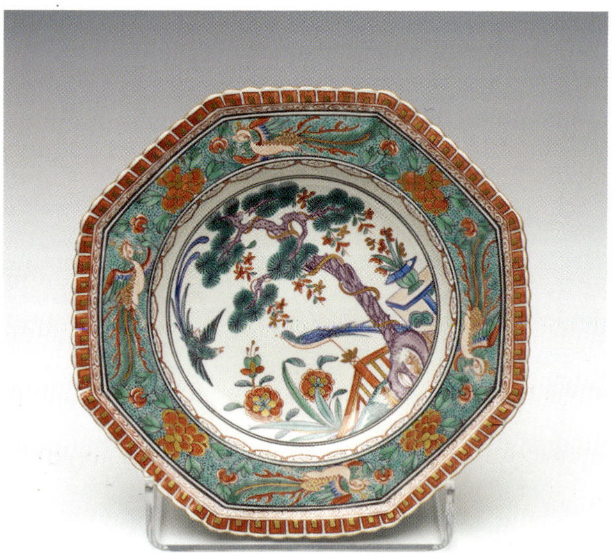

2

2

Dish

1778–80
Diam. 24.5 cm
1957.24.1.158

Close copy of a Chinese original.

REFERENCE
Spero and Sandon 1996, pl. 194.

3

Chinese vase

Early eighteenth century
Ht 29.1 cm
1957.24.1.155

Hexagonal shape with *kylin* handles, based on an ancient Chinese bronze wine vessel, decorated on all sides with Chinese figures, birds and insects. Similar vases can be seen in the British Museum and the Fitzwilliam Museum, Cambridge.

Opposite side shown on p. 28

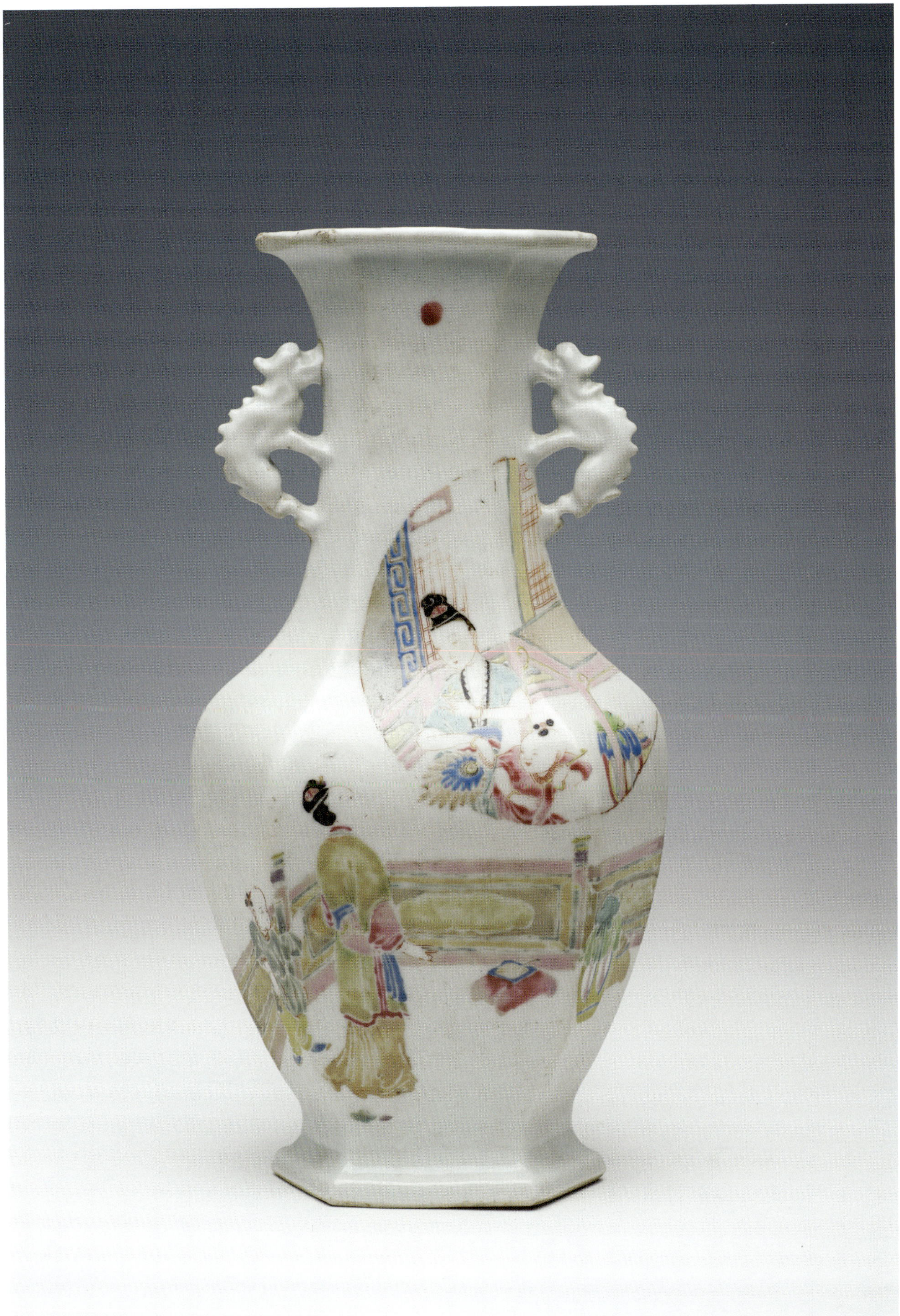

3

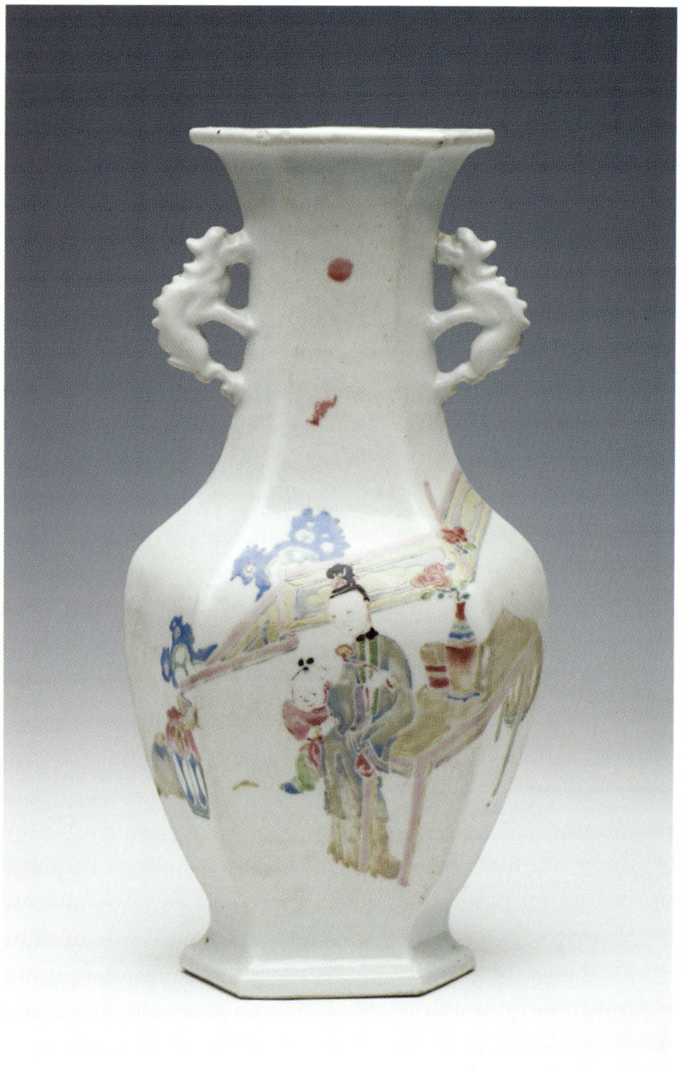

3

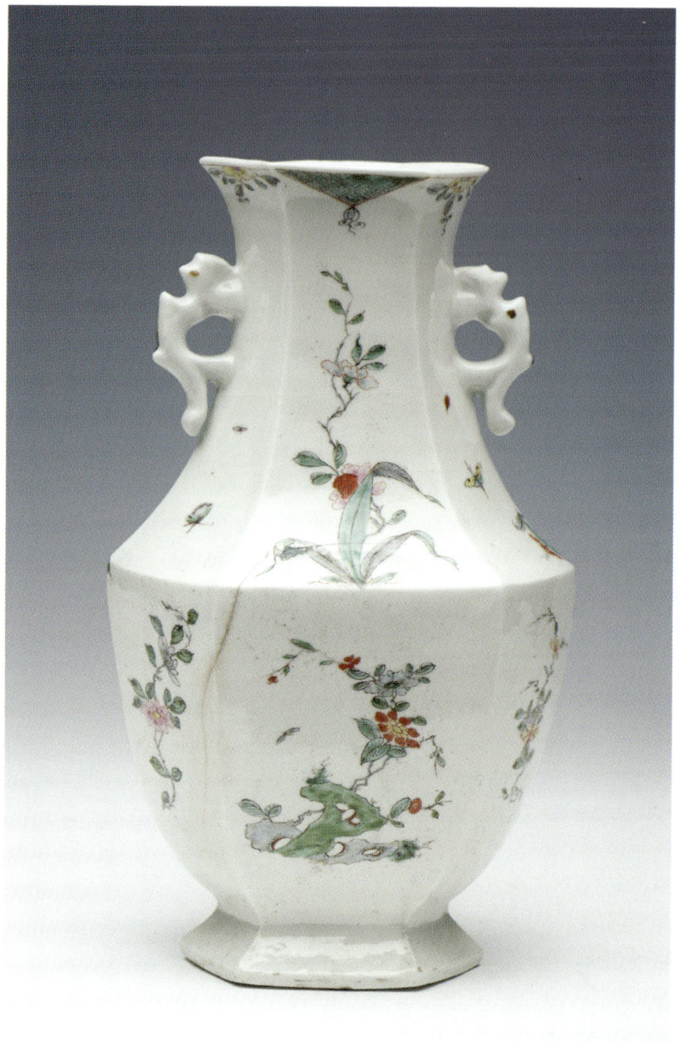

4

4

Vase

1753–4
Ht 26.5 cm
1957.24.1.159

Copy of a Chinese shape, decorated in a *famille rose* palette, with additional shrubs, flowers and insects. Marshall describes the handles as a 'travesty' of the Chinese version. Two other vases with the same decoration are in the British Museum (P&E 1938,3-14, 72, illustrated in Dawson 2007, p. 42) and the Museum of Fine Arts, Boston (1988.1048).

PROVENANCE
Sotheby's, London, 30 January 1942, lot 19.

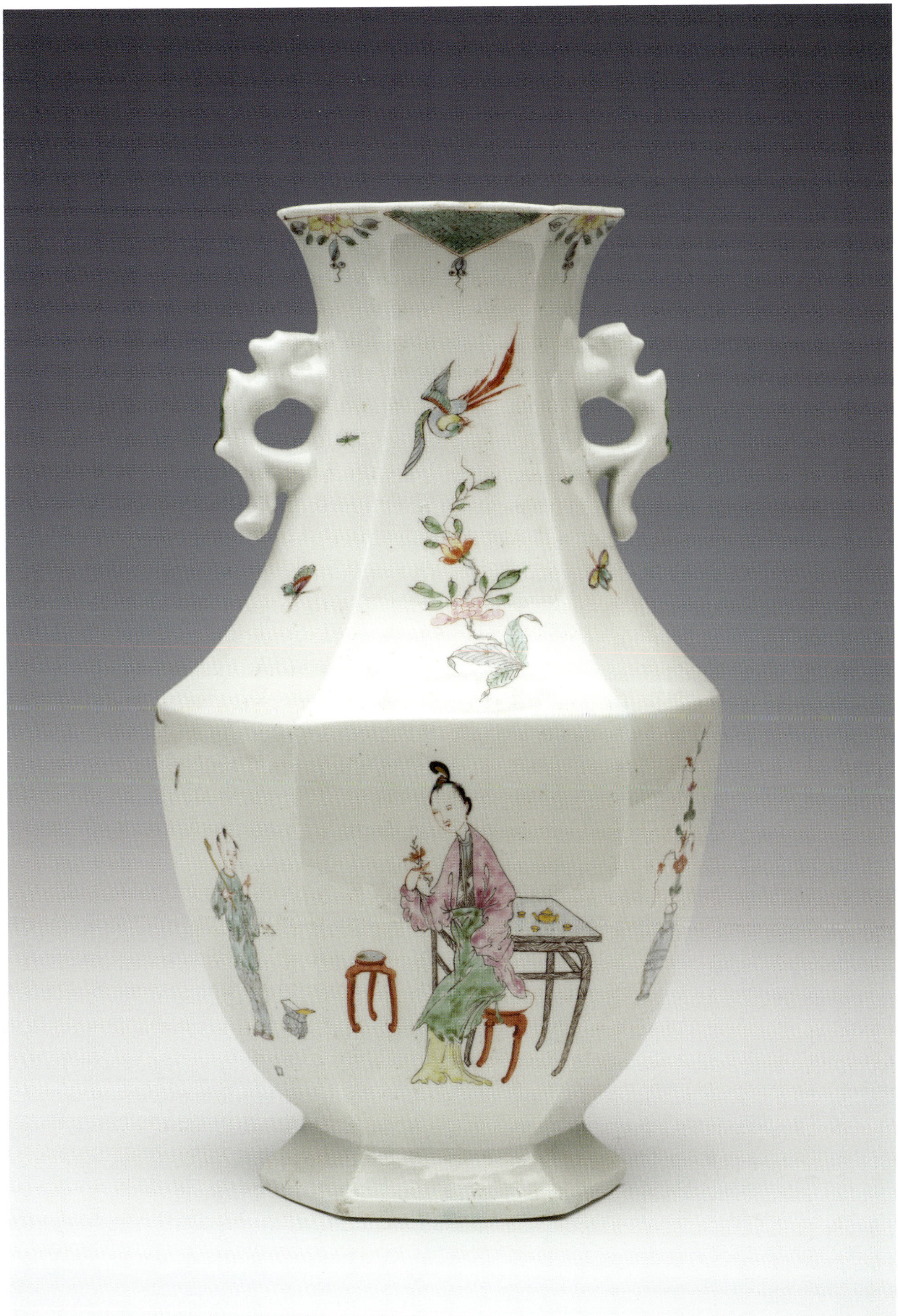

4

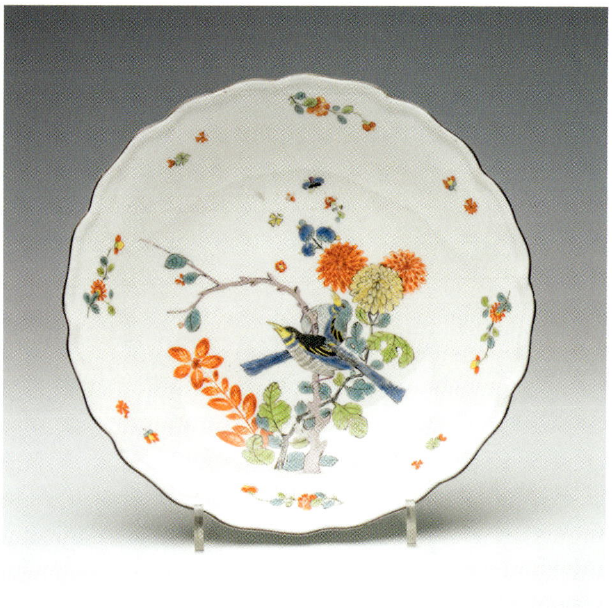

5

5

Meissen dish

1730–35
Diam. 23.9 cm
Mark: crossed swords in blue
1957.24.1.199

Indented rim with brown edge, decorated with two finch-like birds perched on a branch and chrysanthemum sprays on a white background, inspired by Japanese Kakiemon.

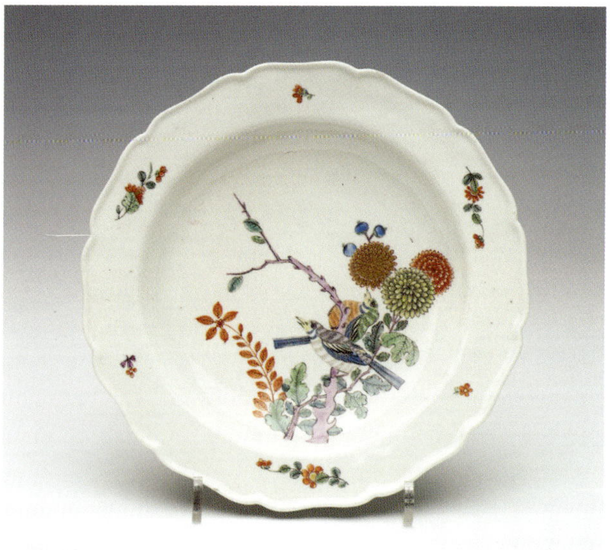

6

6

Deep plate

About 1765
Diam. 23.1 cm
1957.24.1.201

Wavy rim with plain edge, painted with two finch-like birds, possibly made as replacement for a Meissen service. A similar example in the Rode Hall Collection is illustrated in McKeown 2006, pl. 51.

REFERENCES
H. Sandon 1969, pl. 58; Spero 1984, pl. 61.

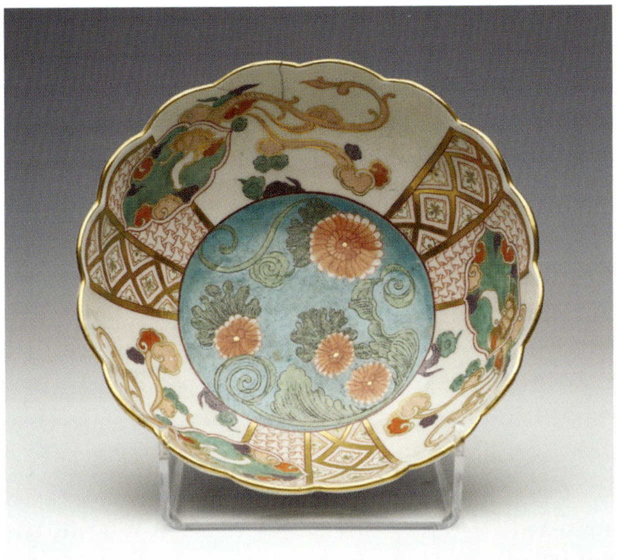

7

7

Chelsea bowl

1765–70
Ht 9.3 cm, diam. 25 cm
1957.24.1.187

Inspired by Japanese decoration but with no recognised pattern.

PROVENANCE
Albert Amor, London, 22 April 1949, £70 (with two Worcester bowls).

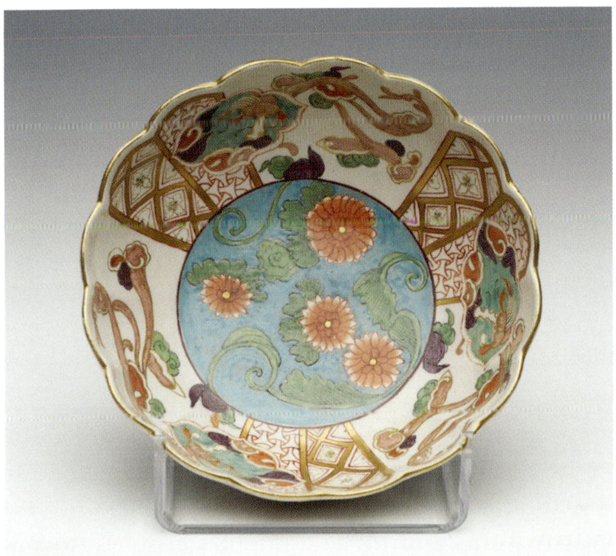

8

8

Bowl

About 1770
Ht 6.9 cm, diam. 19.6 cm
1957.24.1.188

Fluted, moulded body with scalloped gilt rim, painted with an unusual Imari-style design with four red chrysanthemums with green leaves on a turquoise ground in centre. Exterior decorated sparingly with foliage in red and gold with a border of turquoise gadroons.

REFERENCE
Ayers, Impey and Mallet 1990, pl. 351.

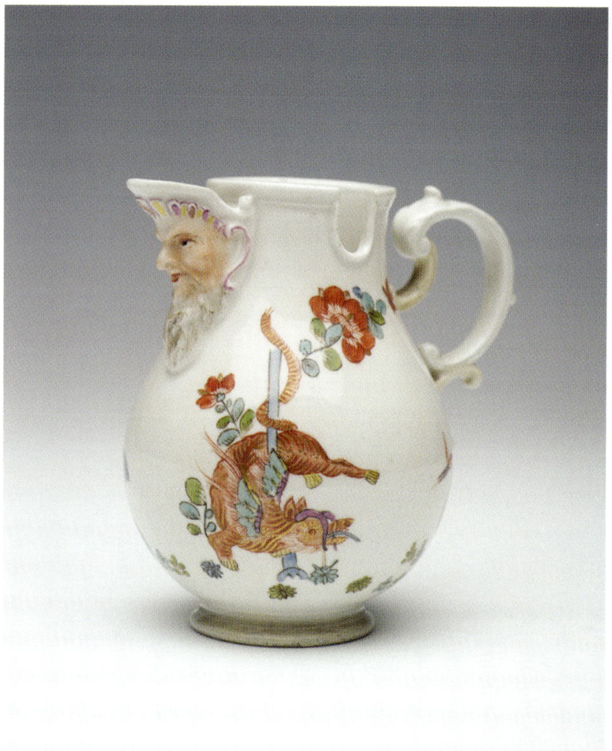

9

9

Meissen condiment pot

1740–50
Ht 12.1 cm
Mark: crossed swords
1957.24.1.233

Lacking cover, with bearded mask spout and aperture for spoon; Japanese-style decoration.

10

Chelsea bowl and Worcester saucer

Bowl 1750–52; saucer about 1770
Bowl ht 6.1 cm, diam. 7.8 cm; saucer diam. 12.9 cm
1957.24.1.225

Japanese-style decoration, mainly in iron red with a tiger and a dragon.

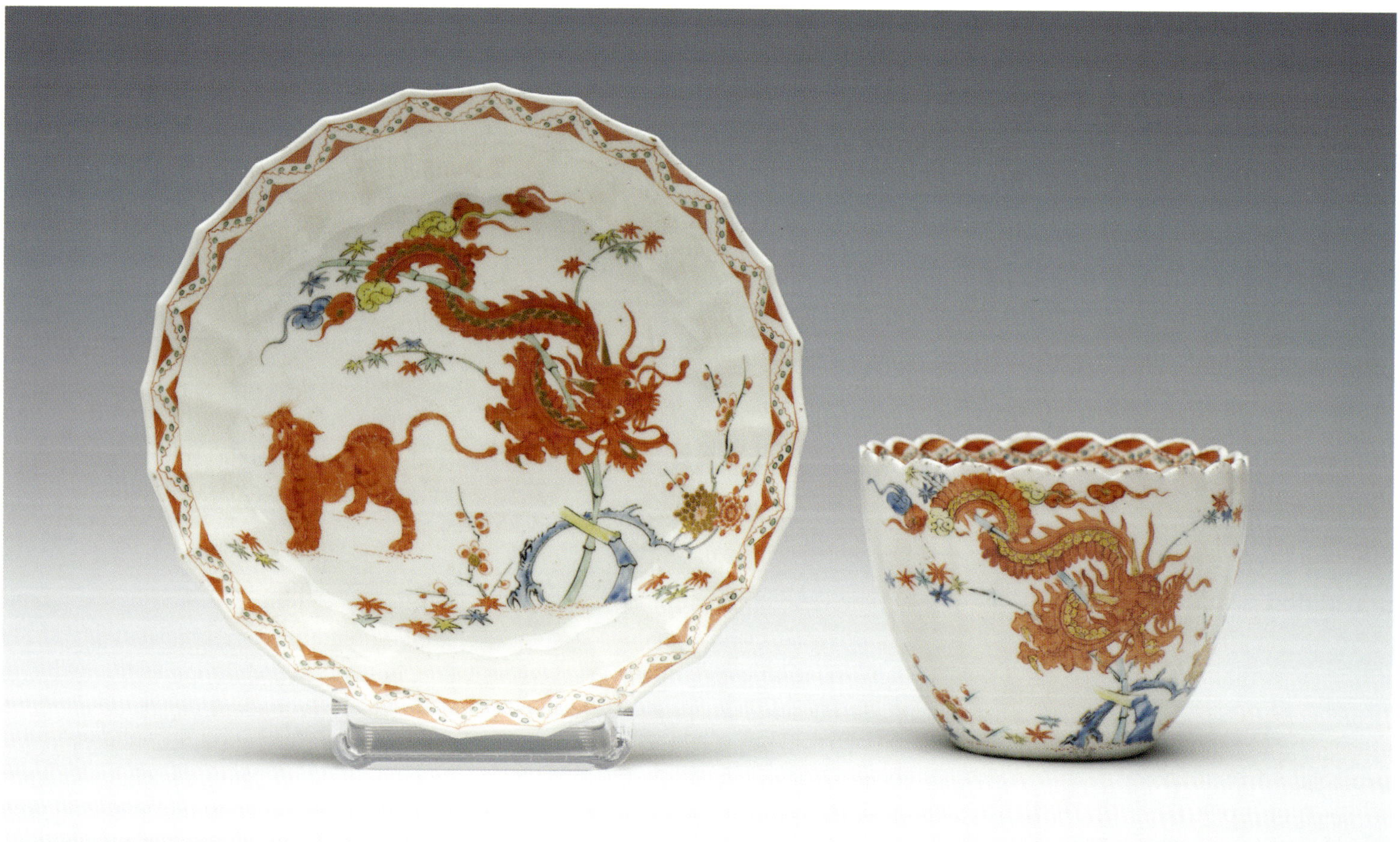

10

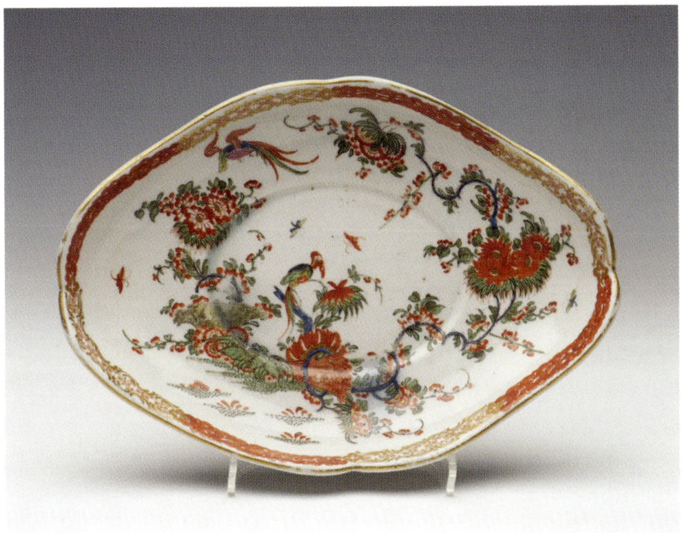

11

11

Chelsea tureen stand

1752–8
Length 23.6 cm, width 16.9 cm
1957.24.1.206

Japanese-style decoration in iron red, green and blue with ho-ho birds, wheatsheaves and chrysanthemums.

12, 13

Tureen, stand and ladle

About 1770
Tureen and stand ht 12.2 cm, length 13.5 cm (without handles); ladle length 16.5 cm
1957.24.1.269 and 275

Quatrelobed oval shape, shell handles, artichoke finial and alternating red and gold scrollwork border. Painted in the Rich Kakiemon palette with the 'Phoenix' pattern. A plate with the same pattern is illustrated in Spero and Sandon 1996, pl. 298, and a similar tureen sold at Bonhams, London, 23 April 2008, lot 195.

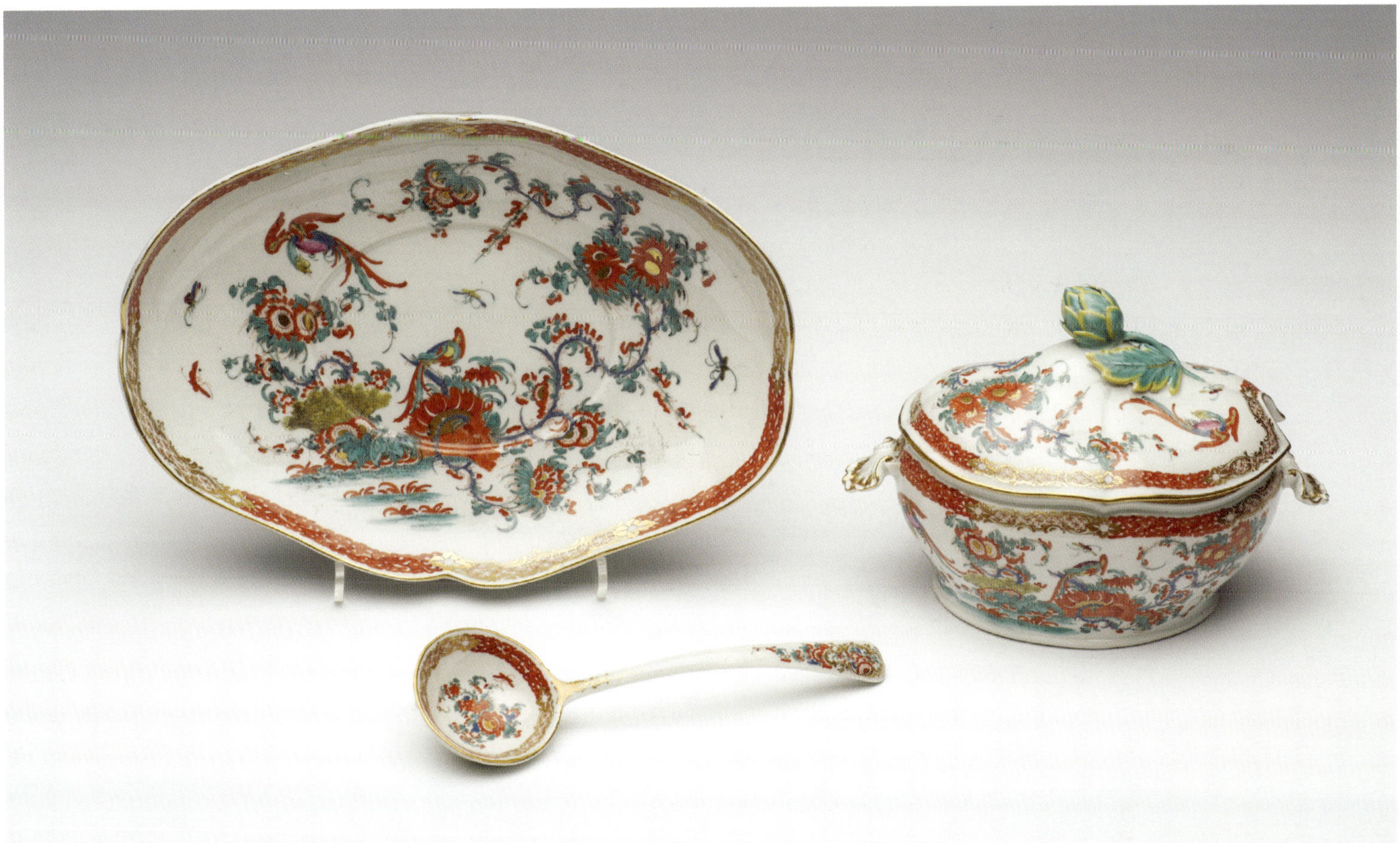

12, 13

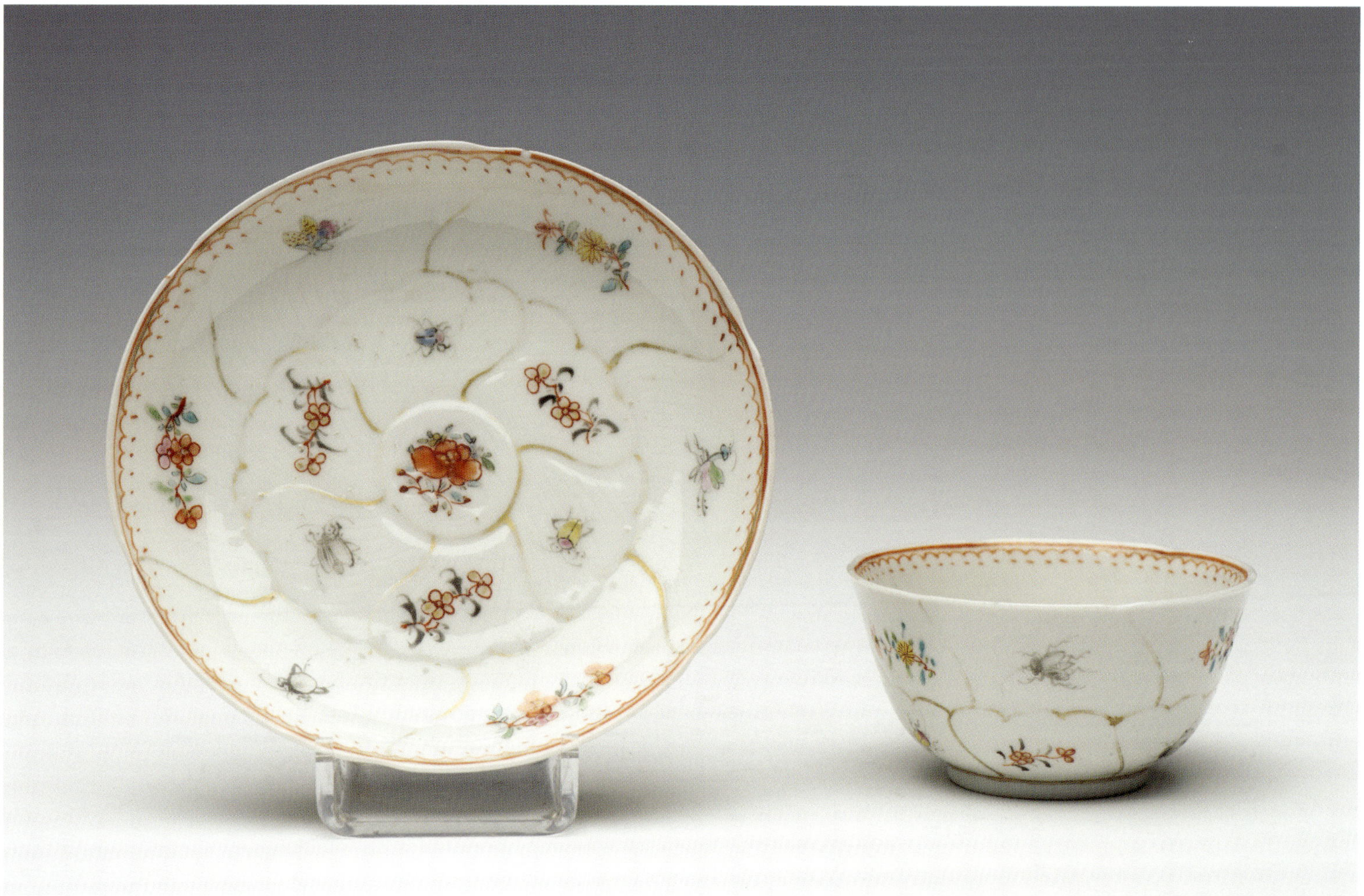

14

14

Chinese teabowl and saucer

Eighteenth century
Bowl ht 3.8 cm, diam. 7.2 cm; saucer diam. 11.5 cm
1957.24.1.232

Qianlong period, gold wavy line decoration, later referred to at Worcester as 'Gold Queen's' pattern, with alternating flower sprays and insects.

15

Bowl

1770–75
Ht 6.6 cm, diam. 14.8 cm
1957.24.1.231

Decorated outside the factory in 'Queen's' pattern with flowers and insects, copied from a Chinese original.

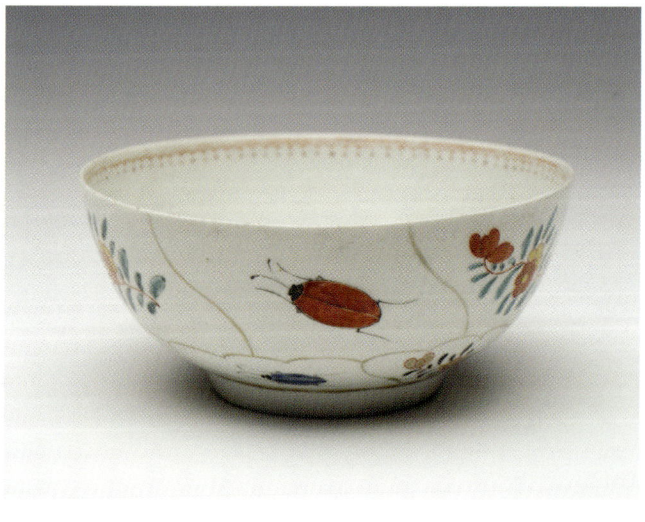

15

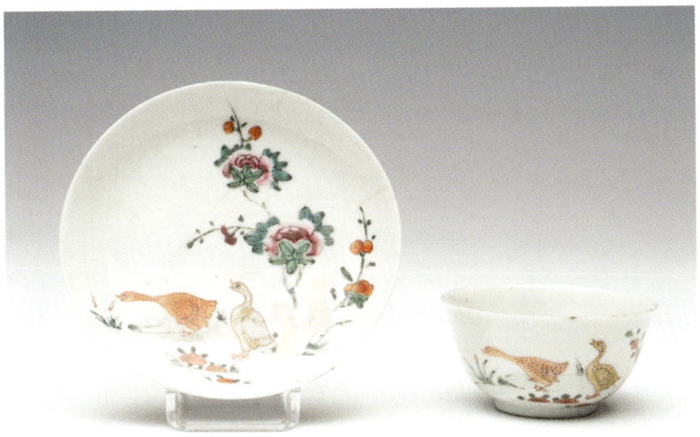

16

16

Chinese teabowl and saucer

Eighteenth century
Bowl ht 3.9 cm, diam. 7.4 cm; saucer diam. 11.6 cm
1957.24.1.197

Qianlong period, decorated with red and gold geese. This pattern was also used at the Longton Hall factory, Staffordshire.

PROVENANCE
H.W. Hughes Collection, 12 February 1944, no. 846.

17

Teabowl, coffee cup and saucer

About 1770
Bowl ht 4.2 cm, diam. 7.6 cm; cup ht 6.5 cm, diam. 6 cm; saucer diam. 12.1 cm
1957.24.1.196

Copy of a Chinese design.

PROVENANCE
H.W. Hughes Collection, 12 February 1944, no. 838.

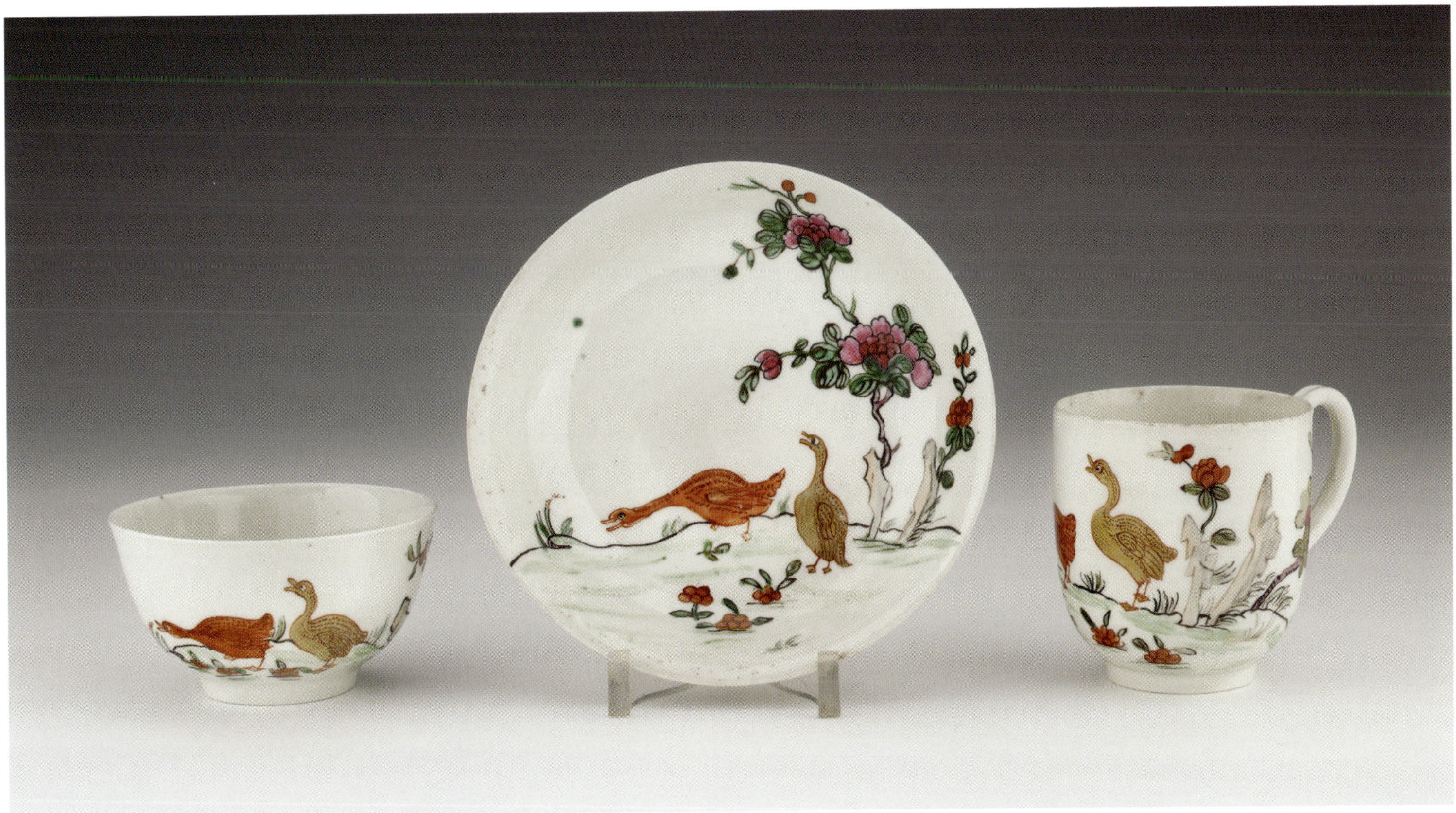

17

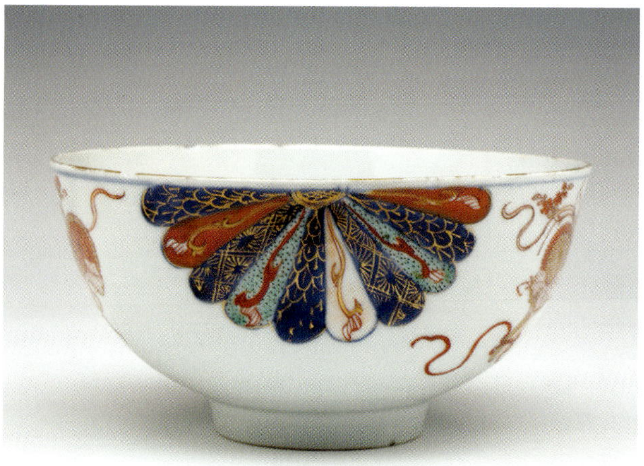

18

18

Chinese bowl

1750–1800
Ht 9.2 cm, diam. 17.9 cm
1957.24.1.170

Decorated on the exterior with two fans of ten leaves in red, blue, green and white, and red and gold chrysanthemum sprays with scrolls between.

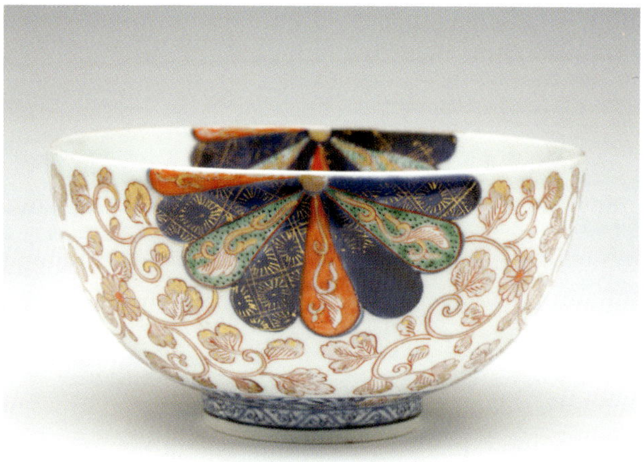

19

19

Japanese bowl

About 1720
Ht 8.1 cm, diam. 15.4 cm
1957.24.1.169

Decorated in Imari style, in strong underglaze blue with red, green and gold; two large stylised chrysanthemum flowers or fans on either side continuing over the rim. Continuous chrysanthemums and scrolls in red and gold on the outside; wavy blue scrolling around foot-rim.

20

Punch pot

About 1775
Ht 22.2 cm
1957.24.1.168

This pot would have been used for punch for drinking after fox hunting: inscribed *Tally Ho* beneath a running fox at base of spout. The Imari-style decoration was referred to as 'Old Japan Fan' pattern at Worcester, where it is mentioned in a sale catalogue of 1769.

PROVENANCE
Tilley & Co., London, 29 October 1949, £60.

REFERENCES
Ayers, Impey and Mallet 1990 pl. 353; Dawson 2007, pl. 37.

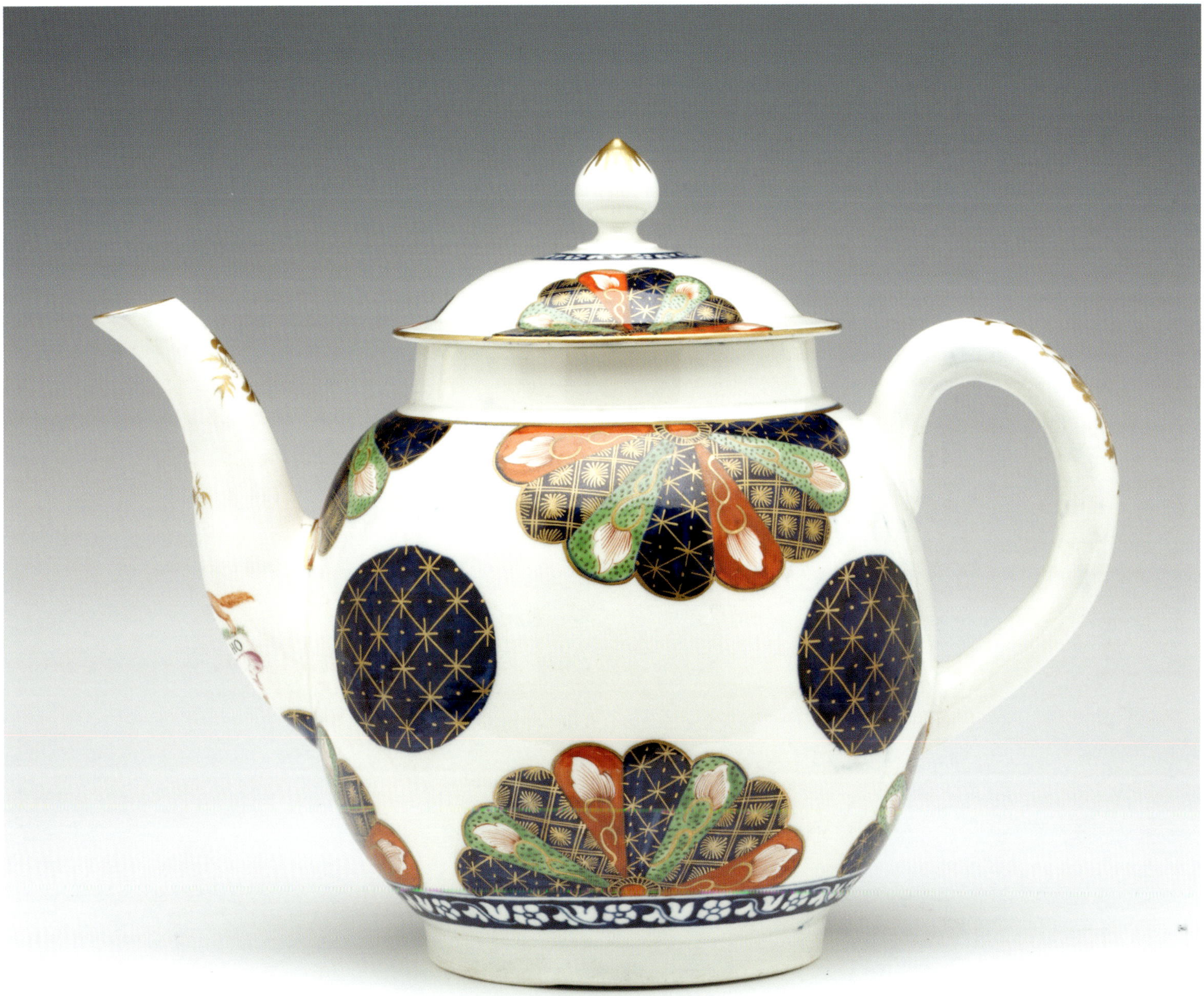

20

20 (detail)

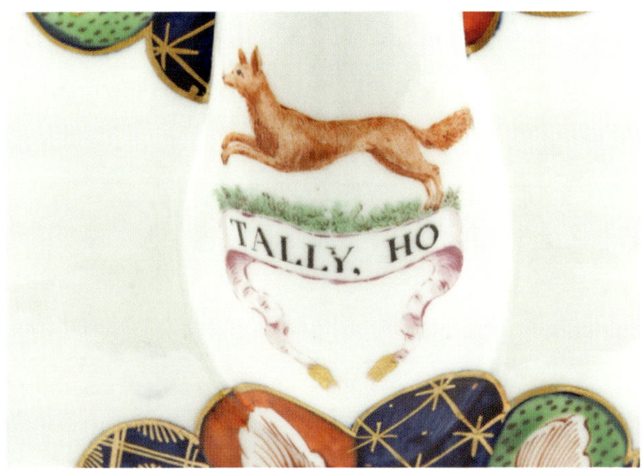

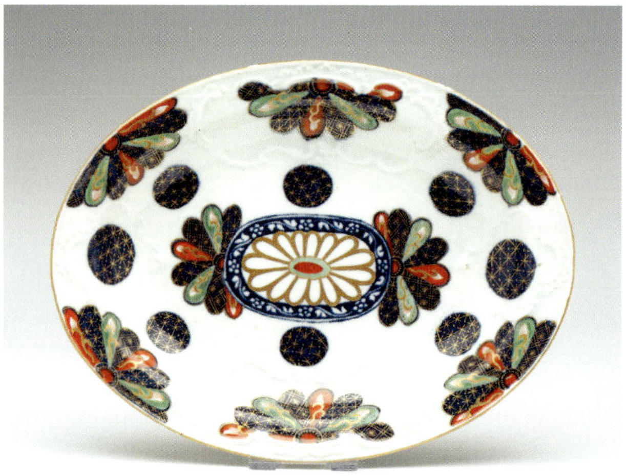

21

21

Dish

1768–75
Length 20 cm, width 15.6 cm
1957.24.1.710

Oval stand with four moulded rococo reserves, decorated in the 'Old Japan Fan' pattern with six fans around the edge, eight diapered blue circles around central underglaze blue oval with a gilt formal chrysanthemum in the centre and a fan at either end.

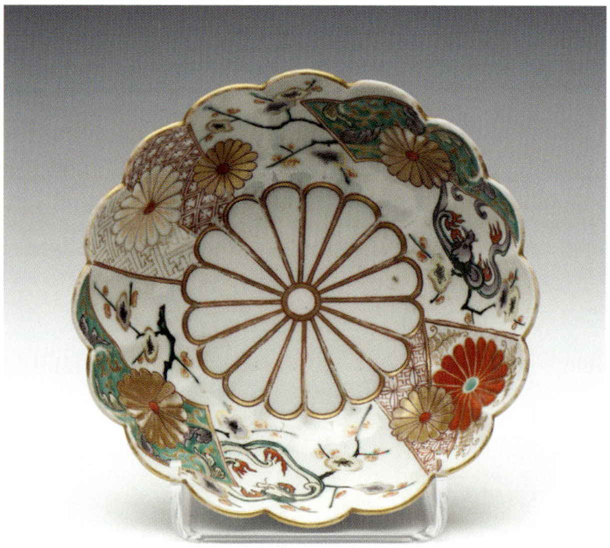

22

22

Japanese bowl

Early eighteenth century
Ht 5.7 cm, diam. 17.8 cm
1957.24.1.166

Moulded, scalloped shape, decorated in Imari style in red, green, pink and black enamels with gold. Central stylised chrysanthemum with moulded panels, outlined in red and gold; larger panels with dragons, prunus and fan-shapes, smaller ones with diapering and fans; red and gold chrysanthemums scattered throughout. Gold floral sprays with coloured accents on underside.

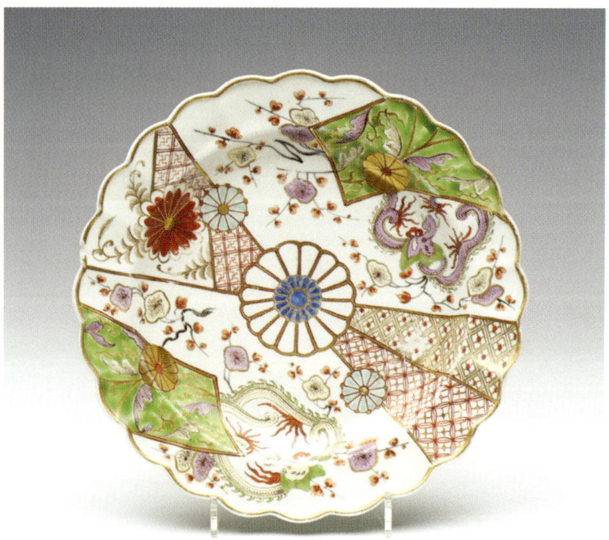

23

23

Plate

About 1772
Diam. 22.4 cm
1957.24.1.165

Adaptation of a Japanese Imari pattern, with irregular panels of dragons, prunus, chrysanthemums and diaper. This is sometimes referred to as the 'Brocade' pattern.

REFERENCES

Spero 1984, pl. 79; Spero and Sandon 1996, pl. 273; Ayers, Impey and Mallet 1990, pl. 352.

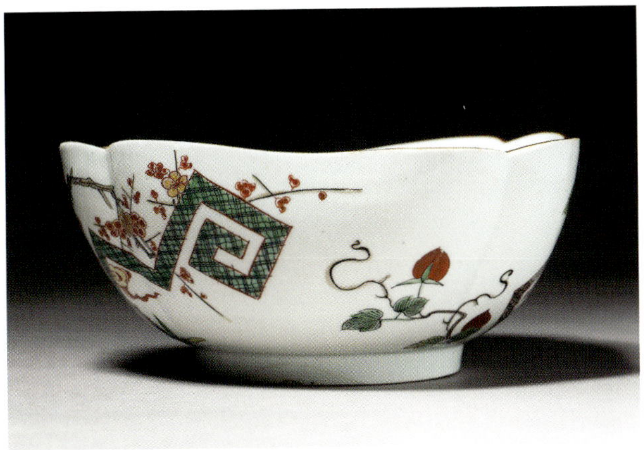

24

24

Japanese bowl

About 1700
Diam. 18.2 cm
EA1985.48

Square, lobed bowl, rounded sides with internal wave moulding in shallow relief around centre. Decorated in dark red, green, yellow, manganese and black enamels with gold, brown rim; two large lightning flashes, prunus tree and flowering plants on exterior, scrolling peony branches descending from interior rim.

REFERENCE
Ayers, Impey and Mallet 1990, pl. 212.

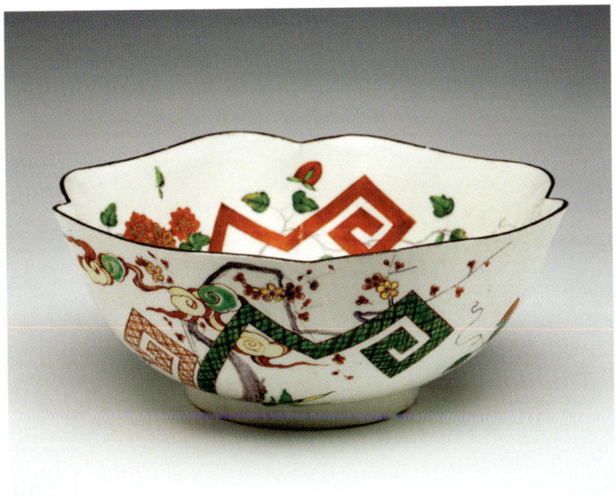

25

25

Derby bowl

1760–65
Ht 9.9 cm, diam. 25.5 cm
1957.24.1.257

Based on a Japanese Arita prototype but lacking the wave moulded interior; the exterior decoration is repeated on the interior. This was previously thought to be Worcester but has now been reattributed to Derby. Originally considered to be unique, other examples are known, including those at the National Trust house, Erddig, near Wrexham (invs. 1145586.1 and 2) and in the Davids Samling Museum, Copenhagen (inv. 23/1971).

PROVENANCE
Leonard Crow, 8 June 1956, £175.

REFERENCE
Ayers, Impey and Mallet 1990, pl. 347.

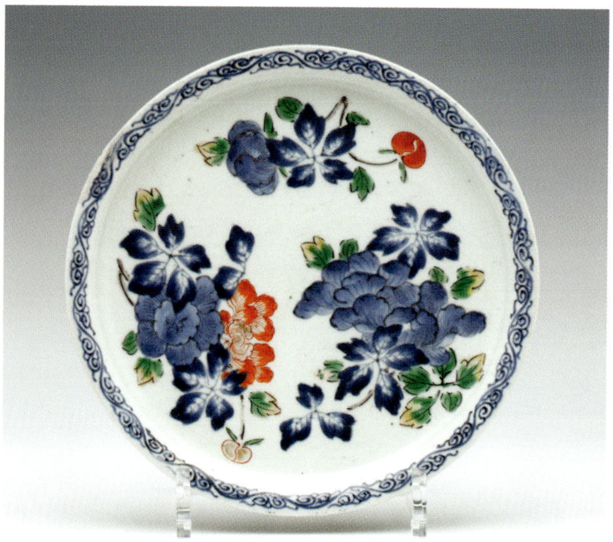

26

26

Japanese plate

About 1700
Diam. 20.5 cm
Mark: six-character Chinese Ch'eng Hua reign mark within a blue circle
1957.24.2.178

Painted in Imari style with two large sprays of peonies in underglaze blue with red, green and yellow flowers and leaves; continuous underglaze blue scroll on rim. On reverse, red flowering scroll with blue flowers and red-washed leaves above blue line.

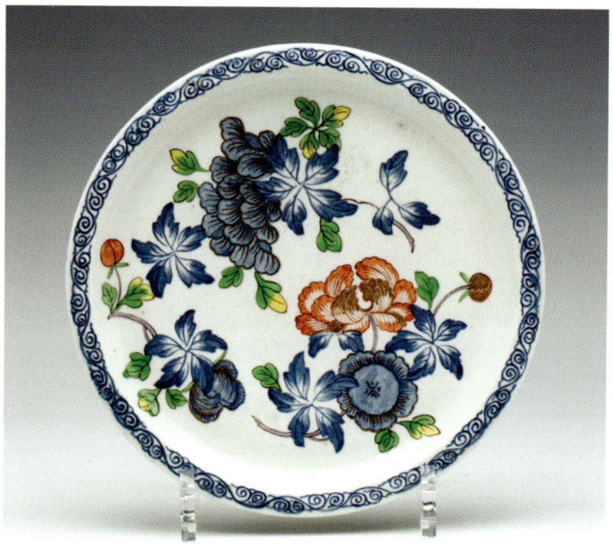

27

27

Plate

About 1770
Diam. 20.2 cm
Mark: simulated Chinese Ch'eng Hua reign mark with six characters
1957.24.1.177

An exact copy of an Arita original in both decoration and form, with an unusual flat rim, made as a replacement for a Japanese service belonging to Sir John Sebright Bt of Worcestershire. A similar plate is in the Museum of Royal Worcester Porcelain.

REFERENCES
Sandon 1993, p. 307; Spero 1984, col. pl. 20.

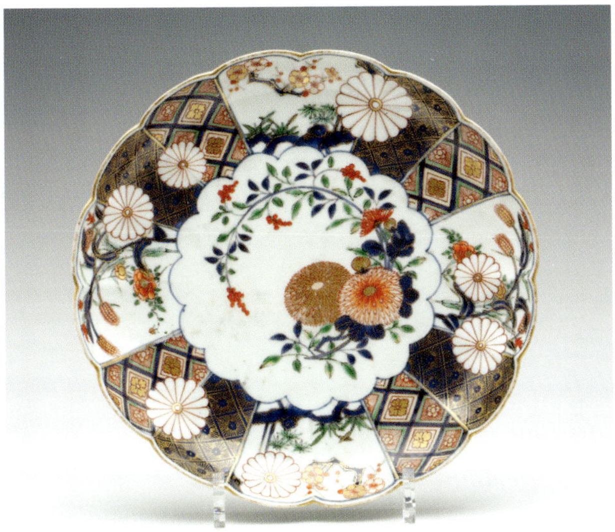

28

28

Japanese plate

About 1700
Diam. 23.4 cm
1957.24.1.189

Lobed plate with curved moulded sides, decorated in Imari style in underglaze blue, red and green enamels with gold; central asymmetric floral spray with chrysanthemums, panelled border with diaper patterns and stylised flowers. Elaborate scrolling with camellia floral decoration on reverse.

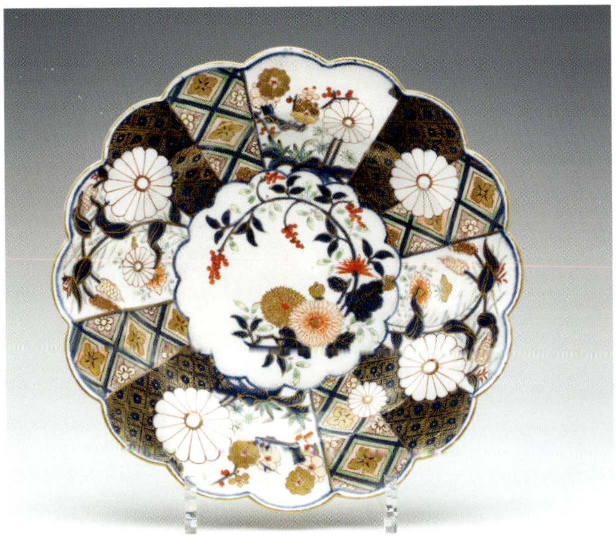

29

29

Chelsea plate

1752–8
Diam. 24.1 cm
Mark: none
1957.24.1.190

Painted after an Imari original in underglaze blue, enamels and gilt on a Meissen shape. Described in the 1756 Chelsea sale catalogue as 'rare (or fine) old japan pattern blue and gold'. Some items in this service bear the Chelsea blue anchor mark.

REFERENCES
Ayers, Impey and Mallet 1990, pl. 345; Bonhams, London, 8 April 2009, lot 62.

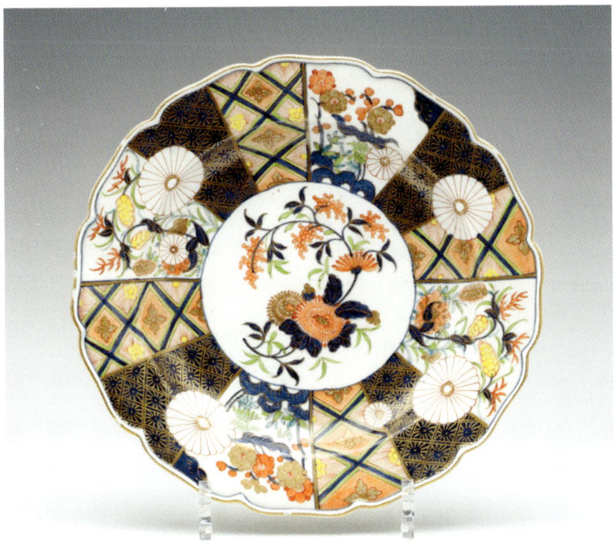

30

30

Plate

About 1772
Diam. 23.8 cm
Mark: underglaze blue anchor
1957.24.1.191

The presence of a blue anchor mark suggests that this may be a copy of or replacement for a Chelsea plate copying a Japanese original. Simple floral decoration on reverse.

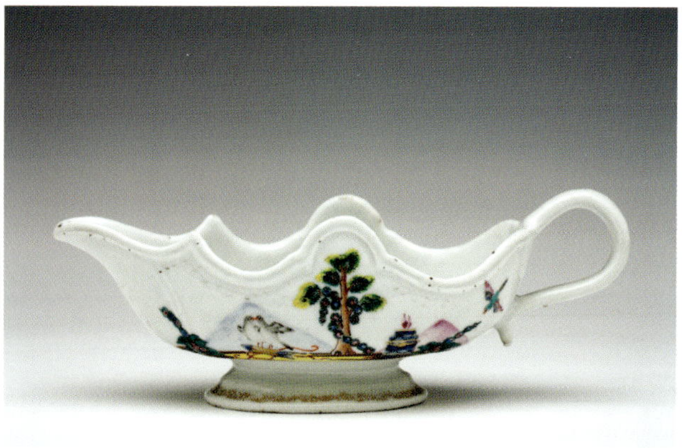

31

31

Chinese sauceboat

Eighteenth century
Ht 9.4 cm, length 24.8 cm, width 10.5 cm
1957.24.1.203

Decorated with the so-called 'Valentine' pattern with a bird of happiness, flaming hearts on an altar, bridal wreath on a tree and two birds billing on a quiver. The original design was drawn by Peircy Brett (1709–1781) for Commodore Anson (1697–1762), depicting a garlanded breadfruit tree on Tinian Island, Pacific Ocean, and was subsequently used on many Chinese export services. It is doubtful whether this is a prototype or an Oriental copy of a Western design, the inspiration for which was originally derived from China.

REFERENCE
Sandon 1993, p. 353.

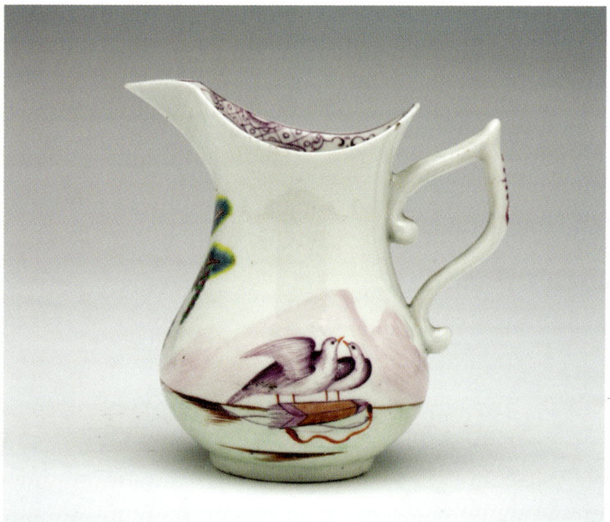

32

32

Cream jug

1758–62
Ht 7.9 cm, max. diam. 8.5 cm
1957.24.1.204

Plain silver shape with peaked handle, purple rococo border inside rim, decorated in a distinctive palette with the 'Valentine' pattern, introduced at Worcester about 1757–8. A teapot in this pattern from the Crane Collection is illustrated in *The Crane Collection of 18th-Century English Porcelain*, auction cat., Bonhams, 31 March 2010, lot 124.

PROVENANCE
Harold Davis, St James's, London, 30 December 1943, £7.

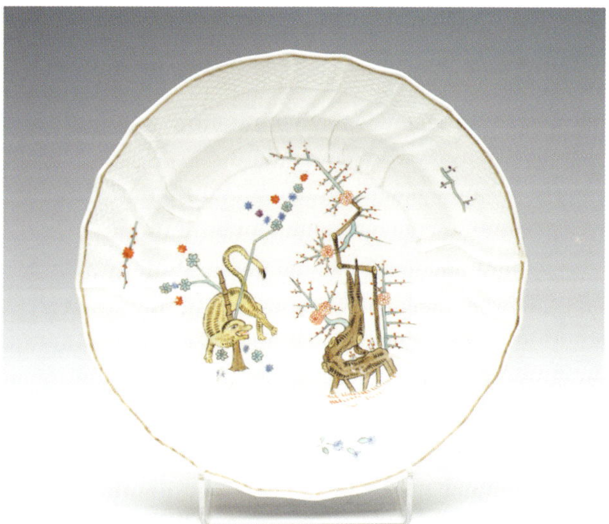

33

33

Caughley plate

About 1780
Diam. 23.1 cm
1957.24.1.181

Although in a different palette, the decoration on this plate and on no. 34 is inspired by Meissen after a Japanese design. A Worcester plate with a similar design and a brown edge is illustrated in Spero and Sandon 1996, pl. 284.

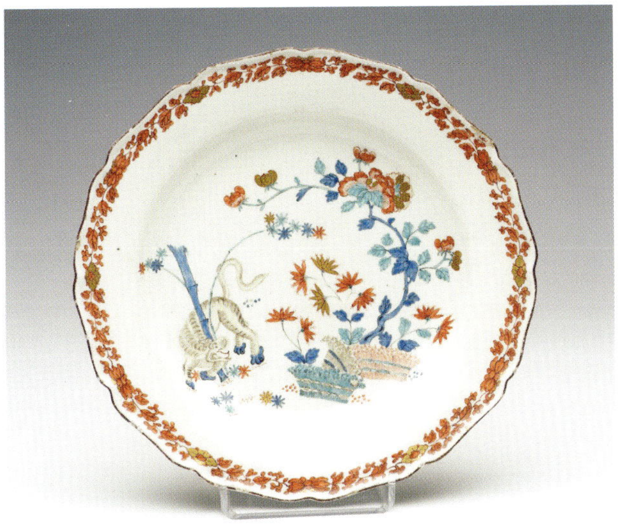

34

34

Deep plate

1770–72
Diam. 22.6 cm
1957.24.1.180

Decorated in Kakiemon style with a tiger and wheatsheaf pattern and an iron red border. Worcester made two distinctly different versions of the 'Yellow Tiger' pattern, one closely following Meissen, as in the Caughley example. The other closely follows Chelsea of the red anchor period and includes banded hedges and a floral border.

REFERENCE
Sandon 1993, p. 372.

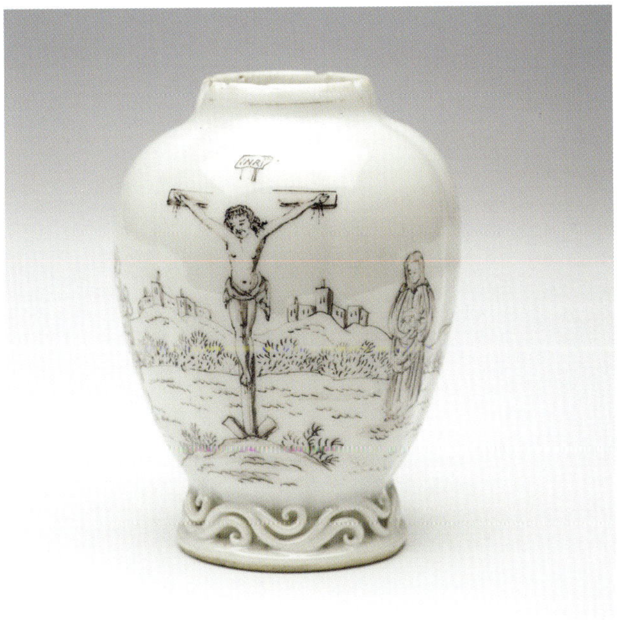

35

35

Chinese tea canister

About 1750
Ht 10 cm
1957.24.1.793

Pencilled decoration of a crucifixion scene with European buildings.

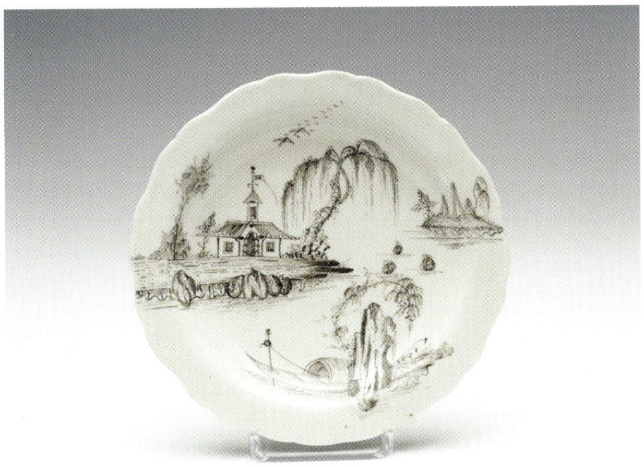

36

36

Fingerbowl stand

1755–8
Diam. 15.5 cm
1957.24.1.792

Pencilled decoration of Oriental landscape with a church, water and boats. A teabowl and saucer with a pencilled church scene is illustrated in Spero and Sandon 1996, pl. 60.

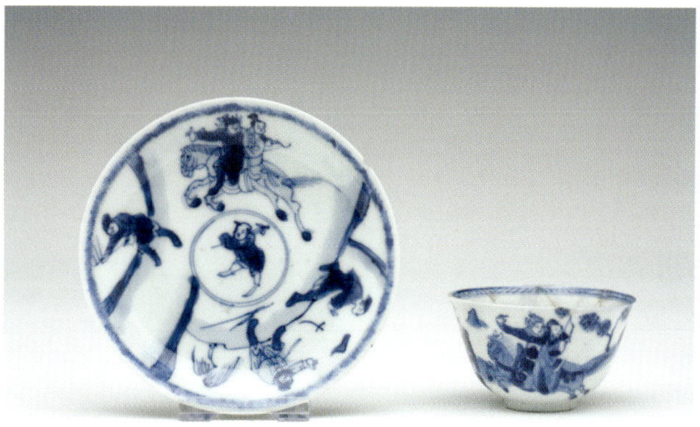

37

37

Chinese teabowl and saucer

1700–30
Bowl ht 3.2 cm, diam. 6 cm; saucer diam. 10 cm
1957.24.1.218

An original Kangxi design from the late seventeenth century in underglaze blue, showing an Imperial hunting scene with attendant figures holding banners. The name 'Eloping Bride' was given to this design by Victorian collectors who misunderstood the pattern.

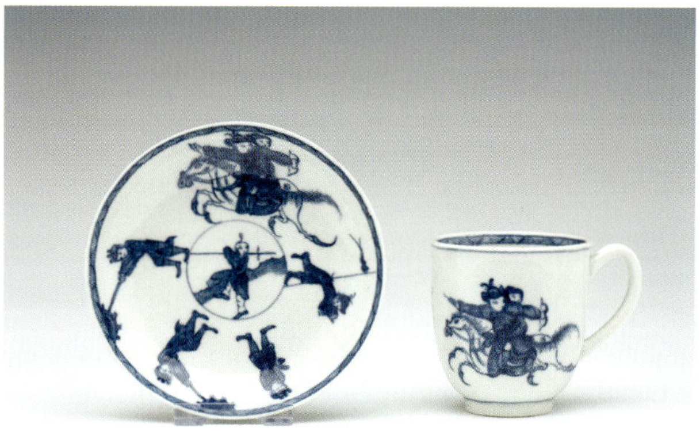

38

38

Coffee cup and saucer

About 1770
Cup ht 6.1.cm, diam. 5.6 cm; saucer diam. 10.3 cm
Mark: workman's mark and pseudo-Chinese mark on both
1957.24.1.219

Based on a Chinese original but slightly simplified by elimination of some of the background, this pattern only appears on teawares. Instead of hooves, the horses now appear to have talons.

REFERENCE

Branyan, French and Sandon 1981, pattern no. I.A.20.

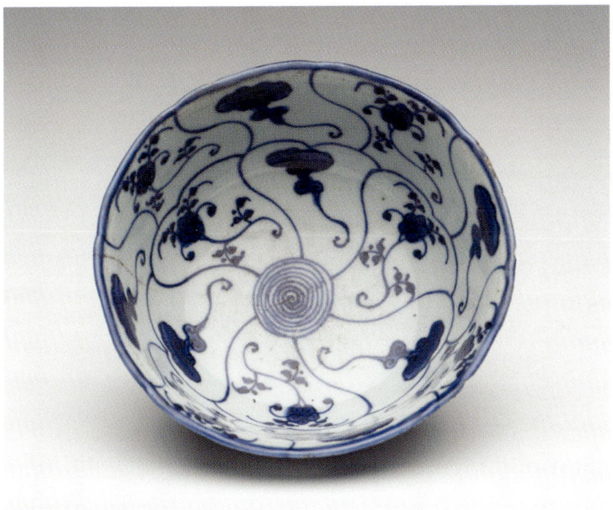

39

39

Chinese bowl

1750–70
Ht 7 cm, diam. 14.7 cm
1957.24.1.1074

Decorated both inside and out in underglaze blue with a double row of flower heads within wavy compartments outlined in blue.

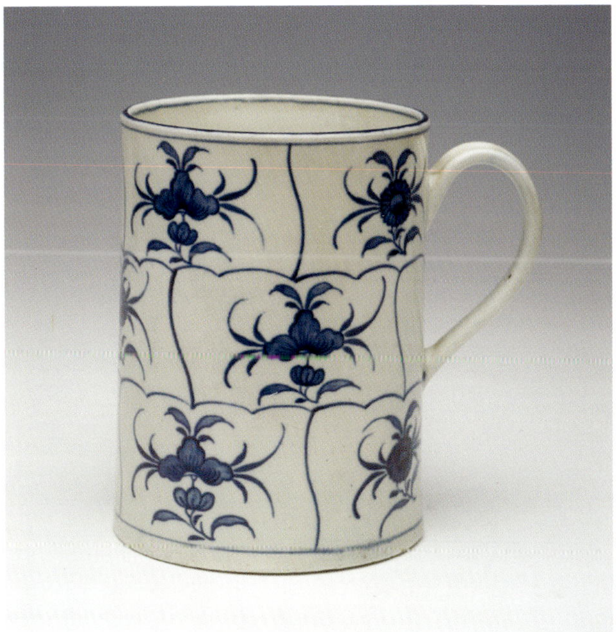

40

40

Mug

About 1770
Ht 14.1 cm, diam. 9.9 cm
Mark: *W* enclosed in an oblong.
1957.24.1.1012

Underglaze blue decoration, derived from a Chinese design, with twelve irregularly shaped panels each containing a formal flower. This is known as the 'Floral Queen's' pattern, in respect of the gold design with petal-shaped panels, called 'Gold Queen's' pattern. A Japanese bowl with the same design is illustrated in Hobson 1910, pl. XXXI, fig. 2.

REFERENCE
Branyan, French and Sandon 1981, pattern no. I.F.5.

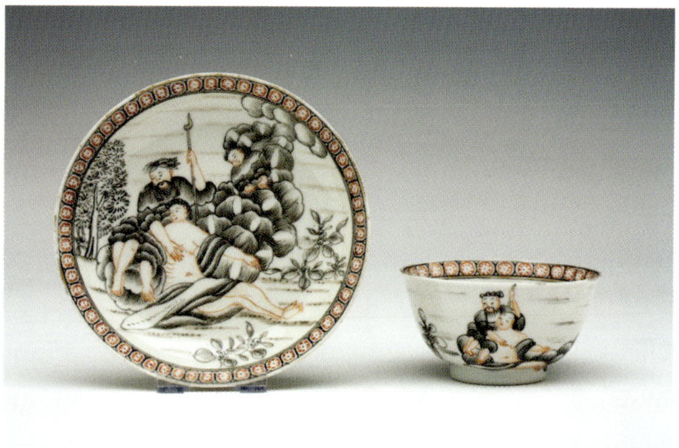

41

41

Chinese teabowl and saucer

Eighteenth century

Bowl ht 4.7 cm, diam. 7 cm; saucer diam. 11.8 cm

1957.24.1.161

Decorated in Jesuit style (see p. 25) with a scene drawn in black and red. Once considered to represent the Good Samaritan, it is now thought to show an episode in Ovid's *Metamorphoses*, possibly after a painting by Bartholomeus Spranger (1546–1611).

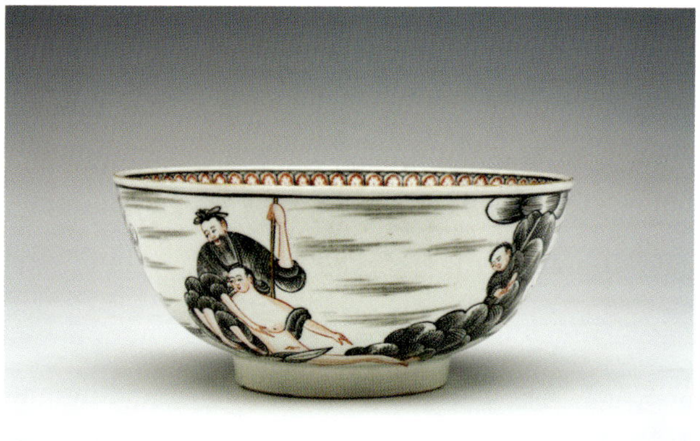

42

42

Caughley bowl

About 1795

Ht 7.4 cm, diam. 16 cm

1957.24.1.162

Painted in Chinese Jesuit style with a repeated scene of the Good Samaritan, possibly decorated outside the factory.

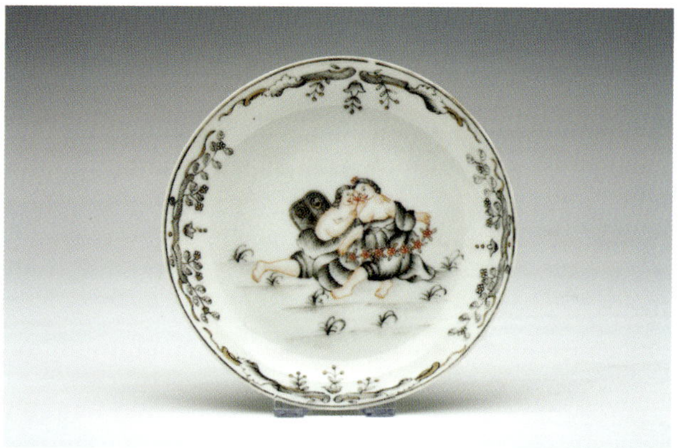

43

43

Chinese saucer

Qianlong period

Diam. 12.1 cm

1957.24.1.163

Pencilled decoration in Jesuit style with two European lovers.

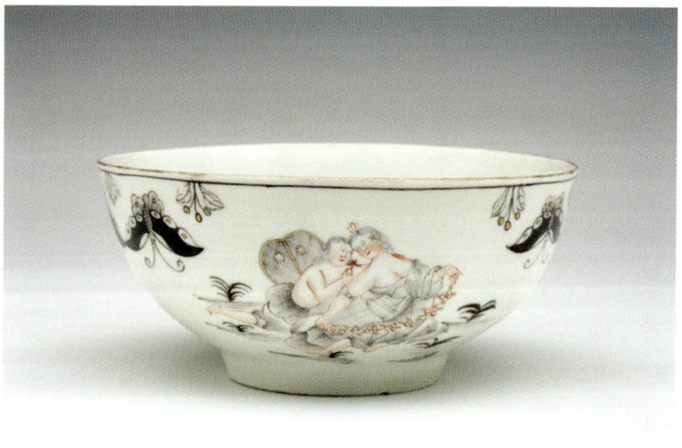

44

44

Bowl

About 1765

Ht 7.2 cm, diam. 15.6 cm

1957.24.1.164

Pencilled decoration in Jesuit style with two European lovers and bold border of three butterflies, wings spread.

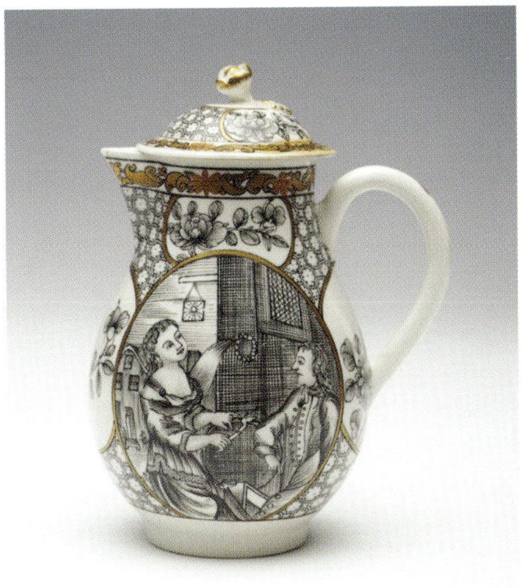

45

45

Covered milk jug

About 1770
Ht 14.1 cm
1957.24.1.785

Decorated in Chinese Jesuit style with European figures, all drawn in black with gilding. On each side is an oval panel with a European man and woman in eighteenth-century costume. Floral decoration at the base of the handle and below spout; the rest of the ground is diapered.

PROVENANCE
Cecil Davis, New Bond Street, London, 6 July 1944, £20.

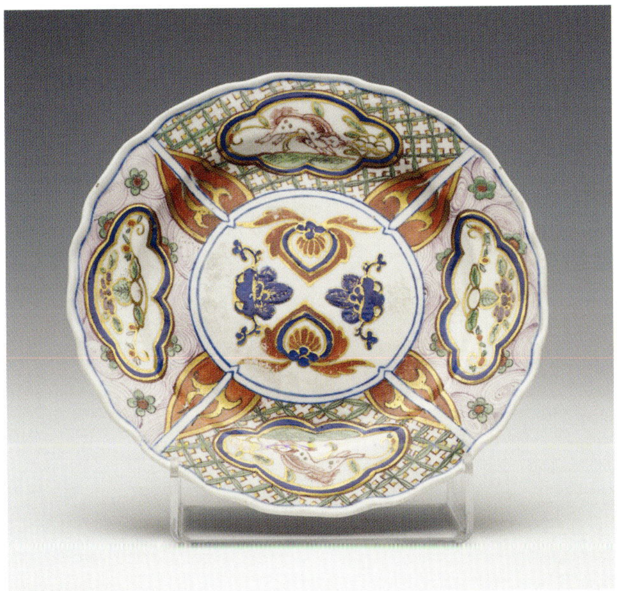

46

46

Derby plate

About 1775
Diam. 17.8 cm
Mark: pseudo-Chinese mark
1957.24.1.184

Decorated in Japanese style with no. 3 from the Derby pattern book.

REFERENCE
Ayers, Impey and Mallet 1990, pl. 356.

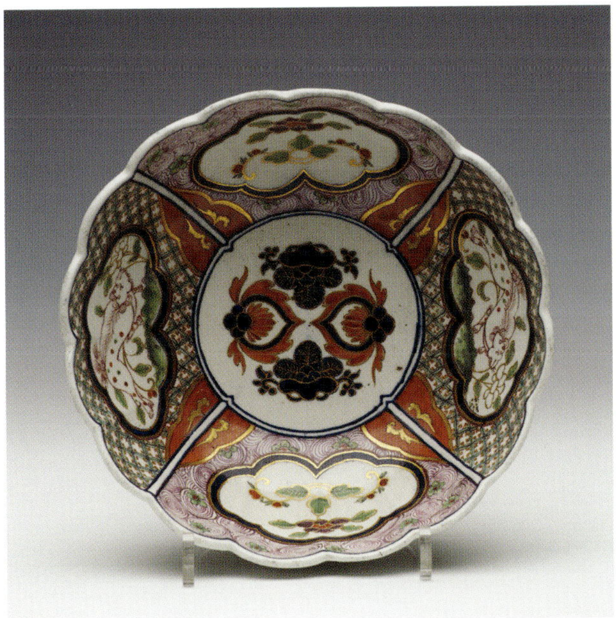

47

47

Bowl

1775–80
Ht 7.7 cm, diam. 21.8 cm
Mark: pseudo-Chinese mark
1957.24.1.179

Directly copied from no. 3 in the Derby pattern book, which is taken from an Arita prototype.

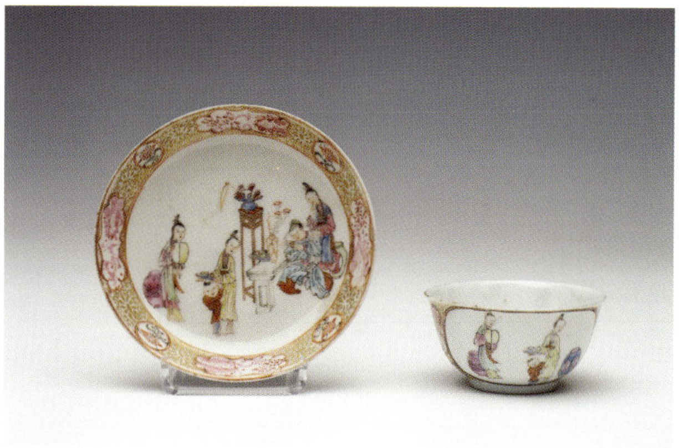

48

48

Chinese teabowl and saucer

Eighteenth century
Bowl ht 3.9 cm, diam. 7.5 cm; saucer diam. 11.4 cm
1957.24.1.172

Qianlong period, arabesque border with Chinese figures in centre.

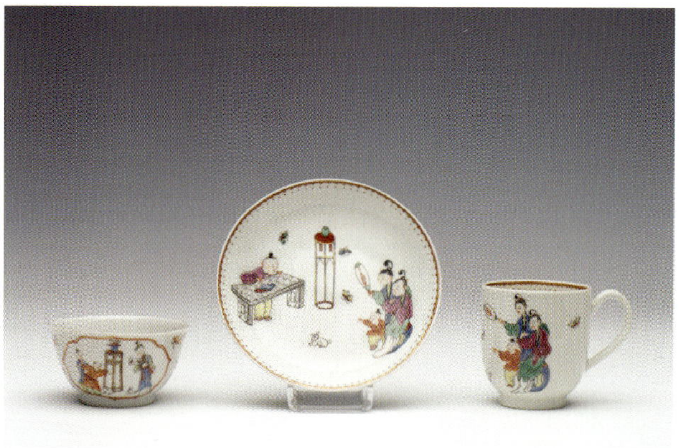

49

49

Chinese teabowl, Worcester coffee cup and saucer

About 1770
Bowl ht 4.1 cm, diam. 7.5 cm; cup ht 6.4 cm, diam. 5.7 cm; saucer diam. 11.8 cm
1957.24.1.228

Decorated with Chinese figural scenes enclosed in irregular cartouche on the Chinese teabowl.

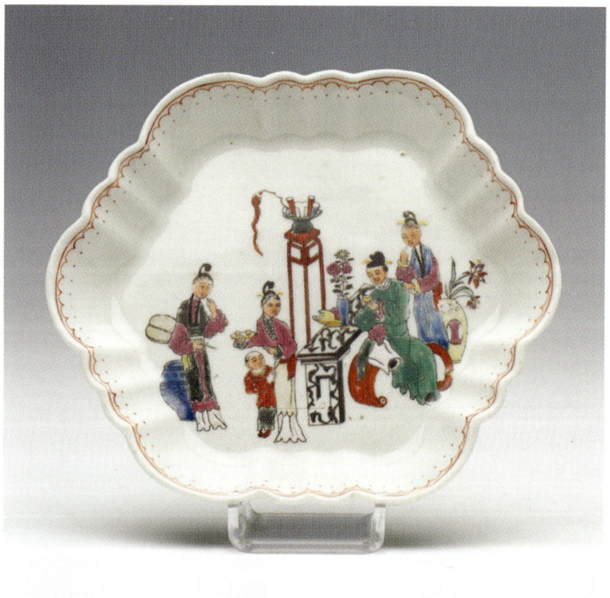

50

50

Teapot and stand

About 1775
Teapot ht 13.8 cm; stand diam. 14.7 cm
1957.24.1.171

Decorated with an outline print of women and child, coloured with enamels. This copy of the 'Chinese Family' design always has a red crowfoot border.

REFERENCE
Sandon 1993, p. 109.

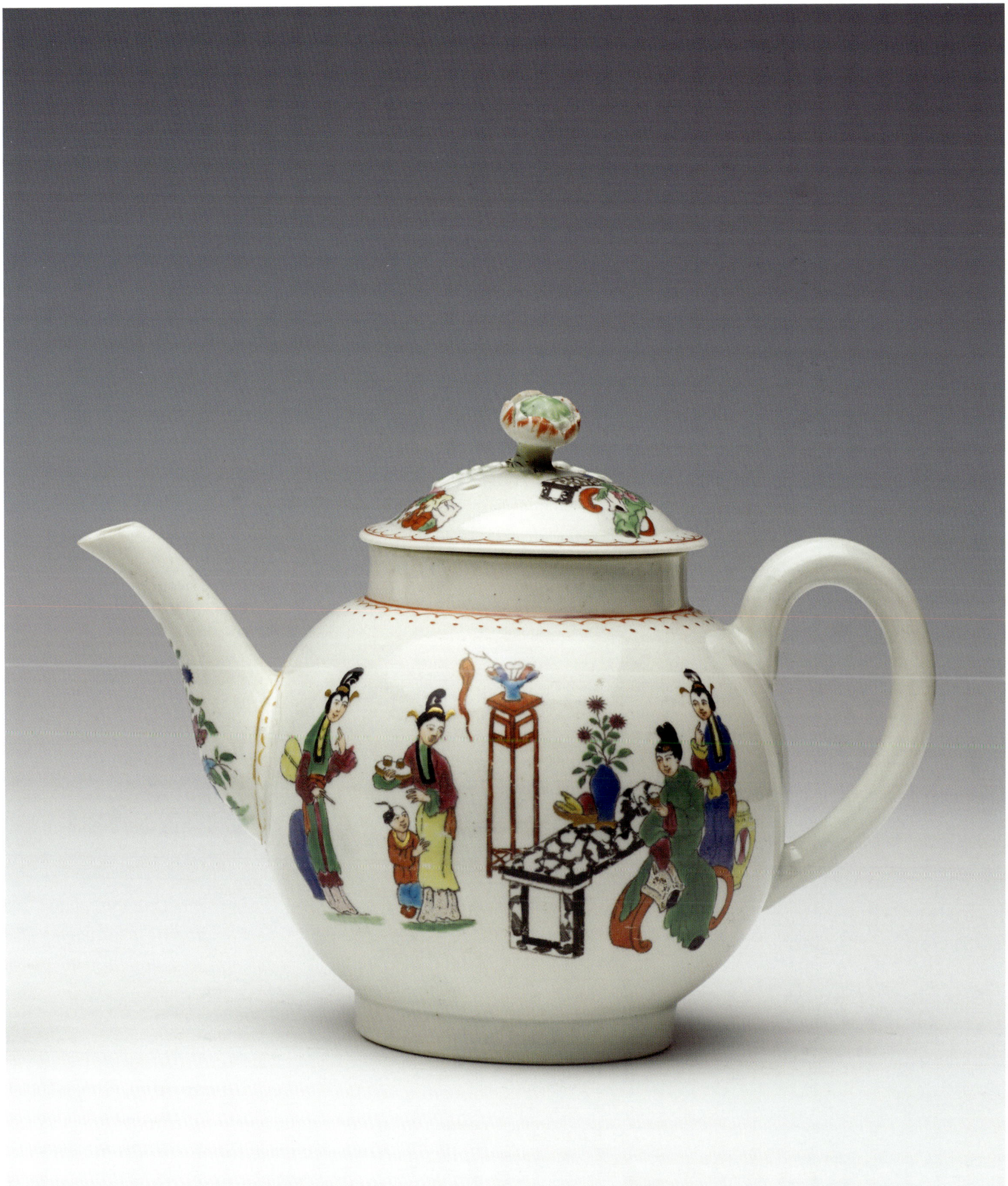

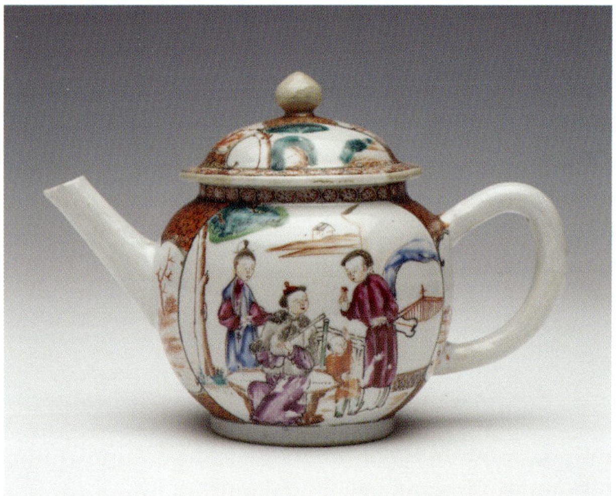

51

51

Chinese teapot

1750–70
Ht 12.9 cm
1957.24.1.236

This design inspired the decoration on no. 52.

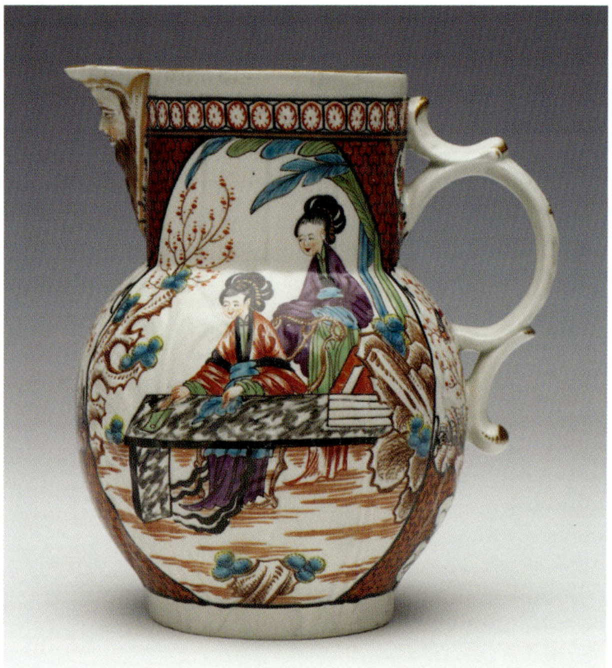

52

52

Jug

About 1770
Ht 18 cm
1957.24.1.229

Cabbage-leaf moulding with a masked spout. Decoration is a Chinese design with a lady seated at a table, another in attendance, flanked by panels of birds in red and black, all in reserves on a red mosaic or scale pattern ground; cell pattern border on rim.

REFERENCES

Sandon 1969, pl. 56; Sandon 1993, p. 91; Bonhams, London, 7 March 2007, lot 84.

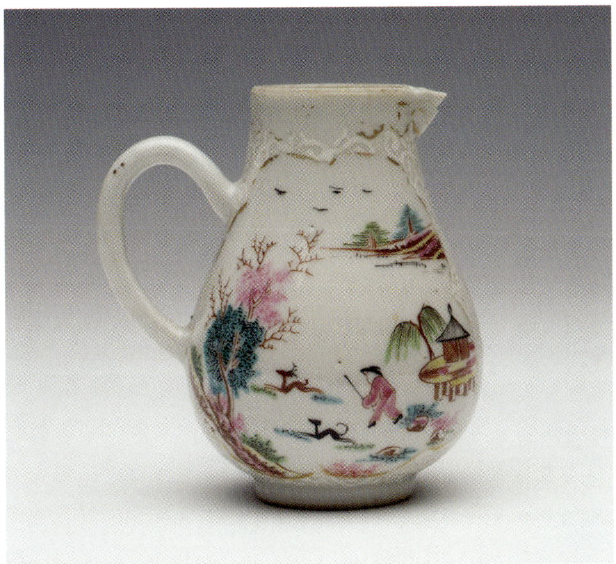

53

53

Chinese cream jug

Late eighteenth century
Ht 9.8 cm
1957.24.1.209

Possibly South Chinese, moulded with white raised decoration forming reserves painted with the 'Stag Hunt' pattern. For a full discussion of this pattern see McNeile 1990.

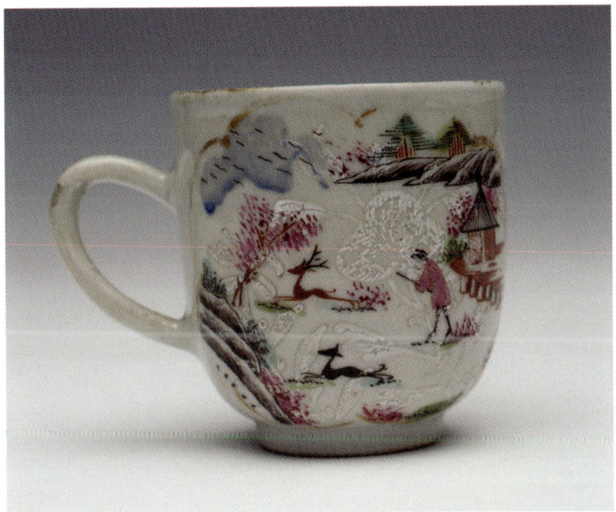

54

54

Chinese coffee cup

Late eighteenth century
Ht 6.6 cm, diam. 5.9 cm
1957.24.1.207

Possibly South Chinese, moulded with white raised decoration, painted with the 'Stag Hunt' pattern. This cup may have been decorated in Europe.

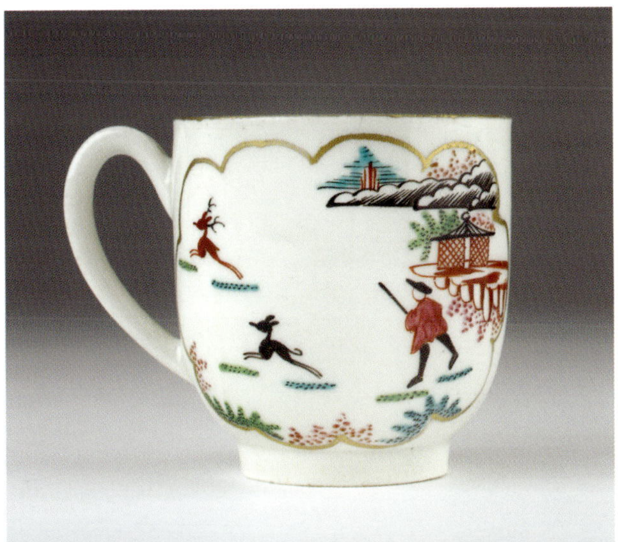

55

55

Coffee cup

1760–65 or possibly Chamberlain's about 1792
Ht 6.5 cm, diam. 5.9 cm
1957.24.1.205

Decorated with a later version of the 'Stag Hunt' pattern.

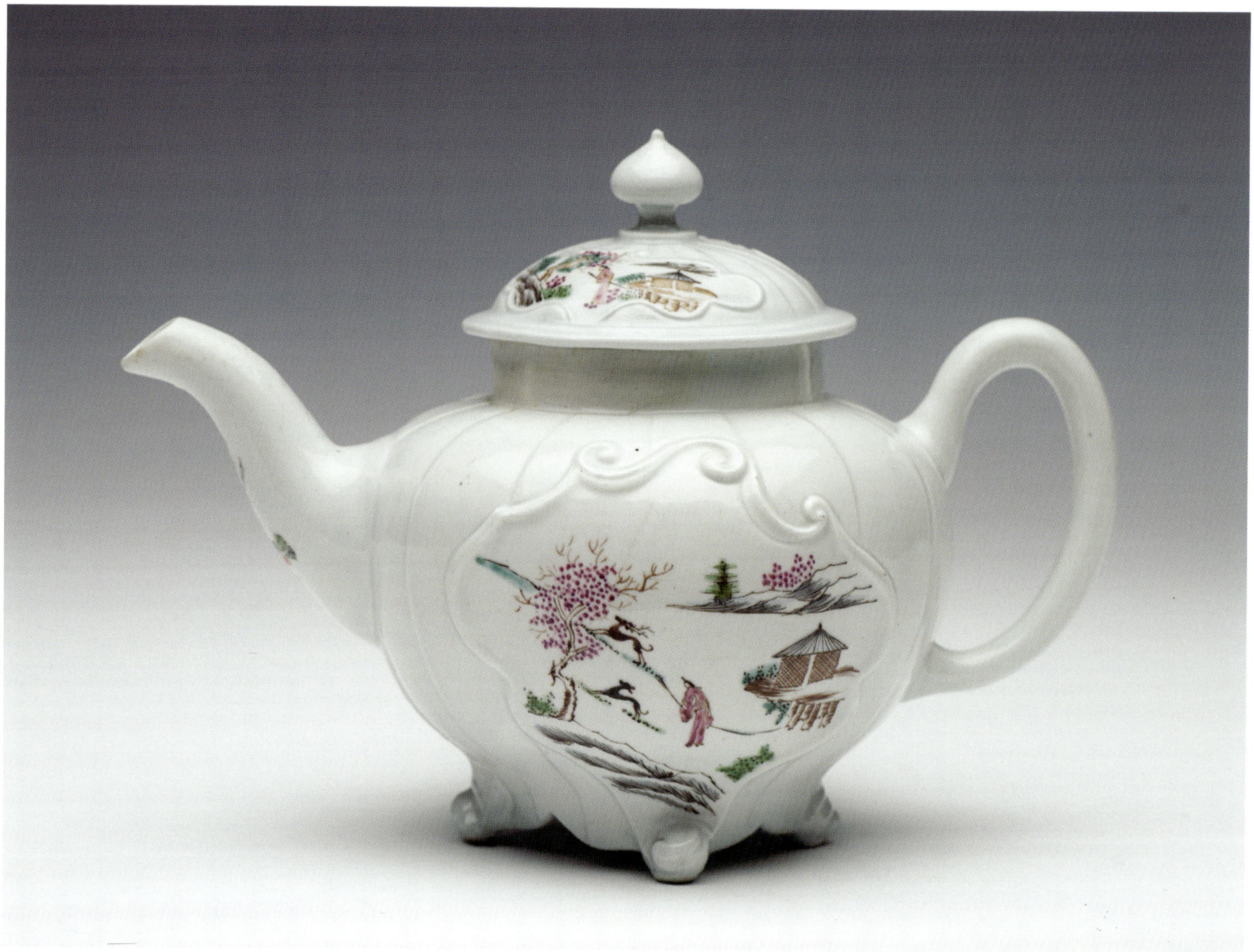

56

56

Teapot

1752–3
Ht 13.1 cm
1957.24.1.294

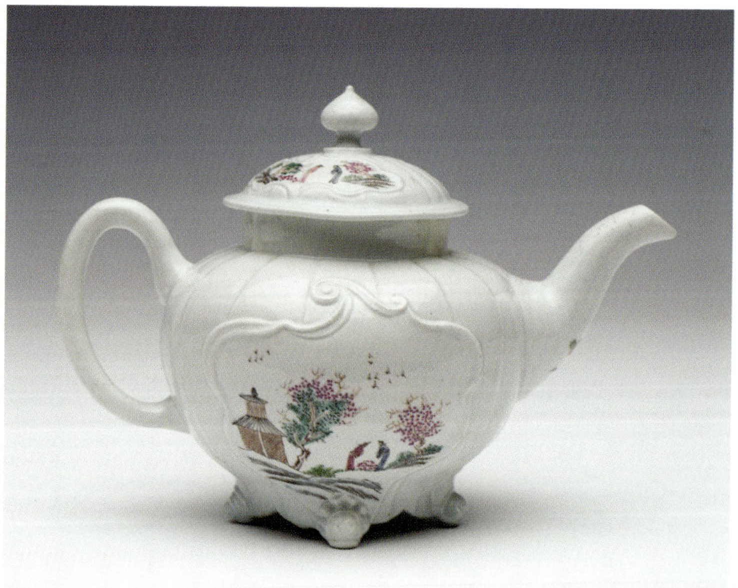

Rare shape showing influence of rococo silver, decorated with the 'Stag Hunt' pattern. Similarly moulded teapots are in the Museum of Royal Worcester Porcelain (no. 57) and the Victoria and Albert Museum (V&A: 414:118/&A-1885).

PROVENANCE
Sotheby's, London, 31 May 1943, lot 163, £16.

REFERENCE
Spero and Sandon 1996, pl. 7.

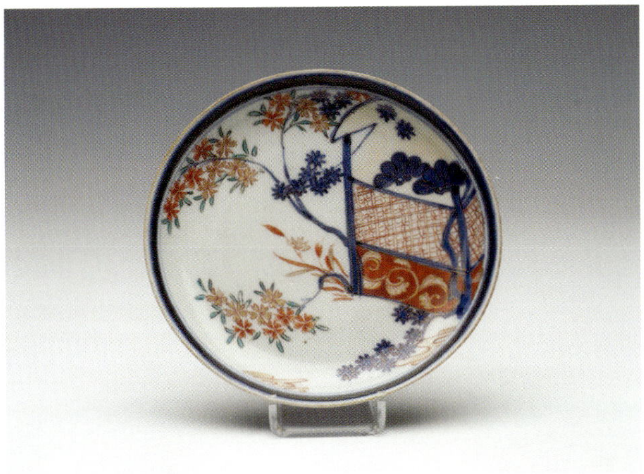

57

57

Japanese saucer

Early eighteenth century
Diam. 14 cm
Mark: gilded blue leaf within a blue circle
1957.24.1.1084

Imari-style decoration, in underglaze blue with overglaze enamels and gilding, showing pine, plum and bamboo growing around fence with clouds. Three plum branches on reverse.

58

Teabowl and saucer

1765–70
Bowl ht 4.4 cm, diam. 7.2 cm; saucer diam. 13.7 cm
Mark: gilded blue leaf within a blue circle
1957.24.1.1084

Close copy of a Japanese original.

PROVENANCE
Sotheby's, London, 20 October 1959, lot 257, £22 (including Japanese saucer, no. 57).

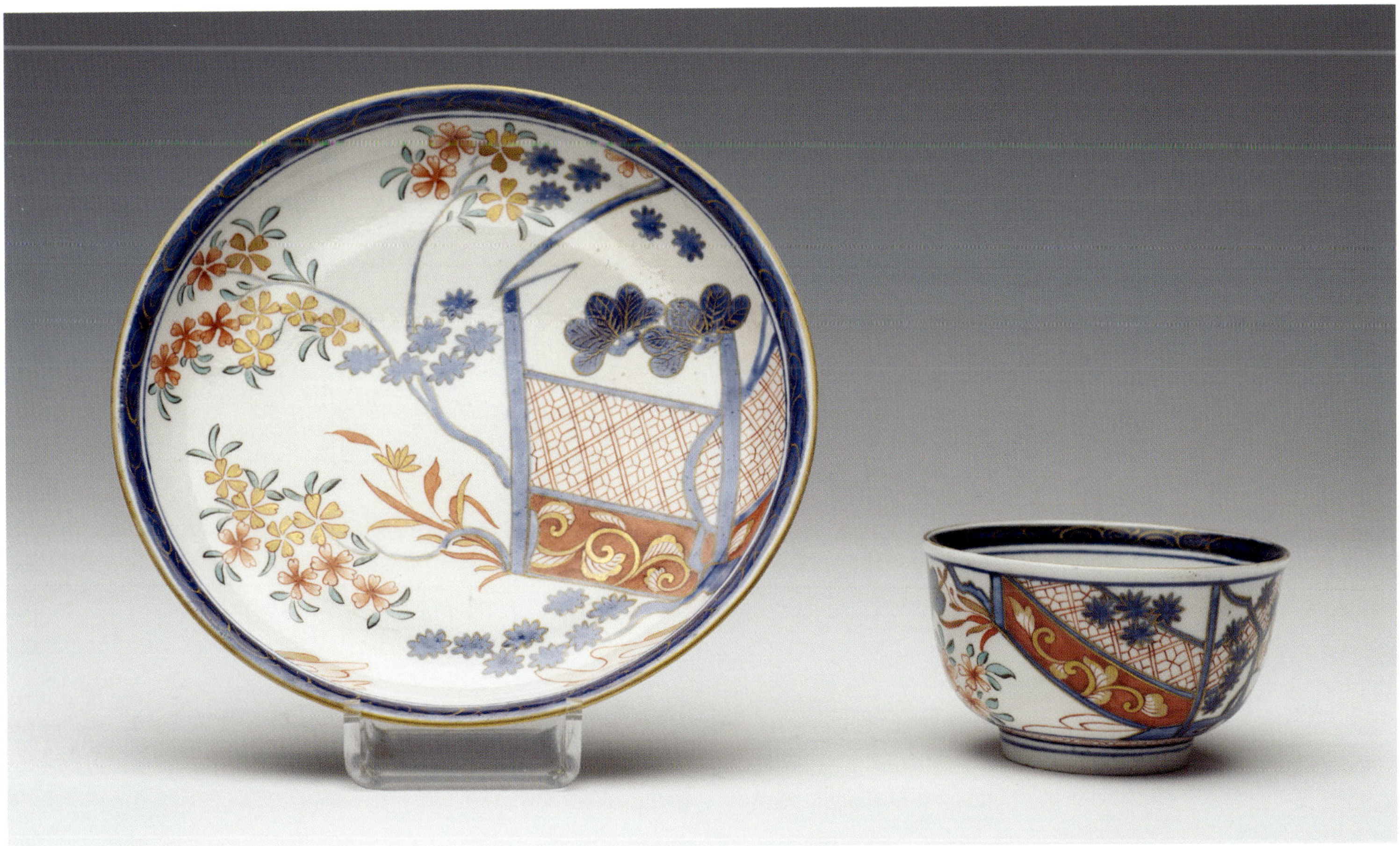

58

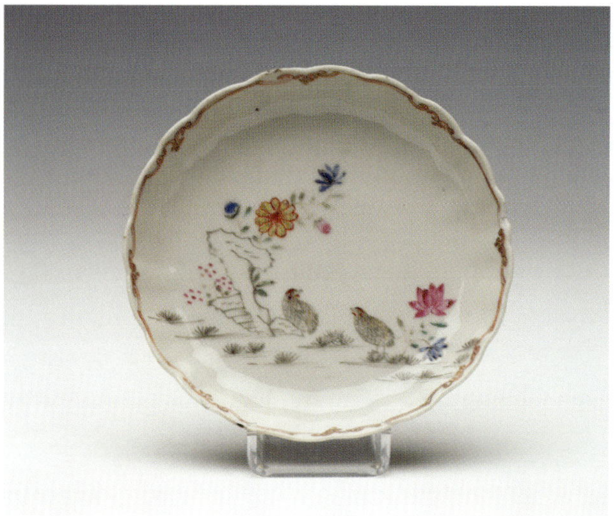

59

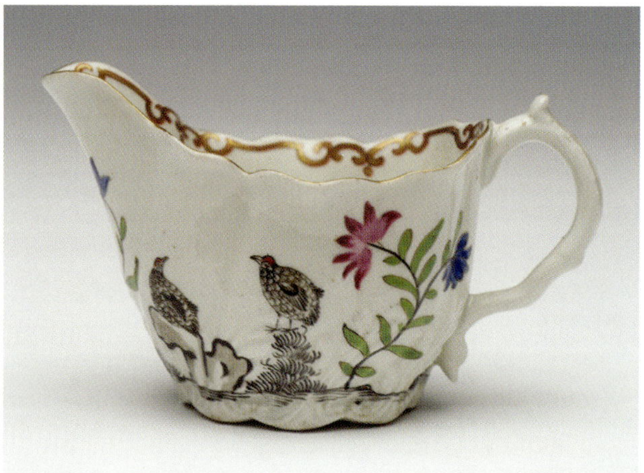

60

59

Chinese saucer

About 1760
Diam. 12.3 cm
1957.24.1.215

Qianlong period, decorated with two black outlined quails on rocks with lotus flowers and other blossom.

REFERENCES

Ayers, Impey and Mallet 1990, chap. XV; Girton 2004, pl. 17.

60

Creamboat

1770–75
Ht 6.6 cm, length 11.3 cm, width 7.2 cm
1957.24.1.216

Chelsea ewer shape, decorated with black quails; possibly by Giles.

REFERENCES

Girton 2004, fig. 42; McKeown 2006, pl. 35.

61

Meissen cup and saucer

About 1740
Cup ht 4.4 cm, diam. 8.1 cm; saucer diam. 12.9 cm
Mark: crossed swords in blue
1957.24.1.186

Cup with everted rim edged in brown, decorated with a 'Quail' pattern.

PROVENANCE

H.W. Hughes Collection, 12 February 1944, no. 395.

62

Teabowl and saucer

1775–80
Bowl ht 5.5 cm, diam. 6.8 cm; saucer diam. 12.6 cm
Mark: red crescent
1957.24.1.185

Decorated in a 'Quail' pattern, similar to that found on Bow and derived from Meissen.

REFERENCE

Spero and Sandon 1996, pl. 294.

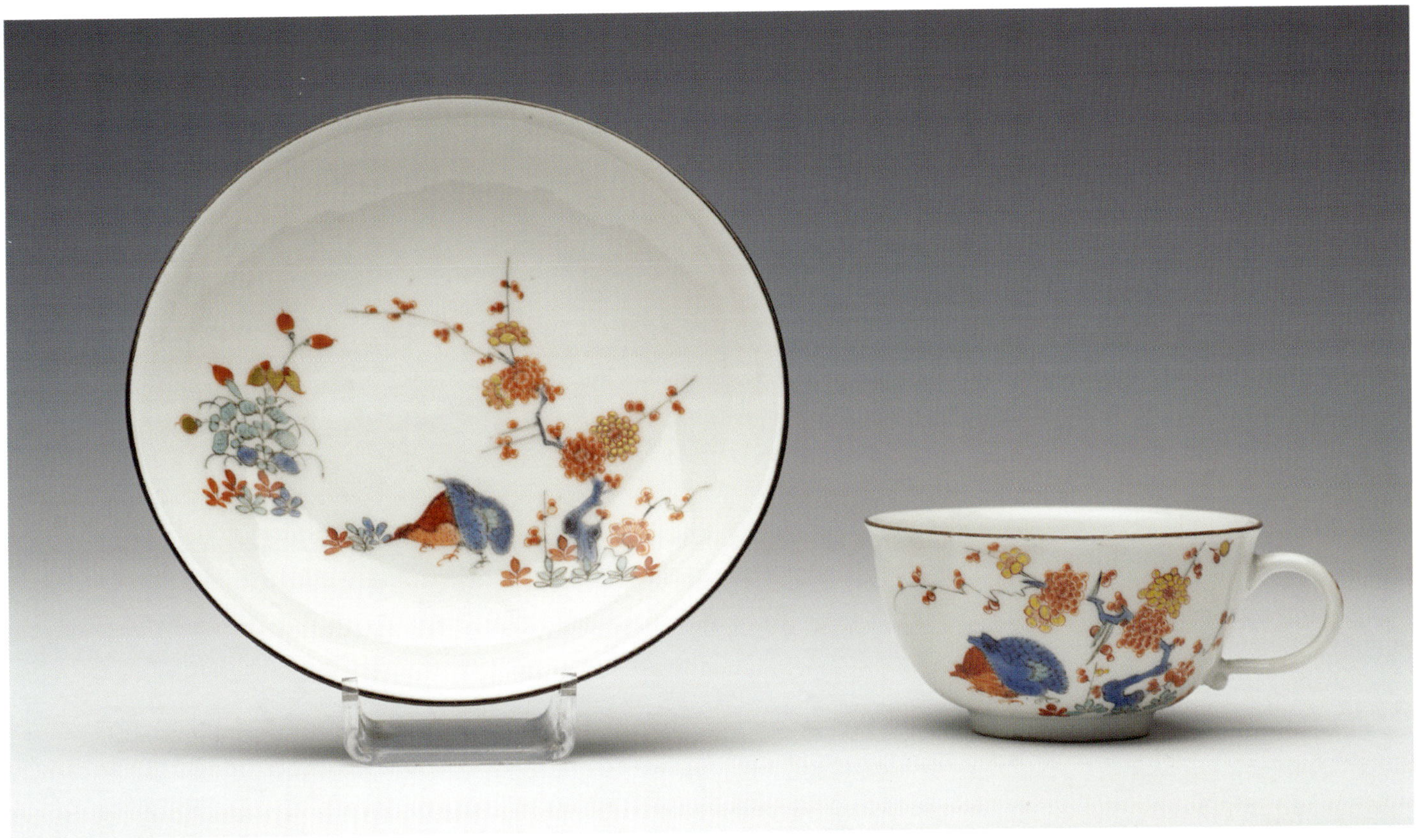

61

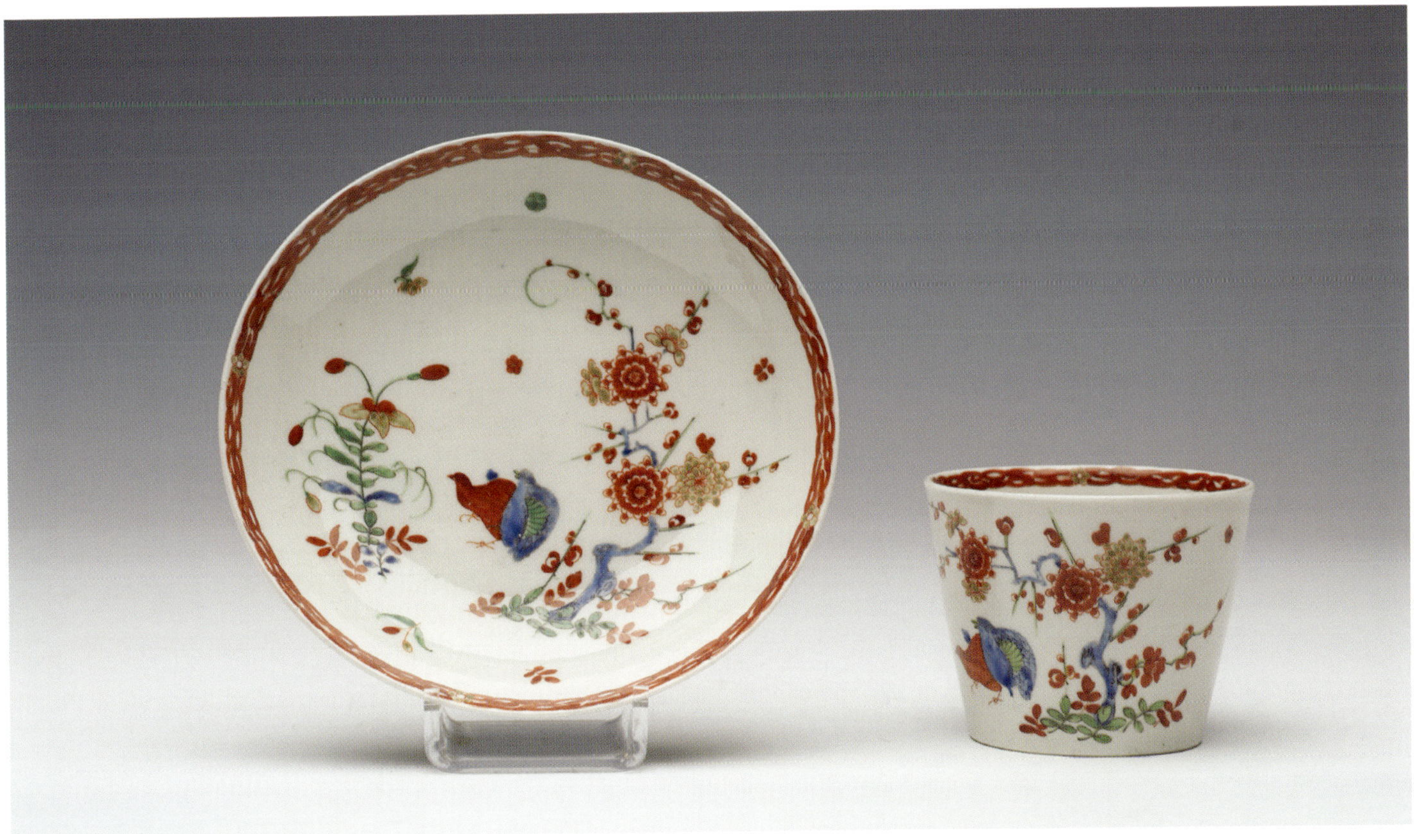

62

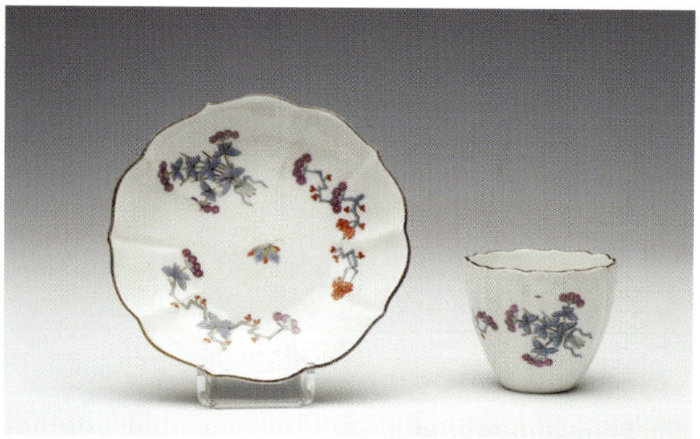

63

63

Meissen teabowl and saucer

About 1750
Bowl ht 5.2 cm, diam. 6.1 cm; saucer diam. 11.9 cm
Mark: crossed swords
1957.24.1.183

From a Japanese Kakiemon original, with typical sprays and bouquets, also copied at the Chantilly, Chelsea and Bow factories.

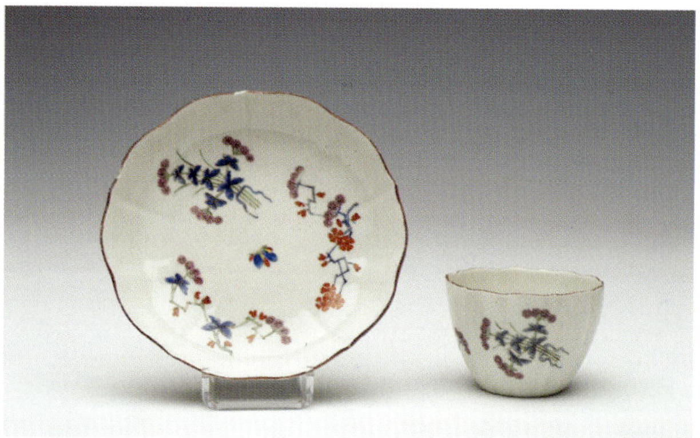

64

64

Teabowl and saucer

About 1772
Bowl ht 4.8 cm, diam. 6.5 cm; saucer diam. 12.3 cm
1957.24.1.182

The lobed shape and decoration are both derived from Meissen, the insect in the centre of the saucer being very typical.

REFERENCE
Spero and Sandon, 1996, no. 288.

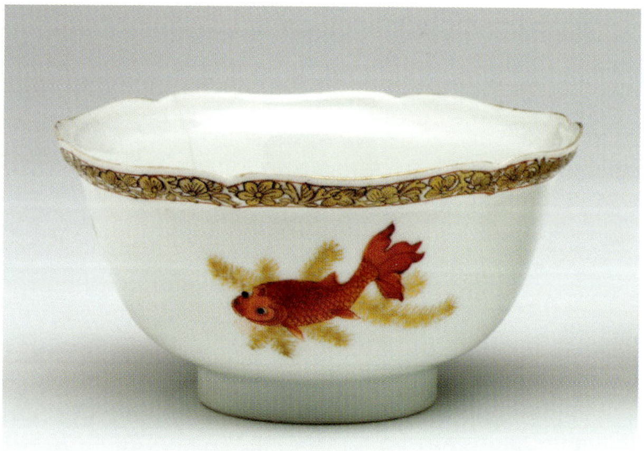

65

65

Chinese bowl

Qianlong 1736–95
Ht 6.2 cm, diam. 11.6 cm
1957.24.1.213

Wavy edge with *rouge de fer* and gold border on outside, decorated with three *rouge de fer* carp with four-forked tails swimming in golden weeds, another carp in base.

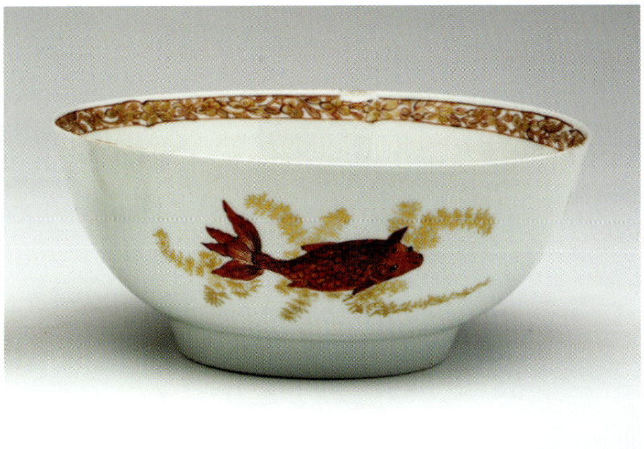

66

66

Christian's Liverpool bowl

About 1765
Ht 6.8 cm, diam. 15.3 cm
1957.24.1.214

Plain edge, *rouge de fer* and gold border inside rim, decorated with carp in a close copy of a Chinese design.

PROVENANCE
Sotheby's, London, 12 March 1957, lot 5, £110.

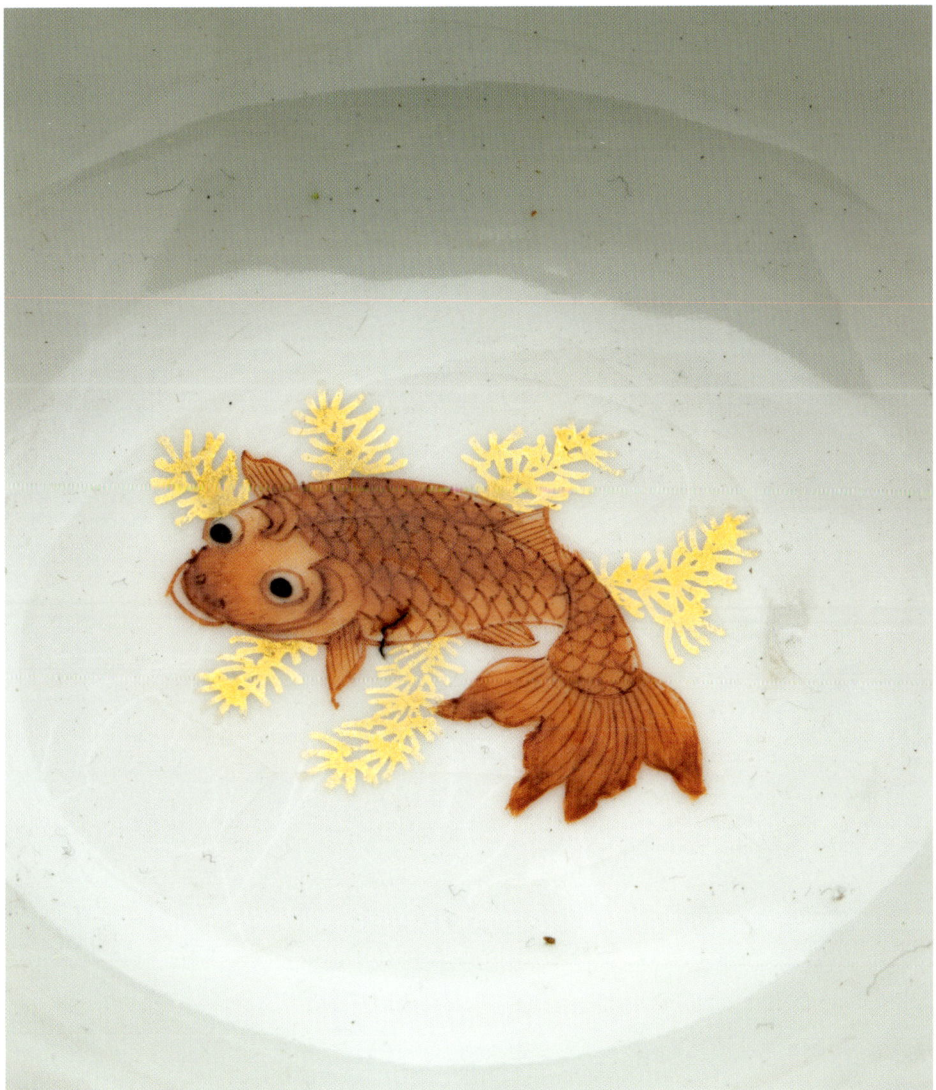

65 (detail)

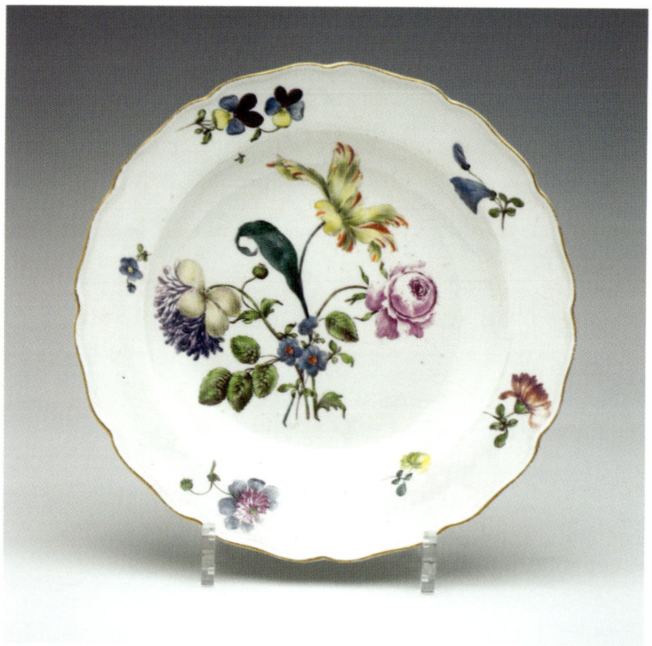

67

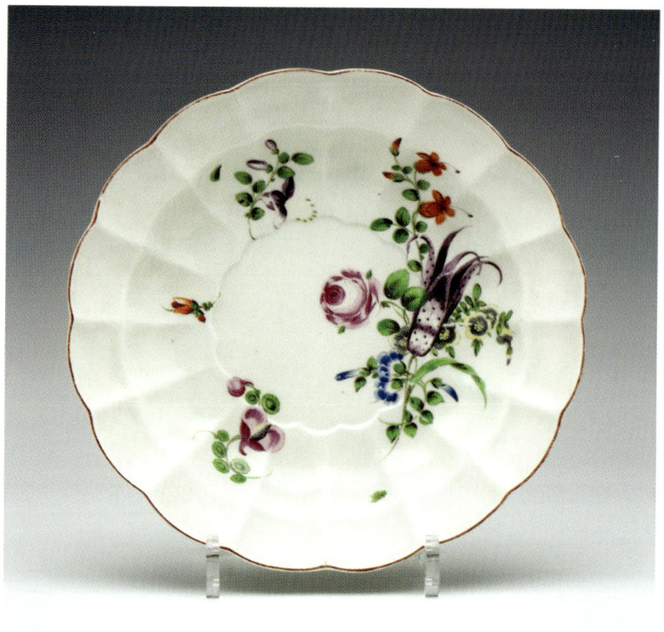

68

67

Meissen deep plate

1740–45
Diam. 23.4 cm
Mark: crossed swords and incised *61*
1957.24.1.202

These typical Meissen floral sprays are the inspiration for much Worcester porcelain decoration.

68

Deep plate

About 1770–72
Diam. 24.2 cm
1957.24.1.198

Fluted with brown rim, decorated with European flowers inspired by Meissen.

69

Meissen teacup and saucer

1770–75
Cup ht 4.8 cm, diam. 8 cm; saucer diam. 13.2 cm
1957.24.1.208

Painted with flowers, fungi and fruit.

70

Teacup and saucer

About 1770
Cup ht 4.4 cm, diam. 8 cm; saucer diam. 13 cm
Mark: crossed swords in blue on the cup with *9* and a dot, and on the saucer without a numeral
1957.24.1.210

Floral sprays with 'cut' fruit, derived from Meissen, probably decorated by Giles.

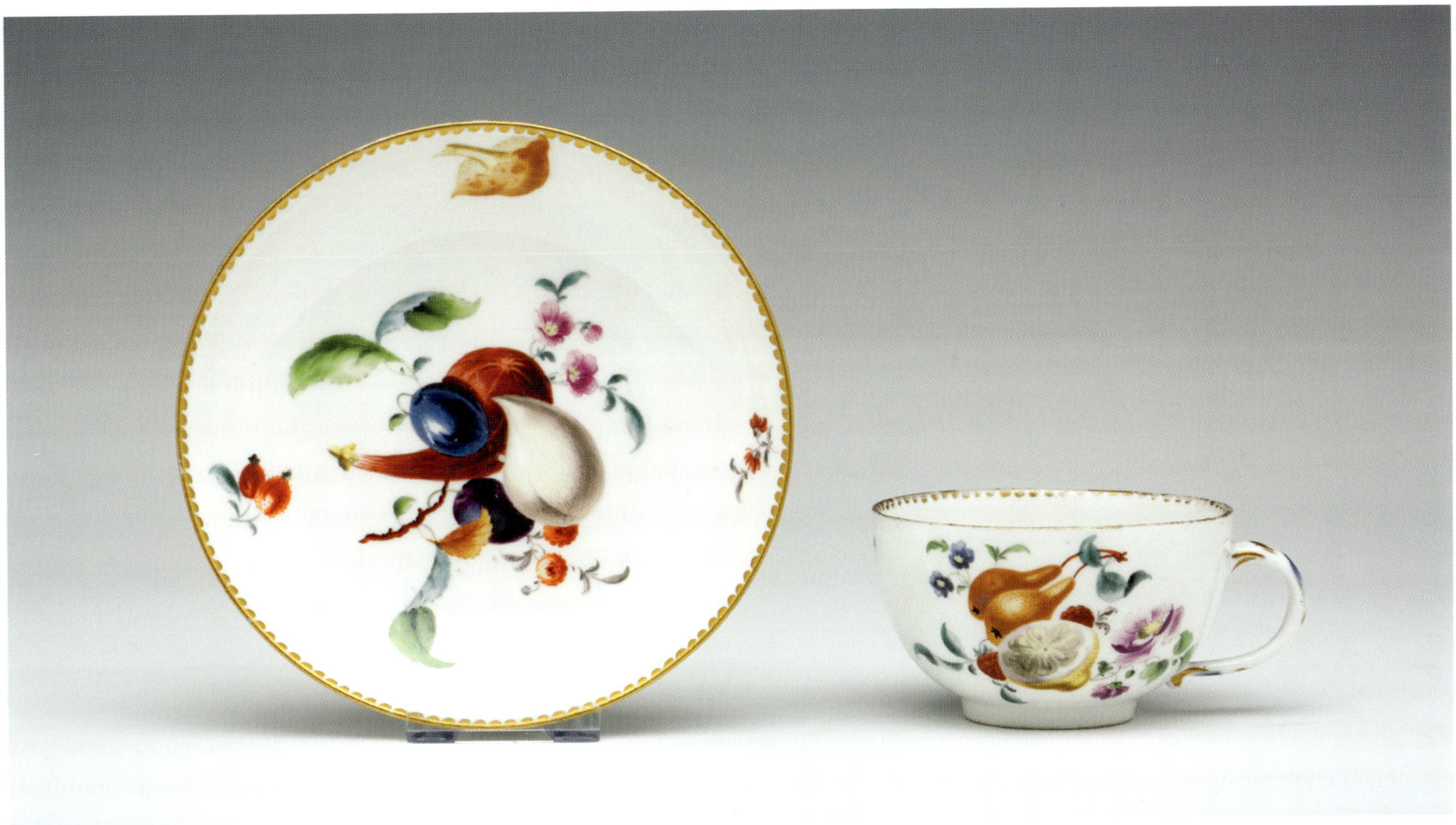

69

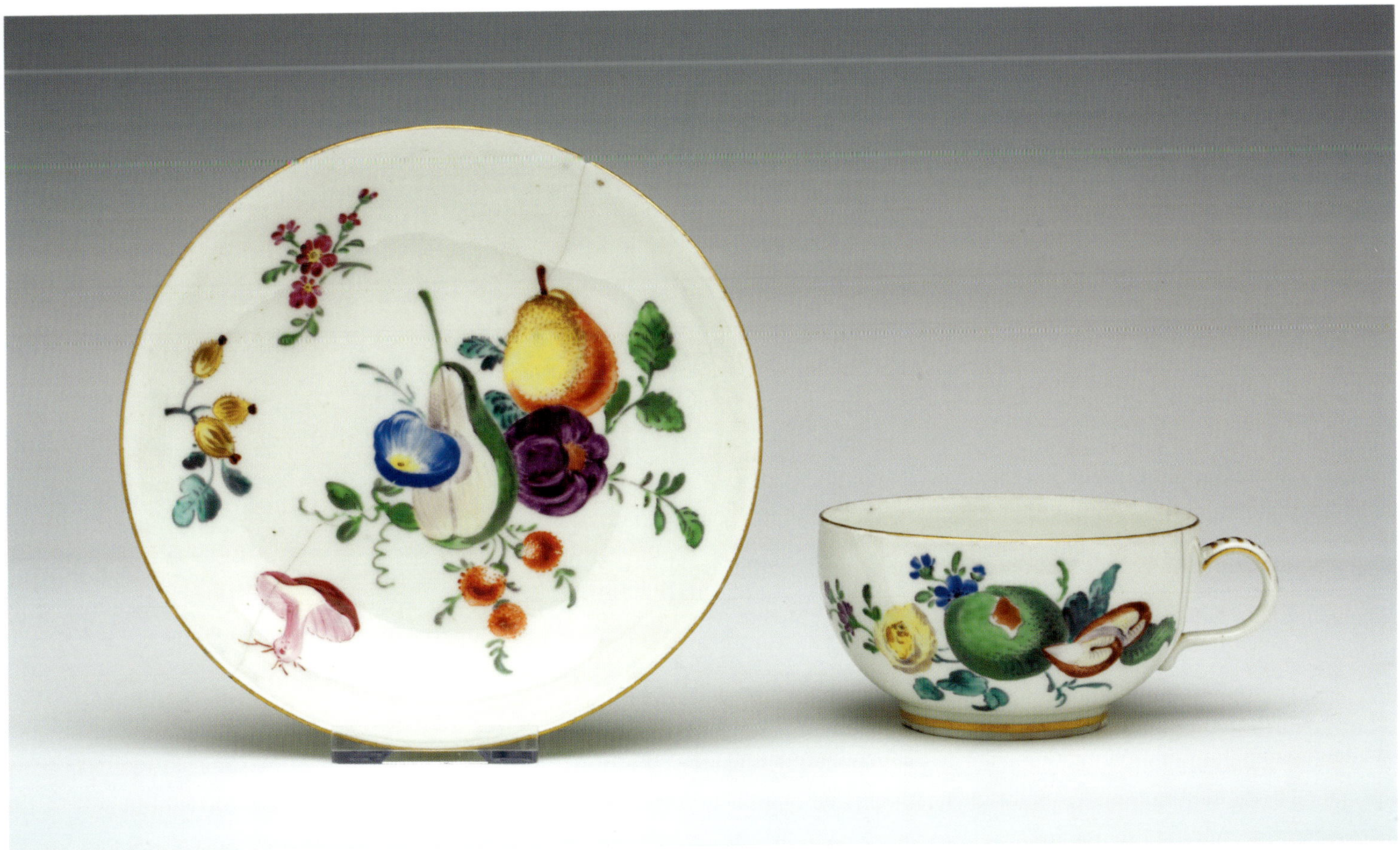

70

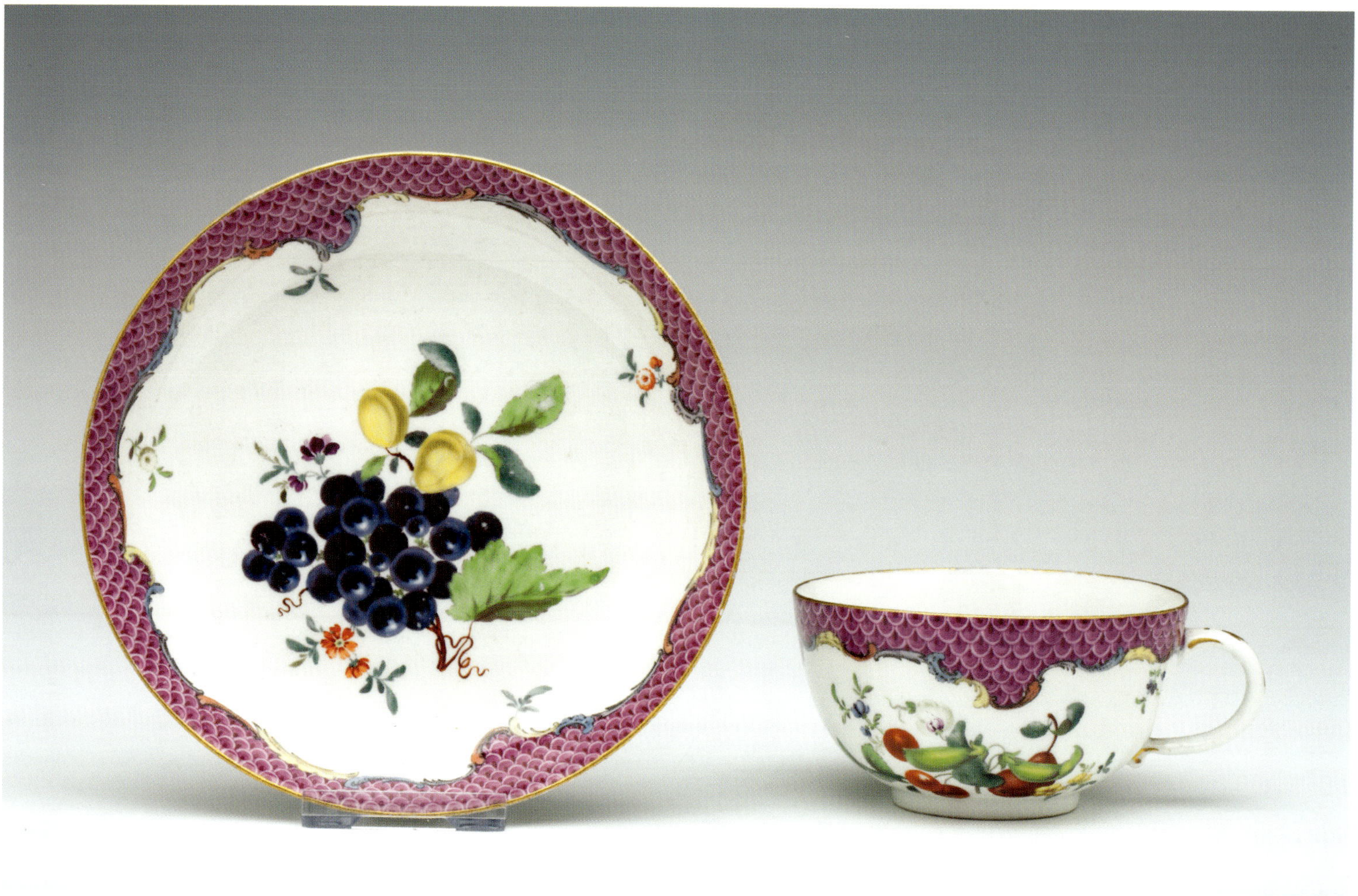

71

71

Meissen teacup and saucer

1770–80
Cup ht 4.6 cm, diam. 7.9 cm; saucer diam. 13.5 cm
Mark: crossed swords on both
1957.24.1.192

Decorated with fruit and flowers within an irregular pink scale border.

72

Worcester teacup

1775–8
Ht 4.9 cm, diam. 8.2 cm
1957.24.1.193

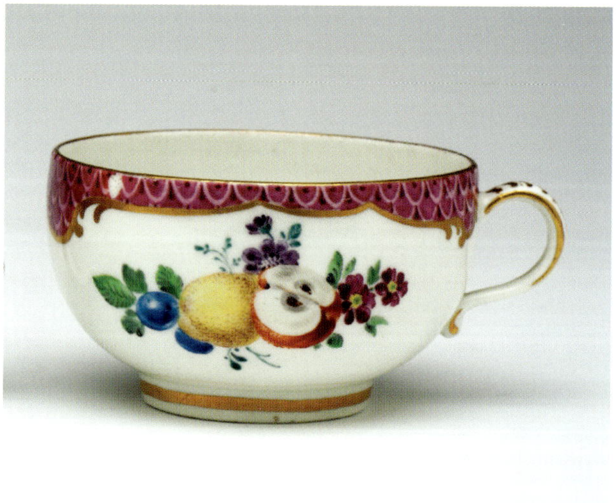

72

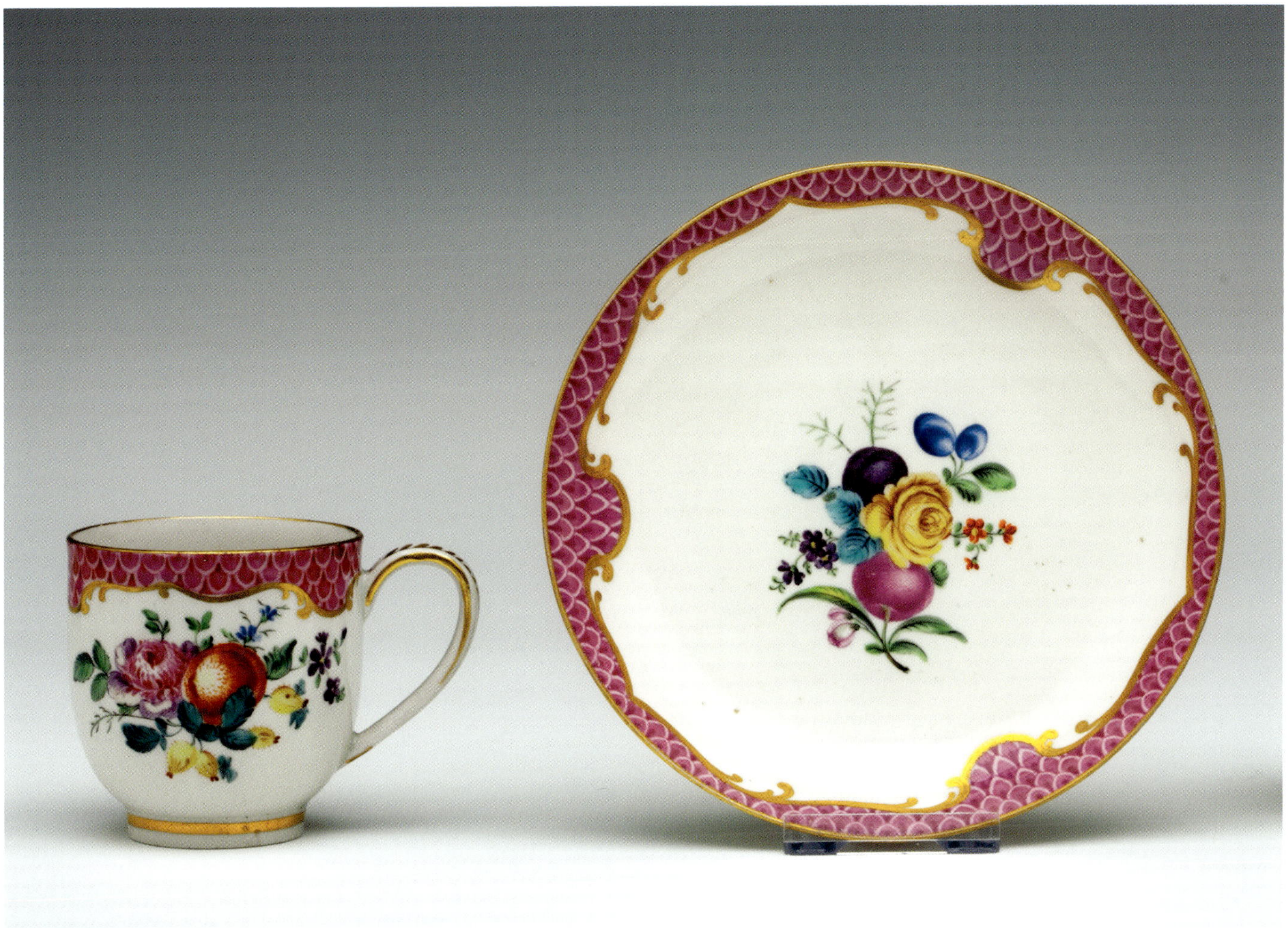

73

73

Neale (Staffordshire) coffee cup and saucer

About 1785
Coffee cup ht 5.9 cm, diam. 5.6 cm; saucer diam. 13 cm
1957.24.1.193

Fruit and flower decoration inspired by Meissen; teacup decorated in the Giles workshop.

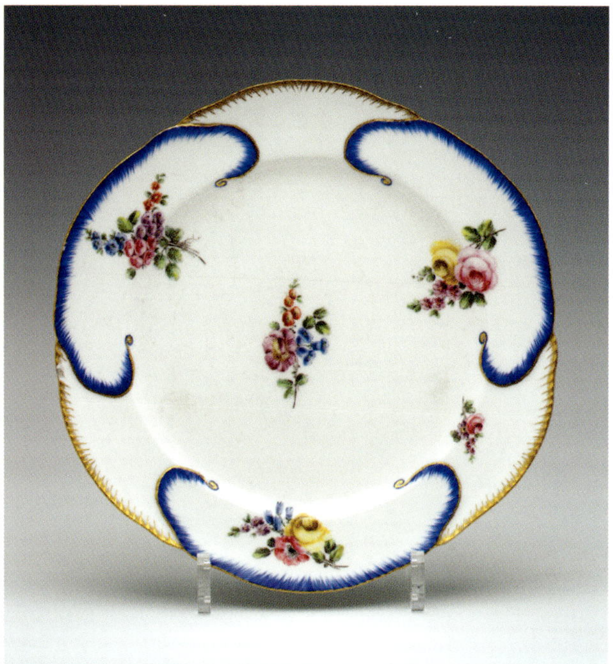

74

74

Sèvres plate

About 1763
Diam. 24.7 cm
Mark: interlaced *LL*, *K* for 1763, cursive *6* and incised *6* and *U*
1957.24.1.156

'*Feuille de Choux*' (cabbage leaf) decoration.

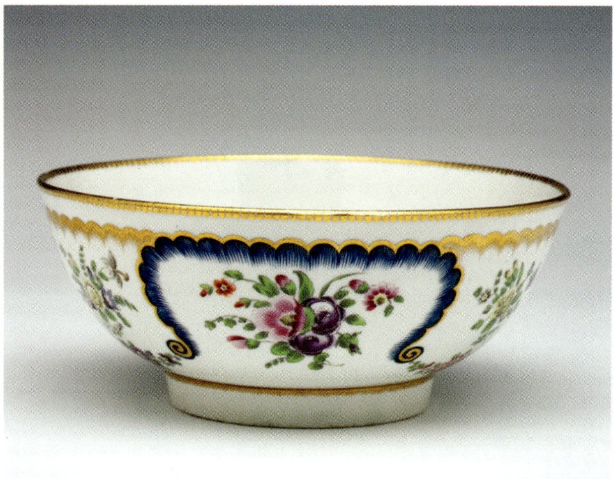

75

75

Bowl

About 1780
Ht 7.5 cm, diam. 17.4 cm
1957.24.1.160

A factory adaptation of a Sèvres design from 1758. Both the Worcester factory and the Giles workshop copied this design. At Worcester the pattern was restricted to tea services.

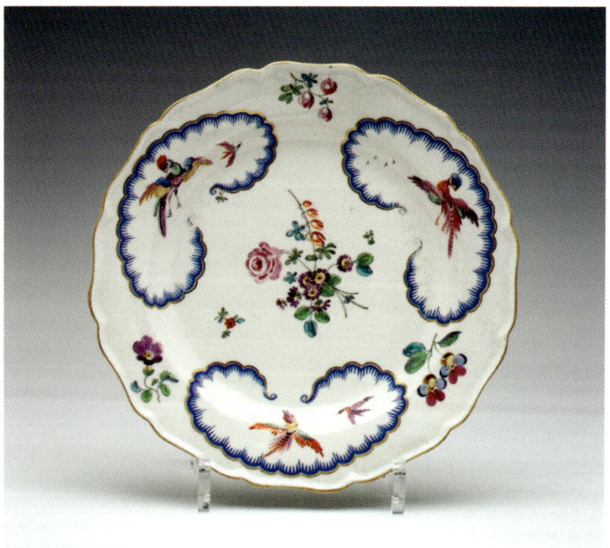

76

76

Plate

About 1770–72
Diam. 22.4 cm
1957.24.1.524

An adaptation of the Sèvres '*Feuille de Choux*' design, used by Giles on dessert wares. In the sale of Giles's wares in March 1774, lot 65 was described as 'six ice cups and covers enamelld blue shell and birds'.

REFERENCE
Spero and Sandon 1996, pl. 415.

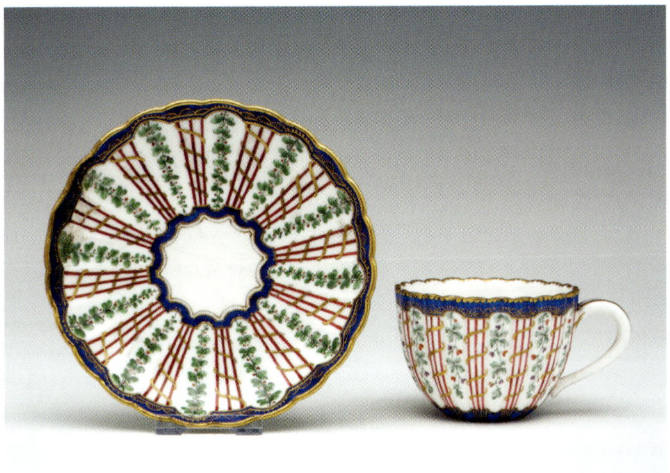

77

77

Sèvres teacup and saucer

1763
Cup ht 5.3 cm, diam. 7.2 cm; saucer diam. 12.8 cm
Mark: on cup interlaced *LL*, *K* for 1763 and pin-shaped mark
1957.24.1.194

Decorated with a 'Hop Trellis' pattern and blue border.

PROVENANCE
H.W. Hughes Collection, 12 February 1944, no. 486.

78

Teabowl, coffee cup and saucer

1778–82
Bowl ht 4.8 cm, diam. 7.6 cm; cup ht 6.5 cm, diam. 6.1 cm; saucer diam. 12.5 cm
1957.24.1.195

This is a close copy of a Sèvres design. A considerable number of so-called 'Hop Trellis' designs, derived from Sèvres, were introduced at Worcester from the mid-1770s until the early 1780s.

REFERENCE
Spero and Sandon 1996, pl. 372.

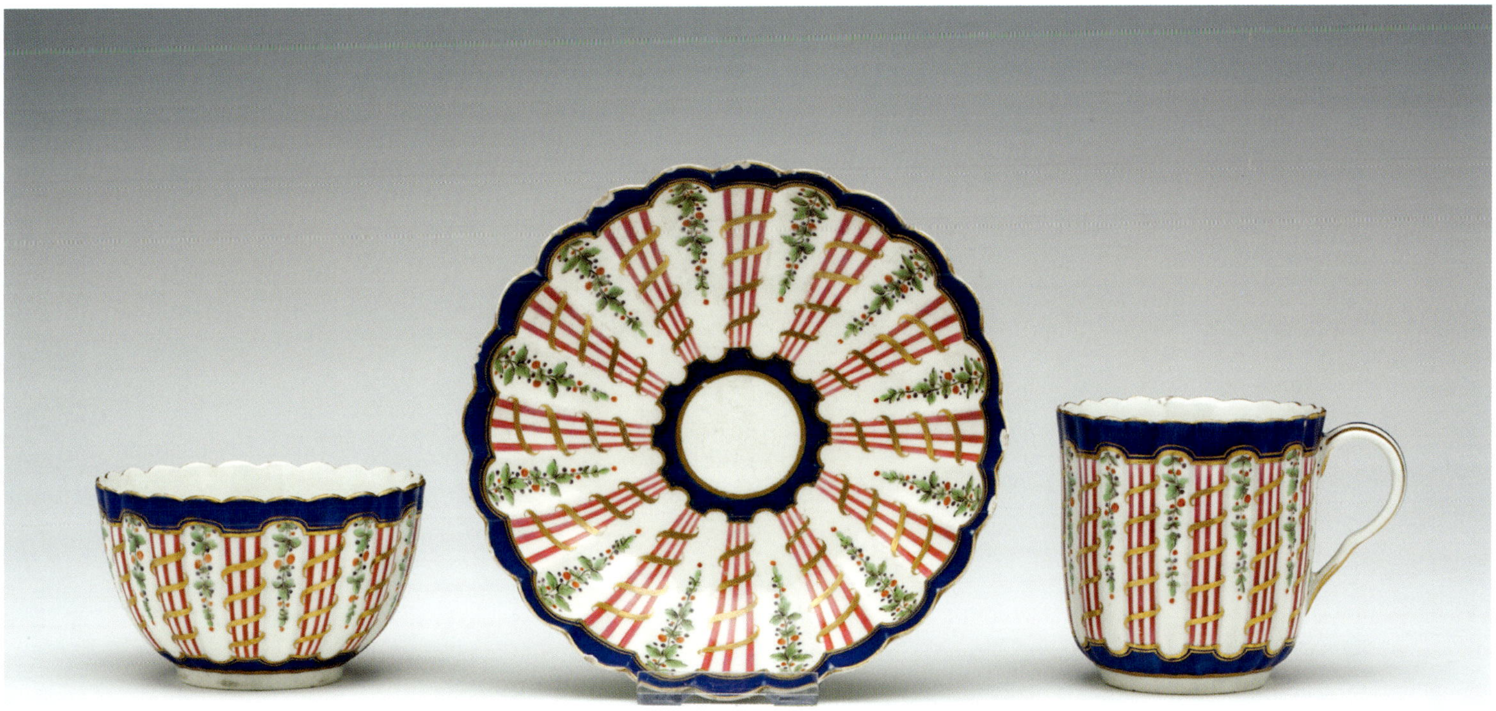

78

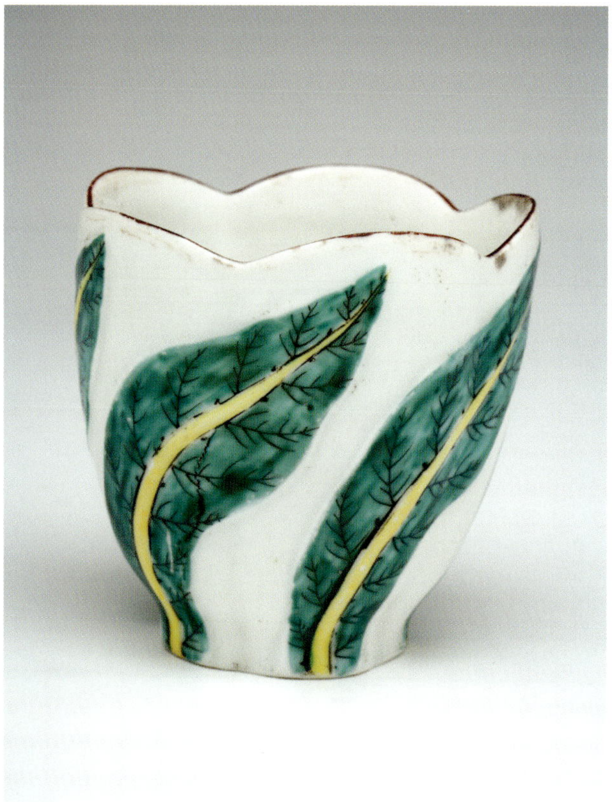

79

79

Chelsea cup

1752–8

Ht 7.3 cm, diam. 7.1 cm

1957.24.1.211

Moulded beaker, scalloped rim with brown edge, painted with five Asplenium scolopendrium (hart's tongue fern) leaves with yellow ribs rising obliquely from the base. This design was first used at Chelsea in the late 1740s and also appears on Chantilly porcelain.

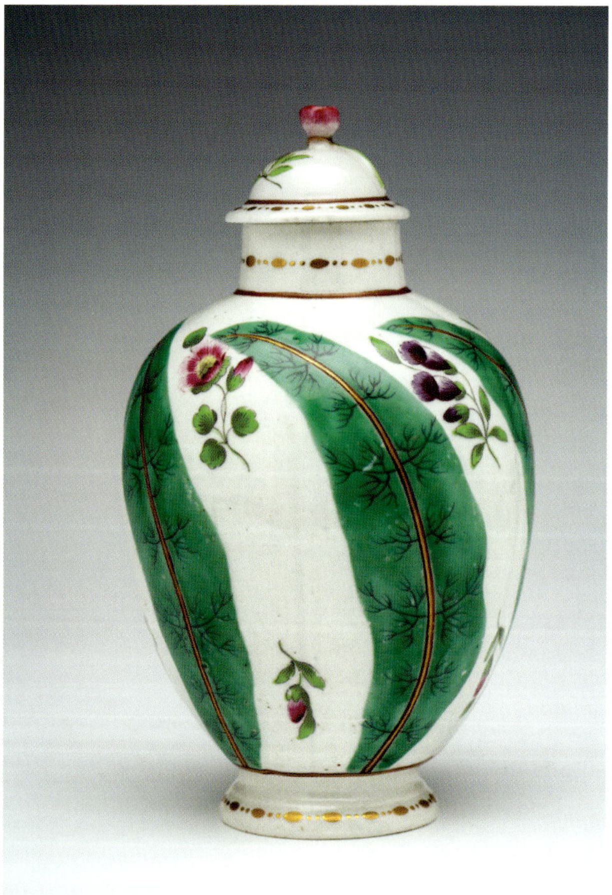

80

80

Tea canister and later cover

About 1772–5

Ht 15.8 cm

1957.24.1.212

Copy of a Chelsea design with cover of a later date. The five moulded Asplenium scolopendrium leaves curve from right to left, the reverse of the Chelsea prototype, with flower sprays painted between them.

REFERENCE

Spero and Sandon 1996, pl. 209.

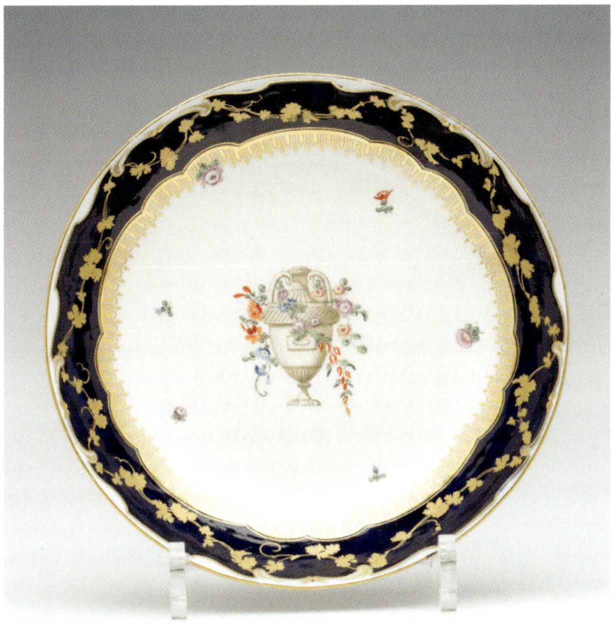

81

81

Chelsea-Derby cake dish

1772–5
Diam. 20 cm
Mark: gold anchor
1957.24.1.999

Decorated by Giles.

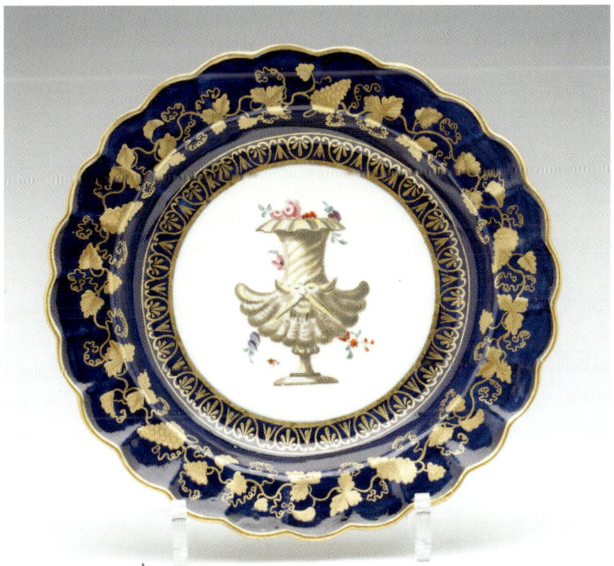

82

82

Plate

1770–75
Diam. 21.9 cm
Mark: crescent
1957.24.1.1004

Wet blue border with gilt wreath of vine leaves and grapes, masked urn garlanded with flowers in centre, decorated by Giles.

REFERENCE
Sandon 2008, pl. 52.

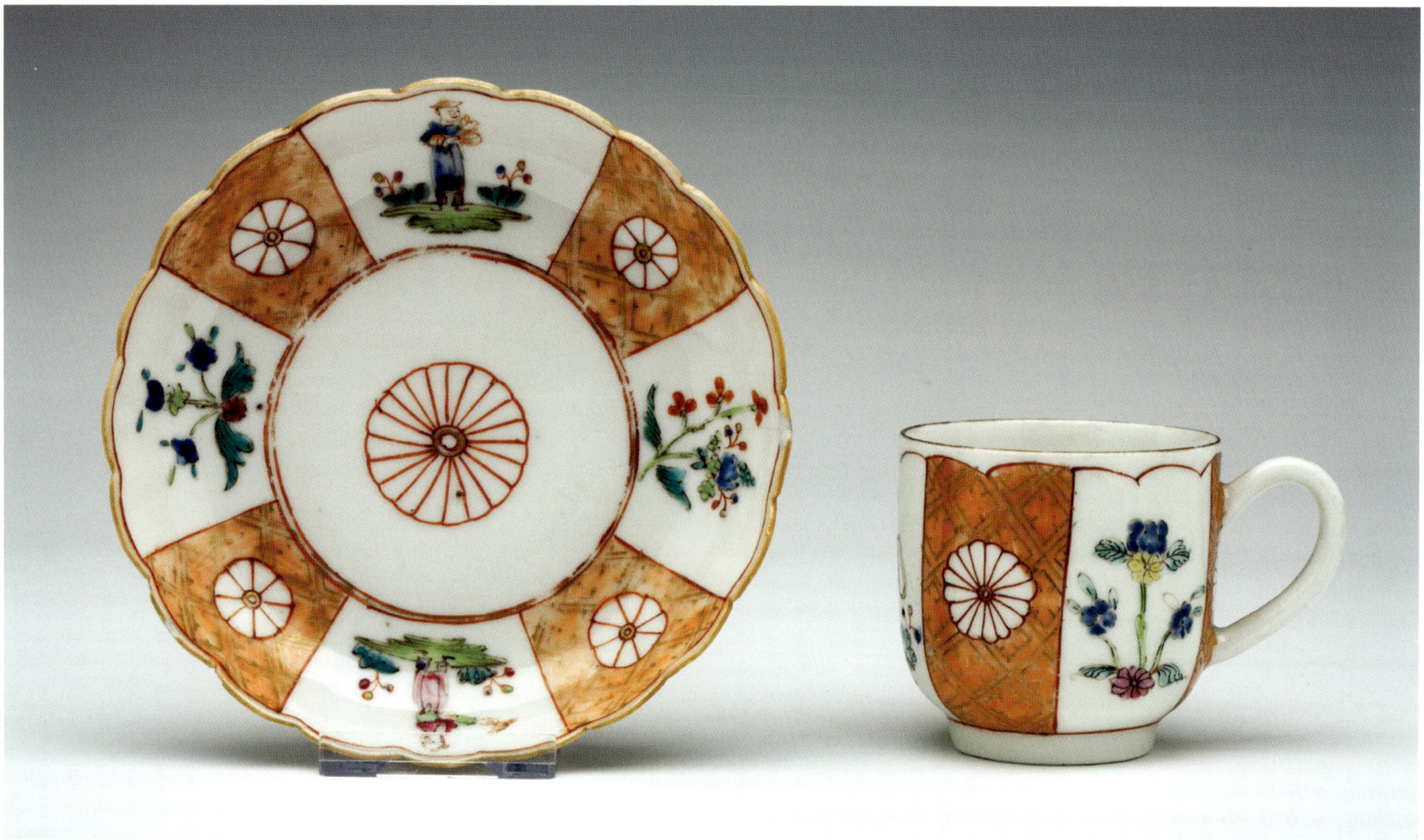

83

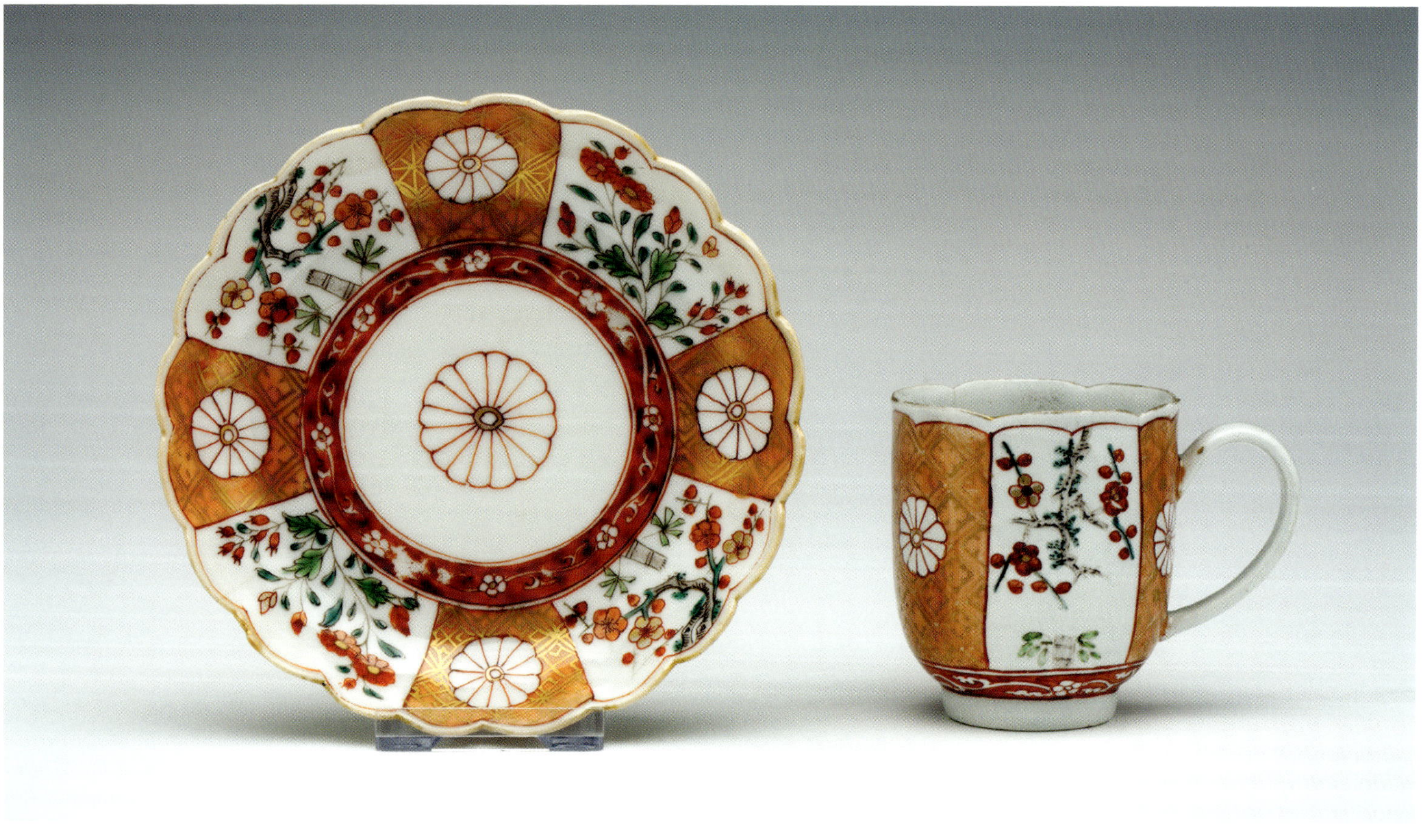

84

83

Worcester coffee cup and Chinese saucer

About 1770
Cup ht 5.7 cm, diam. 5.6 cm; saucer diam. 12.1 cm
1957.24.1.238

Decorated with four orange, gilt-diapered bands, each with a white chrysanthemum, separating two panels with Oriental foliage and two with Chinese figures each holding a bird. Edge is scalloped on saucer, plain on cup.

84

Chaffers, Liverpool, coffee cup and Japanese saucer

1760–65
Cup ht 6.1 cm, diam. 5.2 cm; saucer diam. 11.9 cm
1957.24.1.237

Scalloped edge on both cup and saucer, decorated with four orange, gilt-diapered bands, each with a white chrysanthemum, separating panels of Oriental foliage. A deeper orange border, scrolled in white, around centre of saucer and base of cup. A Liverpool teapot in this pattern is illustrated in Hills 2011, no. 5.35.

85

Worcester teabowl and Chinese saucer

About 1762–5
Bowl ht 3.6 cm, diam. 7.3 cm; saucer diam. 11.7 cm
1957.24.1.221

Decorated in Oriental style with a white bird painted in *bianco sopra bianco* sitting on a brown fence; peony spray and blue rock to the left.

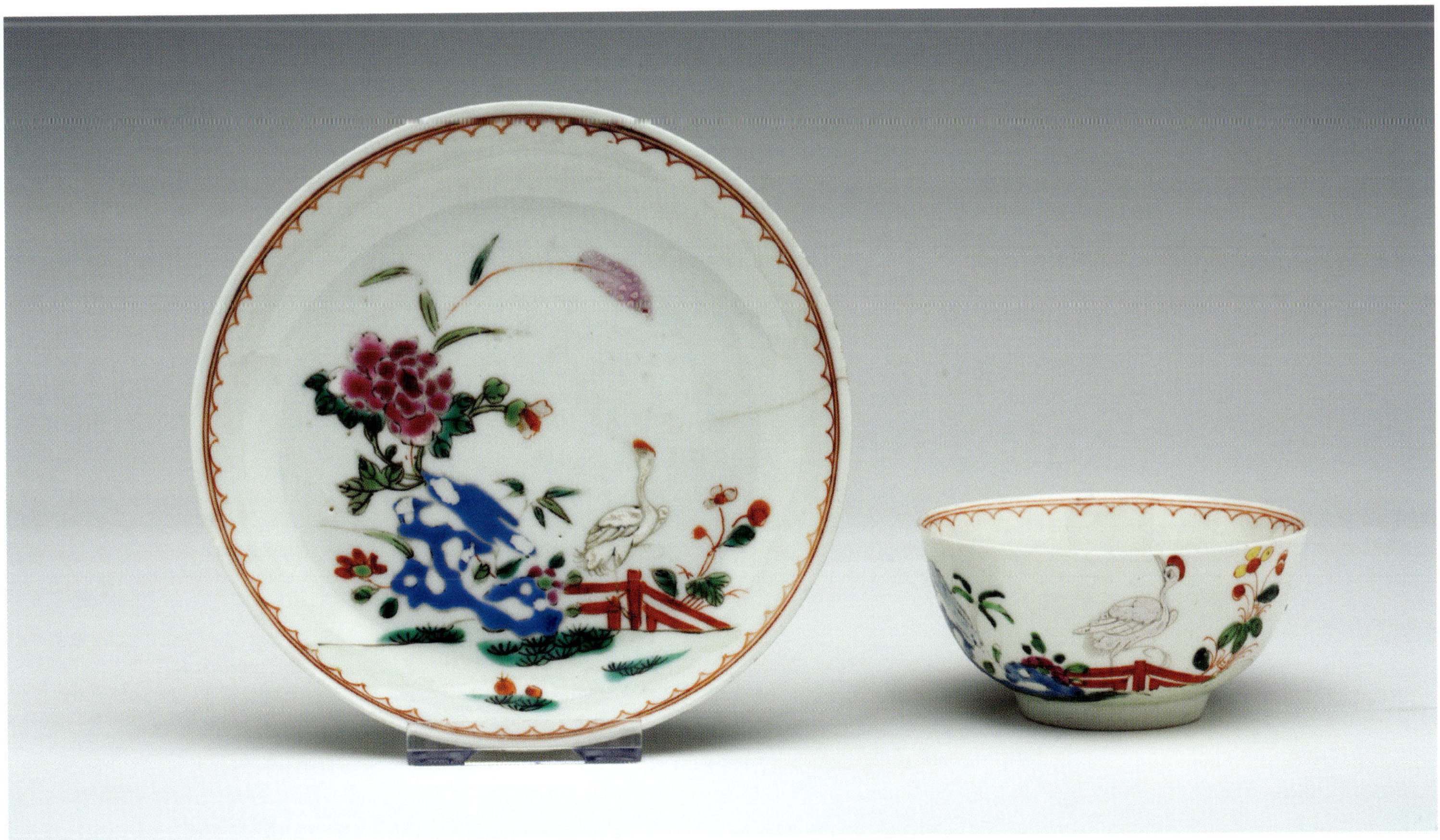

85

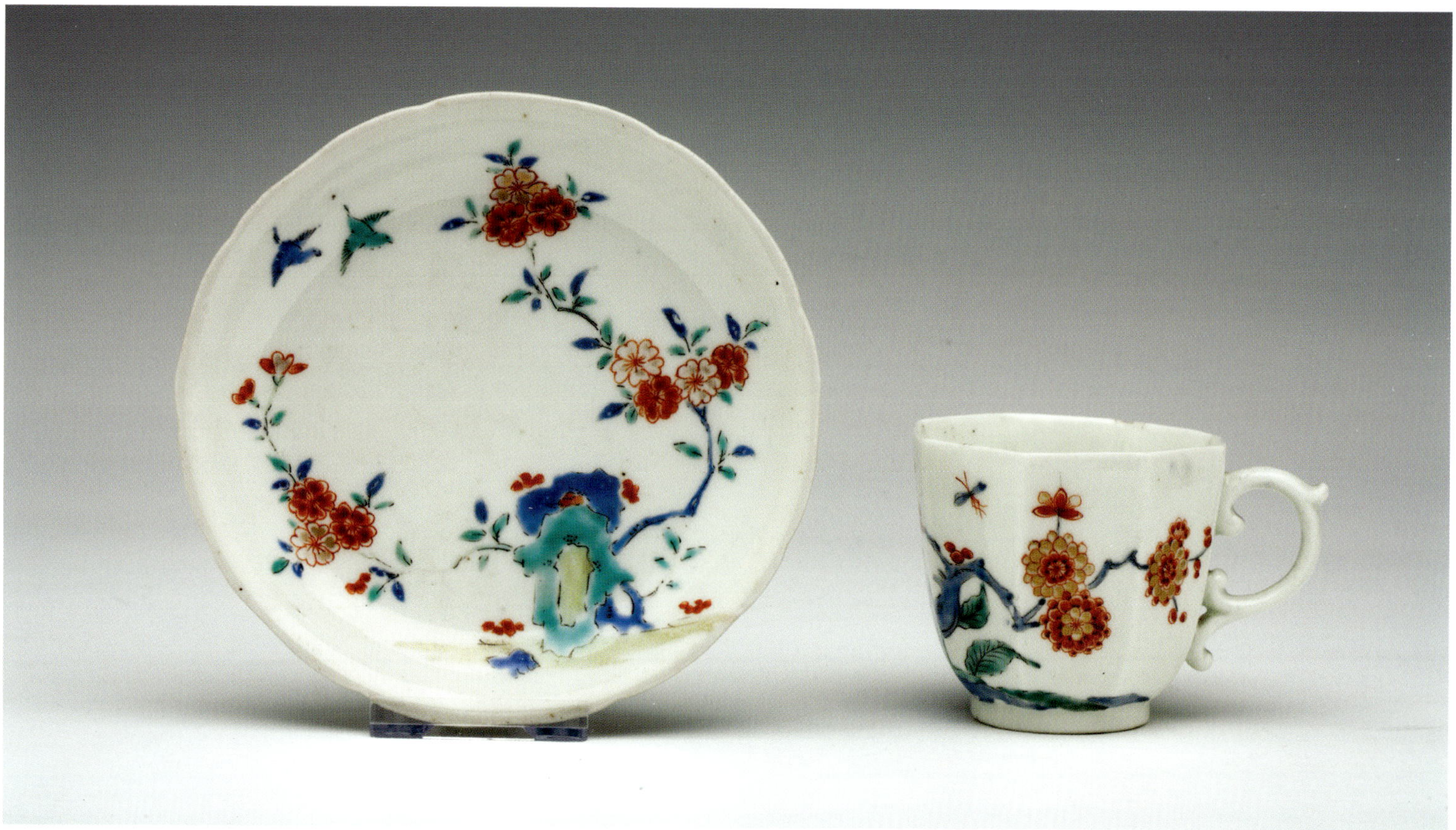

86

86

Chelsea teacup and Japanese saucer

Cup 1753; saucer about 1700
Cup ht 5.7 cm, diam. 5.8 cm; saucer diam. 12.2 cm
1957.24.1.1075

The octagonal cup and saucer are decorated in Kakiemon style with flowering prunus and rocks in red, green, gold and underglaze blue.

87

Worcester coffee cup and Chinese saucer

1770–75
Cup ht 6.2 cm, diam. 5.4 cm; saucer diam. 12 cm
1957.24.1.223

Decorated with the 'Queen's' pattern in underglaze blue on the saucer, with sprays in red and green enamel. On the cup the outlines are in gilt and all the decoration is overglaze, possibly by Giles.

88

Worcester coffee cup and Chinese saucer

About 1755
Cup ht 6.1 cm, diam. 5.4 cm; saucer diam. 11.9 cm
Mark: red annulet and ring under cup handle
1957.24.1.337

Although not a pair, these are decorated with similar scenes with brown-stemmed pine trees on left and, in centre, a Chinese woman holding a fan.

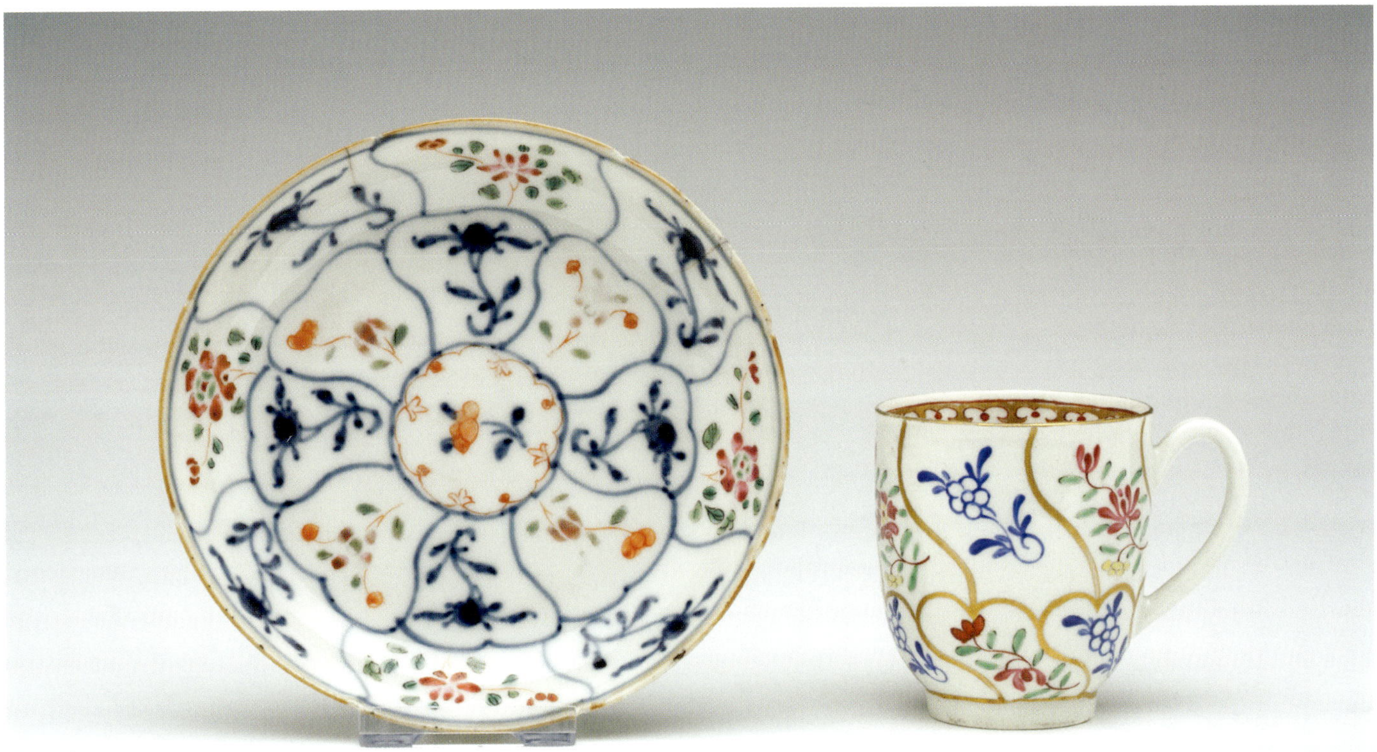

87

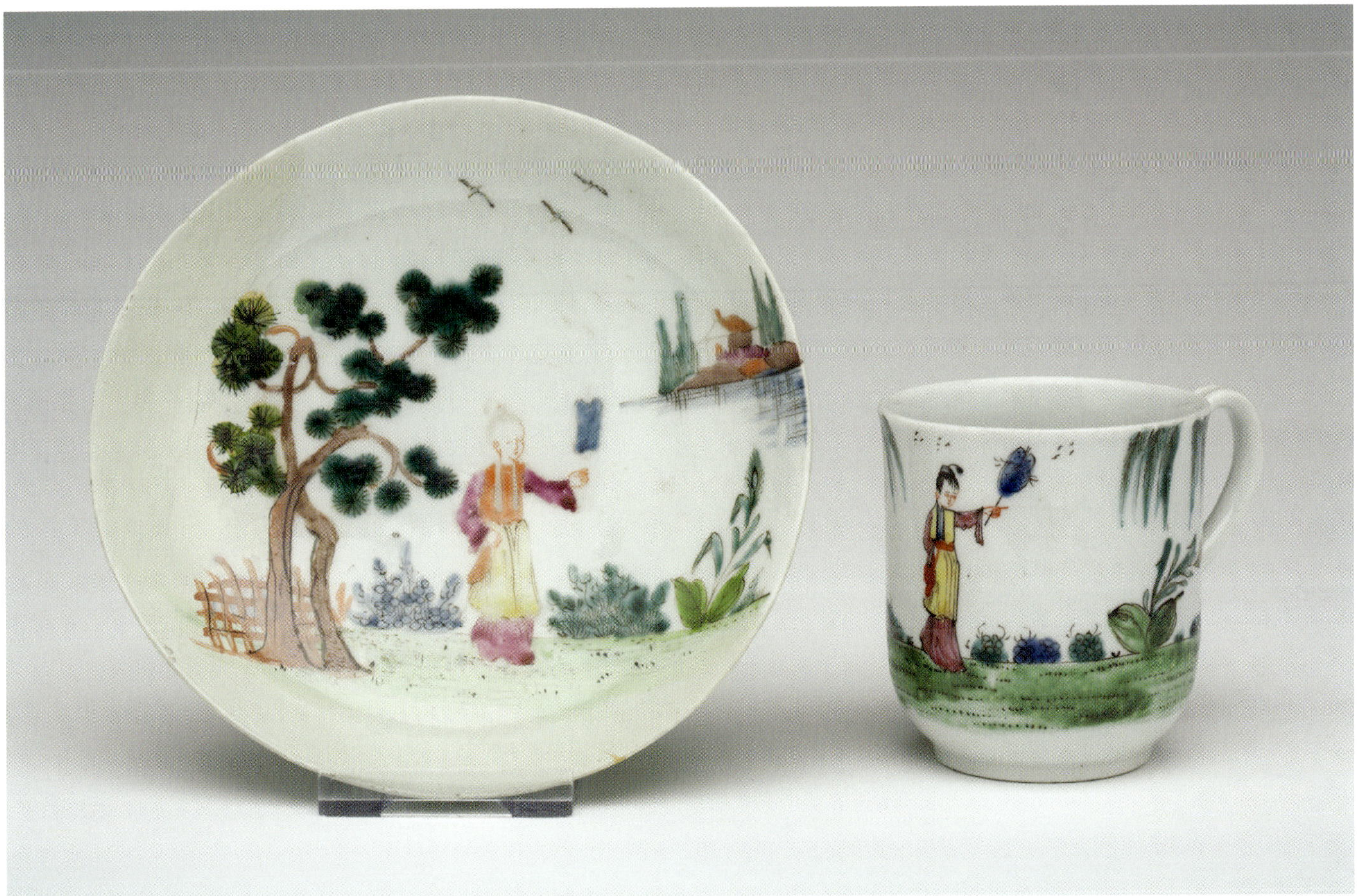

88

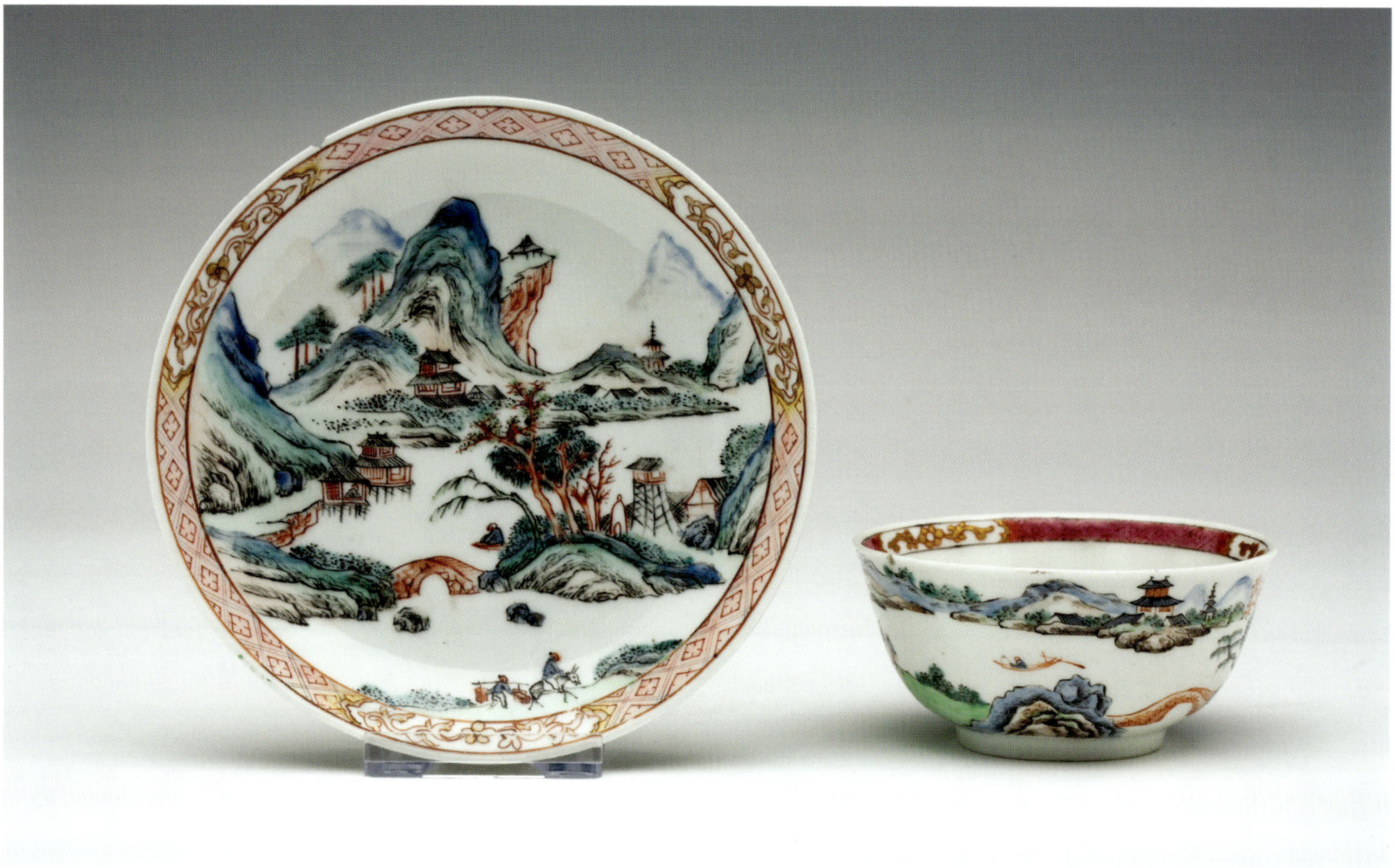

89

89

Worcester teabowl and Chinese saucer

About 1770
Bowl ht 3.7 cm, diam. 7.3 cm; saucer diam. 11.5 cm
1957.24.1.174

Detailed painting on both, with a continuous scene of a prince and his retainers setting out on their travels in the foreground; the border has three red diaper panels separated by gilding.

90

Worcester coffee cup and Chinese saucer

About 1770
Cup ht 6.7 cm, diam. 6.4 cm; saucer diam. 13.4 cm
1957.24.1.226

Decorated with eight main panels, four with wet blue reticulated with gilding, four with red diapering, all with white panel and flower spray, narrow band of flowers between. The cup was possibly decorated by Giles.

91

Worcester coffee cup and Chinese saucer

1770–75
Cup ht 6.4 cm, diam. 5.7 cm; saucer diam. 11.5 cm
1957.24.1.227

Gilt and red dot border, wet blue ground with gilt reticulation, three leaf-shaped reserves defined in green and gold, each containing red and gold flowers. The gilding has worn off the saucer, which was made in South China before 1770.

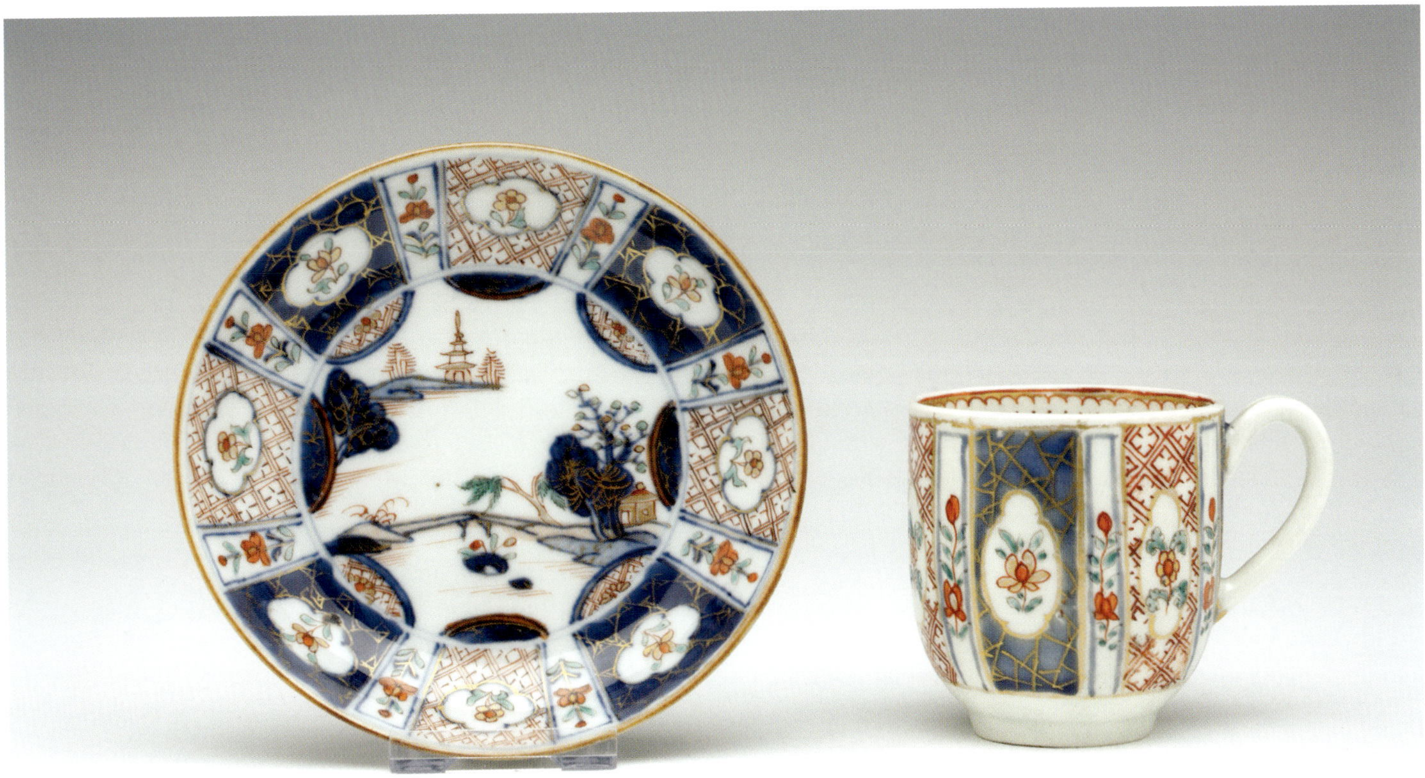

90

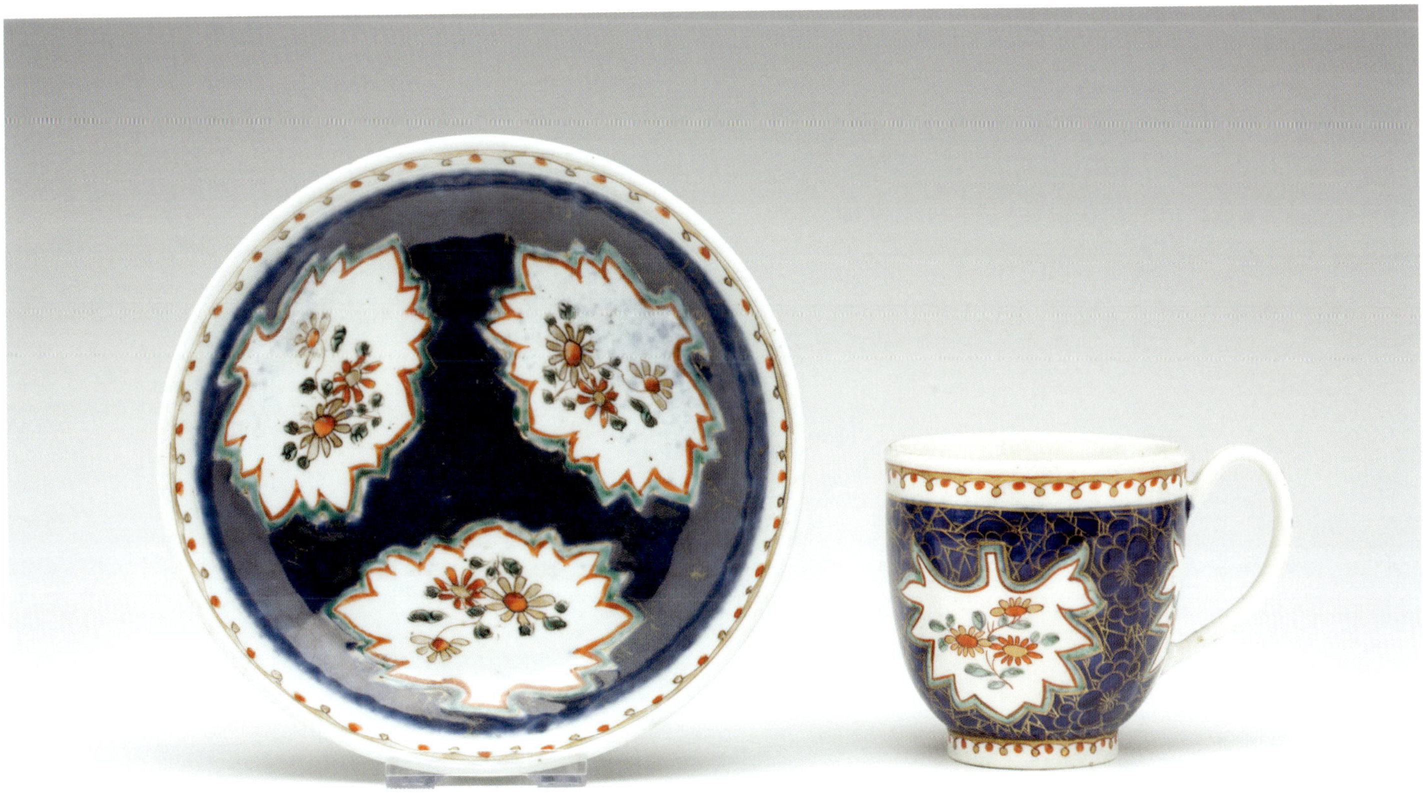

91

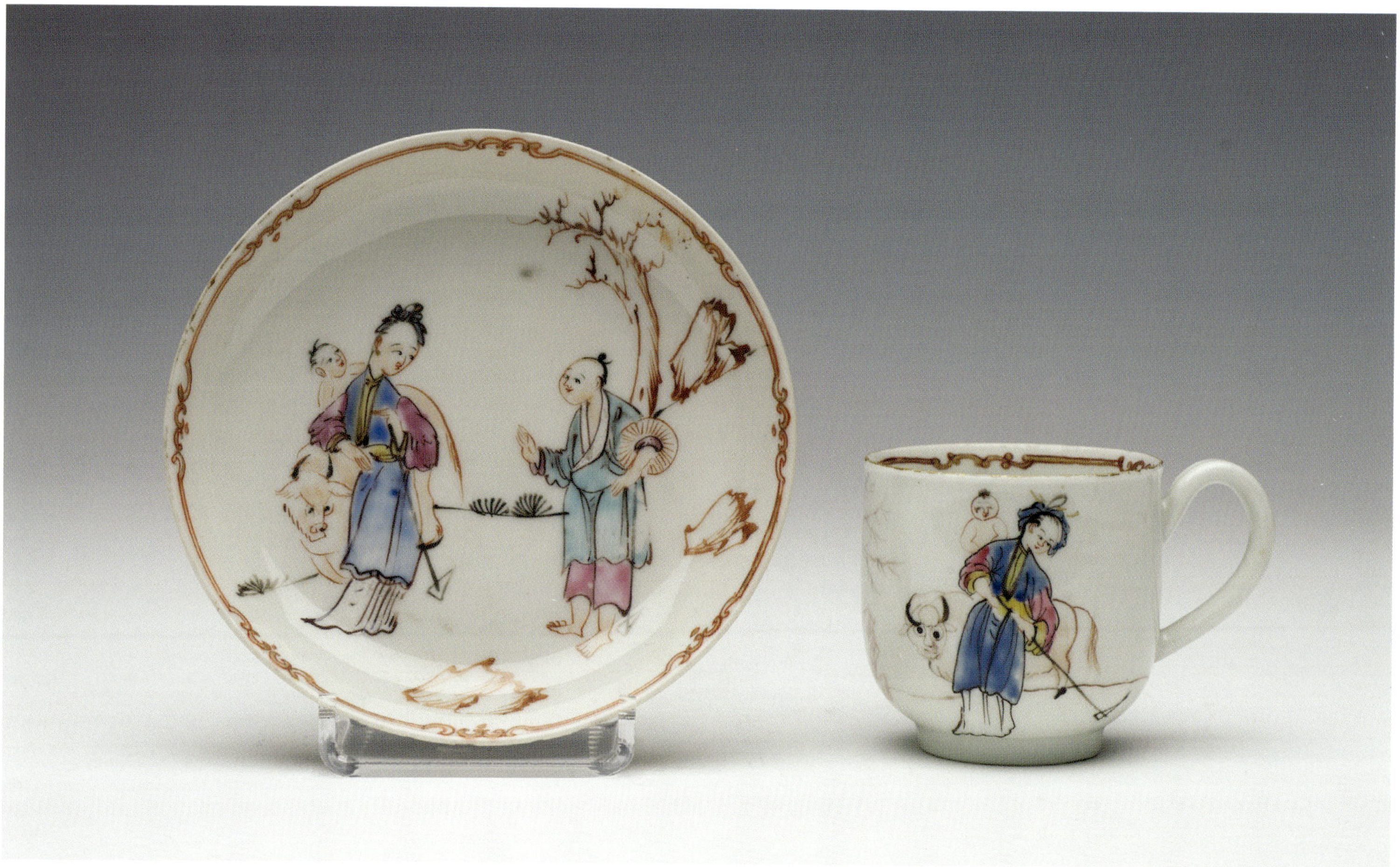

92

92

Worcester cup and Chinese saucer

1760–65
Cup ht 5.7 cm, diam. 5.6 cm; saucer diam. 11.9 cm
1957.24.1.230

Decorated in Oriental style with a woman in front of a cow, man standing on right, each holding a hoe-like implement; a child behind. Simple red and gold border.

93

Worcester cup and Chinese saucer

1778–82
Cup ht 6.1 cm, diam. 5.4 cm; saucer diam. 11.8 cm
1957.24.1. 217

Decorated with an *al fresco* picnic scene taken directly from a Chinese *famille rose* original.

94

Worcester sugar bowl and cover, Chinese stand

Sugar bowl 1755–1760; stand eighteenth century
Sugar bowl ht 10.2 cm, diam. 10.3 cm; stand diam. 15.2 cm
1957.24.1.167

Green diaper border with four formal red chrysanthemums, two seated Chinese figures and one standing beside a child. Marshall considered this to be a replacement as the pattern and grey-green borders are rare at Worcester and closely follow the original.

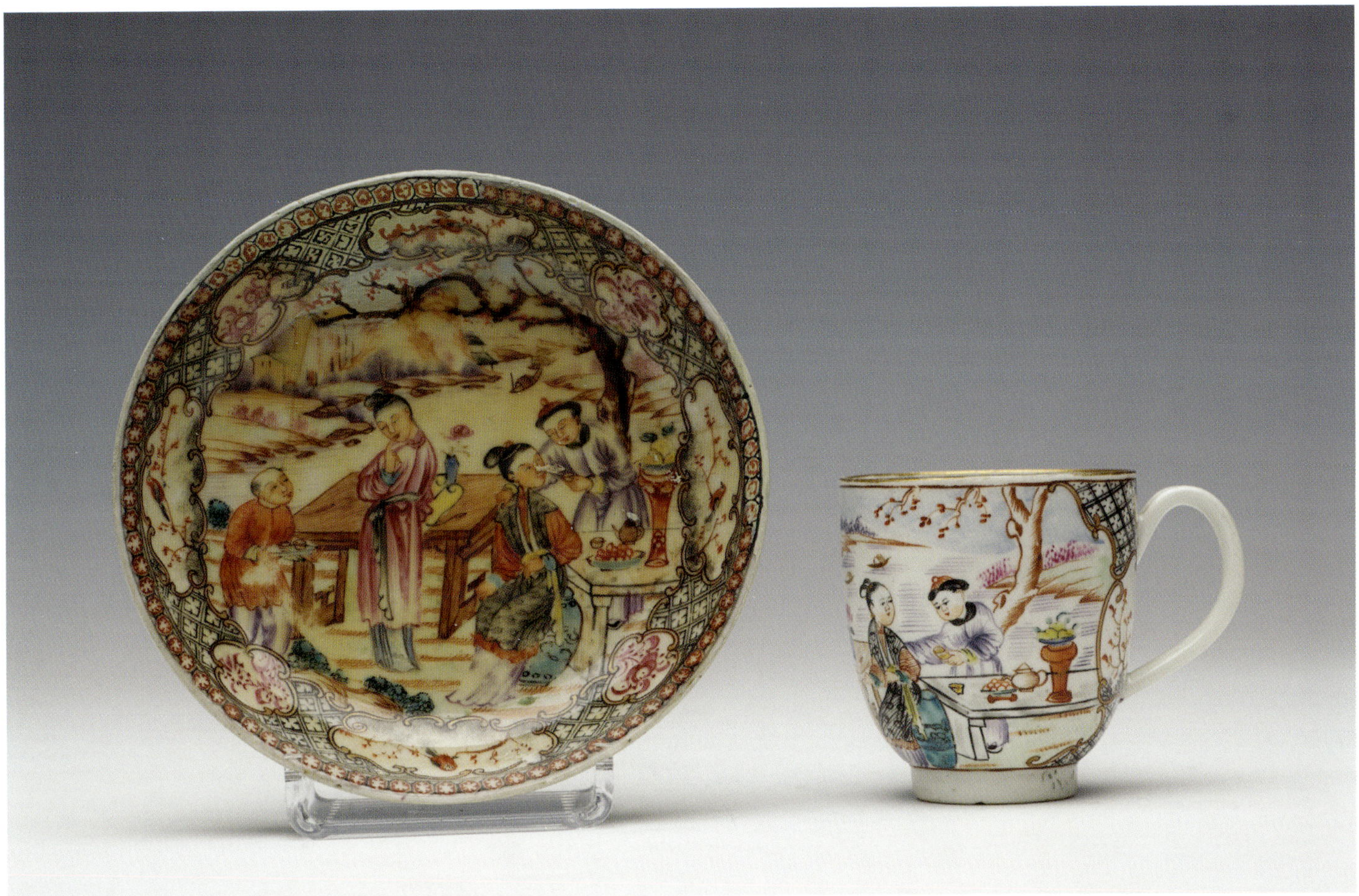

93

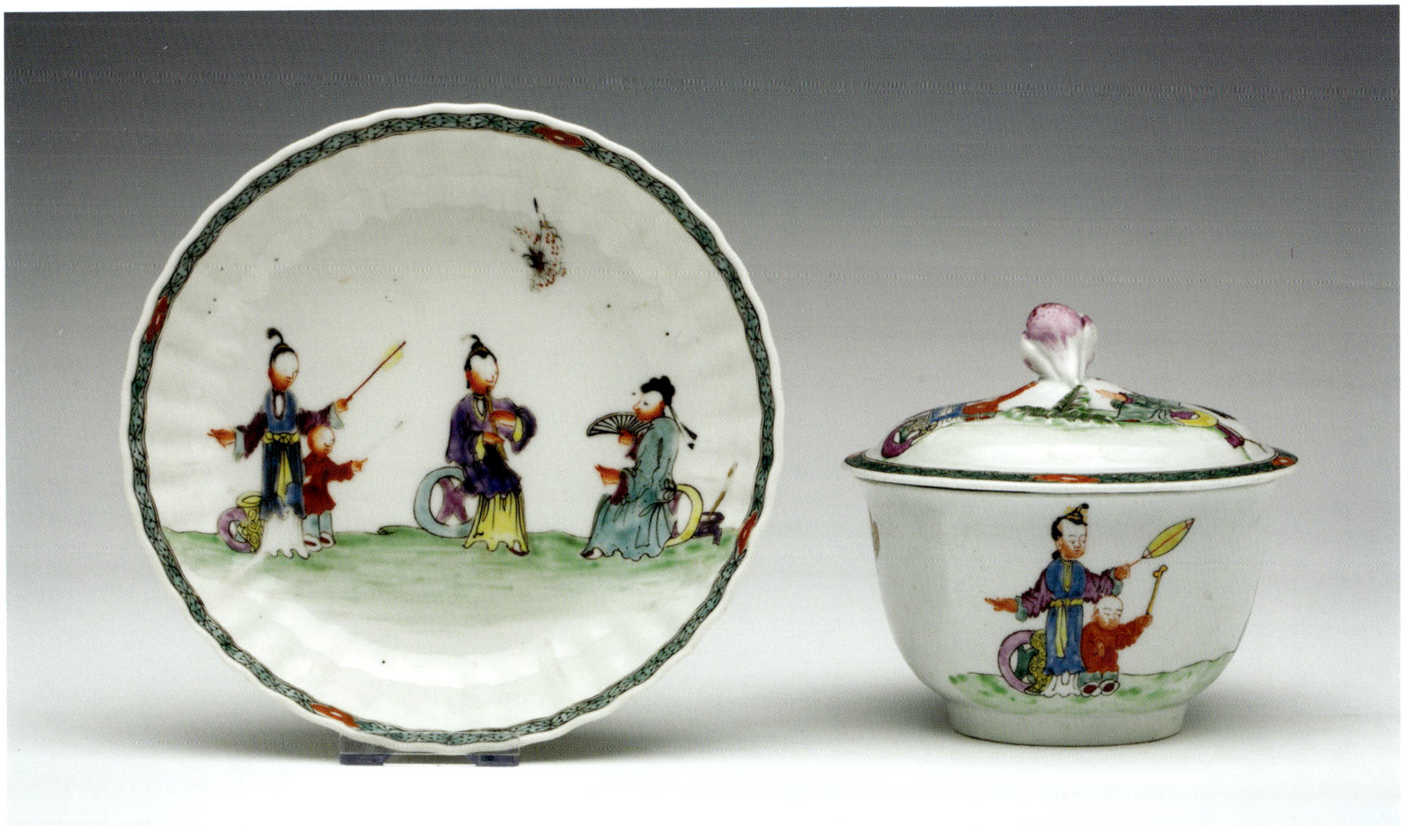

94

2
The Early Period
1751–1756

IN THE FIRST years of the factory, Worcester introduced a chinoiserie style of decoration on porcelain, fusing European and Oriental elements, of which the variety and originality were unsurpassed in England. The essentially European shapes were often derived from silver prototypes. Designs were influenced by Chinese *famille verte* and *famille rose* porcelain and Japanese Kakiemon wares, and the *Indianische Blumen* designs at Meissen. The translucent enamels on many pieces and some of the forms also show close correspondence with salt-glazed stoneware and opaque white glass, which possibly suggests that some Staffordshire workmen with experience in these media worked at Worcester. At the time the Bow porcelain factory, which styled itself 'the new Canton', was concentrating on a more limited range of designs that were closer to the Oriental-style decoration of wares imported by the East India Company. The Chelsea factory, strongly influenced by Meissen and with access to original collections, favoured the Kakiemon style for its Oriental designs and was catering for the more sophisticated aristocratic London market.

The Worcester factory also produced shapes that were less readily available in Chinese porcelain, such as sauceboats, pickle leaves, creamboats and coffee pots. The soapstone body allowed for thinly potted wares, resistant to hot liquids and often having detailed moulding, which were unmatched by other British factories, thus offering the public something entirely new. An advertisement in *The Public Advertiser* of 1 March 1754 for the sale of 40,000 pieces of Worcester porcelain asserts that 'the Commodity will speak for itself'.

The chinoiserie decoration offered a fanciful and idealised view of the Oriental world, with loose compositions of flowering shrubs, decorative rock formations and angular fences, together with Oriental figures and birds. Although there is a great range of designs, individual figures or motifs are often repeated: for example, hollow blue rocks and a crane-like bird, usually with a yellow breast and often standing on one leg, are recurring motifs. Where some patterns appear to be close to the original Japanese Kakiemon or Chinese designs, it is difficult to ascertain whether they were taken directly from the Oriental originals or from Meissen interpretations. Although Meissen was rare in England at this time, it is possible that Worcester had access to some pieces. A few patterns, such as the 'Stag Hunt', probably originated as English designs, were used in China and then re-exported to England.

A group of mainly thrown or turned shapes, often with a characteristic greyish-toned glaze, are known as 'scratch cross' (1753/4–1755/6). These pieces are usually marked with an incised line or cross on the base, sometimes together and occasionally with a painter's mark. The shapes show a more direct link to silver shapes than some of the moulded wares of the same period, which at times appear to be more closely associated with Staffordshire salt-glaze stoneware. Although they are now known to be Worcester products, Marshall believed them to have been made in Liverpool so there are only a few examples in his collection.

Another distinctive group of early Worcester comprises pieces with 'pencilled' decoration. Detailed patterns in monochrome were achieved by using a small pointed brush or 'pencil' with black, manganese or puce enamels. This technique, similar to French *grisaille* and German *Schwarzlot*, is thought to have originated in the Netherlands on stained glass and glass vessels, and then spread to Germany. It was adopted in China, where European engravings were copied in black enamel on export porcelain. The technique was used at Worcester for Oriental scenes, mainly from the late 1750s to the early 1760s, but puce, in particular, may have continued up to about 1770. Of the English factories, the use of pencilling was often thought to be unique to Worcester. However, Derby used a similar technique in puce monochrome.[1] Only a few examples of pencilled decoration on Liverpool porcelain are known, including a William Reid & Co. teapot.[2] Longton Hall also used the technique[3] and the *Salisbury Journal* of 8 September 1790 refers to the sale of the factory stock to include 'pencil'd' wares.

1 See Twitchett 2002, pls. 91, 171, 218.
2 See Hillis 2011, pl. 3.32, p. 34.
3 Watney 1957, pl. 27b.

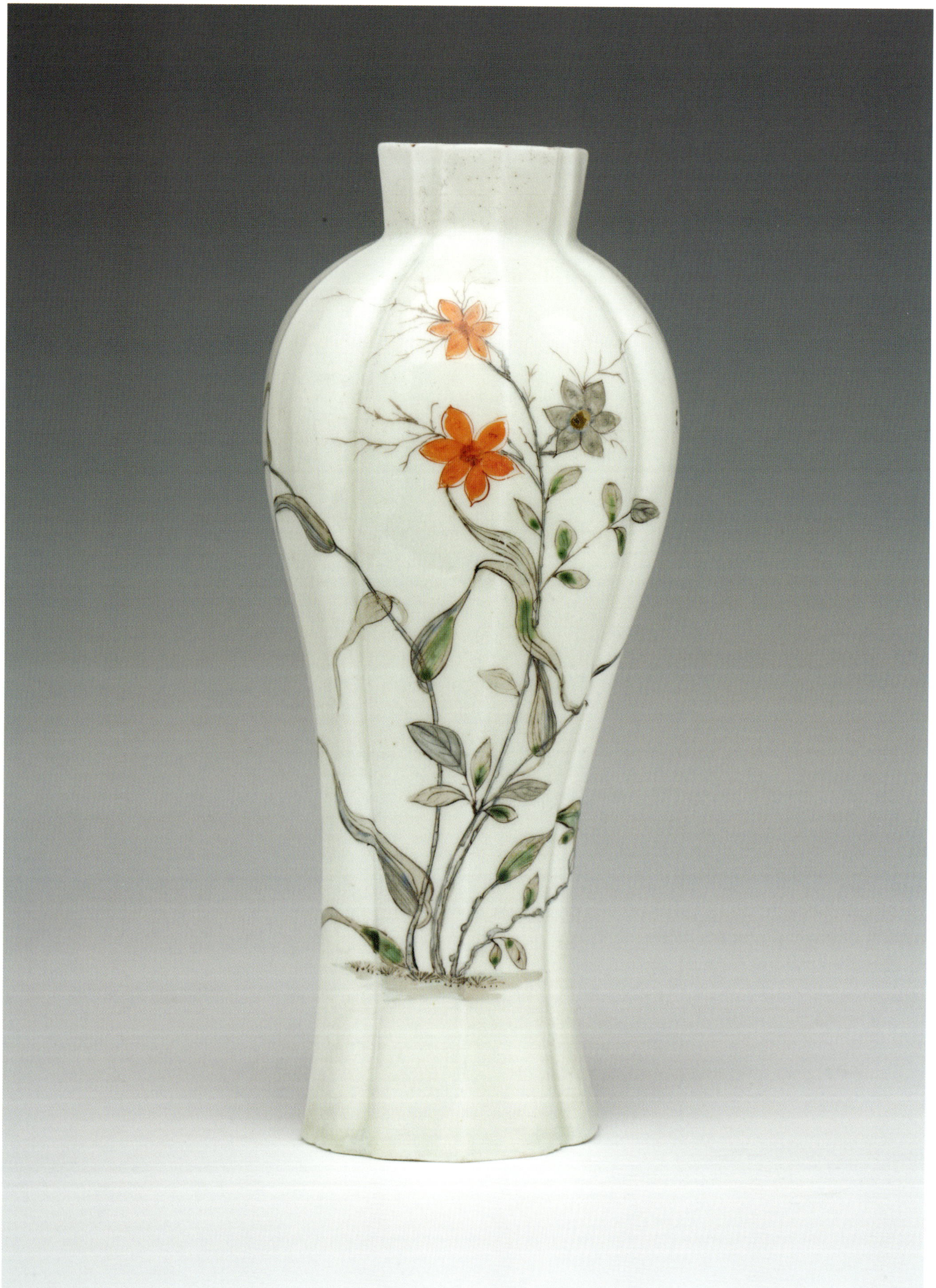

95

95

Vase

About 1752
Ht 19 cm
1957.24.1.773

Lobed baluster shape, derived from Kangxi porcelain, painted in *famille verte* style with flowering plants and grasses and on the reverse with a flying bird and insects.

The companion vase was sold by Mr Marshall, with other duplicates, at Sotheby's on 27 January 1953 and is illustrated in Spero 1984, pl. 1. Two similar vases with covers are in the Museum of Fine Arts, Boston, USA (1988.1052 a-b and 1988.1053 a-b; see fig. 11). A lobed jug with similar decoration is illustrated in Spero 2005, pl. 45.

REFERENCES
Marshall 1954, pl. 3, no. 45; Reynolds 1999, pl. 1.

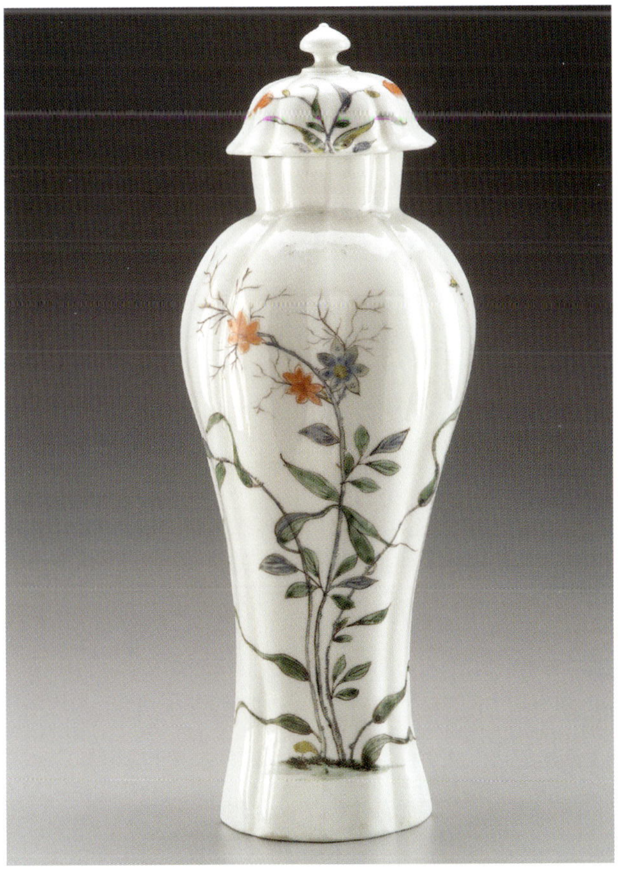

Fig. 11 One of two similar vases with original covers from the Katz Collection, Museum of Fine Arts, Boston, 1988.1052 a-b

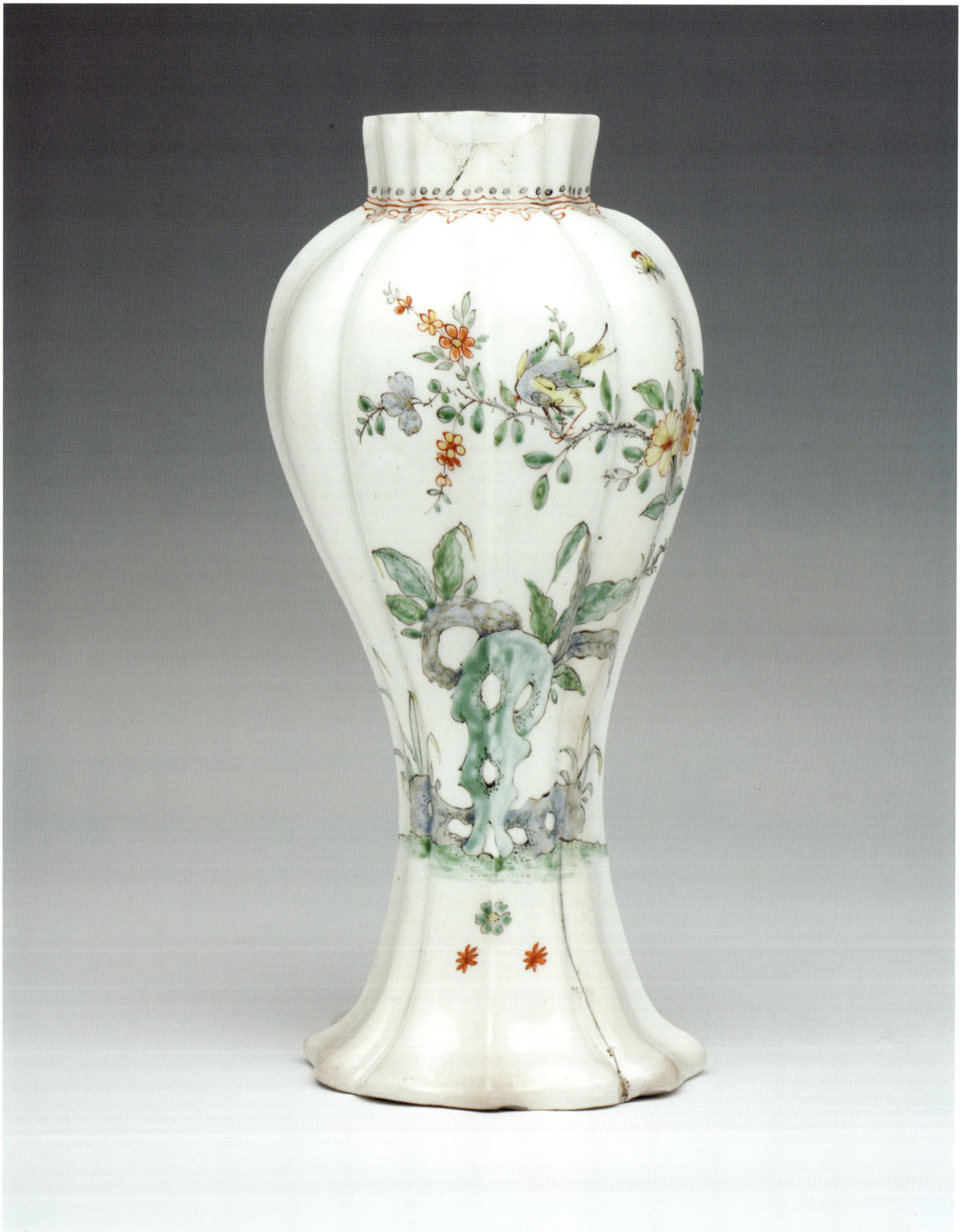

[78] THE EARLY PERIOD: 1751–1756

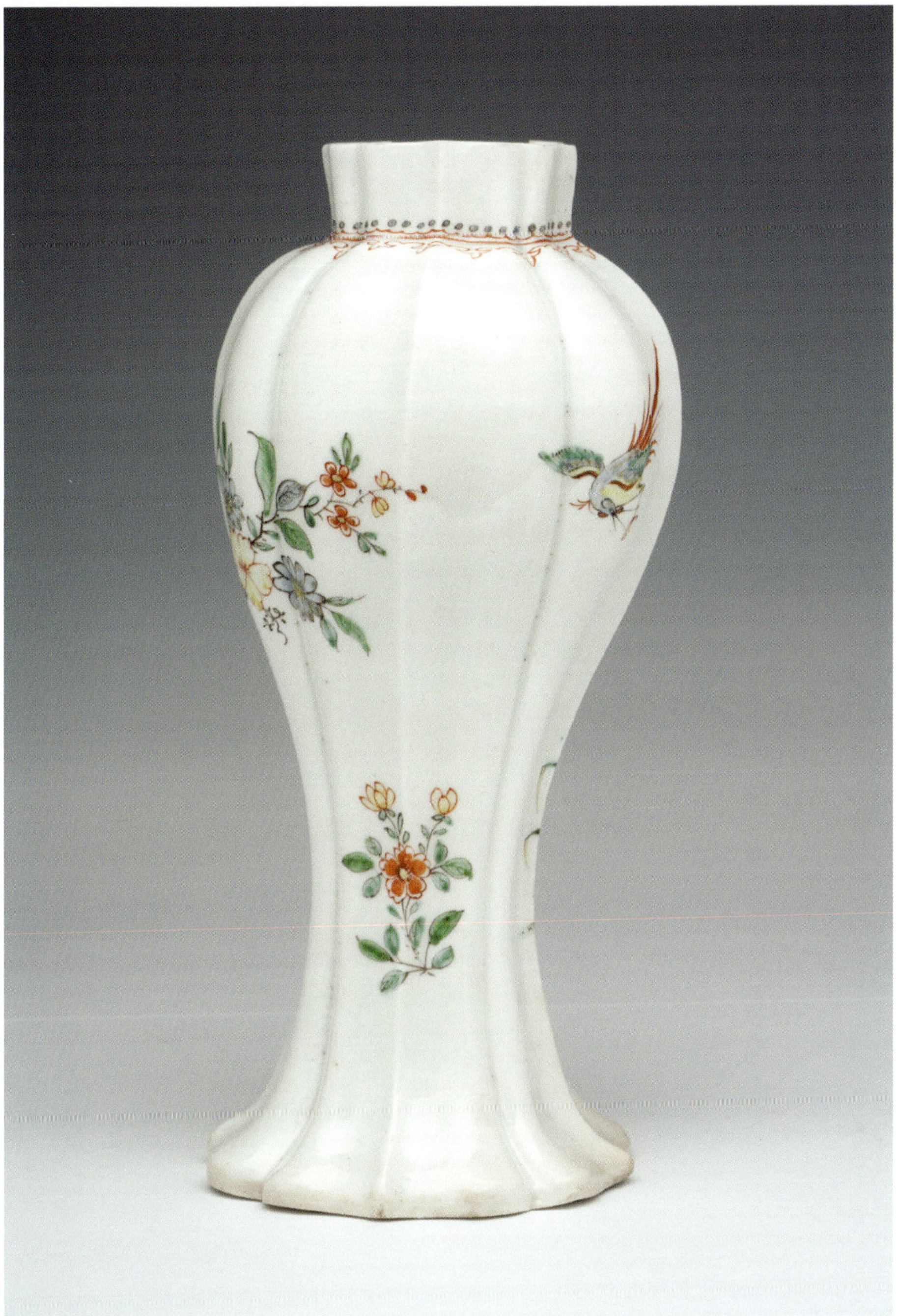

96

96

Vase

1752–3
Ht 22.5 cm
1957.24.1.777

Octagonal, fluted, baluster shape with narrow neck and spreading foot; decorated in green, grey-blue, red and yellow, with plants arising from rocks and one ho-ho bird in flight on reverse; red trefoil border around neck; cover missing.

This vase would have formed part of a garniture of five or seven vases.

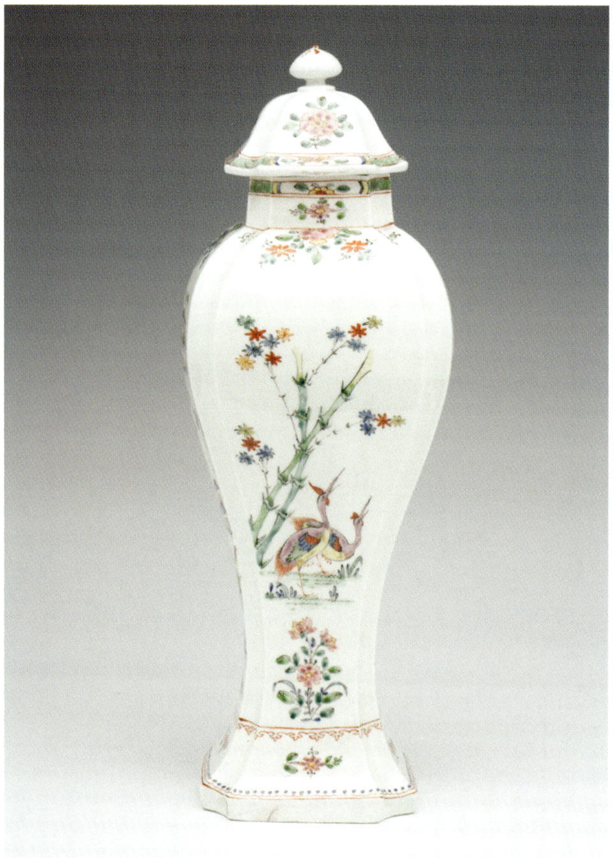

97

97

Vase with cover

1752–3
Ht 32 cm
1957.24.1.532

Baluster shape with chamfered square corners and spreading base, decorated with birds on two sides and Oriental figures in a landscape on the others. Possibly the central vase in a garniture of three, used to decorate the mantel of a chimneypiece. Two similar examples in the Victoria and Albert Museum are illustrated in Marshall 1954, pl. 54, nos. 1104 and 1106.

PROVENANCE
D.M. & P. Manheim, London, 6 June 1951, £350 for a set of three vases.

REFERENCES
Marshall 1954, pl. 43, no. 889; Dawson 2007, pl. 4; Spero 2008, no. 27, p. 44.

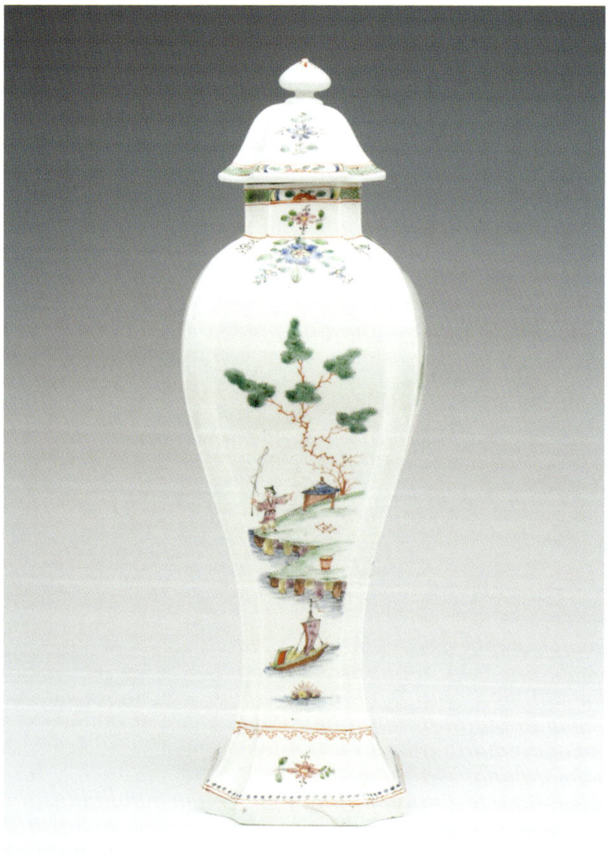

97

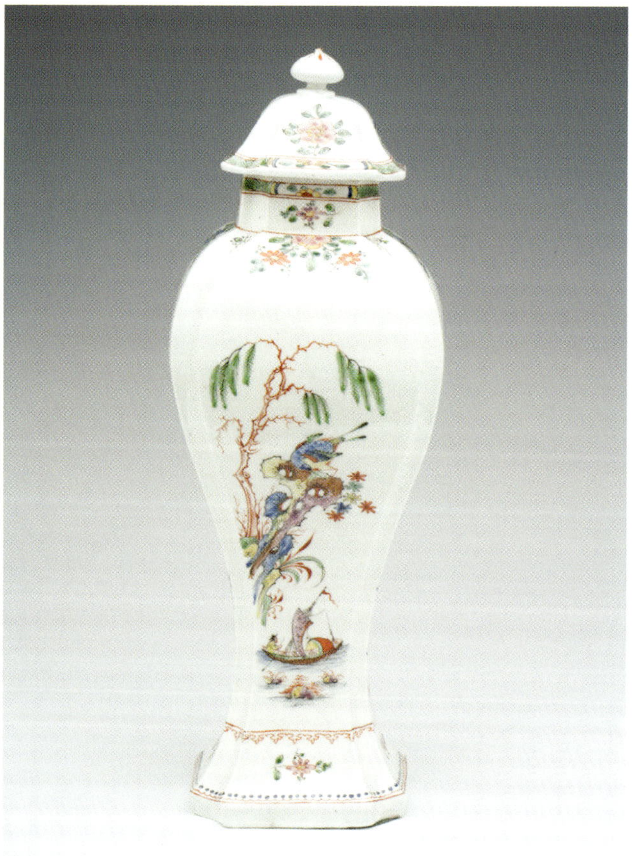

97

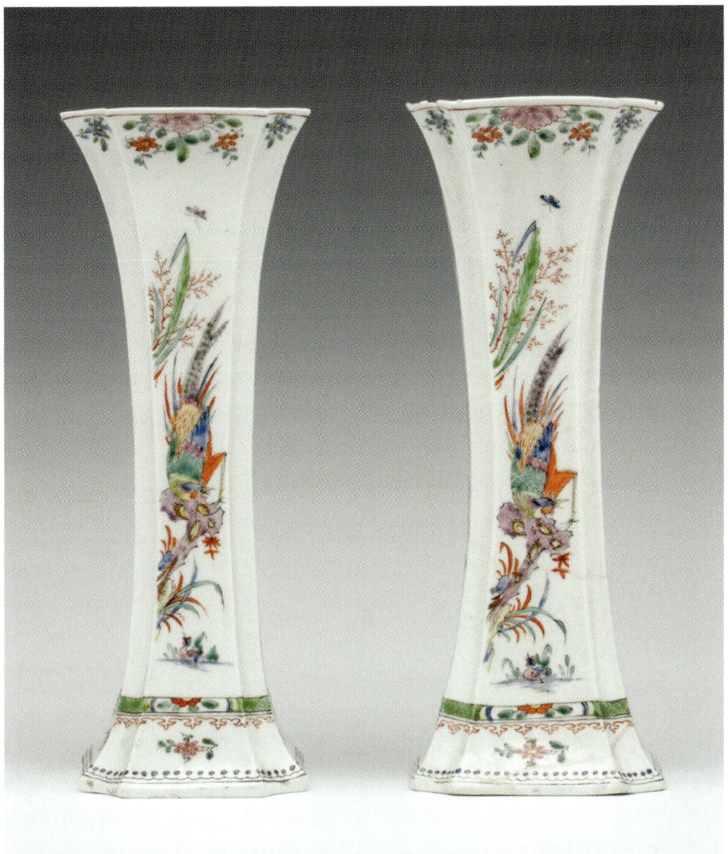

98, 99

98, 99

Pair of vases

1752–3
Ht 24.5 cm and 24.3 cm
1957.24.1.530 and 1957.24.1.534

Chinese bird decoration in a pastel palette; possibly part of a garniture of three vases, with no. 97.

PROVENANCE
Frank Hurlbutt sale, Sotheby's, London, 30 July 1946, lot 14, £75.

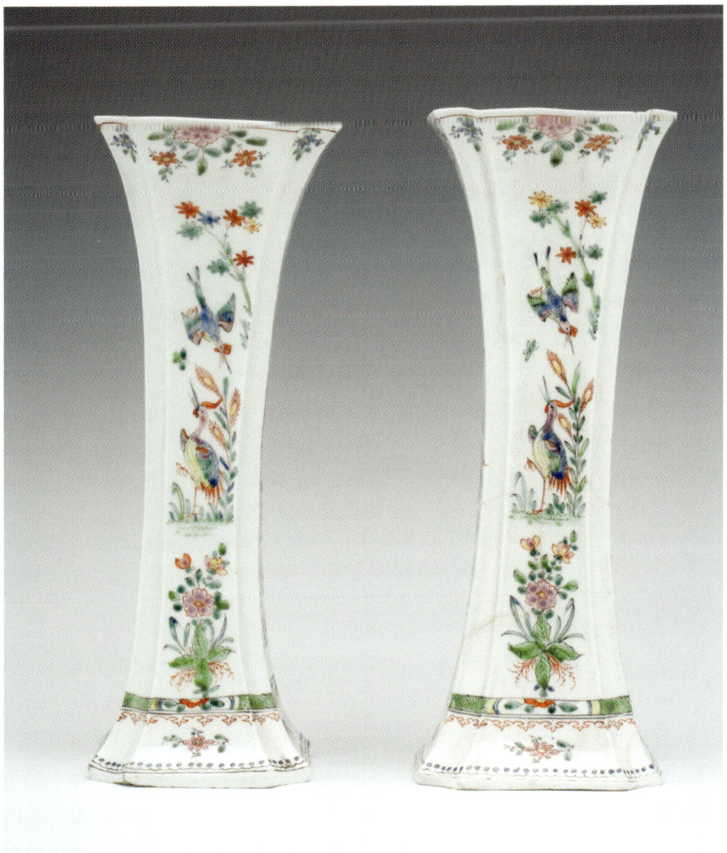

98, 99

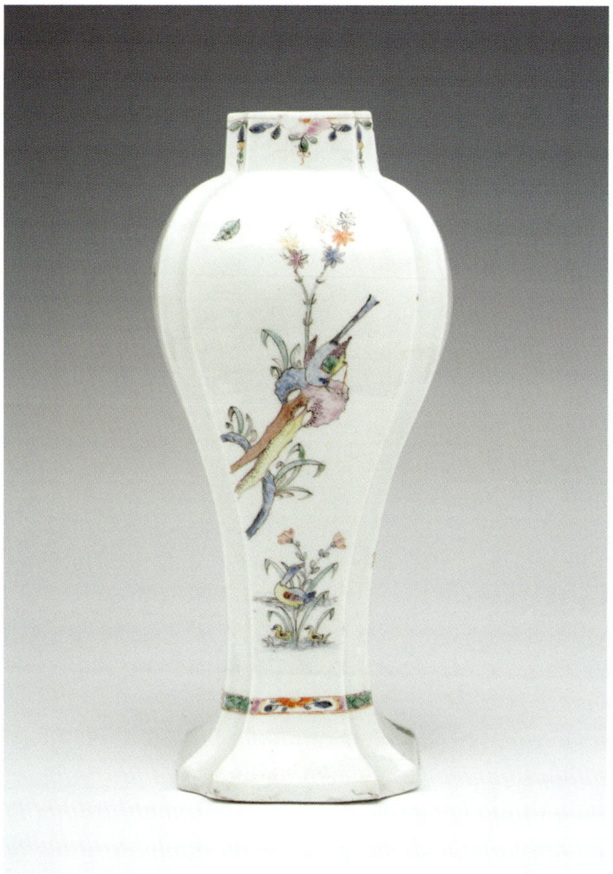

100

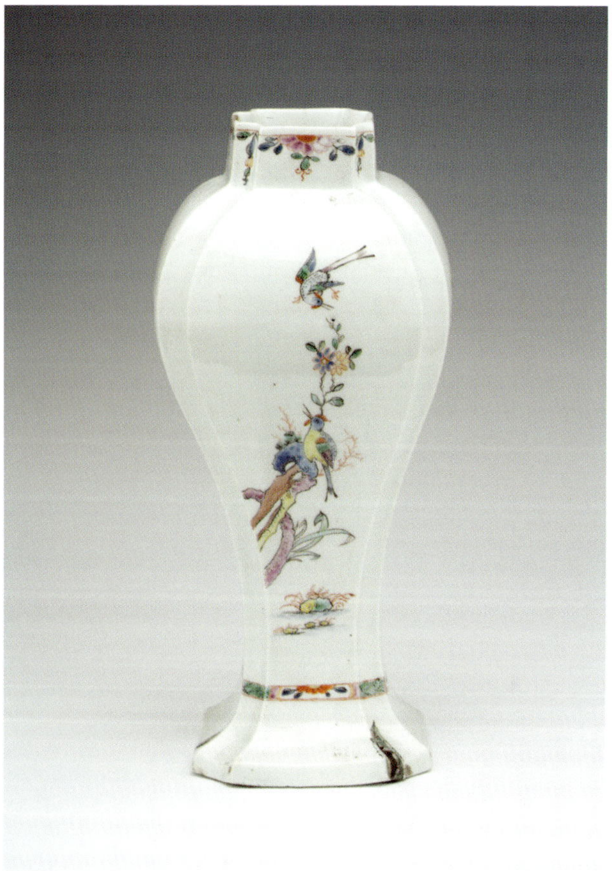

100

100

Vase

Ht 27.1 (without cover)
1957.24.1.528

Quadrangular baluster shape with fluted corners, decorated in Chinese style in pastel colours with exotic birds, flowering trees and plants. Replacement cover.

REFERENCES
Bonhams, London, 10 May 2006, lot 15.

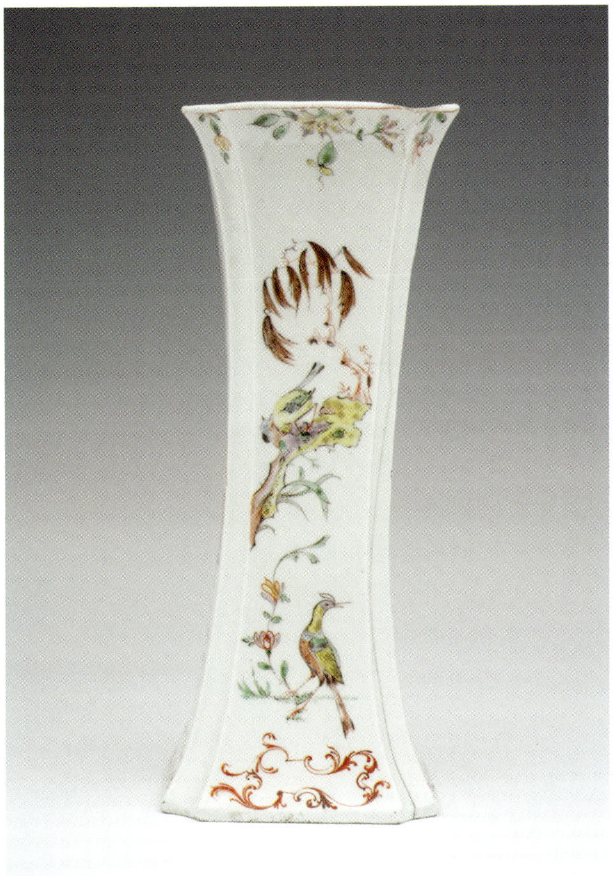

101

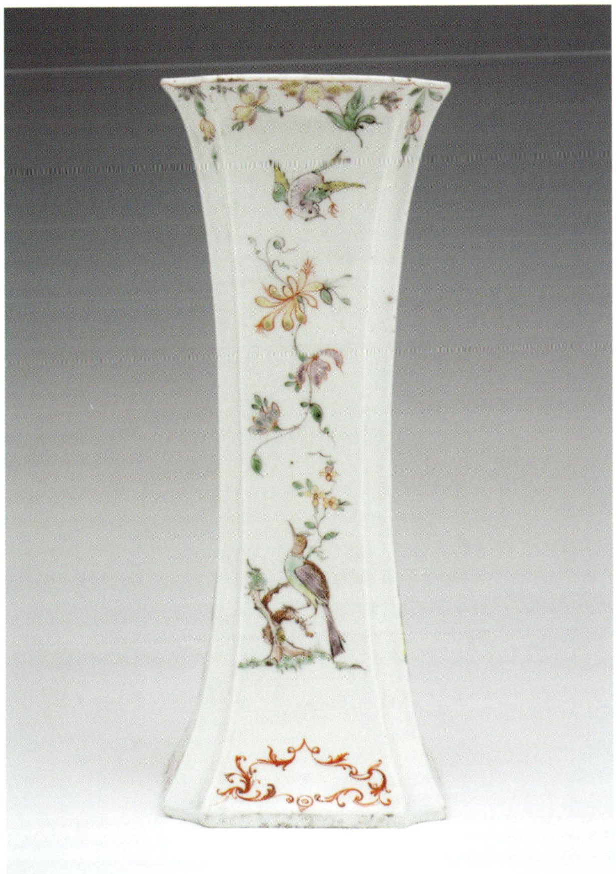

101

101

Vase

1752–3
Ht 25.7 cm
1957.24.1.775

Single vase decorated in Chinese style with birds and foliage in pastel colours and puce scrollwork near base.

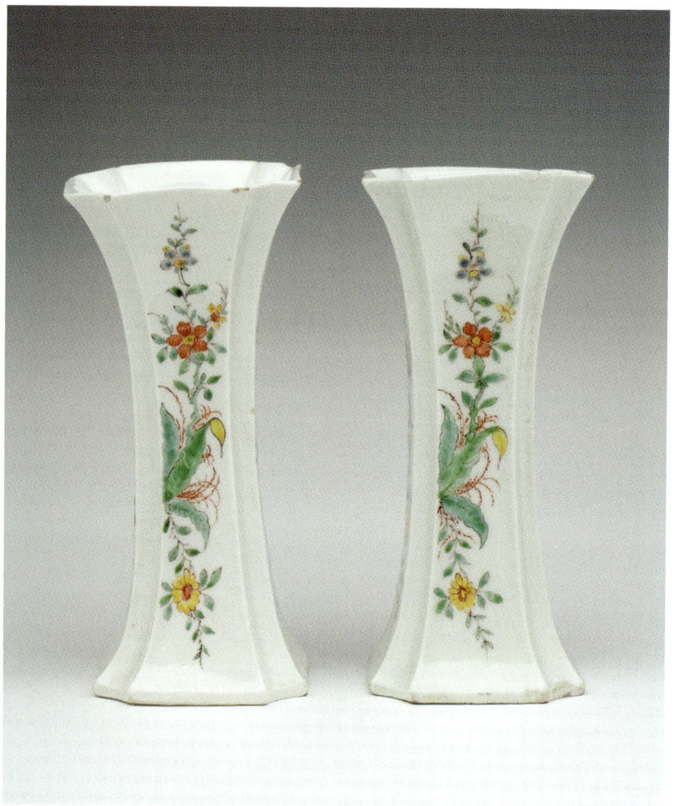

102, 103

102, 103

Pair of vases

1752–3
Ht 18.2 cm and 18.5 cm
1957.24.1.774 and 776

Quadrangular with fluted corners and concave sides, derived from a Chinese form; painted in pastel shades with Chinese flowering plants representing the seasons. A smaller vase of similar form is illustrated in Dawson 2007, pl. 6.

104

Bowl

1752–3
Ht 7.5 cm, diam. 18.4 cm
1957.24.1.845

One of only two recorded examples of lotus-leaf moulded bowls; decorated with floral sprays irrespective of moulding.

PROVENANCE
Arthur Hurst sale part 3, Sotheby's, London, 30 January 1941, lot 108.

REFERENCE
Spero 2005, p. 133, no. 49.

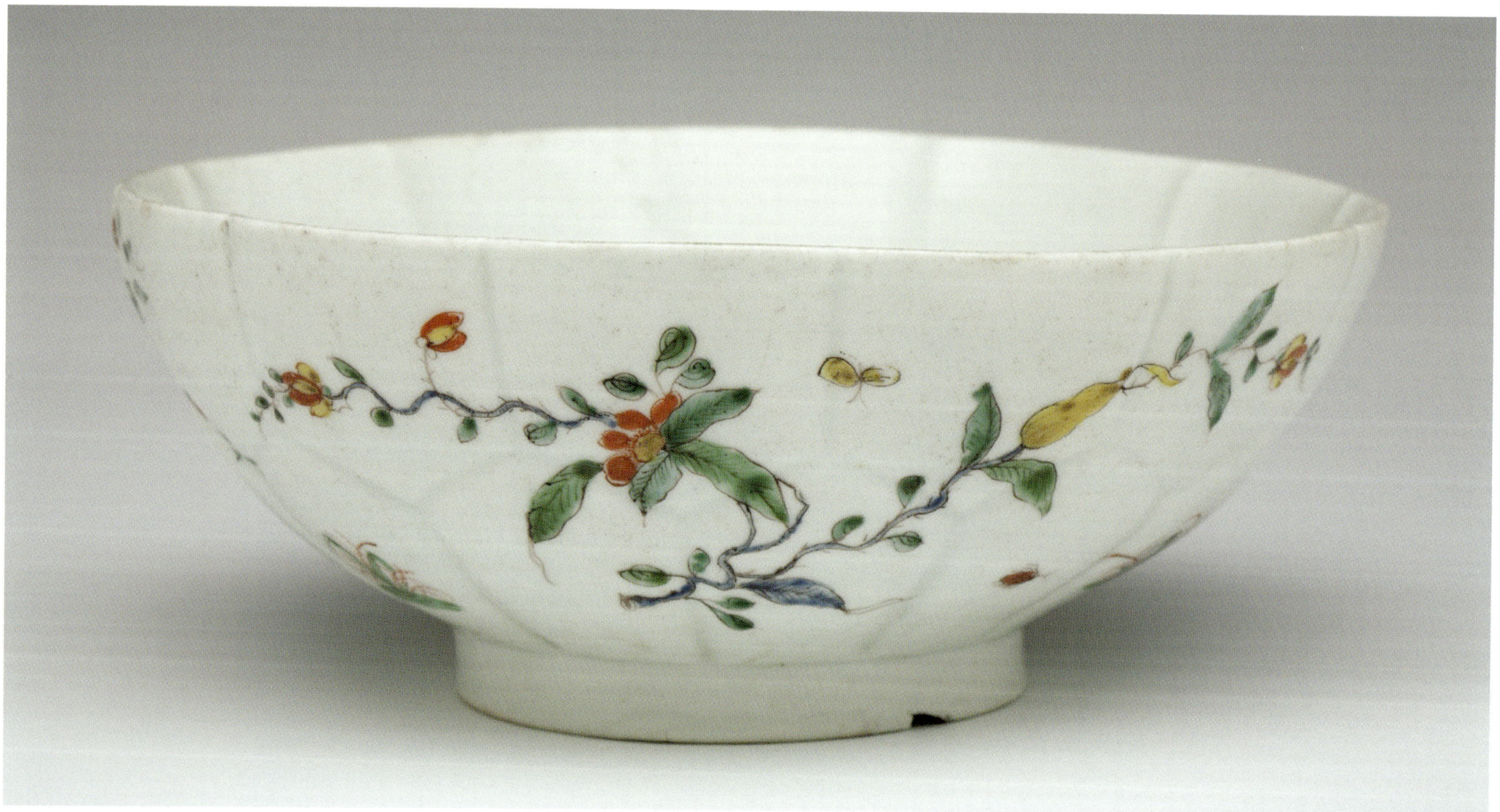

104

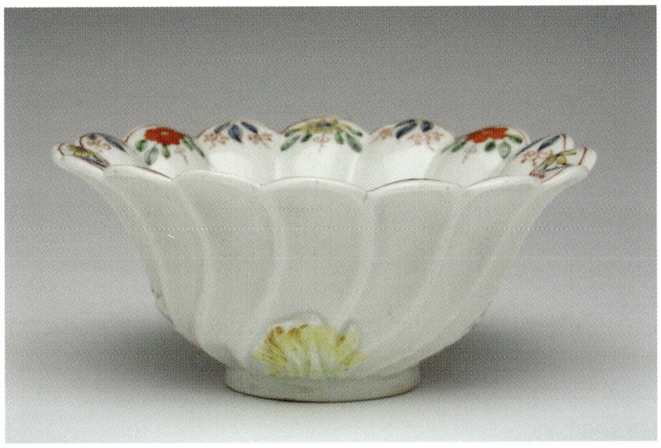

105

105

Bowl

About 1753
Ht 6.7 cm, diam. 14.8 cm
1957.24.1.749

Spirally fluted, scalloped rim; four moulded acanthus leaves at base, coloured alternately yellow and mauve; polychrome floral border inside rim and flower spray in base.

PROVENANCE
Albert Amor, London, 4 April 1956, £48.

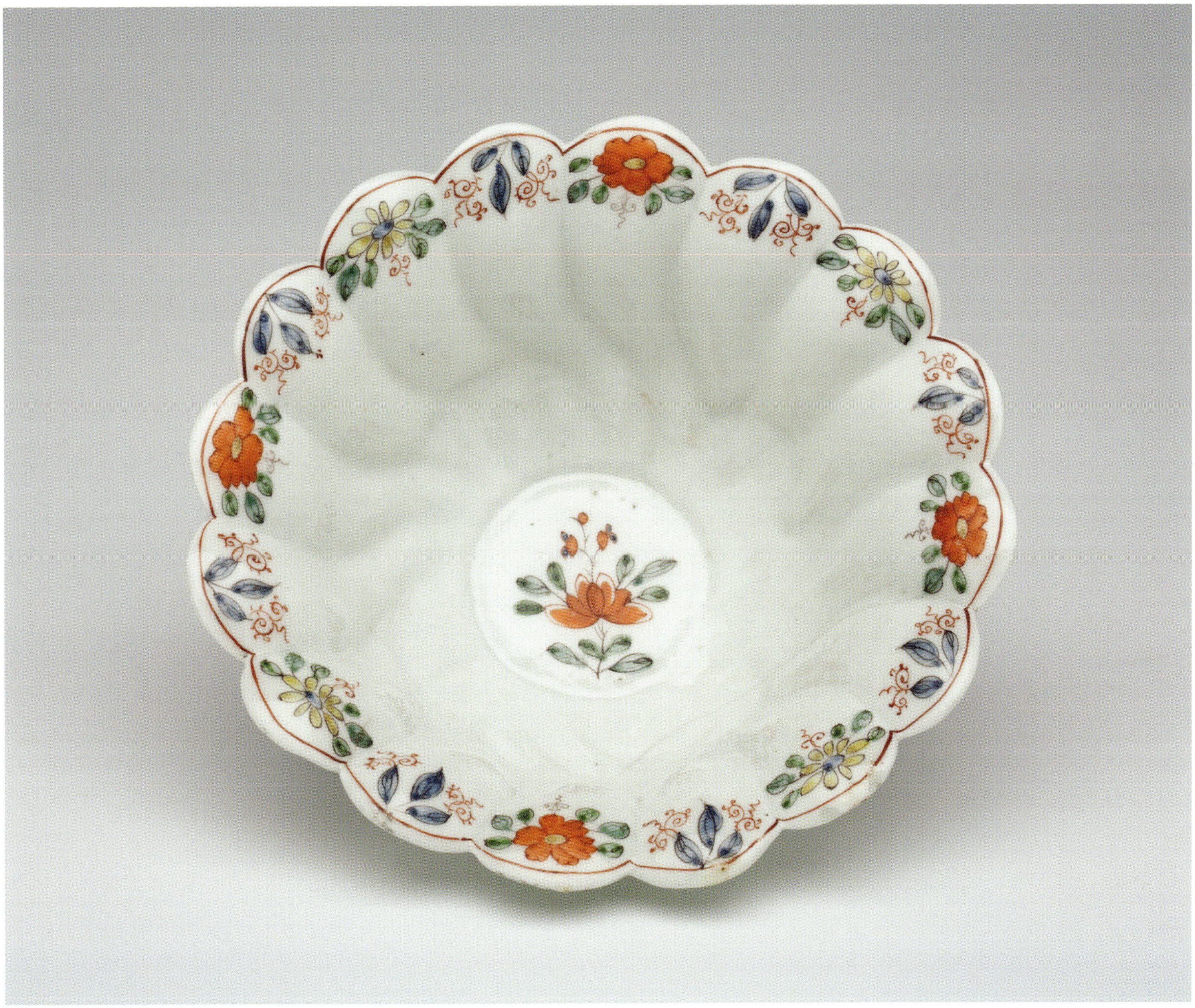

105

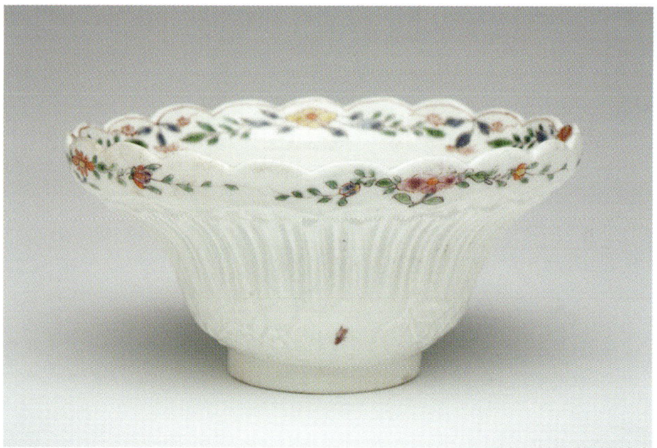

106

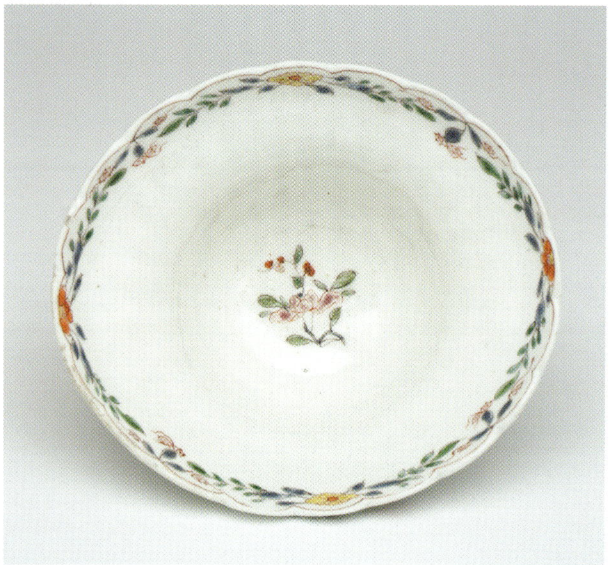

106

106

Sugar bowl
About 1753
Ht 7 cm, diam. 14.1 cm
1957.24.1.751

Moulded silver shape with floral wreath inside and outside rim, flower spray in centre, three minute insects near base. This would originally have had a cover and would have been used for sugar. Sugar was a luxury until the second half of the eighteenth century and many sugar boxes were in silver.

Sugar bowls were not common at Worcester until after 1760, when they started to be supplied with tea services; prior to this, most porcelain examples were Chinese or Bow. The only complete example recorded of a covered sugar bowl of this type is illustrated in Spero 1996, pl. 20. Another example in the Museum of Royal Worcester Porcelain is illustrated in Barrett 1966, p. 6b.

REFERENCES
Clarke 1987, pl. 5; Spero 2005, pl. 53.

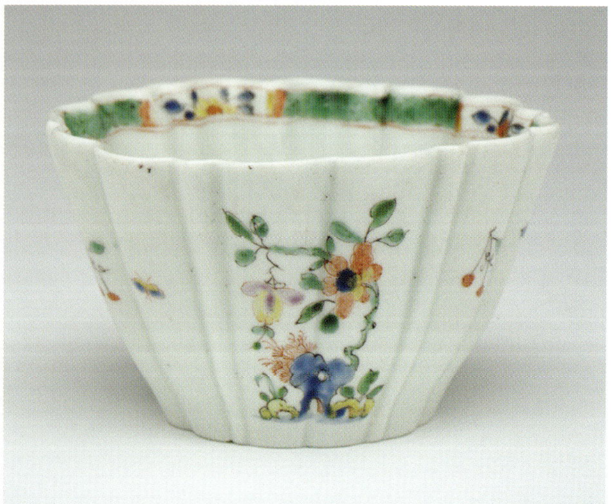

107

107

Sugar bowl
About 1753
Ht 6.8 cm, diam. 11.5 cm
1957.24.1.755

Silver shape, decorated with Oriental-style floral sprays; border of green formalised flowers inside rim; flower spray in base.

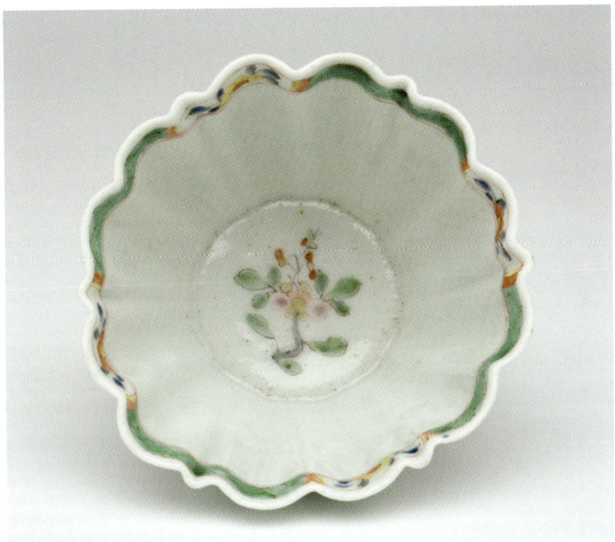

107

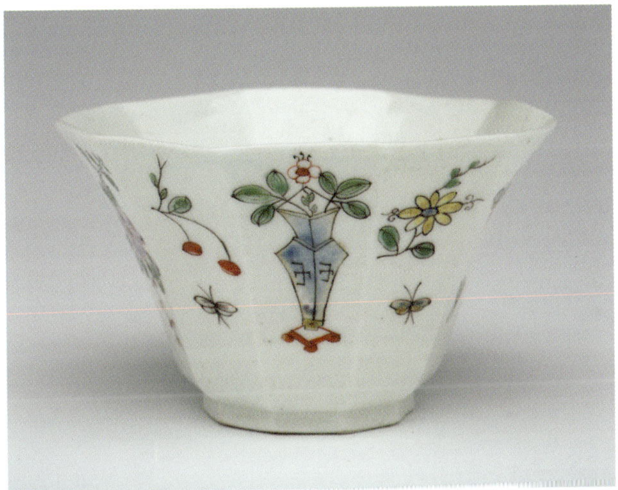

108

108

Wine cup

About 1753
Ht 5.8 cm, diam. 9.3 cm
1957.24.1.752

Decagonal, widening to rim, decorated with vases of flowers, insects and floral sprays; a rare shape, known only at Worcester.

REFERENCE
Spero 2005, pls. 54, 127.

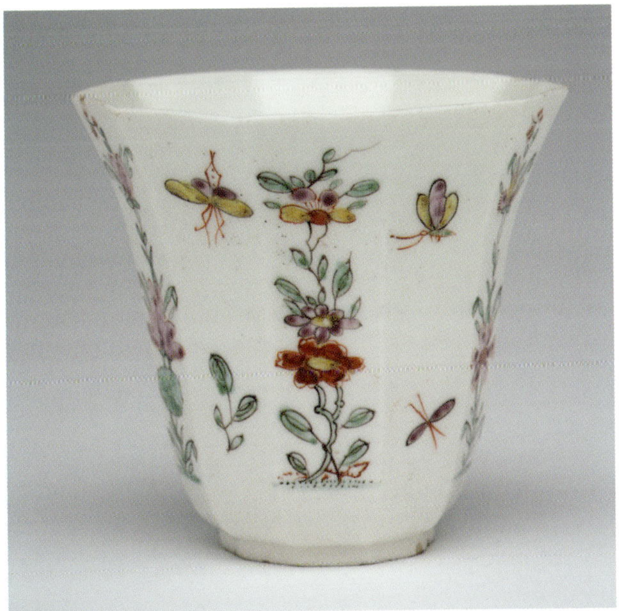

109

109

Wine cup or beaker

1753–4
Ht 6.8 cm, diam. 6.6 cm
1957.24.1.748

Slender, flaring, decagonal shape, decorated with alternating panels of flowers and insects.

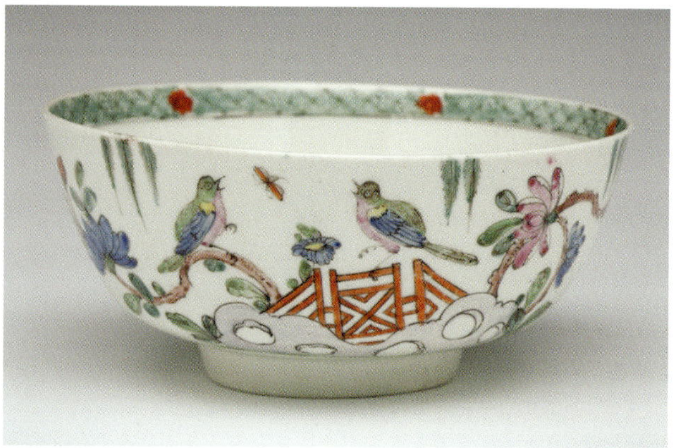

110

110

Bowl

About 1755
Ht 7.1 cm, diam. 15.3 cm
1957.24.1.480

Decorated with two birds perched on a fence on irregular grey rock, floral sprays and insects; green and black diaper border inside rim, with red formal flowers

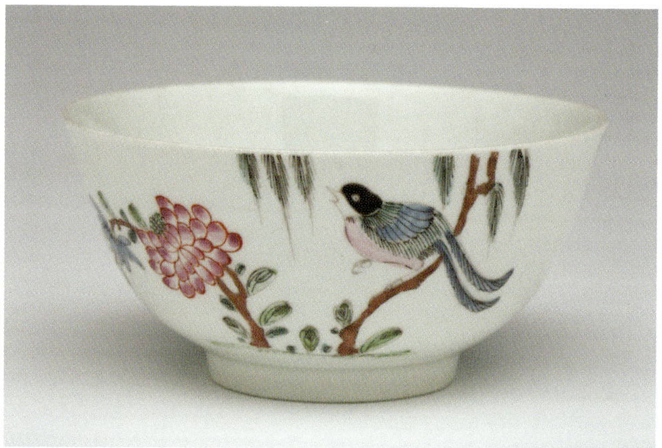

111

111

Bowl

About 1755
Ht 6 cm, diam. 12.1 cm
1957.24.1.481

Painted in Chinese *famille rose* style with an unusually large long-tailed bird perched on a weeping willow, peony spray opposite; decoration extends round the plain rim of the bowl.

PROVENANCE
Sotheby's, London, 18 November 1952, lot 73, £46.

REFERENCES
Amor 1990, fig. 78; Bonhams, London, 12 March 2008, lot 175.

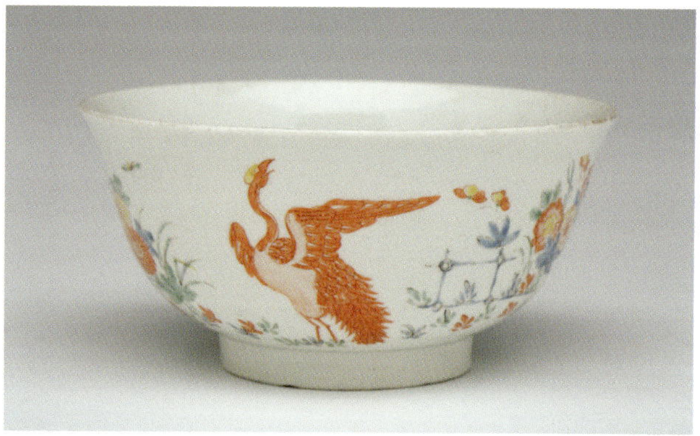

112

112

Bowl

1755–60
Ht 6.2 cm, diam. 12.4 cm
1957.24.1.485

Flared rim decorated with bird in coral red amongst Chinese flowers and foliage.

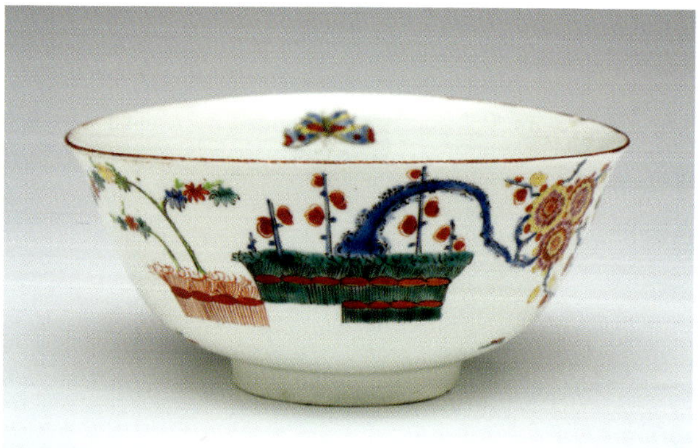

113

113

Bowl

About 1755
Ht 7.4 cm, diam. 15.5 cm
1957.24.1.841

Everted rim with brown edge, decorated in Kakiemon style, with sheaves of wheat and prunus. The Worcester interpretation of the 'Banded Hedge' pattern closely follows Meissen.

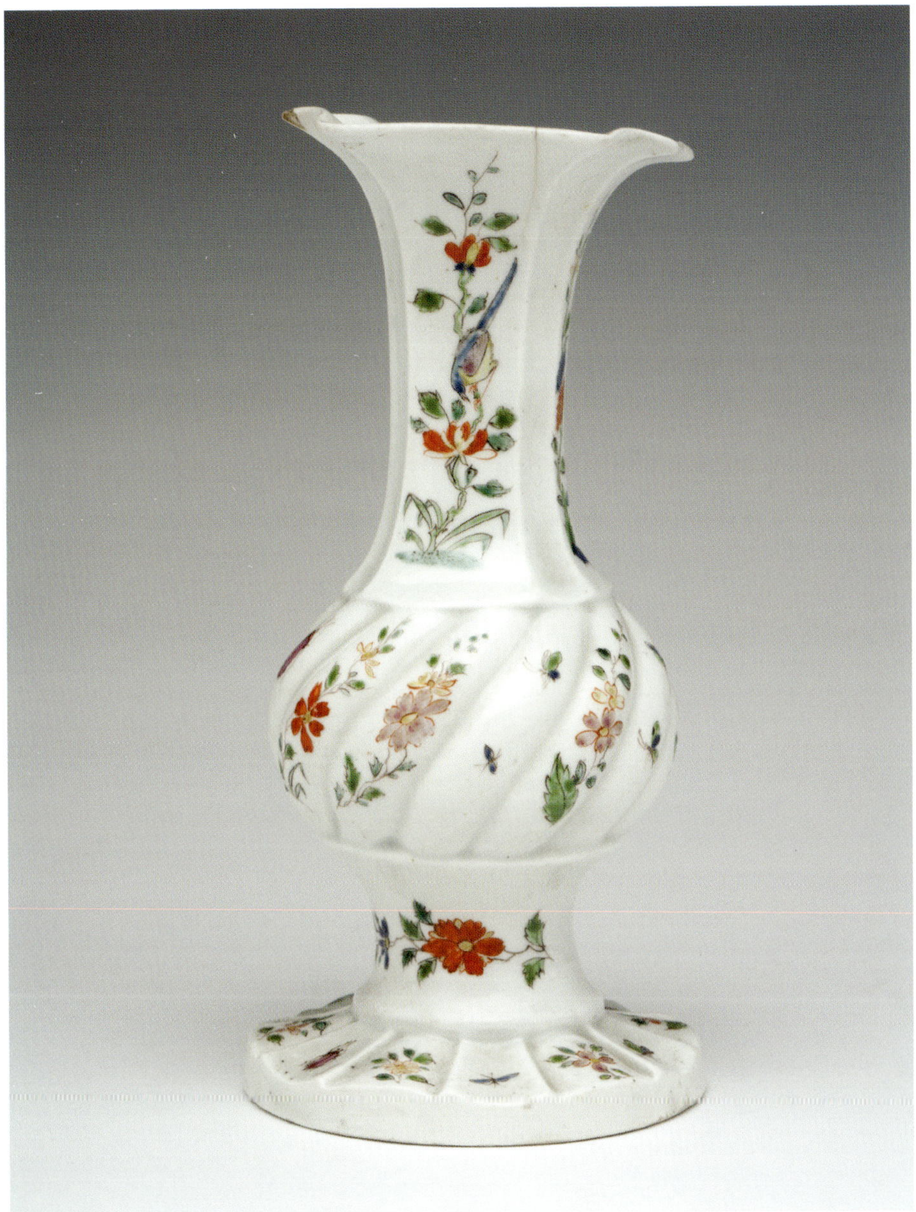

114

114

Vase

1752–3
Ht 15.8 cm
1957.24.1.606

Radially fluted with globular body, octagonal neck and wide fluted rim; decorated alternately with flower sprays and insects, bird decoration on neck. A larger vase of the same shape appears in Robb 2005. Another example is in the Museum of Fine Arts, Boston (inv. 1988.1018).

PROVENANCE
Glendenning Collection; Tilley & Co., London, 26 April 1944, £16.

REFERENCES
Sandon 1993, p. 354; Spero 2005, pl. 67.

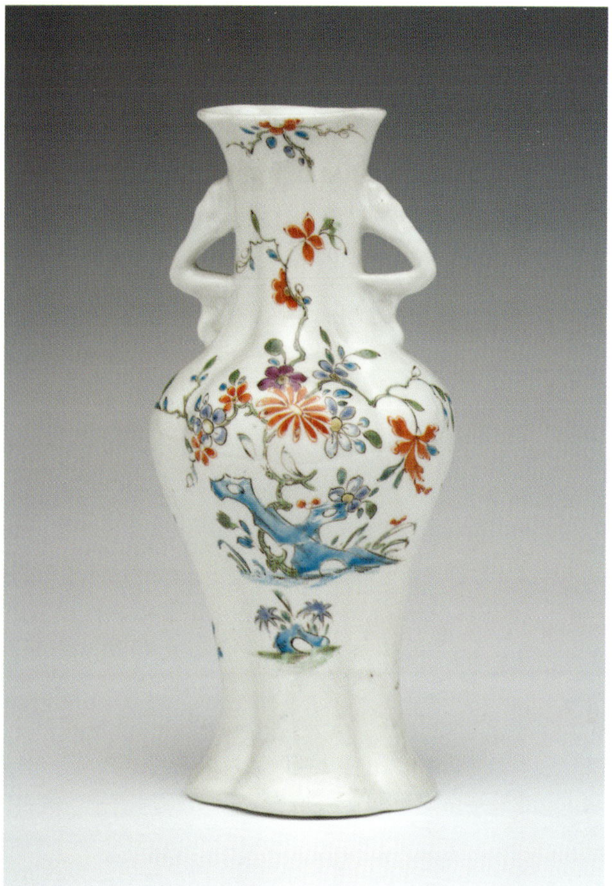

115

115

Vase

About 1754
Ht 16.5 cm
1957.24.1.607

Slender lobed baluster shape with two triangular handles, derived from Chinese porcelain; decorated with Oriental flowers and rockwork.

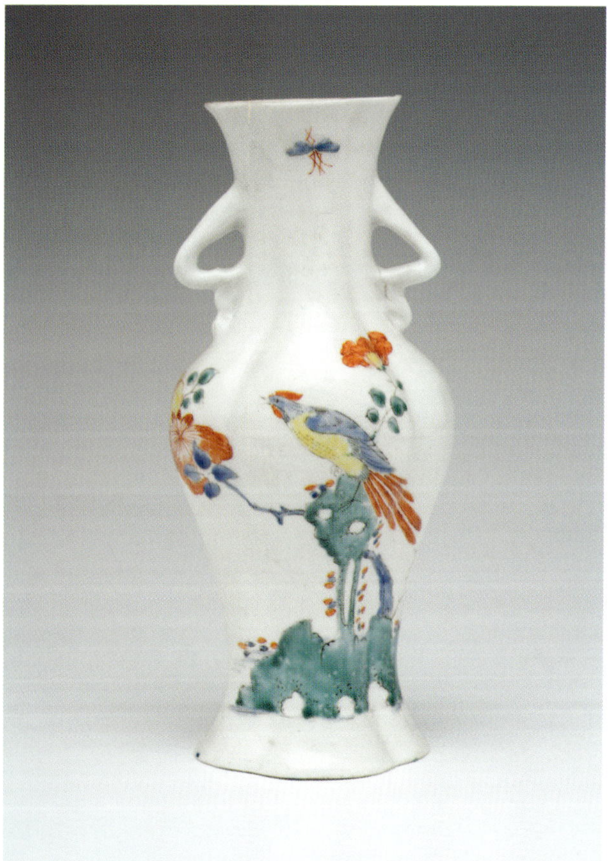

116

116

Vase

1755–6
Ht 16.5 cm
1957.24.1.608

Slender, lobed baluster shape with two triangular handles, decorated on one side with the 'Sir Joshua Reynolds' pattern of a long-tailed ho-ho bird perched on a rock.

REFERENCE
Spero 2005, pl. 125.

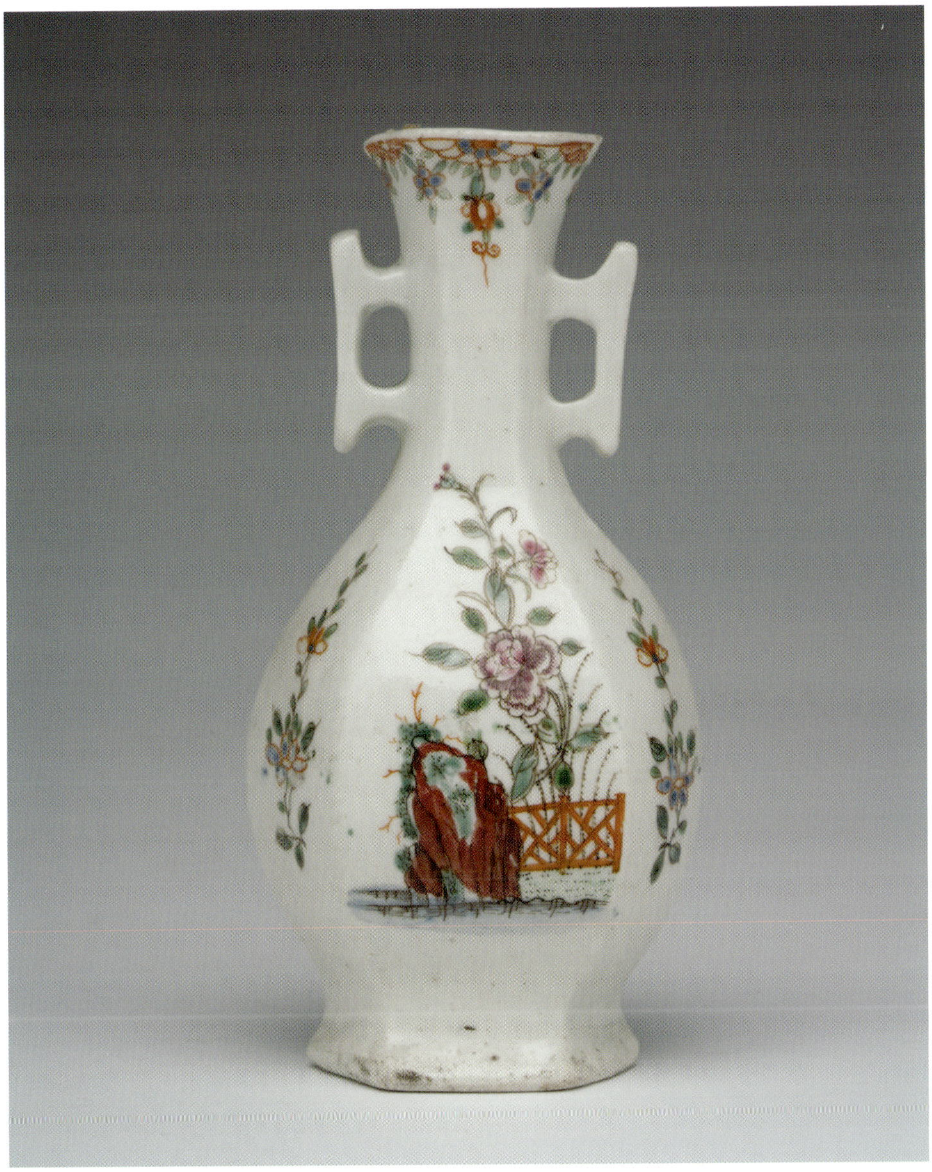

117

117

Bottle

1753–5
Ht 9.8 cm
1957.24.1.589

One of the rarest forms of Worcester vase, baluster hexagonal shape with two bracket handles; decorated with Oriental flowering plants, fence and rocks. A bottle of similar shape, with Oriental figure decoration, is in the Victoria and Albert Museum (C.1344-1924) and another with similar decoration is illustrated in Spero 1984, col. pl. 7, no. 11. A further example, with Kakiemon-style decoration with banded hedge and prunus design, is in the National Museum of Wales, Cardiff (MNW/A.34.925).

REFERENCE
Spero 2005, pl. 55.

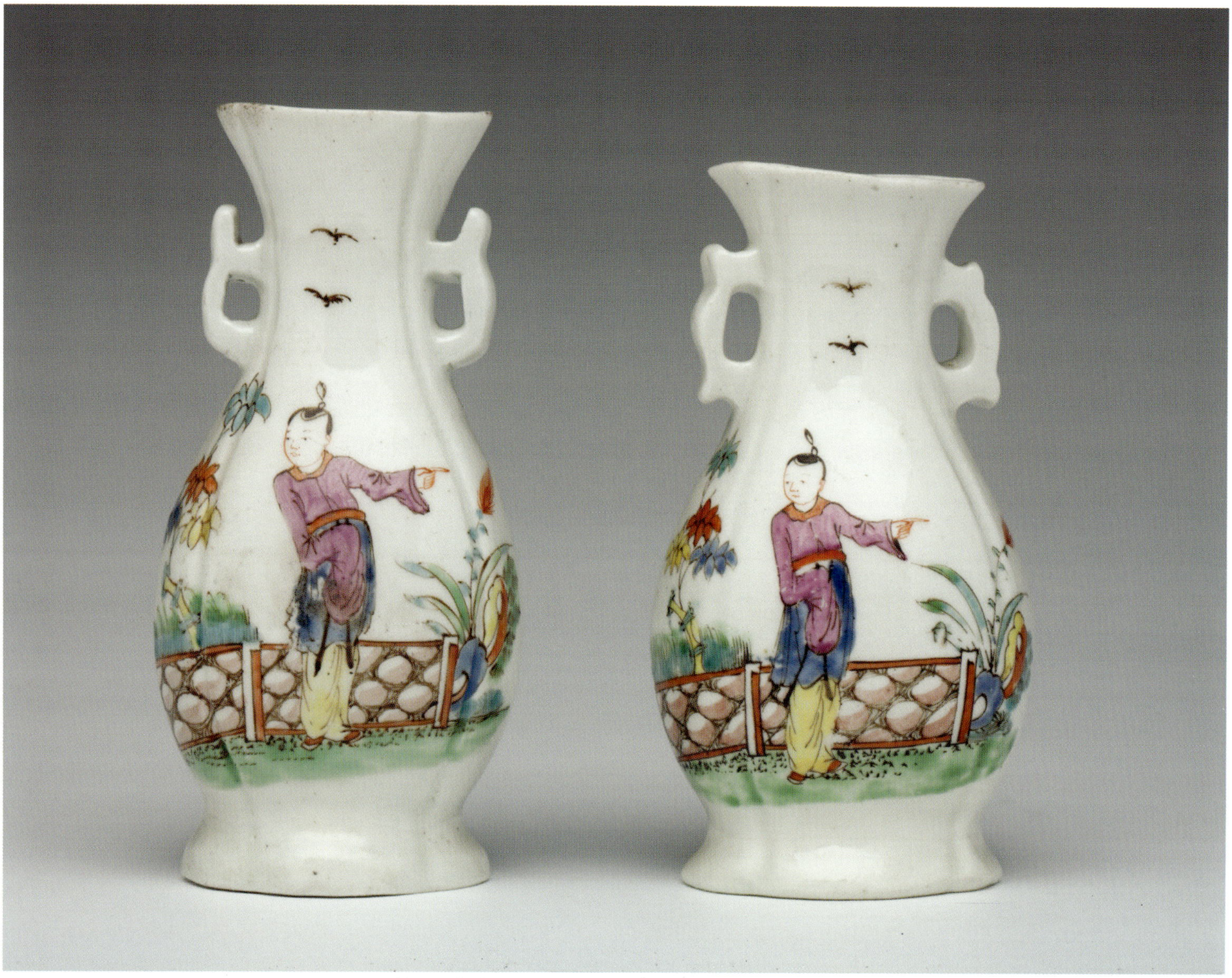

118, 119

118, 119

Pair of vases

About 1753
Ht 9.8 cm and 9.5 cm
1957.24.1.598 and 594

Quatrefoil, lobed baluster shape with oblong stylised handles; painted with a pointing Chinese man in front of a fretwork fence, rocks and flowering plants; floral spray on reverse. Issued at Worcester in only one size, this shape derives from Chinese porcelain where it was produced in a wide range of sizes over a long period.

REFERENCES
Spero and Sandon 1996, pl. 25; Spero 2005, pl. 91.

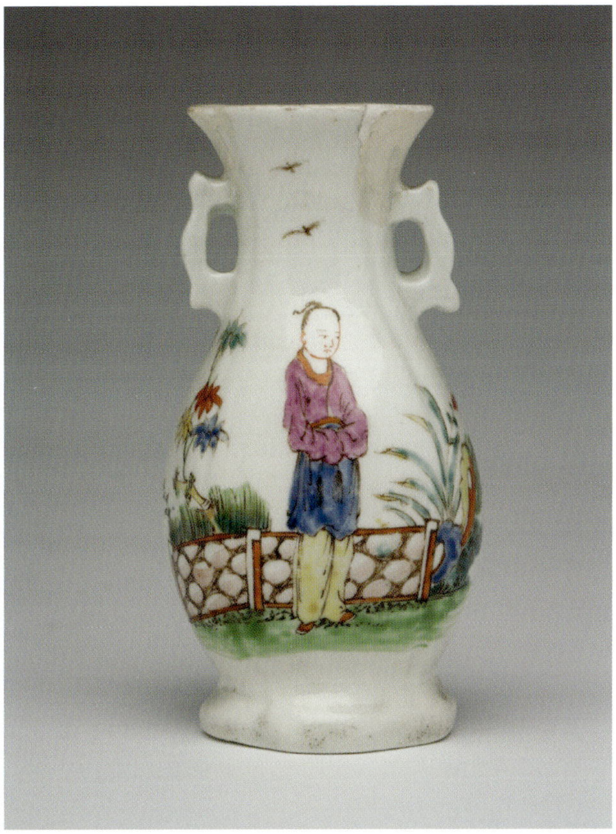

120

120

Vase

About 1753
Ht 9.5 cm
1957.24.1.596

Quatrefoil, lobed baluster shape with oblong bracket handles; decorated with Chinese figure, arms folded, beside fence and flowering plants; floral spray on reverse.

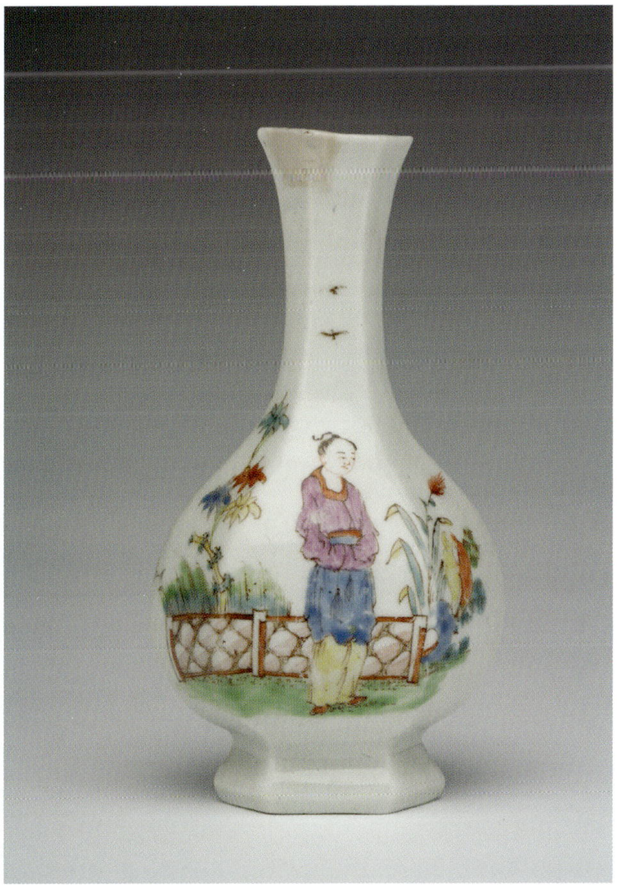

121

121

Bottle

About 1754
Ht 12.1 cm
1957.24.1.609

Bulbous, hexagonal shape; Chinese figure, arms folded, standing before fence, flowering plants at each side. There are no known Worcester bottles decorated in underglaze blue. The shape appears in Staffordshire salt-glazed stoneware.

REFERENCE
Spero and Sandon 1996, pl. 26.

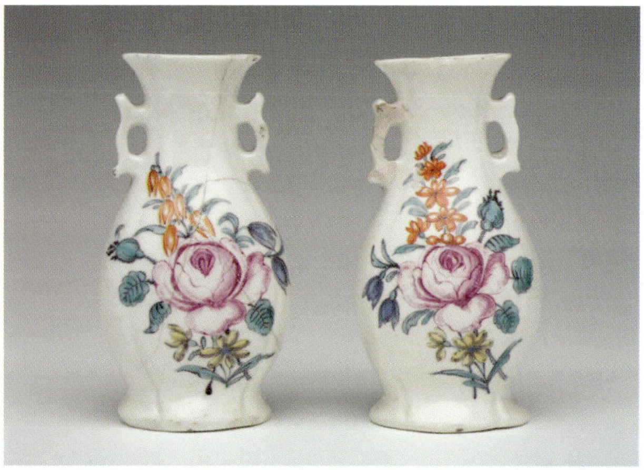

122, 123

122, 123

Pair of vases

About 1758
Ht 8.9 cm
1957.24.1.593 and 597

Quatrefoil, lobed baluster shape with oblong bracket handles; decorated with Meissen-style flowers, a heartsease on the reverse of one bottle, a tiger lily on the other.

REFERENCE
Spero 2005, pl. 90.

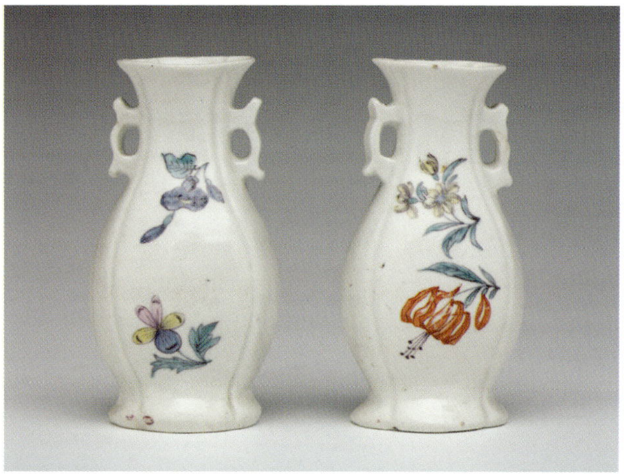

122, 123

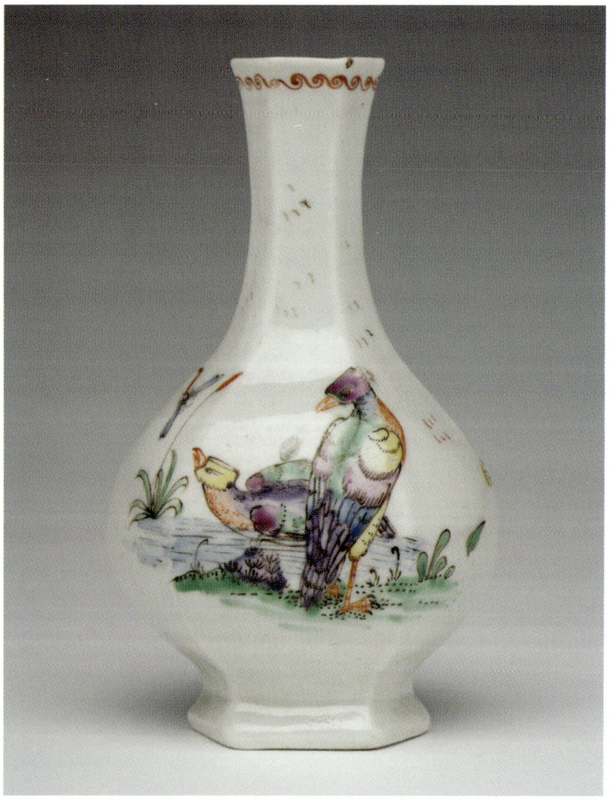

124

124

Bottle

1753–4
Ht 11.4 cm
1957.24.1.600

Bulbous, hexagonal shape, slender neck with red C-scroll border; decorated with two imaginary aquatic birds gazing at a dragonfly. Bottles or vases of this shape are known to have been decorated in about a dozen different patterns.

PROVENANCE
H.W. Hughes Collection, no. 1073, 12 February 1944, £7.

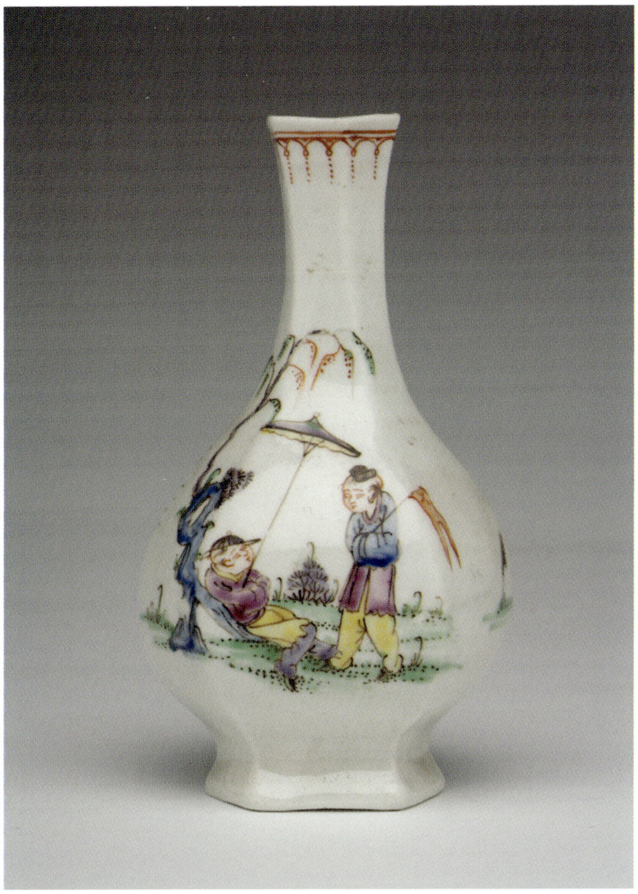

125

125

Bottle

1753–4
Ht 10.8 cm
1957.24.1.612

Bulbous, hexagonal shape, slender neck with *rouge de fer* border; decorated on one side with a Chinese scene with a recumbent man with an umbrella and another man standing by, with a pennant or fly whisk; on reverse, two vases with a bird above.

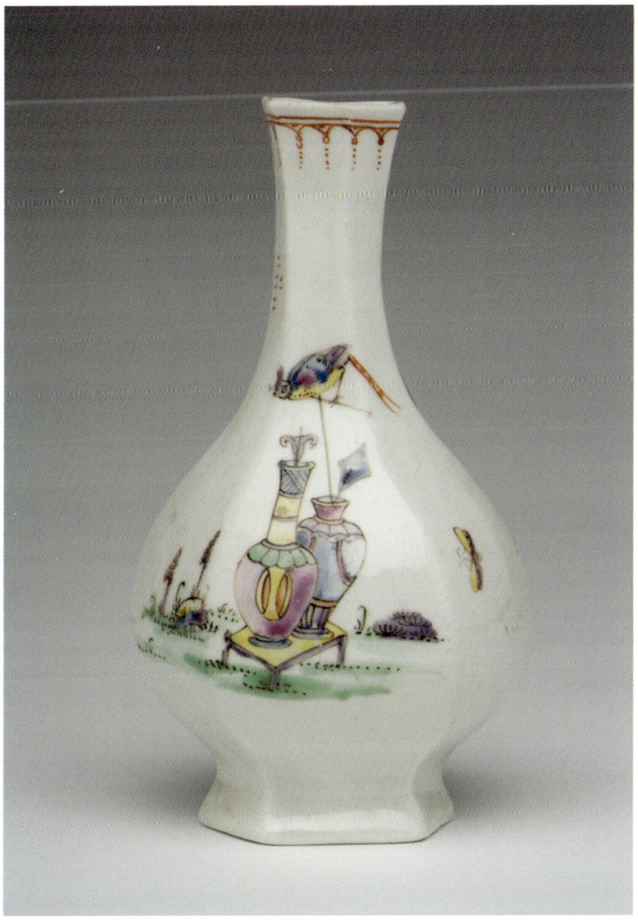

125

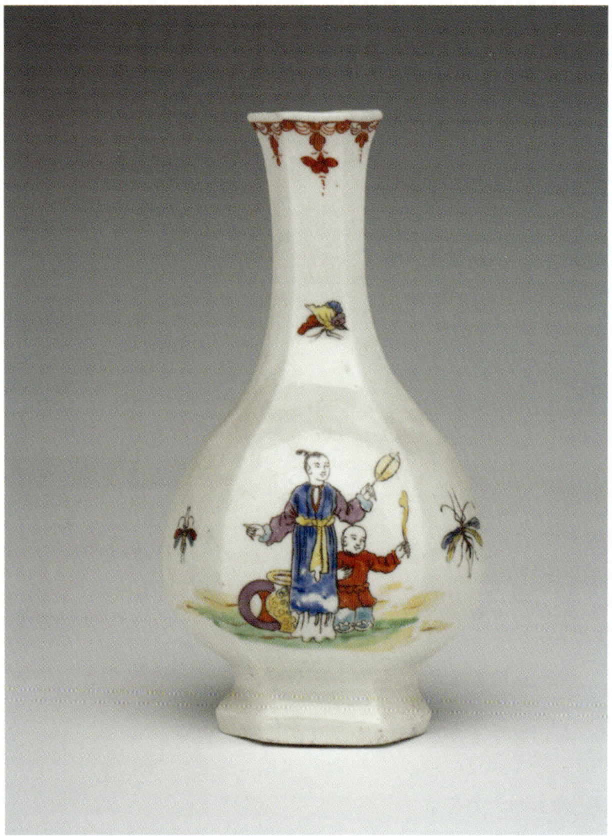

126

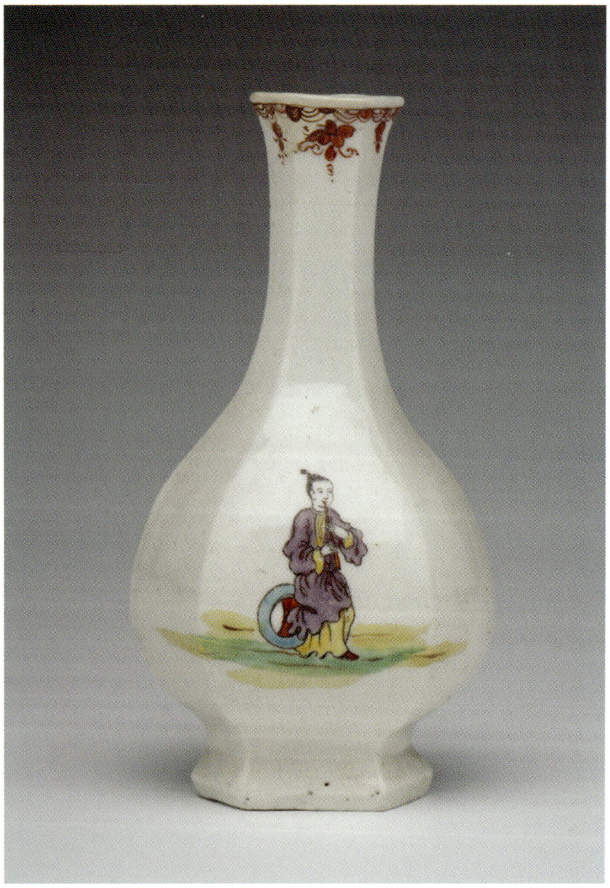

126

126

Bottle

About 1754
Ht 10.5 cm
1957.24.1.613

Bulbous, hexagonal shape, slender neck with *rouge de fer* border with pendants, transfer-printed in black and painted in colours with Chinese figures and various insects.

REFERENCE
Spero 2008.

127, 128, 129

Three bottles

1753–4
Ht 10.5 cm
1957.24.1.602, 610 and 611

Bulbous, hexagonal shape, slender neck with *rouge de fer* border; decorated with a Chinese acrobat balancing on a support held by another Chinese man; on reverse, landscape with house and fence. The acrobat design only appears on bottles such as this, although a version was used on South Staffordshire opaque white glass of the mid-1750s.

REFERENCE
Spero 2005, pl. 47.

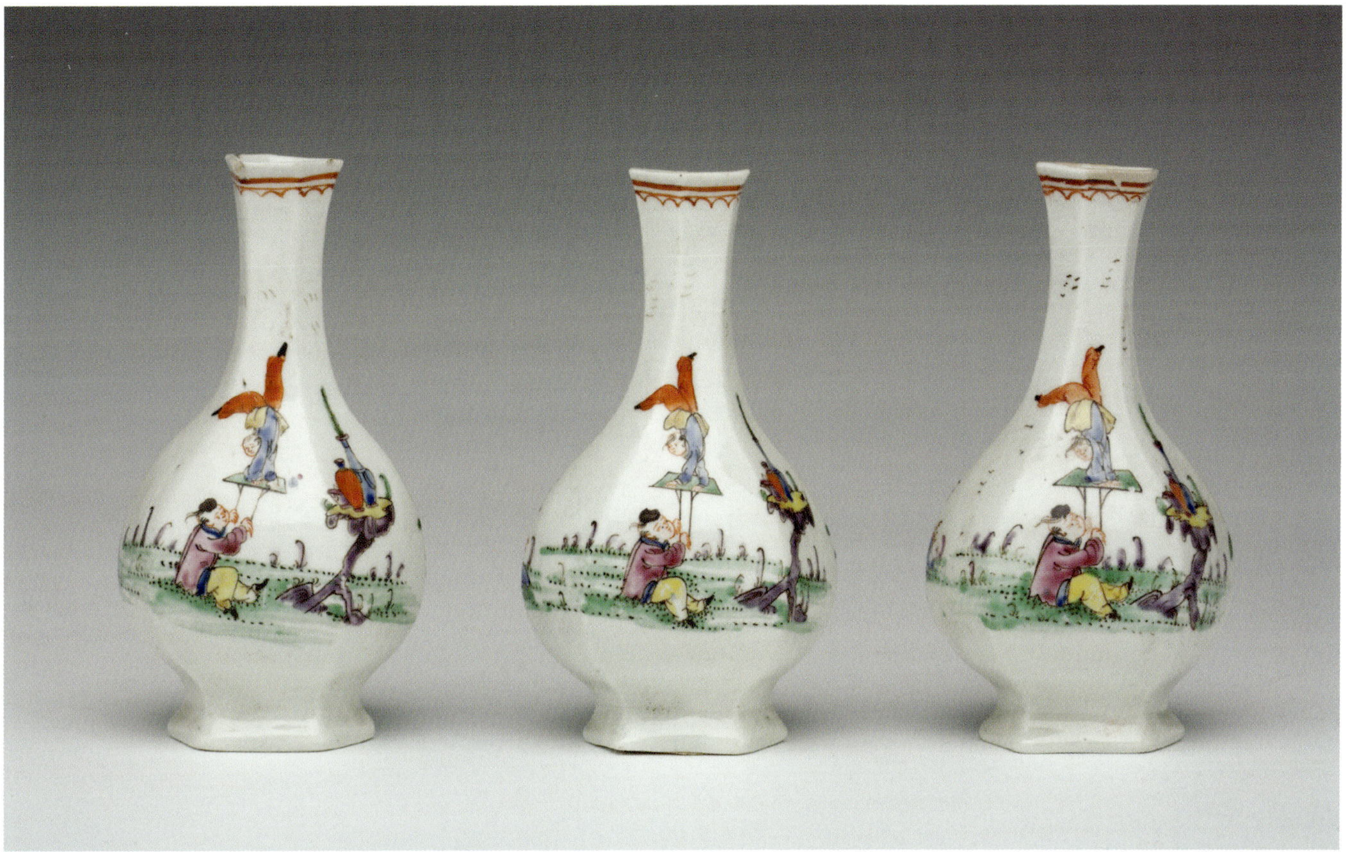

127, 128, 129

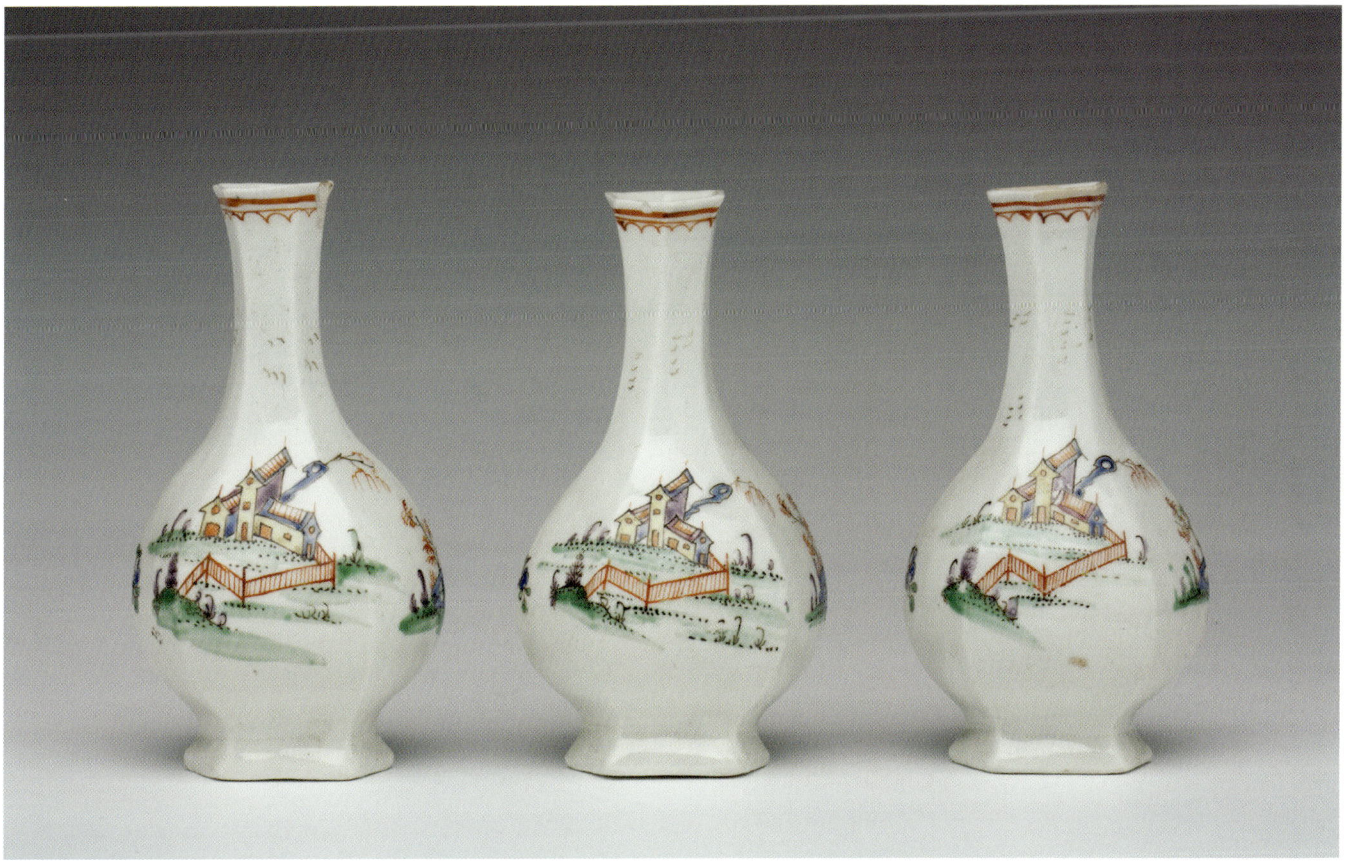

127, 128, 129

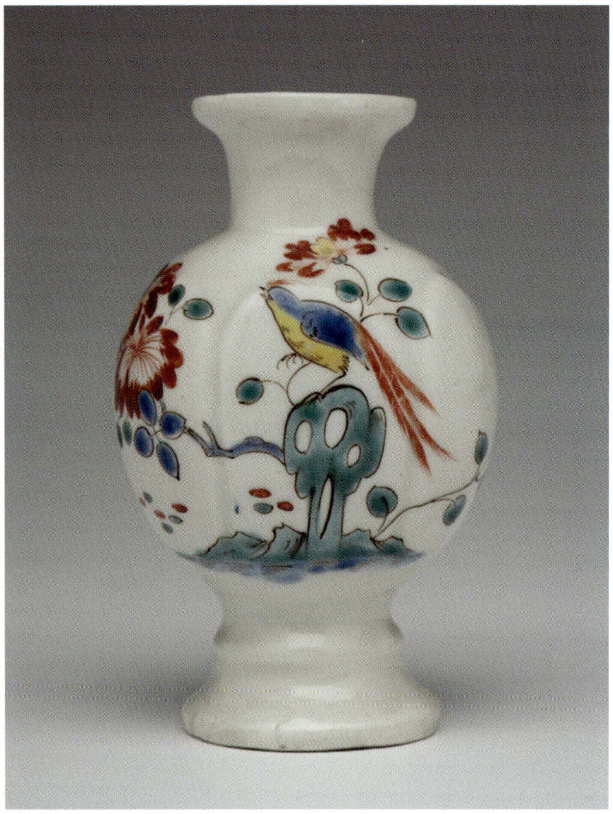

130

130

Vase

About 1754
Ht 8.9 cm
1957.24.1.595

Squat baluster shape, bulbous body lobe moulded with six panels, decorated in Kakiemon style with the 'Sir Joshua Reynolds' pattern of a long-tailed ho-ho bird sitting on a pierced blue rock with trailing flower sprays. The pair to this piece is illustrated in Sotheby's, London, 13 April 2011, lot 136.

PROVENANCE
Sotheby's, London, 16 October 1956, lot 11, £107 5s.

REFERENCE
Amor 1981, pl. 12.

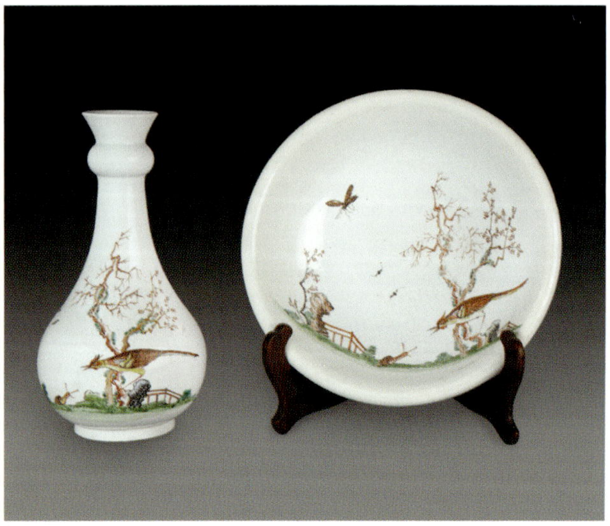

Fig. 12 A water bottle and basin from the Rous Lench Collection. © Museum of Royal Worcester Porcelain, no. 4790

131, 132

Pair of vases

About 1754
Ht 11.4 cm
Mark: both have two parallel incised lines inside foot-rim
1957.24.1.599 and 603

Thinly potted cylindrical shape with concave sides; decorated in brown and green enamels with a bird perched on a tree by a fence, eyeing a large snail on the ground; the reverse with bamboo rising from shaded brown and yellow rocks. This distinctive 'Bird and Snail' pattern is recorded on three early baluster-shaped mugs, each inscribed *E x L 1754* on the base, together with an incised line.

A larger example from the Rous Lench Collection was sold at Christie's, London, 30 May 1990, lot 454 (property of the late T.G. Brown), subsequently in the Sir Jeremy Lever and Paul Crane collections. A water bottle and basin, also from the Rous Lench Collection, are in the Museum of Royal Worcester Porcelain, no. 4790 (fig. 12).

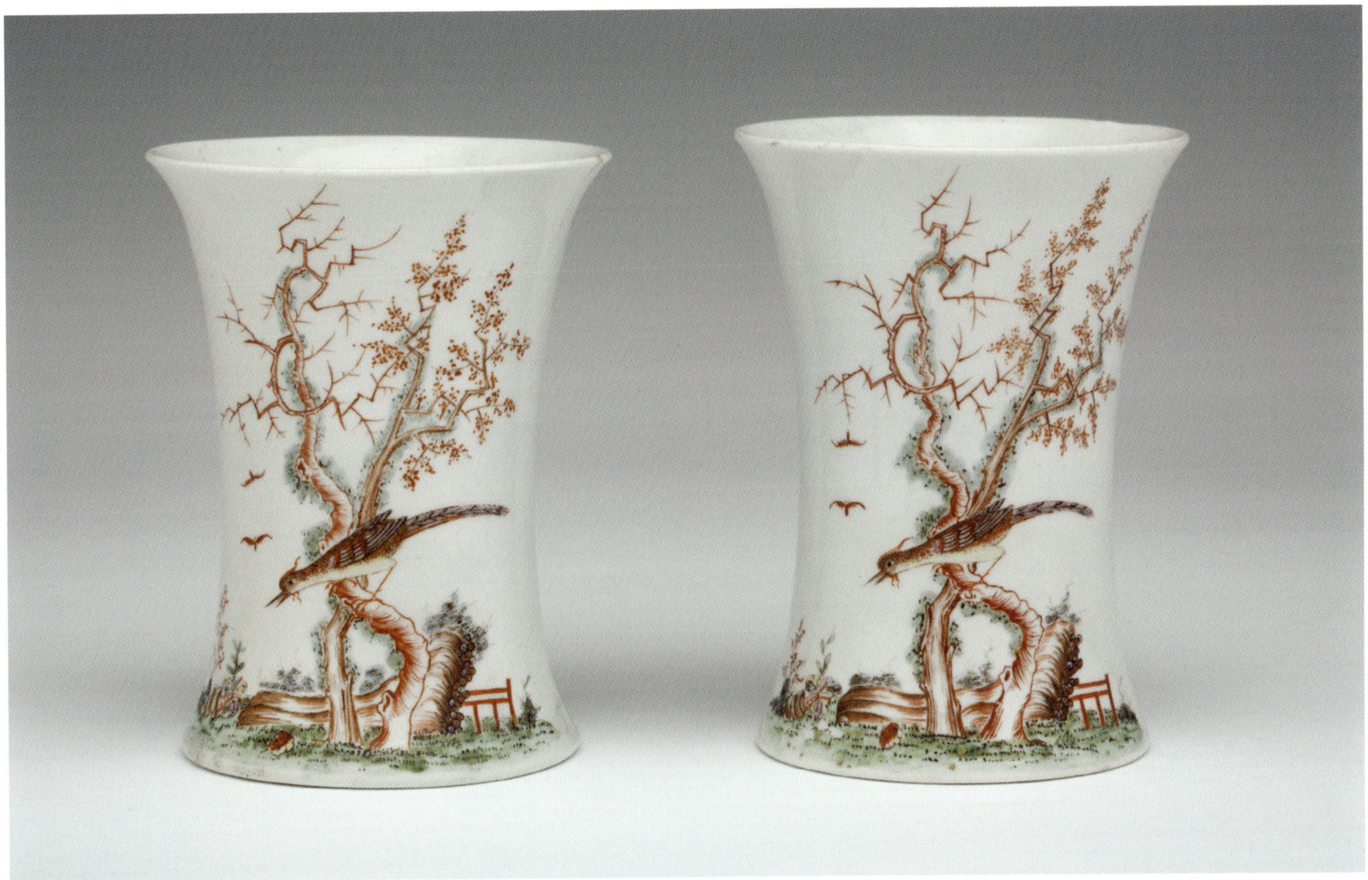

131, 132

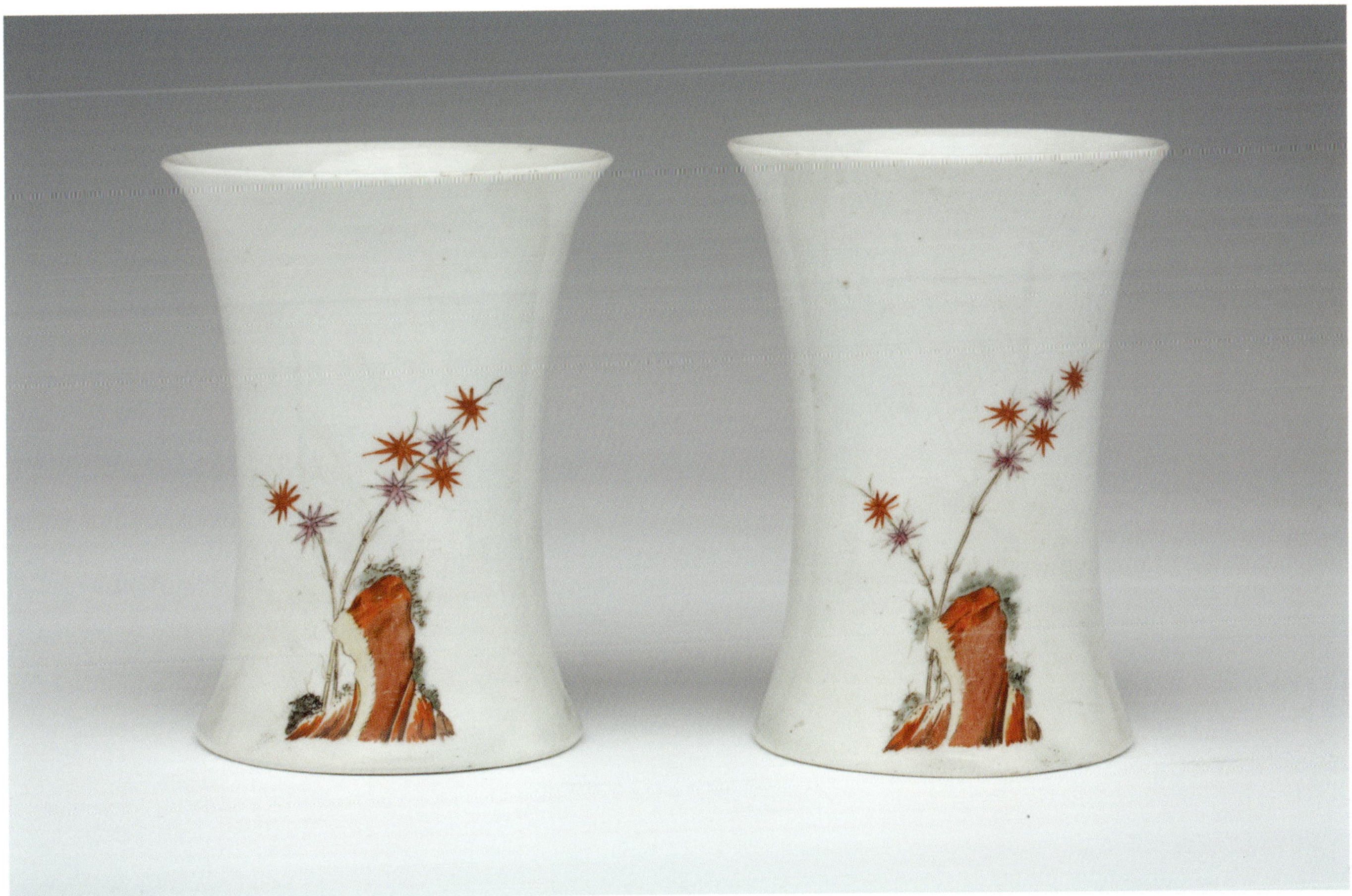

131, 132

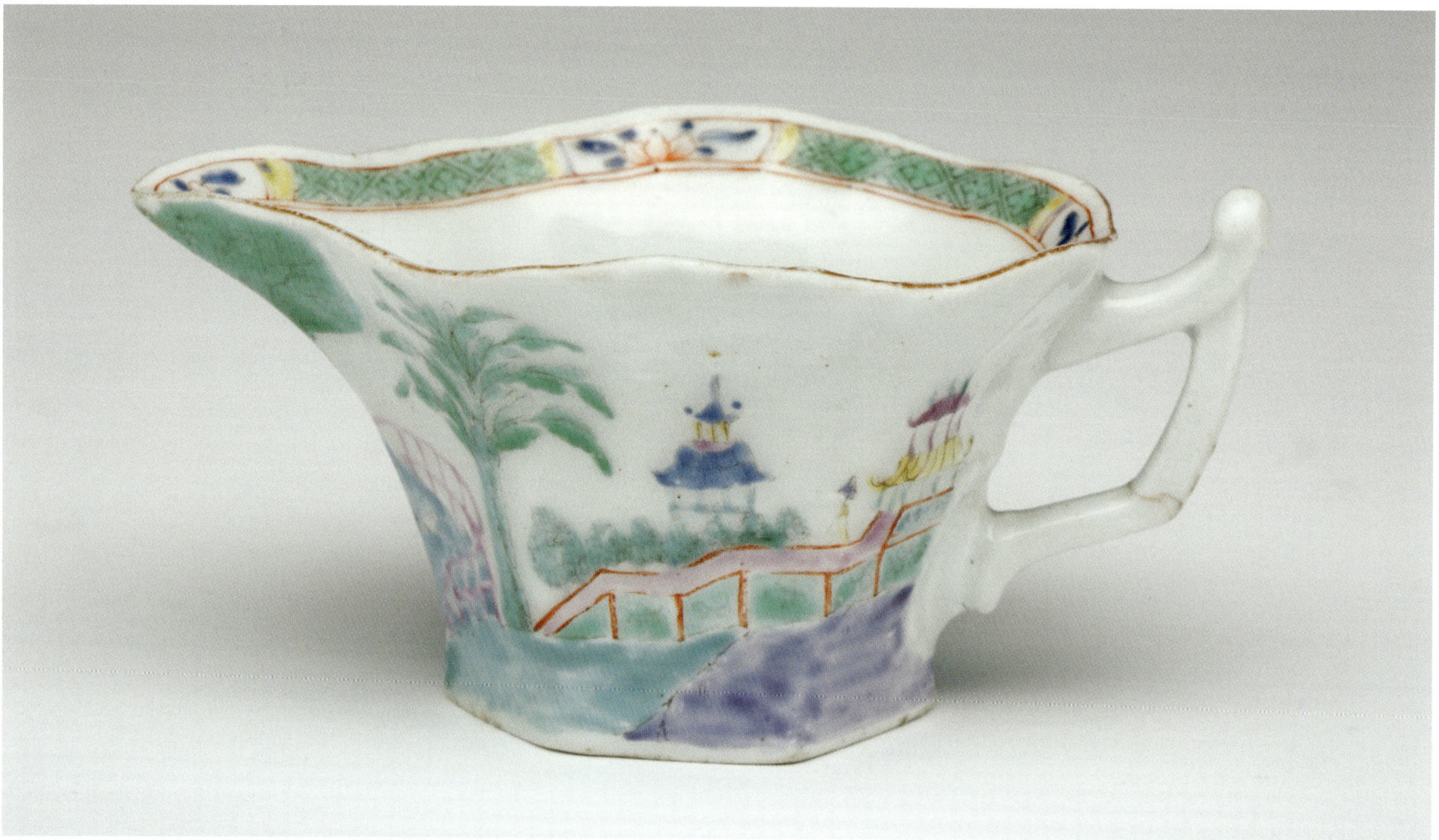

133

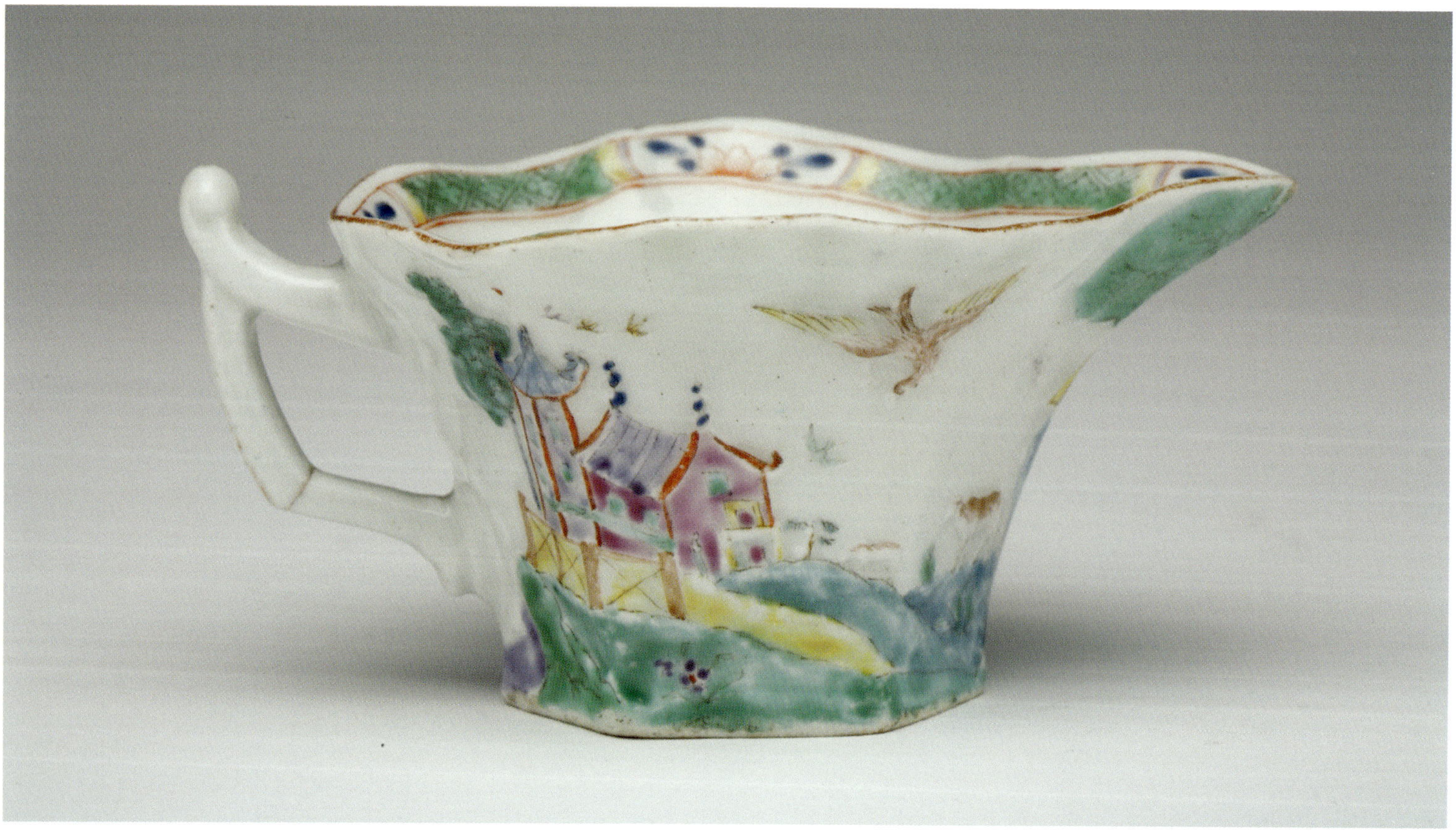

133

133

Creamboat

1752–4
Ht 5.1 cm, length 10.7 cm
Unmarked
1957.24.1.758

Hexagonal shape with an angular handle; moulded exterior with Oriental buildings, fences, trees, birds and cattle in a continuous landscape, picked out in soft colours; narrow inside border of green diaper and floral panels; flowers in base, with a small painted leaf to cover firing crack. The inspiration for this moulded design may have come from Staffordshire salt-glaze stoneware.

This is similar in design to the famous creamboat now in the Museum of Royal Worcester Porcelain, embossed *Wigornia* (the Roman name for Worcester) on the base (figs 13 and 14). The Bishop of Worcester uses the term Wygorn and the old boys of Worcester's Kings School, which Dr Wall attended, are called Old Wigornians.

Sam Clark's research, continued by Dr Paul Riley, identified nine different mouldings, six in polychrome and blue and white and three in blue and white alone. This is an example of moulding F, the only one with an angular handle.

PROVENANCE
Arthur Hurst sale part 3, Sotheby's, London, 30 January 1941, lot 104.

REFERENCES
Reynolds 1998, p. 12; Riley 1989.

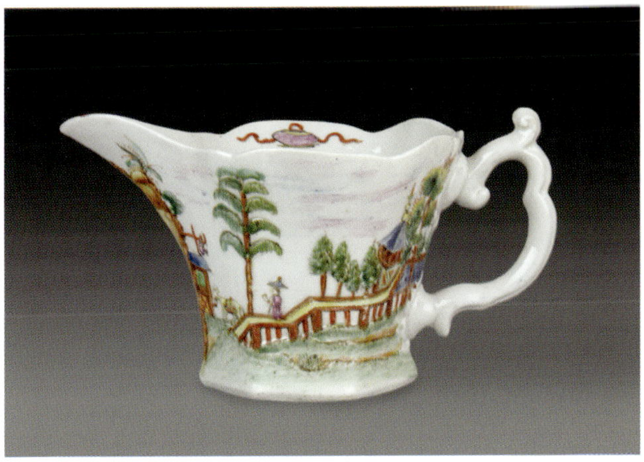

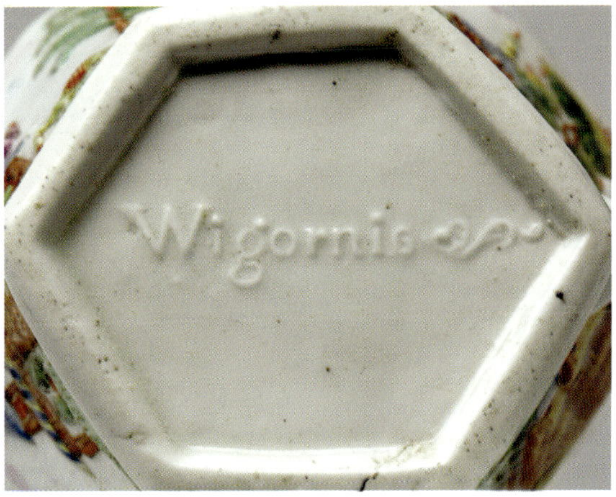

Figs 13 and 14 Creamboat with moulding type 'A' which includes figures, scroll handle. Perhaps the only known example of Worcester porcelain with 'Wigornia' impressed on the base. © Museum of Royal Worcester Porcelain, no. 4184

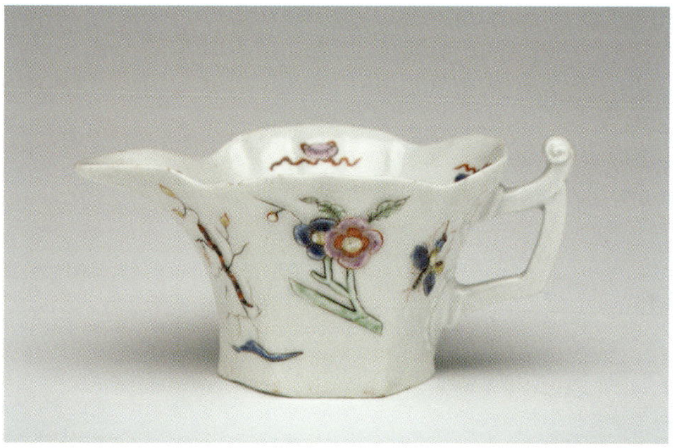

134

134

Creamboat

About 1755
Ht 5.4 cm, length 10.8 cm
1957.24.1.1023

Hexagonal, peaked angular handle with moulded raised insect and floral design picked out in colour; plain lip; four Buddhist symbols inside. An example in the Museum of Royal Worcester Porcelain is illustrated in Barrett 1958, pl. 7b.

PROVENANCE
Filkins & Co., London, 7 July 1944, £9 10s.

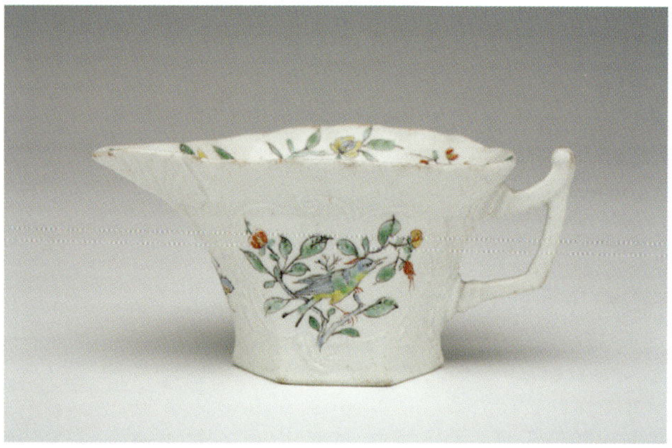

135

135

Creamboat

About 1754
Ht 5.2 cm, length 11 cm
1957.24.1.762

Moulded silver shape with hexagonal base, peaked handle, shell-shaped lip; rococo panels on each side, one with a colourful bird and the other with a floral spray.

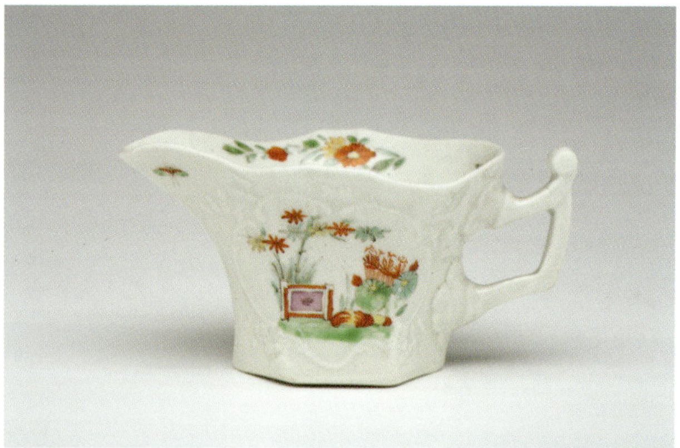

136

136

Creamboat

About 1755
Ht 5.6 cm, length 10.8 cm
1957.24.1.1021

Hexagonal, wavy edge, angular peaked handle; decorated with Chinese flowering plants within rococo moulded panels on both sides, two insects painted below lip.

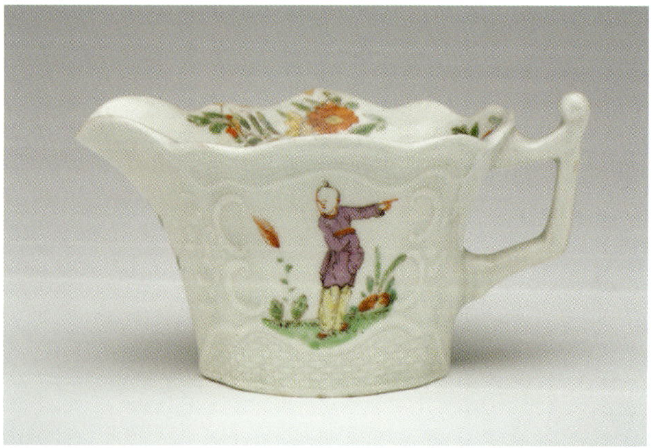

137

137

Creamboat

About 1755
Ht 6 cm, length 10.5 cm
1957.24.1.979

Silver shape with oval base, angular peaked handle, moulded basketwork border below wavy rim; rococo panels decorated with bowing Oriental figure.

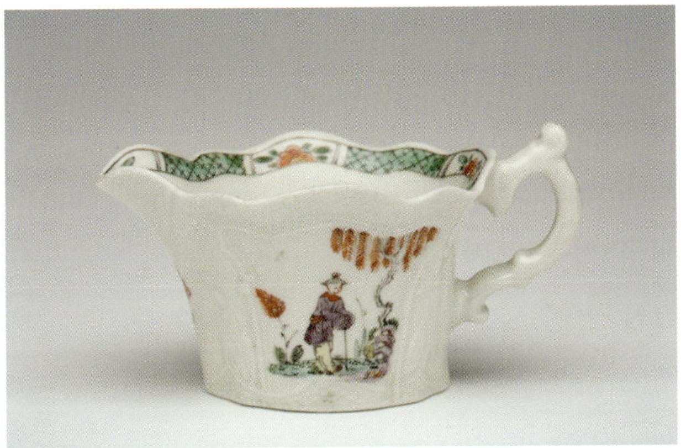

138

138

Creamboat

About 1755
Ht 6.5 cm, length 11.4 cm
1957.24.1.977

Silver form, irregular oval shape, wavy edge moulded with basketwork, scroll handle; side panels decorated with Chinese man beneath a willow tree.

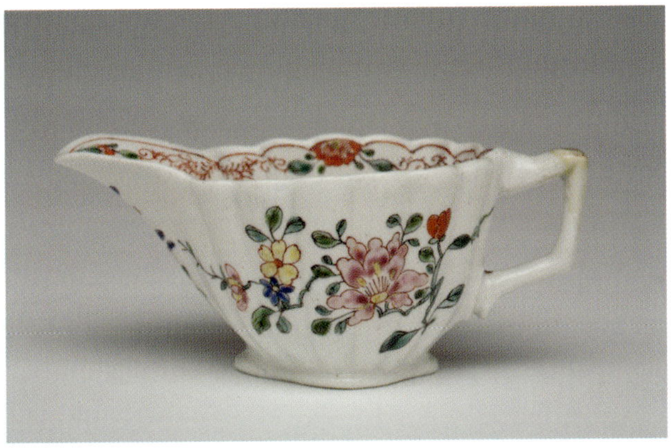

139

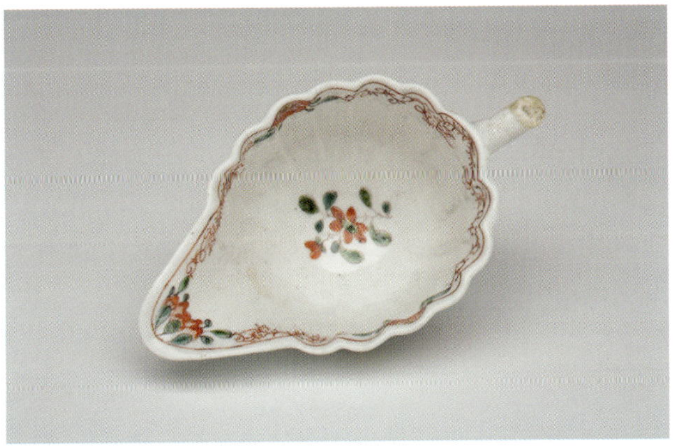

139

139

Creamboat

1752–3
Ht 4.6 cm, length 10.6 cm
1957.24.1.746

Triangular base, vertically fluted with square handle, decorated with Chinese flowers; *rouge de fer* scalloped border with flowers inside rim and in base.

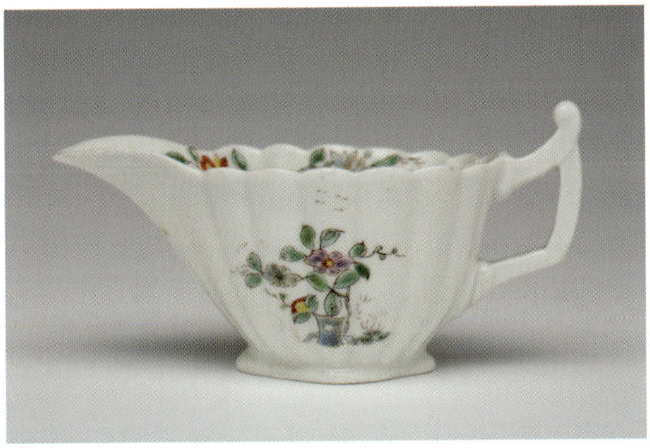

140

140

Creamboat

About 1753
Ht 5.4 cm, length 10.6 cm
1957.24.1.744

Silver shape, triangular base, vertically fluted with angular handle, scalloped rim; light floral decoration with butterfly below spout and flowers inside.

REFERENCE
Spero 2005, p. 162, no. 74.

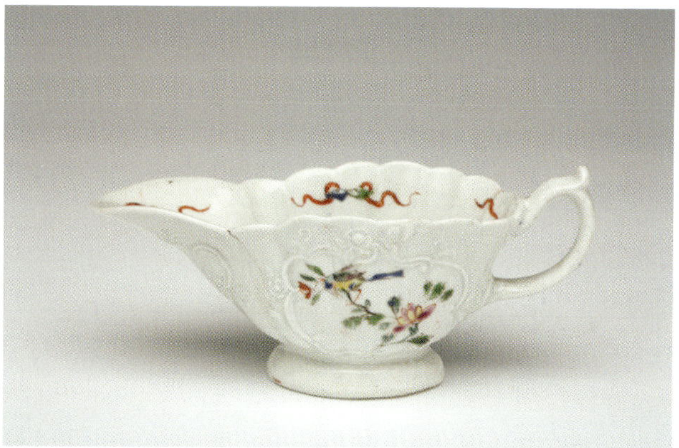

141

141

Sauceboat

About 1753
Length 12.7 cm, width 7.3 cm
1957.24.1.1014
Fluted silver shape, scalloped rim, oval base; floral moulded reserves with bird on one side, flowers on the other, undecorated reserve under spout, rim interior decorated with Chinese symbols.

REFERENCES
Albert Amor 1981, 1992.

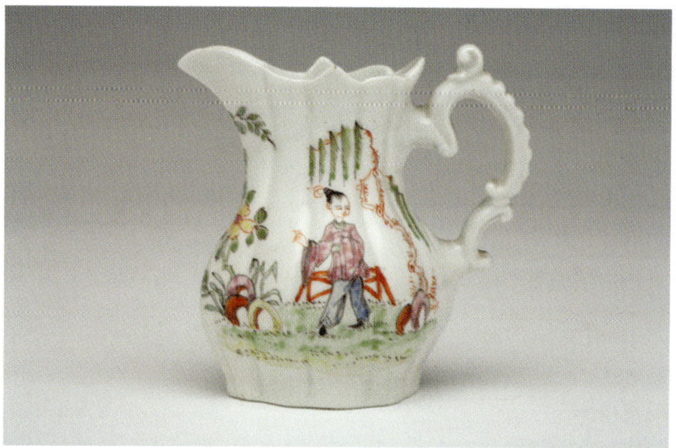

142

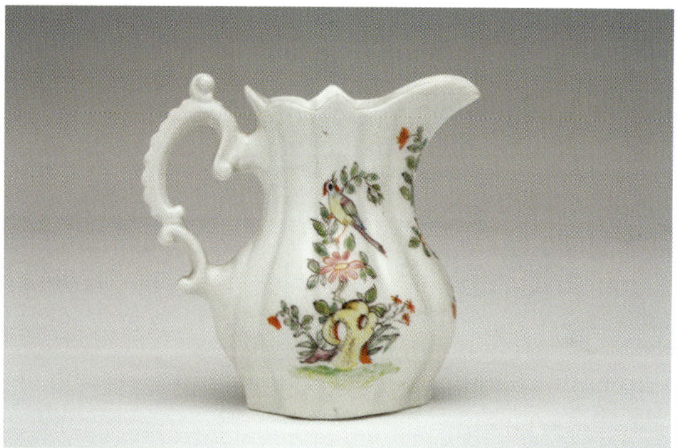

142

142

Cream jug

1753–4
Ht 7.6 cm
1957.24.1.588

Lobed silver shape with vertical fluting, rococo double scroll handle; decorated on one side with Chinese man below willow tree; on reverse, bird perched in foliage. This shape is usually associated with chinoiserie designs and is also found with blue and white and purple or puce camaïeu as well as polychrome decoration.

REFERENCES
Spero and Sandon 1996, pl. 29; Spero 2005, pl. 87.

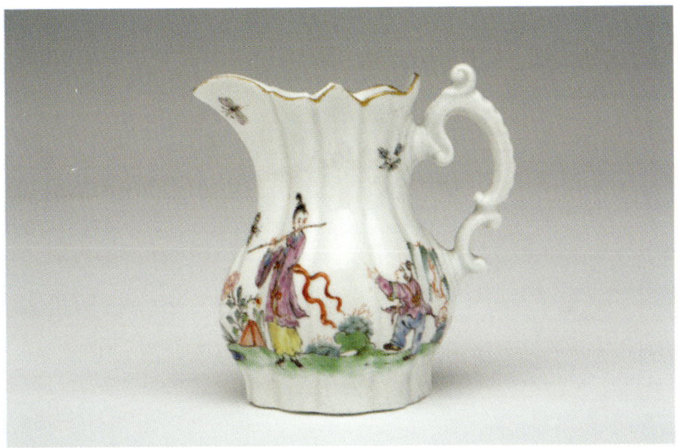

143

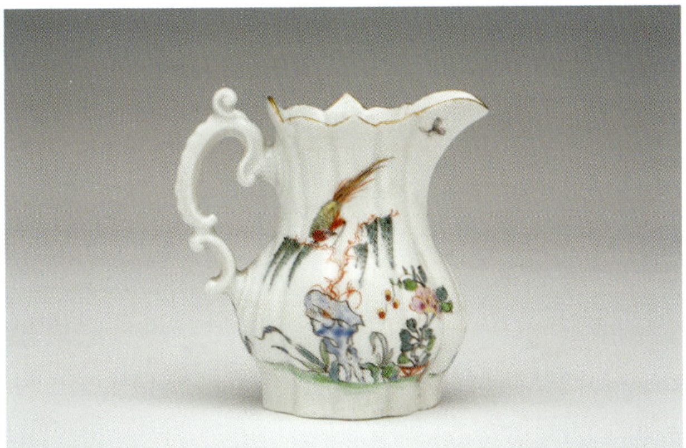

143

143

Cream jug

1753–4
Ht 7.6 cm
Mark: incised stroke on base below handle
1957.24.1.590

Lobed silver shape with vertical fluting, rococo double scroll handle, irregular rim edged in gold. Decorated on one side with Chinese woman playing a flute with a child beside her, and on the other with a pheasant perched in a tree.

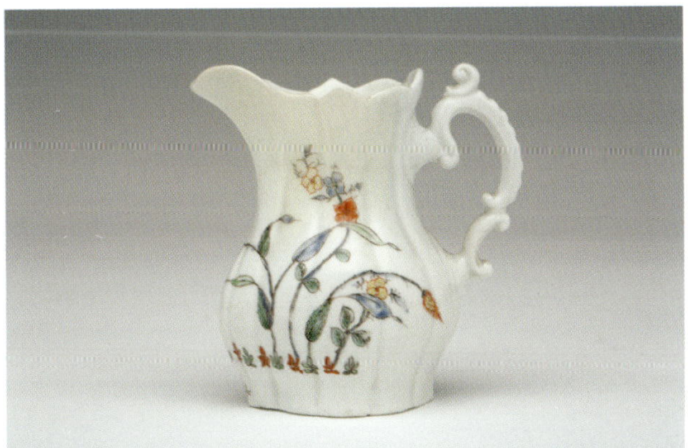

144

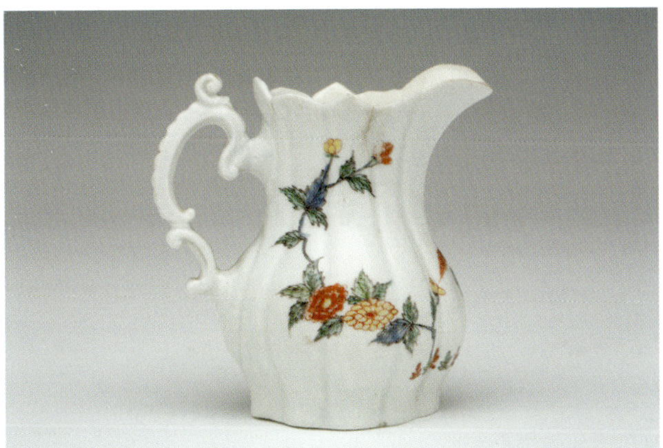

144

144

Cream jug

1753–4
Ht 7.6 cm
1957.24.1.601

Lobed silver shape with vertical fluting, rococo double scroll handle; decorated with Oriental plants in natural colours in a similar style to vase no. 95. A similar jug is in the Fitzwilliam Museum, Cambridge (inv. C.46–1992).

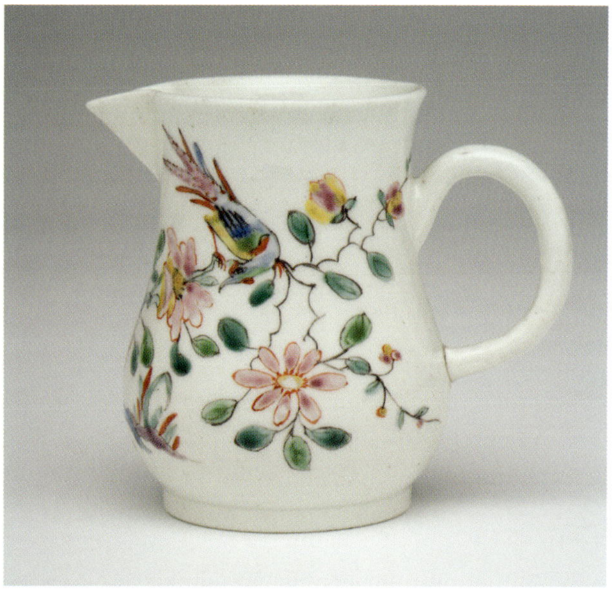

145

145

Cream jug

About 1753
Ht 6.3 cm
Mark: incised line on base
1957.24.1.1043

With 'sparrow-beak' spout and plain loop handle; decorated with a colourful bird perched among sprays of flowers.

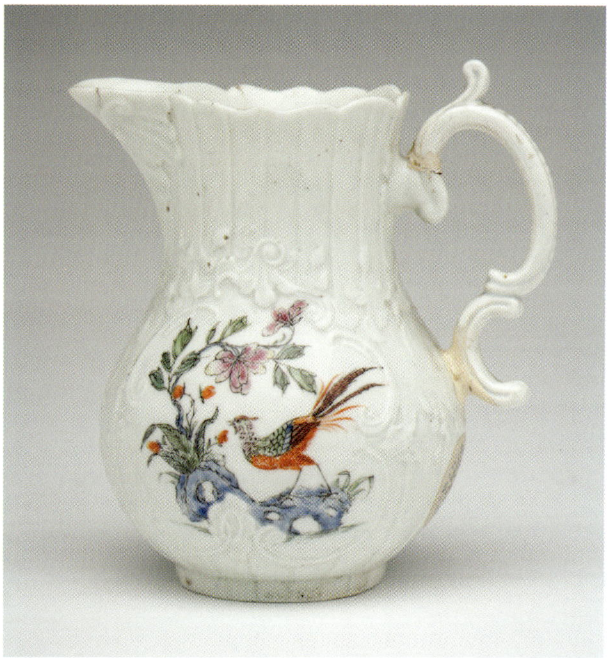

146

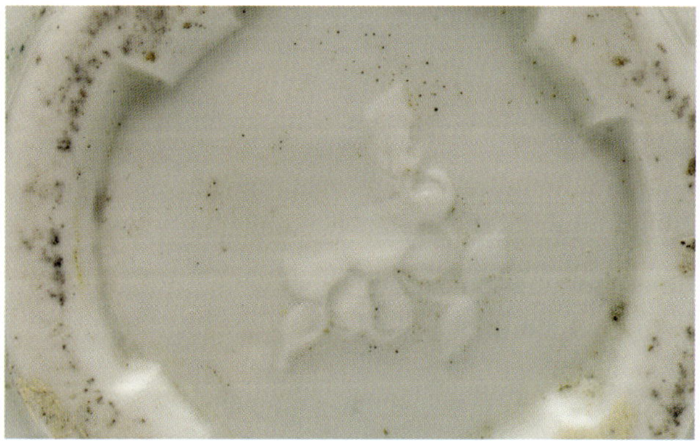

146 (detail)

146

Cream jug

1754–5
Ht 8.9 cm
Mark: moulded leaf spray on base
1957.24.1.495

Pear-shaped silver form with double scroll handle, moulded body; reserves decorated with exotic birds and flowers.

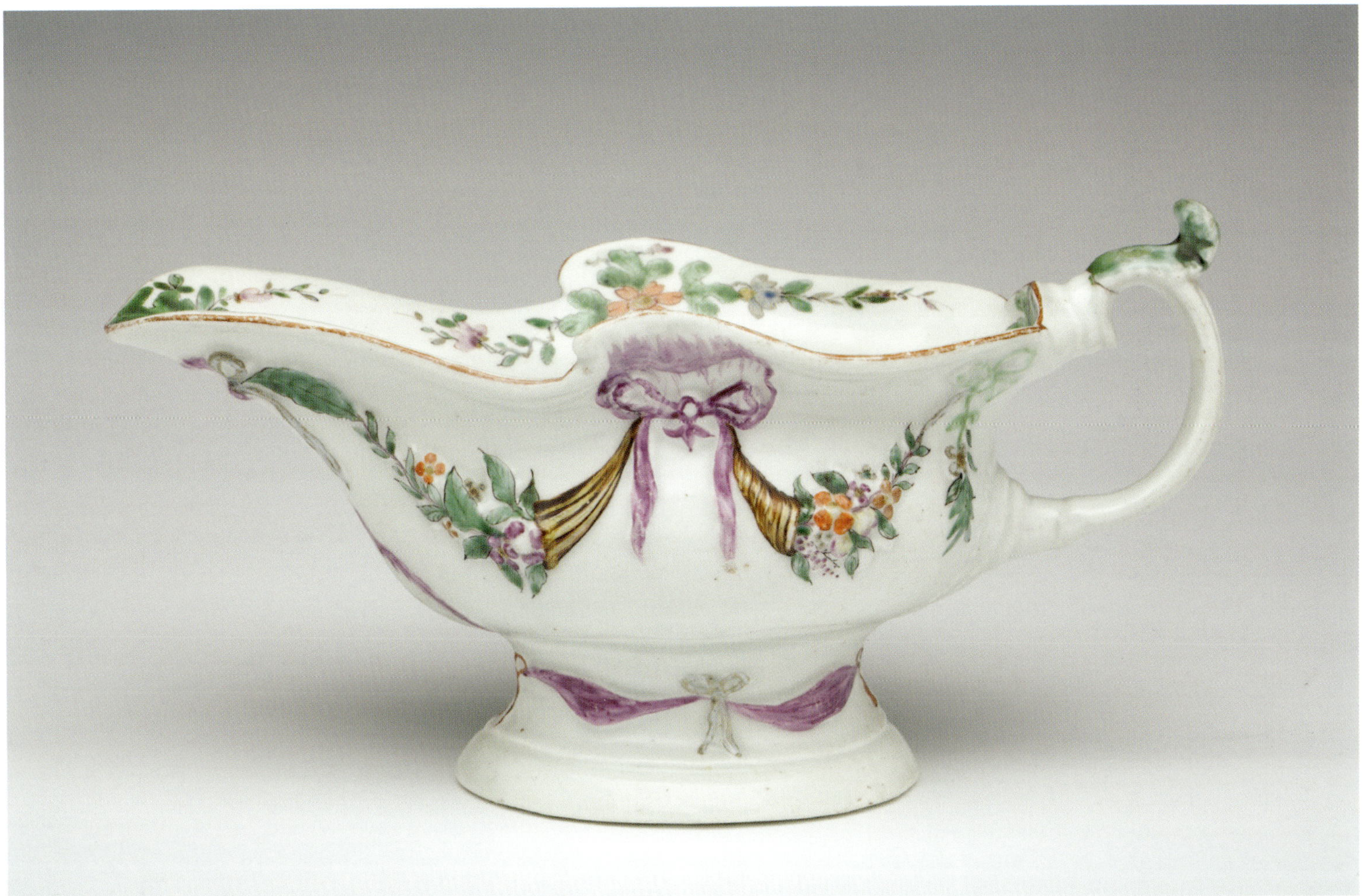

147

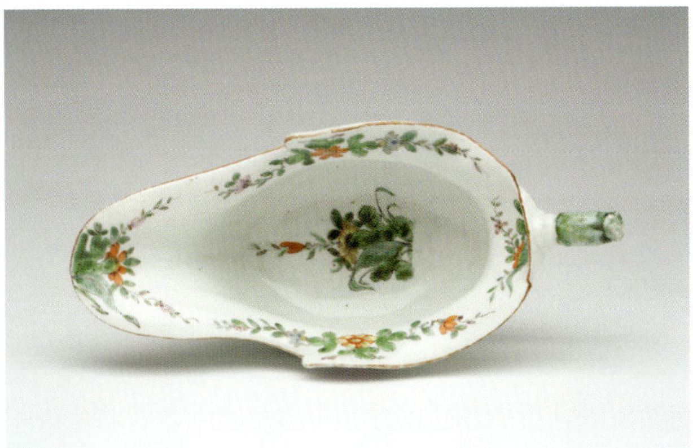

147

147

Sauceboat

About 1753
Ht 11.9 cm, length 22.2 cm
Mark: incised line on base
1957.24.1.857

Moulded silver shape with oval pedestal foot and scroll handle, thumb rest coloured green; decorated with moulded cornucopia swags picked out in colours and purple ribbons; inside border and base decorated with Oriental flowers and foliage.

This is a simplified version of a high scroll handle form first produced at Bristol, an example of which, marked *Bristoll*, is in the Victoria and Albert Museum (V&A: C.1297–1924). The Rienzi Collection, Houston, has an example with a green leaf painted over the *Bristoll* factory mark.

REFERENCES

Reynolds 1999, pl. 5; Barrett 1966, pls. 3a and 3b; Spero 2005, pls. 43, 44.

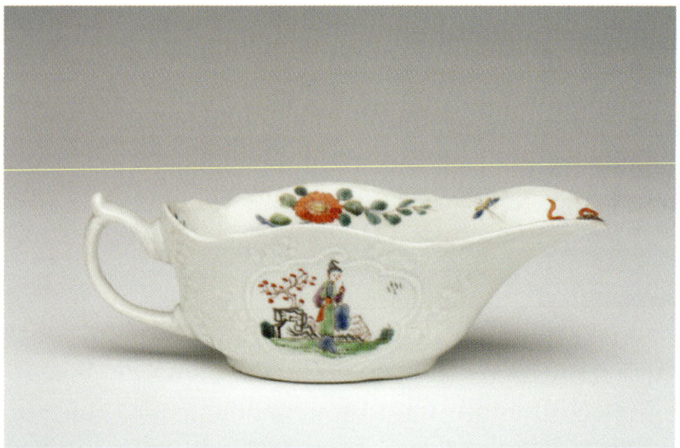

148

148

Sauceboat

1753–4
Ht 5.2 cm, length 15.6 cm, width 7.2 cm
Mark: red annulet and ring
1957.24.1.1022

Flat base, moulded with prunus sprays and rococo-style reserves; decorated with a Chinese woman holding a fan.

REFERENCE
Spero 1984, pl. 26.

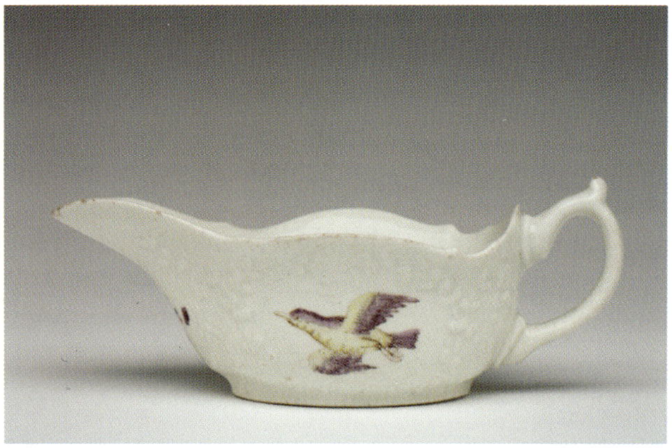

149

149

Sauceboat

About 1755
Ht 5.5 cm, length 15 cm
1957.24.1.518

Flat base, wavy rim, scroll handle; floral moulded panels with unusual decoration of a single mauve and yellow bird in flight on one side, flower spray on the other side and below lip.

REFERENCE
Bonhams, London, 10 December 2008, lot 115.

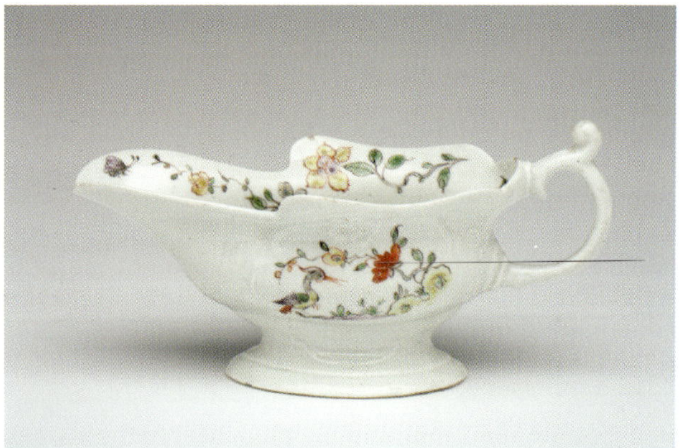

150

150

Sauceboat

About 1754
Ht 8 cm, length 16.7 cm, width 8 cm
1957.24.1.756

Silver shape, moulded reserves painted with typical early stork-like birds standing on one leg, the other raised, with flowers and foliage; internal floral border includes daffodils and butterflies; floral spray in base.

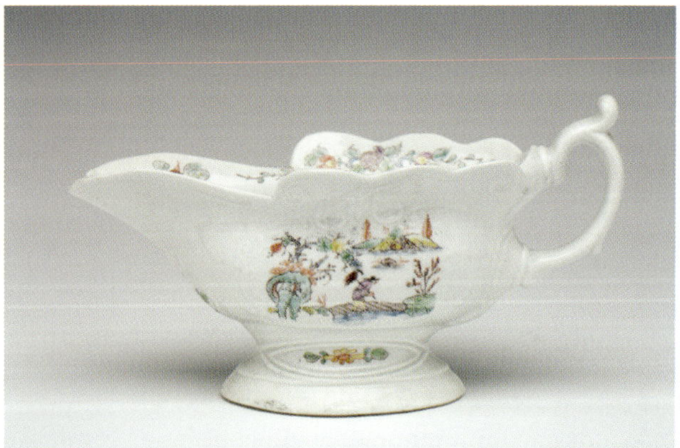

151

151

Sauceboat

1753–5
Ht 10.2 cm, length 19.2 cm, width 9.3 cm
1957.24.1.757

Silver shape with moulded panels decorated with Oriental scenes of Chinese man on bridge with umbrella on one side, junk in full sail on the other; floral wreaths on lip and in base.

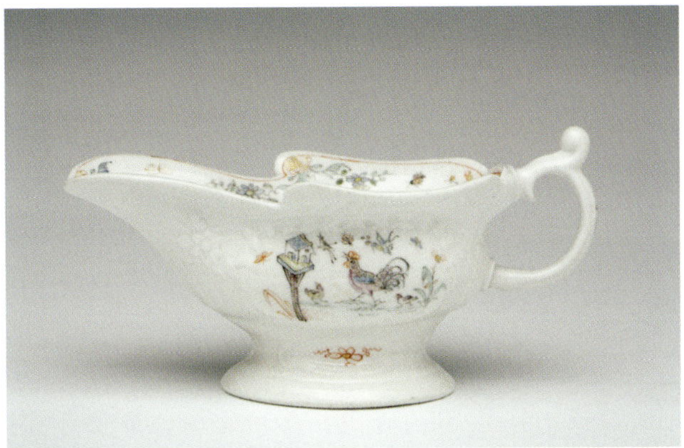

152

152

Sauceboat

About 1754
Ht 8.6 cm, length 17.1 cm, width 8.4 cm
1957.24.1.1067

Floral moulded silver shape; unusual decoration of a dovecote and singing bird, a cock and two hens on one side, a Chinese lake scene on the other; various Oriental flowers and symbols inside.

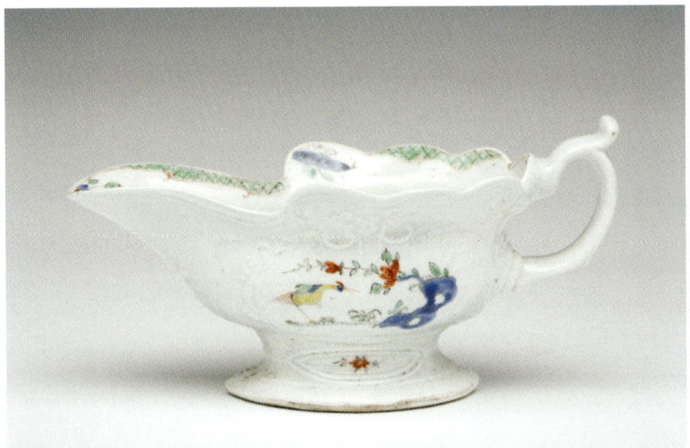

153

153

Sauceboat

About 1753
Ht 10.1 cm, length 19.2 cm, width 9.5 cm
1957.24.1.753

Silver shape, moulded panels decorated with crane-like bird amidst Chinese foliage.

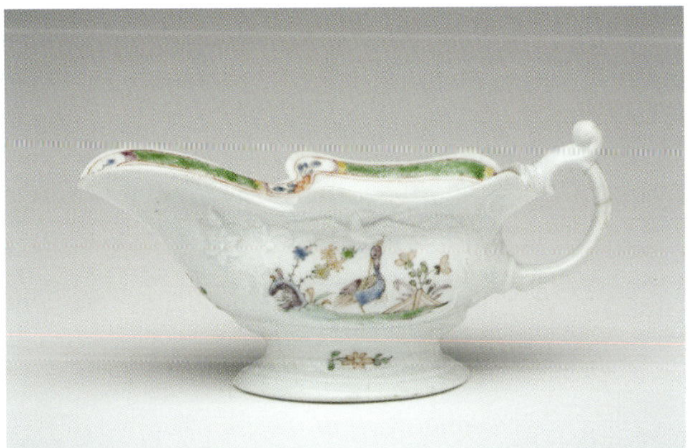

154

154

Sauceboat

About 1755
Ht 8 cm, length 16.4 cm, width 8 cm
1957.24.1.754

Bird decoration within moulded reserves; interior with floral wreaths.

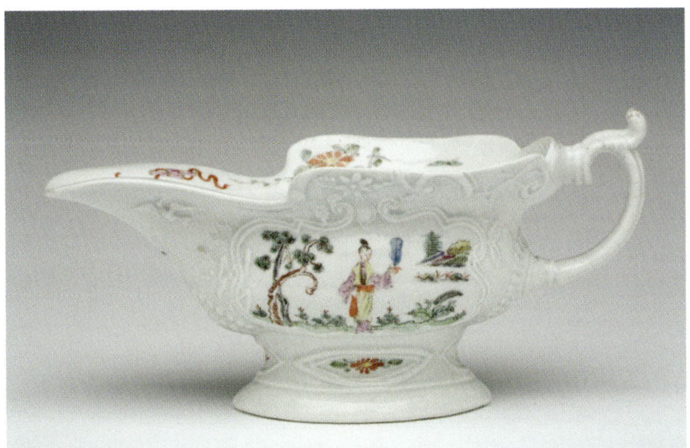

155

155

Sauceboat

About 1754
Ht 11.5 cm, length 23.2 cm, width 11 cm
1957.24.1.290

Silver shape with moulded panels on each side decorated with Chinese woman holding a blue fan; inner rim with flowers and Buddhist symbols.

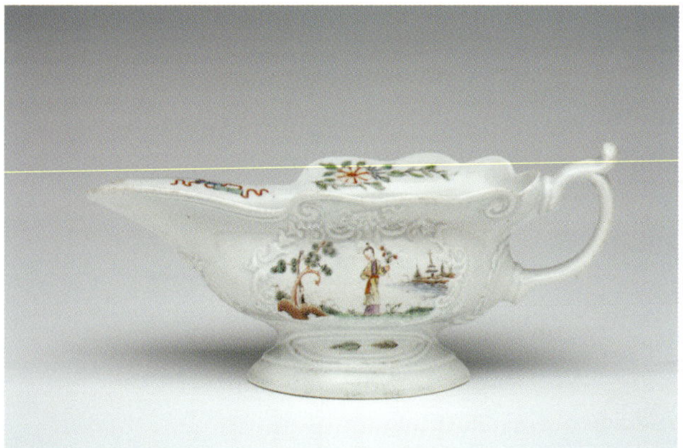

156

156

Sauceboat

About 1754
Ht 8.9 cm, length 19.9 cm, width 9.6 cm
1957.24.1.301

Silver shape; floral moulded panels decorated with an Oriental figure in a landscape, auspicious symbols inside rim.

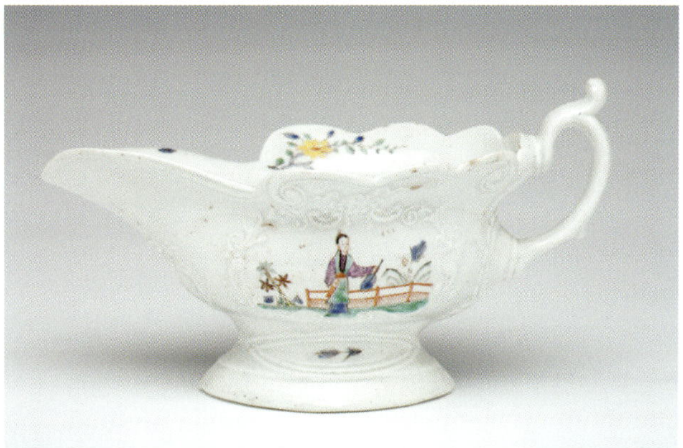

157

157

Sauceboat

About 1754
Ht 10.5 cm, length 18.7 cm, width 10.8 cm
1957.24.1.322

Silver shape on pedestal foot, moulded rosette with pendant acanthus leaf below handle; decorated with a brightly dressed Chinese woman holding a fan by a fence on one side, mauve-clad figure walking over a red arched bridge on the other.

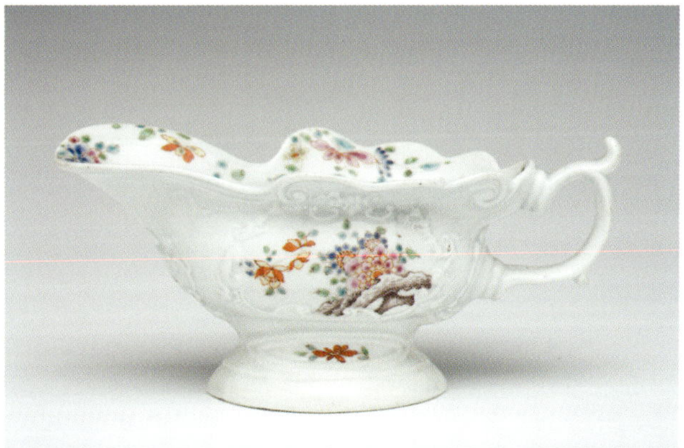

158

158

Sauceboat

1753–5
Ht 9.4 cm, length 19.2 cm, width 9.7 cm
1957.24.1.853

Silver shape with rococo moulded panels, decorated with prunus and other flowers in *famille rose* colours; similar decoration inside rim.

REFERENCE
Amor 1992, p. 8, no. 5.

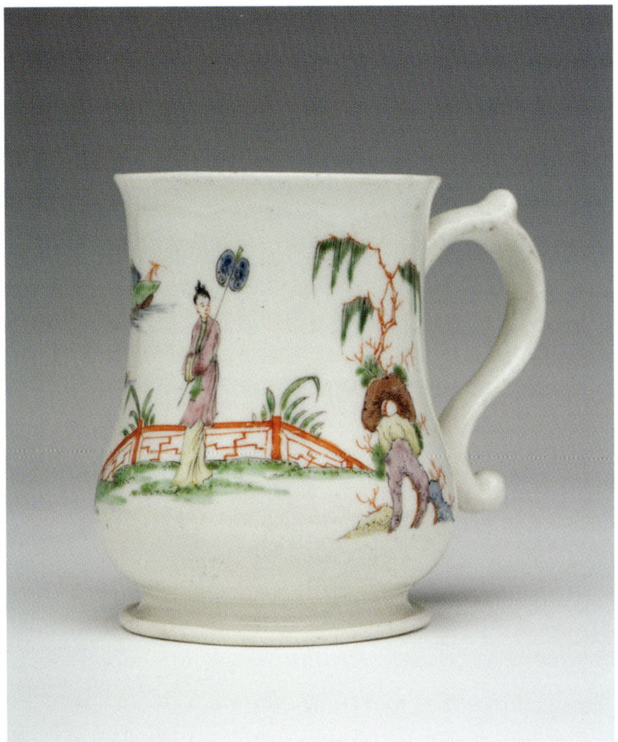

159

159

Mug

About 1753
Ht 9.4 cm
Mark: incised line on base below handle
1957.24.1.1047

Baluster shape with scroll handle; decorated with continuous Chinese scene with sailing ship, island with blue-roofed pagoda, elongated woman holding a blue fan in front of a red trellis and, to her right, an acacia tree rising from coloured rocks.

REFERENCE
Spero 2005, pl. 72.

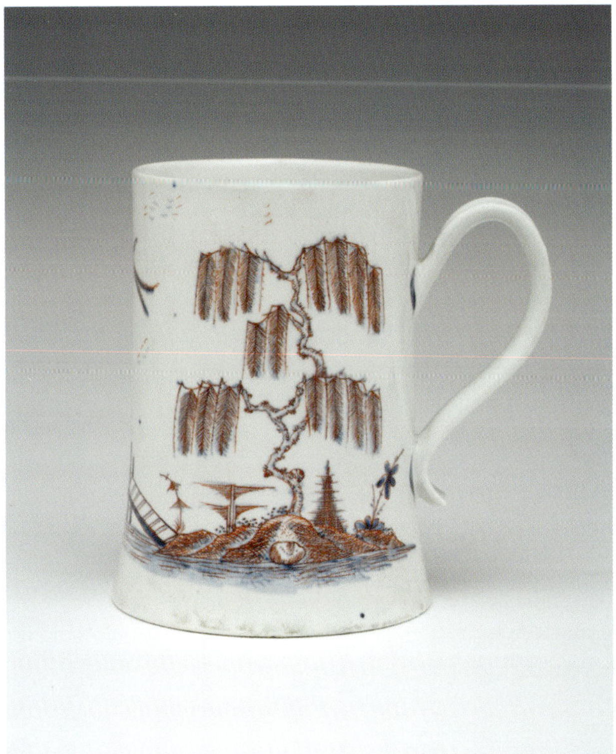

160

160

Mug

About 1754
Ht 14.9 cm, diam. 9.5 cm
Mark: incised line under foot-rim, underglaze blue workman's mark
1957.24.1.1010

Cylindrical with spreading base and ribbed loop handle; decorated in underglaze blue and overglaze red enamel with weeping willows, a Chinese man with a net crossing a footbridge, birds in flight, blue 'commas' beside handle terminal, blue feather decoration on handle. This is known as the 'Question Mark Island' pattern and is one of a few patterns made at the Worcester factory using these colours – the red was not added later. Glazed wasters were excavated on the factory site. A coffee can with similar decoration is illustrated in Spero and Sandon 1996, pl. 42.

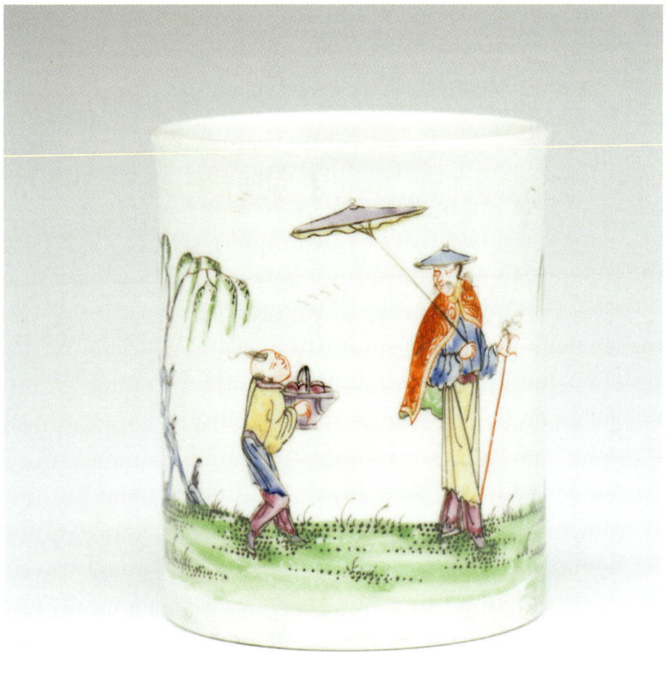

161

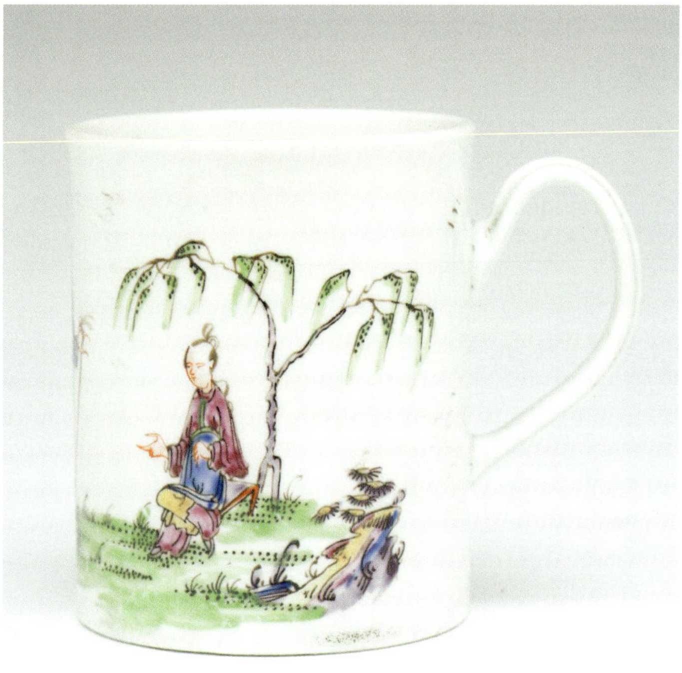

161

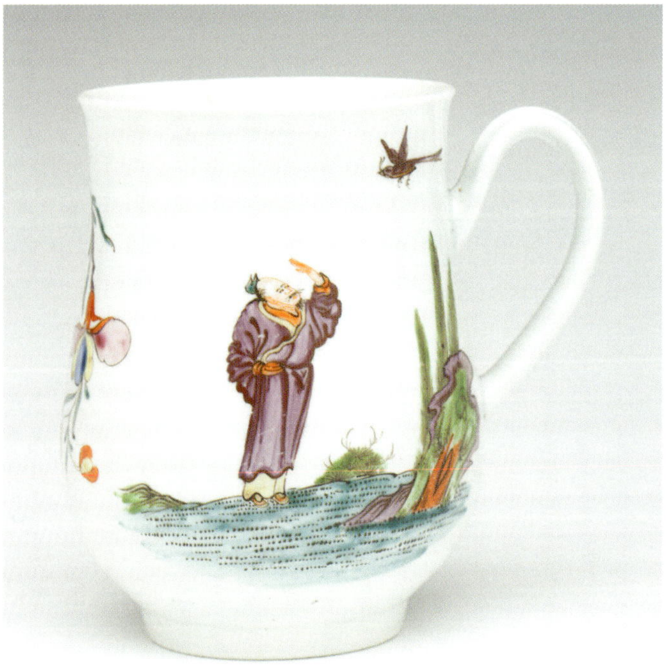

162

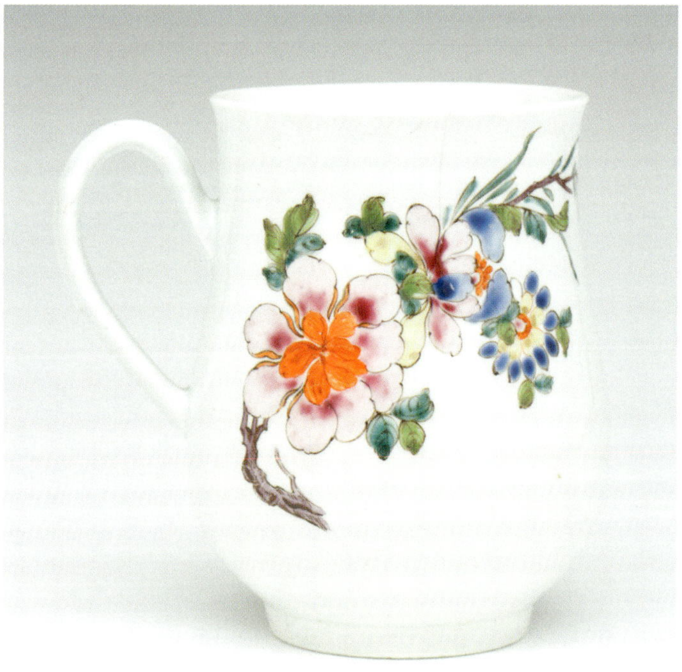

162

161

Mug

1755–6
Ht 8.8 cm, diam. 6.9 cm
1957.24.1.326

Cylindrical with ribbed loop handle; decorated with three brightly dressed Chinese figures, a seated woman under a tree, a man with a stick in his hand holding an umbrella and a boy carrying a basket.

REFERENCE
Spero 2005, pl. 106.

162

Mug

*c.*1756
Ht 11.6 cm
1957.24.1.297

Bell-shaped with ribbed loop handle; decorated with a version of the 'Beckoning Chinaman' pattern; brilliant floral spray on reverse.

REFERENCE
Spero and Sandon 1996, pl. 137.

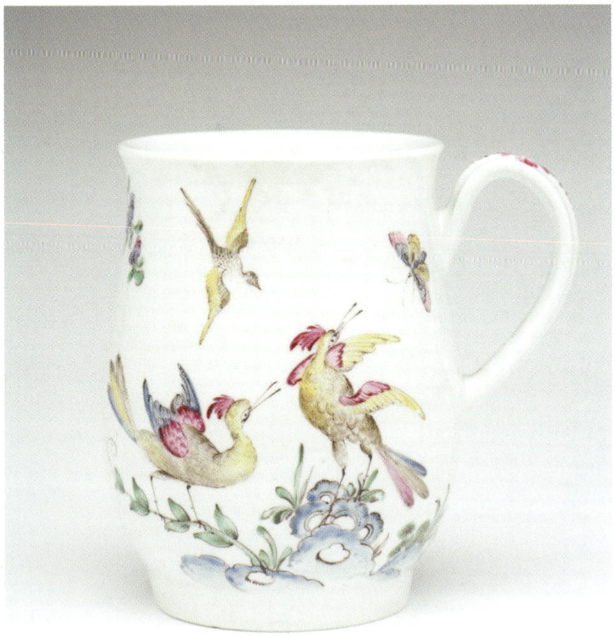

163

163

Mug

1758–60
Ht 12.2 cm
1957.24.1.474

Bell shaped with ribbed loop handle; decorated with one small and two large exotic birds in an unusual palette; large floral spray on reverse.

REFERENCE
Spero and Sandon 1996, pl. 74.

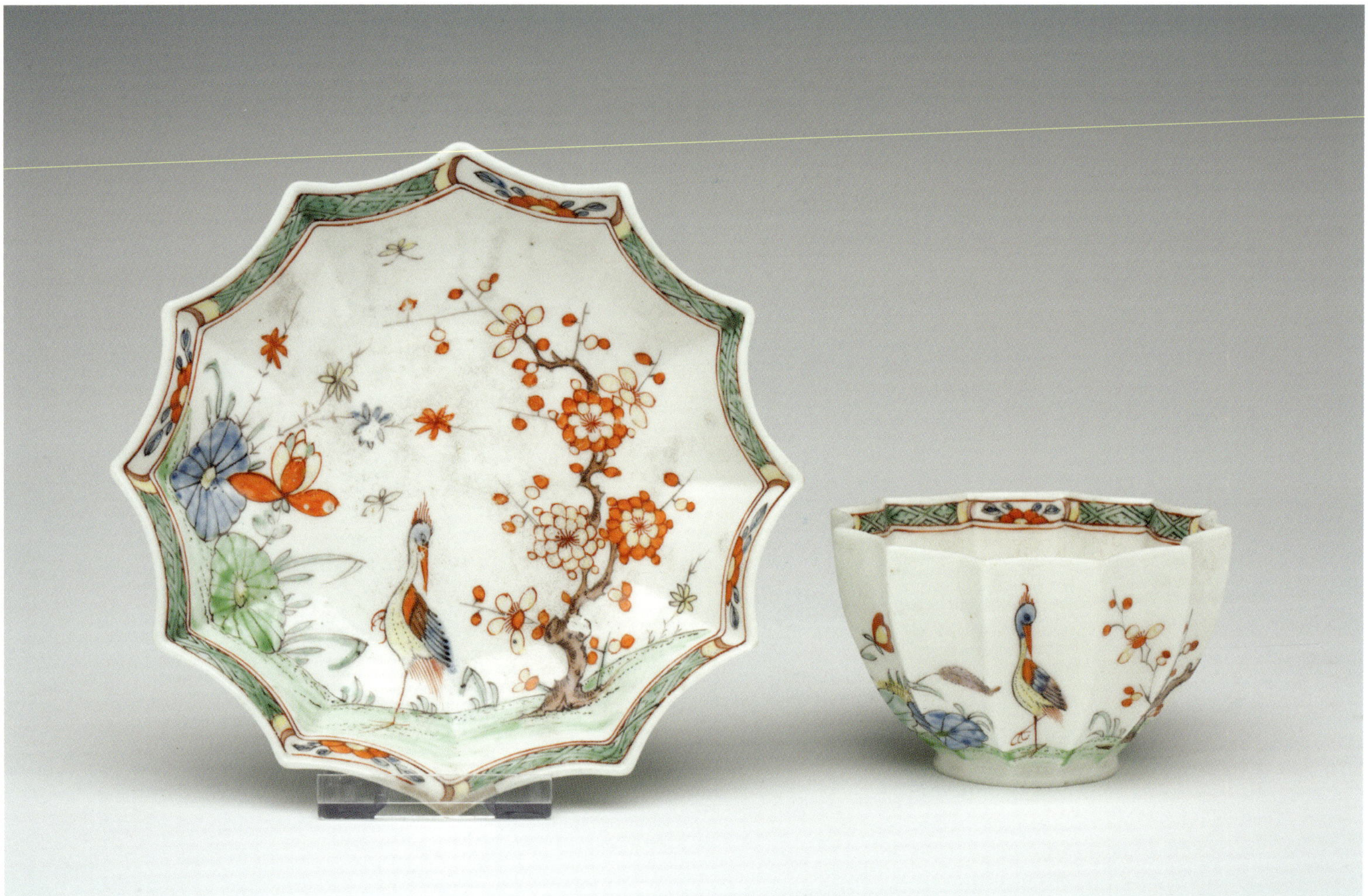

164

164

Teabowl and saucer

About 1752
Teabowl ht 4.7 cm, diam. 7.7 cm; saucer diam. 12.2 cm
1957.24.1.529

Twelve-sided, concavely fluted shape painted with a crane-like bird amongst Oriental flowering plants; border of alternating green diaper and formal flowers. A saucer with similar decoration is illustrated in Spero 2005, pl. 65.

REFERENCE
Bonhams, London, 10 December 2008, lot 98.

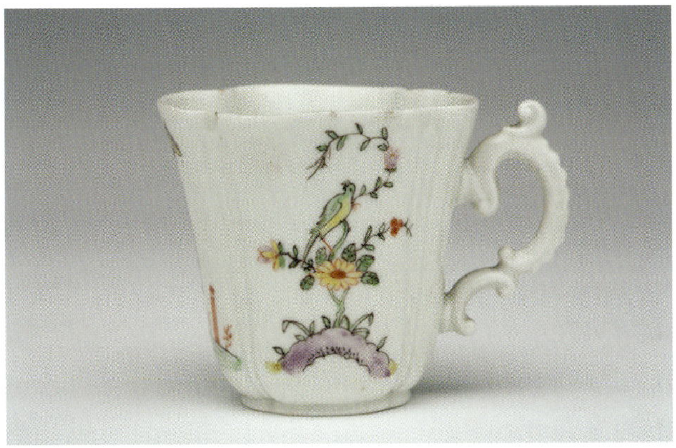

165

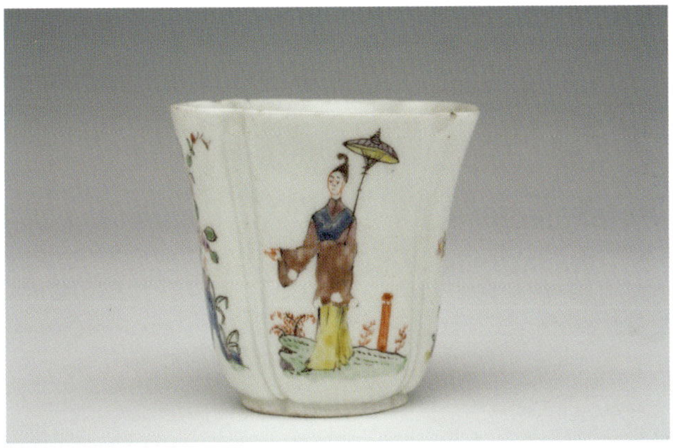

165

165

Coffee cup

About 1753
Ht 6.3 cm, diam. 6.3 cm
1957.24.1.591

Quatrefoil lobed shape with elaborate scroll handle; one panel decorated with a Chinese woman holding a parasol, one with flowers and one with a bird perched amongst flowers and foliage.

PROVENANCE
Glendenning, Tilley & Co., London 26 April 1944, £8 (pair).

REFERENCE
Spero 1984, pl. 13.

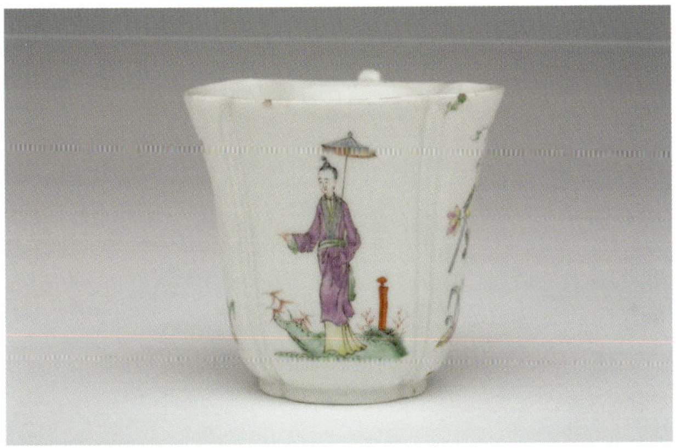

166

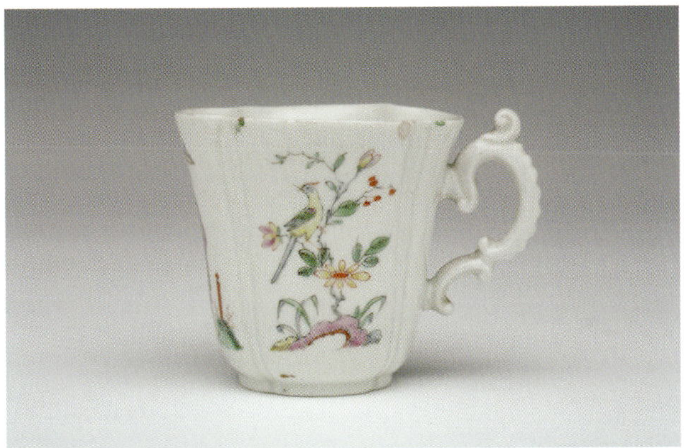

166

166

Coffee cup

1753–4
Ht 6.3 cm, diam. 6.3 cm
1957.24.1.587

Quatrefoil lobed shape with elaborate scroll handle; one panel painted with flowers, one with a Chinese woman holding a parasol and one with a bird amongst flowers and foliage; decorated by a different hand from no. 165.

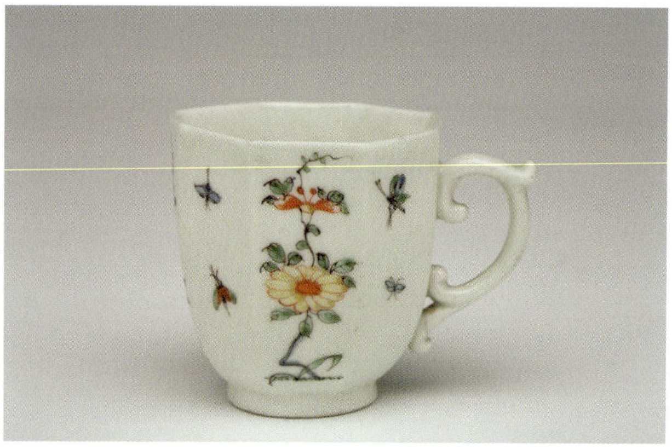

167

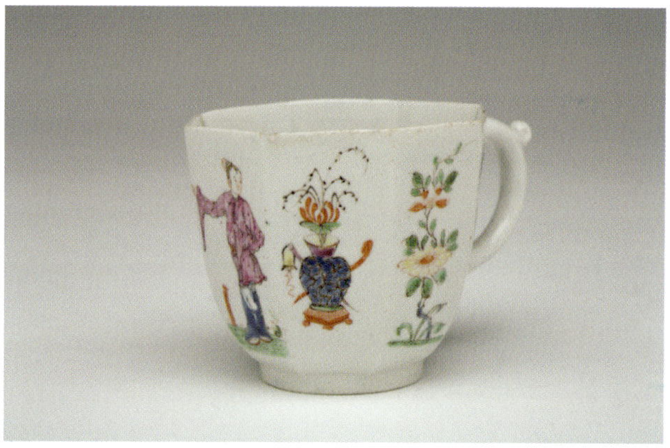

168

167

Coffee cup

1753–4
Ht 5.8 cm, diam. 5.3 cm
1957.24.1.951

Octagonal with scroll handle; alternating panels of Chinese flowers and insects. Only one saucer that matches an octagonal coffee cup is known.

REFERENCES
Spero 2005, pl. 56; Bonhams, London, 10 May 2006, lot 48.

168

Coffee cup

1753–4
Ht 5.7 cm, diam. 6.1 cm
Mark: workman's mark
1957.24.1.952

Octagonal with scroll handle; one panel painted with a Chinese woman, two panels with Chinese flowering plants and two with a vase and floral spray.

REFERENCE
Spero 2005, pl. 94.

169

Teabowl and saucer

1753–4
Teabowl ht 4.6 cm, diam. 7.1 cm; saucer diam. 10.8 cm
Mark: workman's mark
1957.24.1.766

Octagonal, derived directly from a Chinese *famille verte* original; alternate panels of flowers and Buddhist symbols from the 'Hundred Antiques' (a Chinese porcelain design combining a variety of Buddhist symbols with precious objects); red hachured border on saucer and inside rim.

REFERENCE
Spero 2005, pl. 128.

170

Teabowl and saucer

About 1755
Teabowl ht 4.4 cm, diam. 6.7 cm; saucer diam. 10.9 cm
1957.24.1.767

Fluted octagonal shape; enamelled in Chinese *famille verte* style with flowers and butterflies; border of green diaper alternating with floral panels.

REFERENCE
Spero 2005, pl. 115.

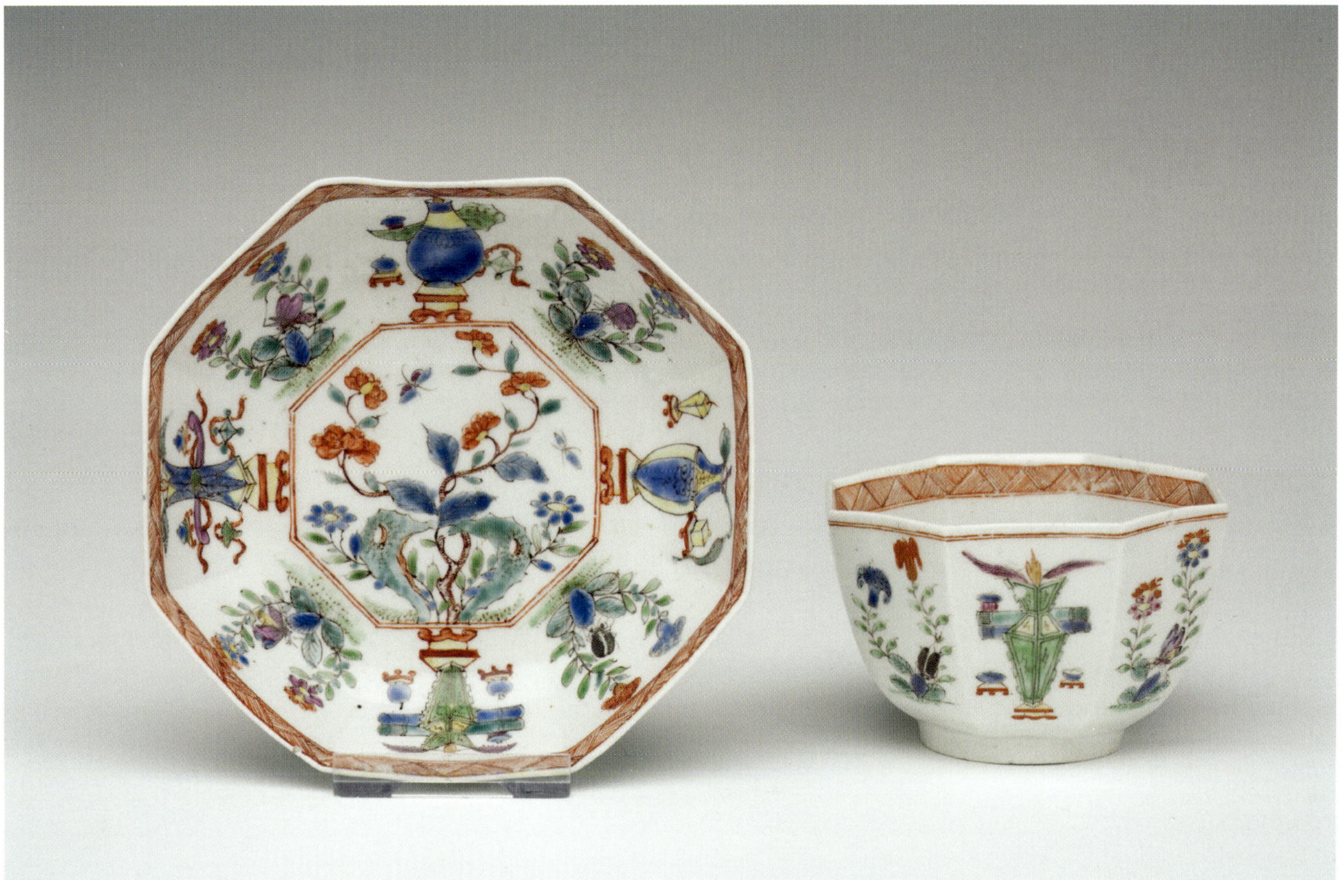

169

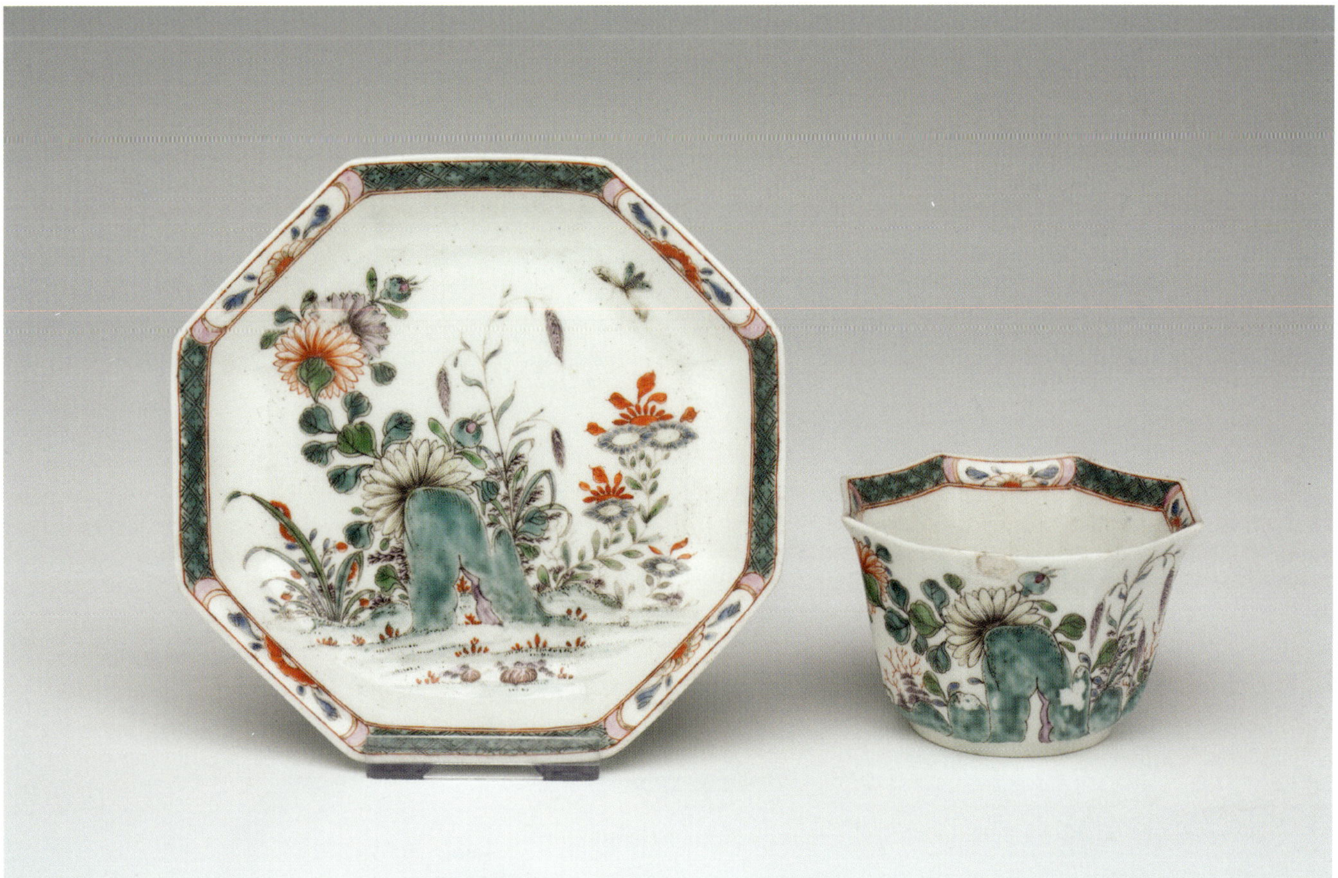

170

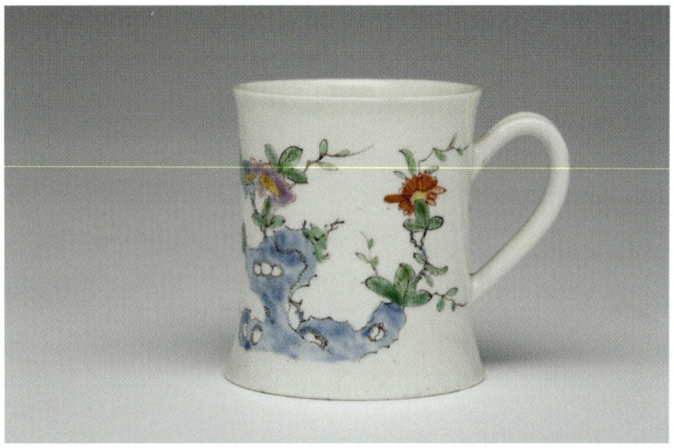

171

171

Small mug

About 1754
Ht 6.2 cm
Mark: incised line inside foot-rim
1957.24.1.1079

Waisted cylindrical shape; painted in Chinese taste with blue holed rocks, flowering plants and two hovering insects.

PROVENANCE
Mrs Geoffrey Hart part 1, Sotheby's, London, 23 June 1959, lot 105, £38.

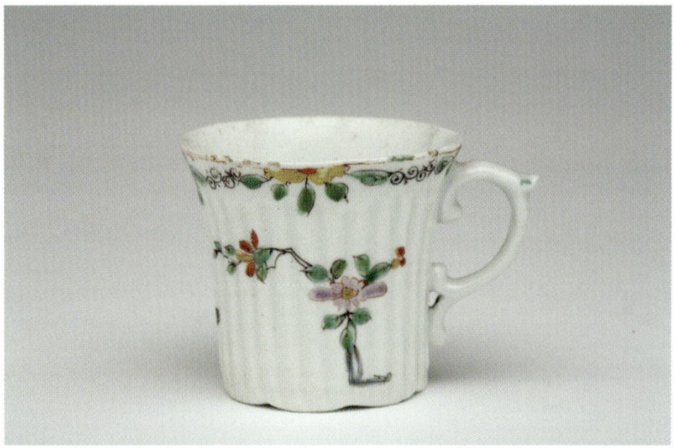

172

172

Coffee cup

1754–5
Ht 5.4 cm, diam. 6.1 cm
1957.24.1.950

Ribbed with scroll handle; decorated with two flower sprays; floral border linked with black scrollwork.

REFERENCE
Spero and Sandon 1996, pl. 22.

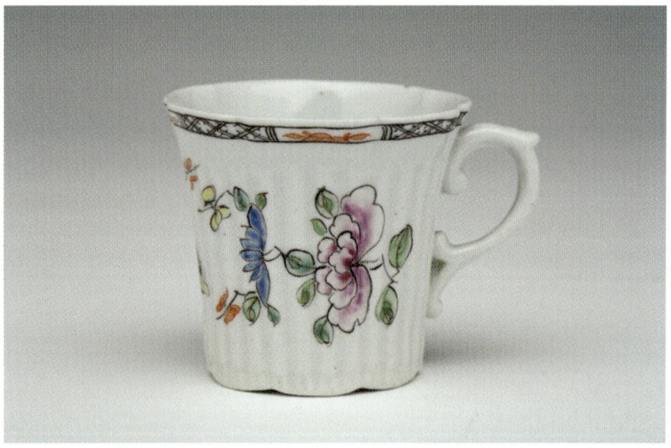

173

173

Coffee cup

1754–5
Ht 5.3 cm, diam. 5.8 cm
1957.24.1.953

Ribbed with scroll handle; decorated with two large floral sprays outlined in black, smaller ones between; border of black diaper alternating with formal red chrysanthemums. A piece with similar decoration is illustrated in Spero and Sandon 1996, pl. 23.

174

Coffee cup and saucer

About 1755
Cup ht 6.5 cm, diam. 5.8 cm; saucer diam. 12.1 cm
1957.24.1.961

Ribbed loop handle; Chinese-style decoration with red fence, peony-type flowers and a ho-ho bird above.

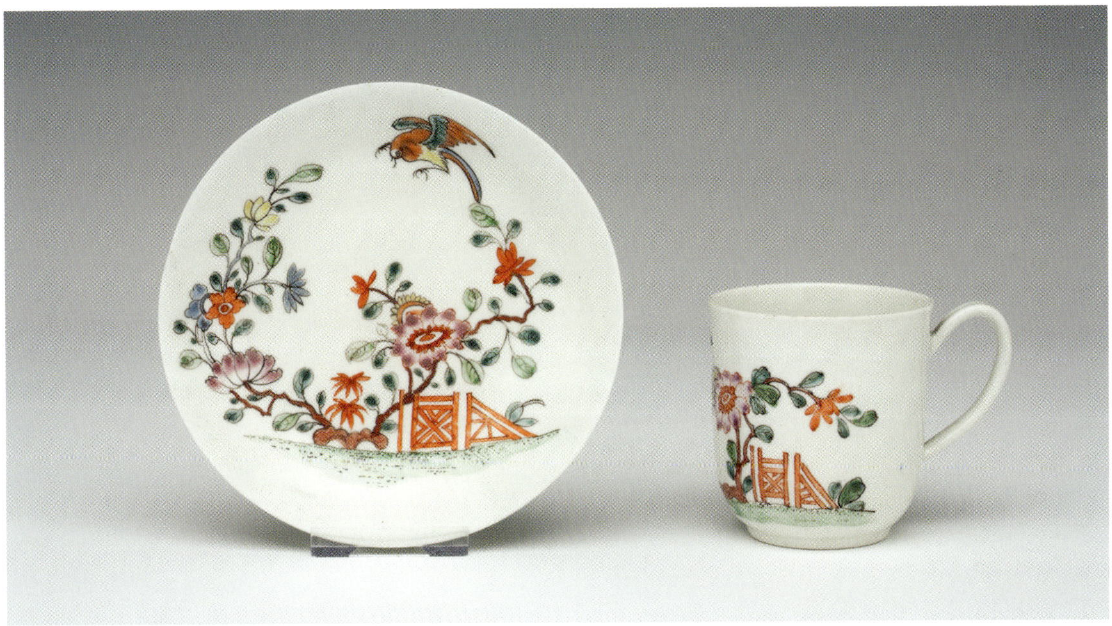

174

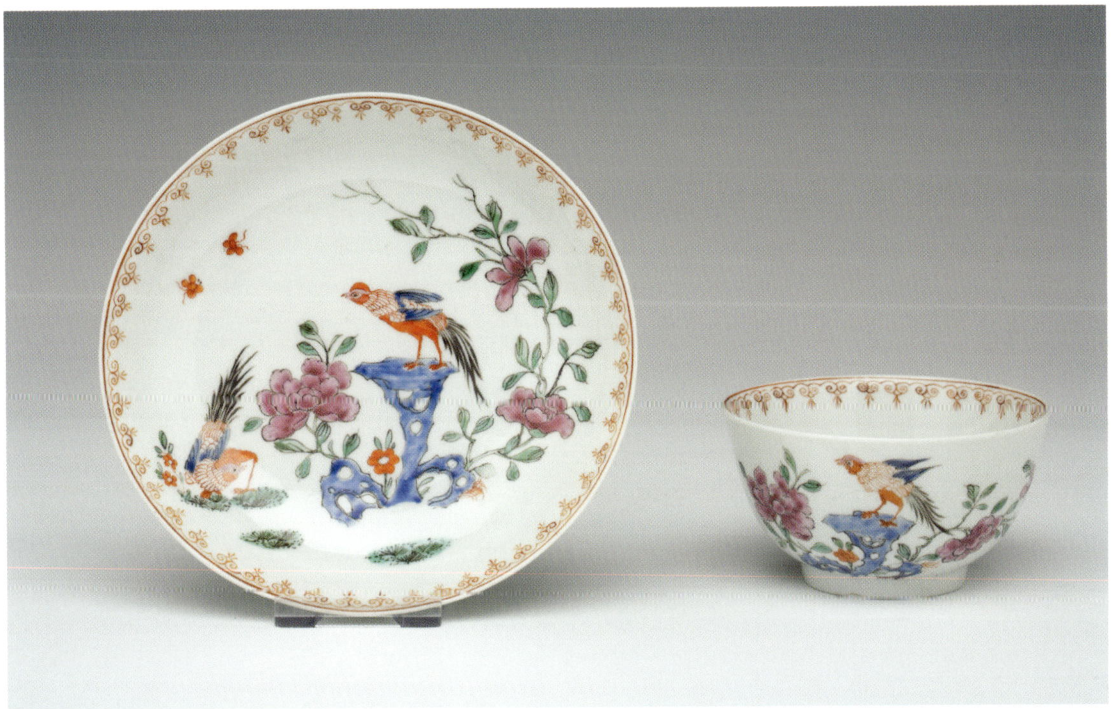

175

175

Teabowl and saucer

1754–5
Teabowl ht 4.7 cm, diam. 8.5 cm; saucer diam. 13.4 cm
1957.24.1.517

Painted in Chinese *famille rose* style with two pheasants, peonies and rocks; formal iron red border.

REFERENCE
Amor 1992, p. 16, no. 27.

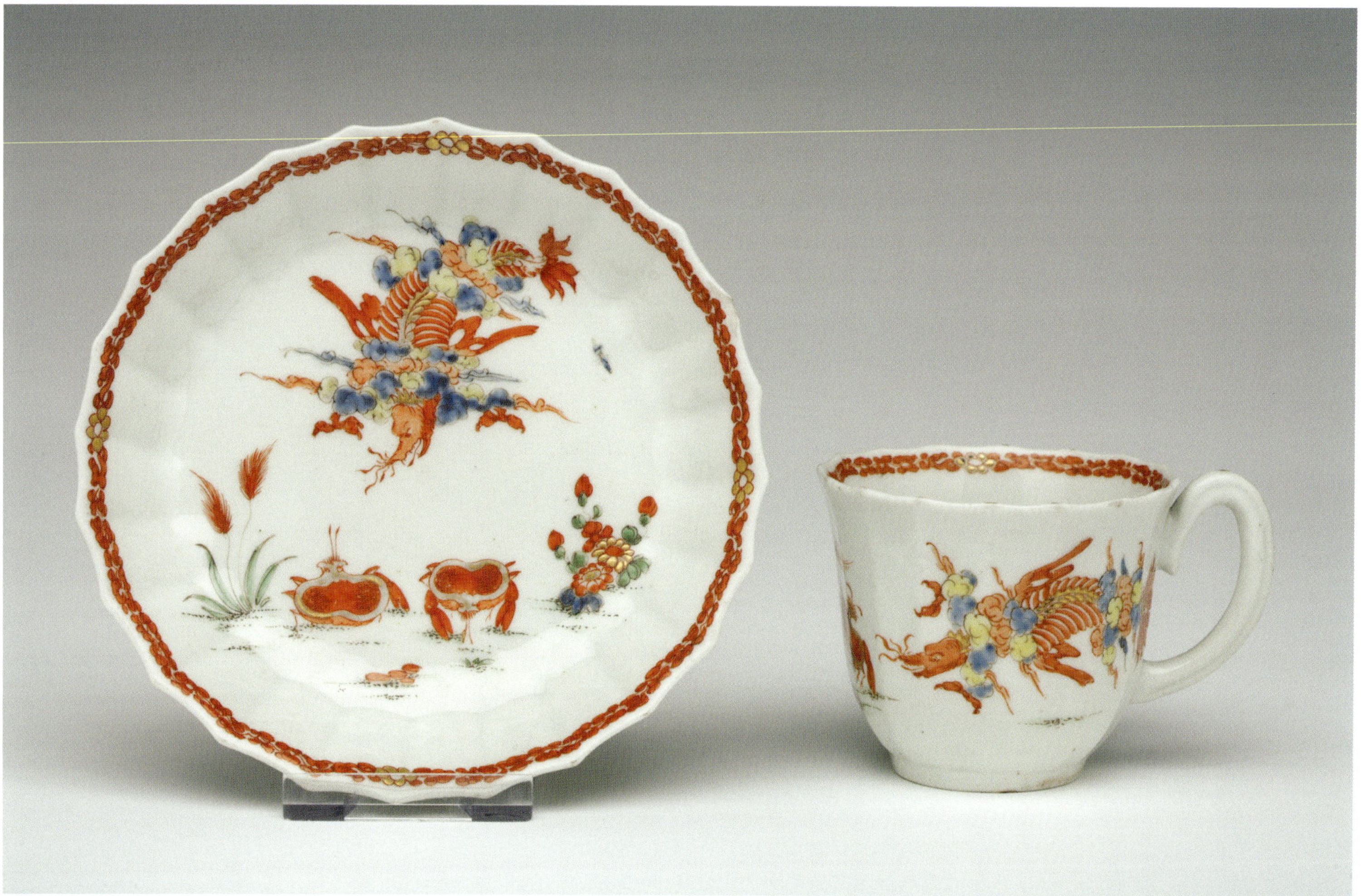

176

176

Coffee cup and saucer

*c.*1755–62
Cup ht 5.3 cm, diam. 6 cm; saucer diam. 11.5 cm
1957.24.1.273

Fluted with scalloped rim, ribbed handle; decorated with a dragon and two crabs, mainly in orange red, with a similarly coloured border. Most likely a Worcester interpretation of a Meissen version of a Japanese design.

REFERENCES
Spero 1984, pl. 63; Spero and Sandon 1996, pls. 125, 126.

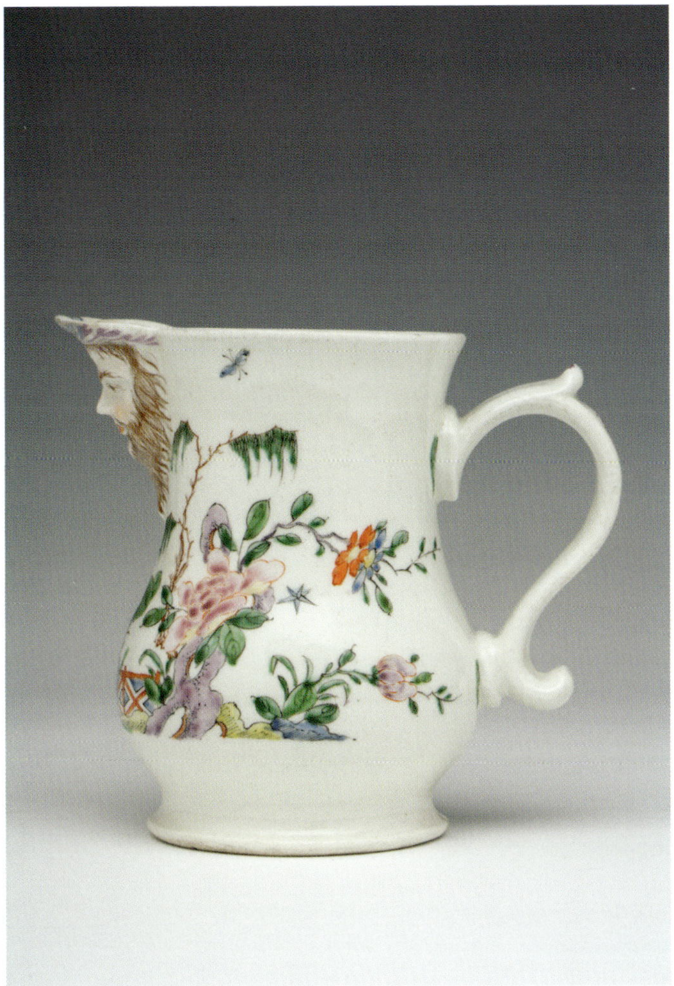

177

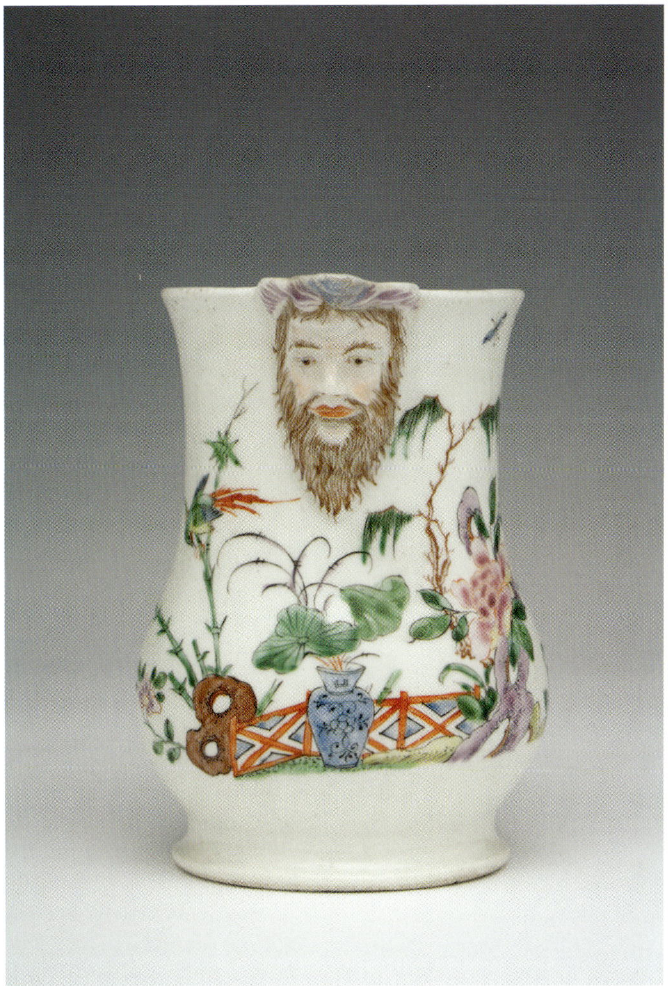

177

177

Jug

About 1754
Ht 12.7 cm
Mark: incised line on base
1957.24.1.861

Baluster shape with coloured masked spout and scroll handle; decorated in the Chinese manner with fence, flowering plants and a bird.

REFERENCES
Spero and Sandon 1996, p. 62; Clarke 1987, p. 22, pl. 8.

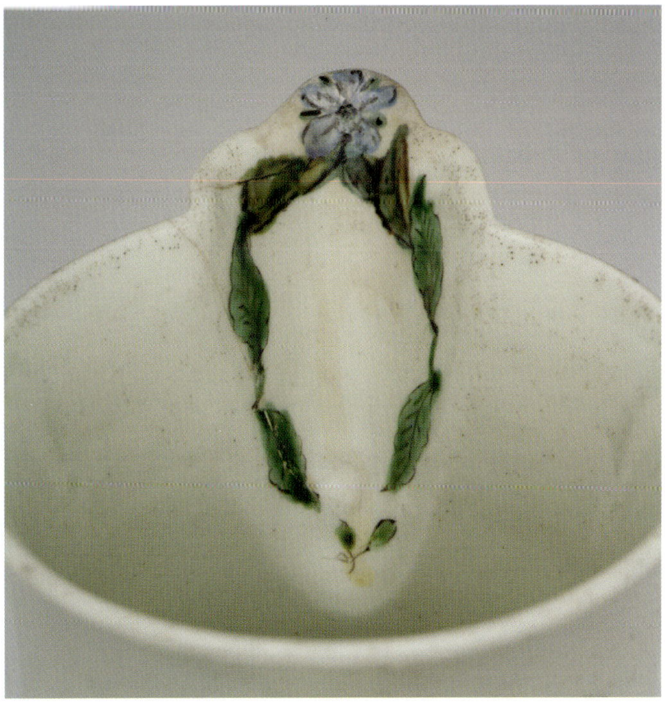

177 (detail)

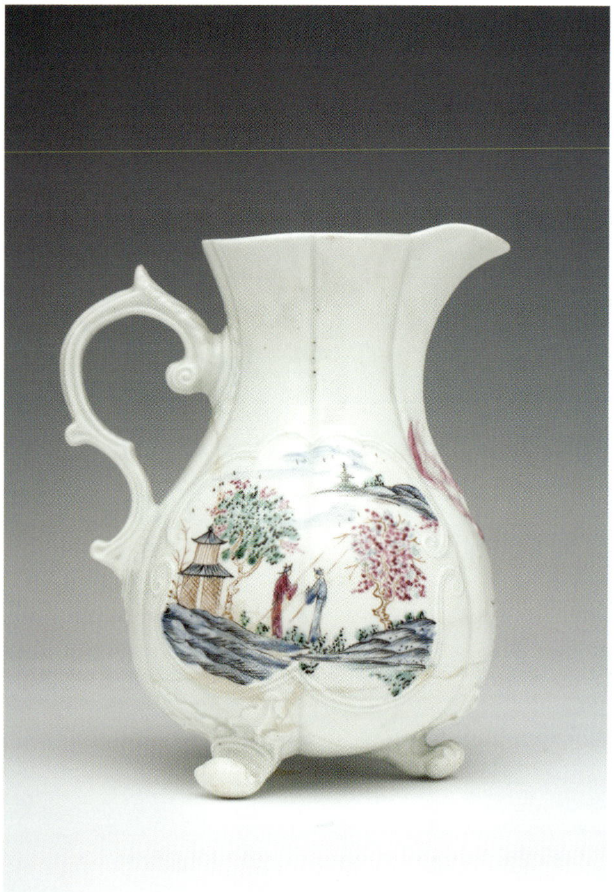

178

178

Jug

1752–3
Ht 18.6 cm
1957.24.1.333

Unusual lobed pear shape with scroll handle, on three scrolled feet springing from moulded cabbage leaves; moulded acanthus leaf picked out in puce below lip; decorated with a version of the Chinese 'Stag Hunt' pattern within moulded panels. The shape is influenced by contemporary silver (fig. 15).

This pattern is always painted in a *famille rose* palette, first adopted at Meissen about 1725. Chinese versions are always enhanced with *bianco sopra bianco*. As the landscape is purely Chinese, it is unlikely to have been taken from a print but may have originated as a landscape with figures in the Kangxi period, influenced by Meissen, for the English market. Worcester produced at least three versions in the 1750s; in this instance the hunter has become a traveller with a bundle on a stick. Derby, Liverpool, Lowestoft and Chamberlain's Worcester also used this pattern. A similar jug decorated with European scenes is in the Victoria and Albert Museum (V&A: 414:543–1885).

REFERENCES

Spero 2005, pl. 45; Barrett 1966, pl. 13; McNeile 1990.

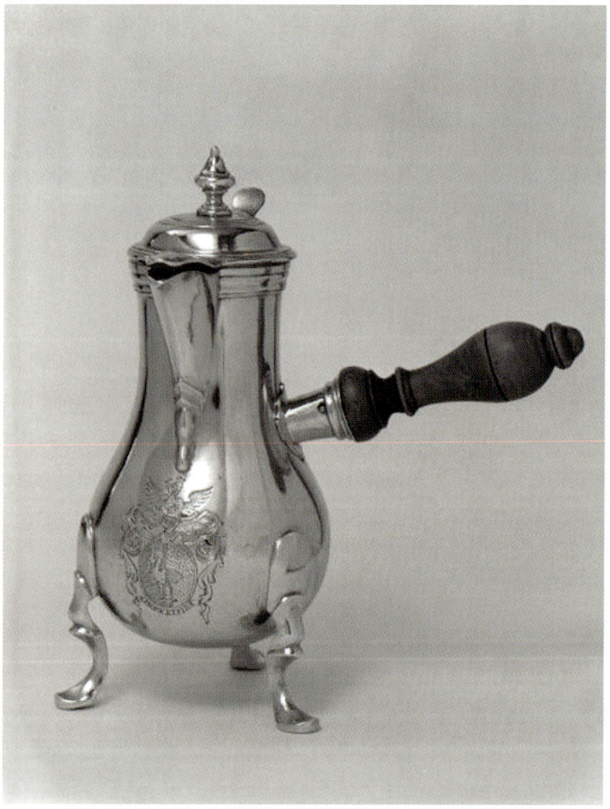

Fig. 15 Silver coffee pot. © Victoria and Albert Museum, London, M.185-1951

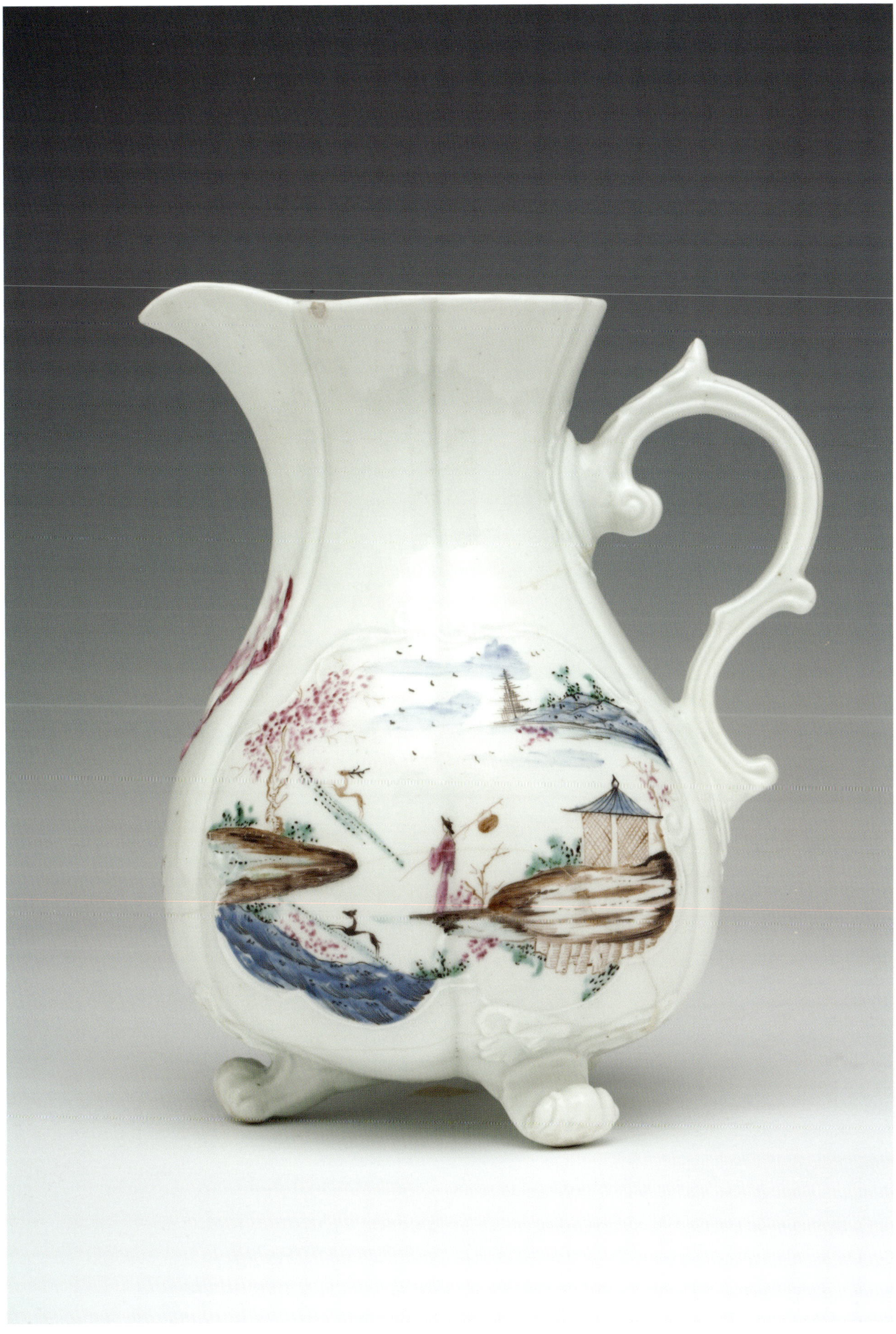

178

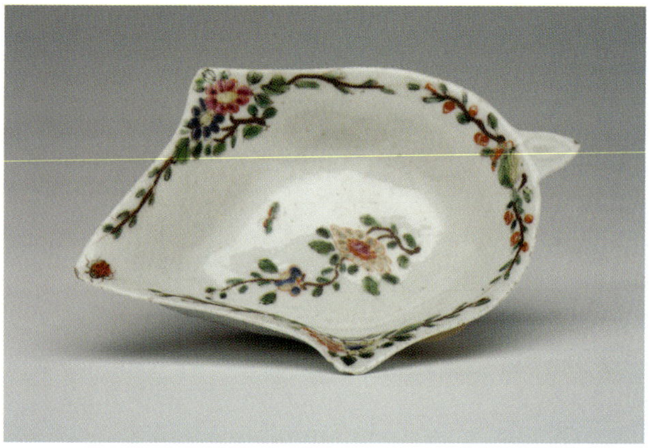

179

179

Pickle dish

1753–4
Length 10 cm, width 7.6 cm
1957.24.1.1013

Leaf shaped with moulded veins on outside; decorated with wreaths of Oriental flowers and insects, ladybird at lip.

REFERENCES
Spero and Sandon 1996, pl. 18; Spero 2005, pl. 58; Clarke 1987, p. 18, pl. 4; Sotheby's, London, 13 April 2011, lot 139; Spero 2008, pl. 33, p. 51.

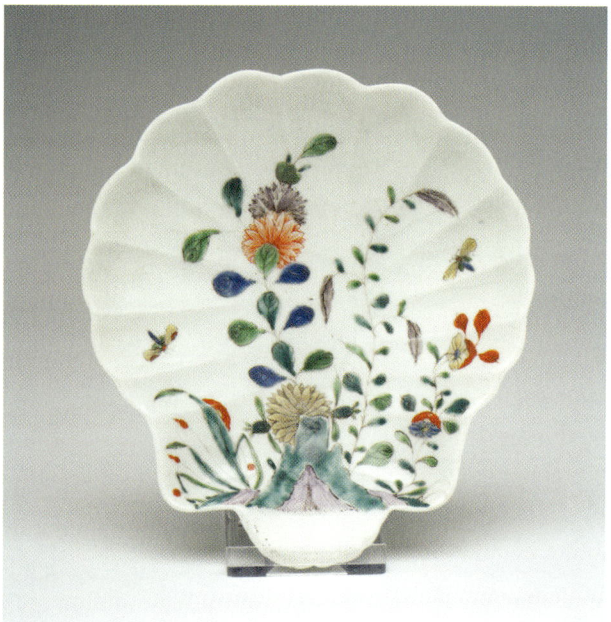

180

180

Sweetmeat dish

1754–5
Length 13.1 cm, width 11.8 cm
1957.24.1.826

Shell shaped; decorated with Chinese flowers, grasses and insects.

REFERENCE
Spero and Sandon 1996, pl. 76.

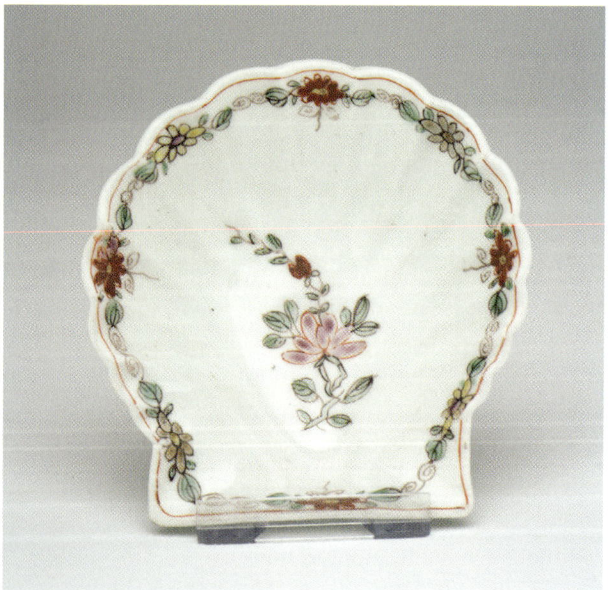

181

181

Pickle dish

About 1754
Length 8.6 cm, width 8.5 cm
Mark: incised line inside foot rim
1957.24.1.1025

Moulded scallop form; formal floral border around edge, flower spray in centre.

REFERENCES
Spero and Sandon 1996, pl. 77; Spero 2005, pl. 59.

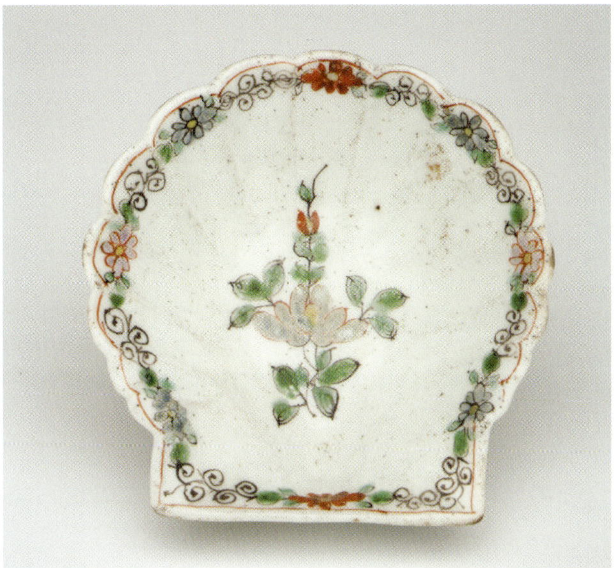

182

182

Pickle dish

About 1754
Length 8.6 cm, width 8.5 cm
Mark: incised line inside foot rim
1957.24.1.1031

Moulded scallop form; formal floral border with black scrolls, flower spray in centre.

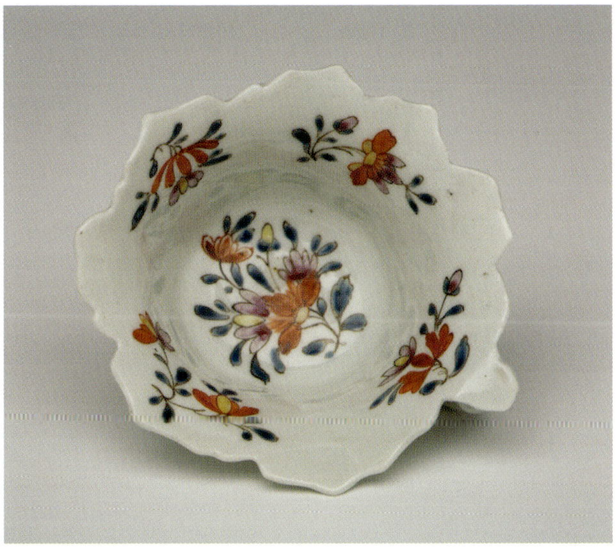

183

183

Butter boat

1755–8
Ht 3.7 cm, length 7.6 cm, width 6.8 cm
1957.24.1.1029

Moulded with three tiers of leaves; decorated inside with five flower sprays in yellow, green, mauve and iron red. Although the precise use is not known, this deep moulded shape may also have been used for pickles.

REFERENCES

Amor 1992, no. 65, Spero and Sandon, 1996, pl. 140.

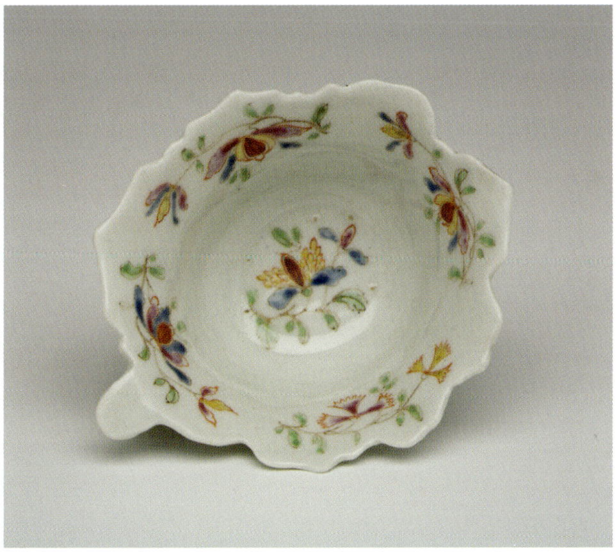

184

184

Butter boat

1755–8
Ht 3.5 cm, length 7.9 cm, width 6.6 cm
1957.24.1.1027

Moulded with three tiers of leaves; decorated in a pale palette with five flower sprays in red, green, blue and yellow.

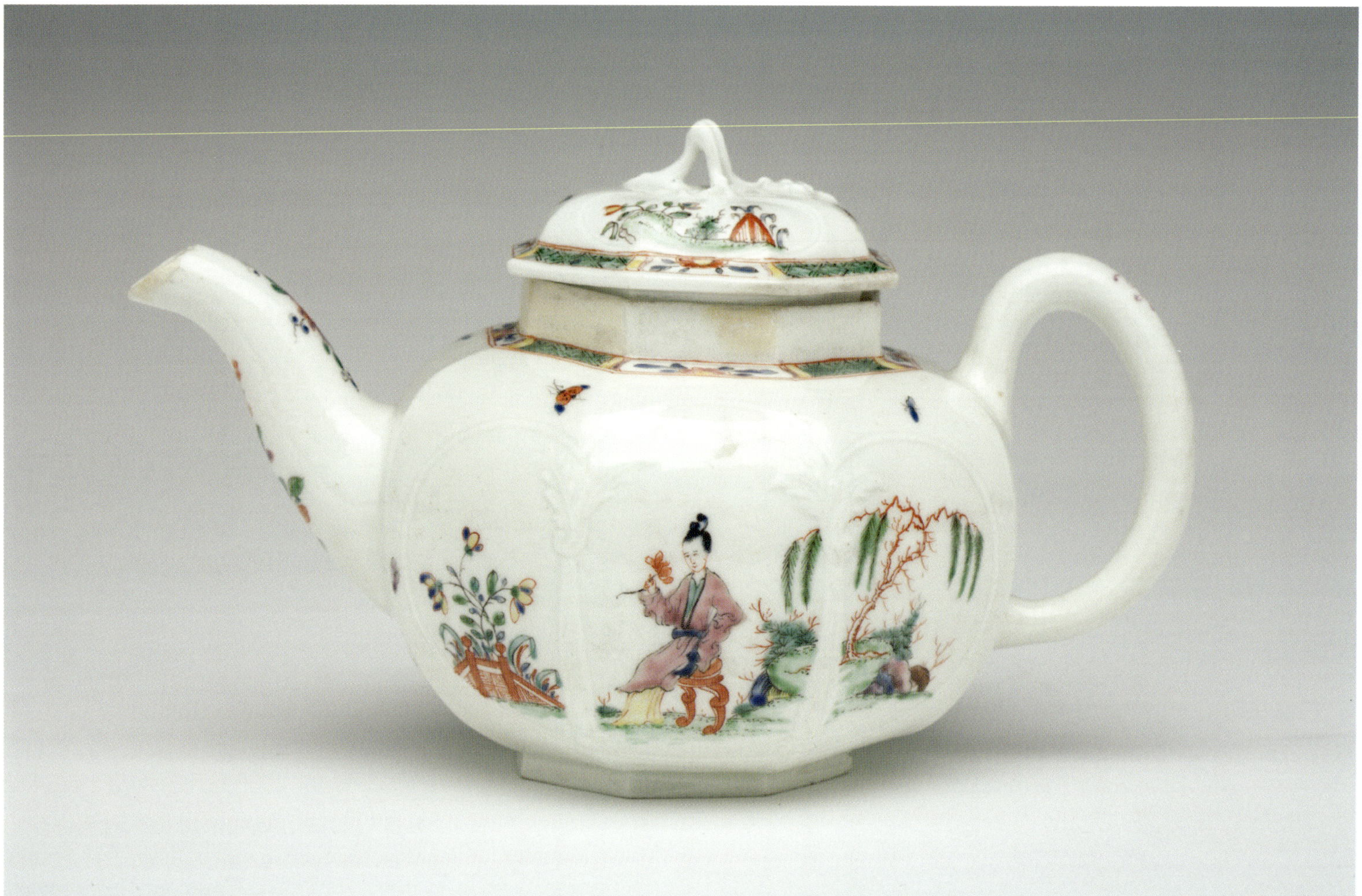

185

185

Teapot and lid

About 1753
Ht 11.2 cm
1957.24.1.307

Squat, octagonal shape, twig knop; three moulded panels on each side decorated with Chinese figures and flowers; borders of diapered green panels alternating with formal flowers.

PROVENANCE
Sotheby's, London, 30 January 1942, lot 41.

REFERENCES
Clarke 1987, p. 19, pl. 5; Spero 2005, pl. 85.

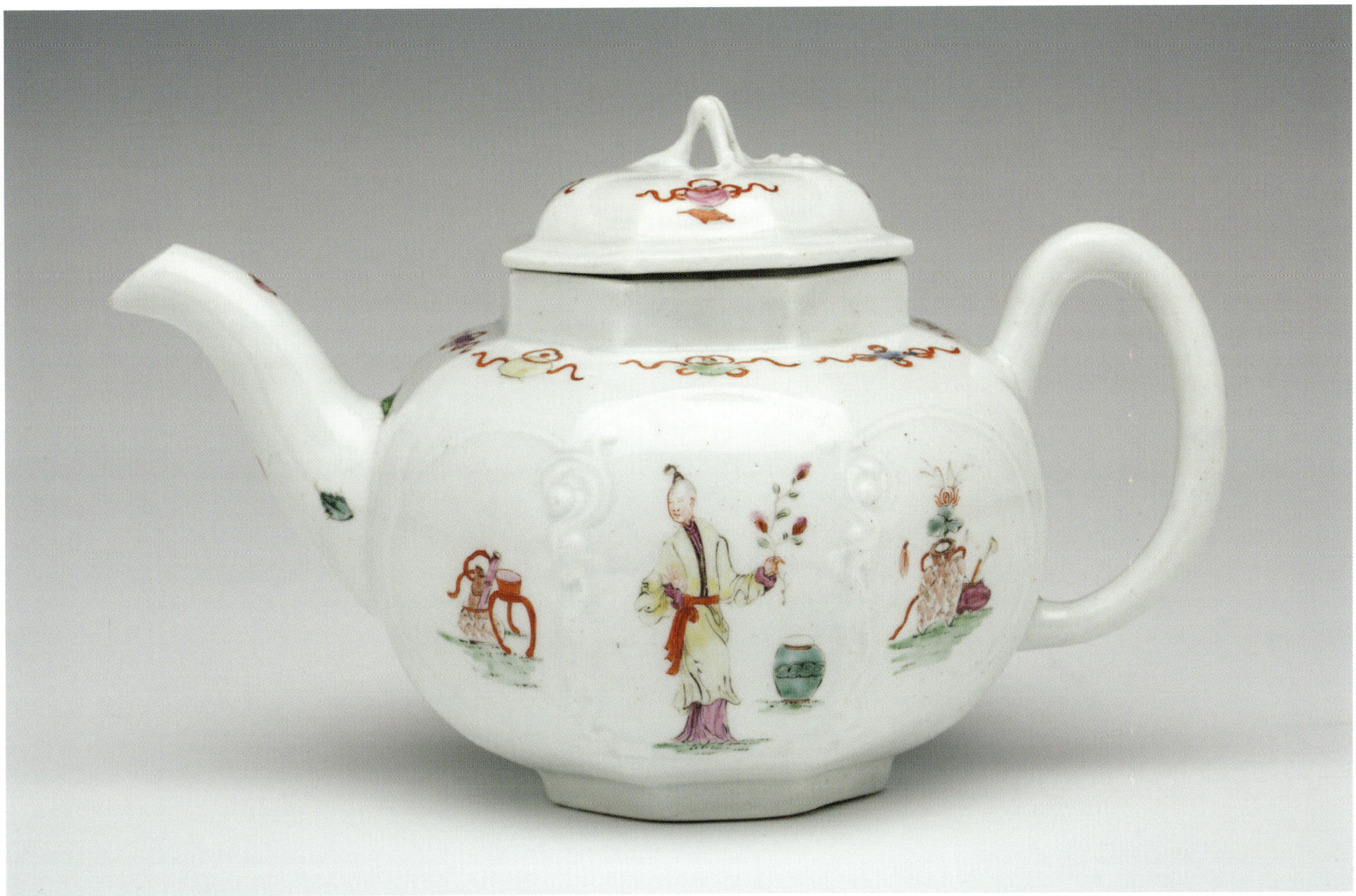

186

186

Teapot and lid

1753–4
Ht 11.8 cm
1957.24.1.309

Squat, octagonal shape, twig knop; three moulded panels on each side decorated with Chinese ladies flanked by utensils; lid and shoulders decorated with Chinese emblems.

REFERENCE
Spero 2005, pl. 93.

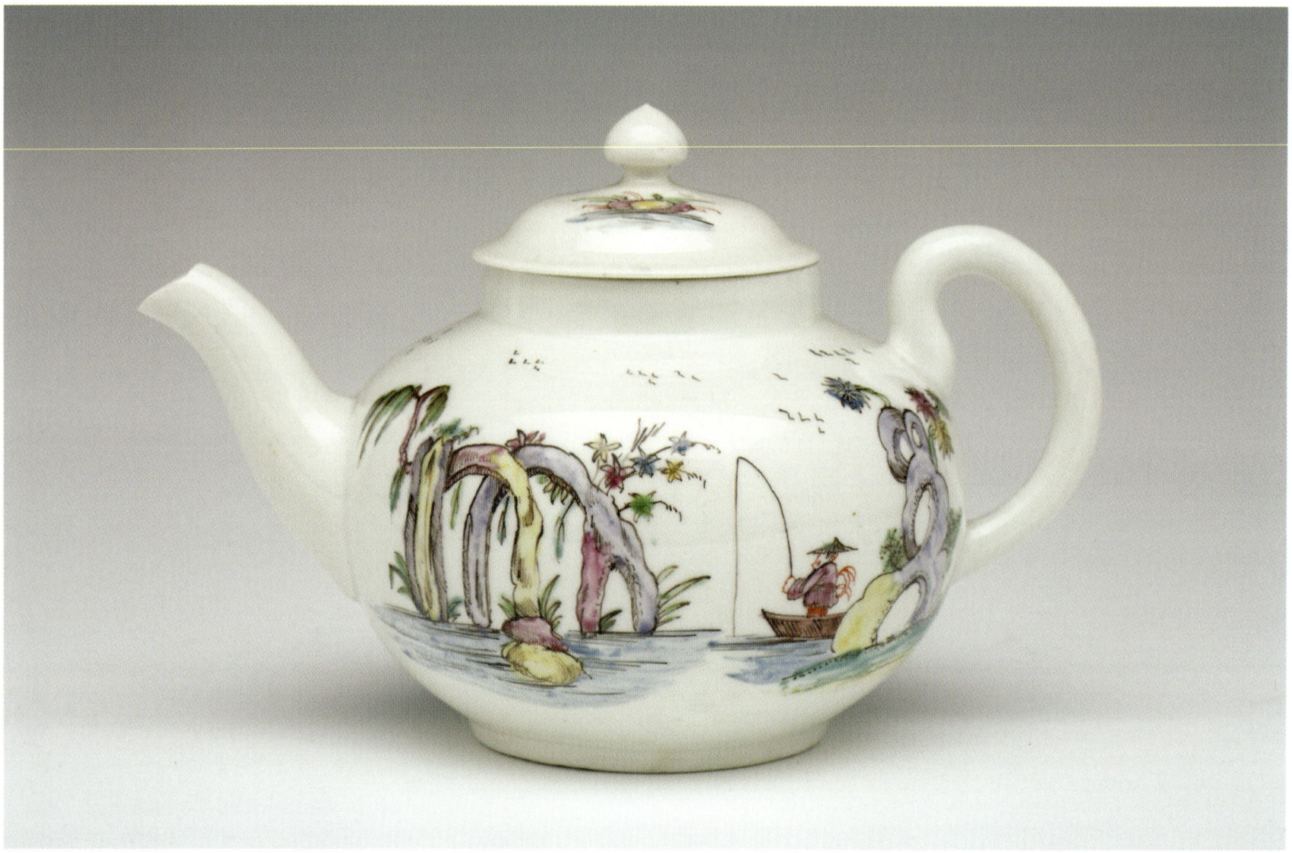

187

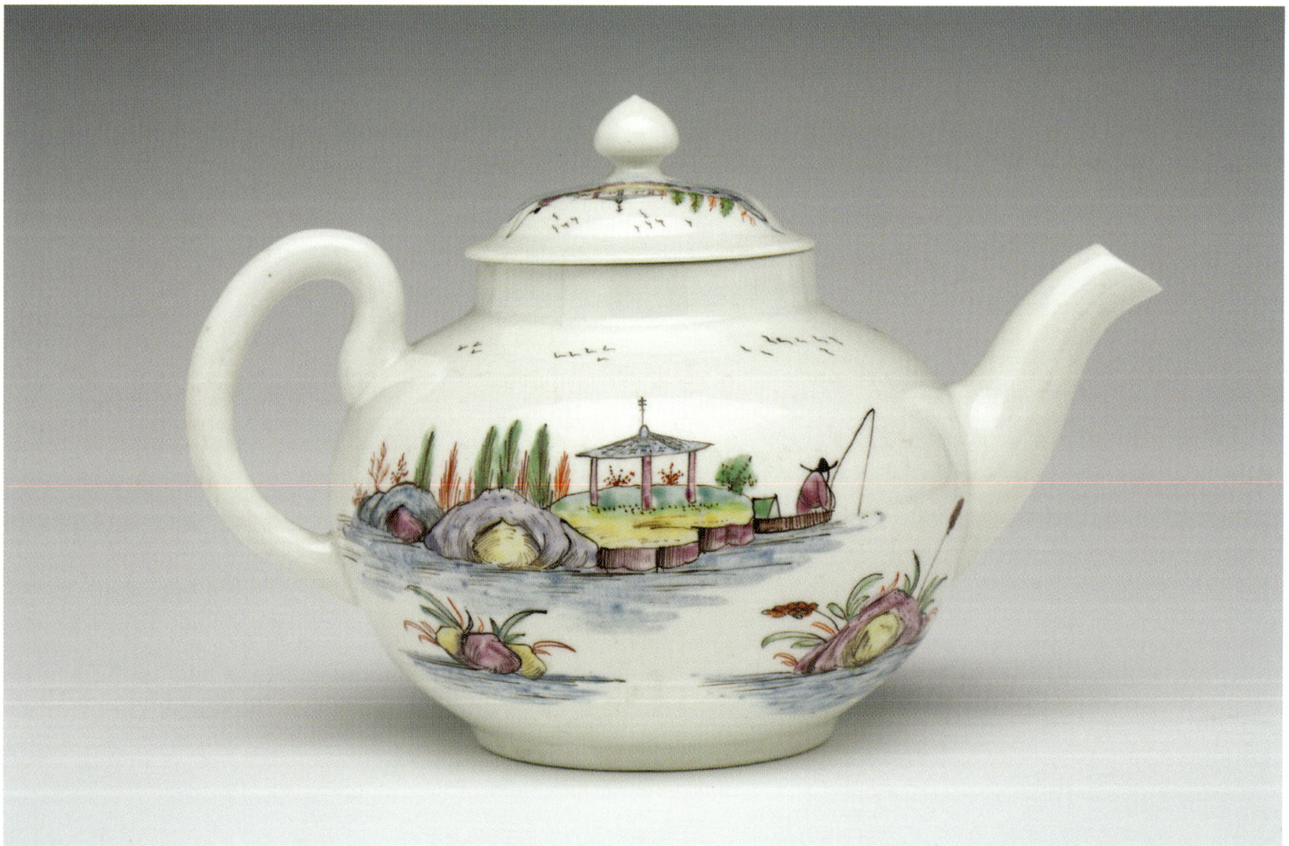

187

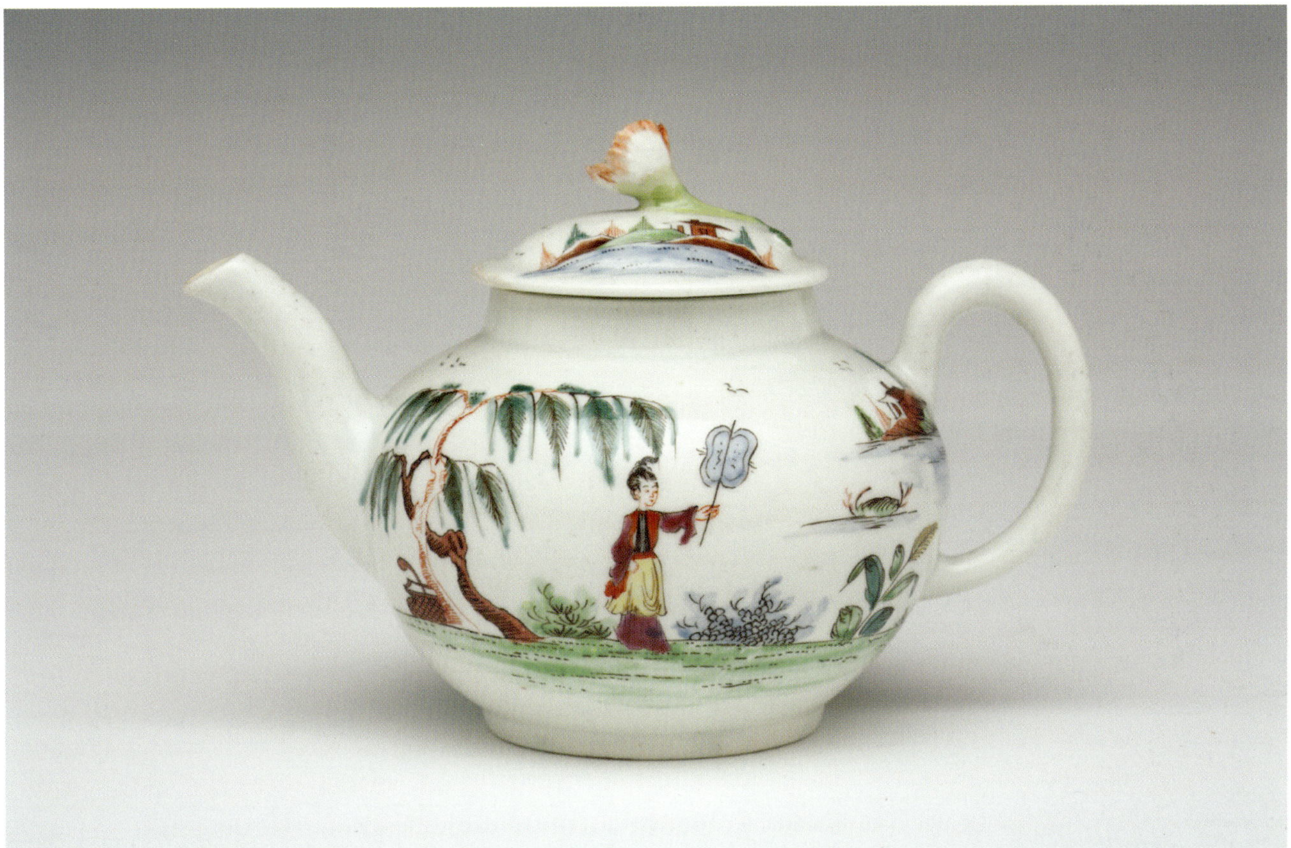

188

187

Teapot and lid

1755–6
Ht 11.7 cm
1957.24.1.317

Squat, globular shape, conical knop, plain loop handle; painted in distinctive colours with a temple on one side and fishermen on a lake on the other. A saucer with similar decoration is illustrated in Spero 2005, pl. 116, and an example from the Museum of Royal Worcester Porcelain in Dreweatt Neate 1995, p. 2, no. 14.

188

Teapot and lid

About 1755
Ht 10.3 cm
1957.24.1.314

Small size with plain loop handle and rosebud knop; decorated in Oriental style with a woman holding a blue fan, standing under a willow tree.

189

Wine funnel
About 1754
Ht 13 cm
1957.24.1.308

Decorated with a 'Long Eliza'-type figure holding blue fan, standing by pine tree; diapered border with formal chrysanthemums inside rim. This shape was probably derived from a George II silver original, issued in three basic sizes, not made at any other factory. Another pattern has flowering peonies and rockwork and a further one is recorded with rococo scrollwork in puce camaïeu. Only fourteen polychrome and four blue and white examples are thought to have survived (figs 16 and 17).

PROVENANCE
Arthur Hurst sale part 3, Sotheby's, London, 30 January 1941, £17.

REFERENCES
Amor 1992, p. 29, no. 67; Spero and Sandon 1996, pl. 86; Spero 2005, pl. 110.

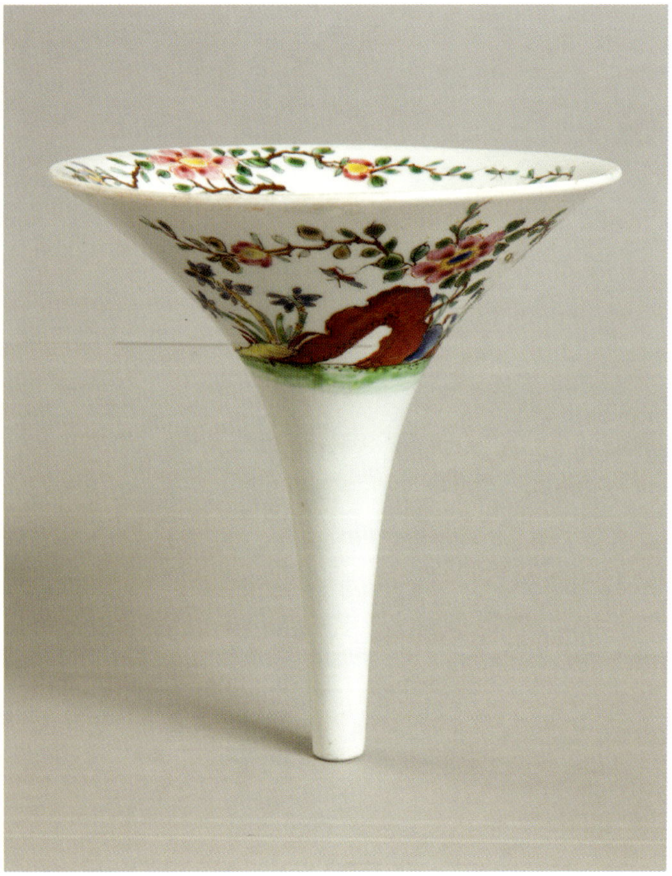

Fig. 16 Wine funnel, *c.*1754. © Bristol Museums, Galleries and Archives

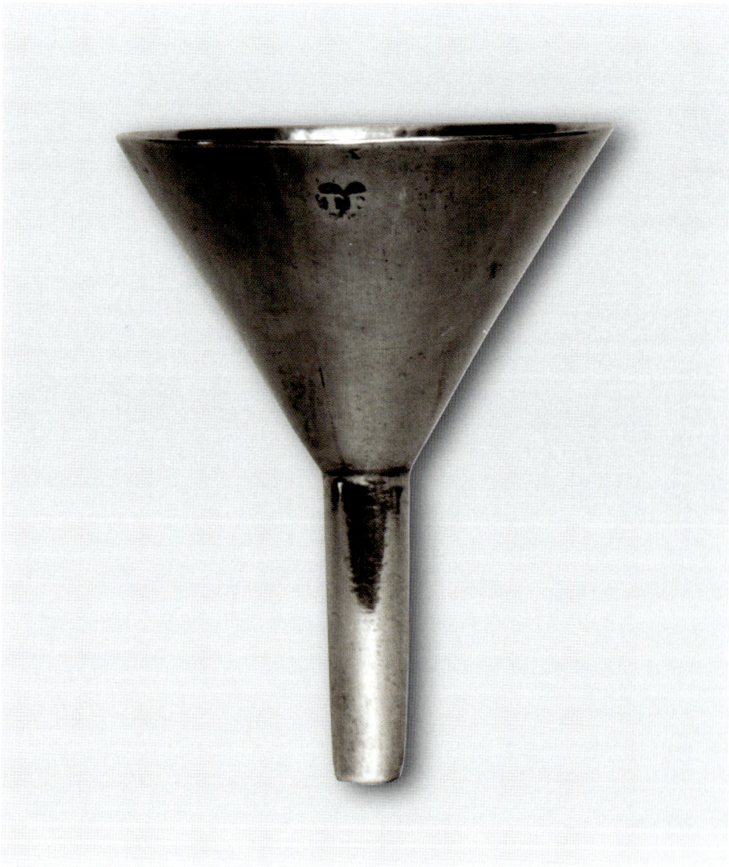

Fig. 17 Silver wine funnel with London maker's mark, TF. © The Trustees of the British Museum, 1944,1001.6

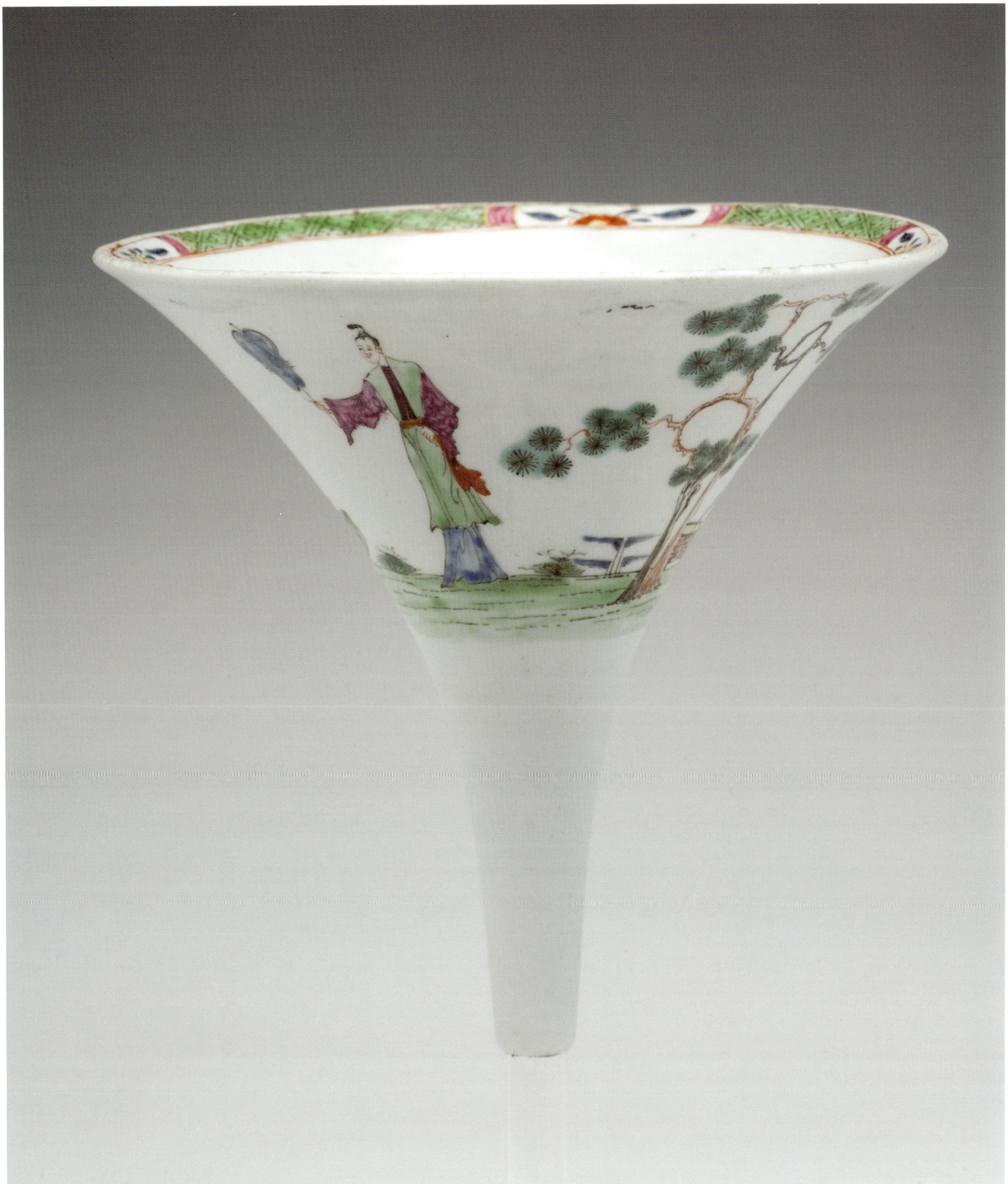

189

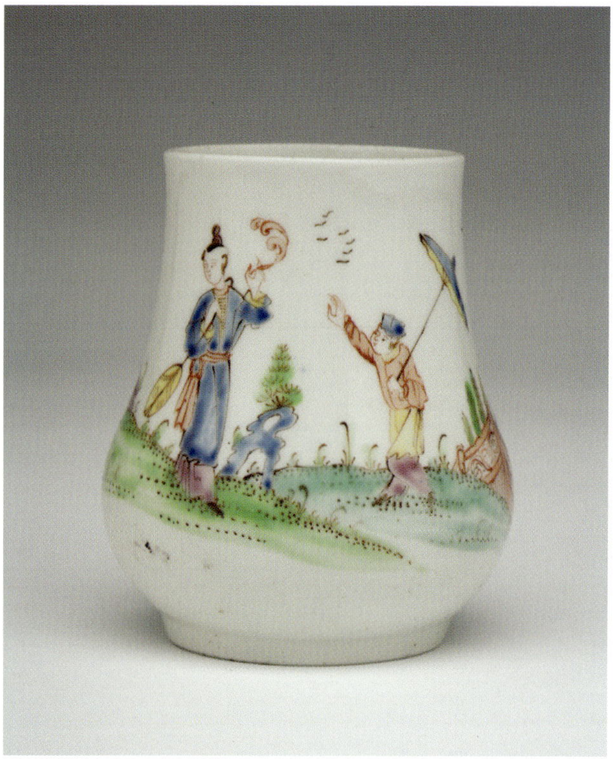

190

190

Dry mustard pot

1753–5
Ht 7.5 cm
1957.24.1.969

Decorated with a Chinese woman holding fan and a boy with umbrella; cover missing.

REFERENCES
Barrett 1966, pl. 7a; Amor 1992, p. 29 no. 66.

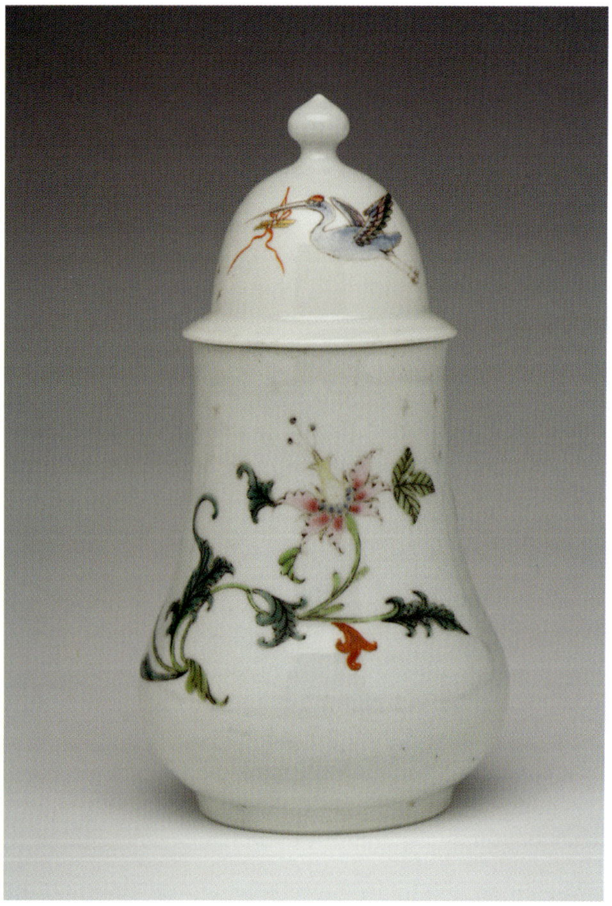

191

191

Dry mustard pot with cover

1755–6
Ht 12.3 cm
1957.24.1.921

Domed cover and conical knop; decorated with Chinese flowers in the 'Honeysuckle' or 'Hibiscus' pattern; bird in flight on cover.

PROVENANCE
Albert Amor, London, 5 January 1954, £120.

REFERENCE
Spero 2008, pl. 33, p. 51.

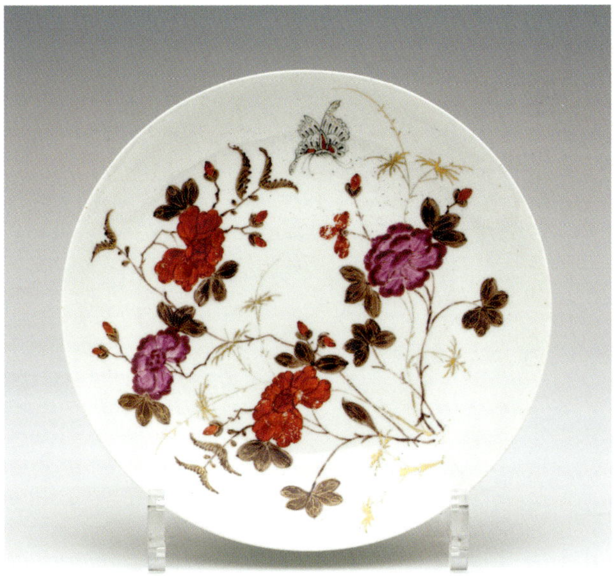

192

192

Cake dish

About 1755–7
Diam. 17.3 cm
1957.24.1.864

Decorated in an unusual palette with two carmine and two red peonies, brown foliage veined in gold; butterfly delicately pencilled in black with red body. A bowl with the same decoration is illustrated in Amor 1981, pl. 42, and a lobed jug in Amor 1992, p. 13, no. 17.

REFERENCE
Spero and Sandon 1996, pl. 130.

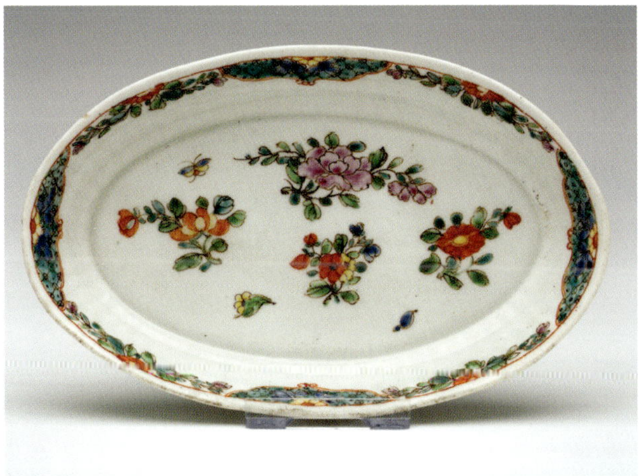

193

193

Spoon tray

About 1755
Length 14.6 cm, width 9.5 cm
1957.24.1.699

Unusual oval shape with moulded ribbed sides; painted in colours with sprays of Oriental flowers and foliage with an irregular floral border. A comparable circular stand is illustrated in Spero 2005, pl. 61, and a similar oval tray in Spero 2007.

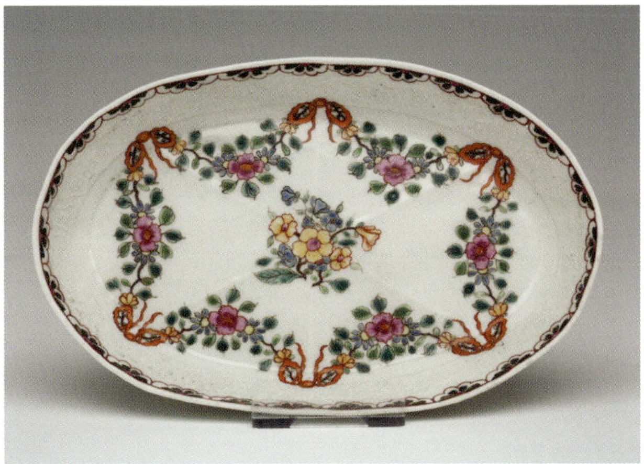

194

194

Spoon tray

About 1756
Length 15.6 cm, width 10.1 cm
1957.24.1.856

Oval, inside rim decorated with half-moons in black with red centre outlined in red; upright border with uncoloured vermicular moulding; oval well or base has mouldings that divide it into six triangular compartments. The decoration of ribbons and floral festoons, disregarding the moulding, is possibly of a later date.

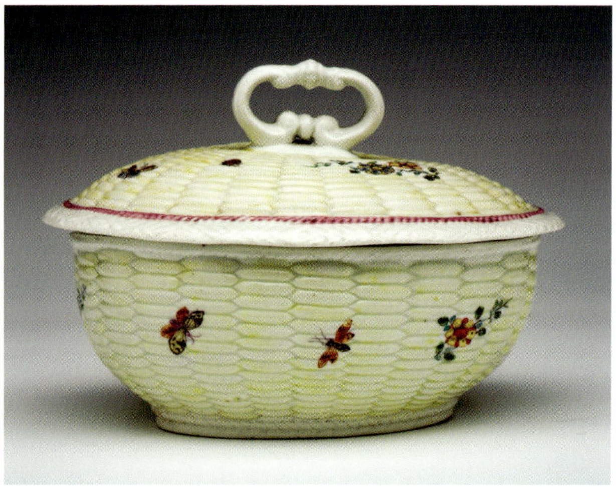

195

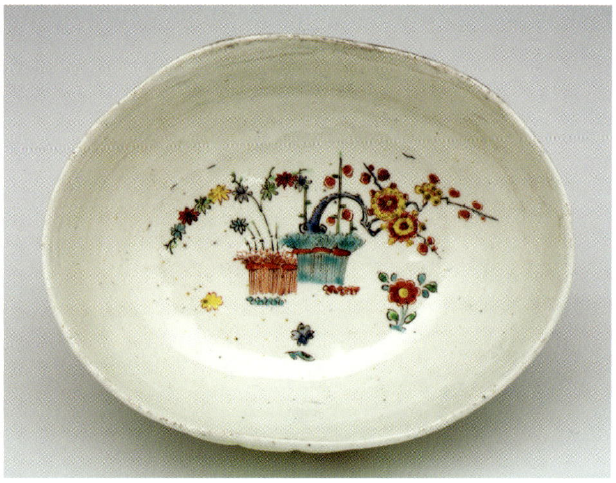

195

195

Tureen with cover

About 1756

Ht 12.9 cm, length 16.1 cm, width 12.5 cm

1957.24.1.674

Oval, vertical moulded basketwork, wide double C-scroll handle on cover; pale yellow ground decorated with insects and floral sprigs; interior painted with Kakiemon-style 'Banded Hedge' pattern; ho-ho bird under cover. A similar tureen with stand is illustrated in Amor 1976, pl. 19.

PROVENANCE

Sotheby's, London, 16 October 1956, lot 69, £143.

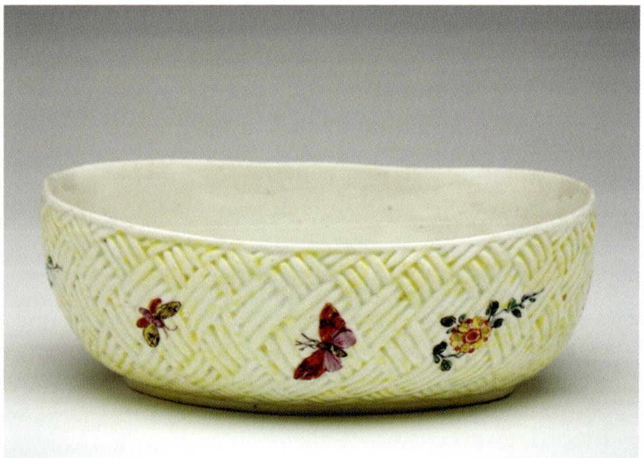

196

196

Tureen (without cover)

About 1755

Ht 5.7 cm, length 16.1 cm, width 12.5 cm

1957.24.1.672

Moulded with diagonal crossing basketwork; pale yellow ground decorated with evenly spaced butterflies, floral sprays and insects; interior with 'Banded Hedge' design.

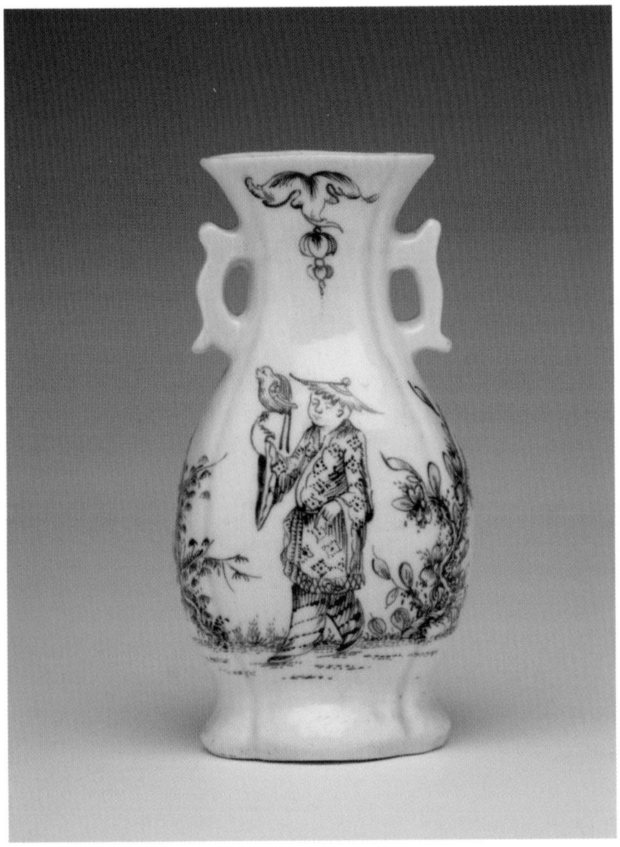

197

197

Vase

About 1755
Ht 9.5 cm
1957.24.1.592

Quatrefoil lobed body with oblong bracket handles; decorated in black pencilling with a Chinese man holding a long-tailed bird on one side, bamboo sprays springing from a rock on the other. A similar vase with a pencilled landscape scene with figures is illustrated in Clarke 1987, p. 20, pl. 6.

PROVENANCE
D.M. & P. Manheim, London, 11 June 1952, £70.

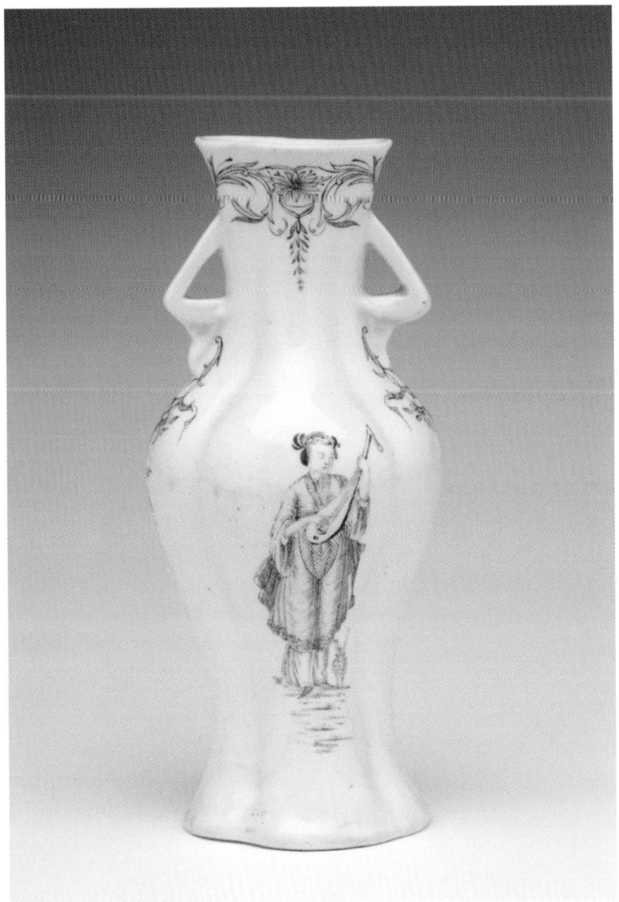

198

198

Vase

About 1756
Ht 16.2 cm
1957.24.1.604

Slender lobed baluster shape with two triangular handles; brown-black pencil decoration of an Oriental woman playing a mandolin.

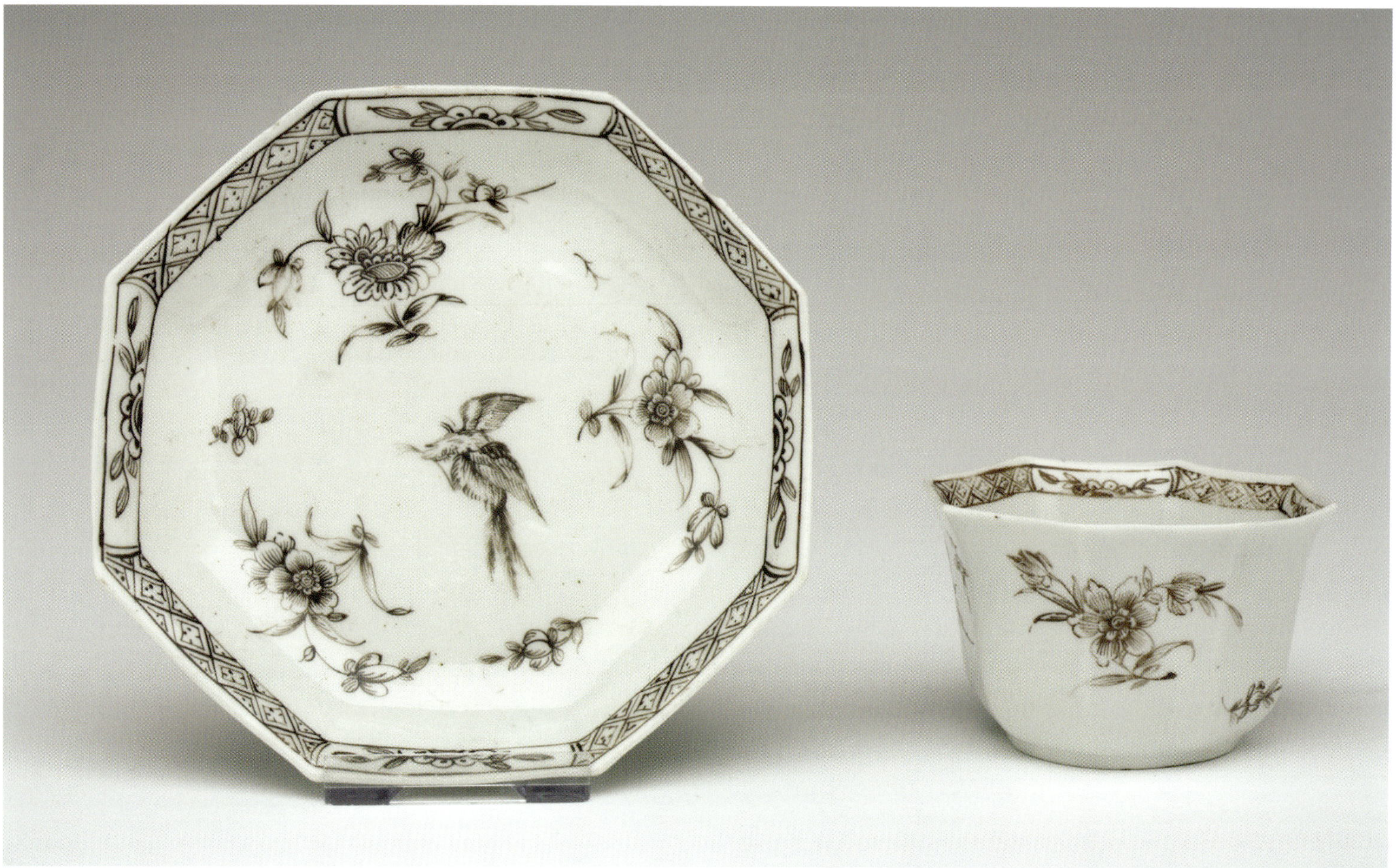

199

199

Teabowl and saucer

About 1755
Bowl ht 4.1 cm, diam. 6.3 cm; saucer diam. 11.3 cm
1957.24.1.788

Octagonal; pencilled with floral sprays and a ho-ho bird, border with diapering and formal flowers.

REFERENCES
Spero and Sandon 1996, pl. 62; Amor 1992, p. 19, no. 30.

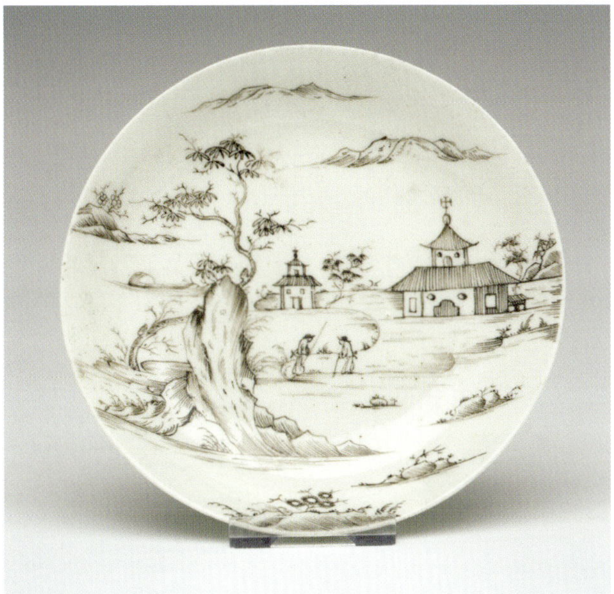

200

200

Saucer

1755–8
Diam. 12.8 cm
1957.24.1.789

Black pencilled Chinese landscape scene with figures and two Christian churches, each surmounted by a cross.

PROVENANCE
D.M. & P. Manheim, London, 11 June 1952, £54.

REFERENCE
Spero and Sandon 1996, pl. 60.

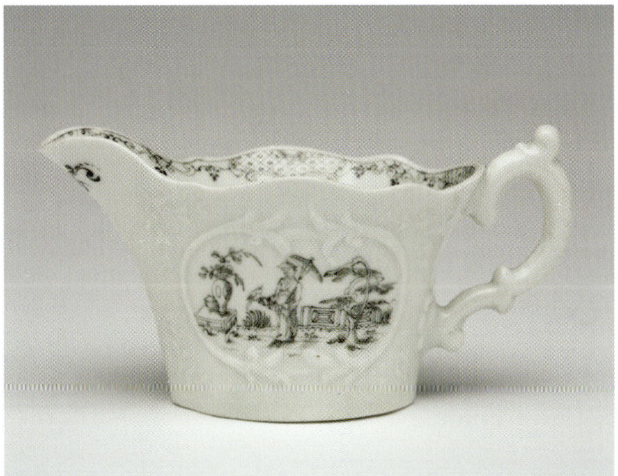

201

201

Creamboat

About 1755
Ht 5.6 cm, length 12.9 cm, width 5.9 cm
1957.24.1.91

Lightly decorated on both sides in black pencilling with a Chinese man in a garden holding an umbrella in one hand, bird on the other; formal spray below lip; diapered border inside rim.

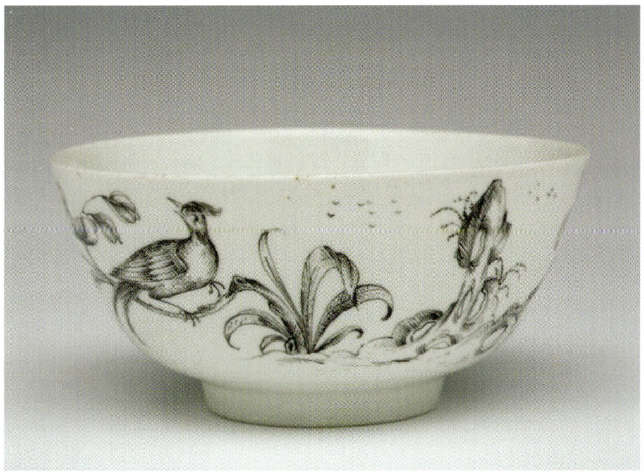

202

202

Bowl

About 1755
Ht 6.5 cm, diam. 13.3 cm
1957.24.1.487

Pencilled in black, crested bird with long forked tail perched on branch among shrubs and rocks.

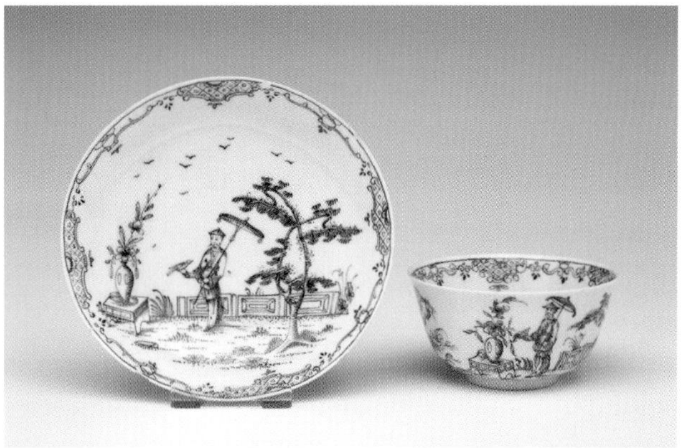

203

203

Teabowl and saucer

About 1756
Bowl ht 4 cm, diam. 7.5 cm; saucer diam. 11.4 cm
1957.24.1.783

Black pencil decoration with Chinese scene of a man under an umbrella holding a bird; border with diapering and scrolls.

REFERENCES
Spero and Sandon 1996, pl. 150; Spero 2005, pl. 137.

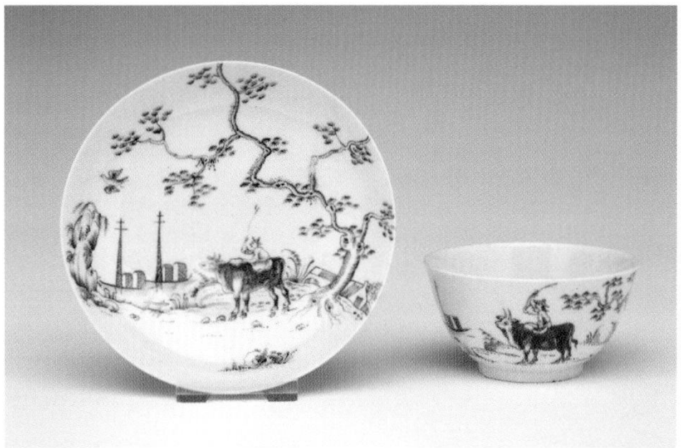

204

204

Teabowl and saucer

1755–60
Bowl ht 4 cm, diam. 7.6 cm; saucer diam. 11.5 cm
1957.24.1.781

Pencilled in black with an oxherd below an acacia tree, with sampans moored in the river alongside – the well-known 'Boy on a Buffalo' pattern.

REFERENCES
Barrett 1966, pl. 35a; Spero 1984, pl. 170.

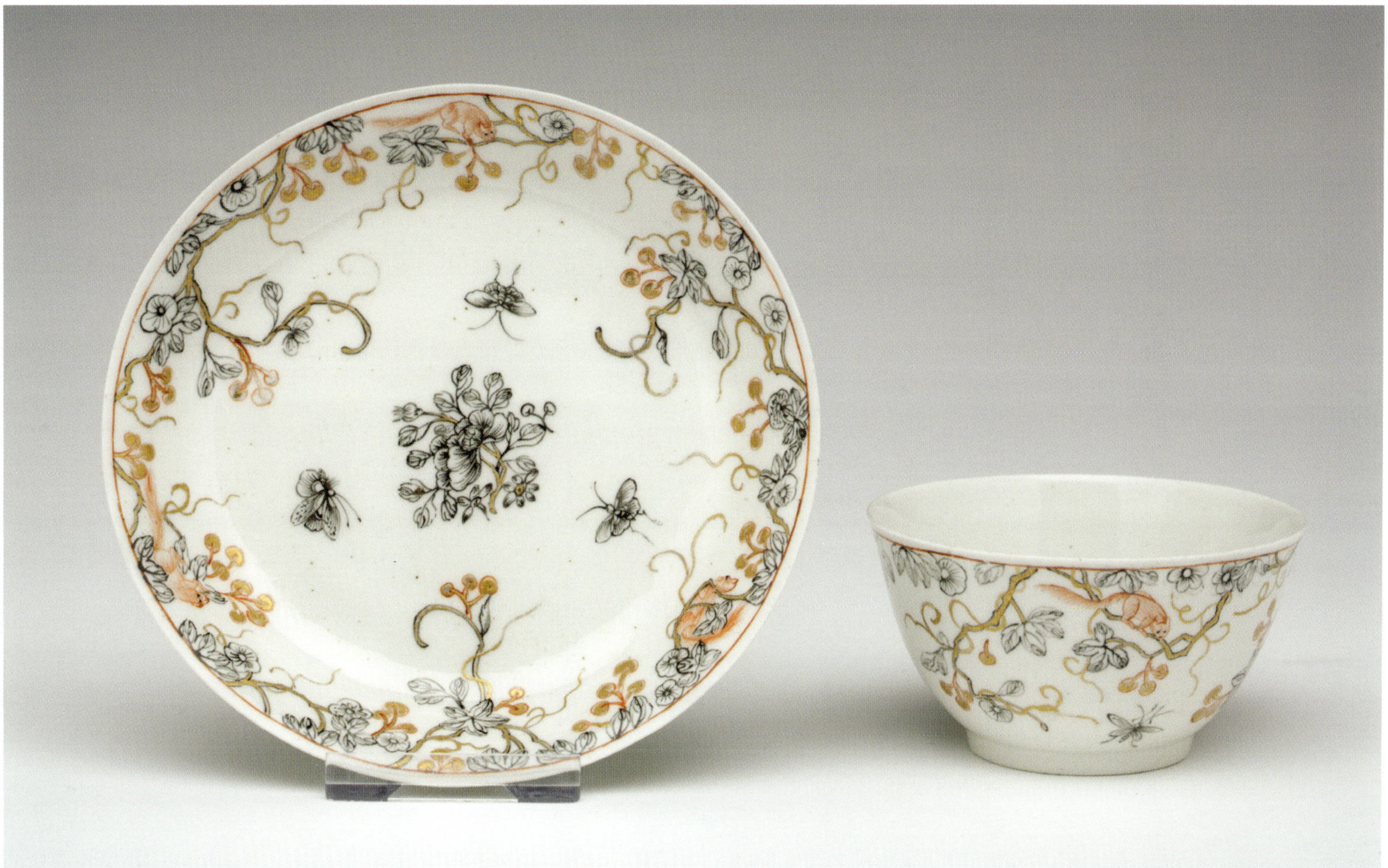

205

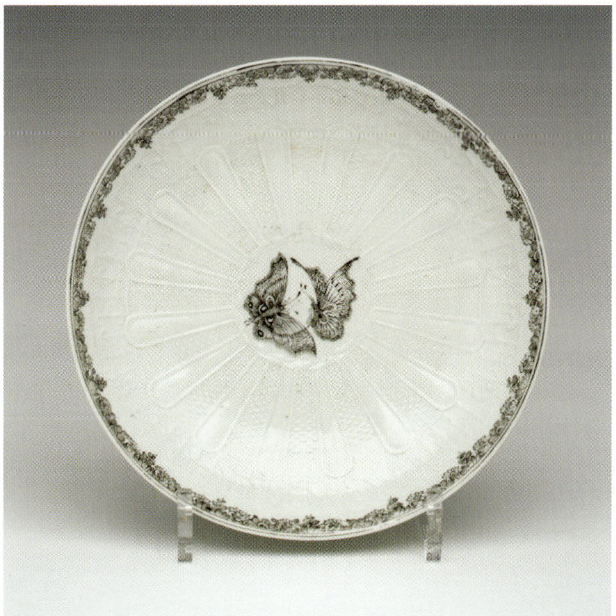

206

205

Teabowl and saucer

1754–5
Ht 4.1 cm, diam. 7.4 cm; saucer diam. 11.8 cm
1957.24.1.784

Pencilled mainly in black with some gilding; 'Rat and Vine' pattern incorporating three red squirrels or rats in a border of fruiting vines; black and gold bouquet in centre with three butterflies around. Rats are associated with good luck and plenty; the rat is also the first of the Chinese Zodiac signs.

206

Cake dish

About 1756
Diam. 20.4 cm
1957.24.1.782

Petal moulded with pencilled floral border and two butterflies in central circle.

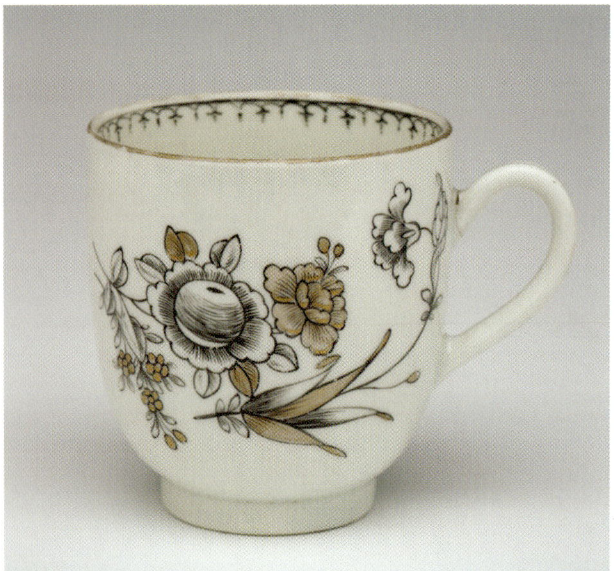

207

207

Coffee cup

About 1765
Ht 6.5 cm, diam. 5.8 cm
1957.24.1.786

Pencilled floral sprays enriched with gilding; black pencilled border of loops and dots inside gold rim. Although of later date, 207 and 208 are included as they show a similar style of decoration.

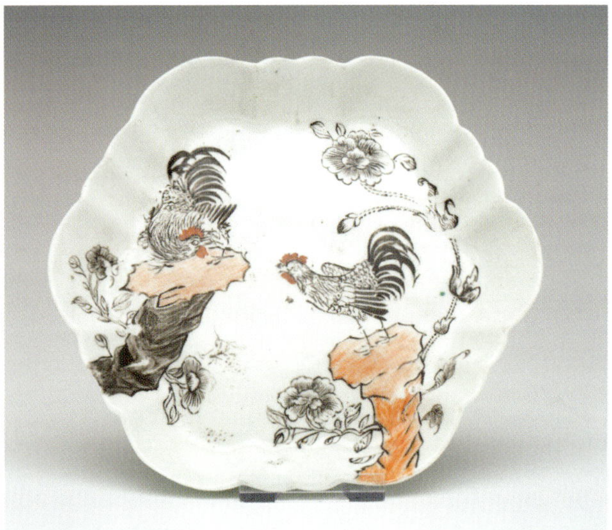

208

208

Teapot stand

About 1765
Diam. 14.3 cm
1957.24.1.794

Fluted hexagonal shape, decorated after a Chinese original with two pencilled cocks with red combs standing on red-brown rocks.

209, 210

Teabowl and saucer, coffee cup

1756–60
Bowl ht 4 cm, diam. 7.6 cm; saucer diam. 11.7 cm; coffee cup ht 5.7 cm, diam. 5.7 cm
1957.24.1 304 and 305

All decorated in mauve pencilling with two Chinese men outside a two-storied house; elaborate border below rim; teabowl with indented rim, coffee cup with plain rim and wishbone handle.

REFERENCES
Spero and Sandon 1996, pl. 148; Spero 2005, pl. 139; Bonhams, London, 12 March 2008, lots 179, 180.

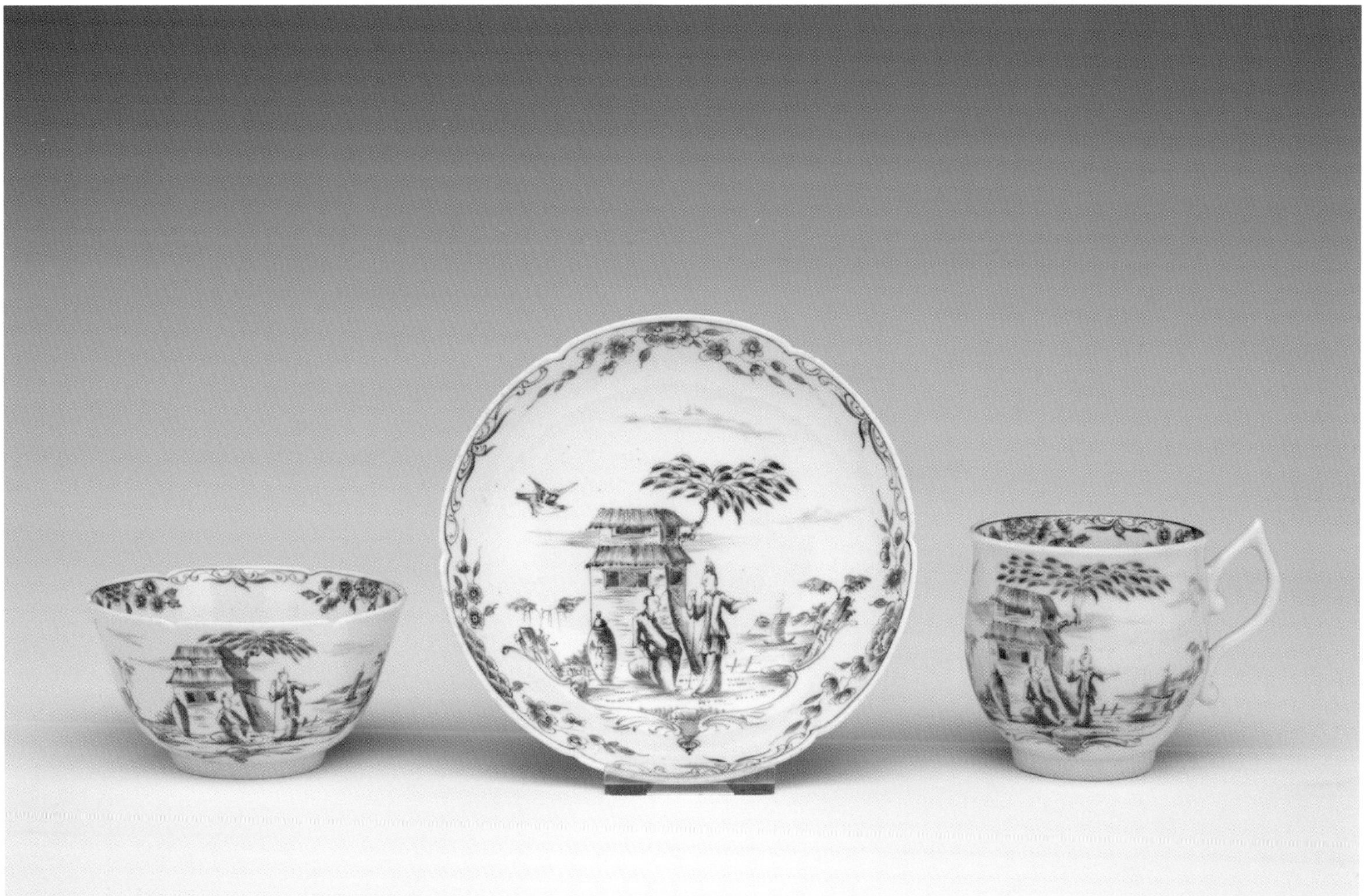

209, 210

3

European Designs 1756–1765

FROM THE MID-1750s Meissen became an increasingly important influence on Worcester porcelain. The 1761 bankruptcy papers of Richard Holdship describe Worcester as 'a porcelain manufactory in imitation of Dresden ware'. It is debatable how much Meissen porcelain workers at Worcester would have actually seen, but they would have been exposed to pieces produced by the Chelsea factory, which for much of the 1750s was producing wares in the Meissen style, and also to prints such as those found in *The Ladies Amusement* and other publications (figs 18 and 19). As well as painted decoration, particularly in the form of large sprays of naturalistic European flowers known as *Deutsche Blumen*, the Meissen influence also extended to shapes of vases, plates, leaf-shaped dishes, openwork baskets, leaf-moulded sauceboats and tureens, including some in the form of partridges and cauliflowers.

Previous difficulties in firing items such as plates and dishes were gradually being overcome and technical advances allowed for larger items to be reliably produced. By the mid-1760s the emphasis began to shift from elaborate moulded shapes, which reflected the late baroque and rococo styles, to decoration on simpler forms.

By the early 1760s the influence of Meissen was beginning to wane. Production at the Meissen factory had been disrupted by the Seven Years War (1756–63) and much of its artistic originality declined. By the end of the decade Sèvres was replacing Meissen as the main influence on Worcester porcelain design, reflecting the change in taste from rococo to neoclassical and a move to simpler and more formal decoration.

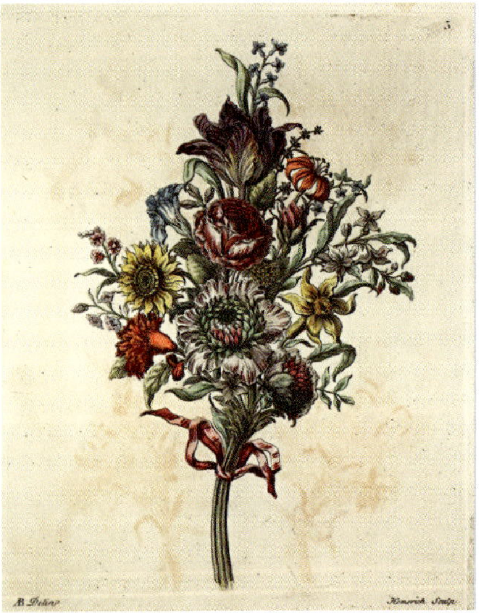

Fig. 18 Plate 23 from *The Ladies Amusement*. © Museum of Royal Worcester Porcelain

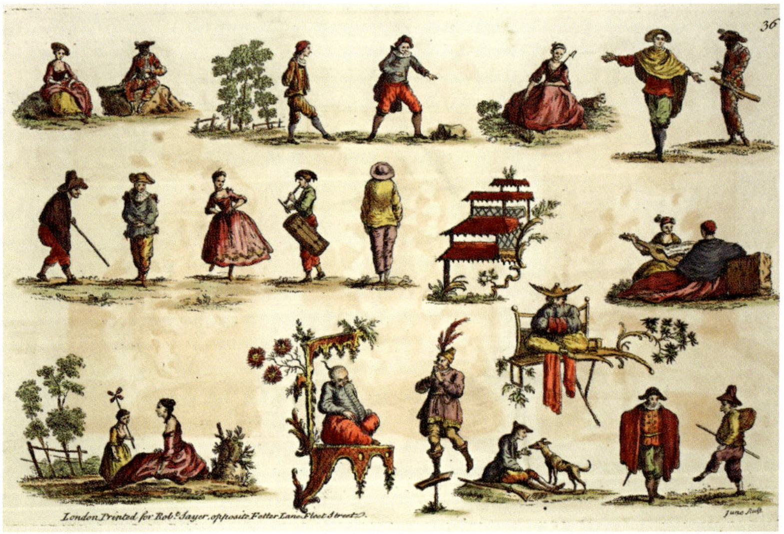

Fig. 19 Plate 36 from *The Ladies Amusement*. © Museum of Royal Worcester Porcelain

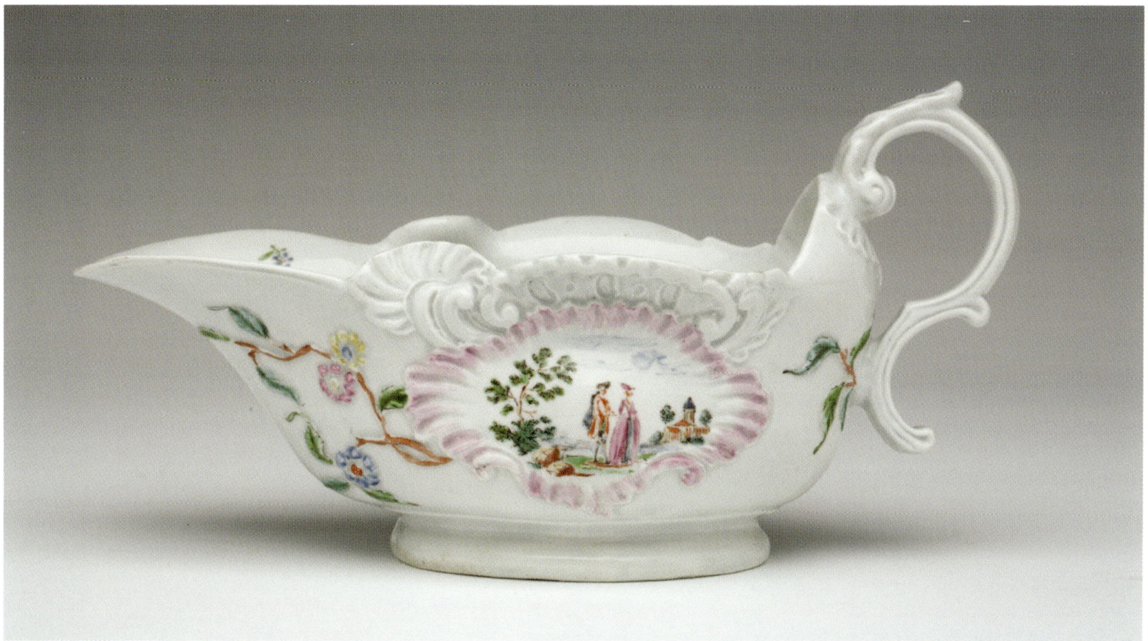

211

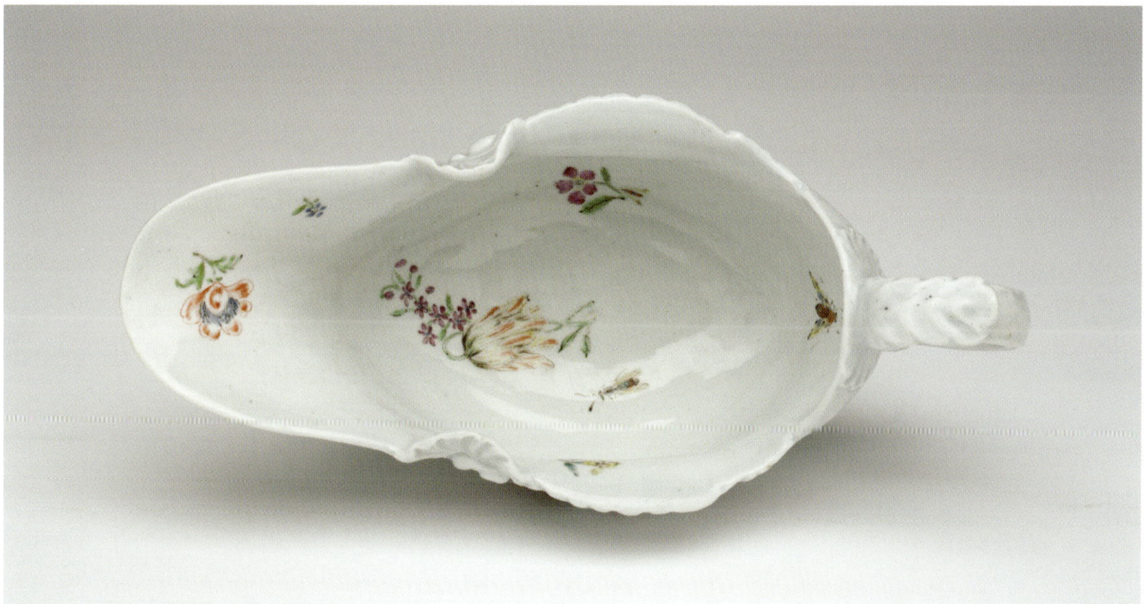

211

211

Sauceboat

1753–4
Length 23 cm
1957.24.1.88

Crisp moulding with rococo panels painted in Meissen style with European figures in landscape; moulded raised flower sprays picked out in colour under spout.

REFERENCES
Amor 1992, p. 10 no. 9; Spero and Sandon 1996, pl. 44; Spero 2005, pl. 132.

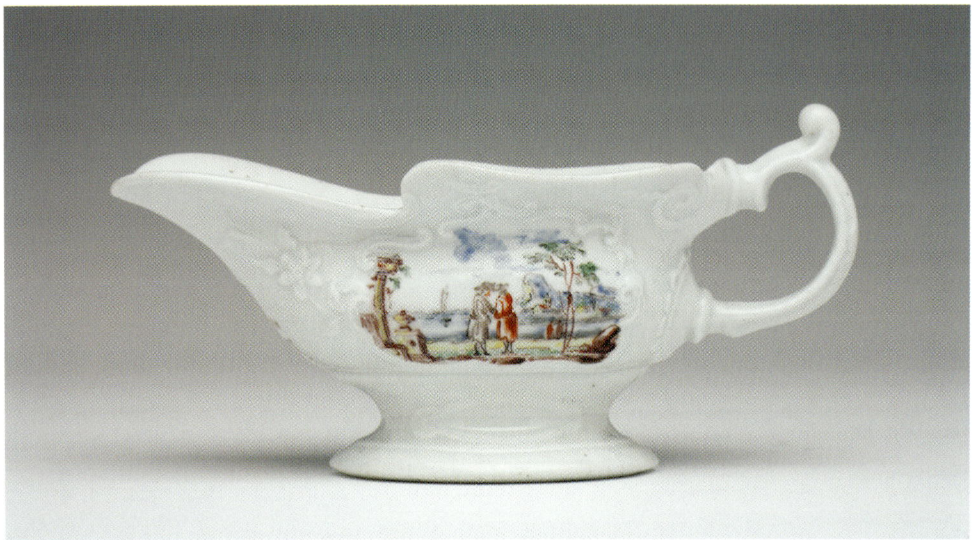

212

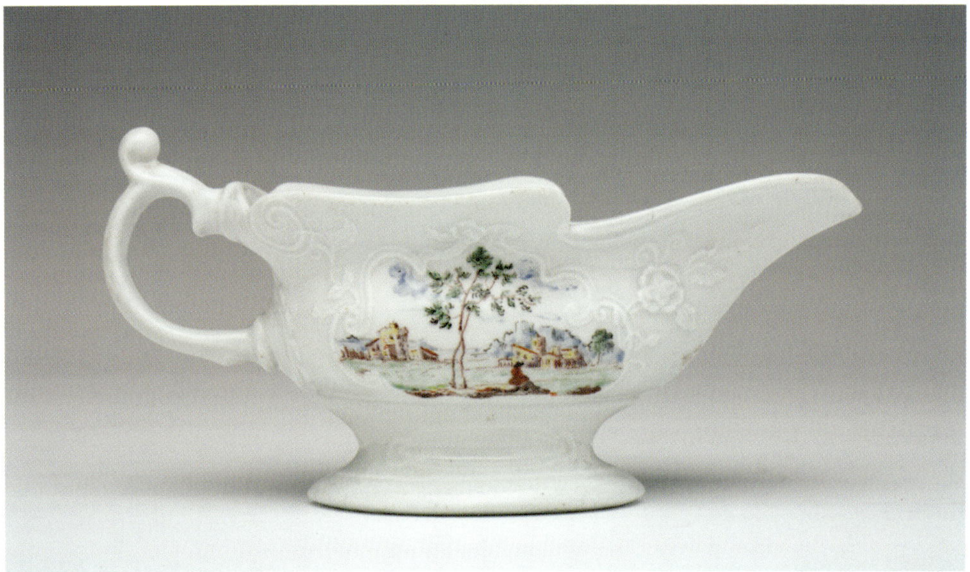

212

212

Sauceboat

1754–5
Ht 8.4 cm, length 16.6 cm
1957.24.1.85

Reserves painted with eighteenth-century figures in a landscape; below lip, two figures under tree in grisaille. This shows the fusion of diverse influences, combining the decorative style of Meissen with an English rococo silver shape of the 1740s.

REFERENCE
Spero and Sandon 1996, pl. 92.

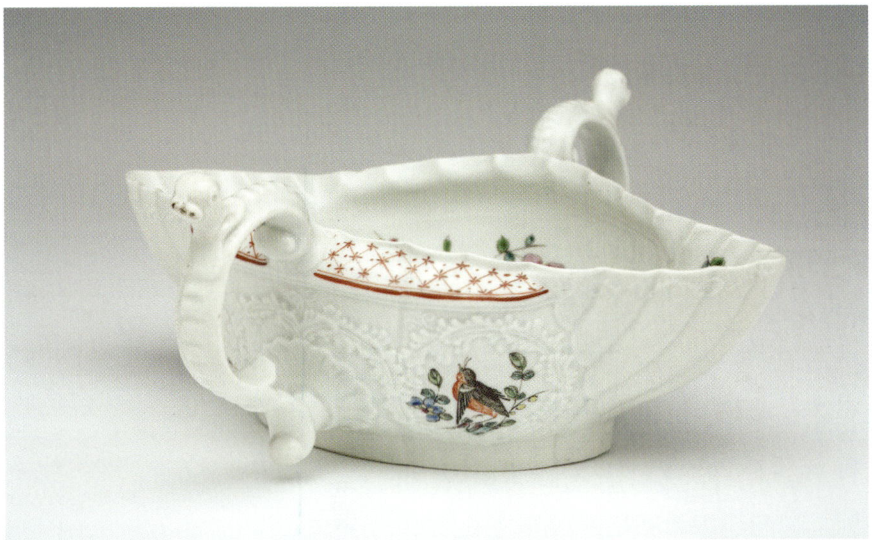

213

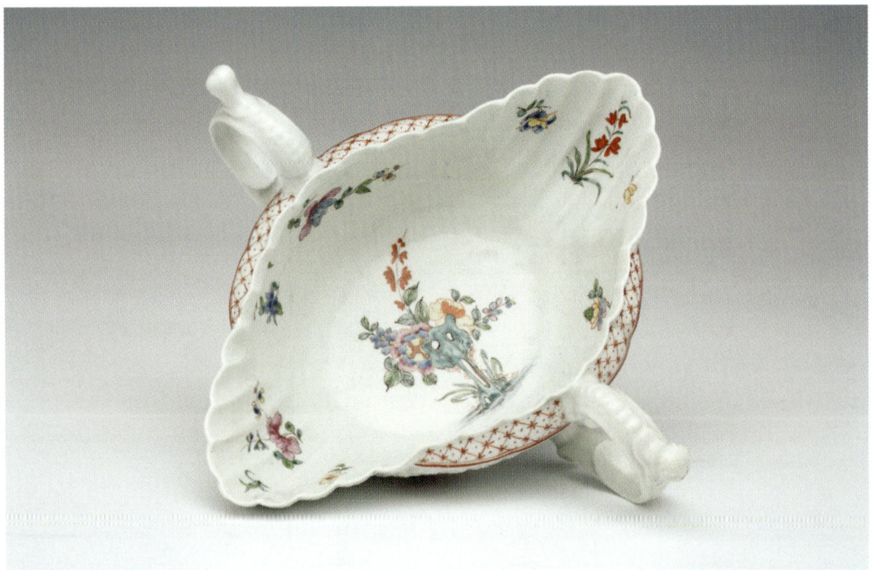

213

213

Two-handled sauceboat

1754–5
Ht 9.5 cm, length 22.4 cm, width 21.6 cm
Mark: red annulet and arrow
1957.24.1.855

Lips moulded as scallop shells; floral moulding around two reserves painted with birds, Oriental flower decoration inside; red diaper border. The scroll handles have unusual pug dog or monkey's head thumb pieces, which only appear on the largest size of this shape.

PROVENANCE
Albert Amor, London, 11 July 1951, £75.

REFERENCE
Spero and Sandon 1996, pl. 31.

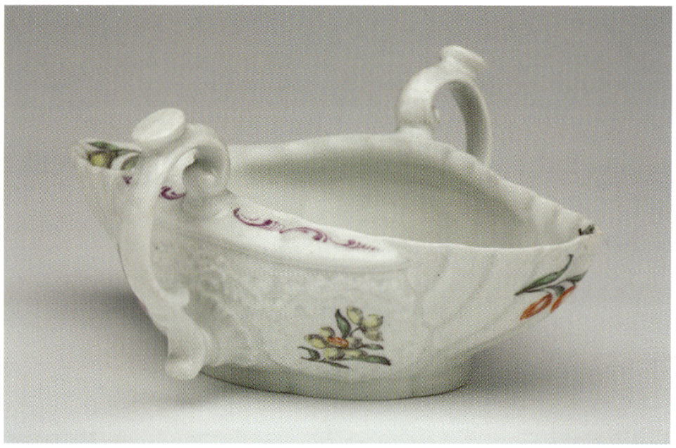

214

214

Two-handled sauceboat

1755–7
Ht 8.4 cm, length 18.7 cm
1957.24.1.397

Four floral moulded reserves, each with different flower sprays, a tiger lily painted between. This shape was made in three sizes and is derived from both silver and Staffordshire salt-glaze shapes.

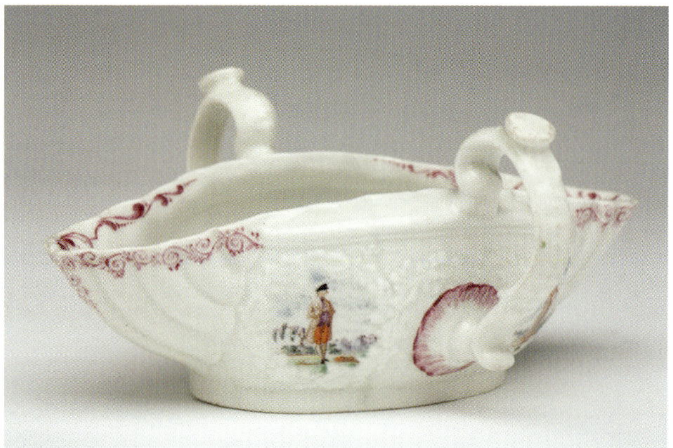

215

215

Two-handled sauceboat

1756–8
Ht 7.1 cm, length 16.3 cm, width 13.7 cm
1957.24.1.79

The smallest size in this shape; decorated with European figures in contemporary costume within four floral moulded panels.

REFERENCE

Spero and Sandon 1996, pl. 102.

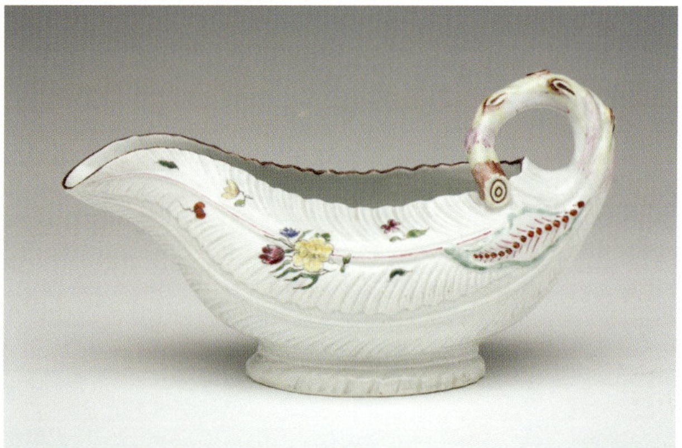

216

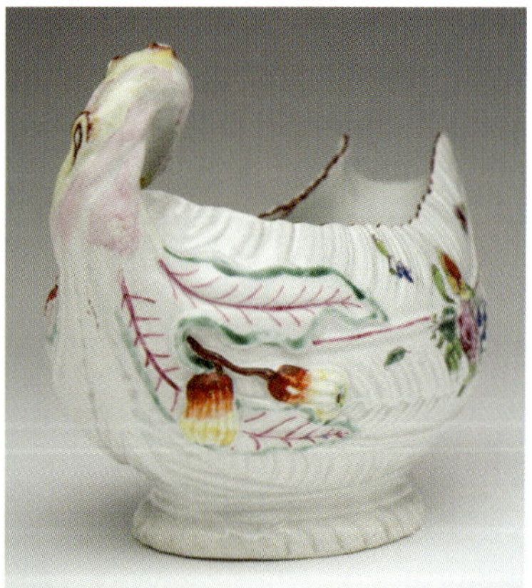

216

216

Sauceboat

1755–7
Ht 12.4 cm, length 21.5 cm
1957.24.1.745

Moulded as overlapping cos lettuce leaves, branch handle with two pears or acorns and leaves, curled for right-hand pouring; gadrooned foot; floral decoration. This shape was made in large quantities over a short period and usually has a brown rim. The basic shape originated at Meissen in the 1740s, was introduced at Longton Hall in 1752–3 and at Derby two years later, and by 1756 was made at Worcester in two sizes. A single Bow model, in white, is known (1758–60), and they were also made at West Pans (1768–75). A pair of sauceboats in Lambeth delftware, with similar moulding and dimensions, is in the Glaisher Collection at the Fitzwilliam Museum, Cambridge (C.1683A and B–1928).

REFERENCES

J. Sandon 1993, p. 219; Archer 2013, no. G.17, pp. 282–3.

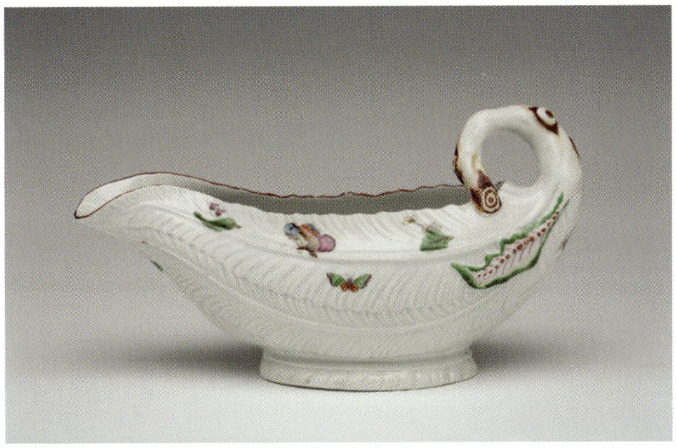

217

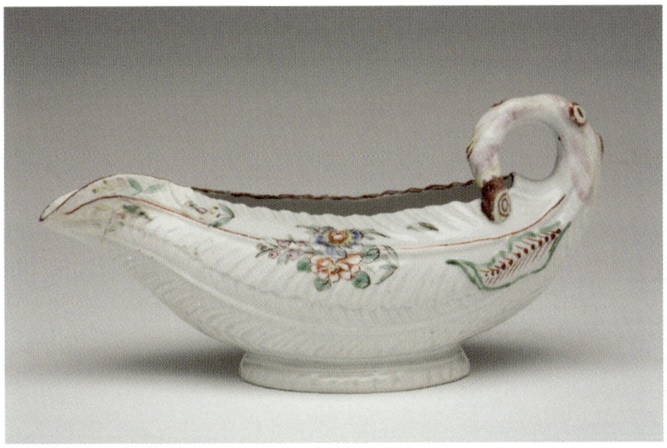

218

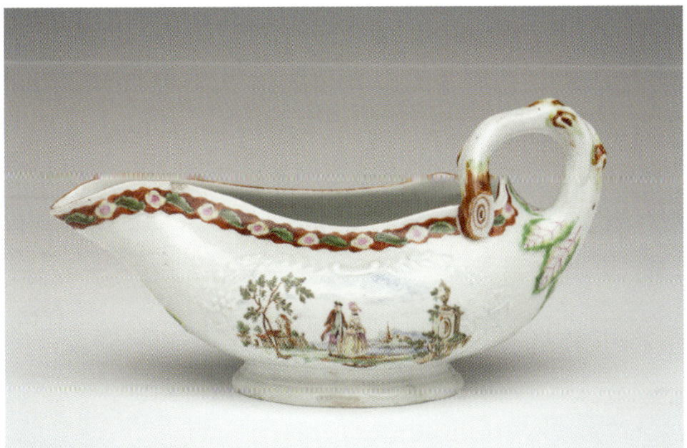

219

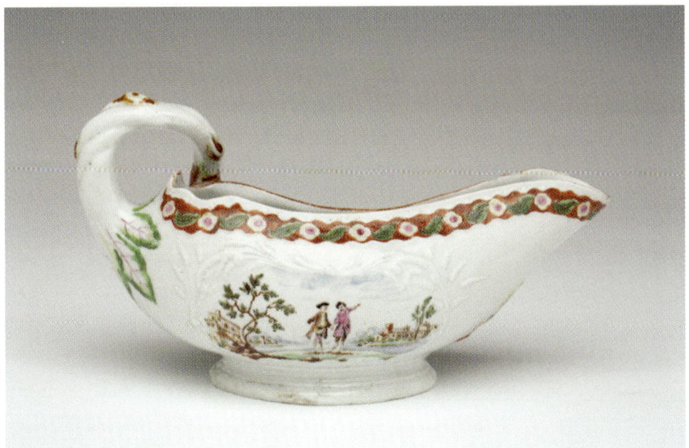

219

217

Sauceboat

1755–7
Ht 10.1 cm, length 18.3 cm
Mark: workman's mark in red
1957.24.1.747

Moulded as cos lettuce leaves, branch handle; decorated with flowers and insects.

218

Sauceboat

1755–8
Ht 9.8 cm, length 19 cm
1957.24.1.743

Moulded as cos lettuce leaves; floral decoration in unusually pale colours; spray of convolvulus and other flowers in base.

219

Sauceboat

1754–5
Ht 11.9 cm, length 22 cm
1957.24.1.90

Moulded as cos lettuce leaves; floral moulded reserves with eighteenth-century figures in landscape. The border decoration may have been added later.

REFERENCE
Sandon 1993, p. 219.

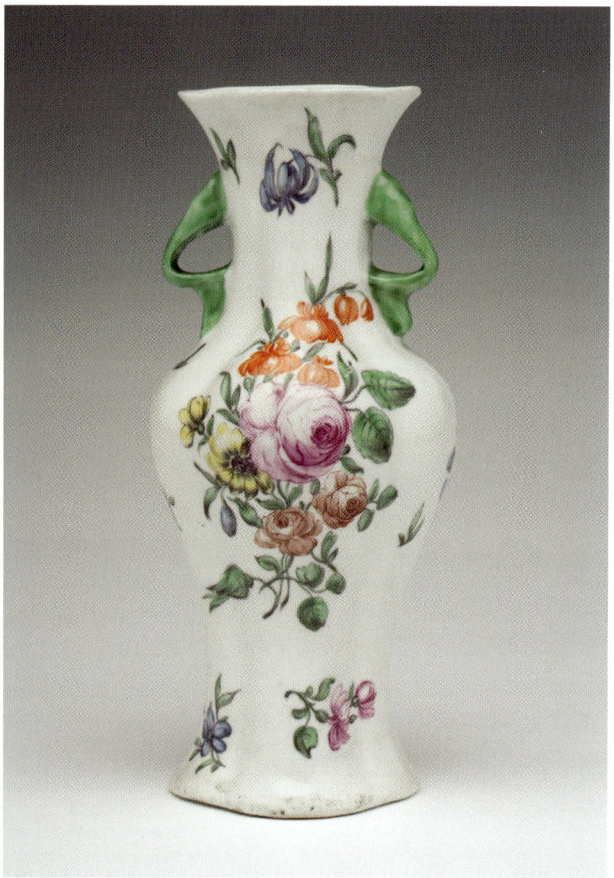

220

220

Vase

1758–60
Ht 16.5 cm
1957.24.1.605

Slender lobed baluster shape with two green triangular handles; decorated with Meissen-style floral bouquets and sprays. An example in the Victoria and Albert Museum is illustrated in Barrett 1966, pl. 22.

PROVENANCE
H.W. Hughes Collection, no. 897 (pair).

REFERENCES
Spero and Sandon 1996, pl. 115; Bonhams, London, 31 March 2010, lot 162.

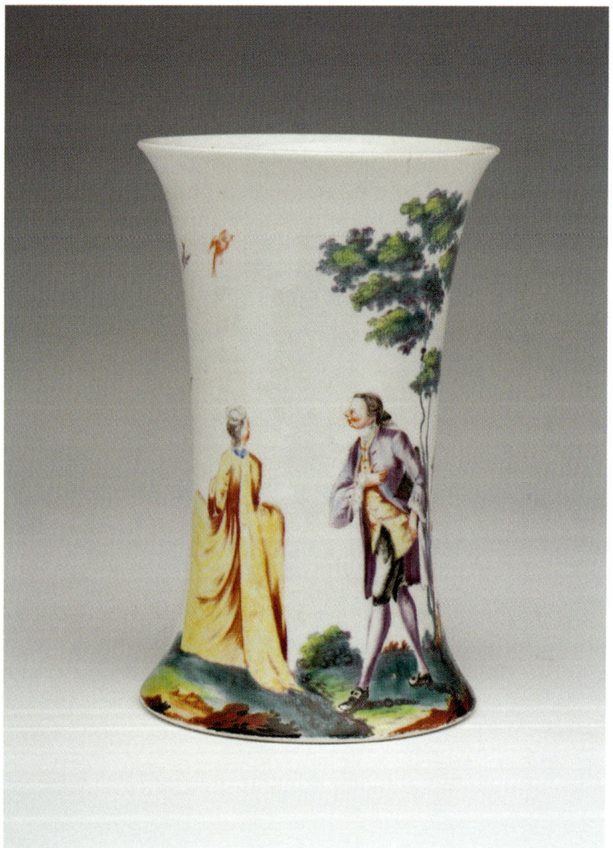

221

221

Vase

1756–8
Ht 14.5 cm
1957.24.1.141

Waisted cylindrical shape; colourfully painted with a gentleman and lady in contemporary dress; exotic birds on reverse. This painting has been attributed to Jefferyes Hammett O'Neale by both Marshall and Barrett.

PROVENANCE
Sir Henry L. Aubrey-Fletcher Collection; Sotheby's, London, 30 May 1947, £68.

REFERENCES
Reynolds 1999, pl. 12; Marshall 1954, p. 43; Barrett 1958, p. 53.

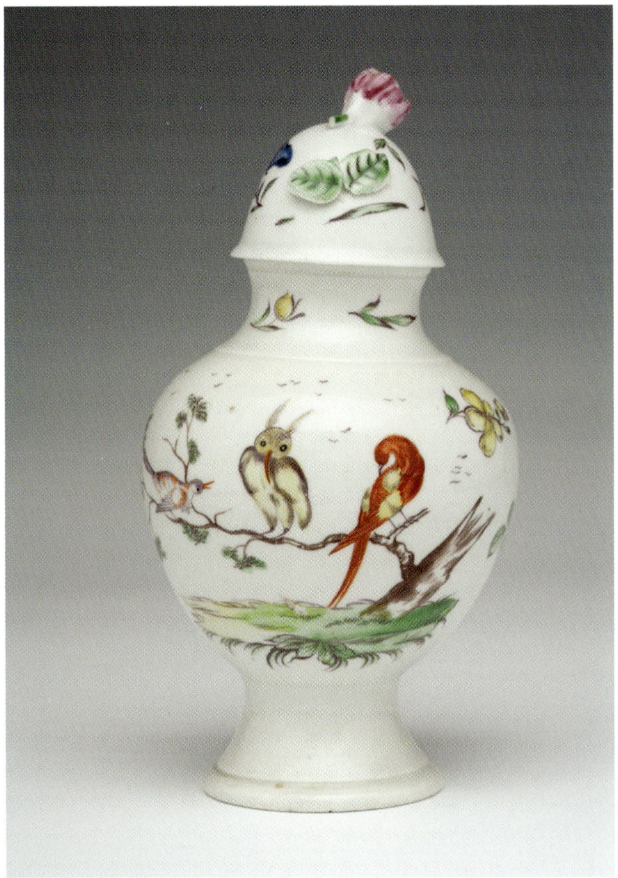

222

222

Vase with cover

1758–60
Ht 16.5 cm
1957.24.1.513

Pear-shaped body with concave neck on a conical foot; domed cover with rosebud knop. The decoration of a long-eared owl mocked by other birds has been attributed to James Rogers. A similar vase in the Victoria and Albert Museum is illustrated in Barrett 1966, pl. 18.

REFERENCE
Reynolds 1999, pl. 10.

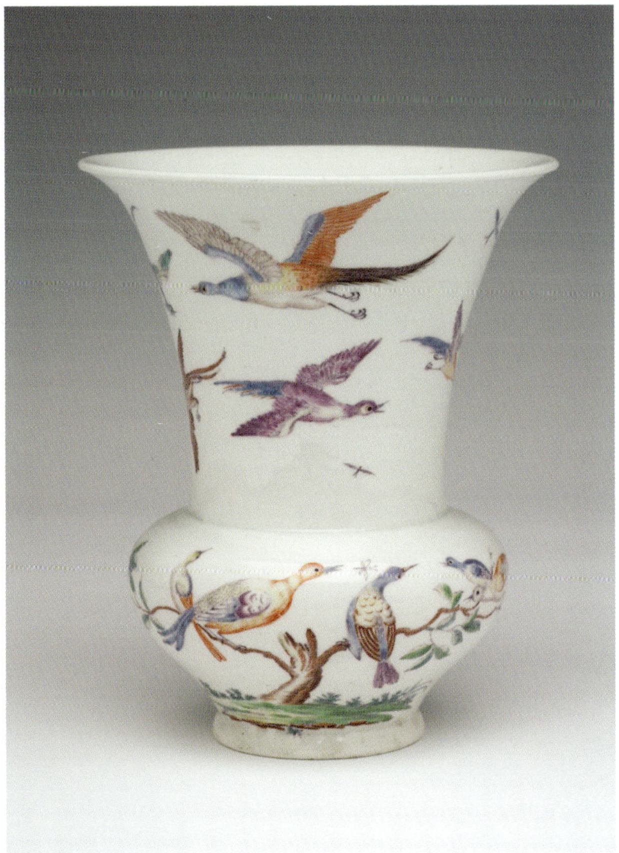

223

223

Vase

About 1758
Ht 14.9 cm
Mark: incised line on base
1957.24.1.501

Low swelling bulbous shape with flared neck and rim; exotic bird decoration, possibly by James Rogers.

PROVENANCE
Tilley & Co., London, 30 April 1950, £50 8s.

REFERENCES
Reynolds 1999, pl. 10; Clarke 1987, pl. 11; Spero and Sandon 1996, pl. 76.

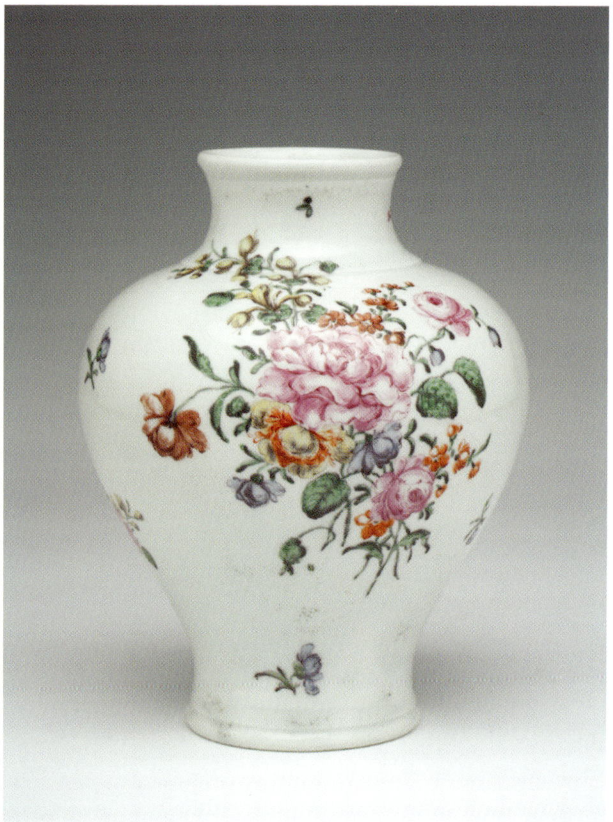

224

224

Vase

1758–60
Ht 16.2 cm
1957.24.1.759

Squat ovoid baluster shape; decorated with floral bouquets and sprays in Meissen style.

REFERENCE
Spero and Sandon 1996, pl. 80.

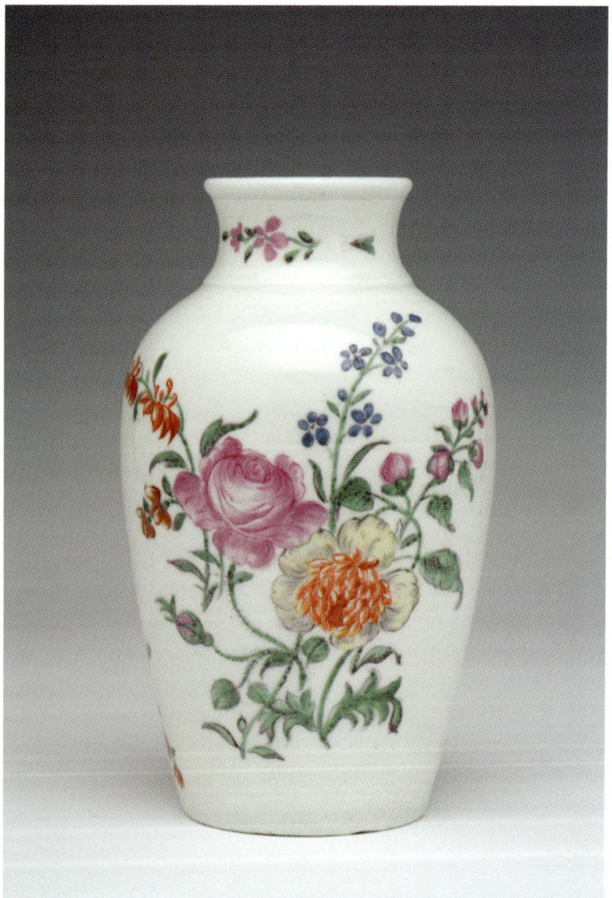

225

225

Vase

About 1760
Ht 17.1 cm
1957.24.1.761

Ovoid shape; decorated with floral bouquets and sprays, a ladybird and two butterflies.

REFERENCE
Spero and Sandon 1996, pl. 81.

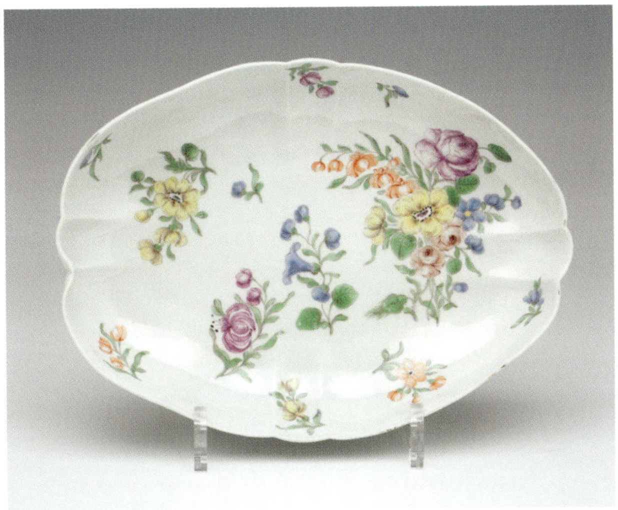

226

226

Dish or stand

About 1760
Length 24.2 cm, width 18.2 cm
1957.24.1.760

Fluted oval shape; decorated with European flowers in Meissen style.

PROVENANCE
A.F. Allbrook, London, 15 June 1951, £35.

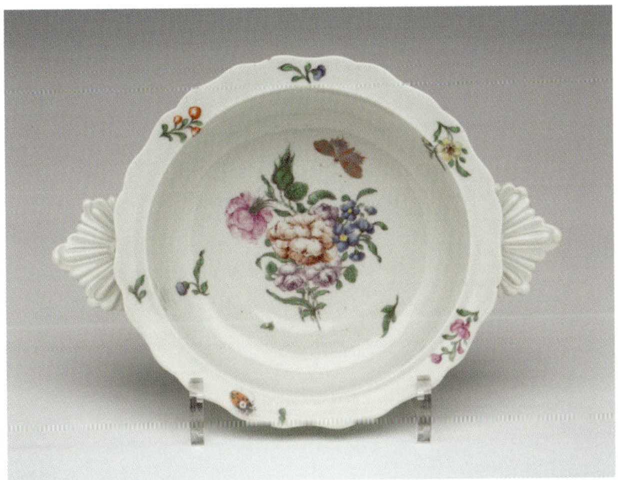

227

227

Porringer

About 1758
Ht 6 cm, diam. 17.6 cm (without handles); length 23.4 cm (with handles)
1957.2.1.750

Circular with wavy edge, acanthus leaf handles; decorated with European flowers and insects.

PROVENANCE
Sotheby's, London, 21 December 1954, lot 151, £36.

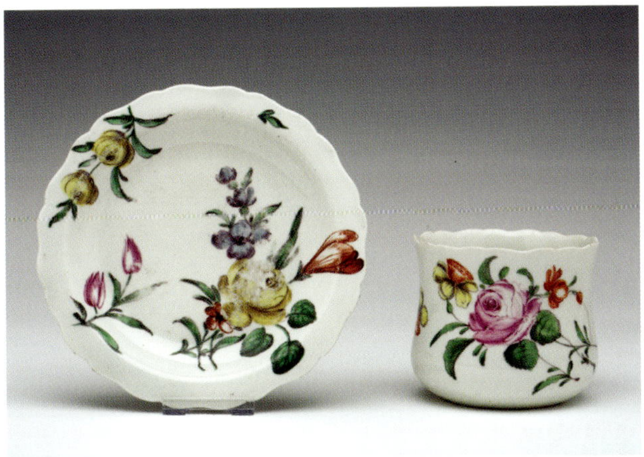

228

228

Fingerbowl and stand

1758–60
Bowl ht 7.5 cm, diam. 8.5 cm; stand diam. 15.1 cm
1957.24.1.411

Waisted cylindrical shape, wavy edge; boldly painted with floral bouquet and detached sprays.

REFERENCES
Spero 1984, pl. 58; Spero and Sandon 1996, pl. 91.

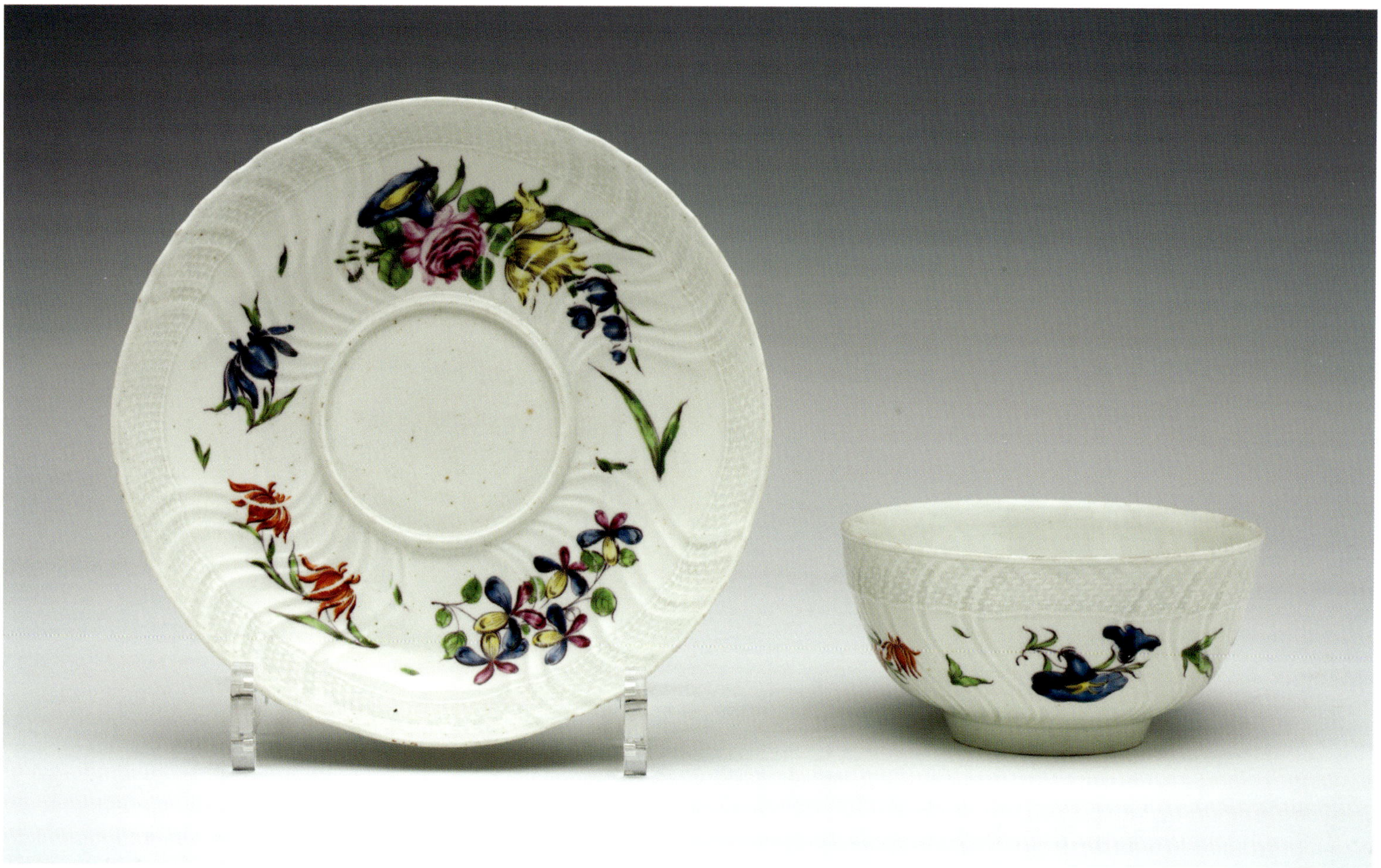

229

229

Bowl and stand

1756–7
Bowl ht 5.9 cm, diam. 11.7 cm; stand diam. 17.6 cm
1957.24.1.1059

Moulded osier pattern around the rim and four spirally fluted mouldings; decorated with European flowers in natural colours; cover missing. This Continental shape was probably derived from Meissen, although a similar form was made at Chantilly.

REFERENCE
Amor 1993, no. 33.

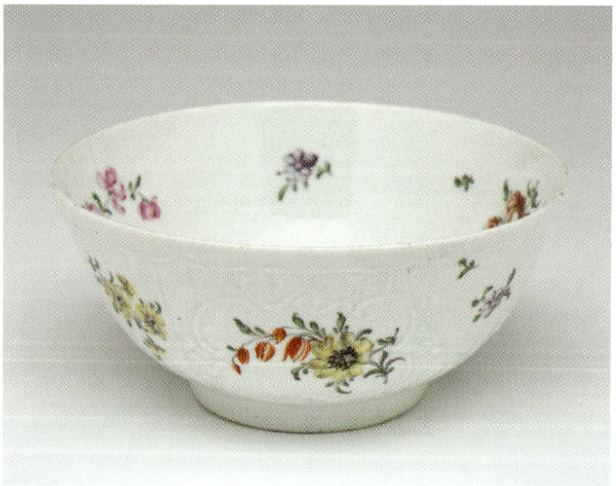

230

230

Bowl

1758–60
Ht 7.1 cm, diam. 15.4 cm
1957.24.1.403

Vertically fluted with rococo moulded panels; decorated with European flowers; further sprays inside bowl.

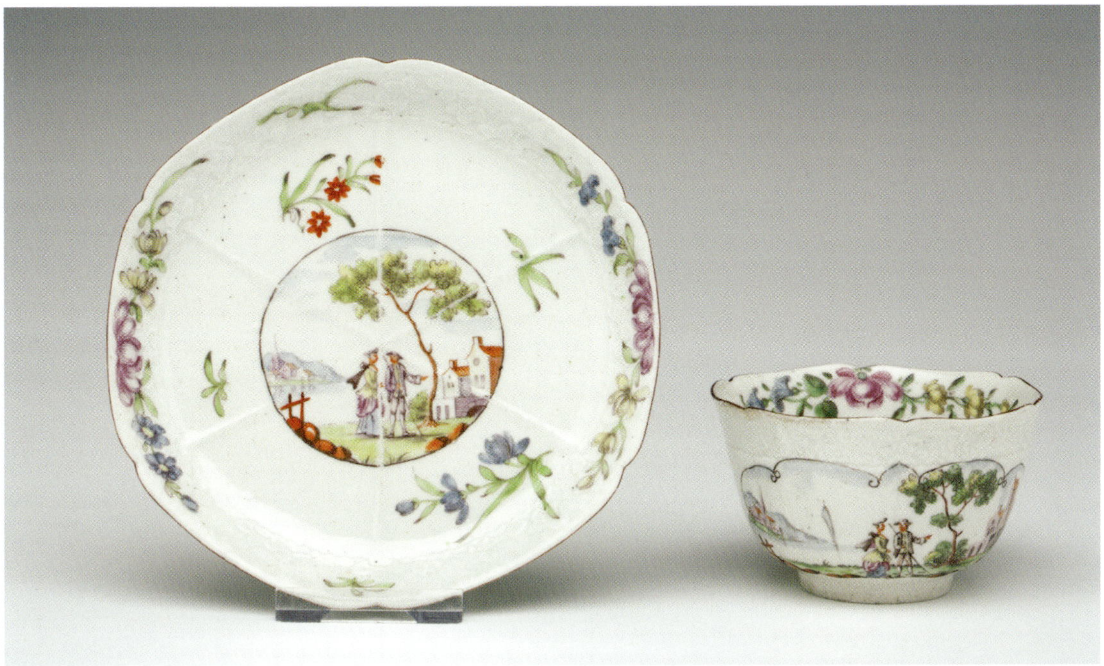

231

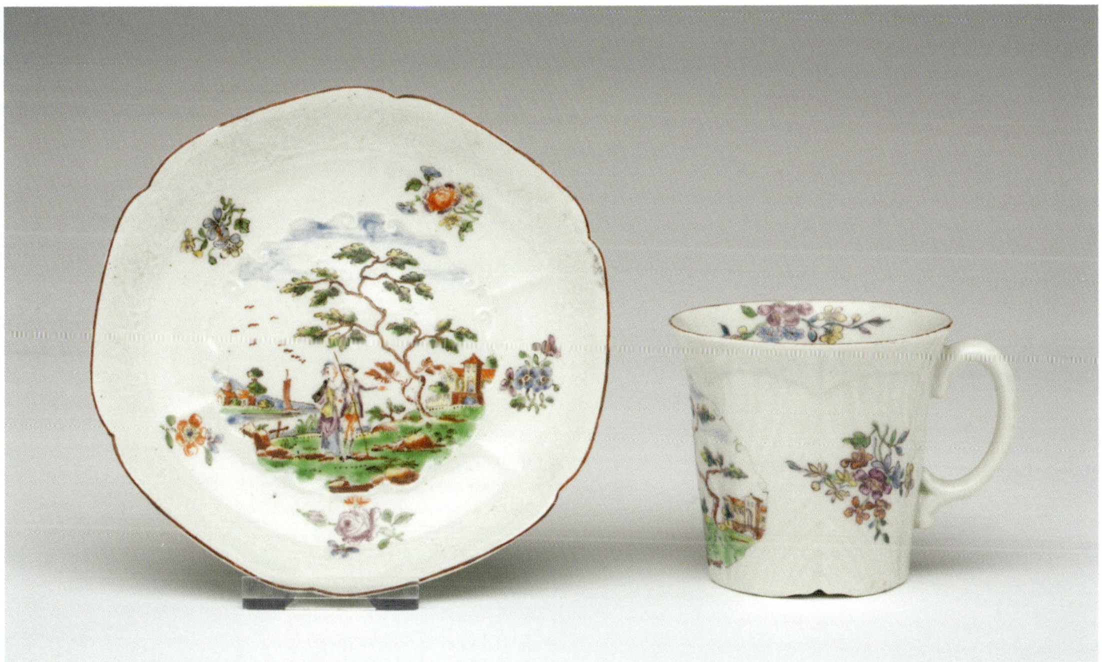

232

231

Teabowl and saucer

1755–6
Bowl ht 4.6 cm, diam. 7.5 cm; saucer diam. 12.2 cm
1957.24.1.84

Indented rim with brown edge; floral moulded borders; decorated in reserves with European figures in a landscape in the style of Meissen. A plate with similar decoration is illustrated in Spero 2005, pl. 135.

232

Coffee cup and saucer

1755–6
Cup ht 6.3 cm, diam. 6.8 cm; saucer diam. 12.2 cm
1957.24.1.80

Feather moulding on cup and floral moulding on saucer; brown rims; both decorated with European figures and floral sprays. A matching teapot is illustrated in Spero and Sandon 1996, pl. 43.

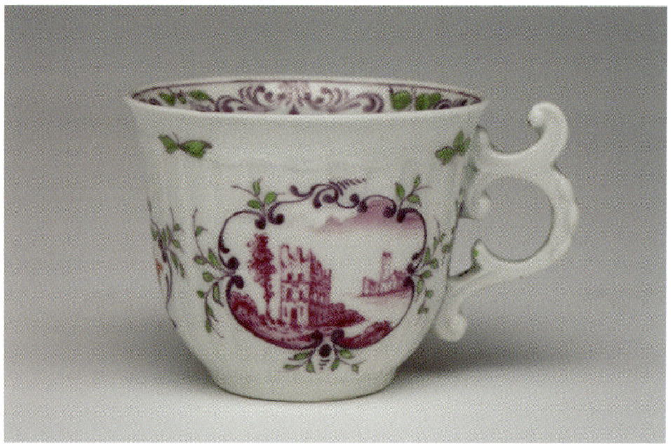

233

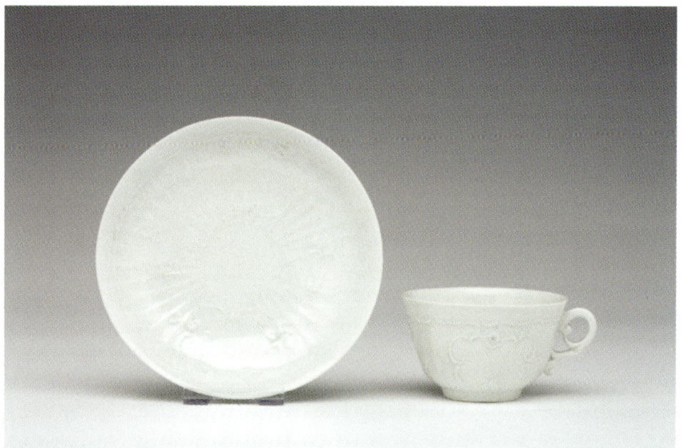

234

233

Coffee cup

1756–7
Ht 5.2 cm, diam. 6.2 cm
1957.24.1.954

Strap moulding with plain everted rim, rococo handle; decorated with landscapes in puce within rococo moulded panels, floral sprays between; border of purple scrolls and four floral sprays inside rim.

REFERENCES
Spero and Sandon 1996, pl.109; Bonhams, London, 10 May 2006, lot 40.

234

Teacup and saucer

1756–7
Cup ht 4.3 cm, diam. 6.9 cm; saucer diam. 11.8 cm
1957.24.1.798

Undecorated strap-moulded shape with rococo reserves, similar to no. 233 but with different handle shape.

REFERENCE
Spero and Sandon 1996, pl. 110.

235

Teabowl and saucer

1758–60
Bowl ht 4.3 cm, diam. 7.1 cm; saucer diam. 11.5 cm
1957.24.1.420

Lobed rim with brown edge; floral decoration similar to Chelsea, inspired by Meissen. A teapot and stand with similar decoration are illustrated in Barrett 1966, pl. 20b, a saucer in Dawson 2007, pl. 19, and a coffee cup, teabowl and saucer in Bonhams, London, 10 May 2006, lot 50.

236

Teabowl and saucer

About 1760
Teabowl ht 3.8 cm, diam. 5.1 cm; saucer diam. 10.4 cm
1957.24.1.418

Decorated in the style of Meissen with a mauve scroll border, half-suns in splendour, floral sprays and insects. A 'Blind Earl' dish with similar decoration is illustrated in Spero 1984, pl. 16, a teabowl and saucer in Spero and Sandon 1996, pl. 98, and a coffee cup and saucer and teapot in Bonhams, London, 10 May 2006, lots 55, 56.

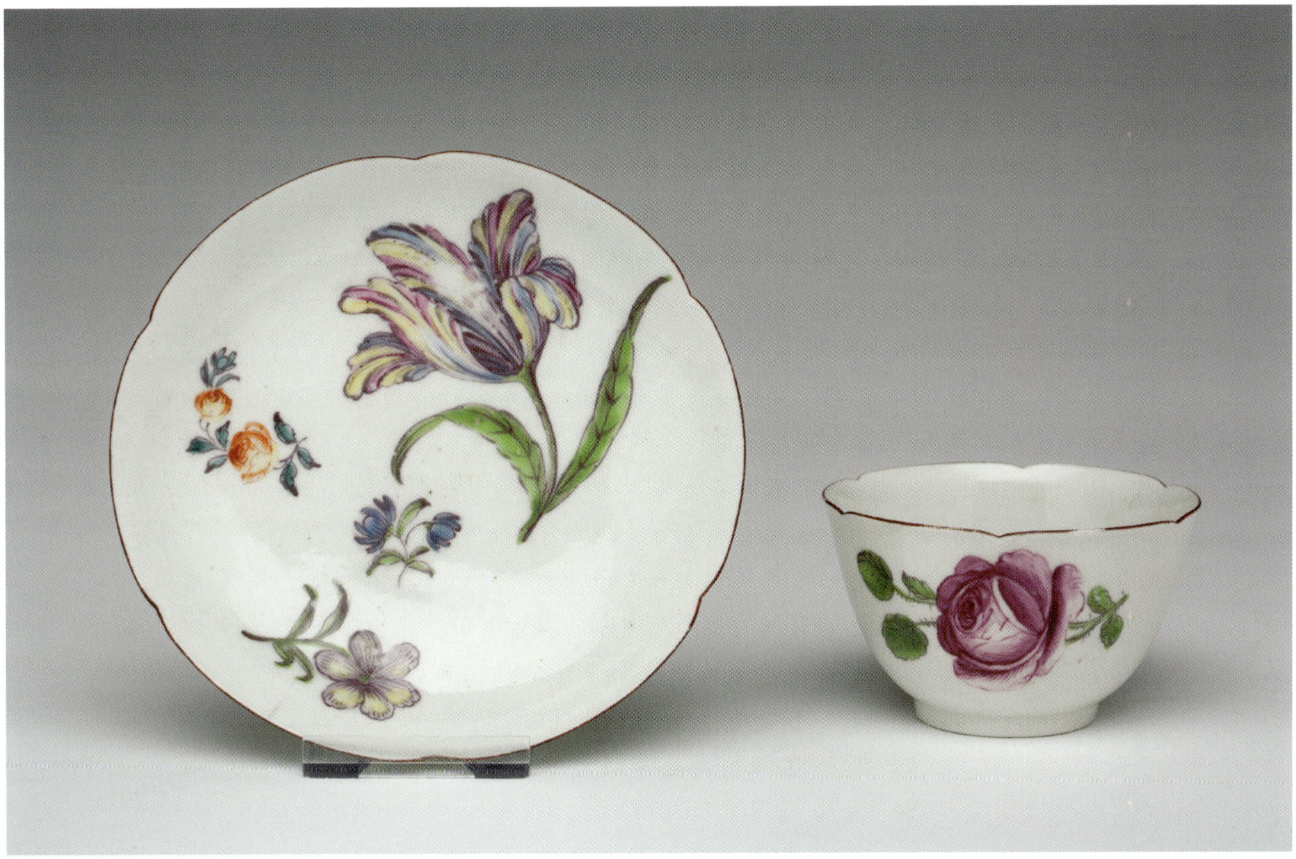

235

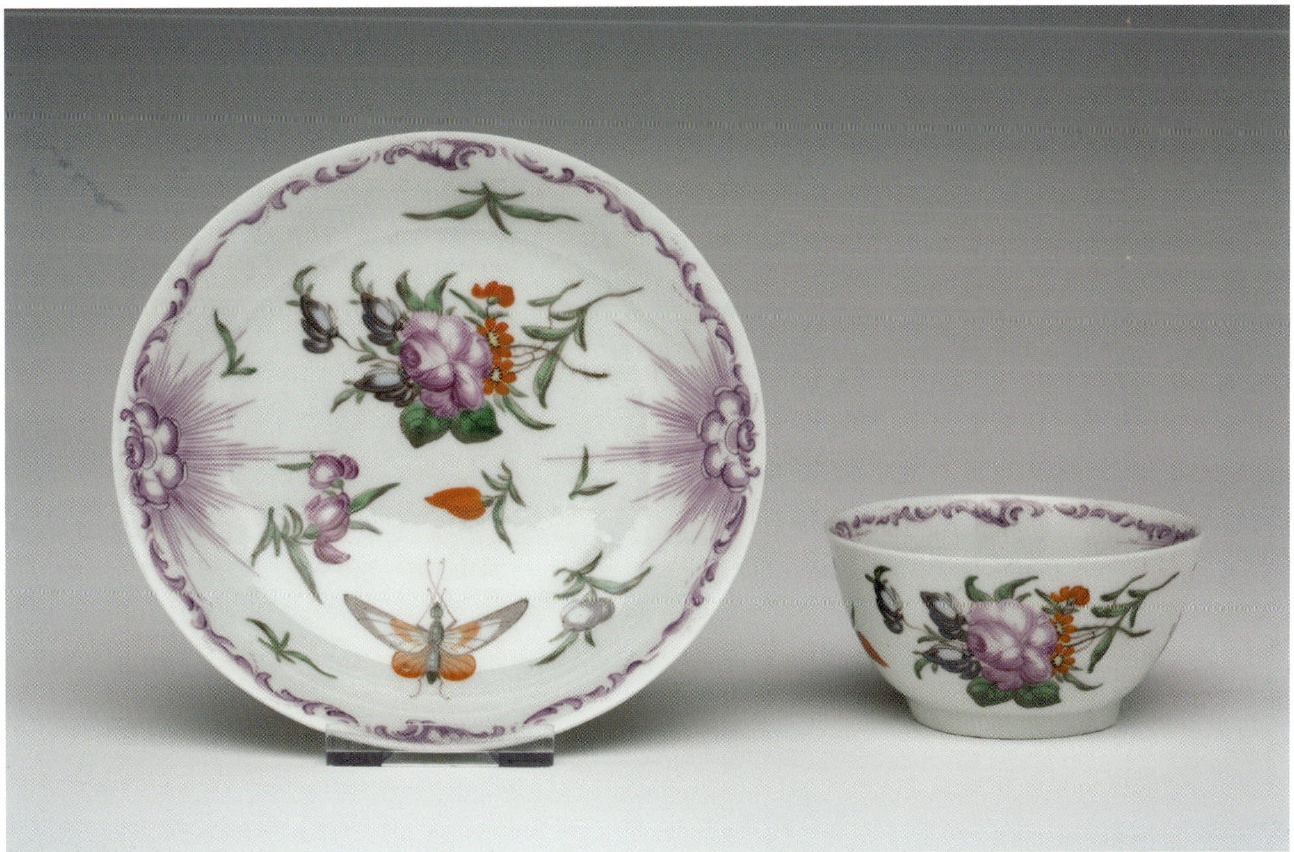

236

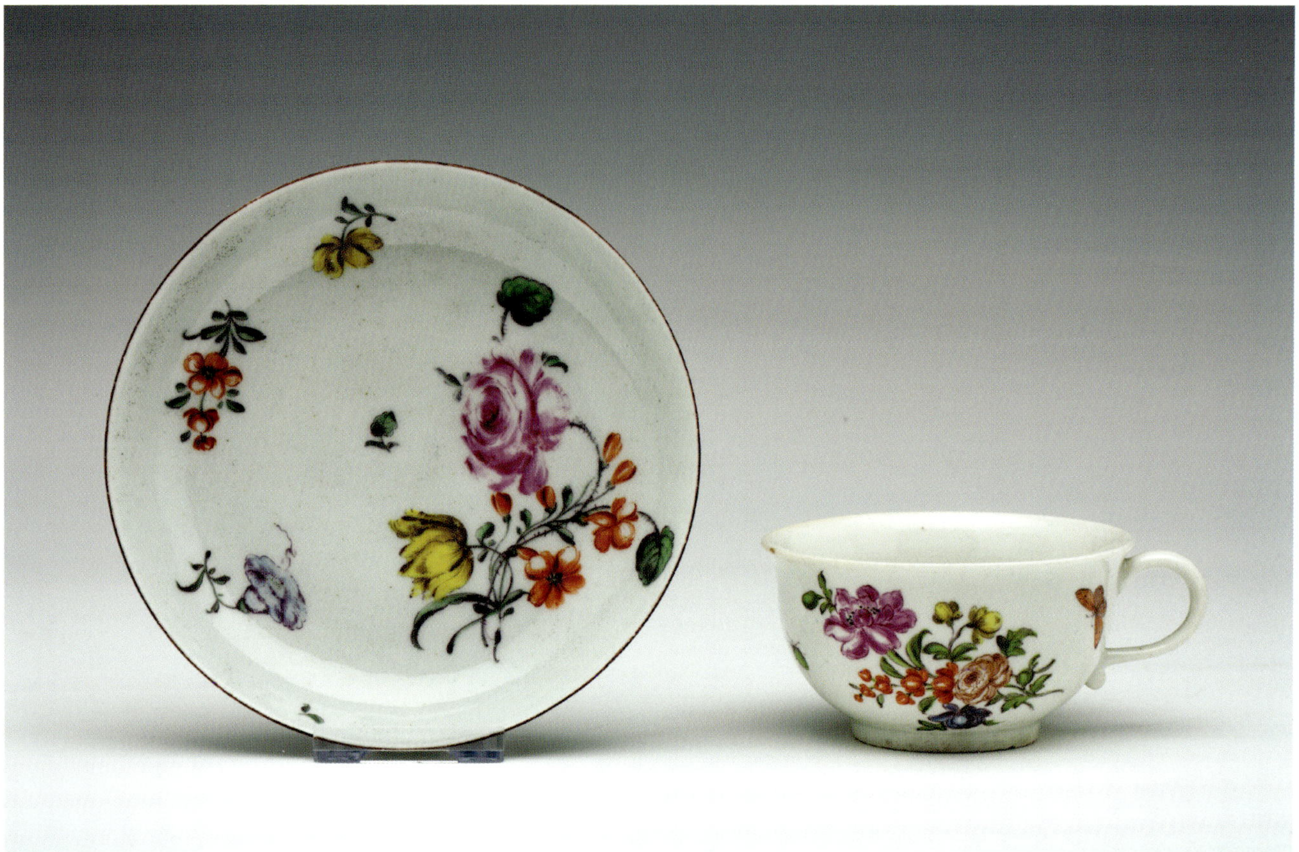

237

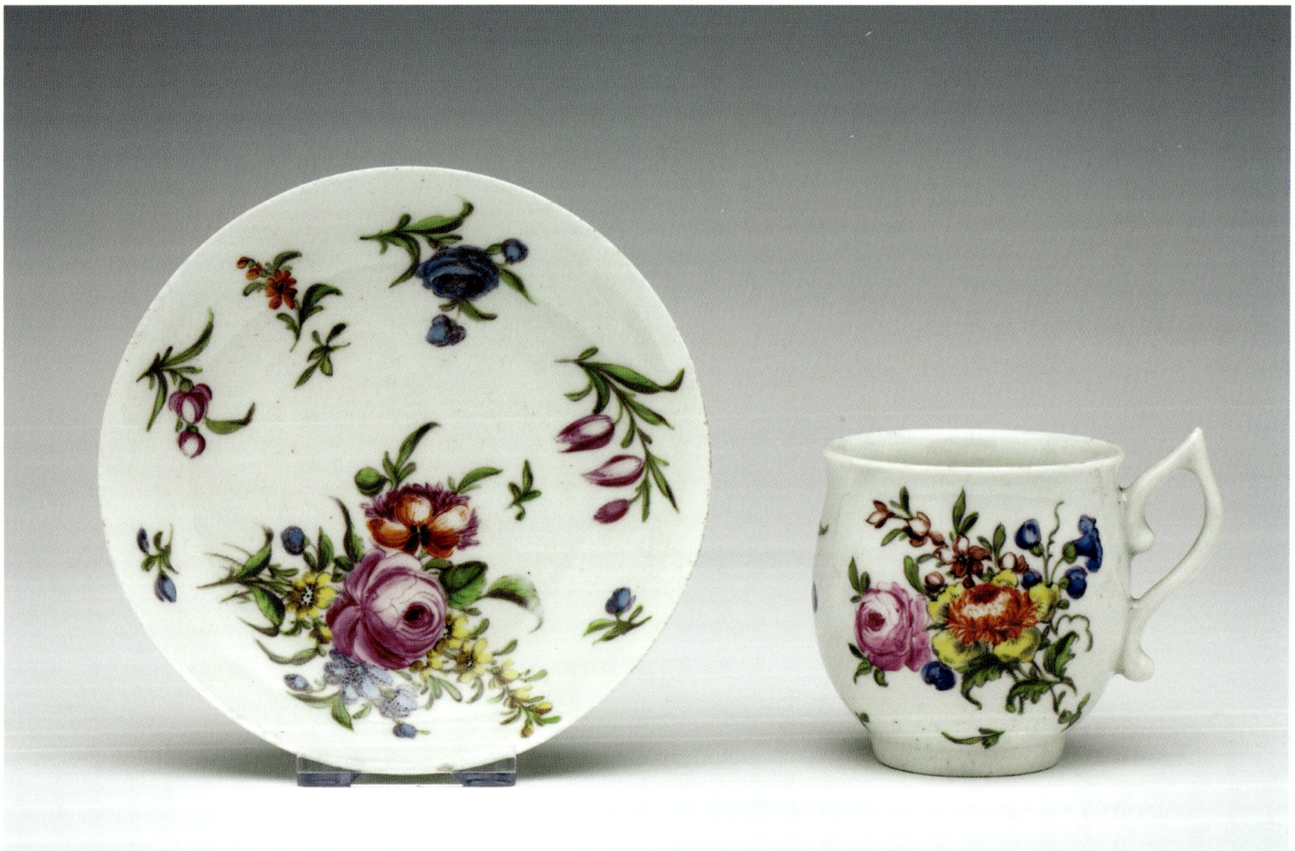

238

237

Teacup and saucer

About 1760
Cup ht 4.4 cm, diam. 8.1 cm; saucer diam. 12.8 cm
Mark: crossed swords and 9 with a dot
1957.24.1.769

Meissen shaped cup with everted rim, brown edge to saucer; European floral decoration.

REFERENCE
Spero and Sandon 1996, pl. 99.

238

Coffee cup and saucer

1758–60
Cup ht 6.1 cm, diam. 5.5 cm; saucer diam. 11.5 cm
1957.24.1.416

Wishbone peaked handle, naturalistic floral decoration; possibly not a pair.

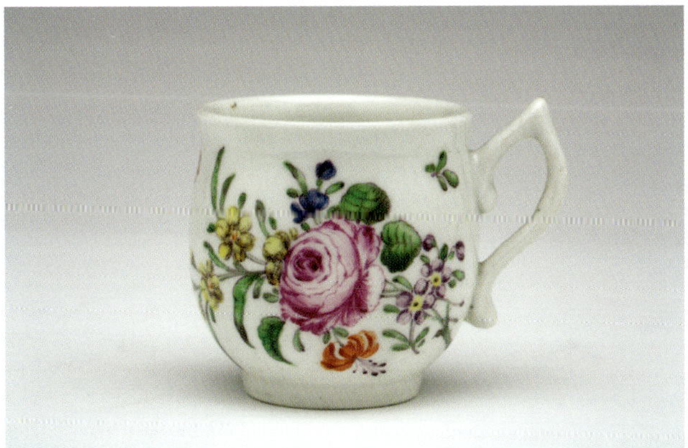

239

239

Cup

1758–60
Ht 5.9 cm, diam. 5.6 cm
1957.24.1.409

Everted rim, wishbone handle decorated with a bouquet of lilies and mixed flowers.

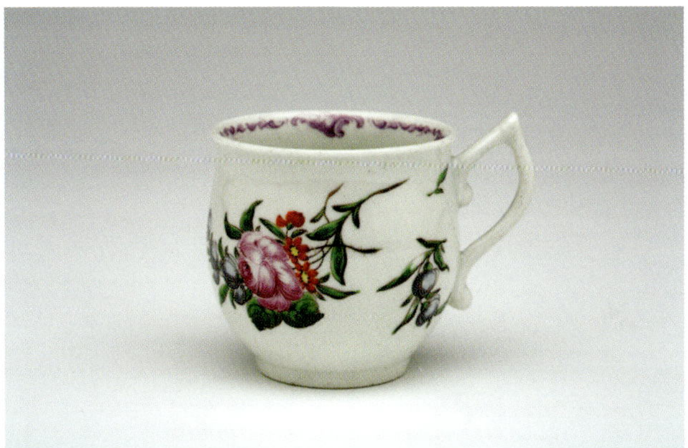

240

240

Cup

1758–60
Ht 5.9 cm, diam. 5.7 cm
1957.24.1.405

Everted rim, wishbone handle; decorated with a bouquet of lilies and mixed flowers, puce scrolls inside rim.

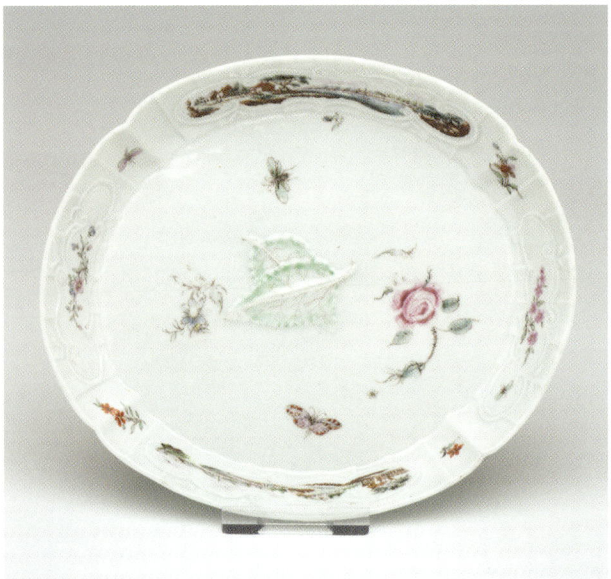

241

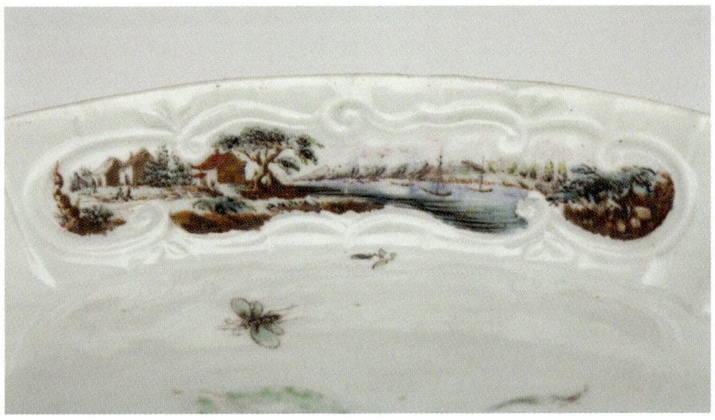

241

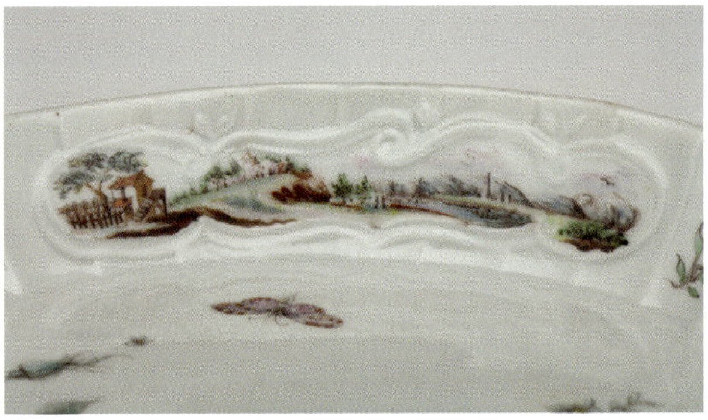

241

241

Dish

About 1756
Length 15 cm, width 13.1 cm
1957.24.1.854

Flat base, moulded rim; panels painted with minutely detailed landscapes and flowers, two moulded rose leaves in centre.

242

Cake dish

About 1756
Diam. 20.3 cm
1957.24.1.96

Radiating basketwork panels within scrolled moulded border; floral sprays around rim and scattered on moulding, central circular panel with European figures in landscape.

REFERENCES
Spero and Sandon 1996, pl. 59; Amor 1981, no. 52.

243

Cake dish

About 1756
Diam. 18.2 cm
1957.24.1.99

Closely fluted with two large rococo panels decorated with mauve landscapes; two smaller panels with butterflies; floral spray in centre, purple scrolling around edge. A similar shaped dish is illustrated in Spero 1984, pl. 34.

PROVENANCE
Harold Davis, St James's, London, 30 December 1943, £11.

REFERENCE
Bonhams, London, 26 November 2003, lot 121.

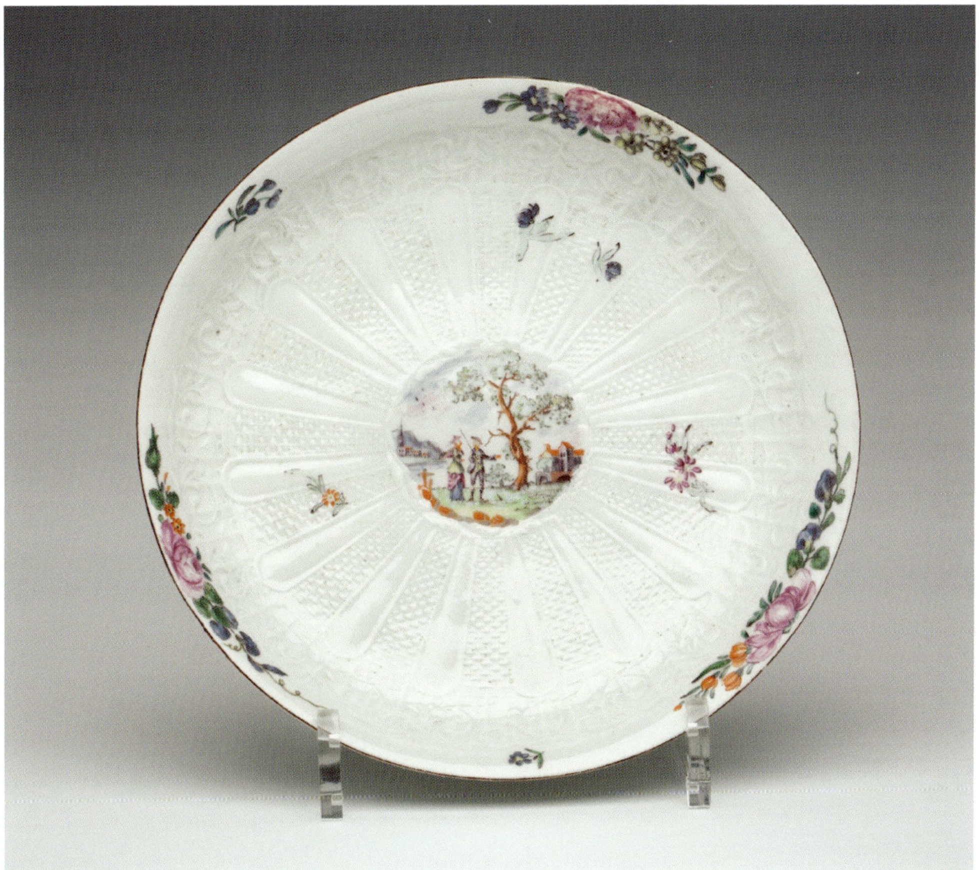

242

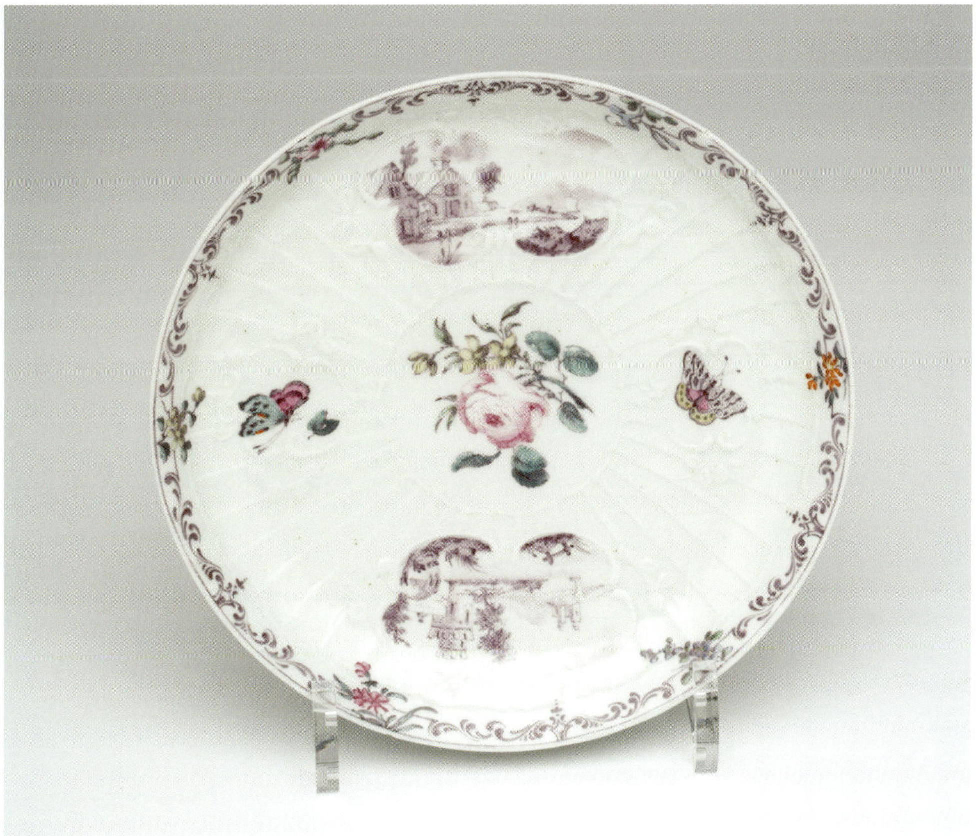

243

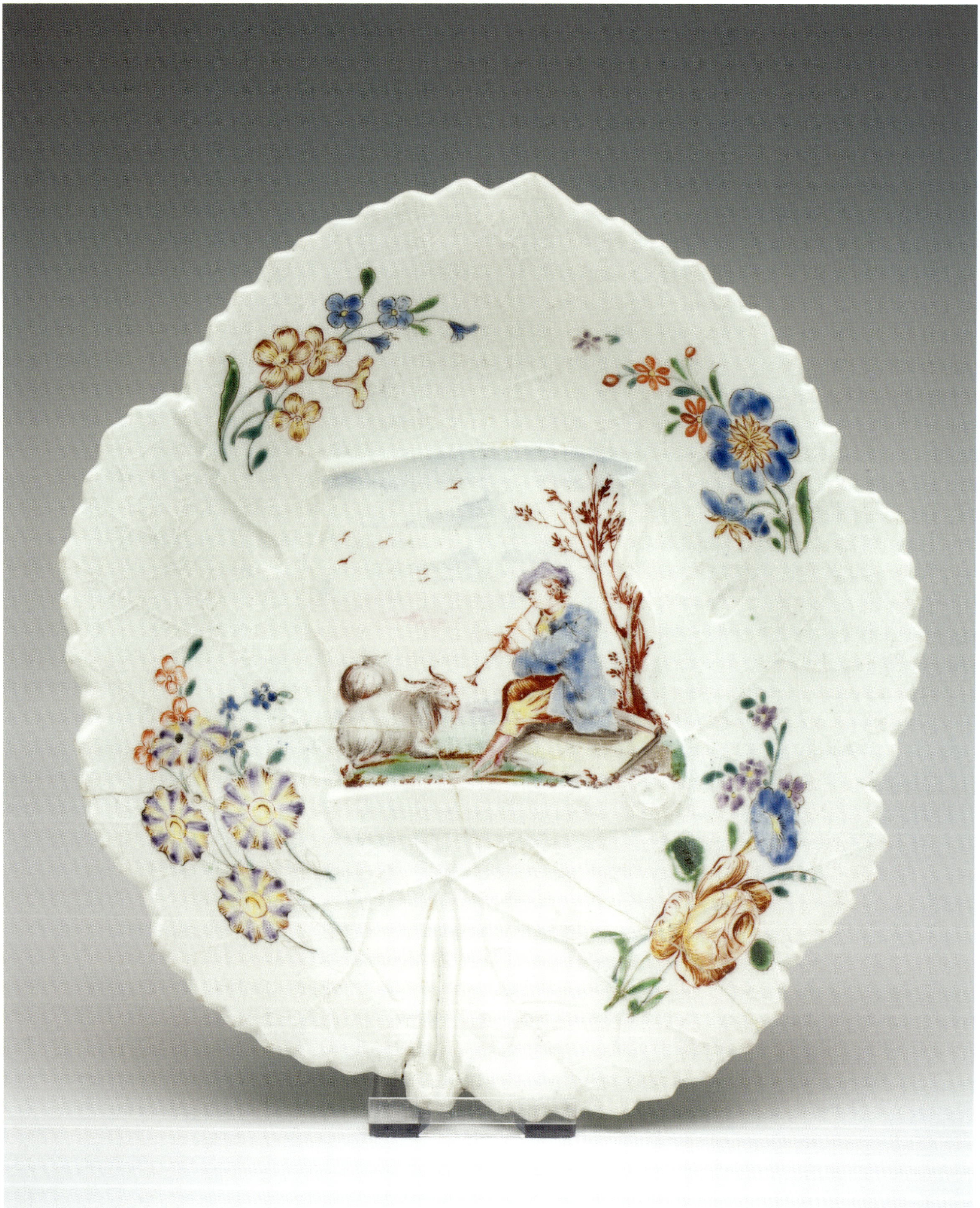

[160] EUROPEAN DESIGNS: 1756–1765

244

Dish

1756–8
Length 19 cm
1957.24.1.920

Fig-leaf shape with moulded veins, plain serrated edge; four bouquets of European flowers, painted in a free and distinctive hand, surround an almost square moulded rococo panel in book form with scene of shepherd in blue coat and hat seated beneath a brown tree, piping to a ram and disappearing ewe, birds in flight above.

Fig leaves are the earliest of a series of leaf-shaped moulded dessert dishes that were a speciality of Worcester from about 1756 to the late 1760s. A similar dish with the central panel decorated in light purple monochrome is illustrated in Amor 1981, no. 57.

PROVENANCE
Tilley & Co., London, 27 September 1954, £35.

REFERENCES
Reynolds 1999, p. 23, pl. 7; Spero 2005, pl. 143; Spero 1984, pl. 41 and col. pl. 14.

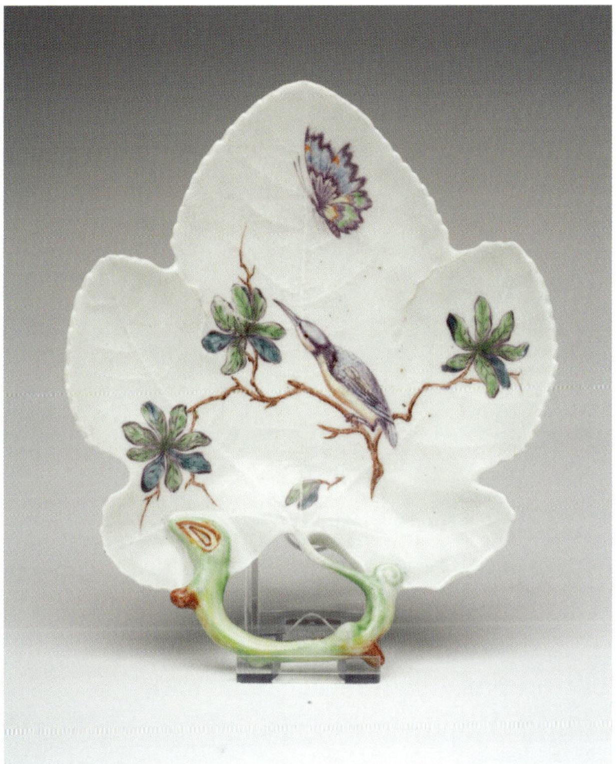

245

245

Sweetmeat dish

1758–60
Length 17.2 cm
1957.24.1.502

Vine leaf shape with serrated edges and moulded ribs, green branch handle, painted in naturalistic tones with bee-eater on leafy branch, a butterfly above. The pair to this was sold by Marshall at Sotheby's, London, on 27 June 1953. The other known example is illustrated in Spero 2007, p. 21.

PROVENANCE
Filkins & Co., London, 7 July 1944, £13 10s (pair).

REFERENCE
Reynolds, 1999, pl. 10.

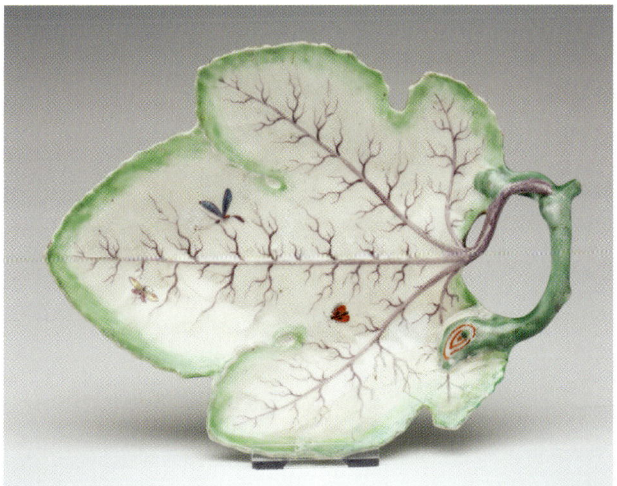

246

246

Sweetmeat dish

1758–60
Length 17.7 cm, width 13.8 cm
1957.24.1.1068

Vine leaf shape with puce veining and green edging, green twig handle; decorated with three insects in colour.

REFERENCE
Bonhams, London, 12 March 2008, lot 185.

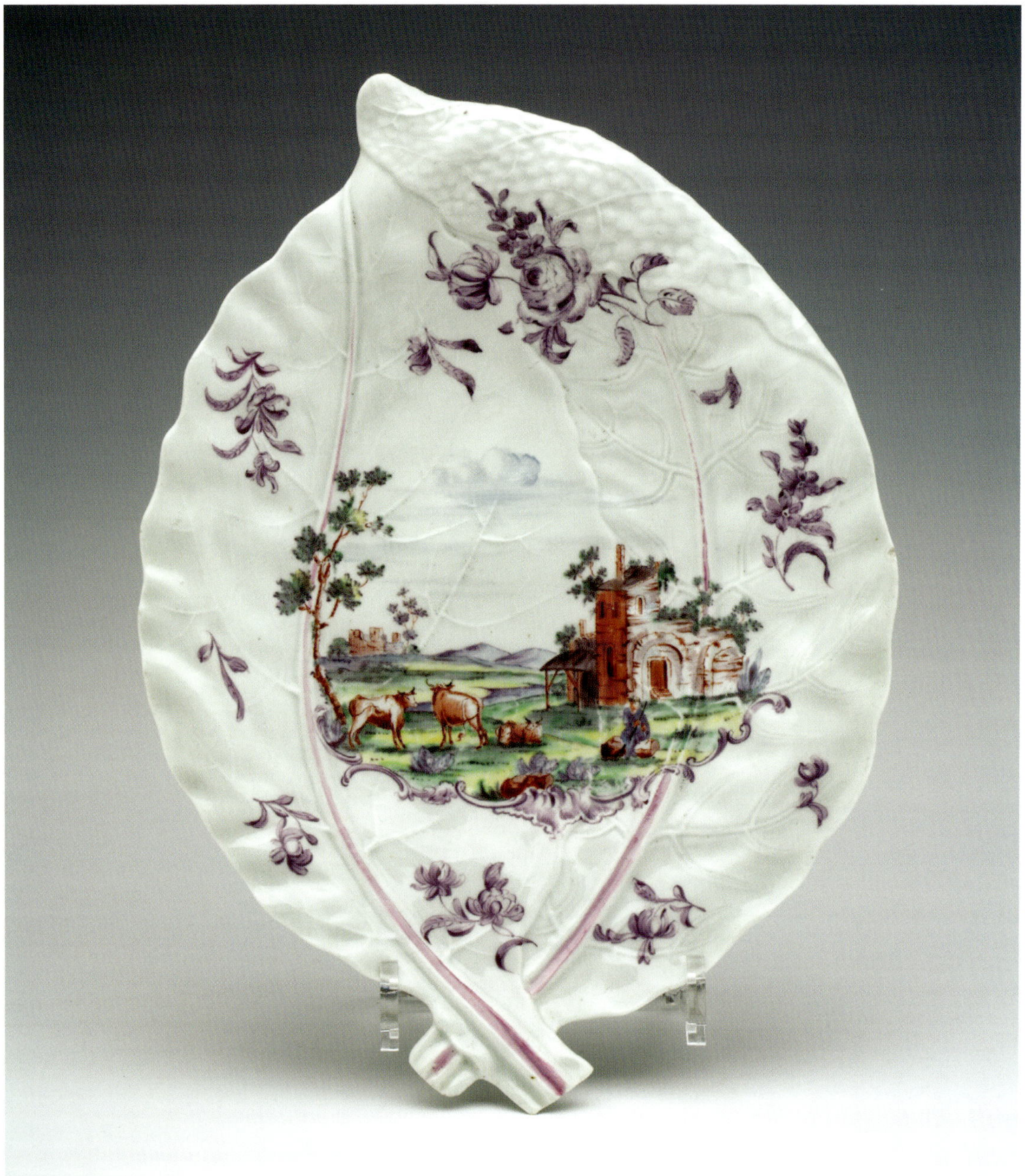

247

247

Dish

1757–8
Length 35.3 cm, width 25.3 cm
1957.24.1.97

Moulded in the form of two overlapping leaves, the crossed stalks with puce central veins; centre painted with rural scene with cows and herdsman, surrounded by flowers in purple monochrome.

REFERENCE
Bonhams, London, 31 March 2010, lot 145.

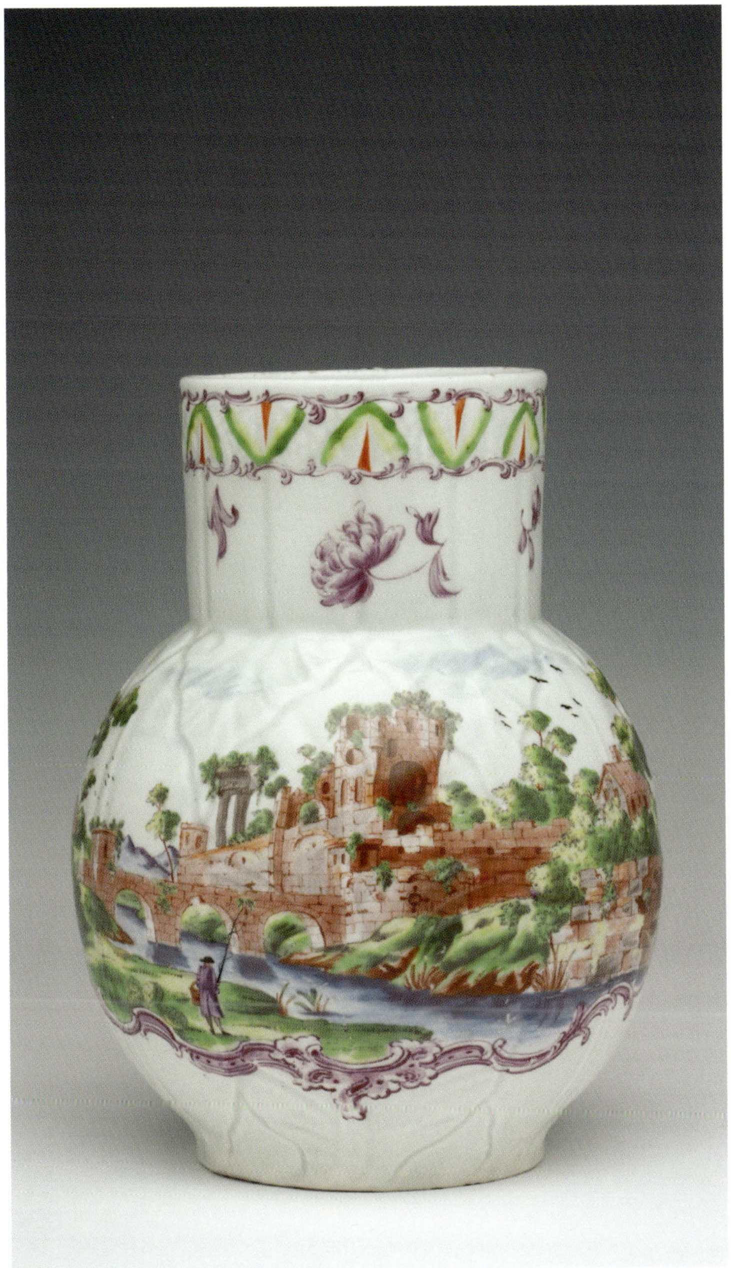

248

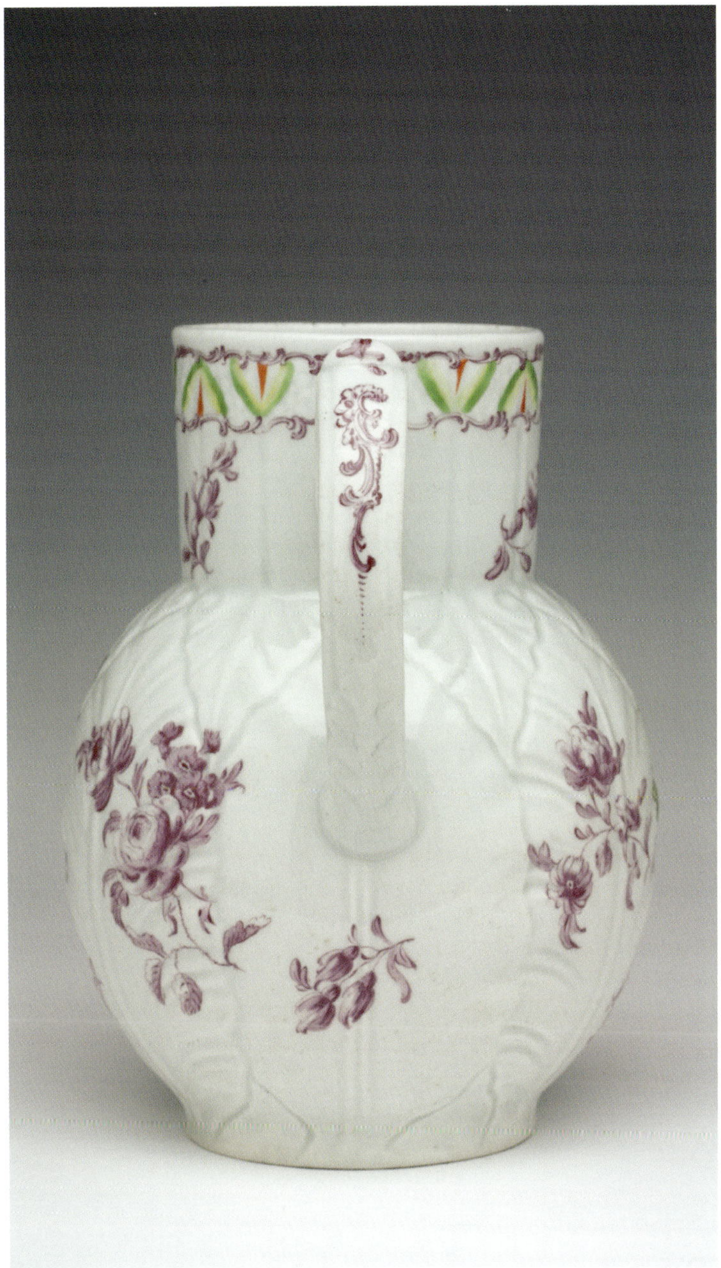

248

248

Jug

About 1758
Ht 20.1 cm
1957.24.1.93

Ovoid body moulded with cabbage leaves, loop handle, cylindrical neck with acanthus leaf border; painted with European scene of fishermen by bridge, ruined castle behind. This shape was known in the eighteenth century as a 'Dutch' jug.

REFERENCES
Barrett 1966, pl. 16; Bonhams, London, 10 May 2006, lot 53.

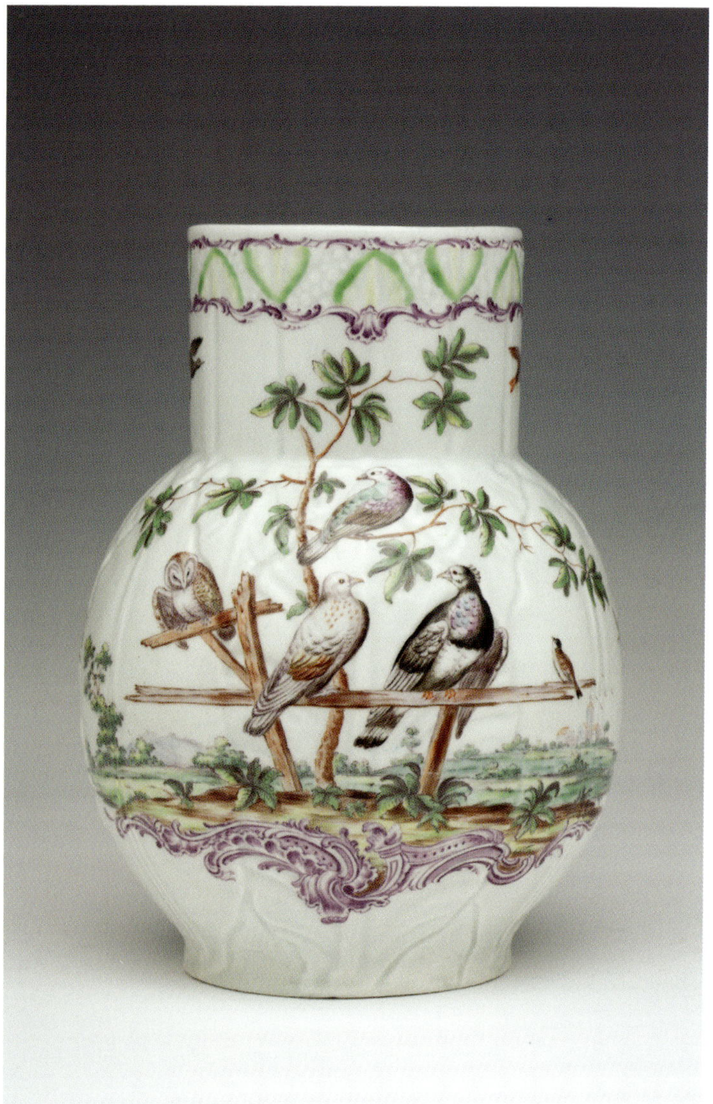

249

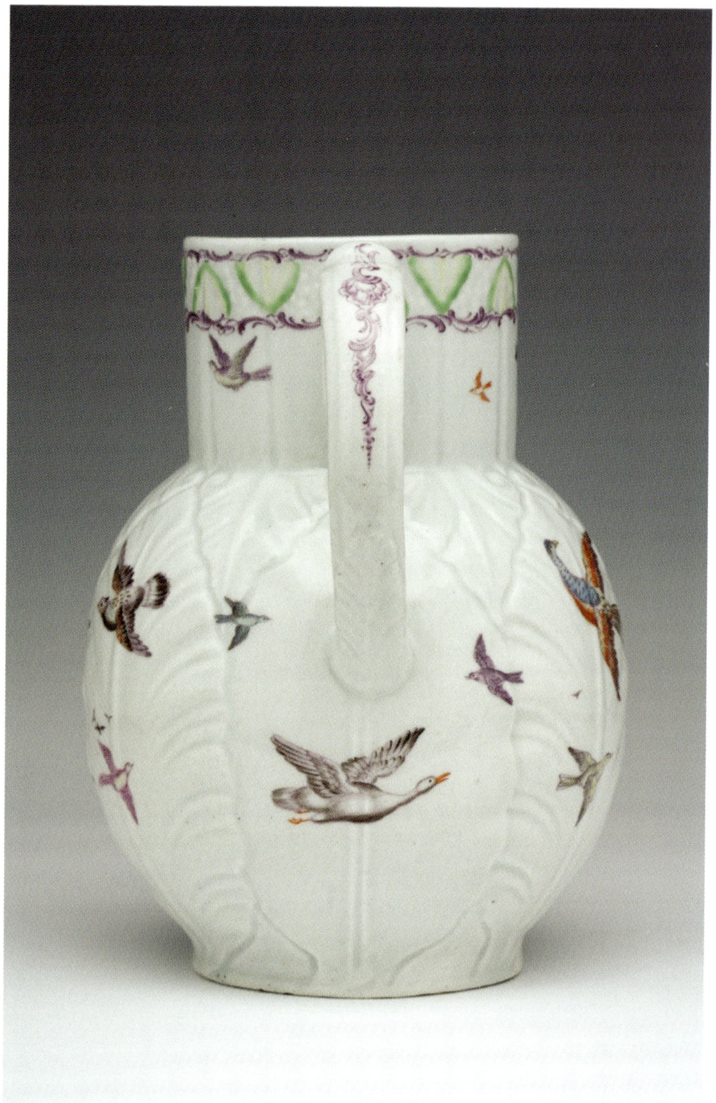

249

249

Jug

1757–8
Ht 20.2 cm
1957.24.1.473

Cabbage leaf moulded body, cylindrical neck and scroll handle; painted with European birds perched in a tree and on a fence, including an owl, pigeons and a pheasant in flight, all within a landscape; above, crimson-pink rococo scrolling. The decoration is possibly by James Rogers. Comparable examples are in the Victoria and Albert Museum (Barrett 1966, p. 15) and the Museum of Royal Worcester Porcelain (Sandon 1969, p. 26); see also a similar jug auctioned at Bonhams, London, 1 May 2013, lot 81.

REFERENCES
Reynolds 1999, p. 26, pl. 9; Spero and Sandon 1996, pl. 68.

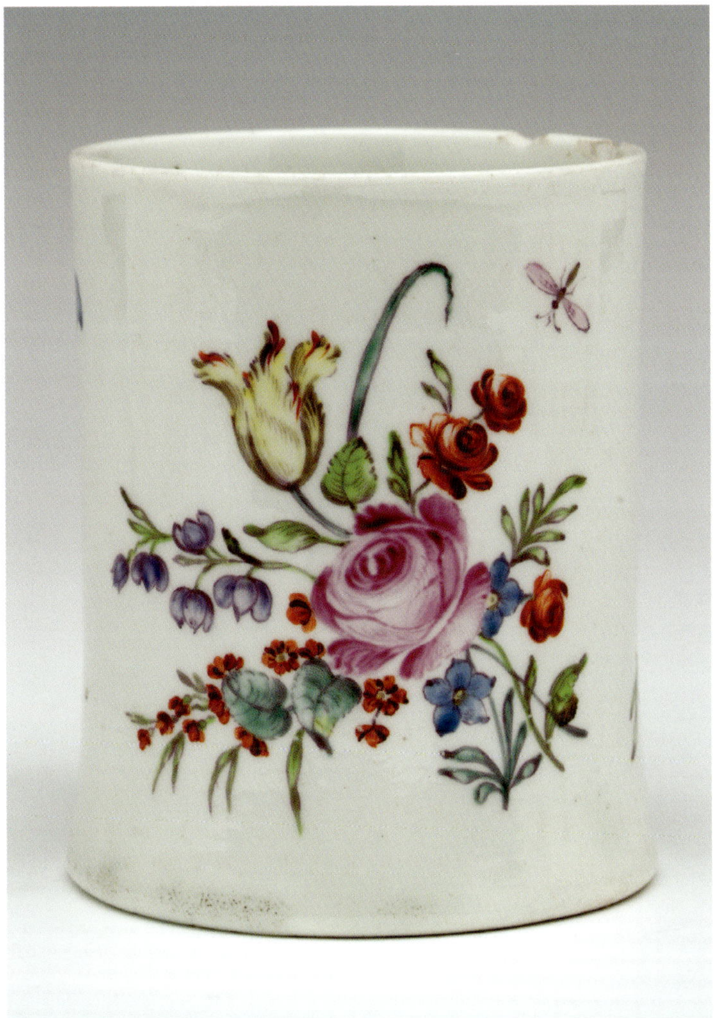

250

250

Mug

1755–60
Ht 8.7 cm, diam. 6.7 cm
1957.24.1.421

Cylindrical shape with slightly spreading base; decorated on either side with naturalistic European flowers and an insect, bouquet on front with roses, tulip and bellflowers.

REFERENCES
Spero and Sandon 1996, pl. 71; Dreweatt-Neate 1995, no. 13; Amor 1973, pl. 31.

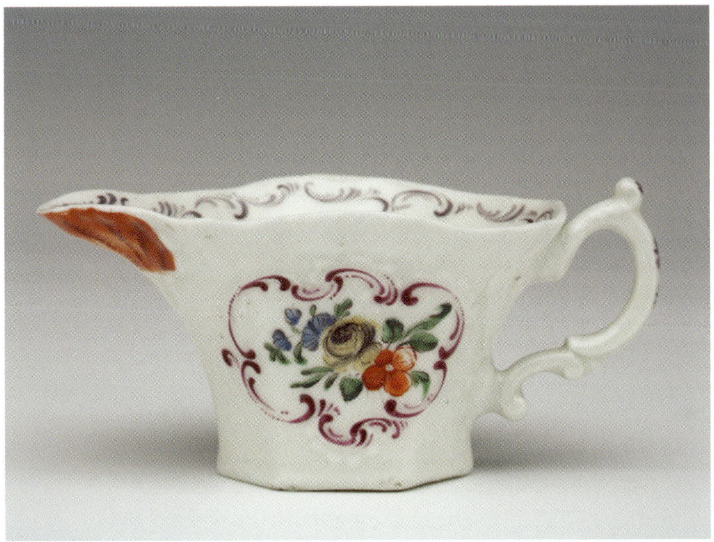

251

251

Creamboat

1758–60
Ht 5.3 cm, length 10.8 cm, width 6.7 cm
1957.24.1.811

Moulded silver shape; shell lip coloured brown, reserves picked out in purple with floral decoration, purple scrolls around inside rim.

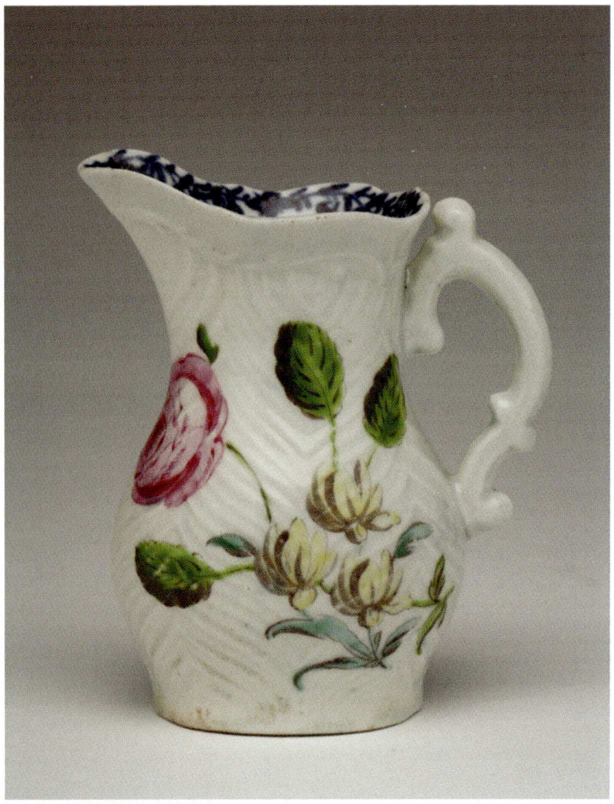

252

252

Cream jug

1758–60

Ht 8.8 cm

Mark: workman's mark

1957.24.1.808

Feather moulding deriving from Doccia porcelain, scroll handle; enamelled over moulding with rose spray on one side, pimpernel and convolvulus on other; underglaze blue border inside rim.

253

Cream jug

1758–60

Ht 9.1 cm

Mark: workman's mark

1957.24.1.519

Feather moulding deriving from Doccia porcelain, scroll handle; enamelled with large peony spray in front, crane-like bird with raised foot to the left, butterflies above; underglaze blue border inside rim. Possibly decorated outside the Worcester factory.

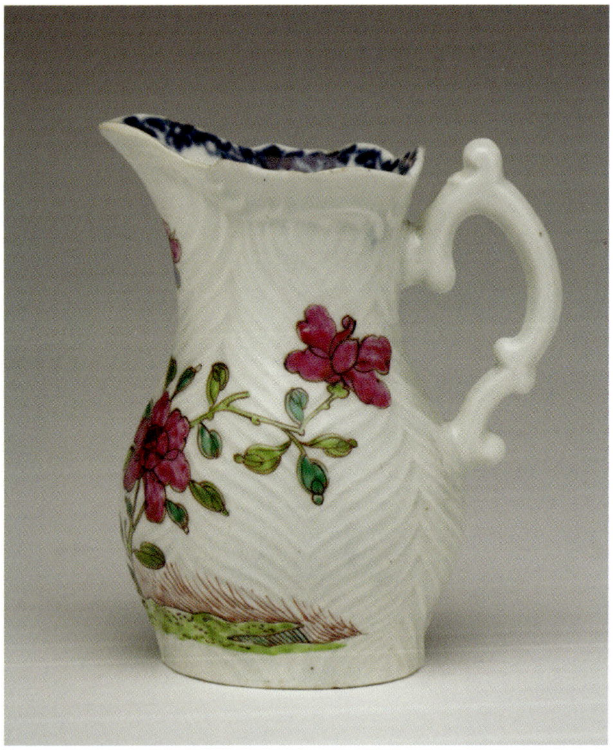

253

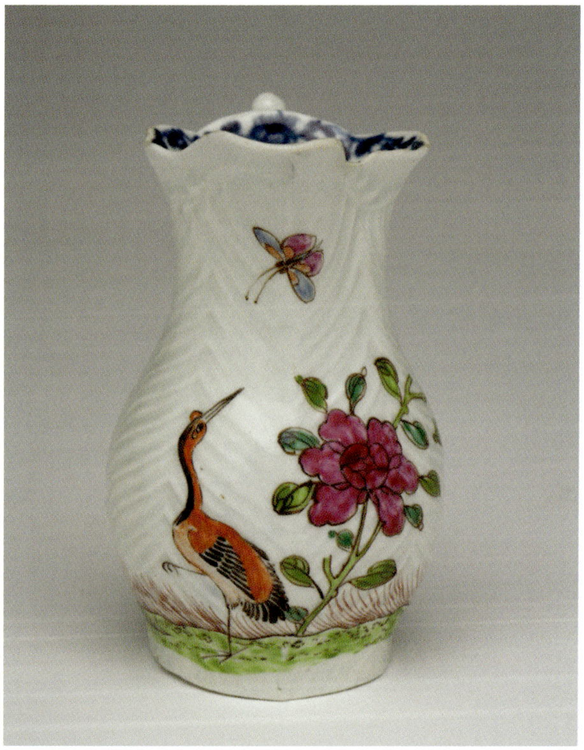

253

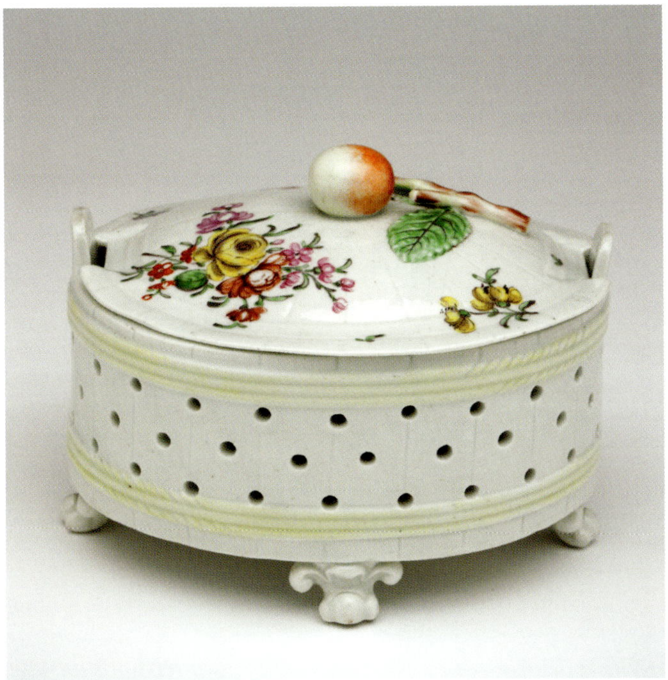

254

254

Butter cooler and cover

About 1758
Length 13.5 cm, width 11.2 cm
1957.24.1.678

Oval pierced moulded shape simulating a section of a wooden barrel, the scroll feet suggesting that it may have had a stand; two lug handles, apple knop, bands of moulded ropework coloured yellow, flower sprays on cover. Originating in silver, this oval shape was derived from an almost contemporary Chelsea red anchor period version.

PROVENANCE
Cecil Davis, New Bond Street, London, 16 June 1952, £14 10s.

REFERENCE
Spero and Sandon 1996, pl. 90.

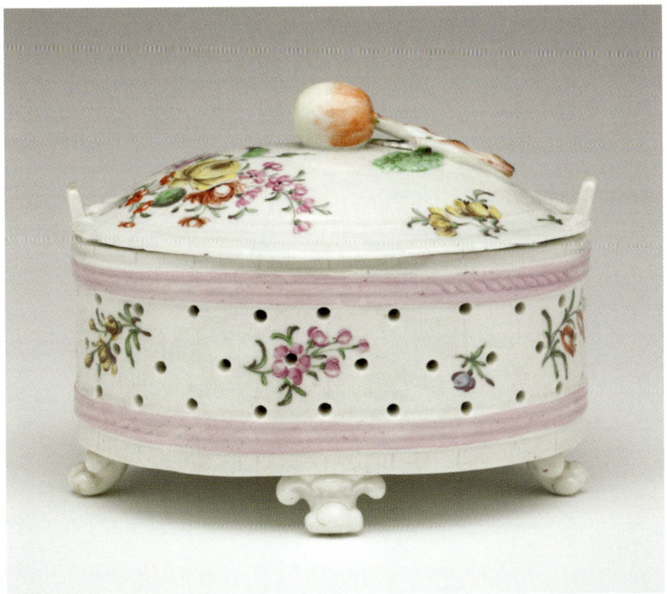

255

255

Butter cooler and cover

About 1758
Length 13.9 cm, width 11.1 cm
1957.24.1.66

As above, with ribbed mouldings coloured in pink, floral sprays on sides and on cover.

REFERENCE
Dreweatt-Neate 1995, p. 8, no. 51.

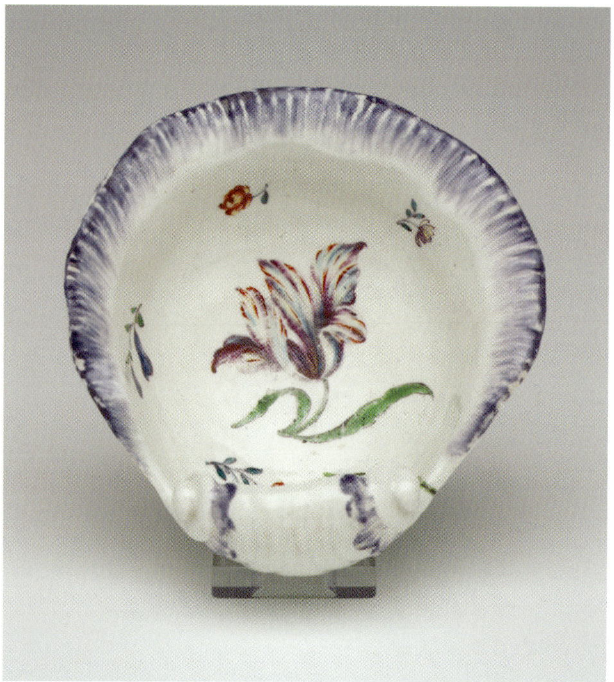

256

256

Sweetmeat dish

1756–8
Length 12.5 cm, width 11.8 cm
Mark: the 4 sign for tin in red
1957.24.1.1058

Moulded shell shape; purple-blue border; multi-coloured full-blown tulip in base; leaf painted at one side to mask firing crack.

PROVENANCE
Albert Amor, London, 3 January 1955, £52.

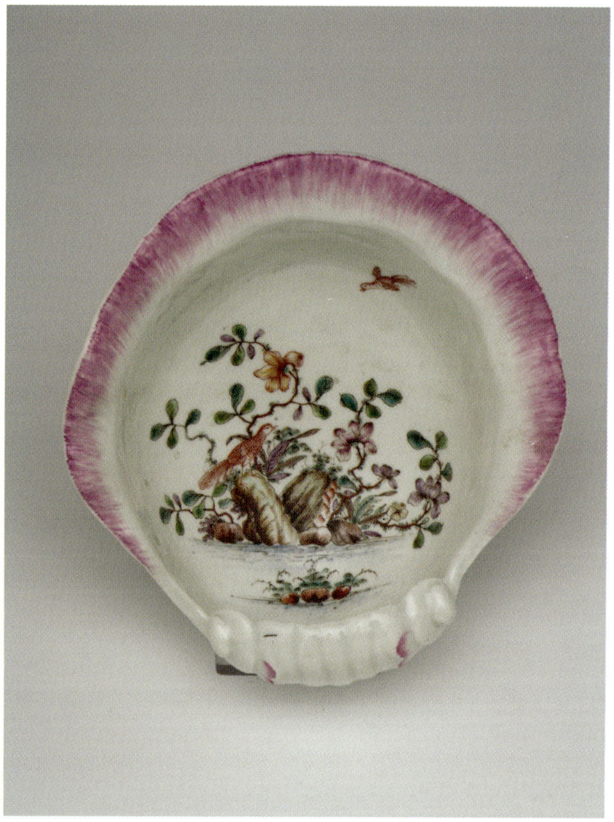

257

257

Sweetmeat dish

1756–8
Length 13 cm, width 11.7 cm, ht 6.3 cm
1957.24.1.1060

Moulded shell shape with pink border; base decorated with scene of bird on rock among Oriental foliage, another bird in flight.

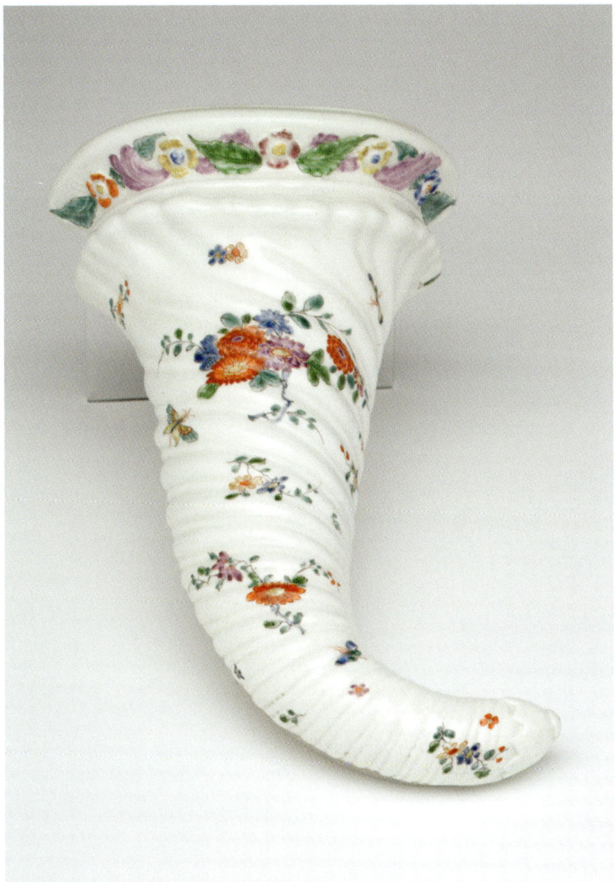

258

258

Cornucopia or wall pocket

1756–8
Length 26 cm
1957.24.1.870

Spiral cornucopia shape with moulded floral border; flower painting is in the style of Meissen Indianische Blumen decoration of twenty years earlier. These were made in pairs, probably inspired by Staffordshire salt-glaze originals. Examples from Bow, Derby, Vauxhall and other English porcelain factories are generally later in date and smaller in size. A few from the period have survived with iron or lead liners, suggesting that they were used for cut flowers or flowering bulbs. These could be hung on the wall by means of suspension holes. The other half of the pair is illustrated in Sotheby's, London, 13 April 2011, lot 145. A similar pair was sold at Bonhams, London, 31 March 2010, lot 142.

PROVENANCE
Filkins & Co., London, 5 February 1942, £11 (pair).

4

Printed Decoration

THE INTRODUCTION OF transfer printing revolutionised the porcelain industry in England. As well as reducing costs, it allowed greater detail and definition in decoration. Prior to this all porcelain had been hand painted, which was labour intensive, sometimes inconsistent and often involved several kiln firings. Surprisingly, although several applications were made, no patents were granted in the eighteenth century for transfer printing on ceramics.

The technique of overglaze printing was probably developed by John Brooks (fl. 1730–1755), the Irish engraver, for use on enamels in Birmingham around 1751. It was subsequently used at Battersea from about 1751–2, on Worcester porcelain two or three years later, and on Bow porcelain by about 1756. At this time the Liverpool firm of Sadler & Green was successfully overglaze printing on tin-glazed earthenware, particularly tiles. However, in England it was only at Worcester that the printing process was developed fully on porcelain, with the advent of underglaze printing in blue in the late 1750s. This technique may have originated at the Doccia factory, near Florence, where a small quantity of underglaze printed wares were produced between about 1749 and 1752.[1]

It is thought that Josiah Holdship, one of the original partners of the Worcester factory, first introduced overglaze printing there. He and his elder brother, Richard, are believed to have developed and overseen the printing department. However, it is the engraver Robert Hancock (fig. 20), arriving at Worcester in 1756, who is most closely associated with the development of underglaze printing. A note said to have been attached to a mezzotint after a portrait of him by Joseph Wright of Derby in the British Museum said 'He discovered the art of Printing on China. He engraved the first plate that was us'd for calico printing. He has engrav'd many Portraits for Countrey Booksellersnd others'. In 1757 he signed an engraved view of the Worcester Porcelain Manufactory. Some items of Worcester porcelain are marked *RH* [for Robert Hancock] *Worcester* with an anchor, a rebus for Holdship. Richard Holdship left Worcester in 1759 and signed an agreement with Derby porcelain manufacturers Duesbury and Heath in 1764. Josiah most likely stayed at Worcester until his death in 1783.

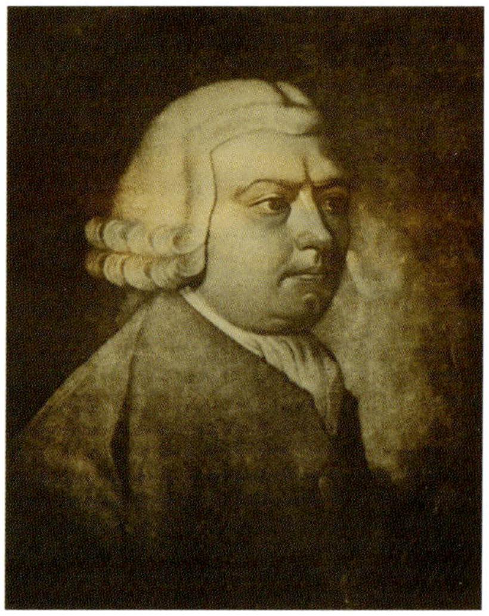

Fig. 20 Robert Hancock after Joseph Wright of Derby, *Portrait of Robert Hancock*, mezzotint, 1770–80. © The Trustees of the British Museum, 1902,1011.2455

'Mr Valentine Green serv'd his apprenticeship to this man. This mezzotinto, from a picture by Mr. Wright, is an essay of his own, but not approving it, he destroy'd the plate, reserving this only impression. There is not another portrait of him.'

In the eighteenth century two methods of printing are thought to have been used, both using a flat sheet of copper, painstakingly engraved by hand using a 'graver', a type of chisel. Designs were created with a combination of punching dots and cutting fine lines. One method, later referred to as 'bat' printing, involved filling the contours of the engraved surface with oil and pressing a thick bat of gelatinous glue on to the plate. The bat and the oil outline were applied to the surface of the porcelain. Finely powdered enamel was then dusted on to the oil before firing. This method could only be used over the glaze. The earliest prints on Worcester porcelain, of 1753–5, which most likely used the bat printing process, were dubbed 'Smoky Primitives' by early collectors. Typically they lack definition and depth and are often of slightly smudgy appearance. It is thought that Robert Hancock may have been involved with producing these prints before 1756. A number of engravings, after the Parisian book illustrator Louis Philippe Boitard (fl. 1734–1760) and engraved by Hancock for book impressions, occur on porcelain made between 1753 and 1755.

The second method involved covering a warmed copper plate with hot oil-based ink, removing the excess and then placing the plate face upward on the bed of a printing press, to be covered with a single sheet of dampened tissue paper. The whole bed was moved between rollers, forcing the ink on to the paper. While the ink was still warm, the tissue was placed, printed side down, on the porcelain and then rubbed with a hard flannel boss until it was free of wrinkles. The tissue was removed by sponging with water and, after drying, the porcelain was then fired in a kiln to fuse the pattern to the glaze. Only about 250 impressions could be taken from one copper plate. Apprentice engravers were employed to re-sharpen used plates, leading to slight variations in the finished print. This second technique allowed the development of underglaze blue printing in the late 1750s, cobalt oxide being able to withstand the temperature in the 'glost' or glazing kiln, unlike other enamels. From about 1757, all printing was done with paper transfers. On her visit to the Worcester factory on 13 July 1770, Lady Shelburne noted that '… Some of their China is painted with a Pencil, Others by Copper Plate, but they made a secret of that Method, & will not let anybody see it done'.[2]

Before the invention of photography, printed illustrations in publications such as *The Ladies Amusement* played an important part in the spread of ideas for decoration. Prints were published on a monthly basis and purchased by subscription, to be collected into a folio or could be bought separately. In his diary on 7 November 1666, Samuel Pepys wrote that he had bought 'some prints for my wife to draw by this winter'.

The first documented printed pieces of Worcester porcelain showing a high level of technical accomplishment are mugs, with a print of the King of Prussia, signed by Hancock and dated 1757.[3] This print was based on a mezzotint by Richard Houston (about 1721–1775) of 1754. From the late 1760s, printing moved away from romantic landscapes, domestic pastimes and bird subjects to scenes of classical ruins, inspired by the Grand Tour and the discovery of Herculaneum.

Excavations at the Worcester factory site show no evidence of underglaze blue and white printed porcelain before about 1757. There is a notable increase in the production of transfer-printed pieces between 1765 and 1775, printing becoming the principal form of decoration on porcelain until the mid-1790s, at which point it almost disappeared. The failure to fully develop printing at the Bow factory, Worcester's main rival at the time, and to recognise it commercial implications, may have been a factor in its decline.

Before arriving at the Worcester factory Robert Hancock had been apprenticed to the Birmingham engraver George Anderton in 1746 and was probably in London by 1753, when the Battersea enamel factory was established. He was strongly influenced by Louis Philippe Boitard and his fellow Parisian Simon-François Ravenet, who engraved copper plates for Battersea. Hancock most likely moved to Worcester in about 1756 but it is not certain whether he was actually employed at the factory or as an independent engraver. He is known to have supplied plates to be used at Bow and probably some for printing in London on Chinese porcelain. Hancock combined his china decoration with work for London publishers; some of his engravings for Worcester were published by Robert Sayer in later editions of *The Ladies Amusement*.

Hancock was not the only engraver at Worcester. Valentine Green (1739–1813) was apprenticed to him in 1760 and James Ross (1745–1821) in 1765. Although he had worked with Hancock as an engraver, it is now known that Thomas Turner was apprenticed to his father, a clergyman, as a 'writing master' in 1761, and is therefore unlikely to have been apprenticed at Worcester; he became a freeman of the city in January 1771, enabling him to trade.

In 1769 Hancock purchased the large house next to the Worcester factory from Richard Holdship and in 1772 briefly became a partner at the factory. However, in October 1774, because of 'certain controversies, differences and disputes', Hancock's share of one sixth of the business was bought out by the remaining partners and he left Worcester shortly after to join Thomas Turner at Caughley, where the exact nature of his involvement is not clear; none of his prints has ever been found on Caughley porcelain.

In 1756 Sadler & Green made an unsuccessful attempt to patent the process of transfer printing on tin-glazed earthenware, its main business being printing on tiles. Their sworn affidavit, dated 2 August 1756, stated that within 'six hours they did print upwards of 1200 earthenware tiles'. In 1762 the firm entered into an exclusive agreement to decorate Wedgwood's creamware. It also printed porcelain from nearby factories, including those of Richard Chaffers (1731–1766) and Samuel Gilbody (fl. 1754–1761), and Longton Hall in Staffordshire as well as Worcester.[4]

The Vauxhall porcelain factory developed a further technique of 'polychrome transfer printing' using different colours for the printed outlines. However, Worcester's strong position in the market for underglaze printing was not seriously challenged until the increased production of Wedgwood's high-quality printing on creamware in the 1770s and the establishment of the Caughley factory in about 1775.

1 Mallet 2011, p. 89.
2 Mallet 1982, p. 109; see also Sandon 1993, Appendix 2.
3 An anonymous contribution to the *Gentleman's Magazine*, dated 20 December 1757, mentions 'an armed bust of the King of Prussia curiously imprinted on a Porcelain Cup of the Worcester manufacture with the Emblem of His Victories'.
4 Hillis 2011, p. 525.

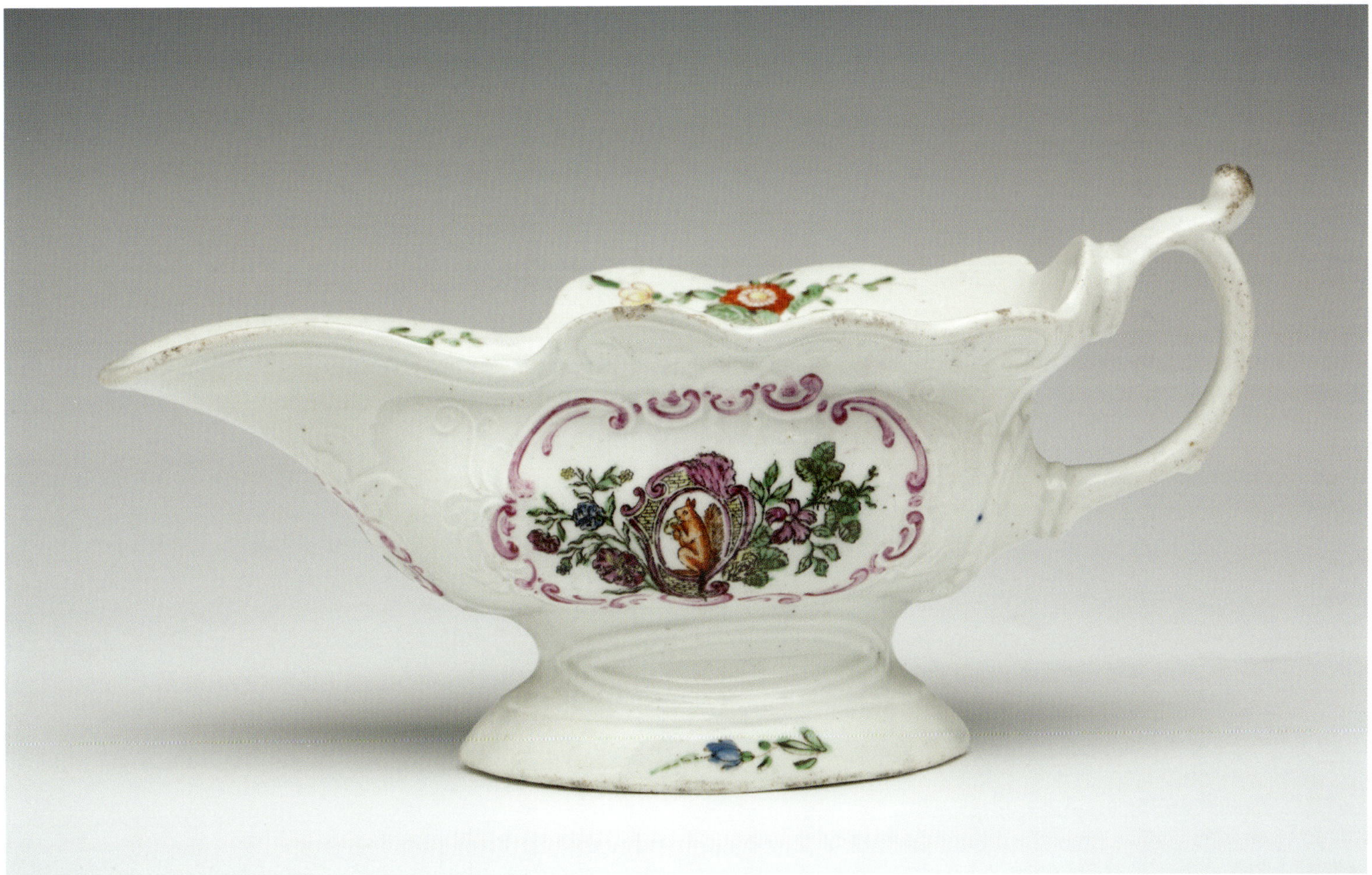

259

259

Sauceboat

About 1754
Ht 10 cm, length 19.3 cm, width 9.4 cm
1957.24.1.1015

Silver shape with moulded panels picked out in puce; on one side, over-glaze print of a squirrel and on the other a pheasant, highlighted in colour; inside the base is a scene of two cows and a herdsman.

REFERENCE
Spero and Sandon 1996, pl. 487.

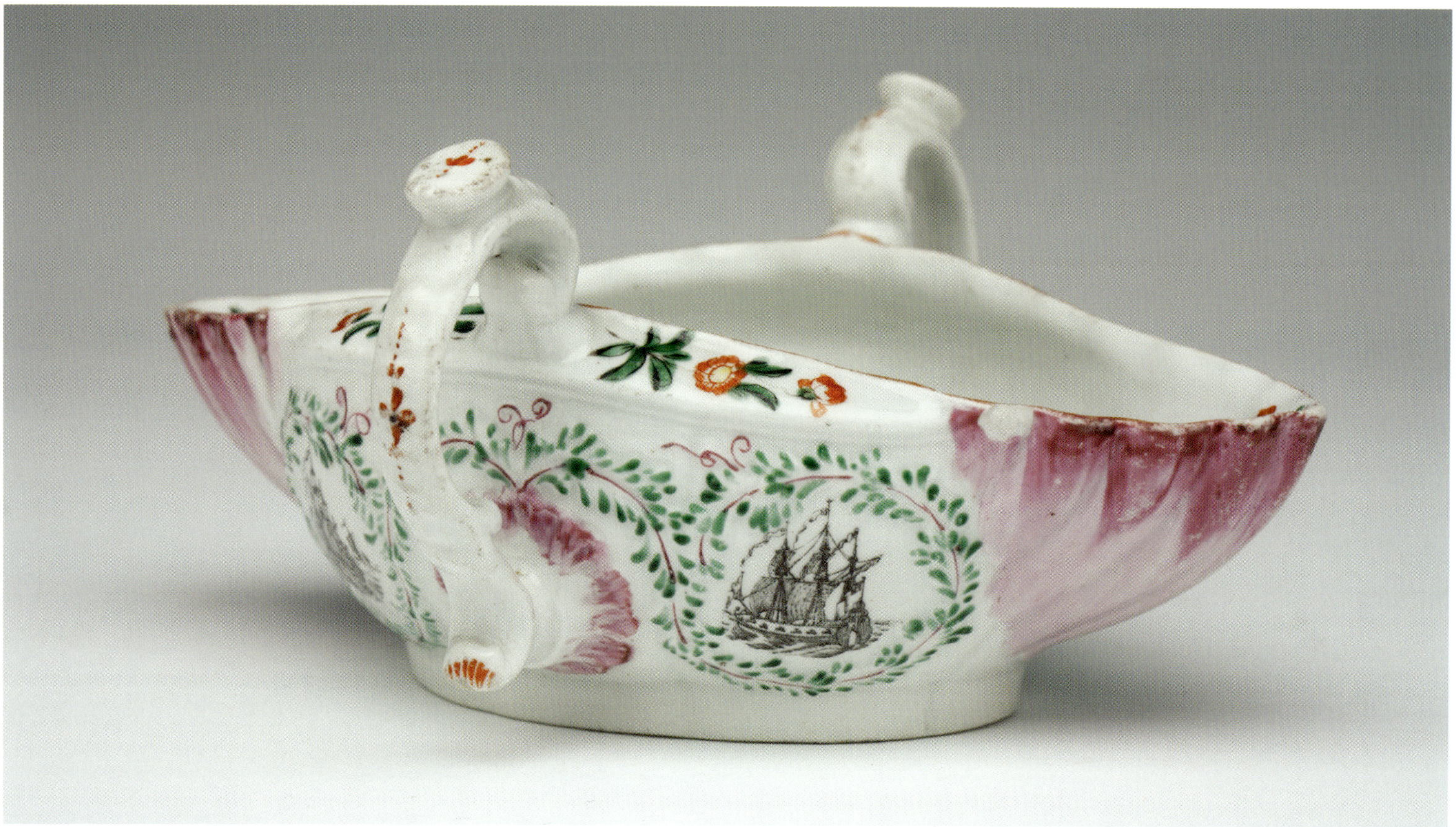

260

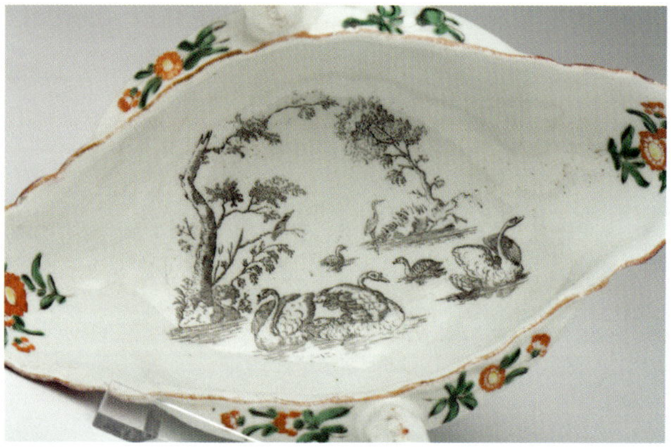

260 (detail)

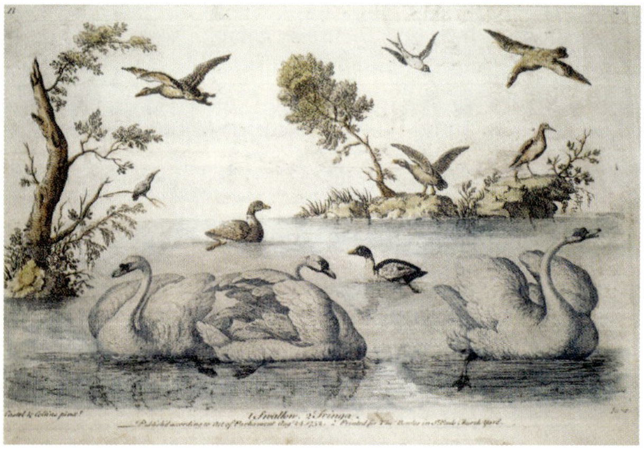

Fig. 21 After an engraving by Robert Hancock, *A River Scene*, print published by Thomas Bowles of St Paul's Church Yard, London, *c.* 1750. Private collection

260

Two-handled sauceboat

About 1756
Ht 8.5 cm, length 18.8 cm
1957.24.1.1017

Moulded body with four panels with over-glaze black prints of ships; polychrome decoration possibly added later. The river scene with swans in the base was possibly derived from a print in a John Bowles drawing book of 1752, signed *Castel and Collins pinxt. June Sc.* (fig. 21). An example without added polychrome decoration is illustrated in Spero and Sandon 1996, pl. 485.

REFERENCE
Handley 1991, p. 119.

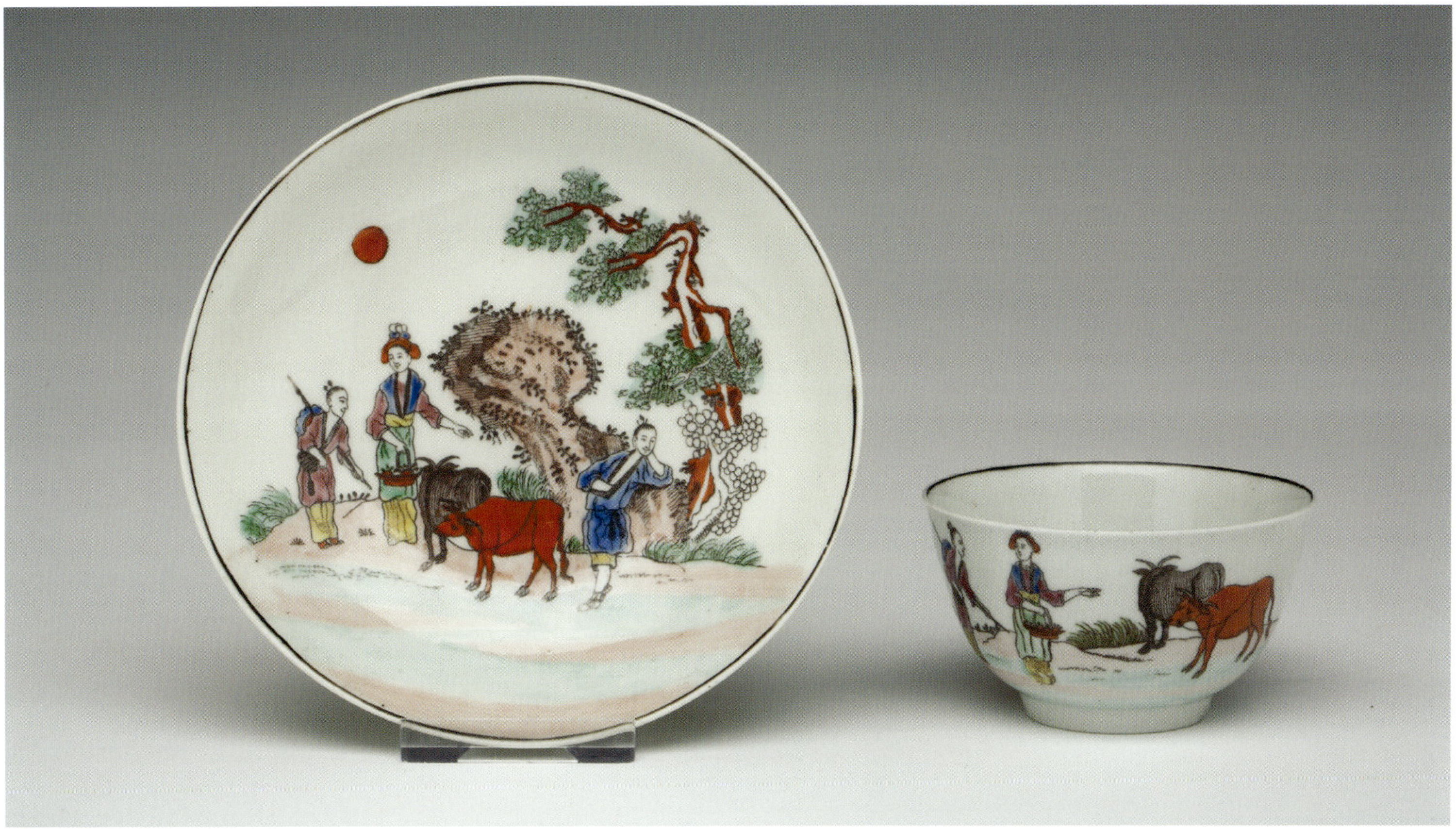

261

261

Teabowl and saucer

1756–60
Bowl ht 4.2 cm, diam. 7.2 cm; saucer diam. 12.1 cm
1957.24.1.340

Colour-washed black transfer print of the 'Red Bull' pattern, with three Chinese figures, two buffalo and a red circular sun.

REFERENCE
Sandon 1993, p. 274.

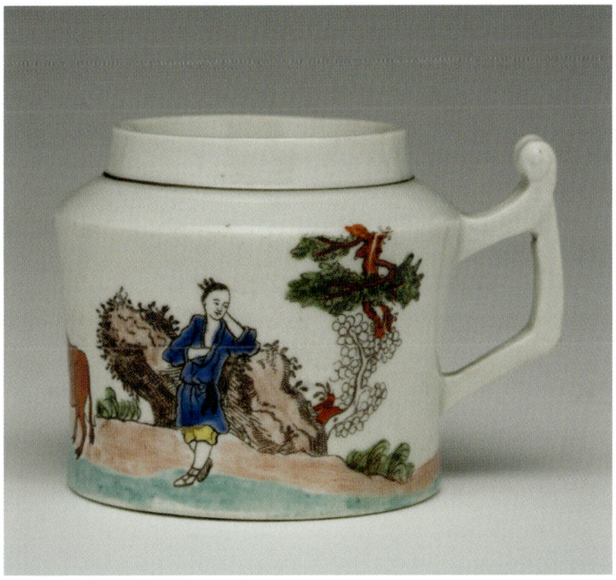

262

262

Wet mustard pot (cover missing)

1755–6
Ht 5.9 cm
1957.24.1.967

Cylindrical, slightly concave sides; colour-washed transfer print of the 'Red Bull' pattern. A similar shape but with cover, printed with a different Oriental figure design, is illustrated in Sotheby's, London, 13 April 2011, lot 134.

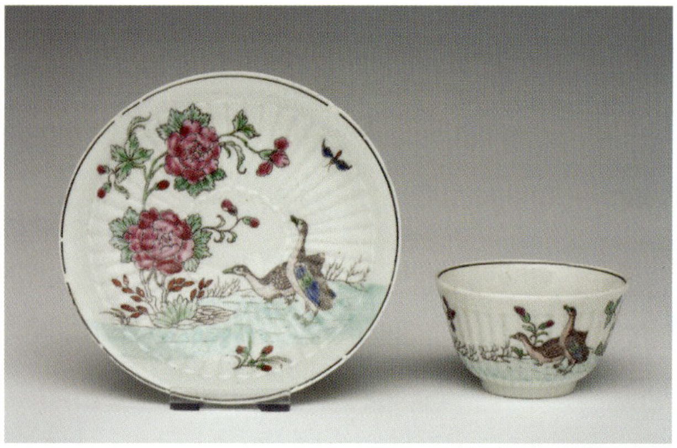

263

263

Teabowl and saucer

1758–60
Bowl ht 4 cm, diam. 6.9 cm; saucer diam. 11.9 cm
1957.24.1.533

Ribbed moulding and plain border; decorated in Chinese *famille rose* colours within a printed outline with a flowering peony plant on the left and two grey geese on the right. This is an early use of a printed outline and is based on a Chinese design – see nos. 16, 17.

PROVENANCE
H.W. Hughes Collection, no. 842; 12 February 1944, lot 842, £2.

REFERENCES
Reynolds 1999, pl. 8; Spero and Sandon 1996, pl. 498.

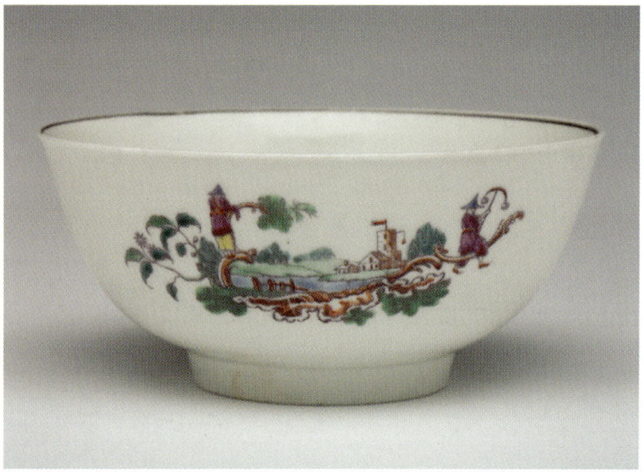

264

264

Bowl

1758–60
Ht 5.6 cm, diam. 12.2 cm
1957.24.1.315

Colour-washed transfer print of 'Les Garçons Chinois', after Jean-Baptiste Pillement; black line inside rim. A pull from the original copper plate is illustrated in Sandon 1993, p. 220.

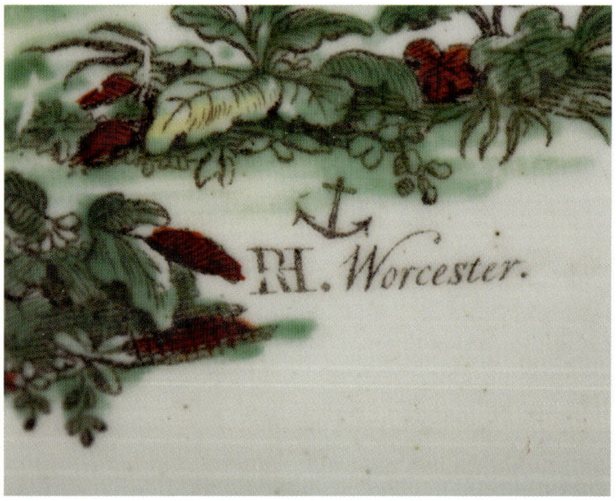

265 (detail)

265

Jug

1760–65
Ht 18 cm
1957.24.1.100

Pear-shaped with scroll handle and mask lip; transfer printed in black and colour washed with a version of 'The Tea Party' on one side and 'L'Amour' on the other; signed *RH. Worcester* with an anchor, a rebus for the name Holdship.

'L'Amour' is after a design by C.N. Cochin *fils* (1715–1790), published by François Vivares (1709–1780) and first used at Bow. Hancock has added the Neptune fountain, garden roller and dog.

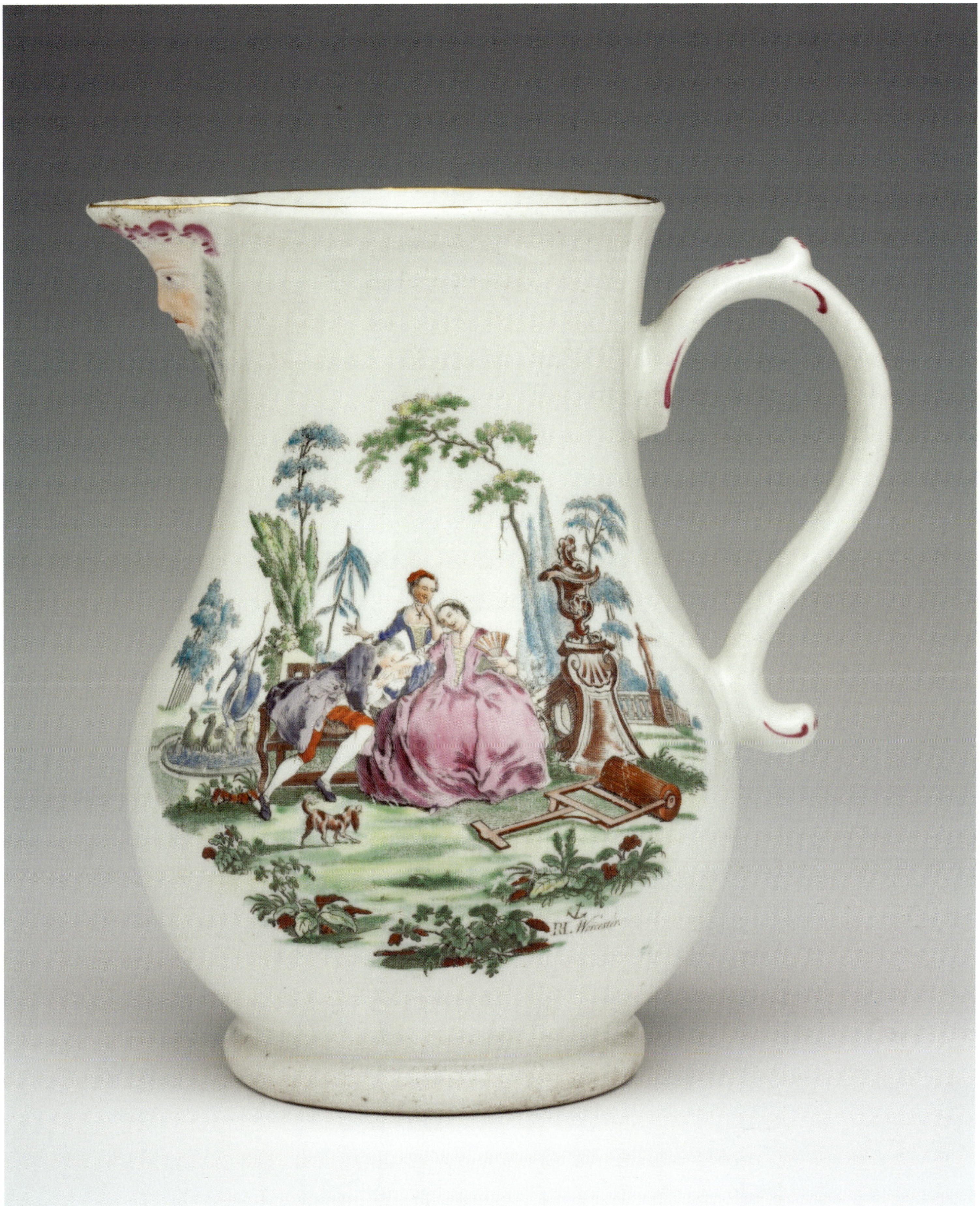

265

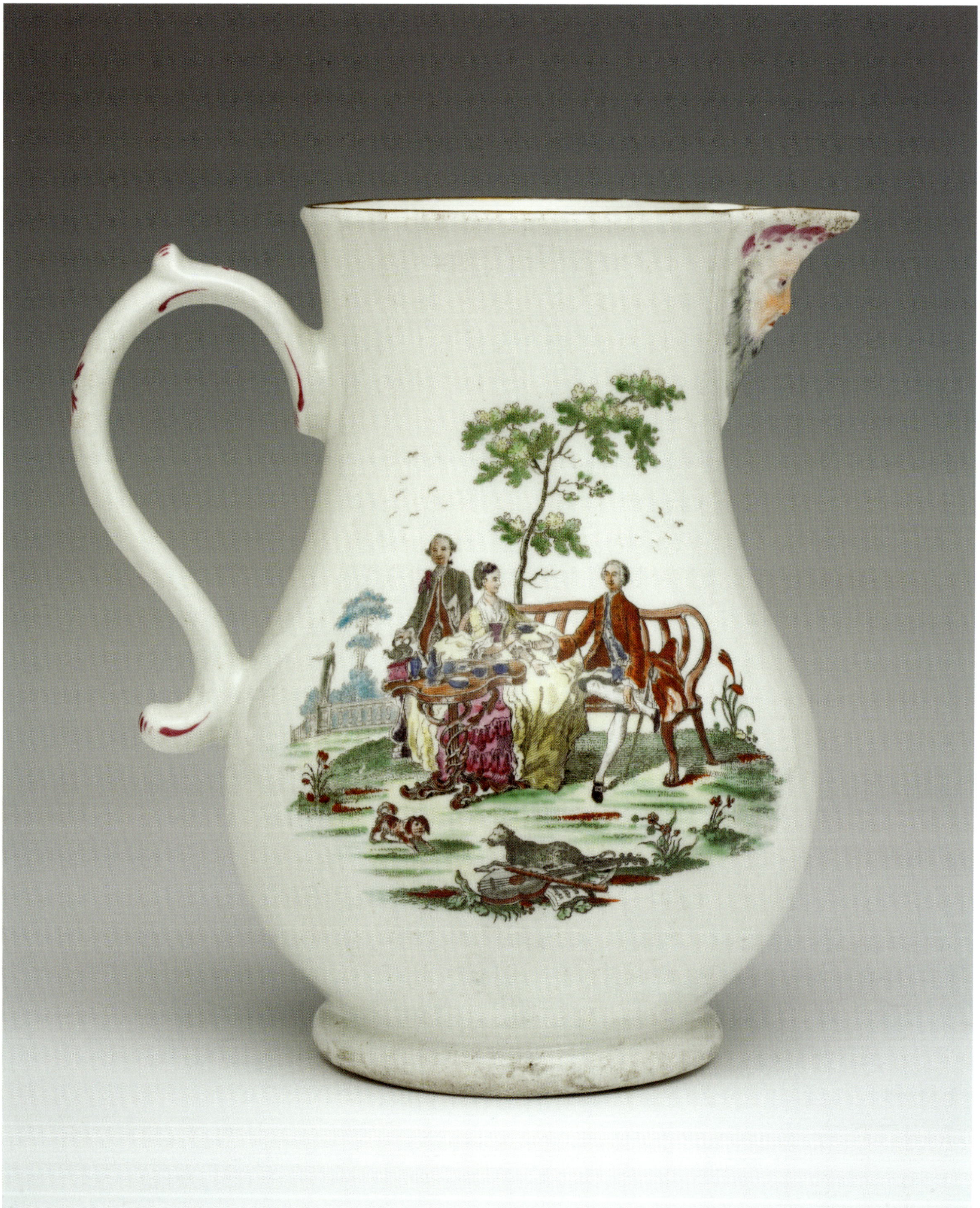

265

'The Tea Party' is the second of three distinct versions, first used at Worcester in 1758–60 and continuing for nearly twenty years. The first and earliest version can be traced to a tea party print, dated 24 November 1756, in a drawing book consisting of a collection of engravings and published by John Bowles & Sons of Cornhill, London, in 1757 or 1758 (fig. 23). The third version is closely based on an engraving by Anthony Walker (1726–1765) to illustrate *The Rape of the Lock* by Alexander Pope (1688–1744), published in 1712 (fig. 24).

REFERENCES

Reynolds 1999, pl. 14; Handley 1991, p. 62; Dawson 2007, p. 160; Guy-Jones 2013, pp. 18, 83.

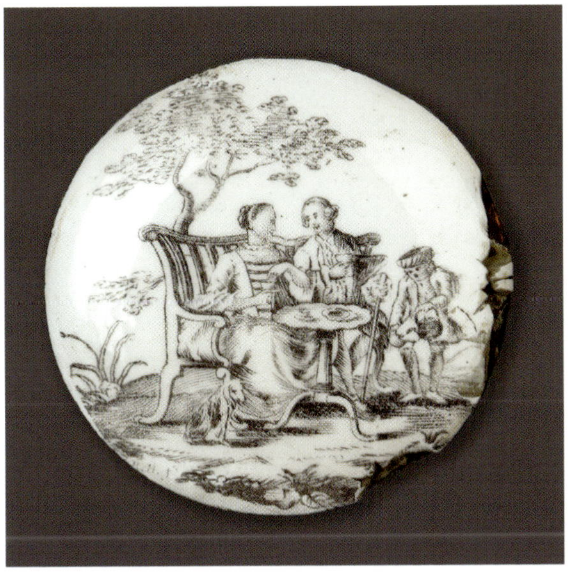

Fig. 22 *Tea party no. 1*, printed enamel watch-back, signed R H f © Museum of Royal Worcester Porcelain

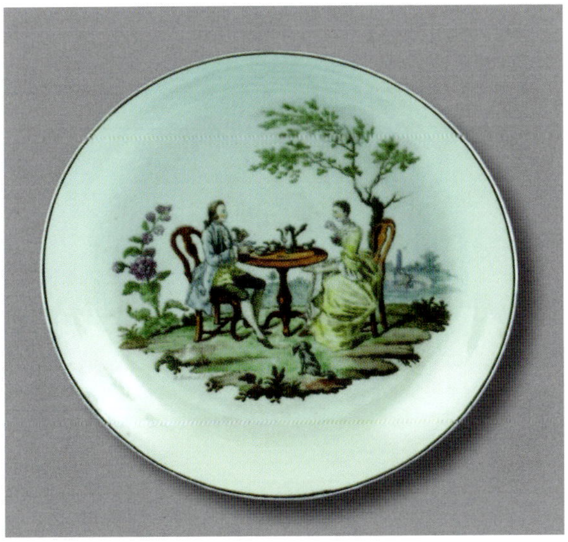

Fig. 23 *Tea Party no. 3*, printed plate. © Museum of Royal Worcester Porcelain

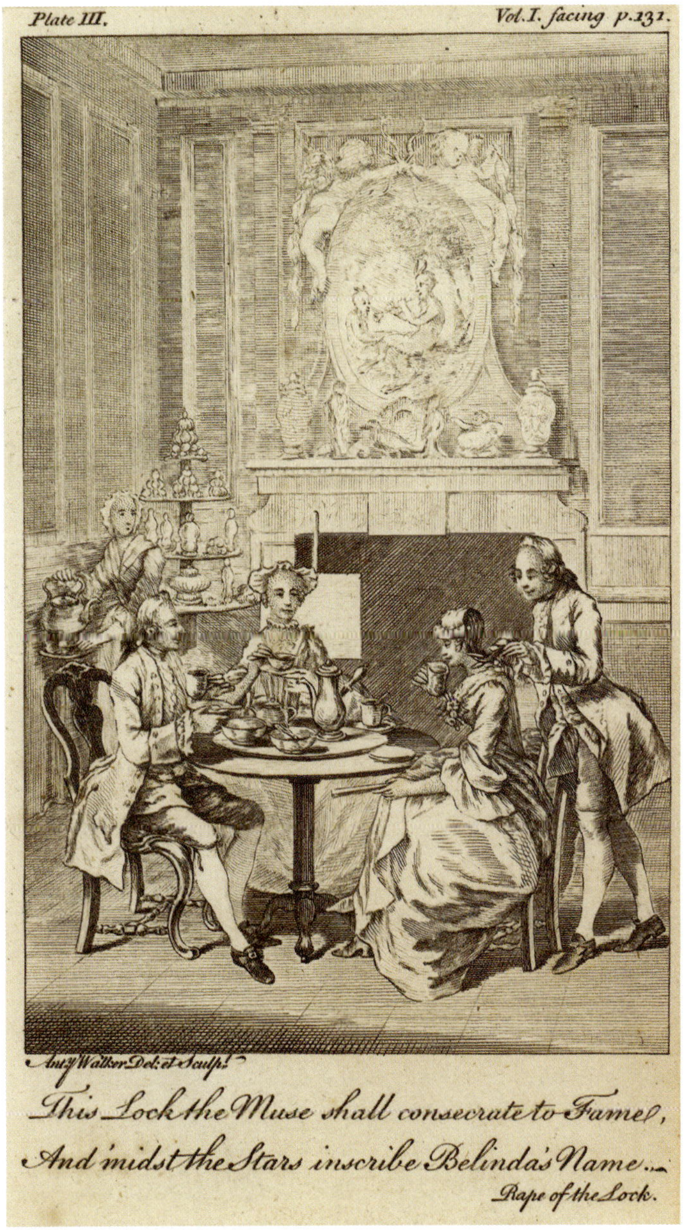

Fig. 24 Anthony Walker, *Tea Party no. 3*, engraving for an edition of *The Rape of the Lock* by Alexander Pope, first published 1712. Private collection

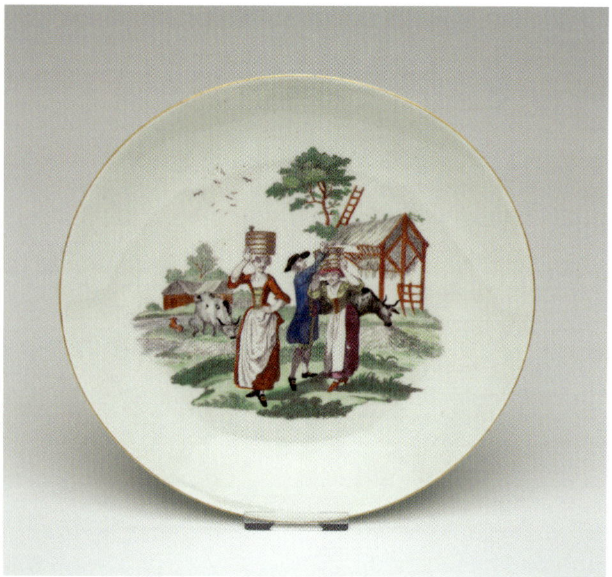

266

266

Cake dish

About 1770
Diam. 18.3 cm
1957.24.1.101

Gilt rim; decorated in a coloured transfer with two milkmaids with pails on their heads, a man with a ladder and two cows; a well-known design by Robert Hancock after a print published in 1766 by Robert Sayer (1725–1794).

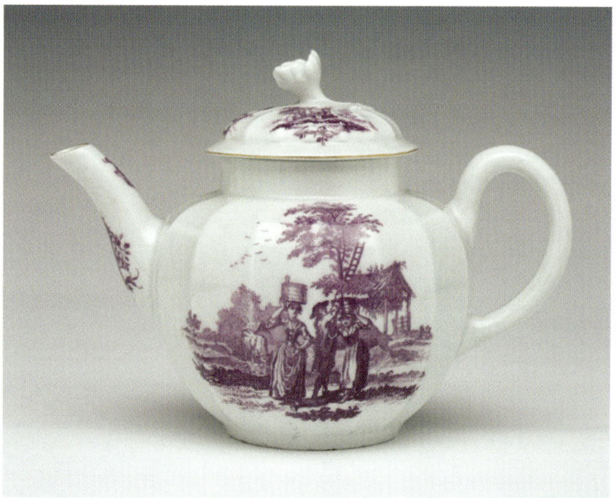

267

267

Teapot

1768–70
Ht 13.6 cm
Mark: fretted square
1957.24.1.92

Fluted, globular shape; printed in mauve with a milkmaid scene on one side and 'Rural Lovers' on the other; patterned escutcheon under spout. Hancock's design source was probably a print called *Rural Lovers*, published by François Vivares in 1760 after a painting by Thomas Gainsborough (1727–1788).

268

Vase with cover

About 1765
Ht 28.8 cm
1957.24.1.661

Hexagonal with conical knop; yellow ground, with panels, outlined in manganese, containing colour-washed prints of classical ruins, possibly inspired by the Grand Tour; *rouge de fer* diapering on neck and edge of cover.

PROVENANCE
H.W. Hughes Collection; Russell, Baldwin & Bright, Worcester, 6 December 1946, £145.

REFERENCE
Spero and Sandon 1996, pl. 265.

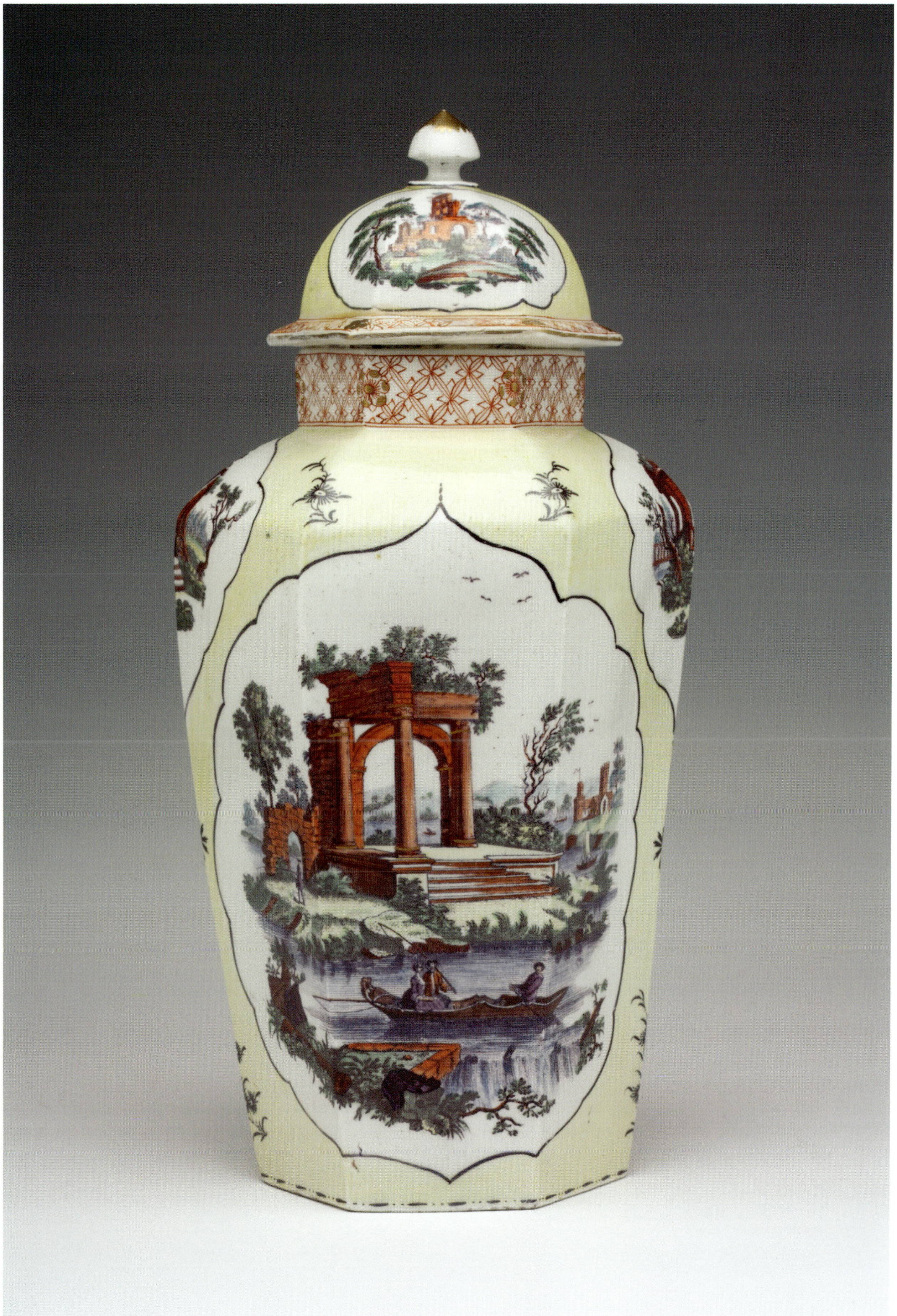

268

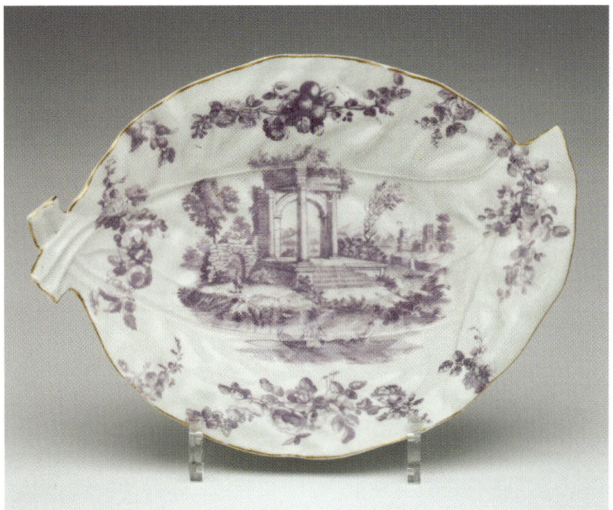

269

269

Dish

About 1765
Length 25.7 cm, width 19.4 cm
1957.24.1.796

Double-leaf form, gilt edge; decorated in mauve transfer print with floral festoons around border and classical ruins in the centre.

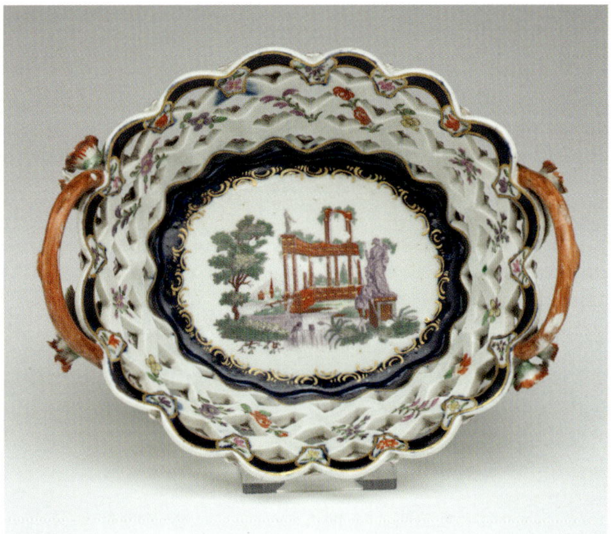

270

270

Oval basket

About 1770
Length 18.4 cm, width 15.4 cm
1957.24.1.571

Wavy edge, brown rustic handles; blue border around rim and well; pierced strapwork sides decorated with flower sprays; coloured transfer print of classical ruins in well.

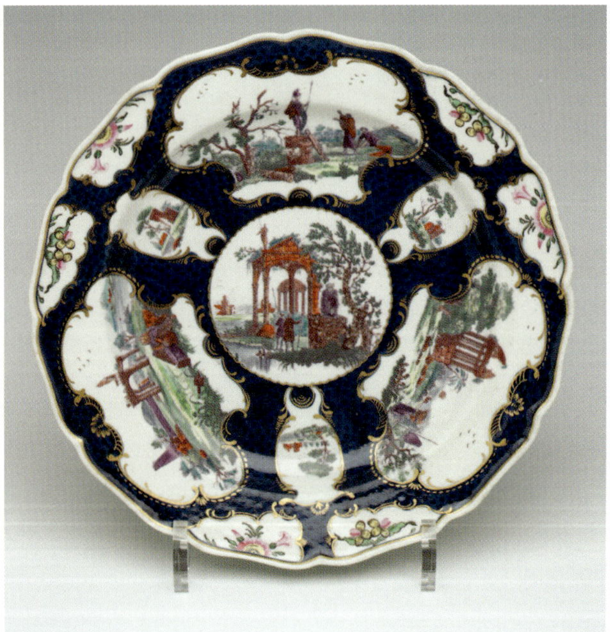

271

271

Plate

About 1770
Diam. 22.5 cm
Mark: fretted square
1957.24.1.153

Wavy rim, blue scale ground, rococo panels defined by scroll gilding, the larger ones with colour-washed transfer prints of classical ruins, the smaller with formalised European flowers.

REFERENCE
Spero and Sandon 1996, pl. 340.

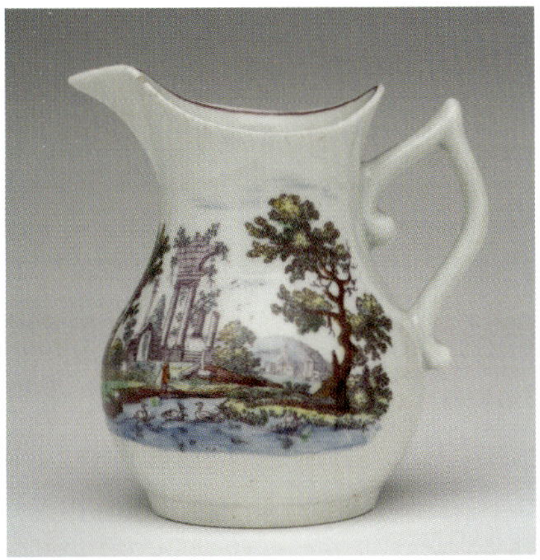

272

272

Cream jug

1760–62
Ht 9 cm
1957.24.1.87

Plain silver shape with peaked or wishbone handle; decorated on both sides with coloured-in printed rural scenes; narrow brown line inside rim.

REFERENCE
Spero and Sandon 1996, pl. 493.

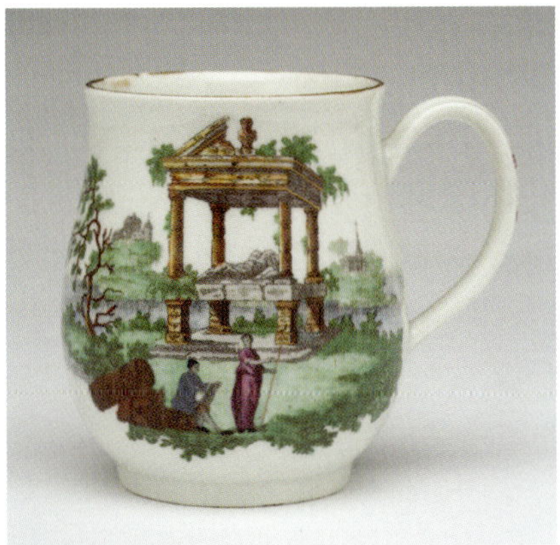

273

273

Mug

About 1768
Ht 8.9 cm
1957.24.1.966

Bell-shaped with ribbed loop handle, decorated in coloured transfer with classical ruins.

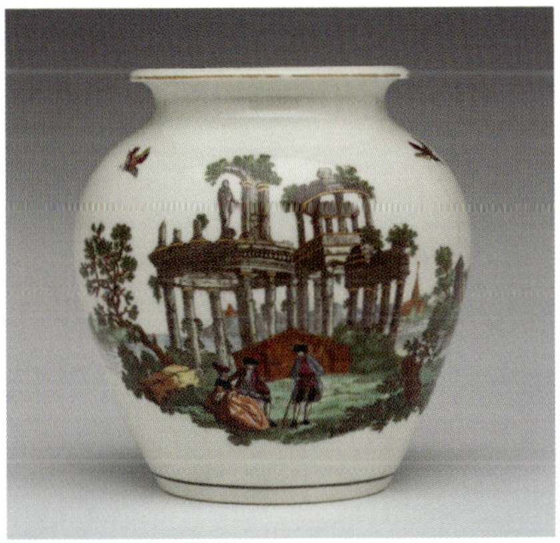

274

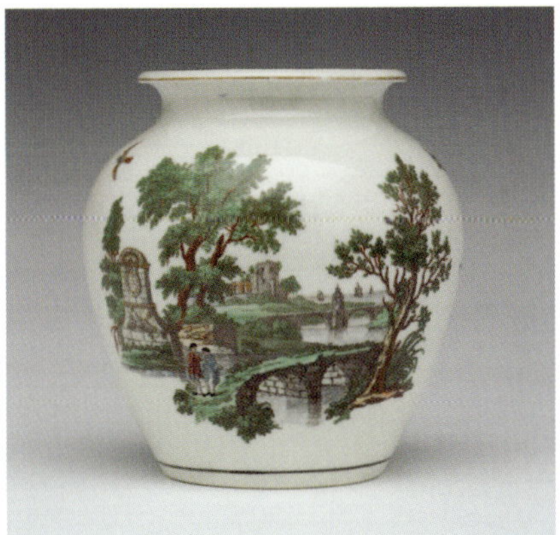

274

274

Vase

About 1768
Ht 12.7 cm
1957.24.1.968

Oviform with wide mouth; black and gilt lines around rim; decorated with coloured prints of classical ruins on both sides.

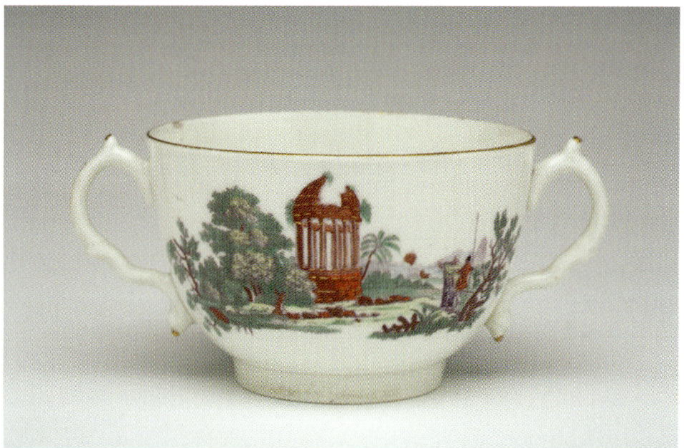

275

275

Broth bowl

About 1770
Ht 6.9 cm, diam. 10.4 cm
1957.24.1.970

Scroll handles and gilt rim; decorated on either side with classical ruins, figures and landscape in coloured transfer; cover and stand missing.

276

Dish

About 1768
Length 19.9 cm, width 16.4 cm
1957.24.1.790

Oval with gilt edge, rococo panels outlined with gilding; decorated with black prints of classical ruins, four printed floral sprays between.

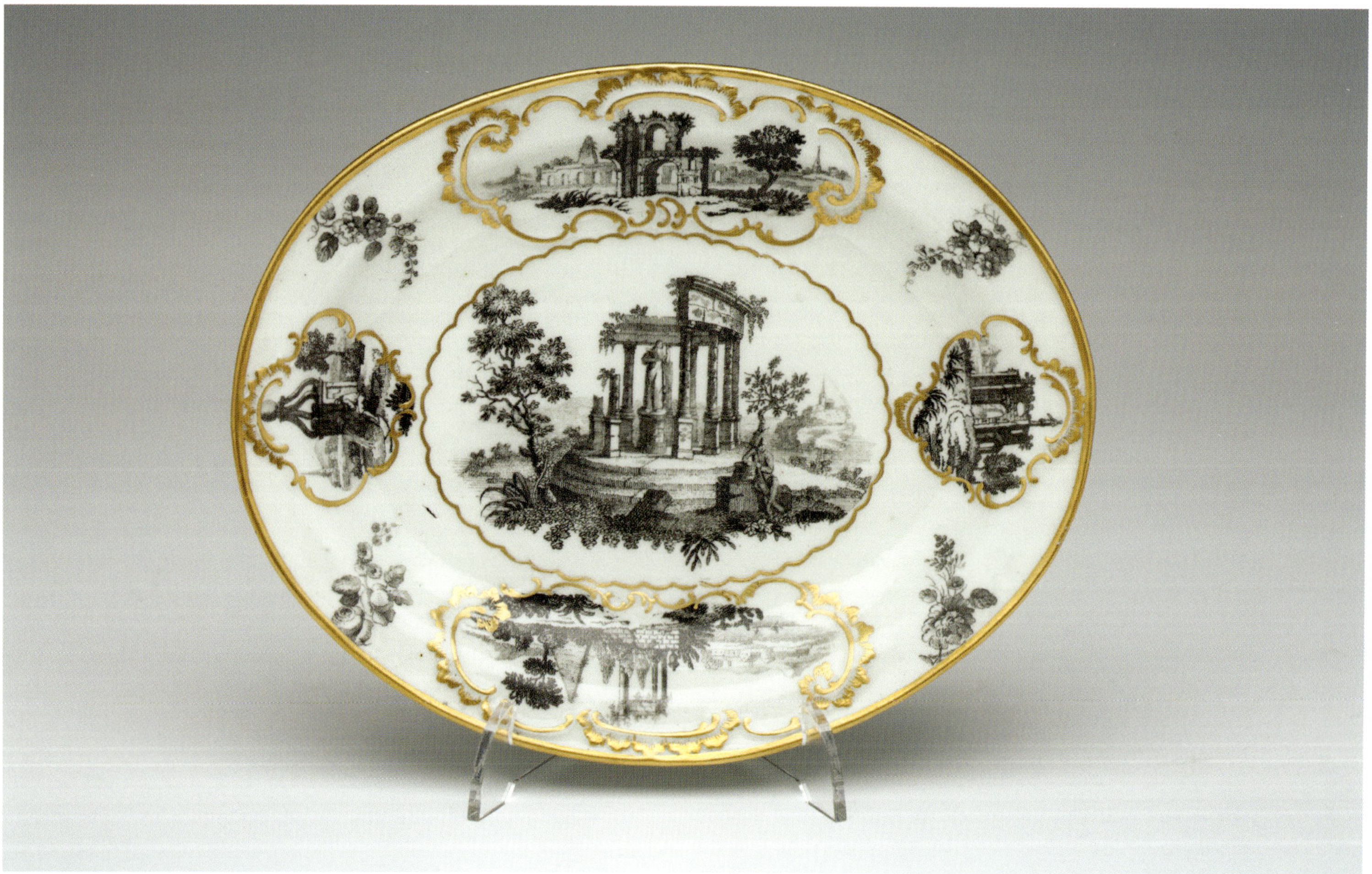

276

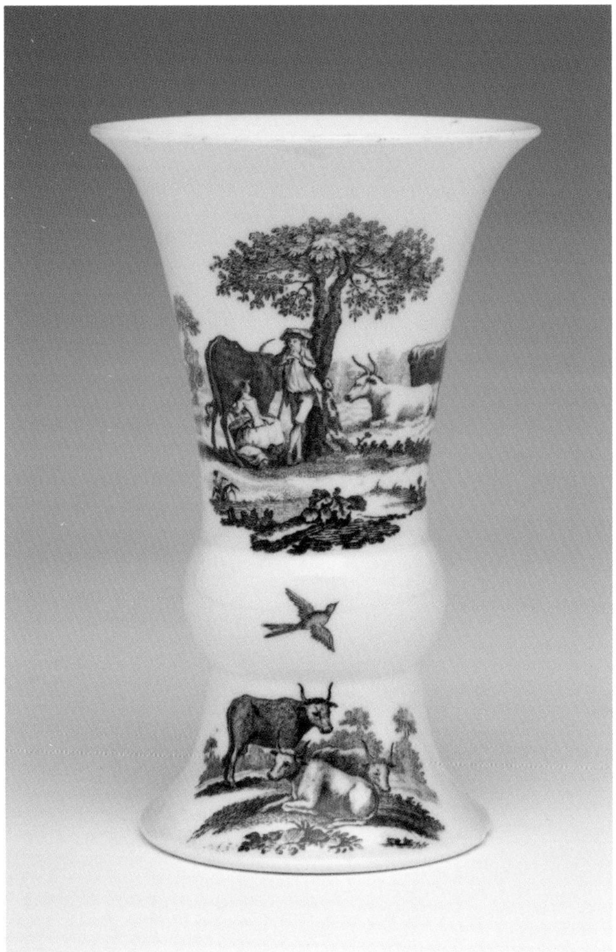

277

277

Vase

About 1772
Ht 15.3 cm
1957.24.1.799

Chinese bronze shape with print of milking scene by Robert Hancock,; after an engraving by Luke Sullivan (about 1725–1771), published in 1759.

278

Two porcelain tokens

1775–85
Diams. 3 cm and 2.6 cm
Mark: embossed letters *WPC*
1957.24.1.927

White, circular shape, inscribed in black, one for a shilling and the other for two shillings; probably issued about 1780, when there was a national shortage of coins. Similar tokens are in the Museum of Royal Worcester Porcelain (inv. 649).

REFERENCES
Spero and Sandon 1996, pl. 510; Sandon 1993, p. 340.

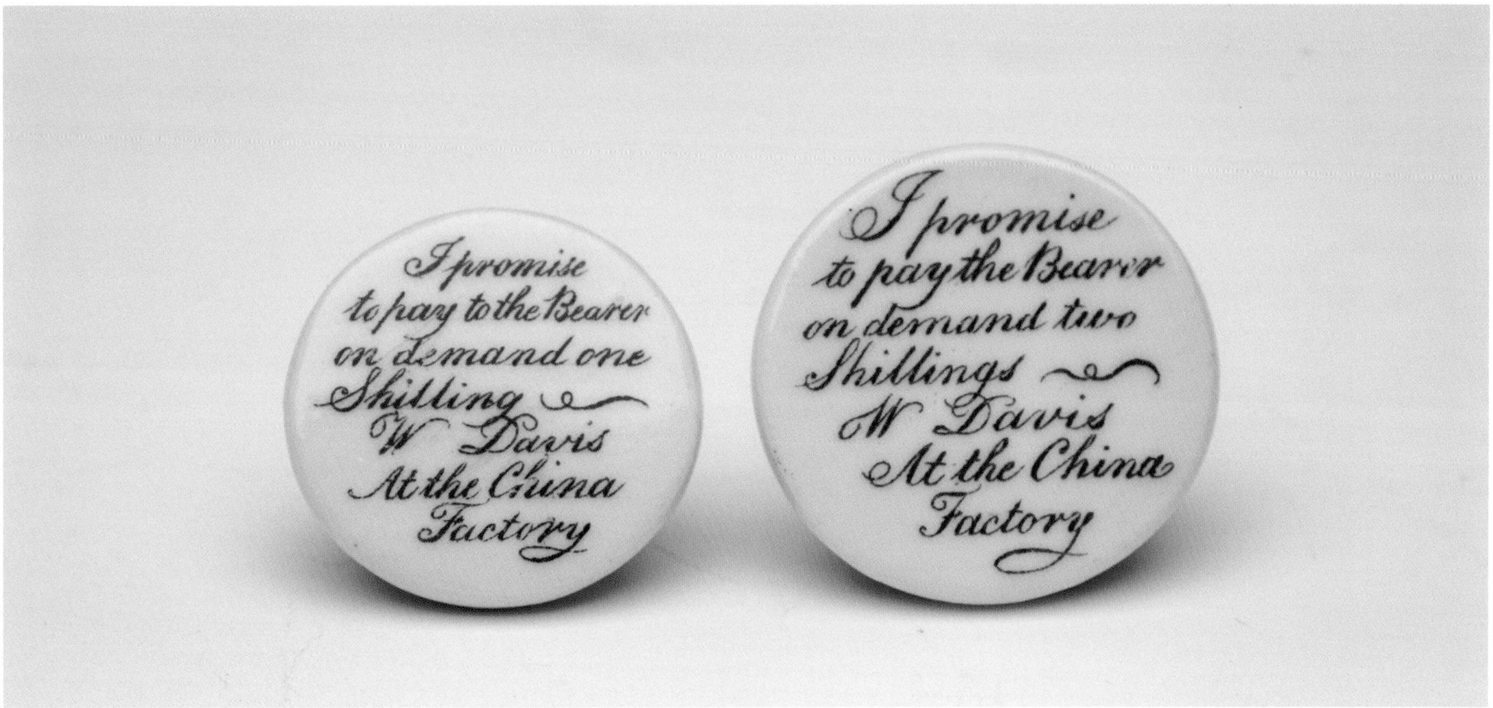

278

5

Chinese Influences from about 1760

WITH CHANGING TASTES, the earlier use of chinoiserie decoration gradually gave way to more patterns being made at Worcester that were direct copies of imported Chinese porcelain. The earlier Worcester designs of the 1750s relied heavily on *famille verte* and *famille rose* wares for inspiration, while those of the 1760s looked to Qianlong wares. This newer decoration lacked the spontaneity of previous designs and the palette was stronger and brighter.

Shapes became less elaborate as the fashion for the rococo faded. This was particularly noticeable in teapots, where the simple globular shape now prevailed and the pointed finial gave way to the flower knop. Worcester teapots were now considered to be superior to Chinese ones: the curved spout, which replaced the straight Chinese shape, poured well and the body was resistant to hot liquids and did not crack, unlike those from other English factories. It is known from contemporary invoices that teapots were often sold by themselves, as well as being part of full tea services.

Detailed designs with Chinese figures painted in a *famille rose* palette on teawares became known in the eighteenth century as 'Mandarin' style, usually having a different scene on either side of each piece. In the Netherlands, 'Gentleman's Mandarin' referred to designs with elaborate gilding and 'Peasant's Mandarin' to a simpler style. Originally the subjects were probably borrowed from Chinese literature, folklore and theatre, but the meaning would usually have been lost on British tea drinkers.

Numerous Chinese patterns were produced at Worcester but by the 1780s figure patterns had declined in favour of more formal floral designs, a style often referred to as *Compagnie des Indes* after the British East India Company, which continued to import Chinese export porcelain into England in large quantities.

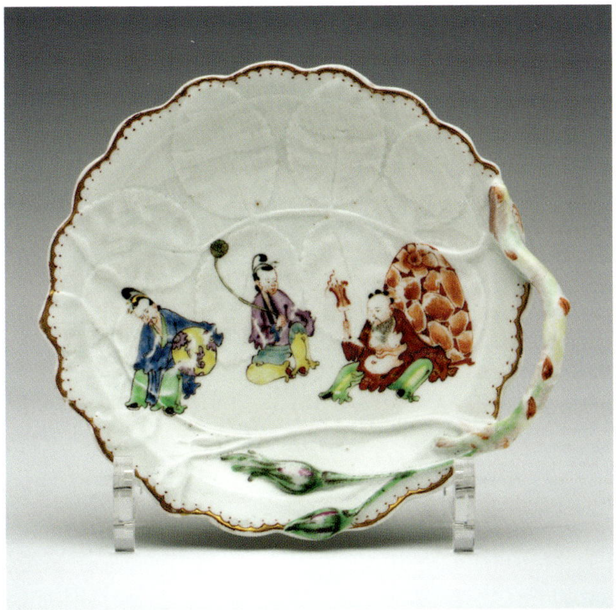

279

279

Sweetmeat dish

About 1760
Length 16.1 cm, width 14.7 cm
1957.24.1.336

'Blind Earl' moulded shape; enamelled in Chinese taste with three seated figures, including Pu-Tai, a Buddhist monk, Ho-Shang and Guan-Yin, symbolising compassion. For a teapot in the same pattern see Spero and Sandon 1996, no. 116.

280

Leaf-shaped dish

About 1760
Length 21.2 cm, width 15.8 cm
1957.24.1.332

Narrow red and gold border; decorated with a Chinese magician and other figures with a table between. This 'Magician' pattern is mainly found on various leaf-shaped dishes.

REFERENCE
Spero and Sandon 1996, no. 139.

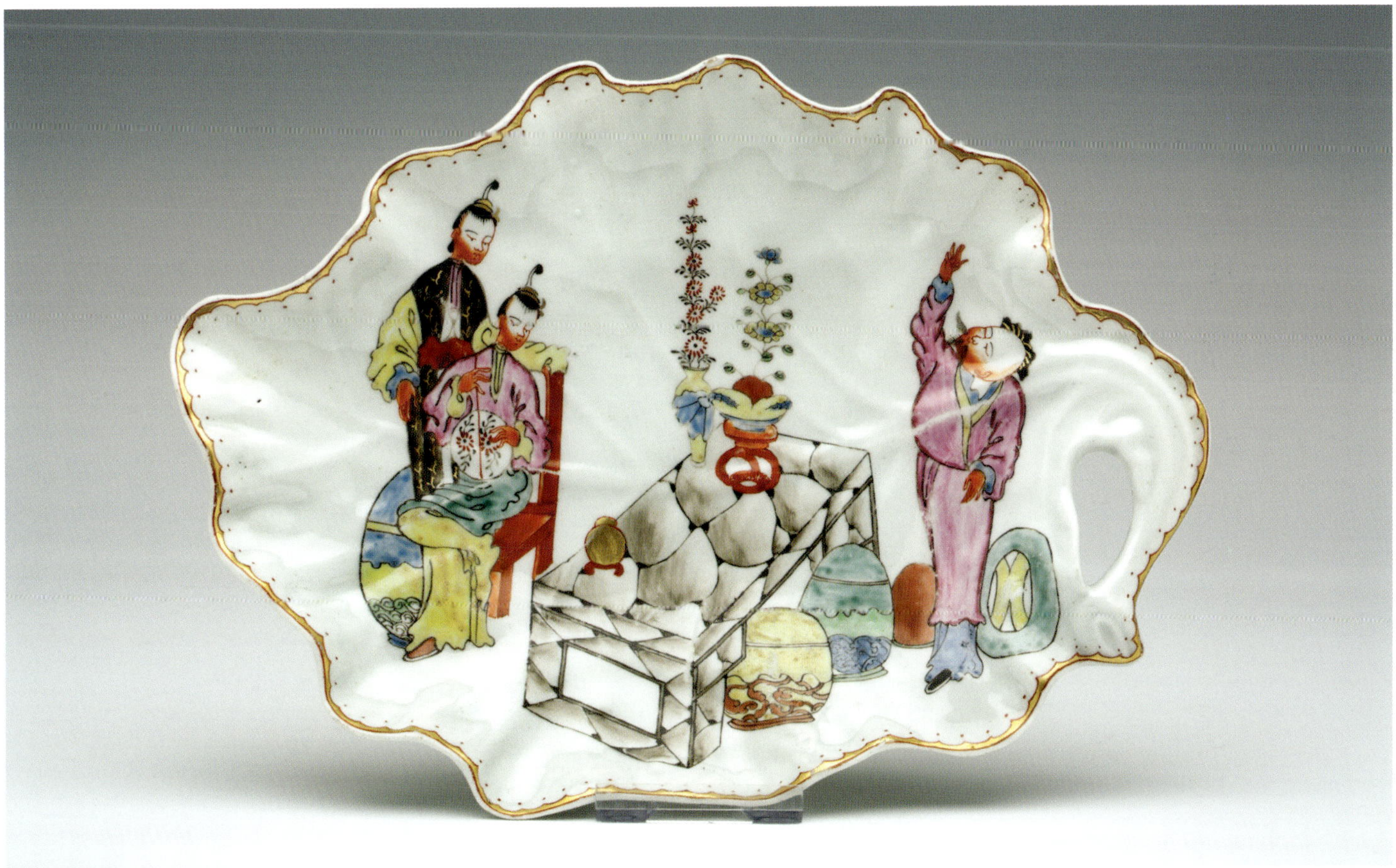

280

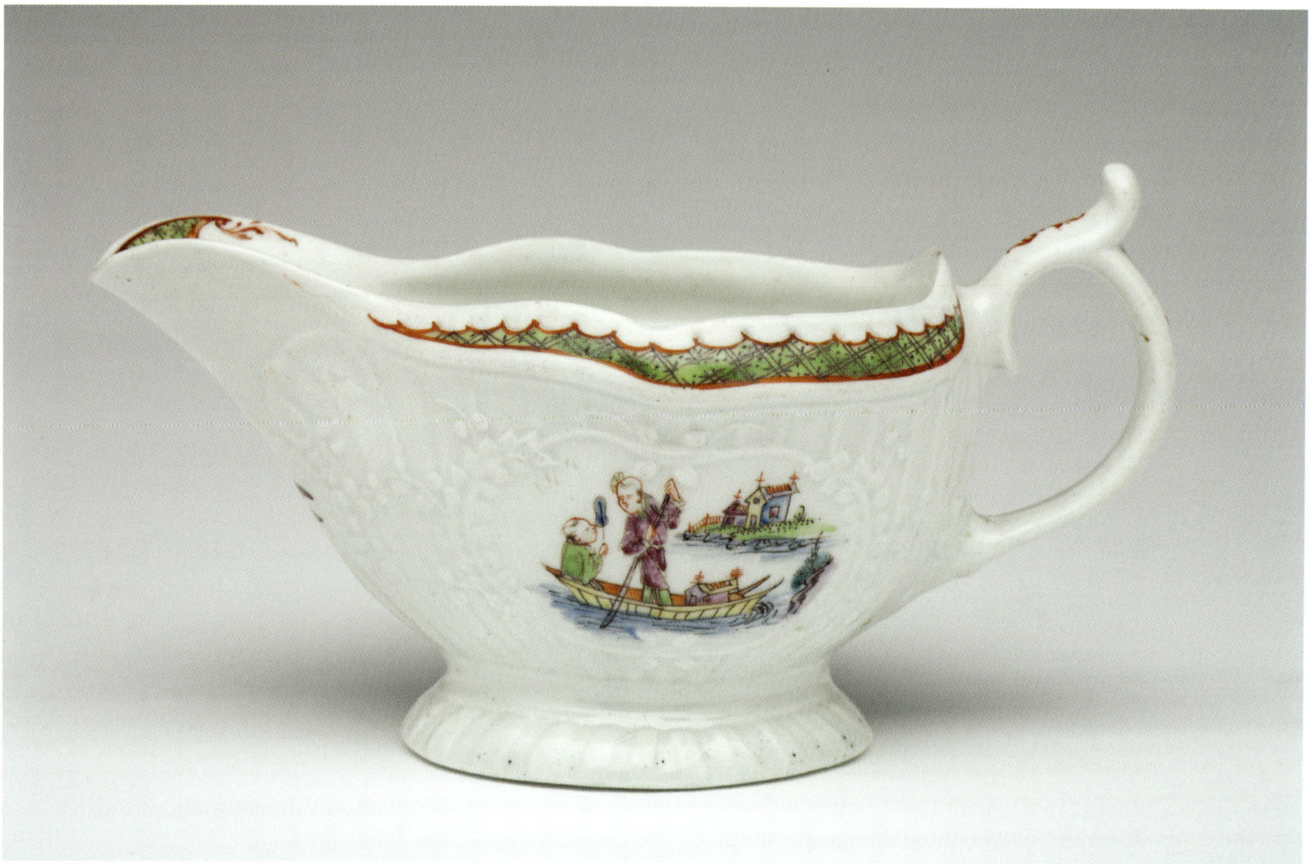

281

281

Sauceboat

About 1758
Ht 9.3 cm, length 17.3 cm, width 9.8 cm
1957.24.1.318

Irregular wavy rim, scroll handle, moulded panels with a Chinese man punting a boat on one side, and a landscape on other.

282

Sauceboat

About 1758
Ht 10.4 cm, length 19.8 cm, width 10.4 cm
1957.24.1.286

Scroll handle, vertical moulding; purple outlined cartouches decorated on one side with a gardener attending a plant and on the other with Chinese plants.

283

Teapot and lid

About 1768
Ht 13.5 cm
1957.24.1.325

Plain loop handle, decorated on both sides with a woman seated at a loom; replacement brass knop.

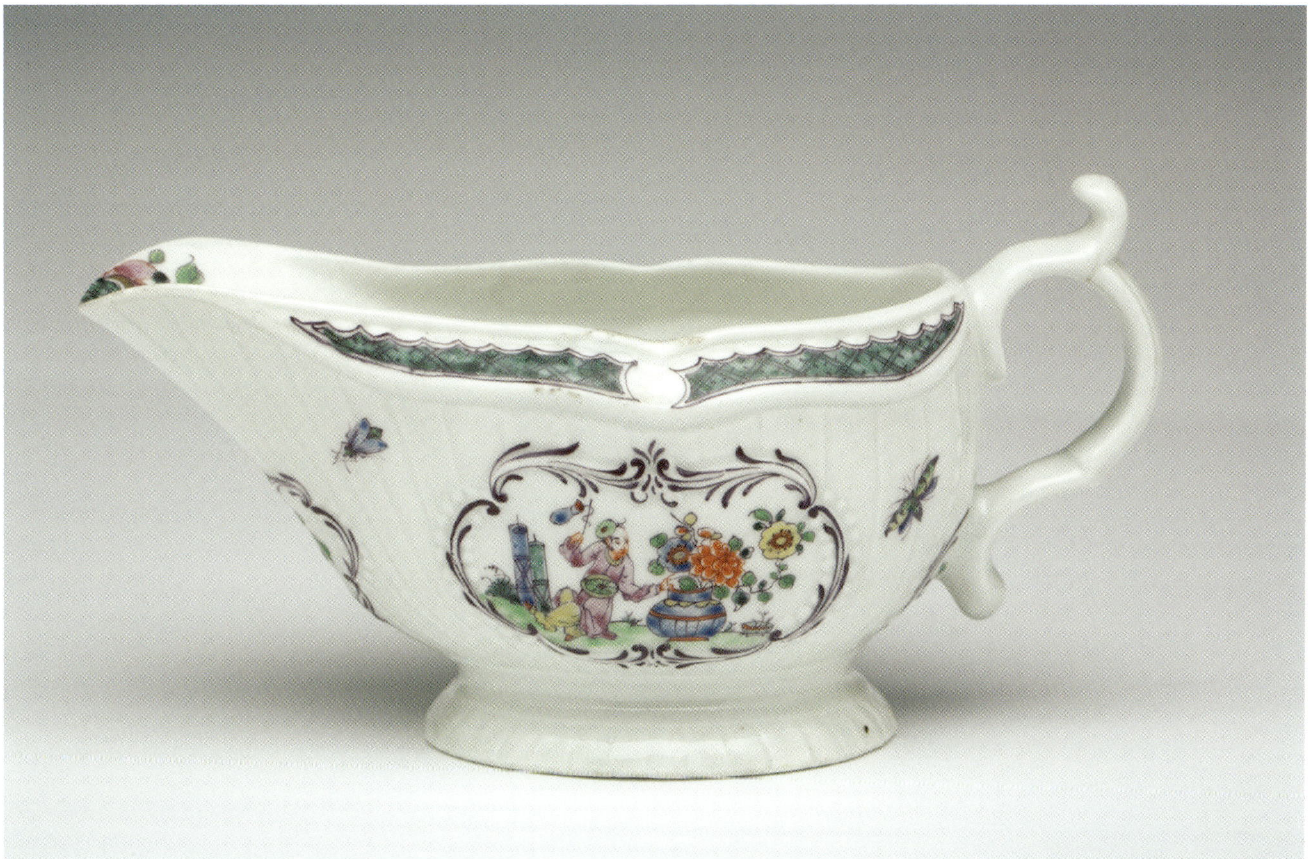

282

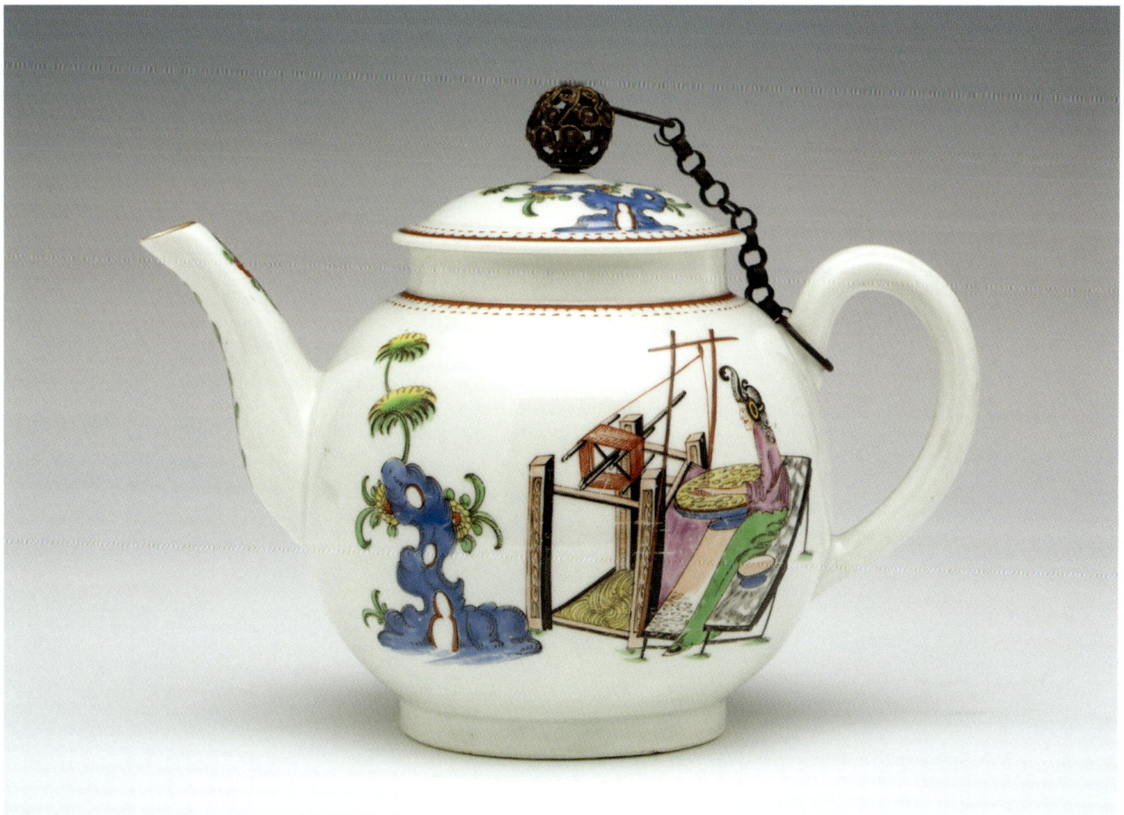

283

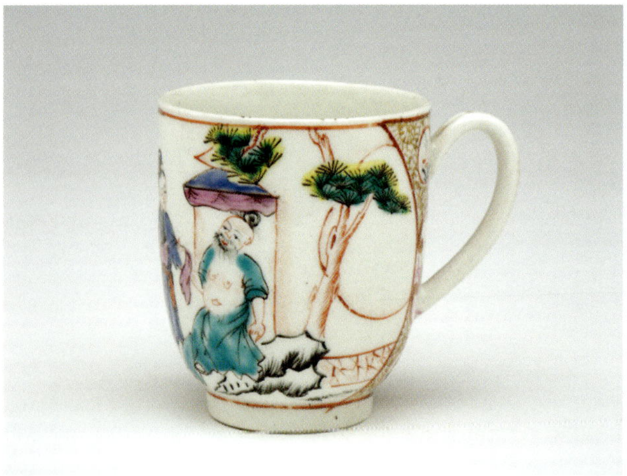

284

284

Coffee cup

1765–70
Ht 6.5 cm, diam. 5.2 cm
1957.24.1.949

Ribbed loop handle surrounded by arabesque gilding; front painted with scene of an elderly Oriental man, partially dressed, and a female attendant nearby holding out mauve cloth.

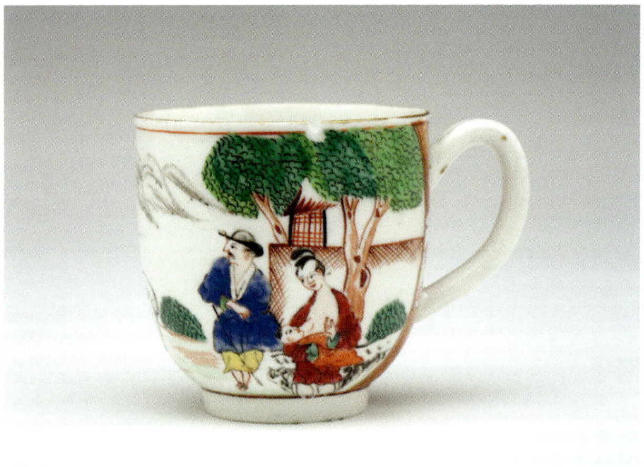

285

285

Coffee cup

1768–78
Ht 6.4 cm, diam. 6.1 cm
1957.24.1.956

Ribbed loop handle surrounded by *rouge de fer* border diapered in gold; painted with a seated woman suckling a baby, and a man in blue beside her gazing out at two sepia sheep.

286

Teabowl and saucer

1780–85
Bowl ht 4.4 cm, diam. 7.9 cm; saucer diam. 11.9 cm
1957.24.1.338

Border of arabesque gilding, with panels of black and red flowers and foliage surrounding Chinese figures.

287

Cake dish

1775–80
Diam. 17.9 cm
1957.24.1.330

Broad border with panels of carmine flowers alternating with scroll gilding; central scene with three Chinese women and two children with two white rabbits.

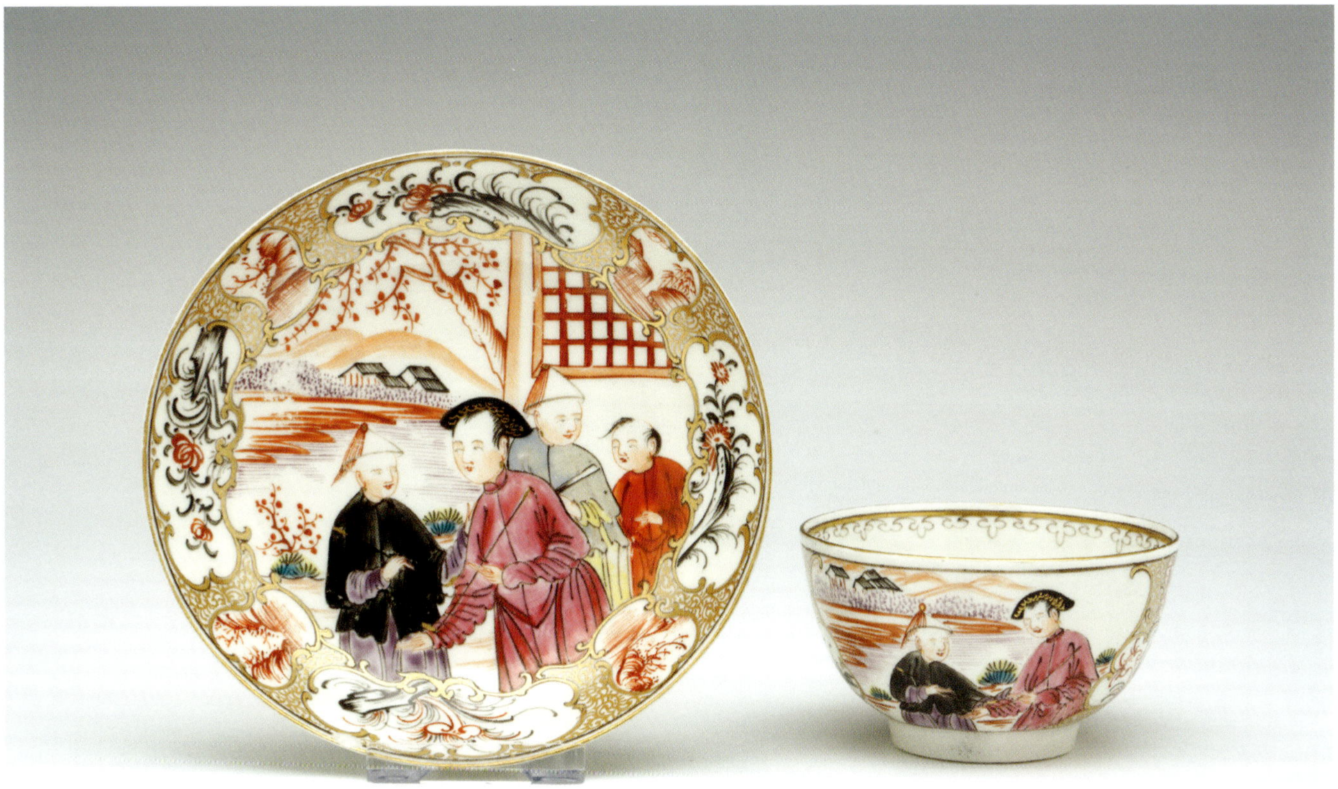

286

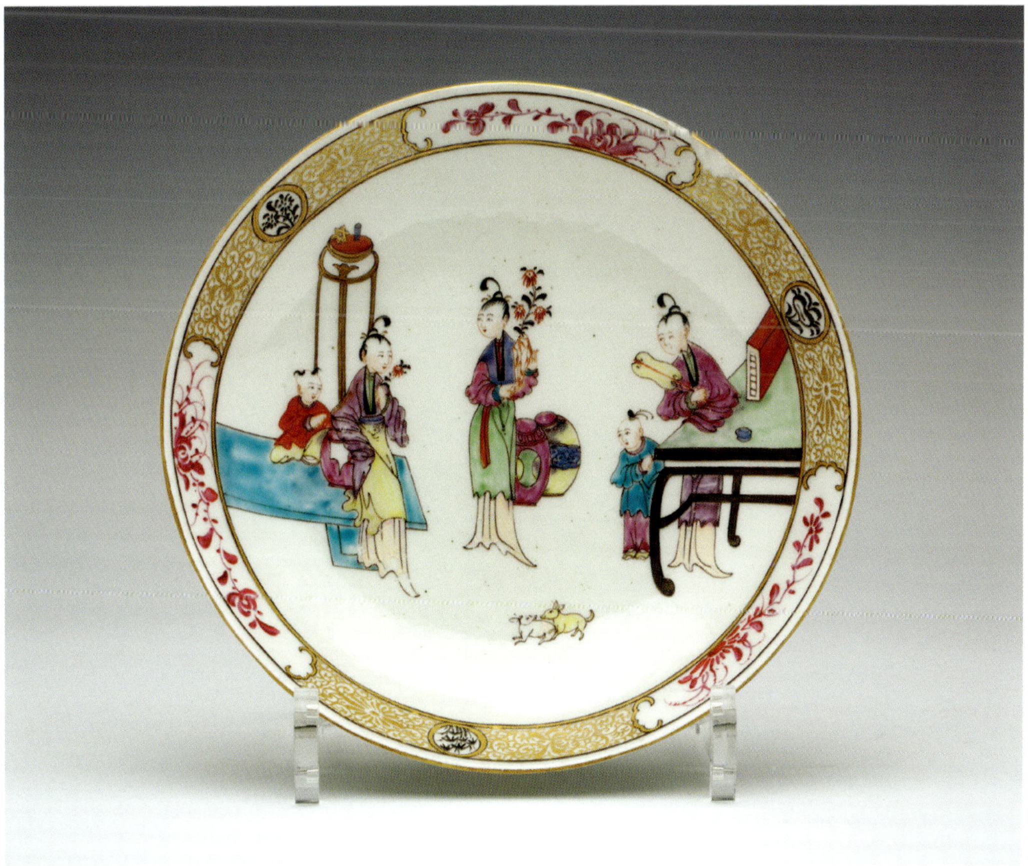

287

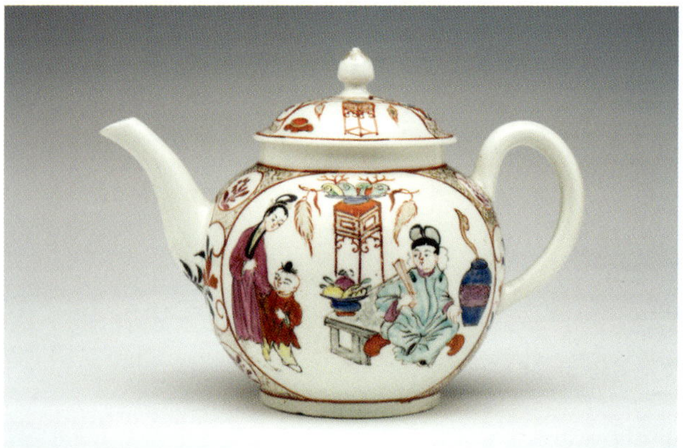

288

288

Teapot and lid

About 1770
Ht 13.8 cm
1957.24.1.323

Globular, plain loop handle, conical knop; decorated with panels of Chinese figures, arabesque gilding between.

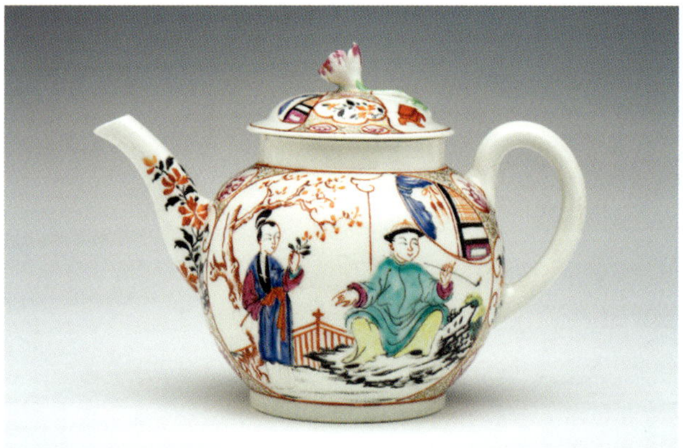

289

289

Teapot and lid

About 1765
Ht 13.9 cm
1957.24.1.329

Globular, plain loop handle, rosebud knop, arabesque gilding with carmine sprays around spout and handle; decorated with Chinese figures including a man smoking a pipe.

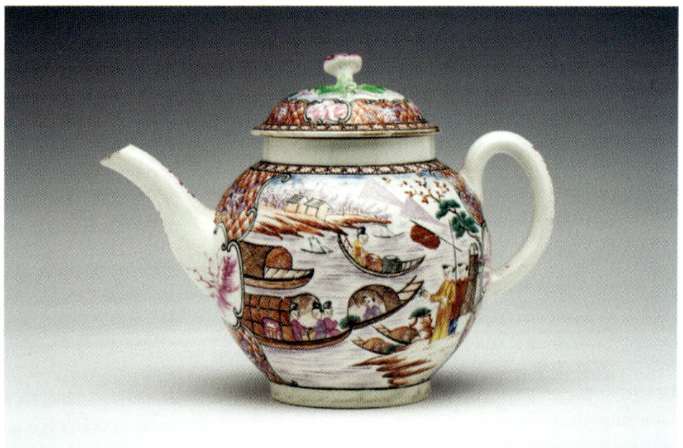

290

290

Teapot and lid

About 1775
Ht 16.6 cm
1957.24.1.911

Brick-red scale ground, reserves with busy Chinese river scenes with sampans and canoes; panels with carmine landscapes below spout and handle.

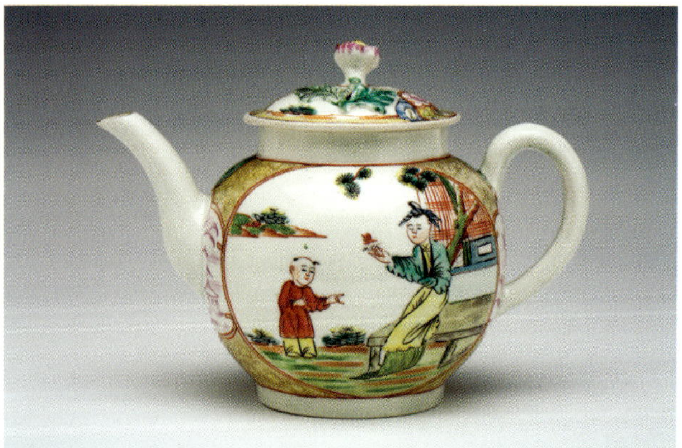

291

291

Teapot and lid

1775–80
Ht 13.1 cm
1957.24.1.676

Unusual yellow scroll ground, with panels of carmine landscape scenes around reserves painted with seated Oriental woman and child; possibly decorated outside the Worcester factory.

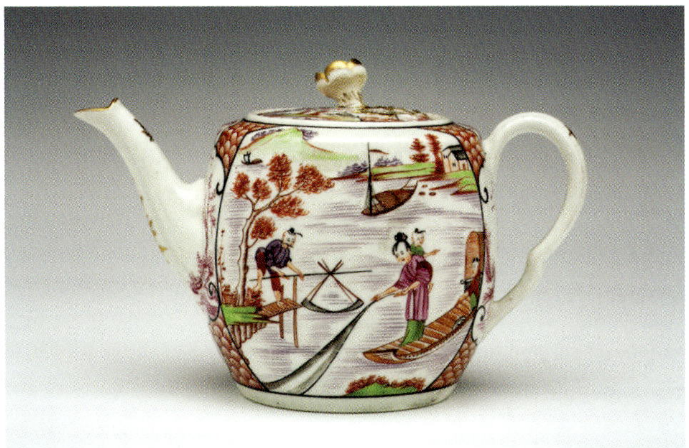

292

292

Teapot and lid

1770–75
Ht 12.8 cm
1957.24.1.913

Barrel shaped with flush lid, rosebud knop; upward red scale ground around panels with river scenes of a woman with child on her back fishing with a net from a sampan, man fishing from jetty.

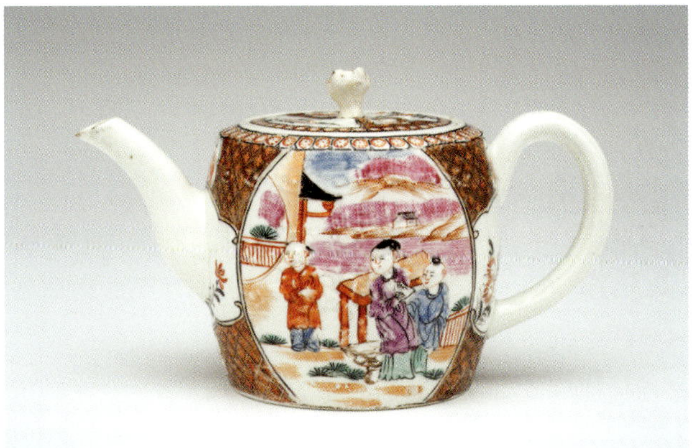

293

293

Teapot and lid

1760–70
Ht 9.5 cm
1957.24.1.306

Barrel shaped, flush lid, rosebud knop; Chinese figure decoration ignores florally moulded body; orange ground colour diapered with black diamonds.

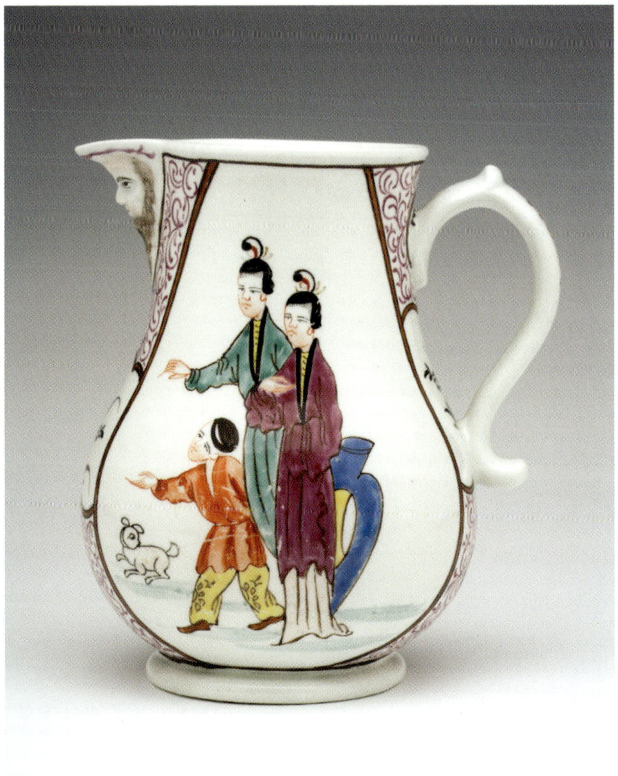

294

294

Jug

About 1765
Ht 17.1 cm
1957.24.1.331

Puce scrolling and oval reserves with black flower sprays around masked spout and handle; on either side, large pear-shaped reserves with elongated Chinese figures and a boy with a small white dog.

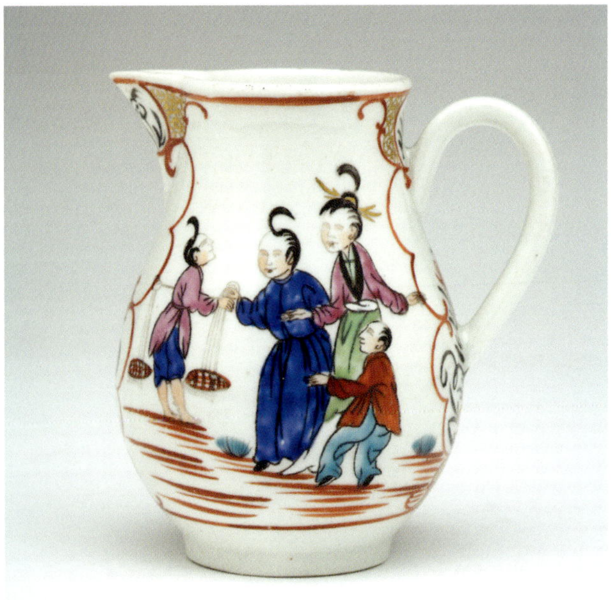

295

295

Cream jug

1768–75
Ht 8.9 cm
1957.24.1.312

Ovoid with ribbed loop handle; decorated on one side with two Chinese women and a child bargaining with a man holding scales; on reverse, a woman looking through latticed window at a child.

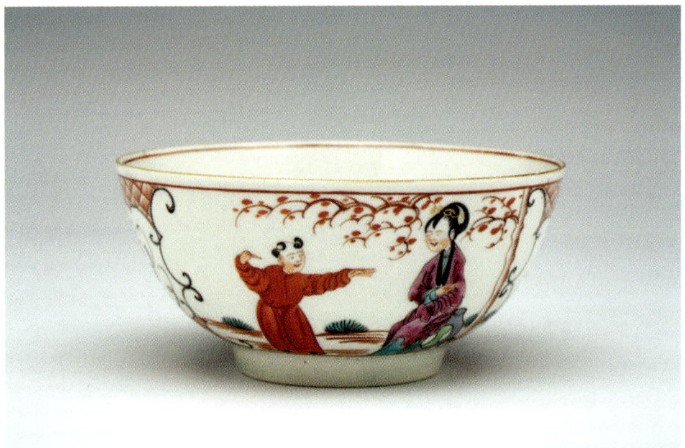

296

296

Bowl

1770–80
Ht 5.4 cm, diam. 11.5 cm
1957.24.1.313

Two large panels outlined in black scrolls, with Chinese figures; two smaller ones with red, lozenge scale ground and black and red flower sprays.

297

Tea canister and cover

About 1765
Ht 15.2 cm
1957.24.1.291

Arabesque gilding and formalised brick-red leaves surround panels of Chinese figures; on one side a tall woman with a man seated beside her, spotted dog at her feet, and on the other a woman holding a tumbler and salver, with a child clutching her dress.

Worcester started to make tea jars or canisters in about 1760–62 but their inclusion in a tea service was very much an exception. They became more common in the 1770s, but were still not always included; it is thought that they were not often made after 1780.

PROVENANCE
H.W. Hughes Collection; Russell, Baldwin & Bright, Worcester, 6 December 1945, £21 (pair).

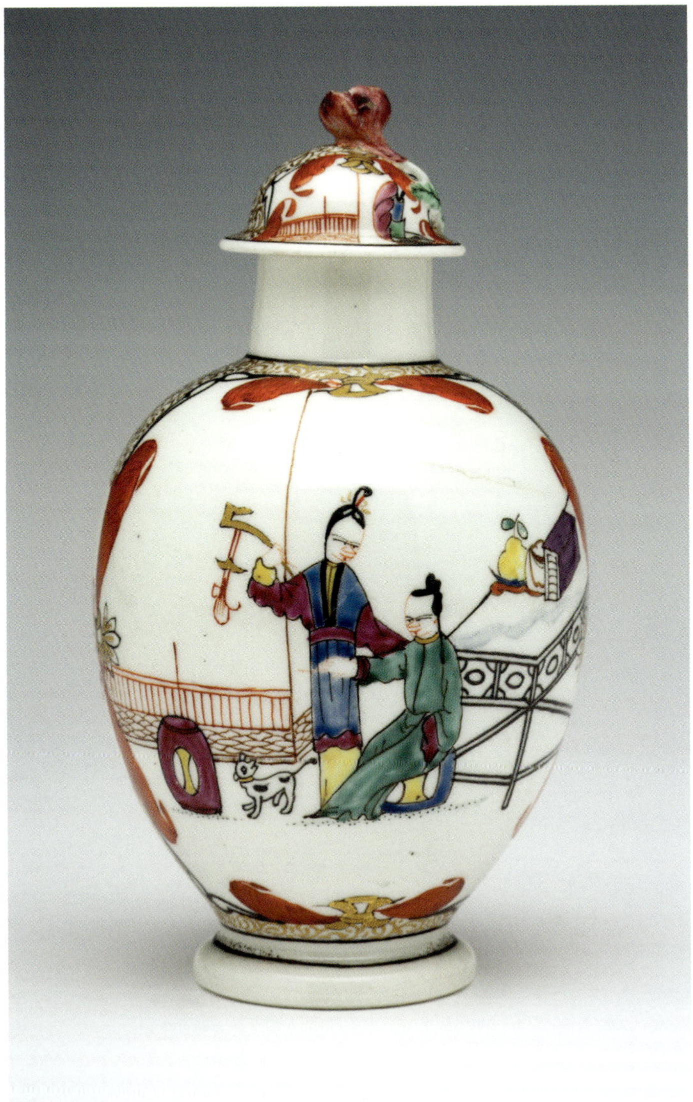

297

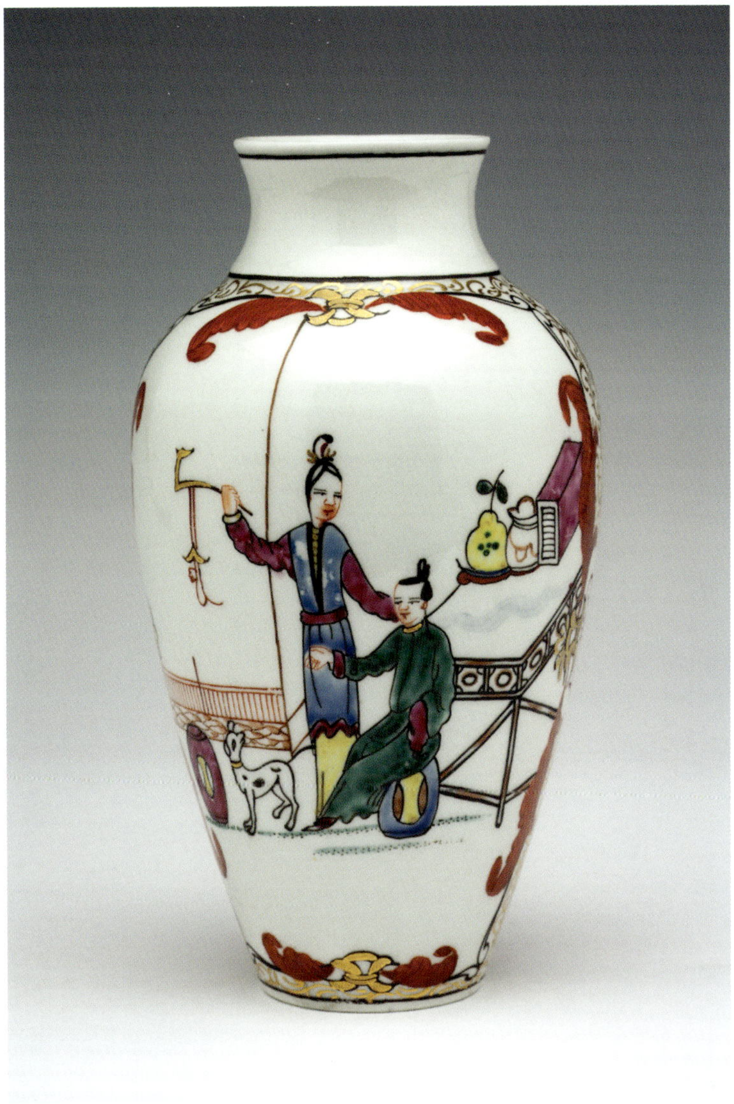

298

298

Vase

1765–70
Ht 18 cm
1957.24.1.281

Slender ovoid shape; two main panels with 'Long Eliza' figures and a spotted dog, separated by elaborate gilding with brick red formalised leaves; the same decoration as no. 297.

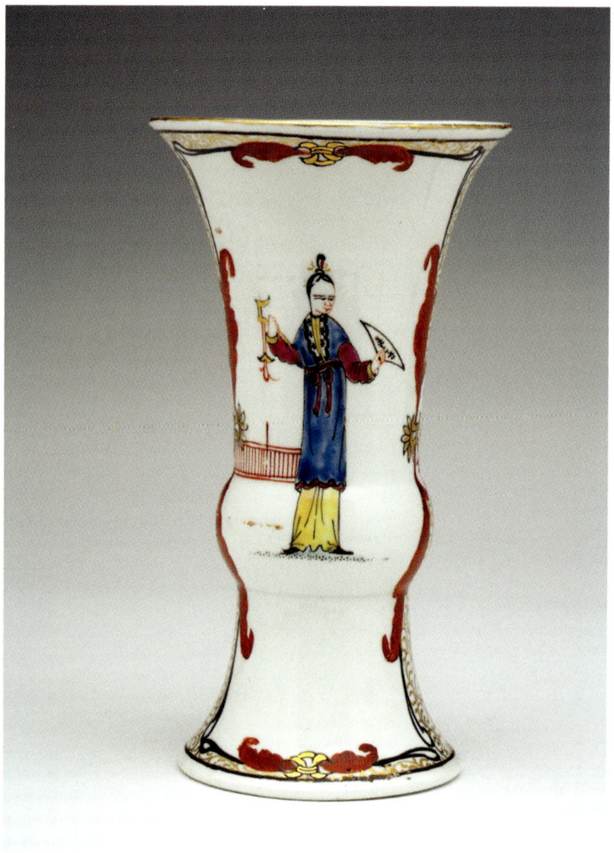

299

299

Vase

1765–70
Ht 16.3 cm
1957.24.1.285

Chinese bronze beaker shape; decorated with panels of 'Long Eliza' figures, separated by brick-red leaf-scroll borders.

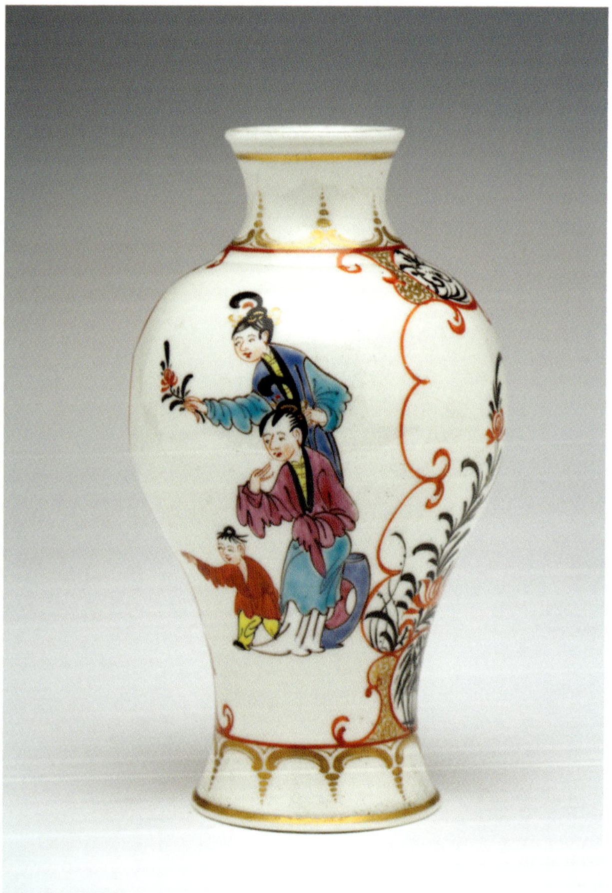

300

300

Vase

About 1780
Ht 12.8 cm
1957.24.1.327

Baluster shape with narrow neck; painted with Chinese figures in panels, separated by red and black feathery plants.

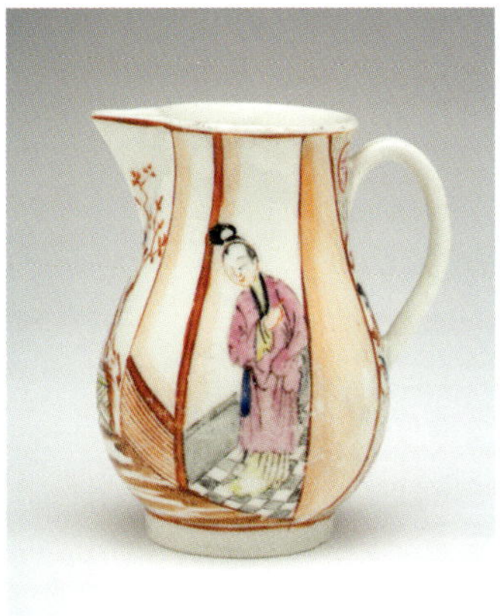

301

301

Cream jug

1770–75
Ht 9.3 cm
1957.24.1.1044

Ovoid, plain loop handle; painted with Oriental figures, a gardener tending plants with a woman looking on.

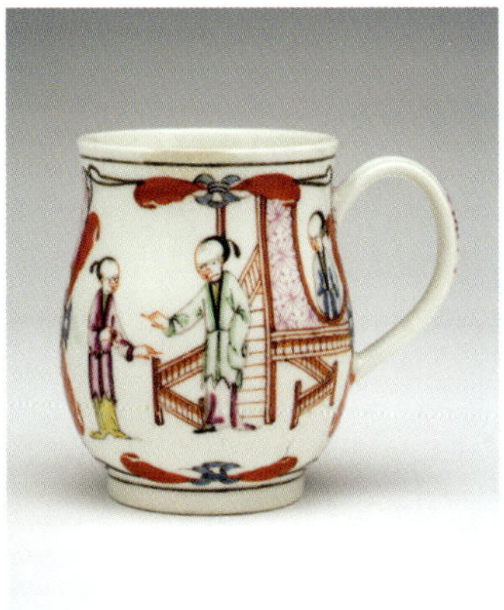

302

302

Mug

1765–70
Ht 8.9 cm
1957.24.1.328

Bell-shaped, ribbed loop handle; decorated on each side with a Chinese man at foot of stairs holding out right hand to a woman, another woman looks through window behind him.

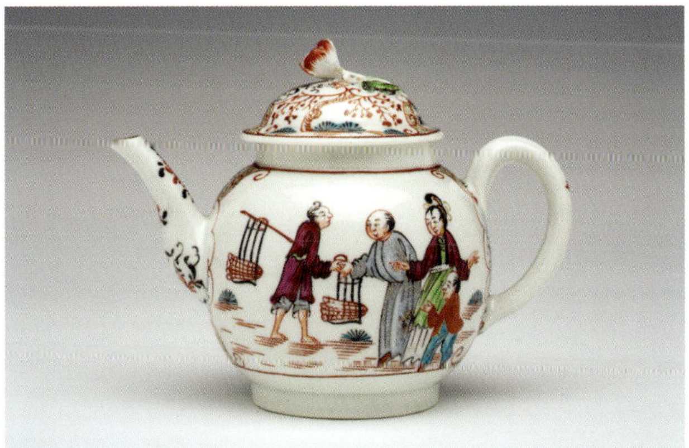

303

303

Teapot and lid

1768–75
Ht 12.6 cm
1957.24.1.311

Plain loop handle, rosebud knop; decorated with a fisherman selling his wares to a family; on reverse, a Chinese woman looking through a latticed window at a child.

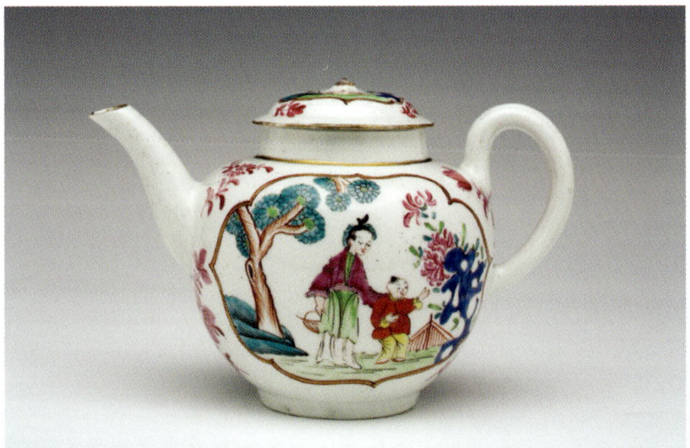

304

304

Teapot and lid

About 1765
Ht 12.7 cm
1957.24.1.288

Cartouches outlined in red and gold, each with a woman standing below a tree, holding a basket in her right hand and clutching a child in her left, red fence and blue holed rock with pink flowers to right; carmine foliage around spout and handle.

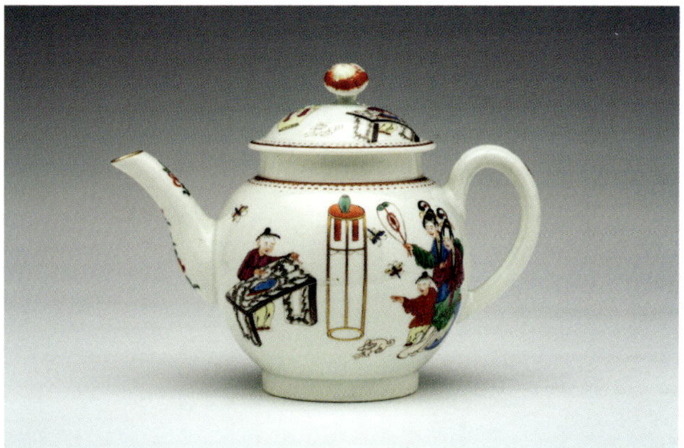
305

305

Teapot and lid

About 1770
Ht 13.6 cm
1957.24.1.282

Plain loop handle, rosebud knop; decorated with two Chinese women and children chasing butterflies, with a small white dog at their feet.

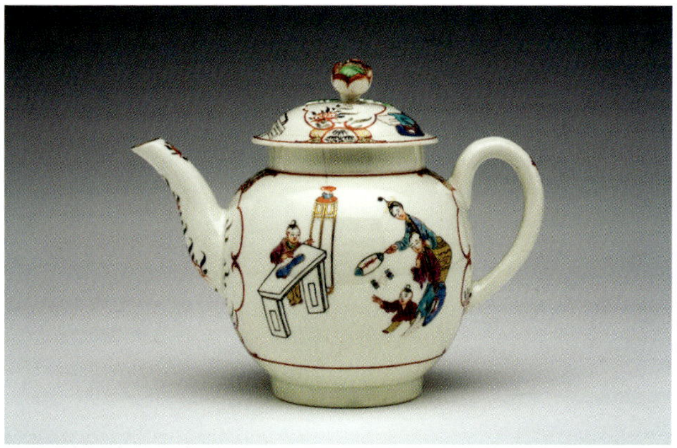
306

306

Teapot and lid

1765–70
Ht 14.8 cm
1957.24.1.284

Plain loop handle, rosebud knop; decorated with a Chinese scene including a mother and child playing with butterflies.

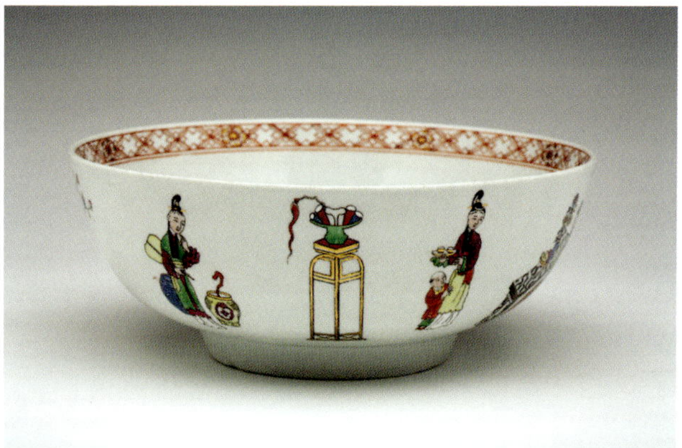
307

307

Bowl

1768–70
Ht 8.4 cm, diam. 20.8 cm
1957.24.1.283

Hand-coloured outline print of Chinese figures, red and gilt diaper border inside rim; very worn decoration of figures and foliage inside bowl.

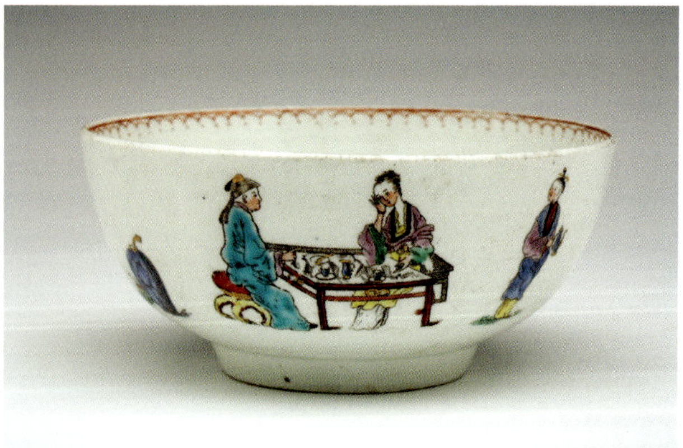
308

308

Bowl

1768–79
Ht 7 cm, diam. 15 cm
1957.24.1.287

Red loop and dot border inside rim; hand-coloured outline print of Chinese man and woman sitting at glass-topped table with an array of coffee cups, servant holding coffee pot beside them.

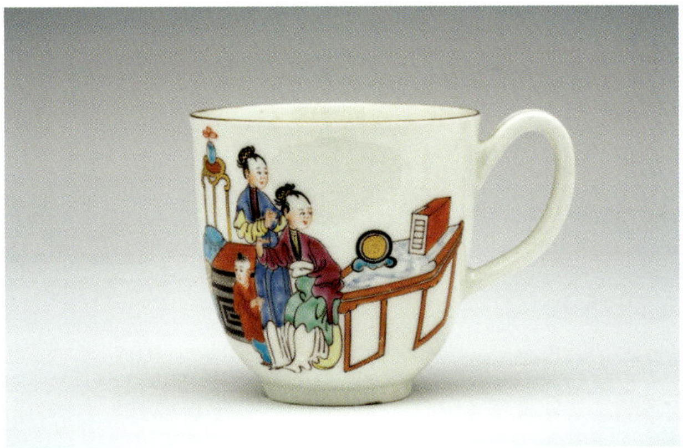

309

309

Coffee cup

1768–78
Ht 6.4 cm, diam. 6.2 cm
1957.24.1.946

Ribbed loop handle, gilt edge; decorated with a scene of two Chinese women, one seated, and a child near a table on one side, two boys before four large vases on the other.

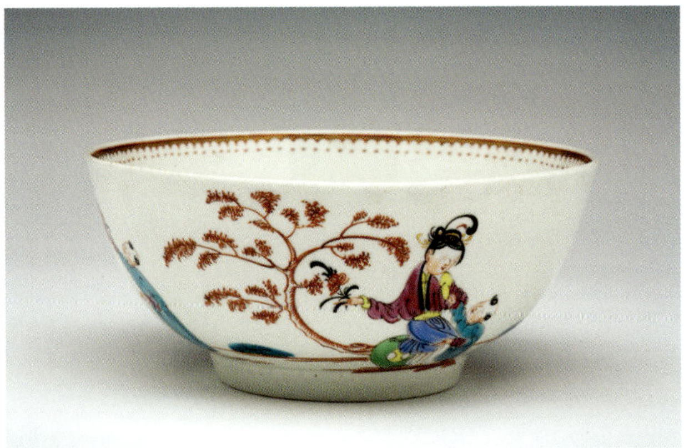

310

310

Bowl

About 1770
Ht 7.3 cm, diam. 15.9 cm
1957.24.1.289

Red and gilt scalloped border inside rim; decorated with five variously clad women in different poses, some with a child.

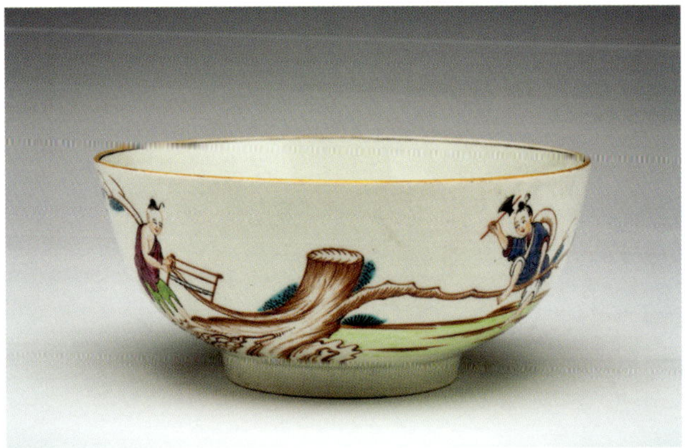

311

311

Bowl

About 1770
Ht 7 cm, diam. 15.4 cm
1957.24.1.310

Yellow rim with black line; decorated with a scene of men sawing wood from a large tree stump.

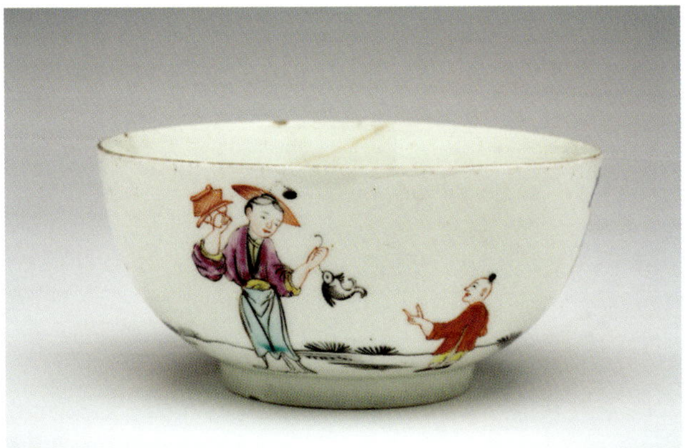

312

312

Bowl

1765–70
Ht 6.1 cm, diam. 11.9 cm
1957.24.1.299

Decorated on one side with a seated figure of a fisherman, caricatured as 'Bodhai', a corpulent monk; on the reverse a lady holding a fish with another looking on.

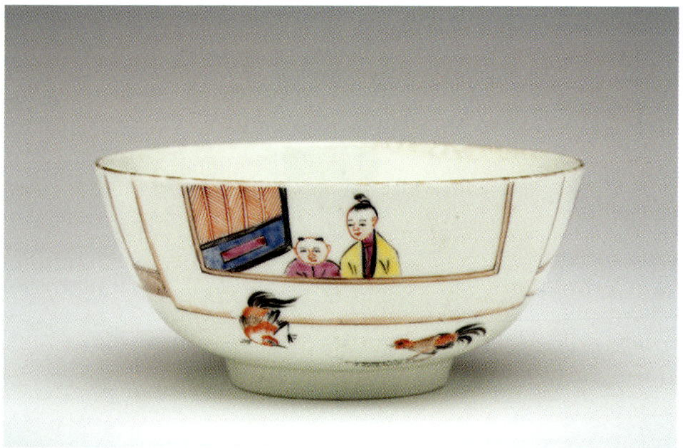

313

313

Bowl

About 1770
Ht 5.4 cm, diam. 11.9 cm
1957.24.1.303

Decorated with Chinese scenes of two men watching cockfighting and two winnowing corn.

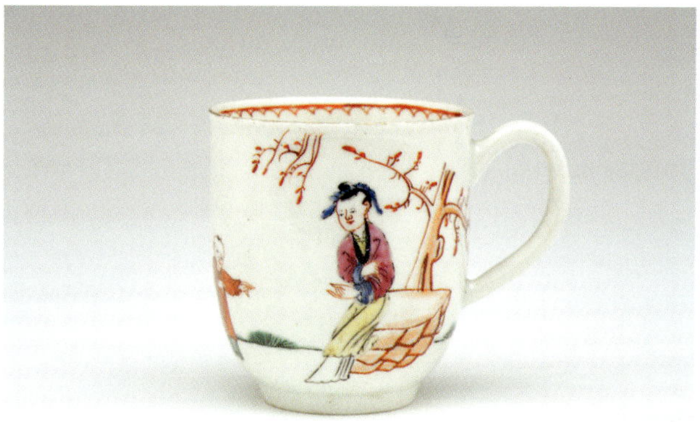

314

314

Coffee cup

1768–78
Ht 6.7 cm, diam. 5.8 cm
1957.24.1.955

Ribbed loop handle, scalloped red line border inside rim; decorated with Chinese scene of a woman and child and two red and green vases.

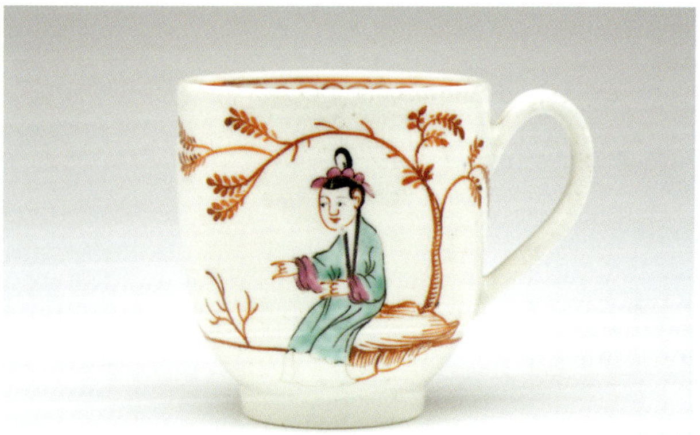

315

315

Coffee cup

1768–78
Ht 6.3 cm, diam. 5.7 cm
1957.24.1.948

Ribbed loop handle, red scalloped line border inside rim; unfinished decoration of seated Chinese figure below tree; plant with star-like flowers on reverse.

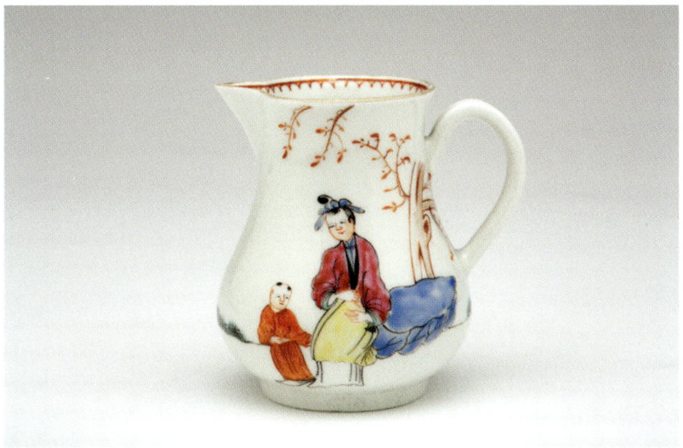

316

316

Cream jug

About 1765
Ht 8.1 cm
1957.24.1.316

Ovoid, ribbed loop handle; painted with two Chinese women and a boy.

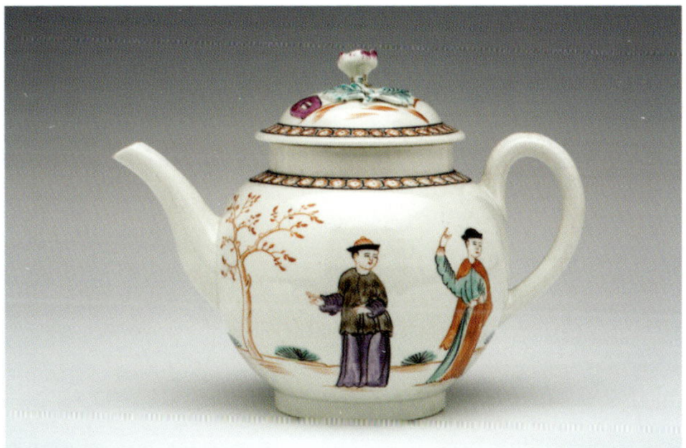

317

317

Teapot and lid

1770–72
Ht 14.7 cm
1957.24.1.320

Plain loop handle, rosebud knop; painted with two Chinese men and a spindly tree.

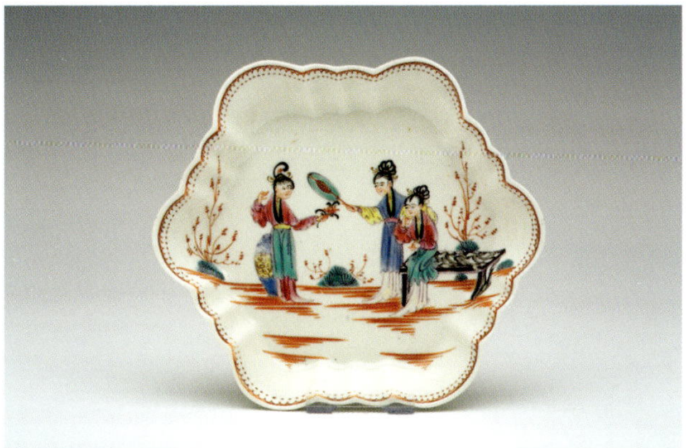

318

318

Teapot stand

About 1775
Width 15 cm
1957.24.1.339

Hexagonal, wavy rim, border of red-brown loops; decorated with three Chinese women.

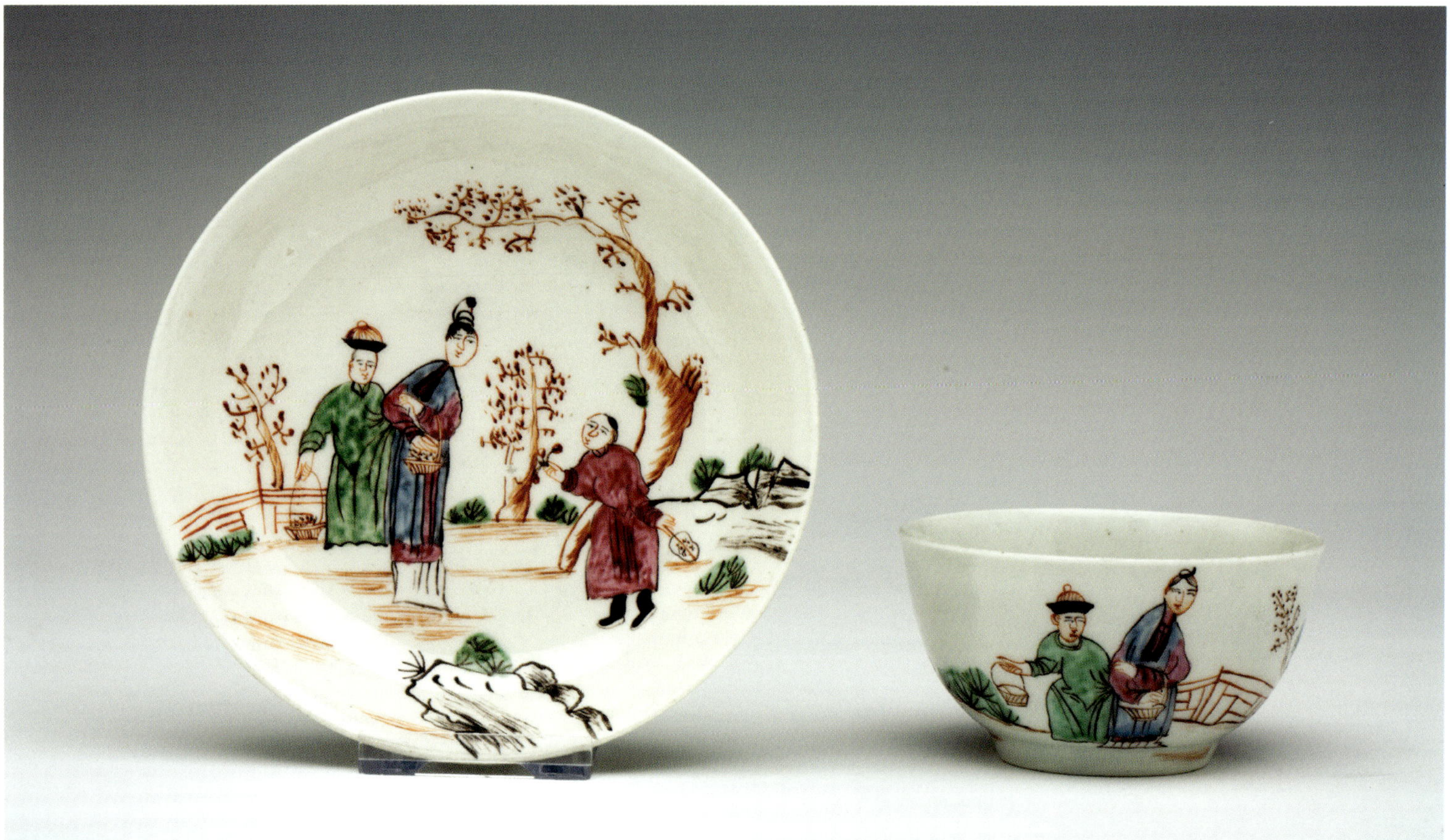

319

319

Teabowl and saucer

About 1775
Bowl ht 4.2 cm, diam. 7.6 cm, saucer diam. 12 cm
1957.24.1.335

Decorated with two Chinese women carrying baskets and a man holding a fan.

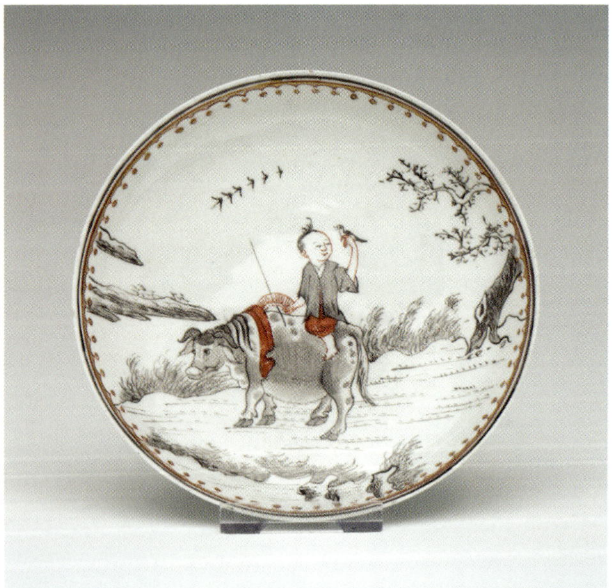

320

320

Saucer

About 1768
Diam. 12 cm
1957.24.1.787

Pencilled, with some red enamelling. The decoration, showing an oxherd holding a bird, with further birds in the sky, is inspired by the Chinese legend of the 'Spinning Maiden': a weaving girl and and an oxherd fall in love, but because they neglect their work, the gods separate them by 'the River of Heaven' (the Milky Way). They are permitted to meet on the seventh day of the seventh month, and on that day all the magpies on earth spread their wings so that the lovers can cross.

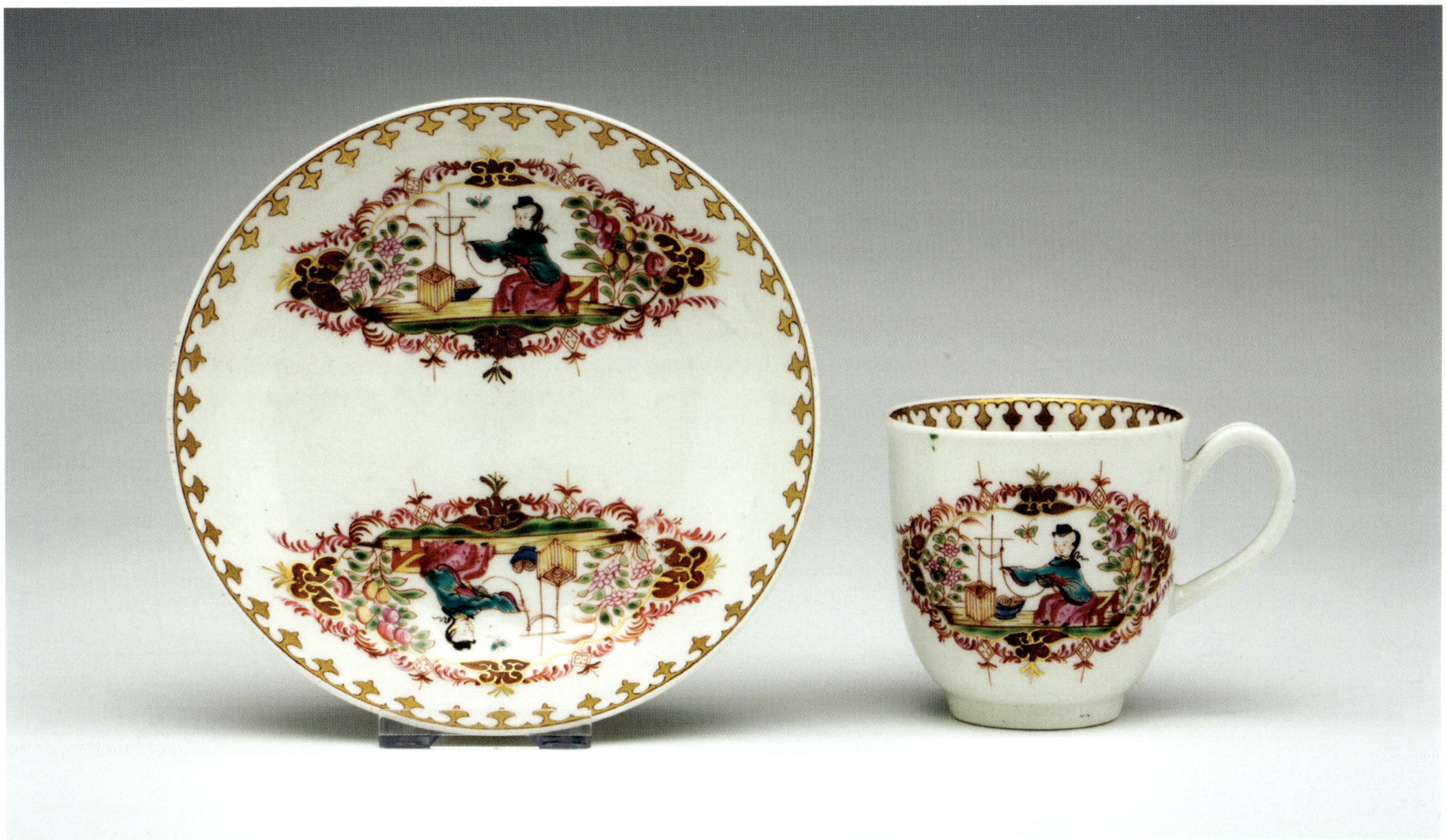

321

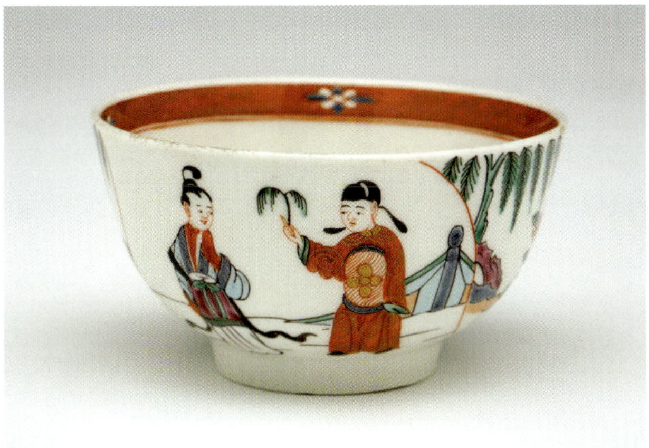

322

321

Coffee cup and saucer

1768–70
Cup ht 6.1 cm, diam. 6 cm; saucer diam. 12.7 cm
Mark: crossed sword and 9 on saucer
1957.24.1.295

Ribbed loop handle; gilt and red dagger border, decorated with the 'Spinning Maiden' pattern (see no. 320) within a scrollwork frame; the design was probably taken from a Chinese export copy of an earlier Meissen chinoiserie design. A teacup and saucer of the same design are illustrated in Spero and Sandon 1996; a tea canister of the same design is in the Museum of Royal Worcester Porcelain.

322

Teabowl

About 1770
Ht 4.3 cm, diam. 7.4 cm
1957.24.1.266

Landscape with Chinese figure decoration; orange border inside rim.

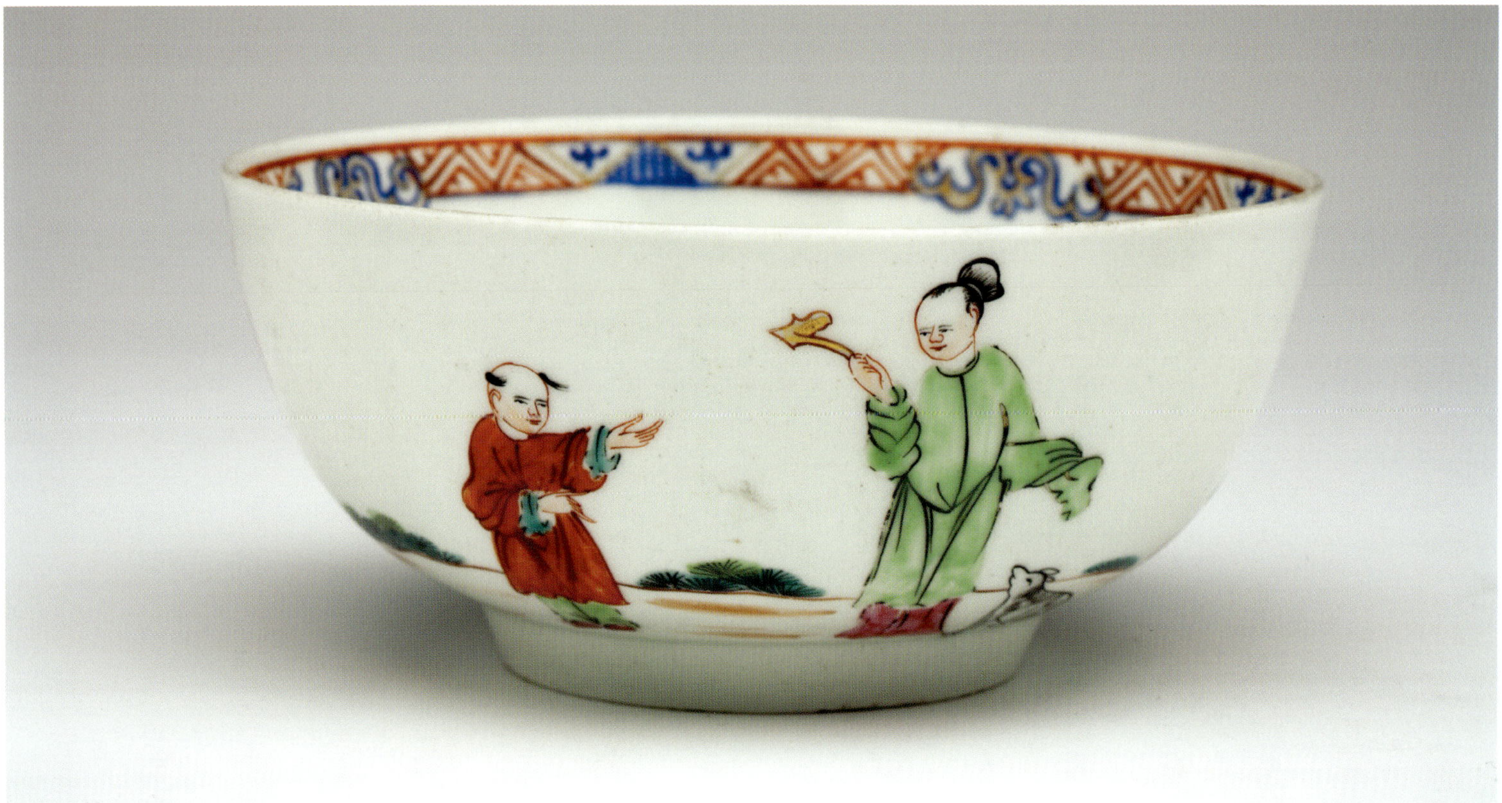

323

323

Bowl

About 1770
Ht 5.7 cm, diam. 12.1 cm
1957.24.1.296

Border inside rim alternately hachured in red and scrolled in blue and gold; various Chinese figures on outside, including a woman in green holding a gold chopper, seated dog beside her.

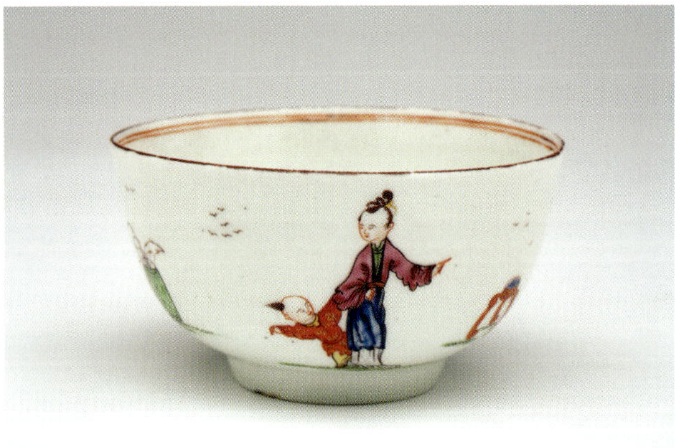

324

324

Bowl

1768–78
Ht 5.2 cm, diam. 9.1 cm
1957.24.1.957

Decorated with Chinese figures including a magician; double red line inside rim.

325

Teabowl and saucer

1770–75
Bowl ht 4.2 cm, diam. 7.1 cm; saucer diam. 12 cm
1957.24.1.298

Decorated with a mandarin smoking a pipe, seated beside a table with a bowl of Buddha's hand citrons (Citrus medica var. sarcodactylis), another figure holding flowers approaching; strong underglaze blue border with trefoils inside rim of cup and around saucer.

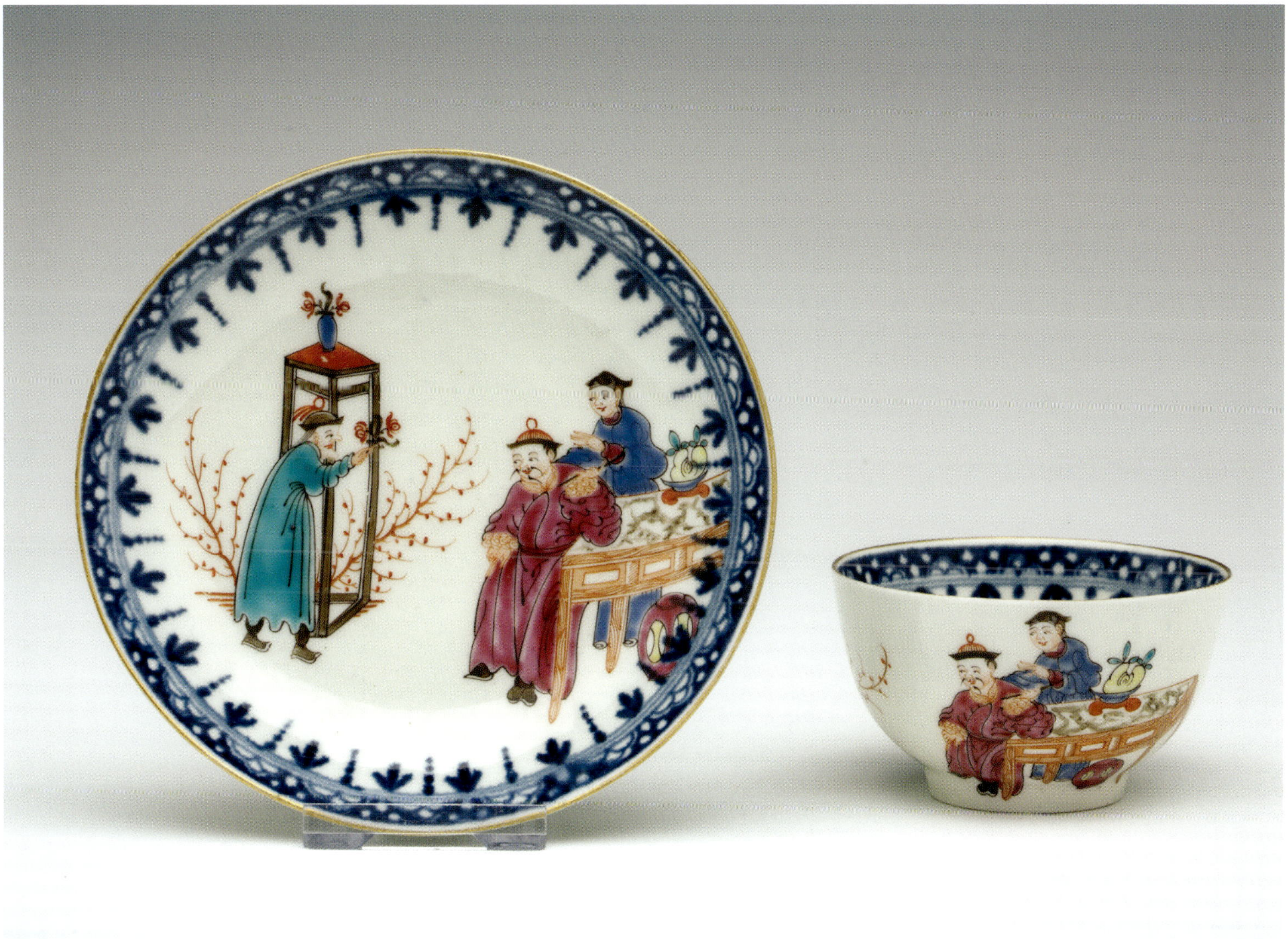

325

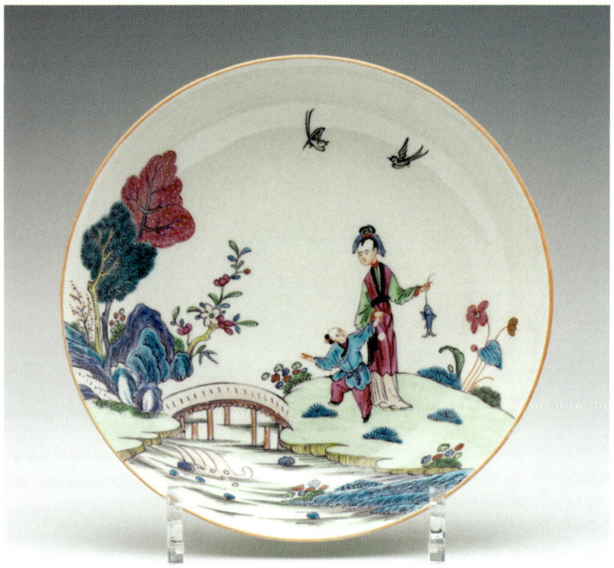

326

326

Cake dish

1770–75
Diam. 19.2 cm
1957.24.1.334

Brown edge; decorated in a striking Chinese palette with a woman, holding on to a small boy and dangling fish in one hand, standing on a grassy mound by a bridge across a river; highly coloured trees with gilding on left. Possibly decorated outside the Worcester factory.

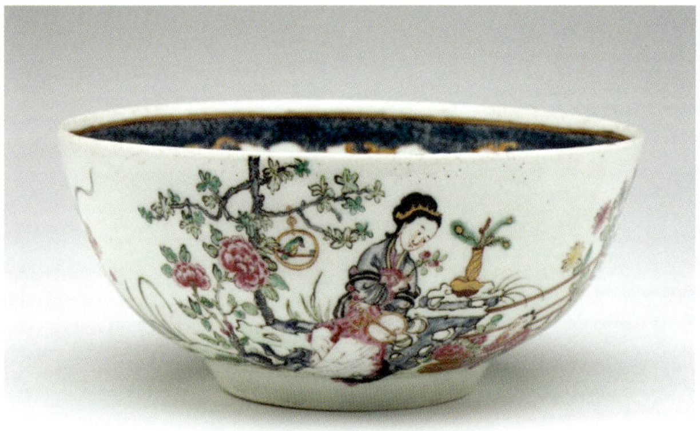

327

327

Bowl

1760–65
Ht 7 cm, diam. 15.3 cm
1957.24.1.321

Irregular overglaze blue 'Y'-scaled border with gilding inside rim, decorated on the outside with a seated lady and child in a fenced garden. Probably inspired by a Chinese original and decorated outside the Worcester factory.

328

Coffee pot and lid

1770–72
Ht 23.6 cm
1957.24.1.1078

Pear-shaped with loop handle and small thumb piece; broad bands of arabesque gilding by handle and spout outline; two large panels, one with a Chinese pedlar with a tray of wares or possibly a game using counters, the other with two Chinese figures; distinctive pale blue ground with brown waves below, possibly outside decoration. A similarly decorated teapot is illustrated in Spero and Sandon 1996, pl. 175.

PROVENANCE
Mrs Geoffrey Hart part 1, Sotheby's, London, 23 June 1959, lot 90, £135.

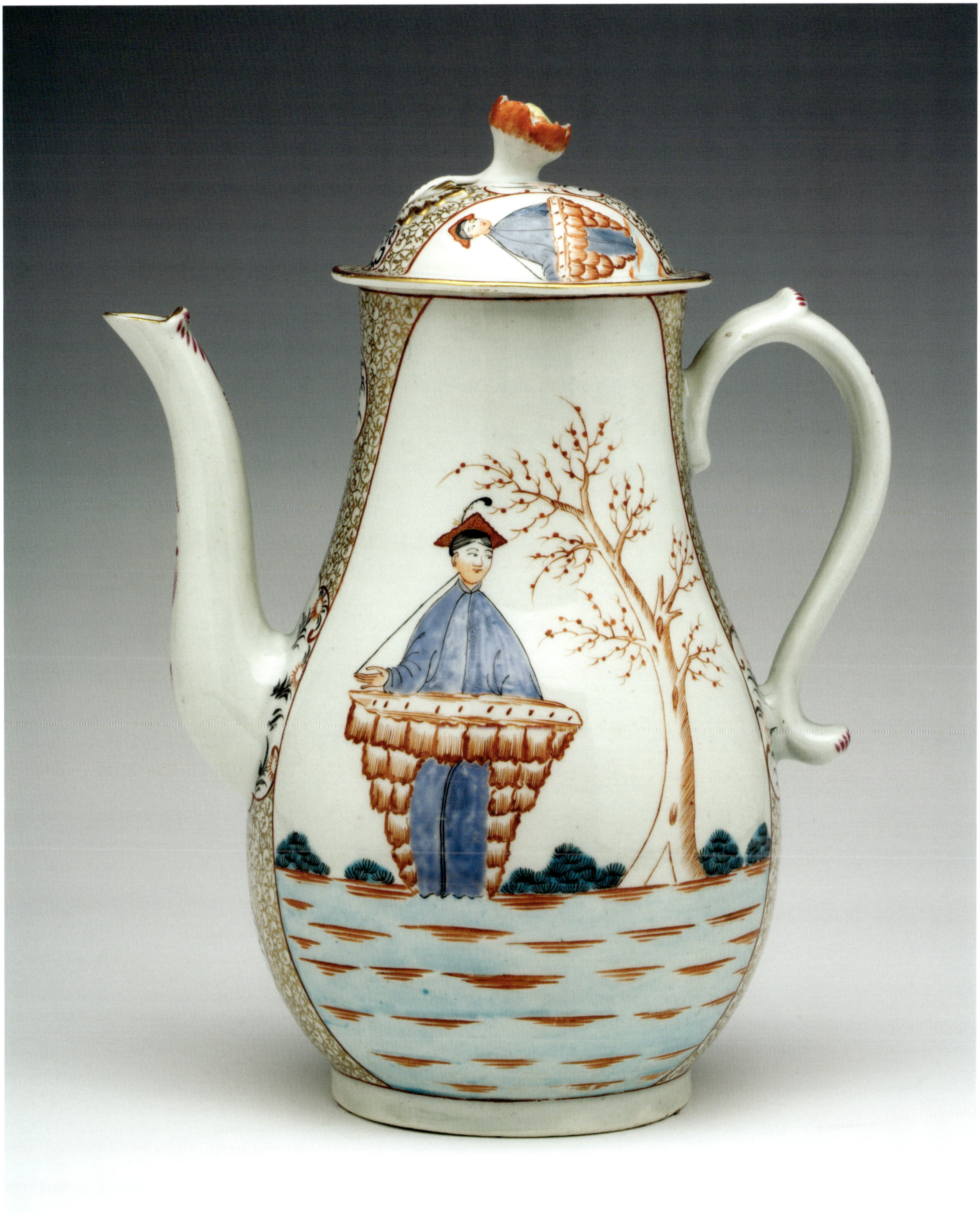

328

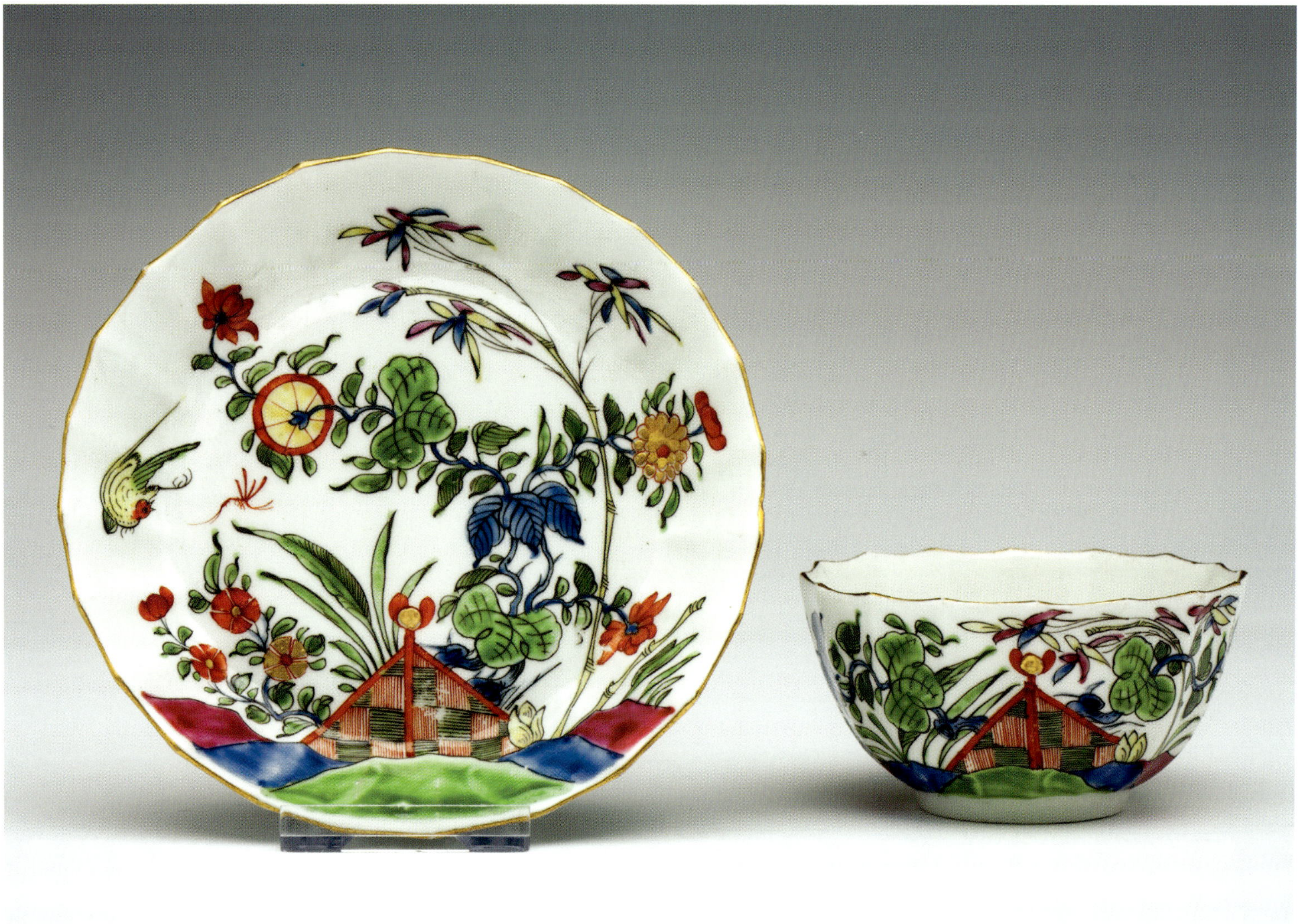

329

329

Teabowl and saucer

1768–72
Bowl ht 3.9 cm, diam. 7.6 cm; saucer diam. 11.8 cm
Mark: fretted square on both
1957.24.1.709

Fluted with wavy gilt rim; decorated in Chinese style in bright colours with a chequered triangle amongst exotic Oriental flowers and foliage with insects; sometimes referred to as the 'Chequered Tent' pattern.

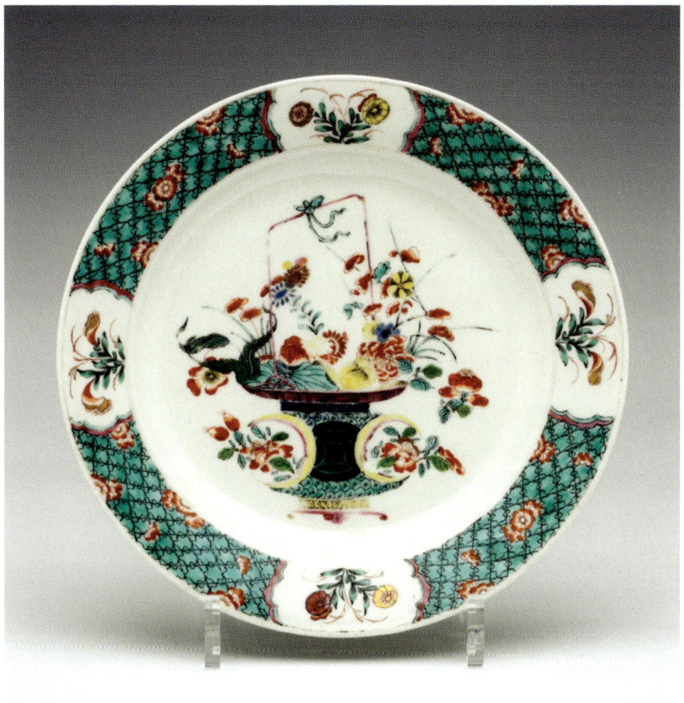

330

330

Plate

About 1765
Diam. 22.3 cm
1957.24.1.742

On the rim are four panels of strong green, diapered black with scattered formal chrysanthemums, foliage and flower sprays between; pedestal dish in centre, with Oriental flowers and foliage.

REFERENCE
Spero and Sandon 1996, pl. 742.

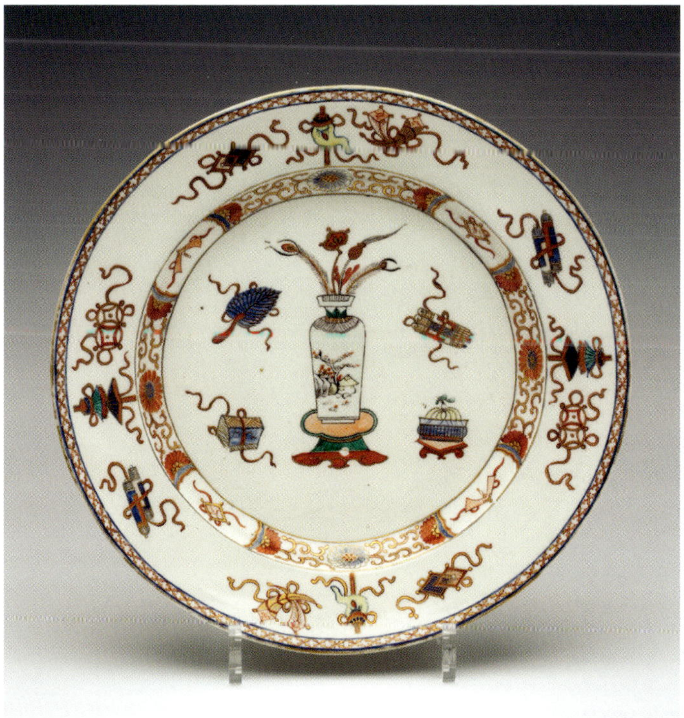

331

331

Dish

1795–1800
Diam. 27.6 cm
1957.24.1.736

Decorated in the centre with a vase on a stand surrounded by Chinese symbols; red, blue and gold borders on rim and around well; four red and blue flowers on reverse.

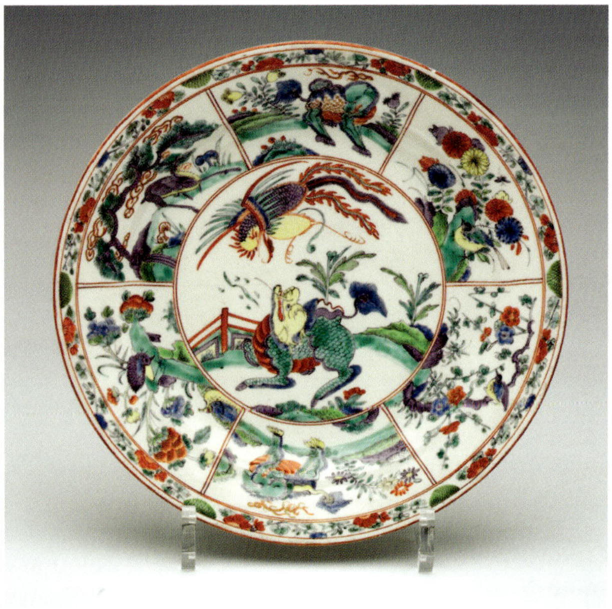

332

332

Plate

About 1775
Diam. 22 cm
Mark: open gold crescent
1957.24.1.903

Close copy of a Chinese design, decorated in *famille verte* style in the 'Bishop Sumner' pattern with *kylins* and a phoenix; three floral sprays on reverse.

333

Two-handled cup and saucer

About 1770
Cup ht 7.7 cm, diam. 6.6 cm; saucer diam. 13 cm
Mark: crossed sword and 9 on both
1957.24.1.711

Cup with entwined twig handles, gilt rim on saucer; decorated in the 'Bengal Tiger' pattern.

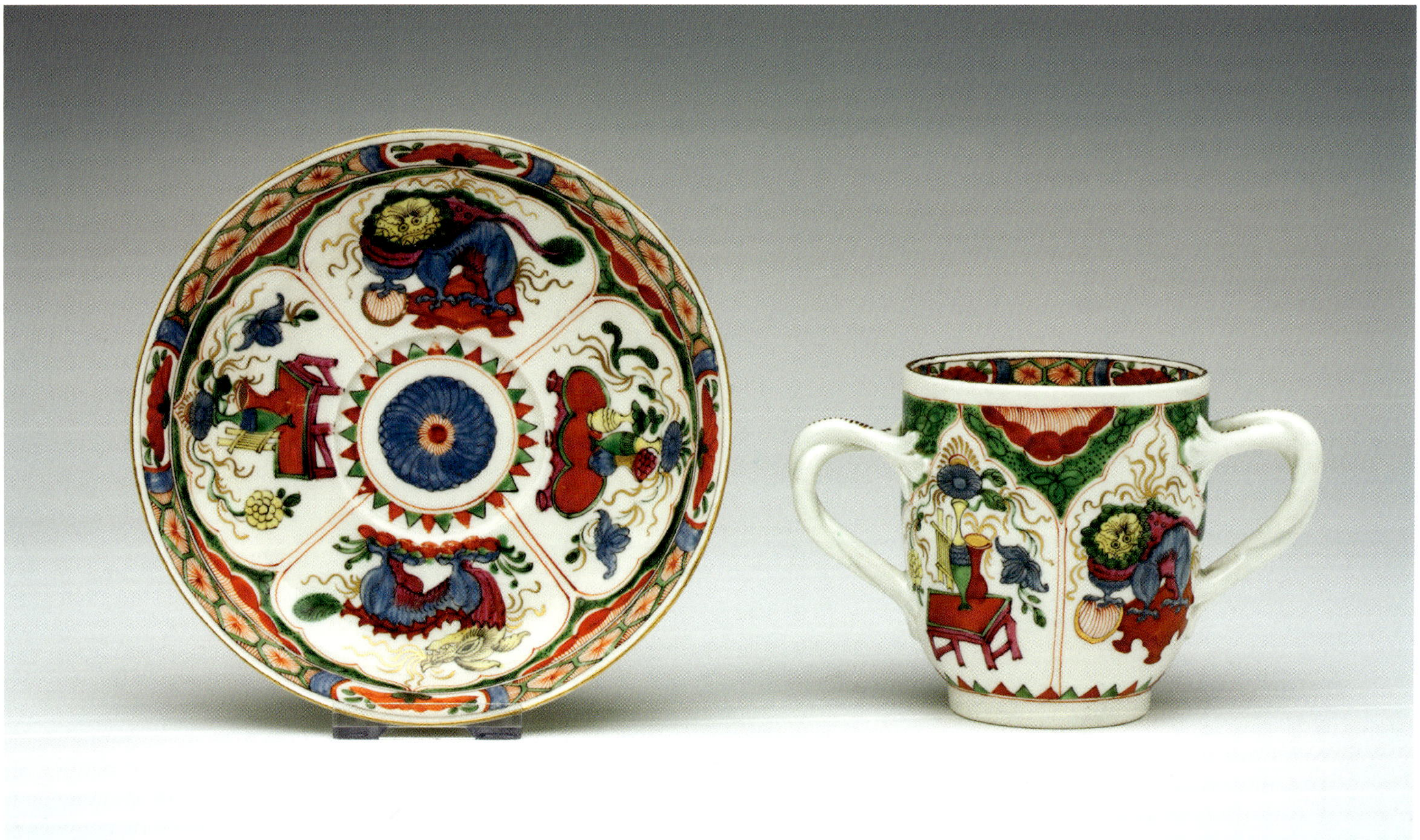

333

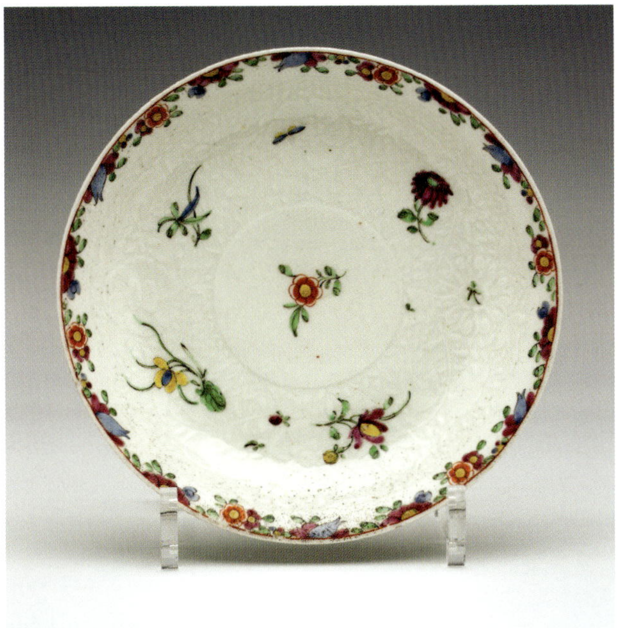

334

334

Cake dish

About 1765
Diam. 17.9 cm
1957.24.1.866

Multicoloured floral border; moulded below with floral wreaths, five small floral sprays with insects in centre.

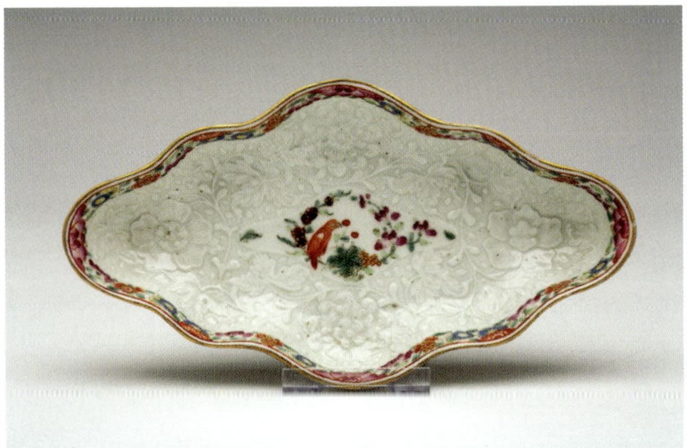

335

335

Spoon tray

About 1765
Length 16 cm, width 8.9 cm
1957.24.1.695

Elongated lozenge shape with wavy edge; narrow polychrome floral border body moulded with roses and leaves, except for central reserve which is painted with a parrot pecking fruit.

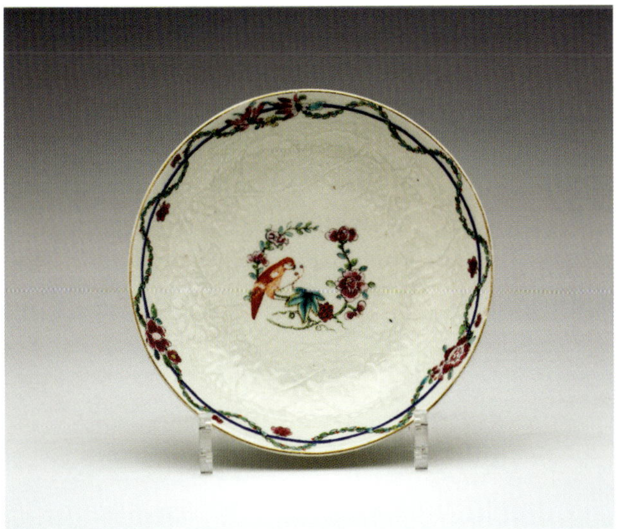

336

336

Cake dish

About 1765
Diam. 17.8 cm
1957.24.1.525

Gilt rim; moulded with intricate pattern of leaves and flowers, centre painted with a parrot pecking fruit, blue line entwined with wreaths of berries and flowers on border.

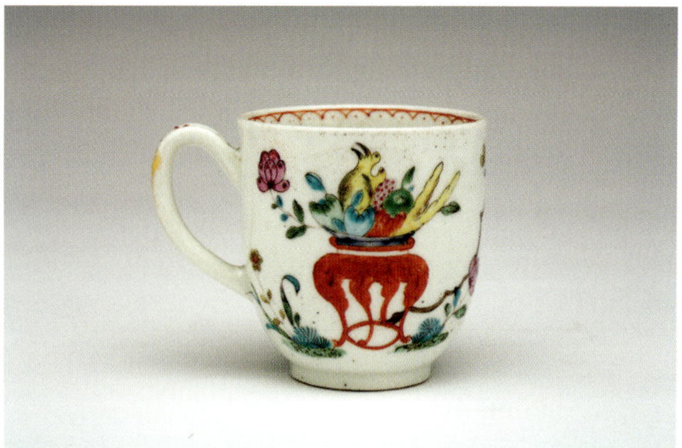

337

337

Coffee cup

About 1768
Ht 6.4 cm, diam. 5.8 cm
1957.24.1.947

Ribbed loop handle; red line scalloped border inside rim; decorated on one side with a four-legged stand in red-brown supporting a black dish with various foliage and fruit, including a finger citron, a symbol of Buddha's hand grasping money, a sign of wealth; continuous flower spray and two insects around rest of bowl.

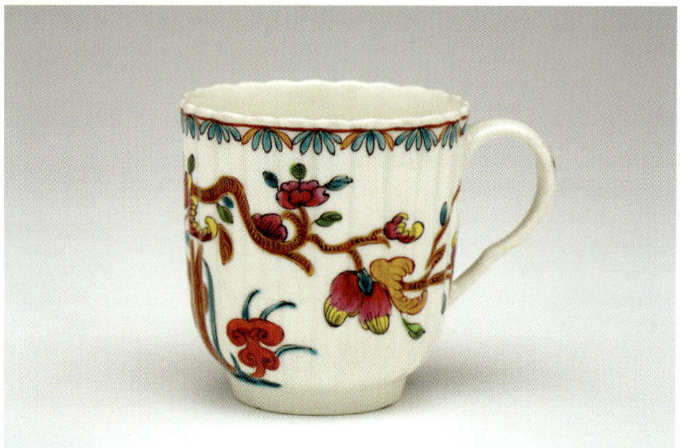

338

338

Coffee cup

About 1775
Ht 6.3 cm, diam. 5.8 cm
1957.24.1.268

Ribbed with broken looped handle; border of leaves in sky blue and gold, continuously decorated with a brown tree trunk and branches with Oriental flowers and foliage.

339

Teabowl and saucer

About 1770
Bowl ht 3.9 cm, diam. 6.8 cm; saucer diam. 12 cm
1957.24.1.270

Gilt edge, red diapered border, sprays of red and gold flowers, blue and green foliage; formalised red and gold flower in centre, within a circle of similar diapering.

340

Teabowl and saucer

1780–85
Bowl ht 4.9 cm, diam. 7.6 cm; saucer diam. 12.9 cm
1957.24.1.274

Boldly decorated with chrysanthemums and prunus blossom, red and gold border; probably copied from a Chinese original.

REFERENCE
Spero and Sandon 1996, pl. 184.

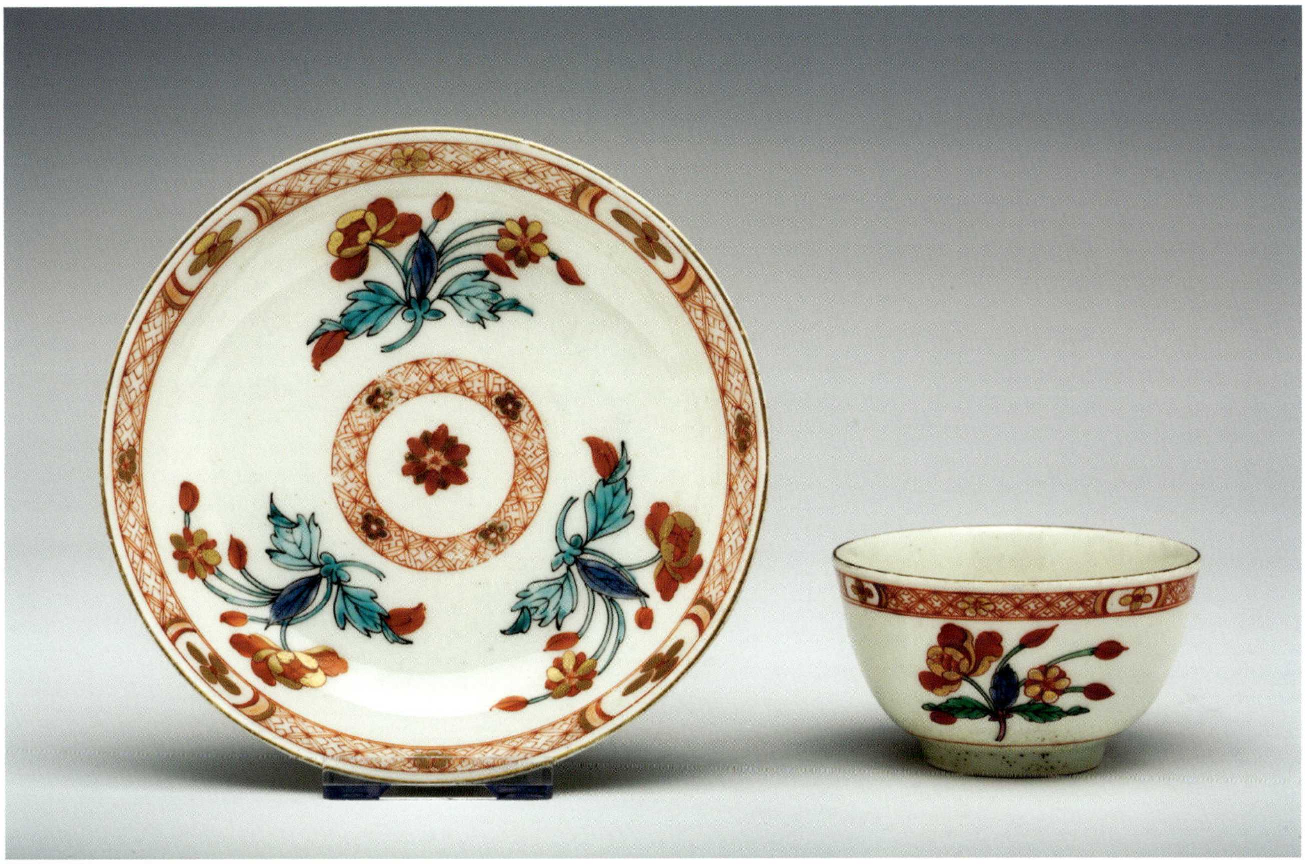

339

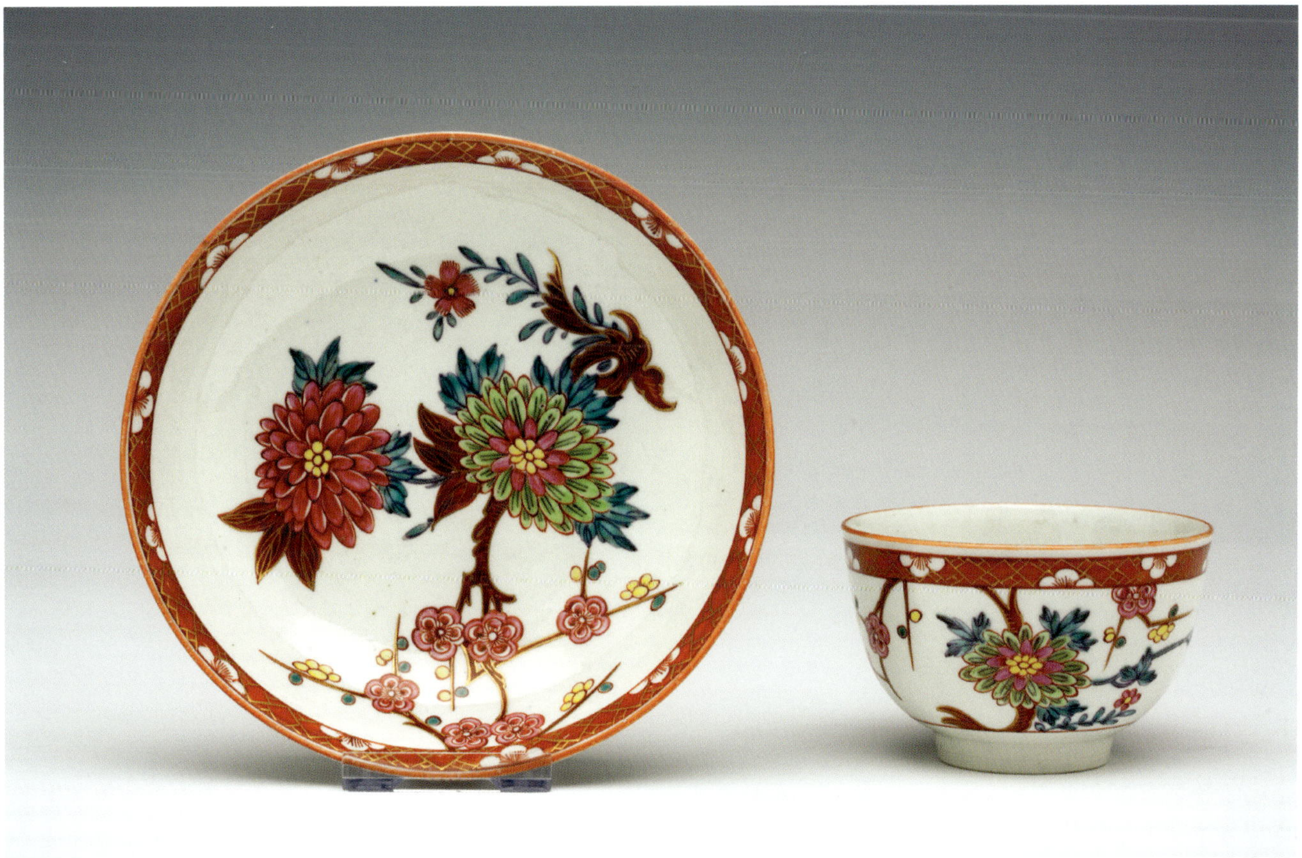

340

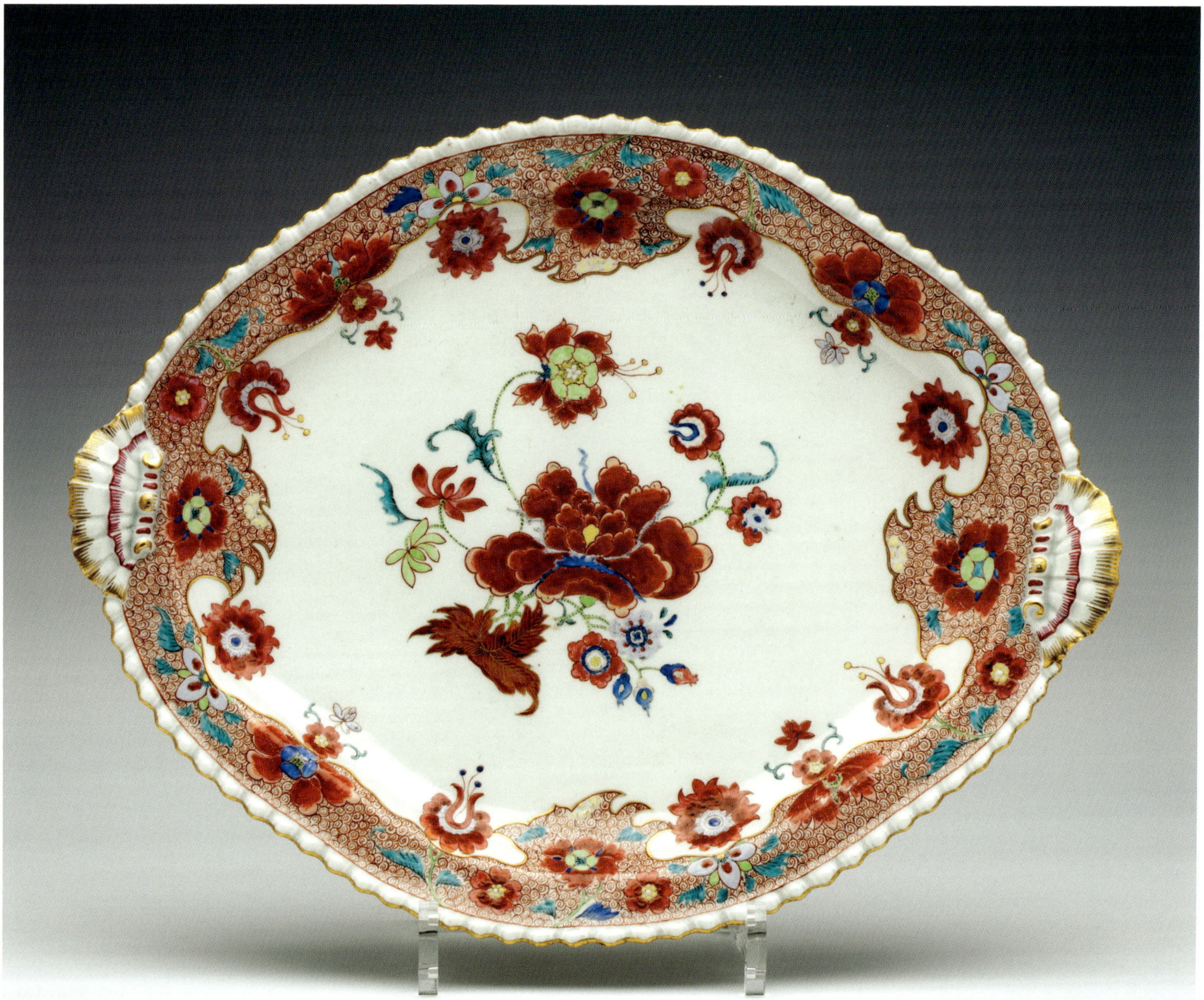

341

341

Tureen stand

1775–80
Length 32.8 cm, width 26.7 cm
1957.24.1.735

Gilt gadroon edge, shell handles picked out in puce and gilding; decorated in the *famille rose* style with irregular gilt-edge vermicular border with small flowers, large peony spray in centre; probably a replacement for a Chinese service.

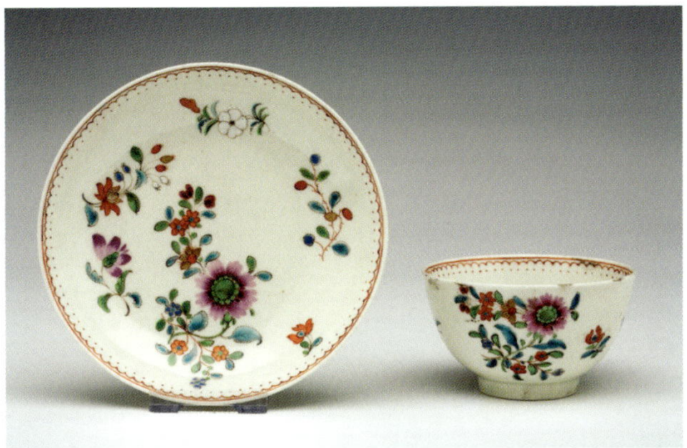

342

342

Teabowl and saucer

1770–72
Bowl ht 4.6 cm, diam. 7.6 cm; saucer diam.12.1 cm
1957.24.1.868

Scalloped red line border with dots; decorated with Chinese-style flowers in brick red, puce, turquoise and gold; one spray has a five-petalled white flower with a dark centre.

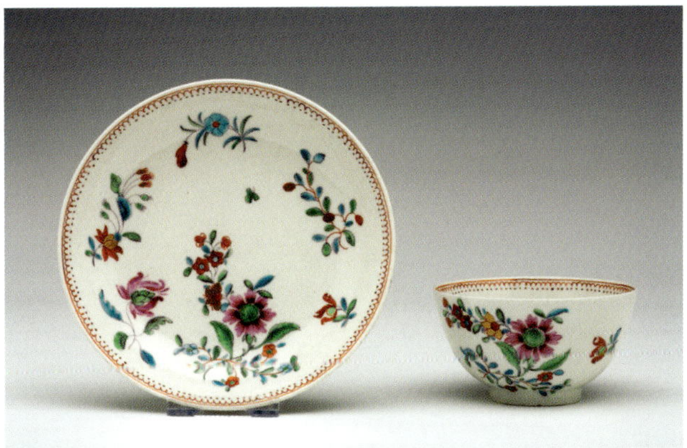

343

343

Teabowl and saucer

1770–72
Bowl ht 4.3 cm, diam. 7.6 cm; saucer diam. 12.5 cm
1957.24.1.869

Similar decoration to no. 342 but with a turquoise flower instead of a white one.

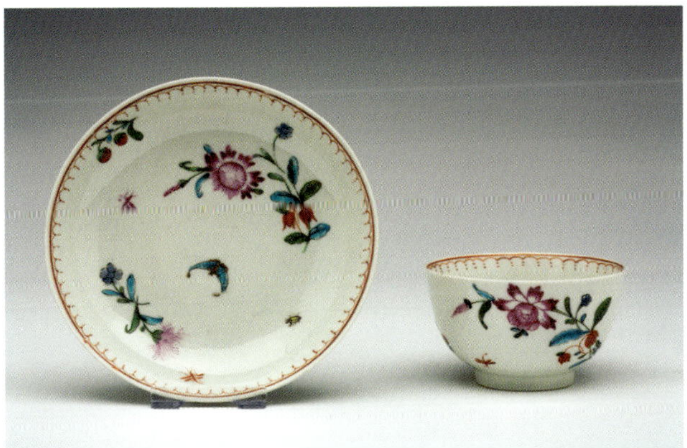

344

344

Teabowl and saucer

About 1770
Bowl ht 4.5 cm, diam. 7.4 cm; saucer diam. 11.8 cm
1957.24.1.988

Red scallop and dot border; decorated with Oriental floral sprays with insects; flying bat in centre.

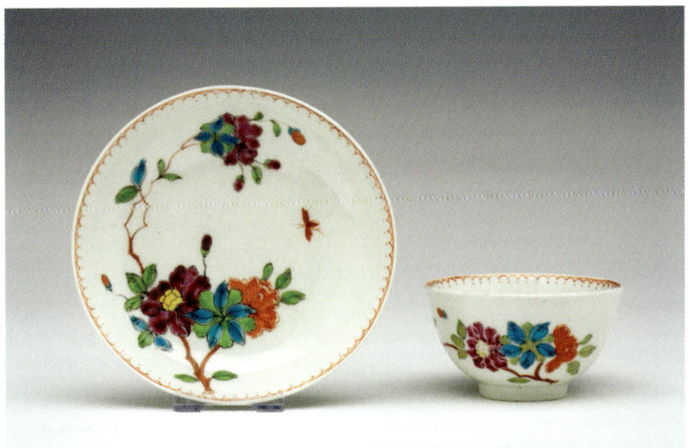

345

345

Teabowl and saucer

About 1765
Bowl ht 4.3 cm, diam. 7.4 cm; saucer diam. 11.9 cm
1957.24.1.871

Thin red scalloped border; boldly decorated with an asymmetric Oriental floral spray in carmine, green, blue and red; one small butterfly.

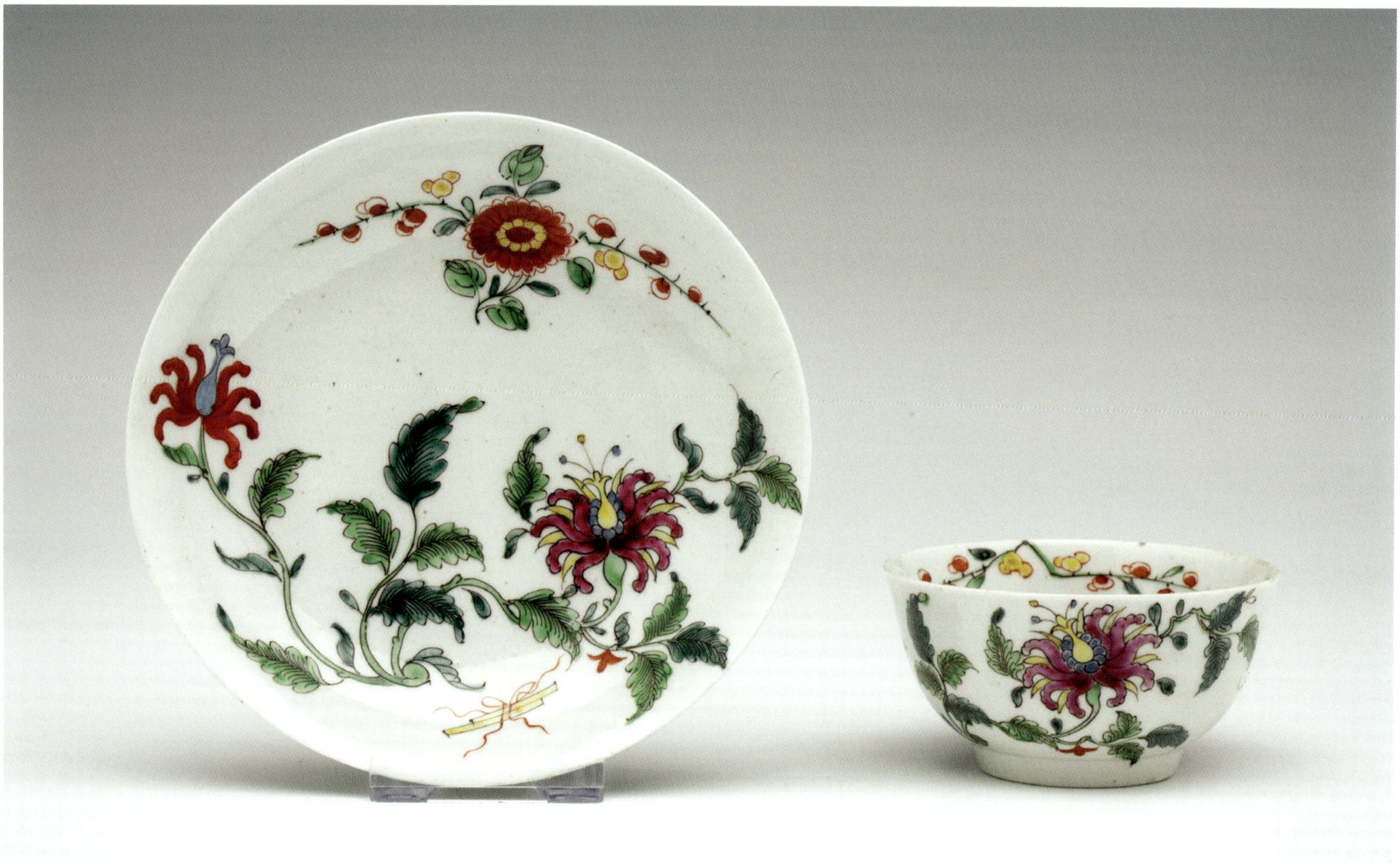

346

346

Teabowl and saucer

1758–60
Bowl ht 3.7 cm, diam. 7 cm; saucer diam. 12 cm
1957.24.1.962

Decorated with the 'Honeysuckle' pattern with three flowering plants, mainly in red, green and yellow.

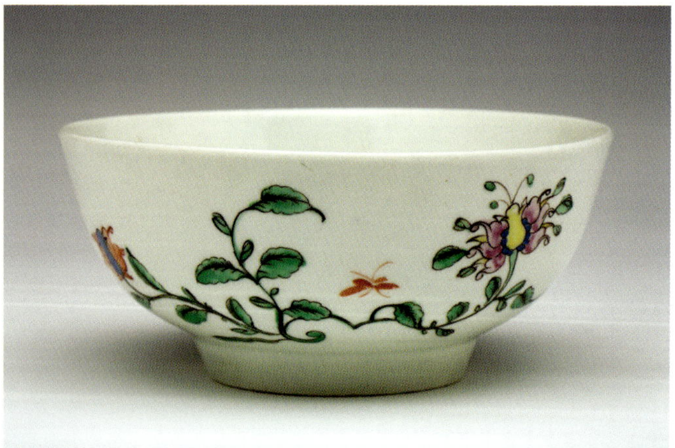

347

347

Bowl

1760–65
Ht 6.9 cm, diam. 15.3 cm
1957.24.1.837

Decorated in Chinese taste with a double peony spray and brown insect on one side, a chrysanthemum spray on the other.

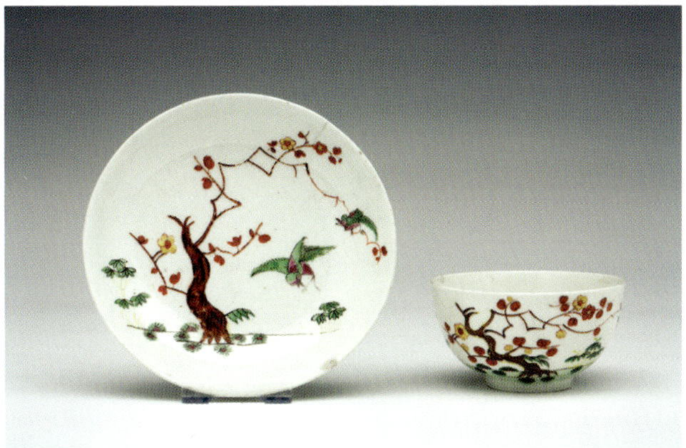

348

348

Teabowl and saucer

About 1770
Bowl ht 4.2 cm, diam. 7.6 cm; saucer diam. 11.9 cm
1957.24.1.991

Decorated in Oriental style with prunus tree with thick dark brown trunk, thin branches with red and yellow foliage and flowers; two green and carmine birds.

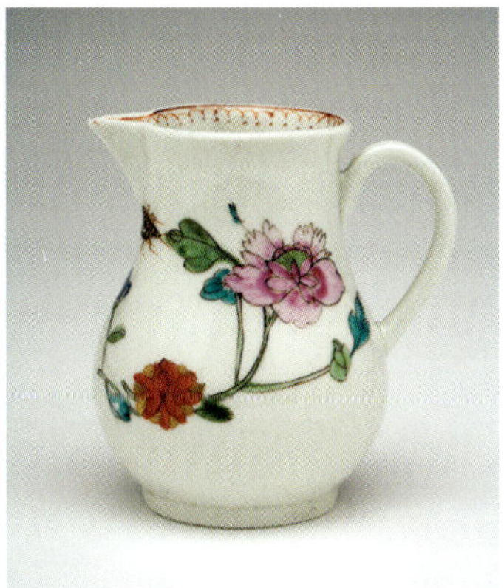

349

349

Cream jug

1768–70
Ht 8.3 cm
1957.24.1.850

Ovoid, ribbed loop handle; red scalloped and dot border inside rim, decorated with strong floral sprays and black beetle or harvest bug speckled in gold; the 'Astley' pattern.

REFERENCE
Spero 1984, pl. 75.

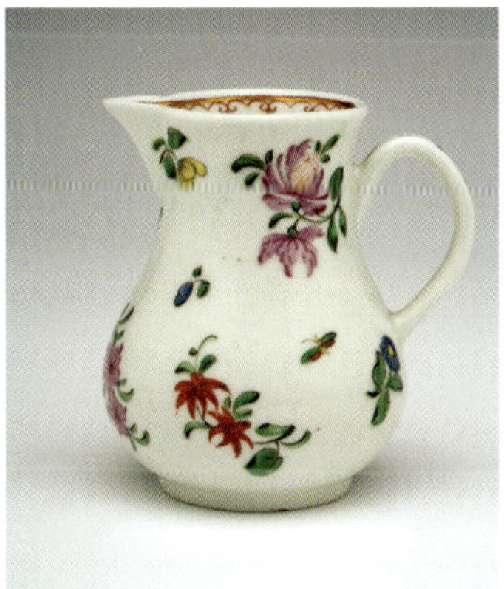

350

350

Cream jug

About 1770
Ht 8.5 cm
1957.24.1.1037

Decorated with floral sprays and minute insects; red and gilt dagger border inside rim.

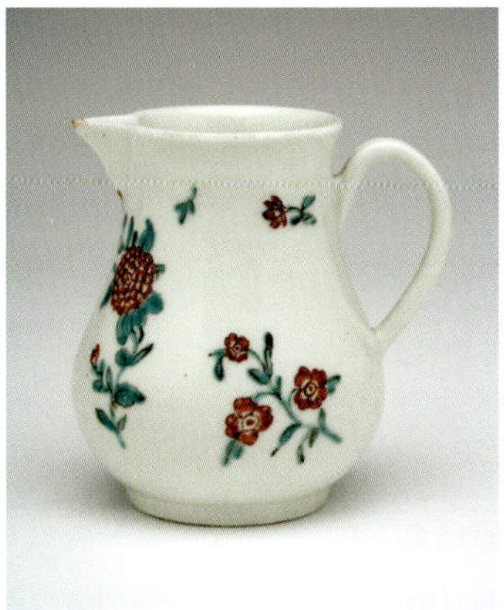

351

351

Cream jug

1770–75
Ht 8.1 cm
1957.24.1.981

Ribbed loop handle; decorated with iron red flowers and blue-green leaves.

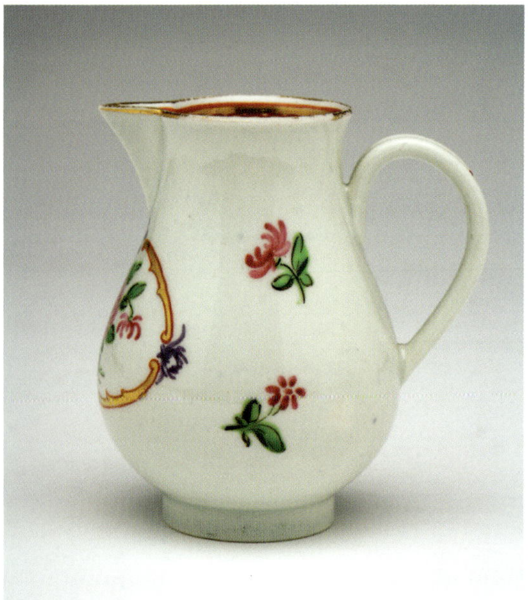

352

352

Cream jug

1775–80
Ht 8 cm
1957.24.1.987

Ovoid, ribbed loop handle; decorated with flower spray within gilt cartouche, and four other small sprays.

353

Bowl

1772–5
Ht 5.9 cm, diam. 11.8 cm
1957.24.1.842

Oriental-style floral decoration, including an unusual curly five-petalled flower in mauve with yellow centre; other flowers include roses and pimpernels.

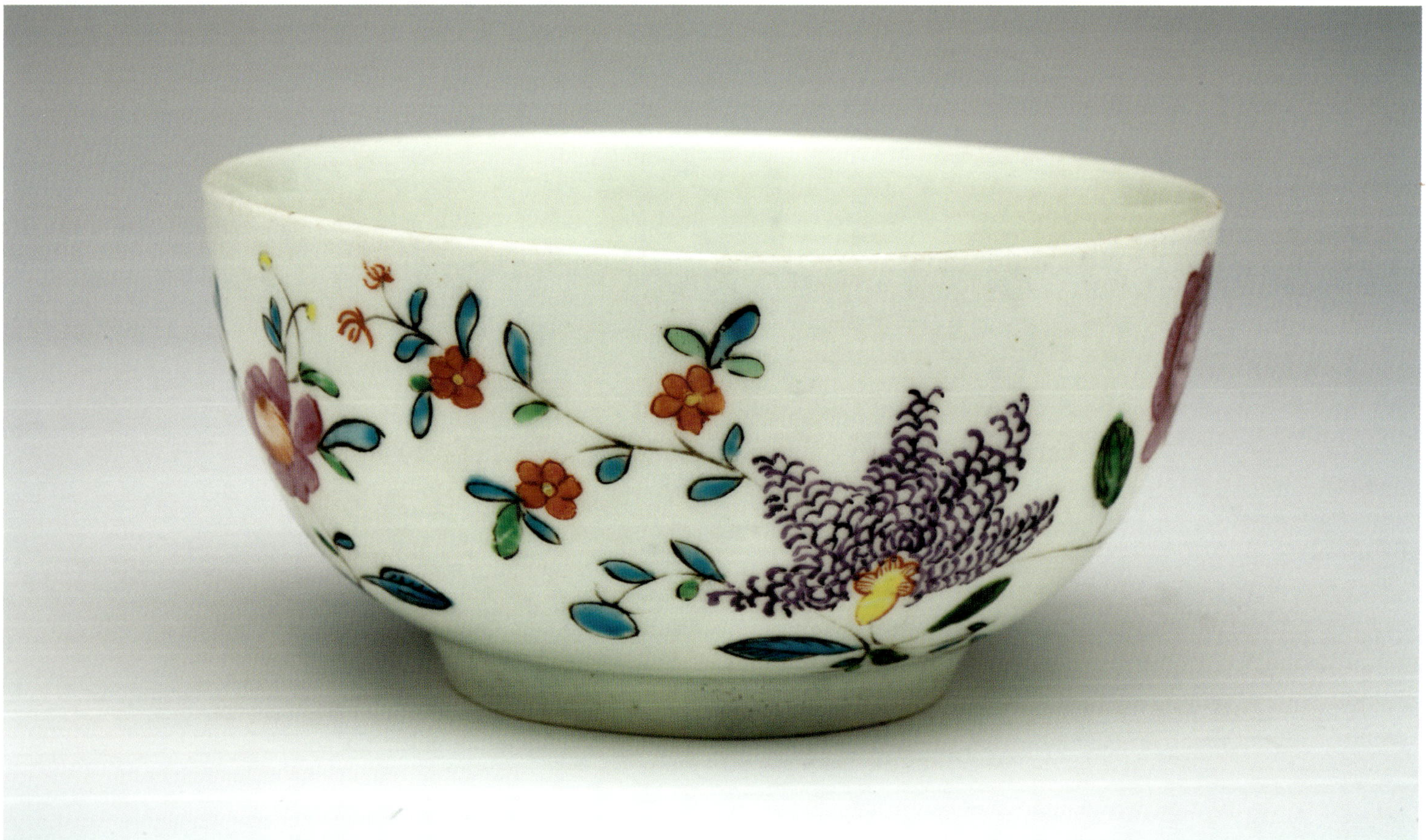

353

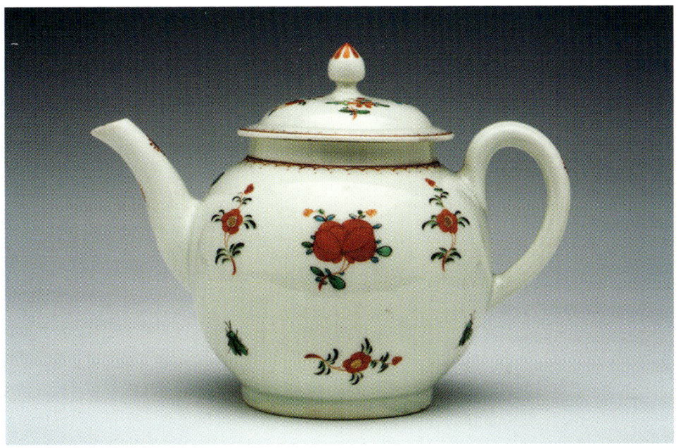

354

354

Teapot and lid

About 1775
Ht 14 cm
1957.24.1.862

Globular, loop handle; scattered Oriental flowers in orange and gold with four small blue and green beetles.

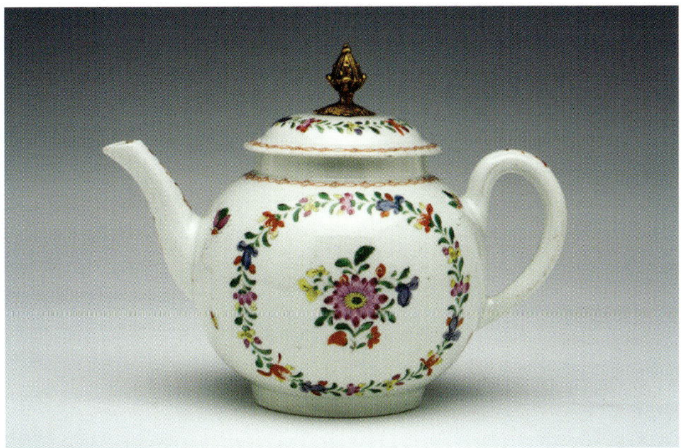

355

355

Teapot and lid

1770–80
Ht 14.9 cm
1957.24.1.840

Globular, loop handle; decorated on each side and on lid with circular wreath of formal flowers with a posy in centre; brass replacement for porcelain knop.

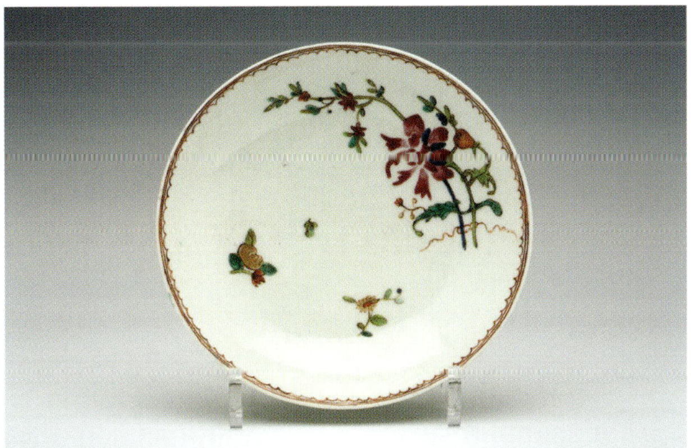

356

356

Cake dish

1770–75
Diam. 17.9 cm
1957.24.1.867

Scalloped red line border; decorated with an asymmetric Oriental spray with one large flower, and two other smaller sprays.

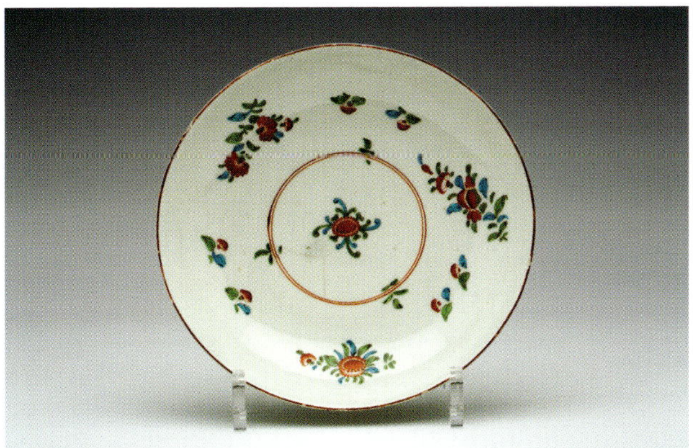

357

357

Cake dish

1772–5
Diam. 18 cm
1957.24.1.863

Red edge, Oriental-style decoration with three large and six small sprays of formal chrysanthemums, and a double red line circle with leaves around central posy.

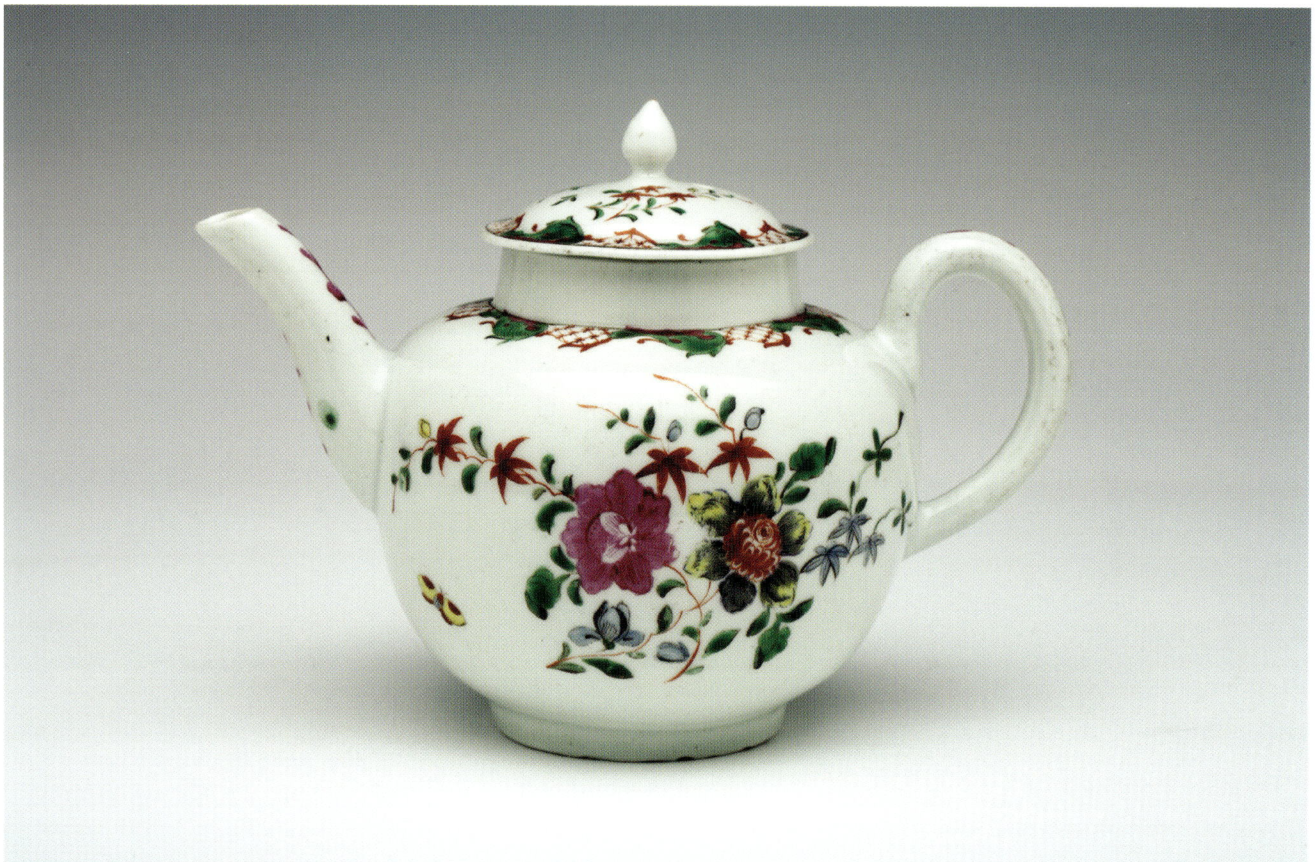

358

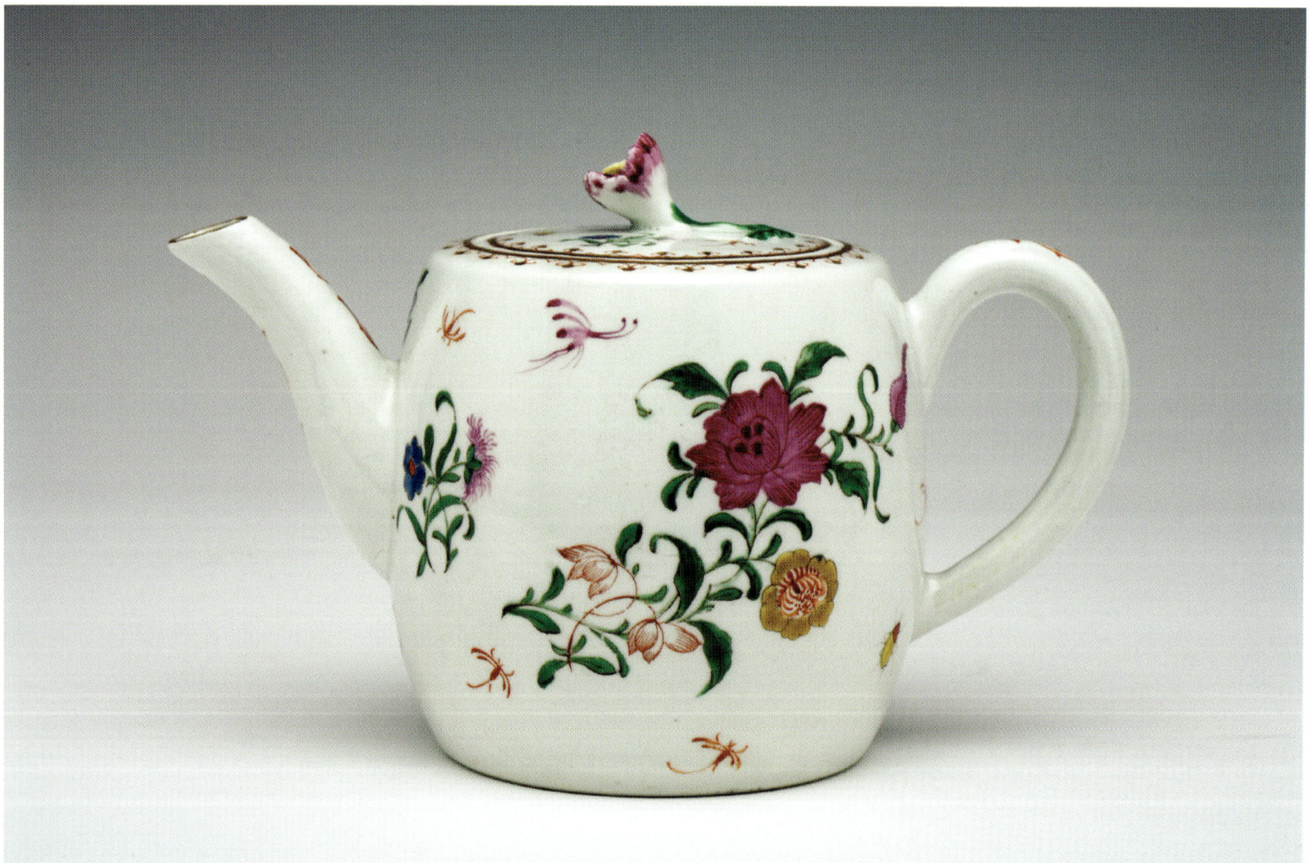

359

358

Teapot and lid

1768–70
Ht 13.8 cm
1957.24.1.836

Globular, plain loop handle, conical knop; decorated with a bouquet of Oriental foliage and flowers; border of green and purple alternating with red diaper around lid and neck.

359

Teapot and lid

About 1770
Ht 10.9 cm
1957.24.1.858

Barrel shaped, loop handle, flush lid with rosebud knop; gilt and red dagger border around lid and top of teapot; similar Oriental floral decoration with a ladybird on both sides.

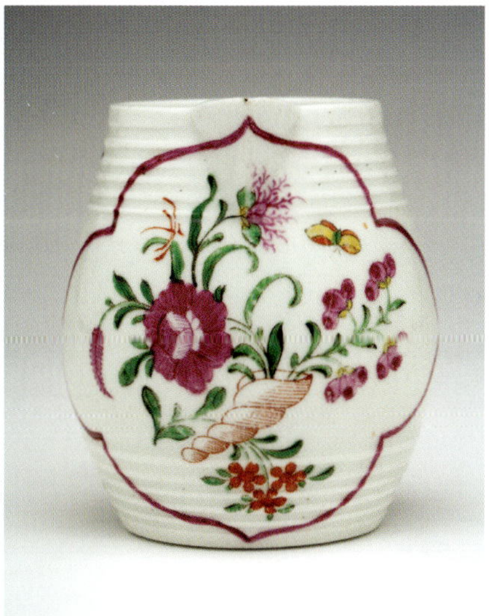

360

360

Cream jug

About 1765
Ht 8 cm
1957.24.1.1046

Barrel shape; predominately pink floral bouquet within puce barbed quatrefoil cartouche. A teapot with similar decoration is illustrated in Spero and Sandon 1996, pl. 147.

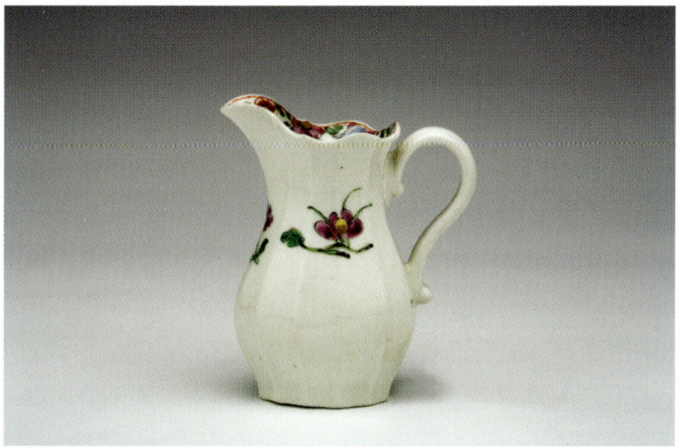

361

361

Cream jug

About 1765
Ht 9.4 cm
1957.24.1.984

Fluted, elongated bell shape, slightly ribbed handle with shell moulding at top; decorated with three small carmine flower sprays; multicoloured formalised floral border inside rim.

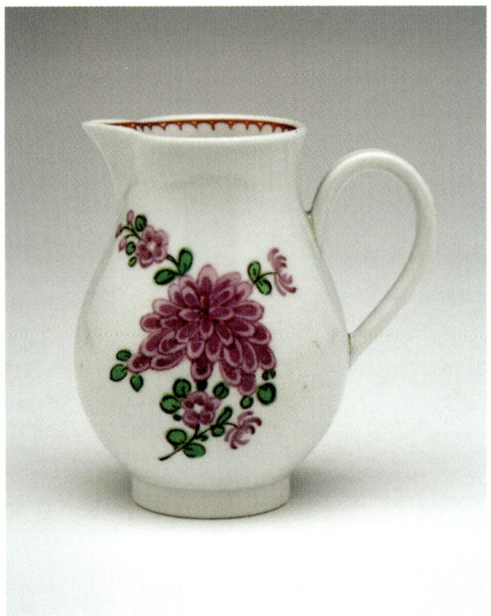

362

362

Cream jug

About 1780
Ht 8.4 cm
1957.24.1.810

Ribbed handle, red loop border inside rim; decorated with a bold posy of purplish flowers.

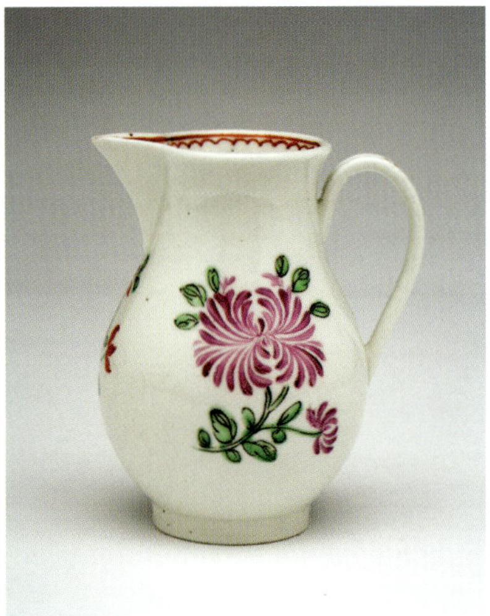

363

363

Cream jug

About 1780
Ht 9.4 cm
1957.24.1.1045

Ribbed loop handle, red loop border inside rim; decorated with pink aster-type flowers; scarlet pimpernel spray below spout.

364

Teapot and lid

1780–85
Ht 13.5 cm
1957.24.1.56

Globular, ribbed loop handle, rosebud knop; decorated with floral bouquets and sprays; pink scale border around neck and lid.

365

Teapot stand

1780–85
Width 14.8 cm
1957.24.1.1036

Hexagonal, fluted; iron red line on rim, below which are six reserves with pink scale; floral spray in centre.

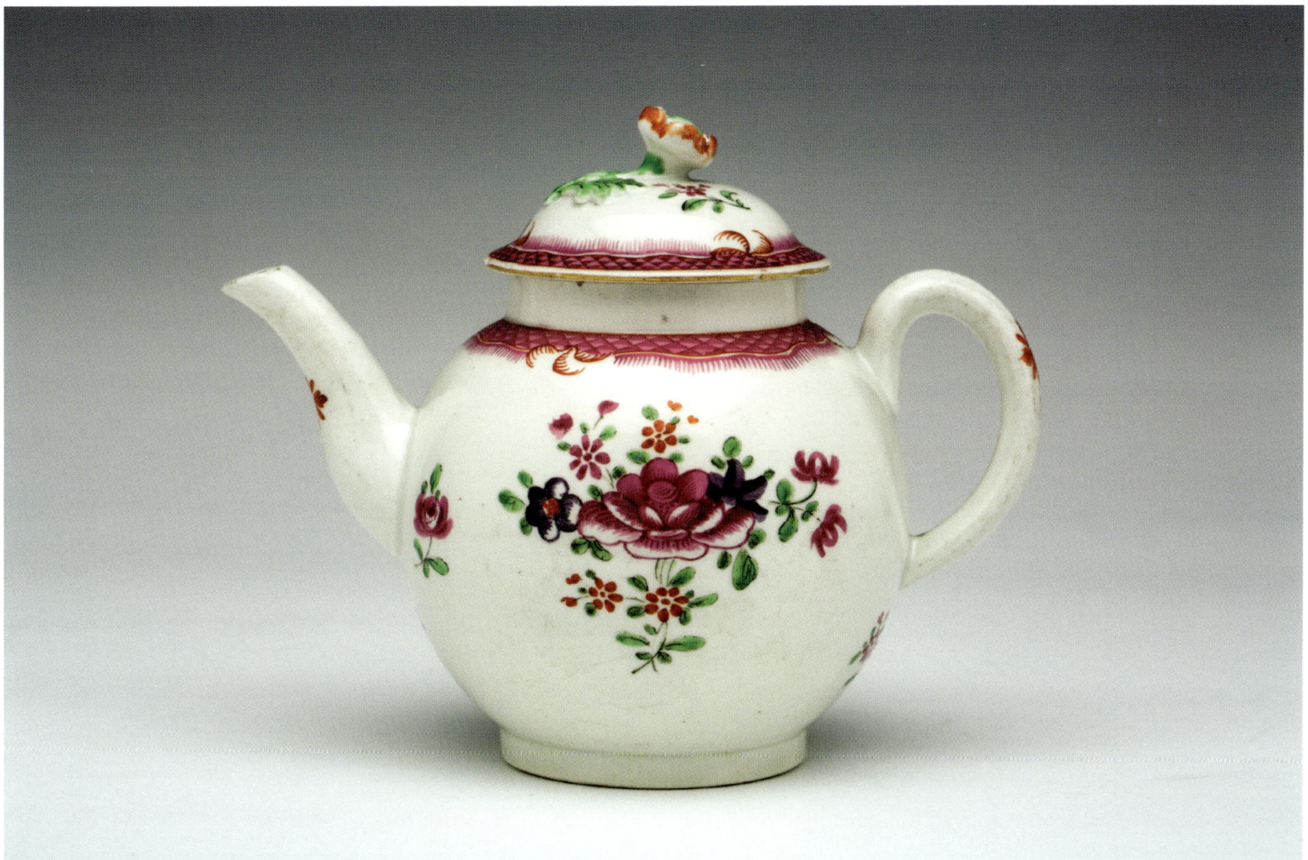

364

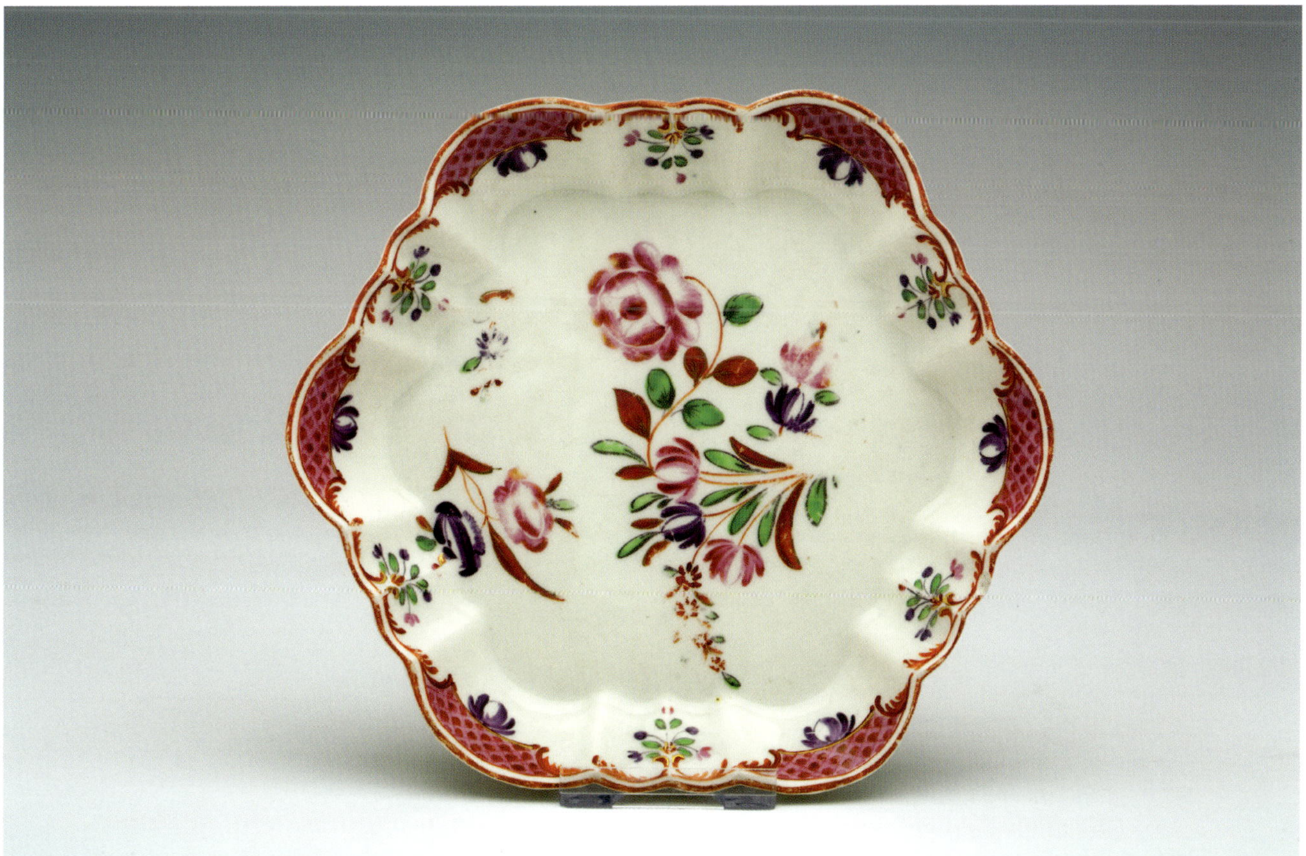

365

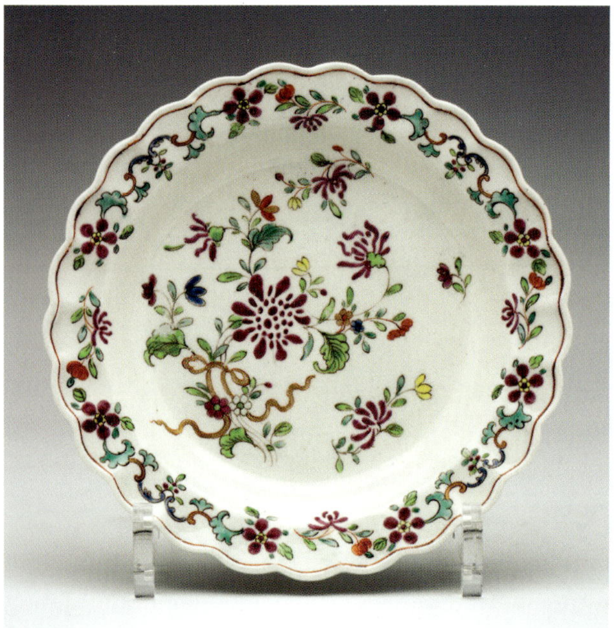

366

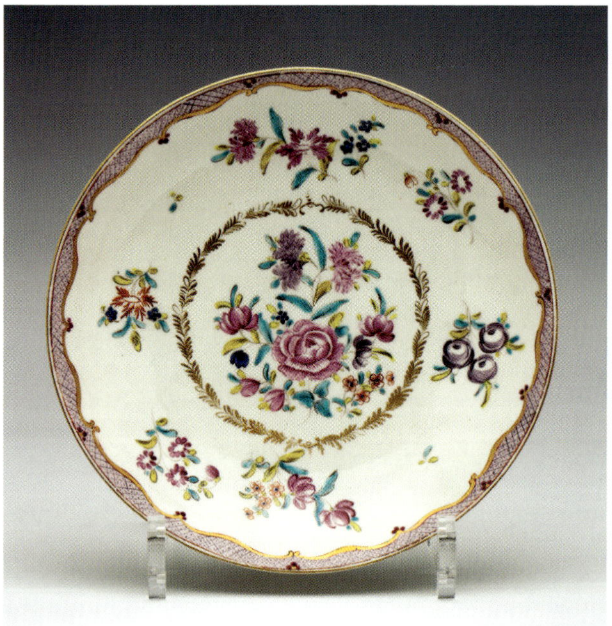

367

366

Plate or stand

1775–80
Diam. 16.3 cm
1957.24.1. 865

Scalloped edge; fluted border with wreath of formalised green and red flowers; further red, green and blue flower sprays tied with gilt bow in centre.

REFERENCE
Spero and Sandon 1996, pl. 156.

367

Cake dish

About 1780
Diam. 18 cm
1957.24.1.1064

Irregular mauve diaper border, with darker spots defined by gilt line; gilt wreath surrounds central bouquet of flowers; smaller sprays around.

368

Teapot and lid

1770–75
Ht 14.9 cm
1957.24.1.176

Globular, ribbed loop handle, conical knop; decorated on each side with a central bouquet, entirely in carmine and gold, and smaller sprays surrounded by scroll gilding.

369

Covered milk jug

1765–70
Ht 12.7 cm
1957.24.1.62

Ovoid, rosebud knop; carmine floral decoration with one spray below spout within gilt cartouche.

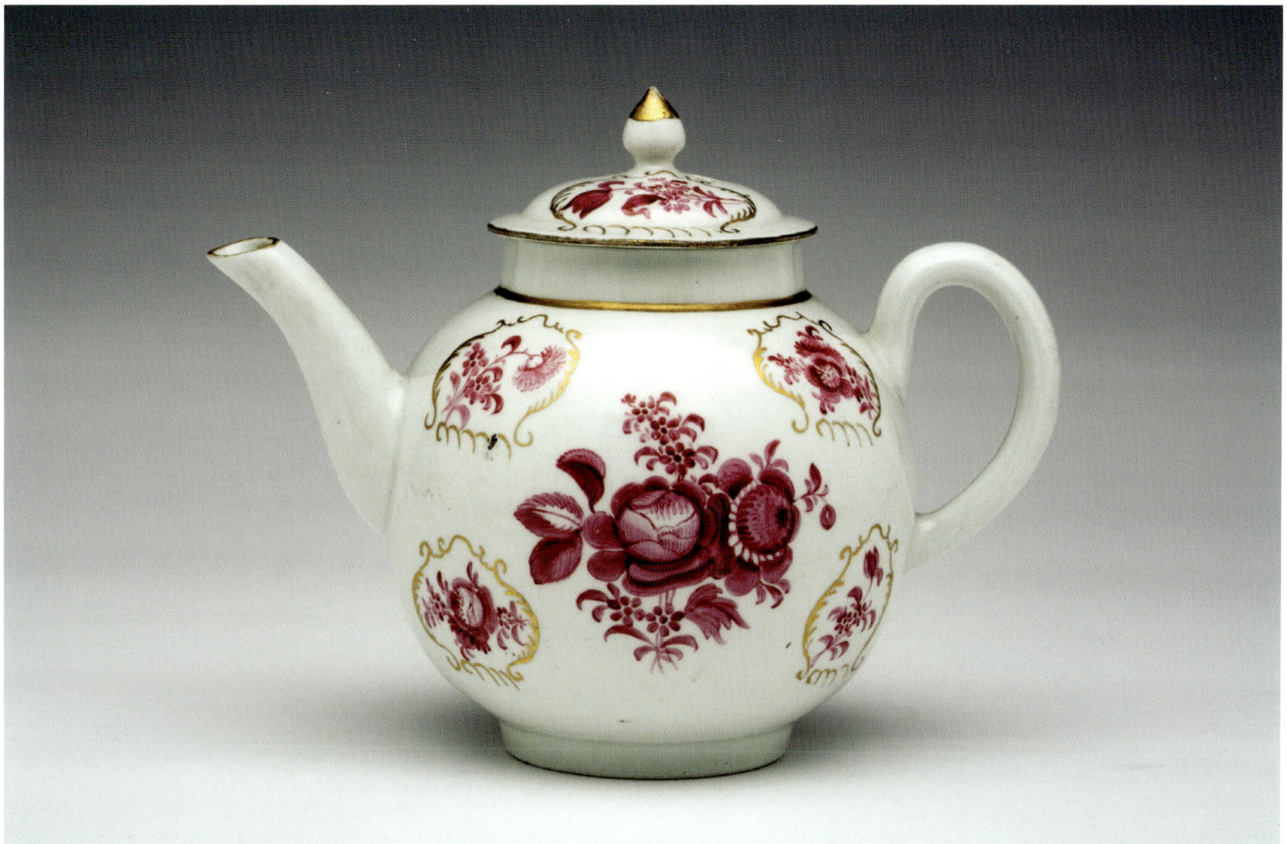

368

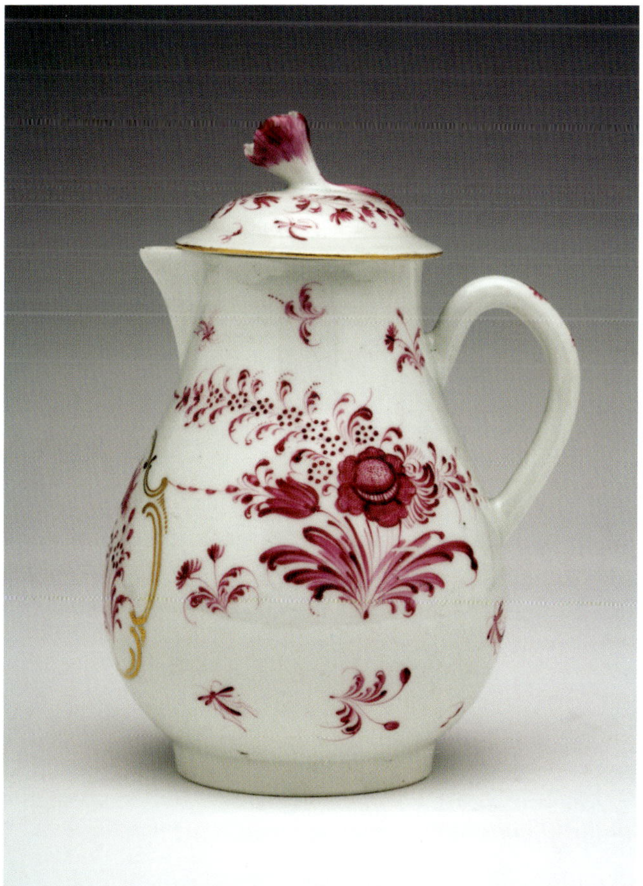

369

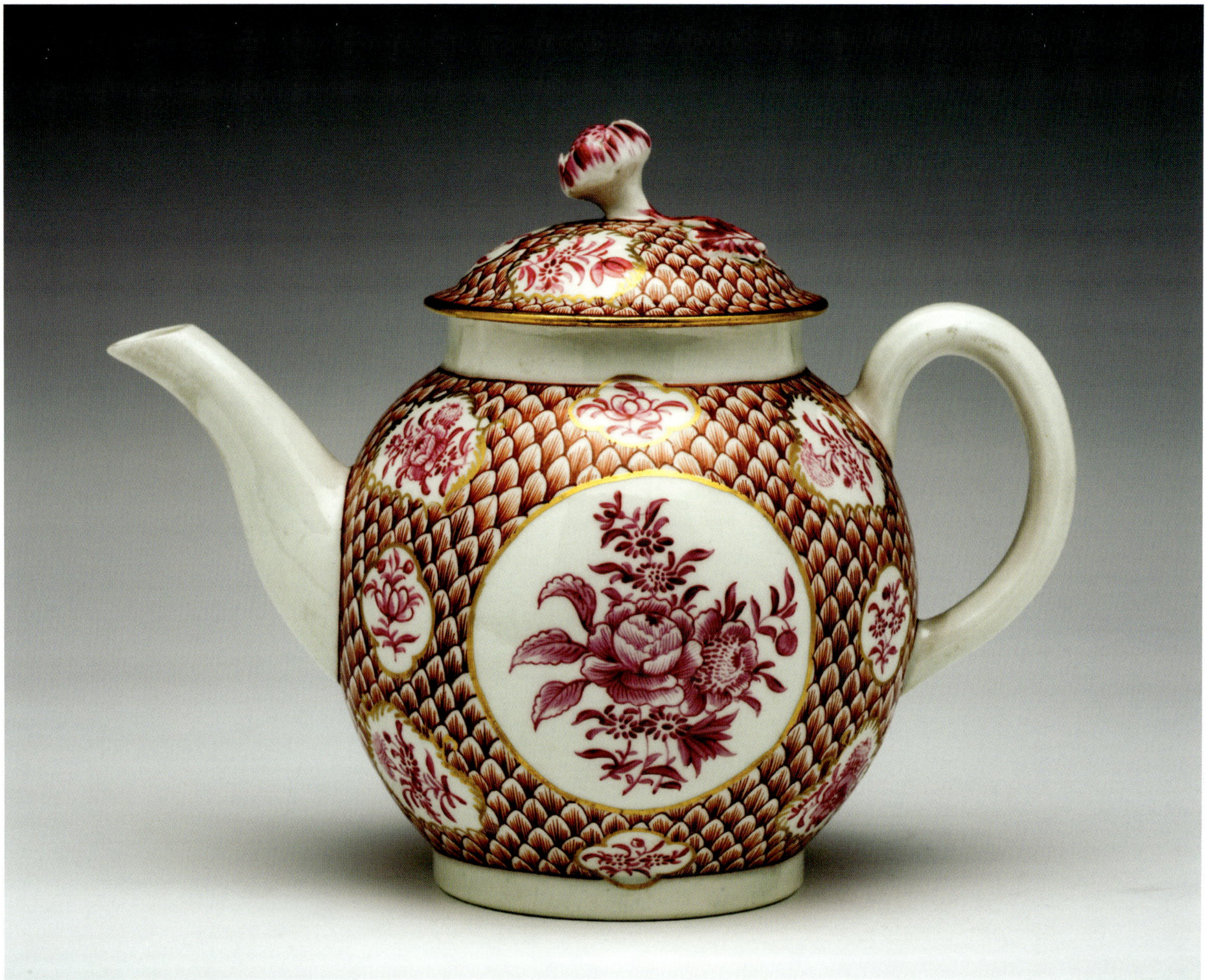

370

370

Teapot and lid

1770–75
Ht 16 cm
1957.24.1.912

Globular, plain white loop handle and spout, rosebud knop; upward red scale ground around one large circular reserve and seven smaller ones, defined by gilding, all with puce flowers; copy of a Chinese design.

PROVENANCE
Hengrave Hall sale 1897, lot 850; Collins and Clark, Cambridge, 17 September 1952, £290.

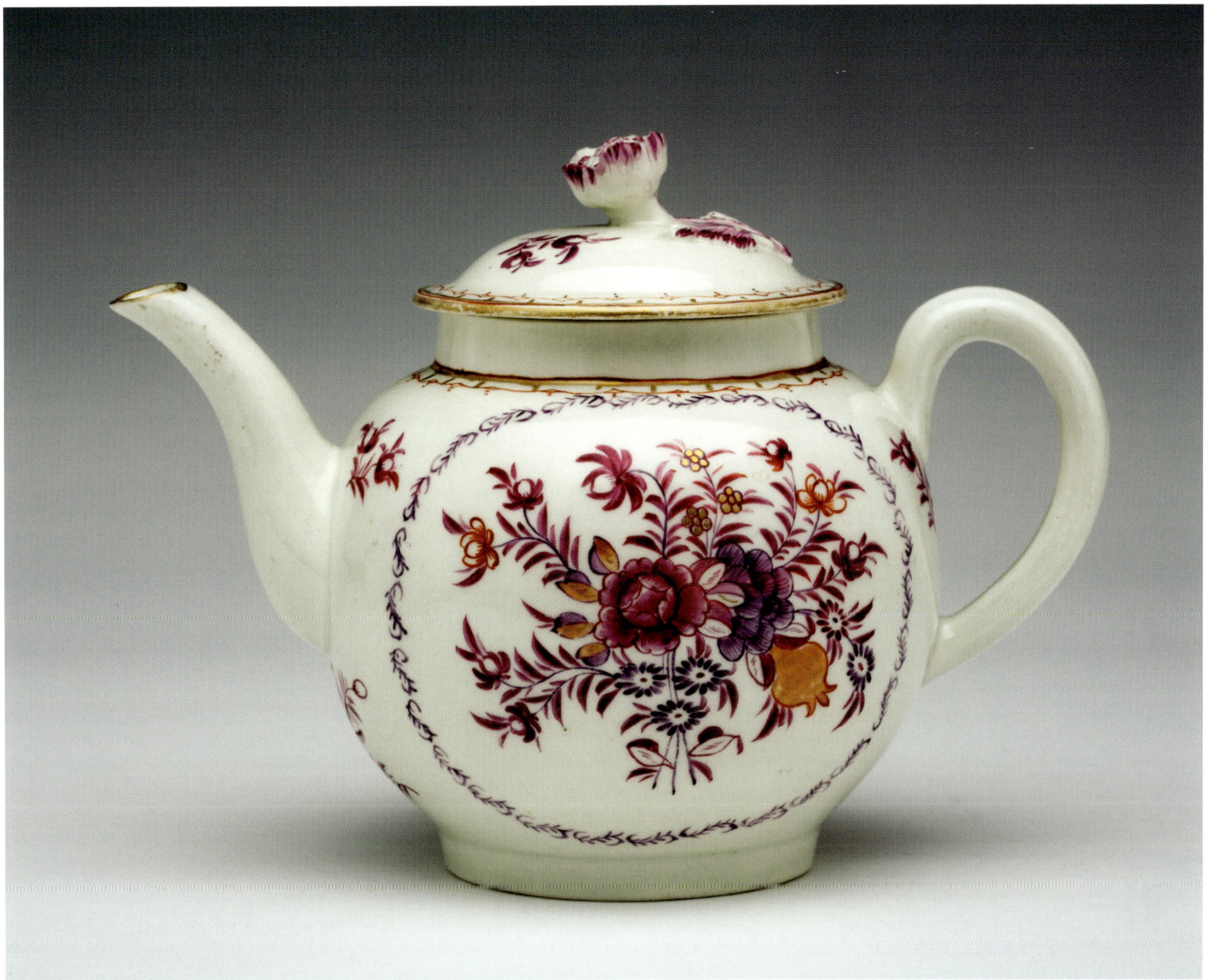

371

371

Teapot and lid

1780–85
Ht 12.9 cm
1957.24.1.60

Globular, plain white loop handle, rosebud knop; simple red and gilt border around lid and base of neck; on either side, a large bouquet of flowers in pink, purple and brown with gold touches, within narrow purple scrollwork; six other small carmine floral sprays.

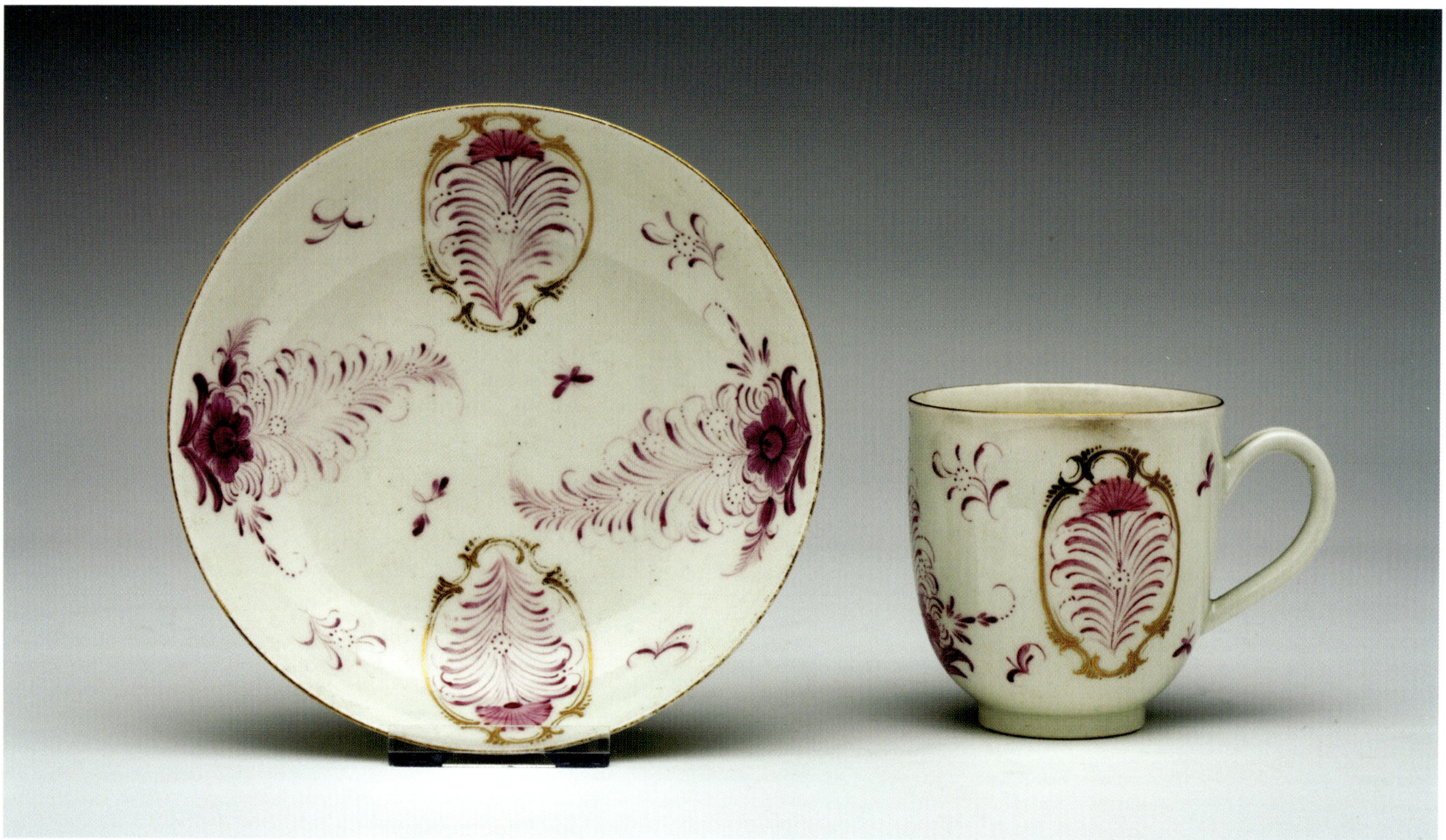

372

372

Coffee cup and saucer

1780–85

Cup ht 6.5 cm, diam. 5.9 cm; saucer diam. 12.2 cm

1957.24.1.1065

Decorated entirely in carmine and gilt with floral sprays, two within gilt cartouches.

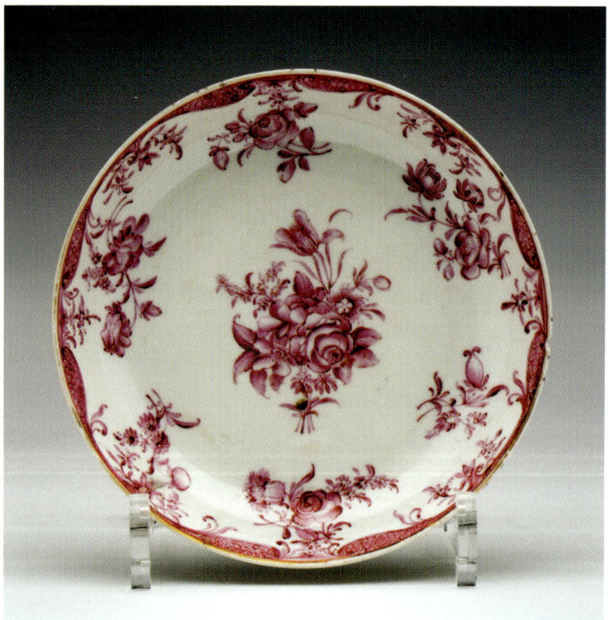

373

373

Chinese saucer dish

Eighteenth century

Diam. 15.5 cm

1957.24.1.175

Painted in London with puce floral decoration.

6

Japanese Influences 1765–1790

BY ABOUT 1639 Japan had ceased trading with the English and the Portuguese, and only traded directly with the Dutch (from a trading post on Deshima Island on Nagasaki Bay) and the Chinese. Most Japanese Kakiemon porcelain that went to China was bought by the English East India Company, but large quantities were also directly exported to Europe through the agency of the Dutch East India Company (VOC). The Dutch preferred blue and white decoration but also imported many pieces in the bold red, blue and gold Imari style, named after the port from which it was shipped to Nagasaki for further distribution. Although exports to Europe from Japan only lasted from 1659 (the year of the first large order placed by the VOC) until about 1745, China made a large quantity of copies from then until the 1770s.

Two distinct types of enamelled decoration were favoured by the VOC, a delicate Kakiemon style and a more richly decorated Imari style. Kakiemon decoration is sparse and asymmetric, with a limited palette of blue, turquoise, iron red, yellow and occasionally manganese on a milky white body. It was particularly sought after by European aristocracy. Its name, meaning 'persimmon' (Japanese *kaki*), can be used to refer to a type of Japanese porcelain made mostly for the export market, or to a particular kiln-site in south-west Arita. Alternatively, it may be used as a name or 'title' by the Sakaida family of potters working at Arita, possibly from the mid-seventeenth century, honouring their development of this distinctive palette, including an orange-red enamel the colour of persimmon. Imari decoration, characterised by dense patterns and underglaze blue, is often used for borders and backgrounds, with coloured enamels added over the glaze. The typical palette is blue with iron red and gold. The chrysanthemum is a frequent motif, symbolising autumn, and was the emblem of the Japanese imperial family.

Much Meissen porcelain was decorated in Kakiemon style between the 1720s and the 1740s, initially under the patronage of Augustus the Strong (1670–1733), Elector of Saxony. In France, Kakiemon decoration was used frequently at Chantilly, where the nearby chateau of the Prince of Condé housed an extensive collection of Japanese porcelain. Diplomat and merchant Sir Everard Fawkener (1694–1758) and Sir Charles Hanbury Williams (1708–1759), British Ambassador to Dresden 1747–50, provided the Chelsea factory with imported porcelain to copy, mostly from Meissen. Japanese porcelain in England was found mainly in great houses during the eighteenth century, so it is likely that the Worcester factory copied a number of patterns from more easily obtainable Chinese copies of the Imari style, rather than from Japanese originals.

Some patterns, for example the 'Quail', 'Kempthorne', 'Fan' and 'Brocade', derive closely from Japanese Kakiemon and Imari designs, although the immediate source was probably Meissen or a Chelsea interpretation. A frequently used image is a phoenix, known in Japan as *ho-o*, later interpreted in England as a 'ho-ho bird'. A well-known pattern with a long-tailed bird perched on a rock is now named by collectors after Sir Joshua Reynolds, although there is no evidence to link it with the painter. This derives from a Kakiemon pattern originating about 1700; a similar decoration appears on Meissen, Chantilly, Chelsea and elsewhere. Worcester first used a version of this pattern in the mid-1750s and it was then reintroduced in about 1768

Another design from a Japanese original, used at Meissen, is based on a phoenix rising from the ashes. The 'Jabberwocky' pattern name, a modern term, derives from Lewis Carroll's nonsense poem in *Through the Looking Glass and What Alice Found There* (1871), illustrated by Sir John Tenniel with a dragon-like creature writhing around forest trees (fig. 25):

> Beware the Jabberwock, my son!
> The jaws that bite, the claws that catch!…
> … the Jabberwock with eyes of flame
> Came waffling through the tulgey wood

By combining motifs such as birds and wheatsheaves into more flamboyant and elaborate patterns, Worcester developed its own rich Kakiemon style, reinterpreting it in a stronger palette, often with gilding, to appeal to the taste of the 1760s.

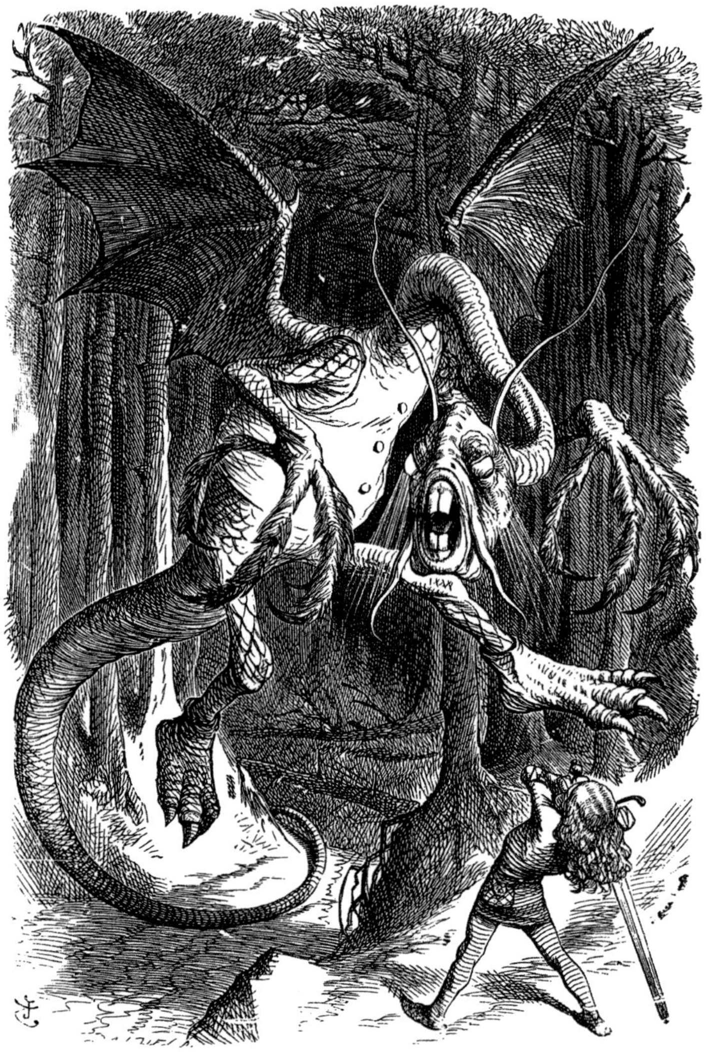

Fig. 25 Sir John Tenniel, *The Jabberwock*, illustration for *Through the Looking Glass and what Alice Found* by Lewis Carroll, 1871

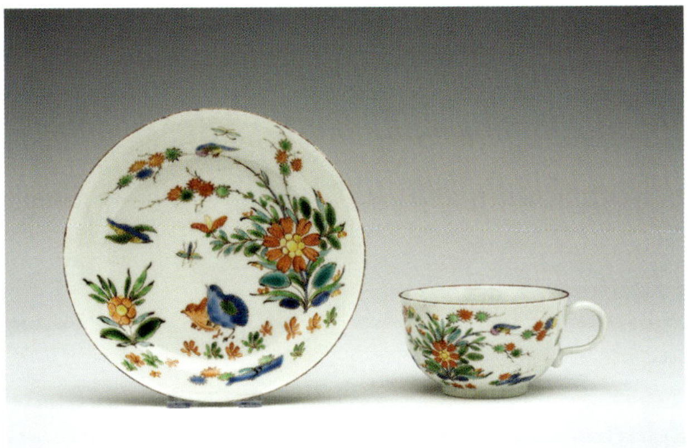

374

374

Teacup and saucer

About 1765
Cup ht 4.6 cm, diam. 7.6 cm; saucer diam. 12.9 cm
Mark: crossed swords and 9 with a dot on both
1957.24.1.527

Everted rim on cup, brown edge; decorated with a version of the 'Quail' pattern with an additional songbird in flight, unusual foliage and flowers. There may be as many as thirteen variations of this pattern on Worcester porcelain associated with a number of different marks. Although the original design is Japanese, the Worcester version was probably inspired by Meissen, filtered through Chelsea and Bow.

REFERENCE
Girton 2004.

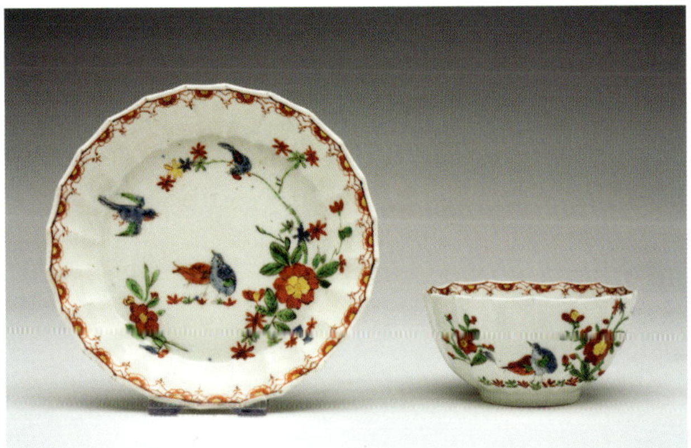

375

375

Teabowl and saucer

1765–70
Bowl ht 4.2 cm, diam. 7.8 cm; saucer diam. 11.8 cm
Mark: fretted square on bowl
1957.24.1.272

Fluted with scalloped edge; irregular red patterned border, decorated with a version of the 'Quail' pattern

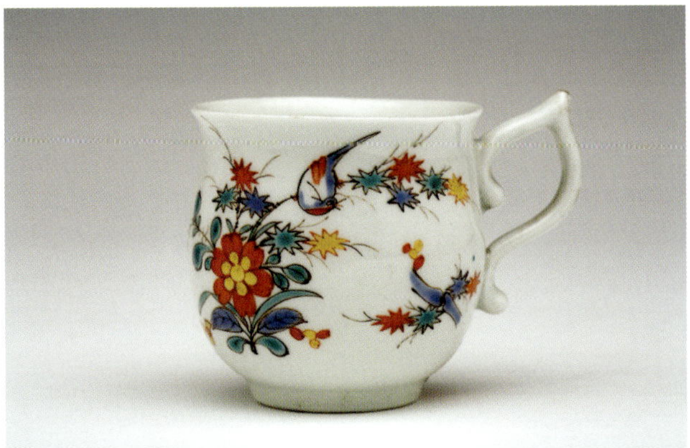

376

376

Coffee cup

1760–62
Ht 5.7 cm, diam. 5.4 cm
1957.24.1.486

Bulbous body, everted lip, peaked or wishbone handle; decorated with the 'Quail' pattern; Oriental flowers and two quails with dark brown backs, light brown breasts and turquoise wings; possibly by Giles.

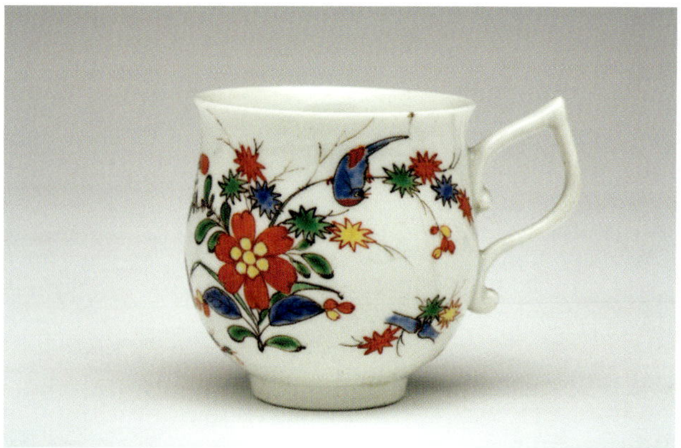
377

377
Coffee cup
1760–62
Ht 5.9 cm, diam. 5.3 cm
1957.24.1.482

Similar to no. 376 but with green wings; possibly by Giles.

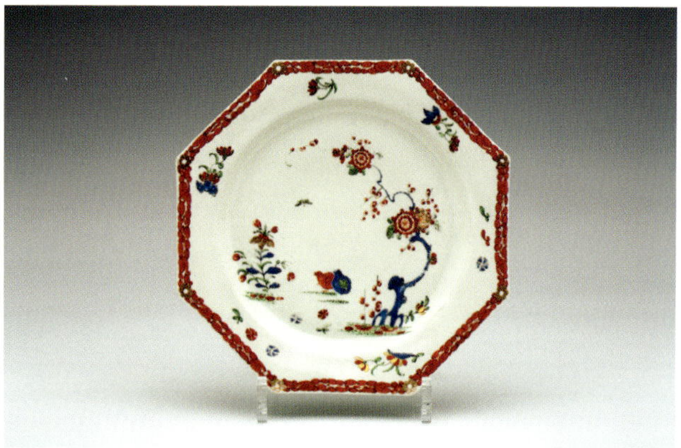
378

378
Plate
1770–80
Width 21.1 cm
1957.24.1.278

Octagonal; iron red and gilt border, painted in a version of the 'Quail' pattern, similar to Chelsea and Bow.

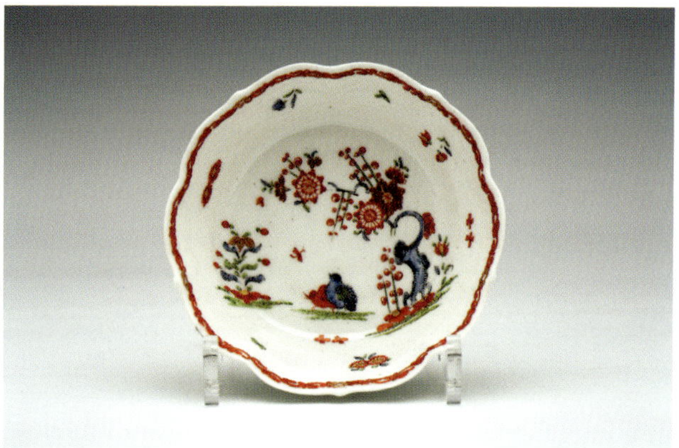
379

379
Saucer
1775–80
Ht 4.7 cm, diam. 14 cm
Mark: incised *W* and double cross
1957.24.1.531

Deep shape to hold a caudle cup; iron red border, decorated with the 'Quail' pattern.

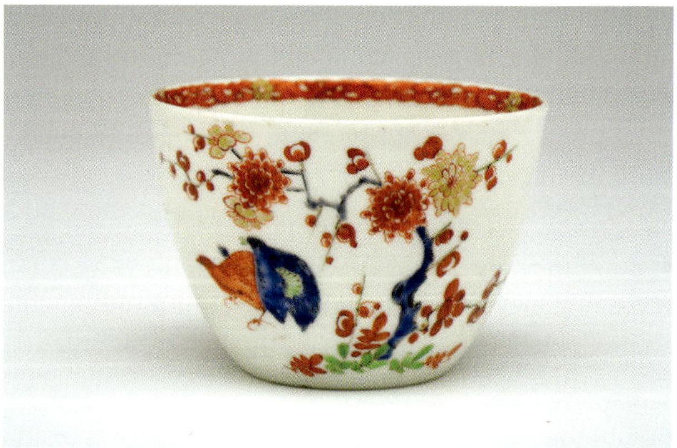
380

380
Teabowl
1770–80
Ht 4.9 cm, diam. 6.8 cm
Mark: open gold crescent
1957.24.1.959

Conical shape; iron red border inside rim, decorated with the 'Quail' pattern.

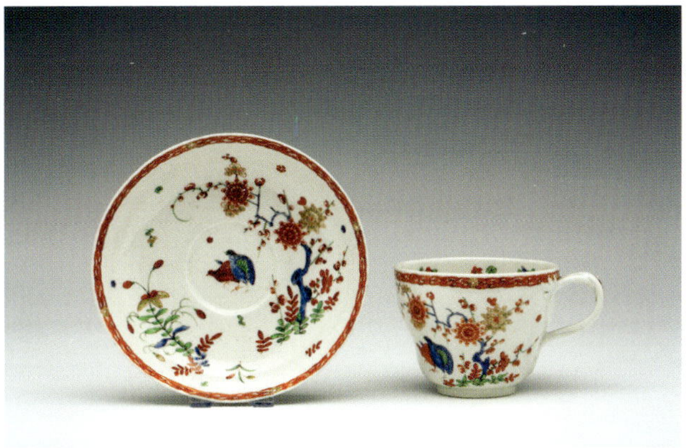

381

381

Teacup and saucer

1770–80
Cup ht 6.5 cm, diam. 8 cm, saucer diam. 13.3 cm
Mark: open red crescent on both
1957.24.1.535

Cup of ogee form with entwined branch handle; iron red border; decorated with the 'Quail' pattern.

382

Sugar bowl and cover

1765–75
Ht 12.4 cm, diam. 10.4 cm
1957.24.1.381

Sky blue border interrupted with iron red diaper, half-chrysanthemums and flowers below; decorated with the 'Quail' pattern.

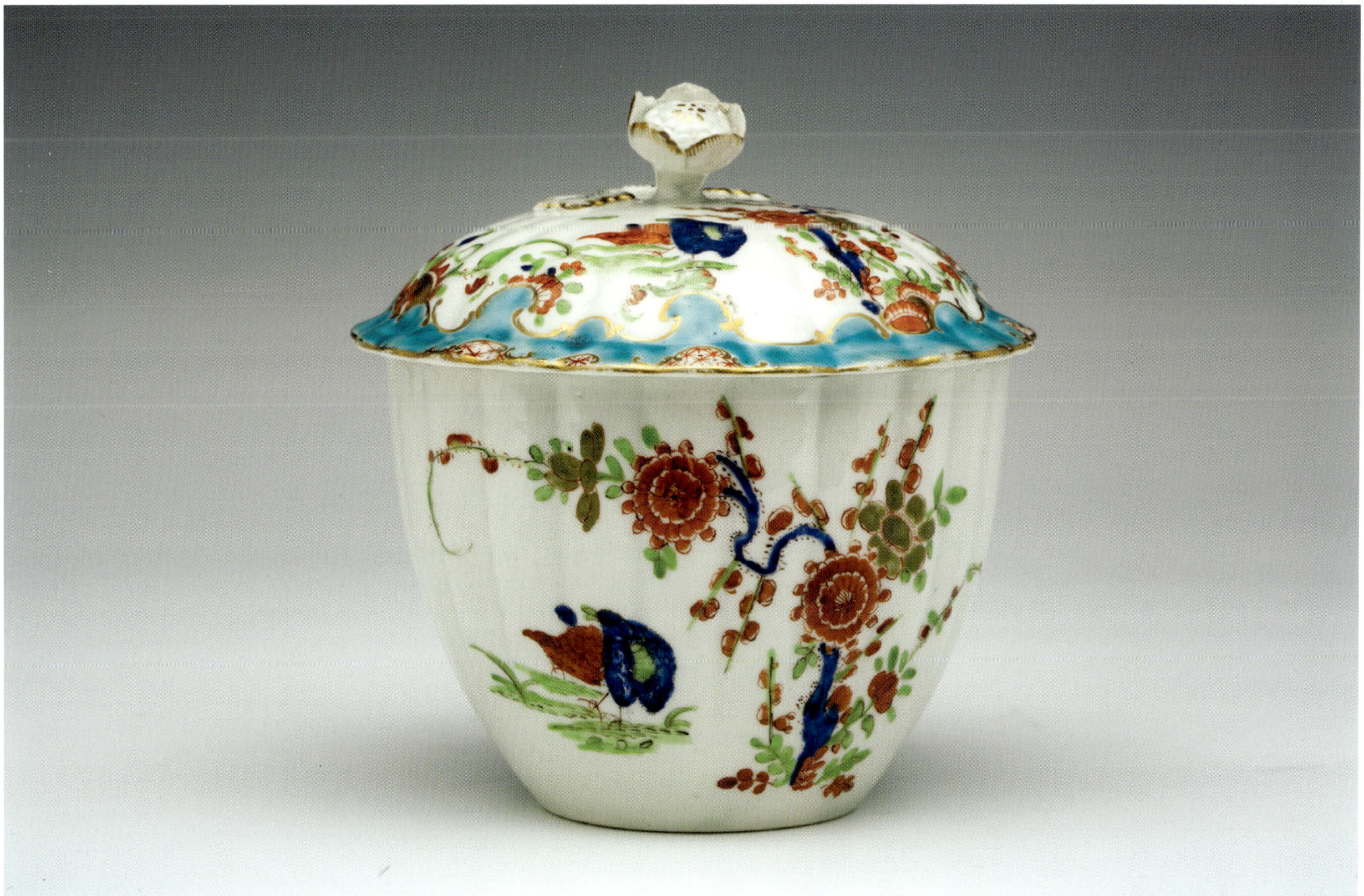

382

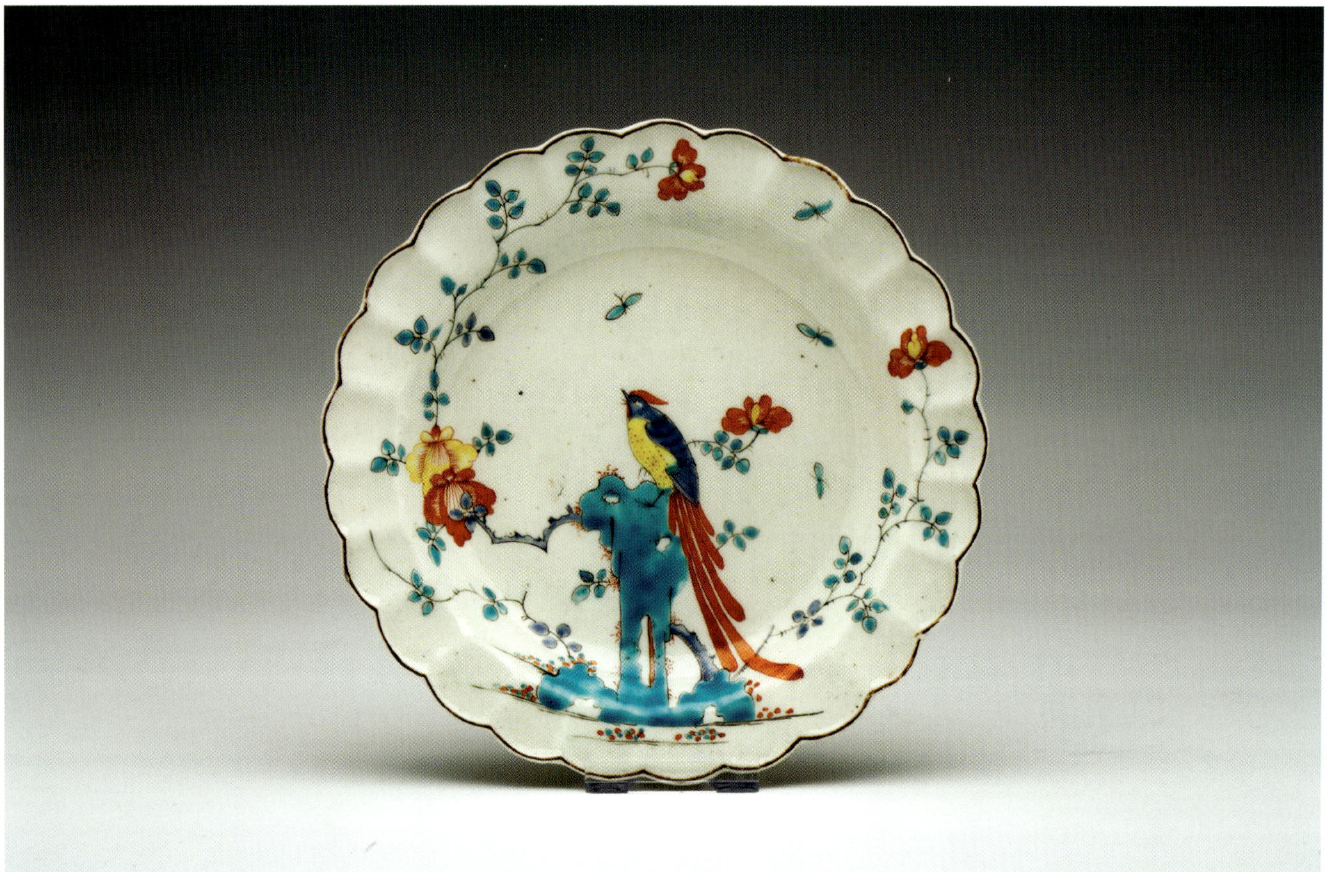

383

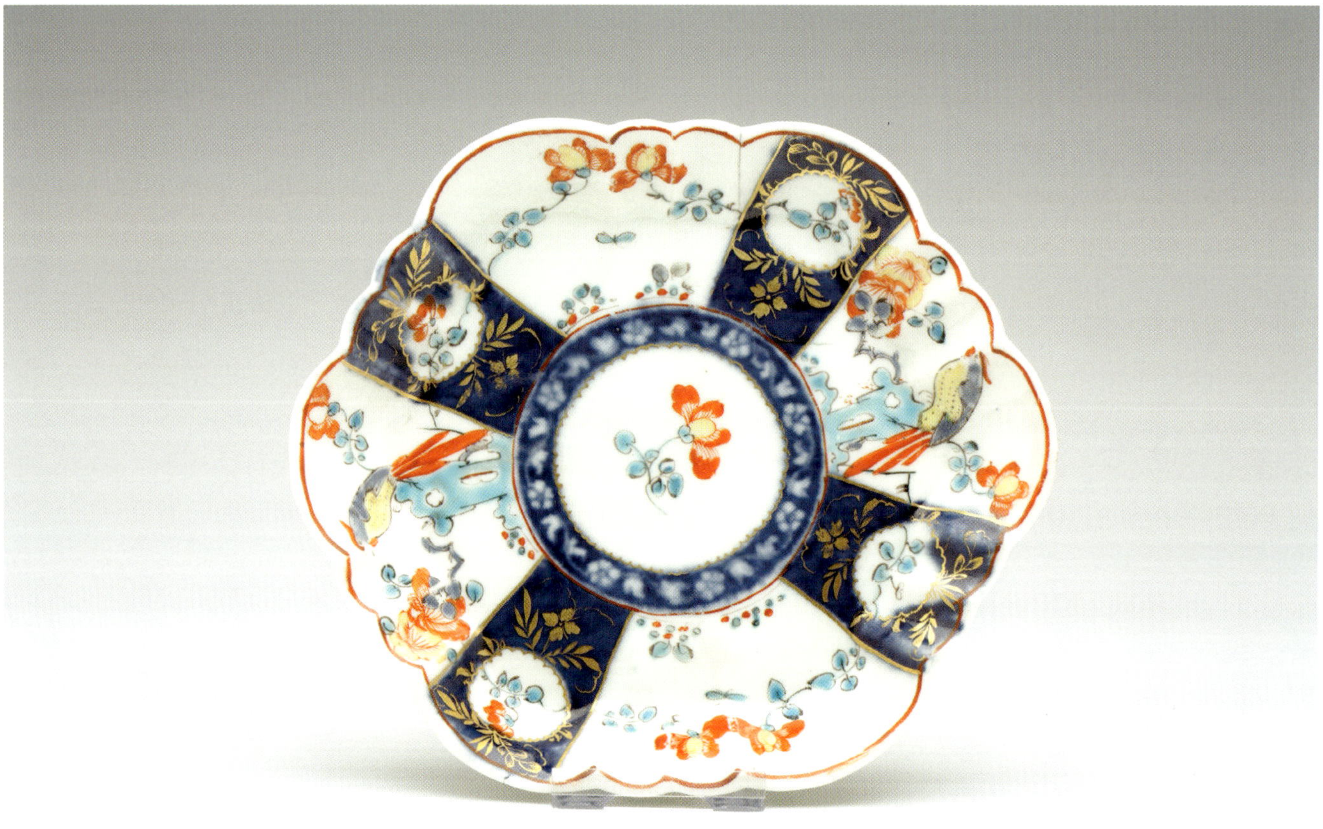

384

383

Plate or stand

About 1768
Diam. 15.7 cm
1957.24.1.494

Brown edge to wavy rim; decorated with the 'Sir Joshua Reynolds' pattern, a long-tailed bird perched on a turquoise rock, possibly corresponding to the 'fine old pheasant pattern' listed in Christie's 1769 sale of Worcester porcelain.

384

Teapot stand

1765–70
Diam. 14.4 cm
Mark: fretted square
1957.24.1.739

Hexagonal; fluted wavy edge with red line, four underglaze blue bands radiating from circle; decorated with the 'Sir Joshua Reynolds' pattern.

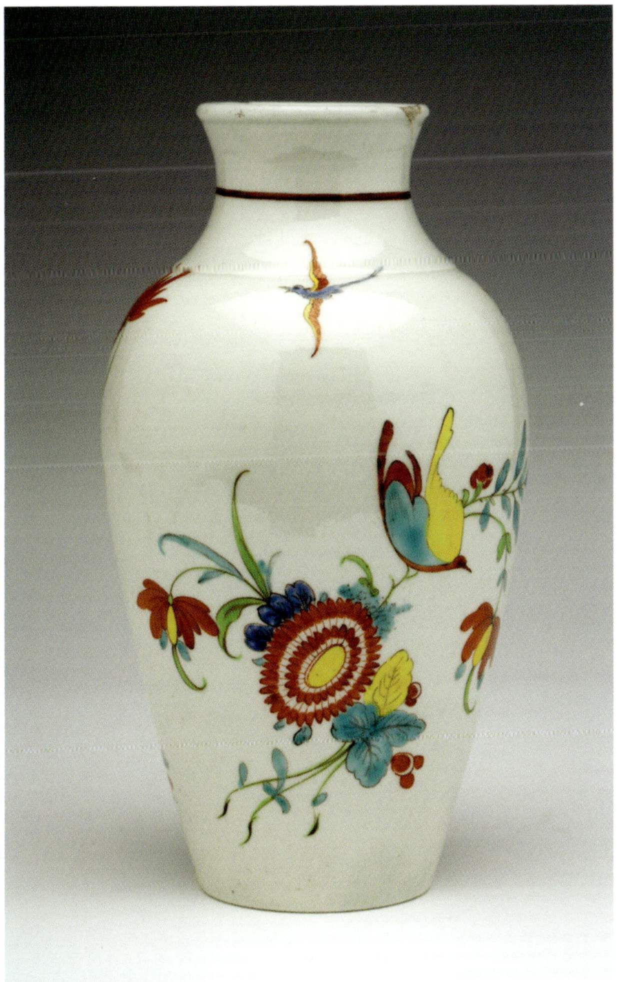

385

385

Vase

1768–70
Ht 17.6 cm
1957.24.1.849

Ovoid; no gilding, brown line around neck, decorated with chrysanthemums and other Oriental plants and foliage in an unusually bright palette. A bowl with similar decoration is illustrated in Spero and Sandon 1996, pl. 296.

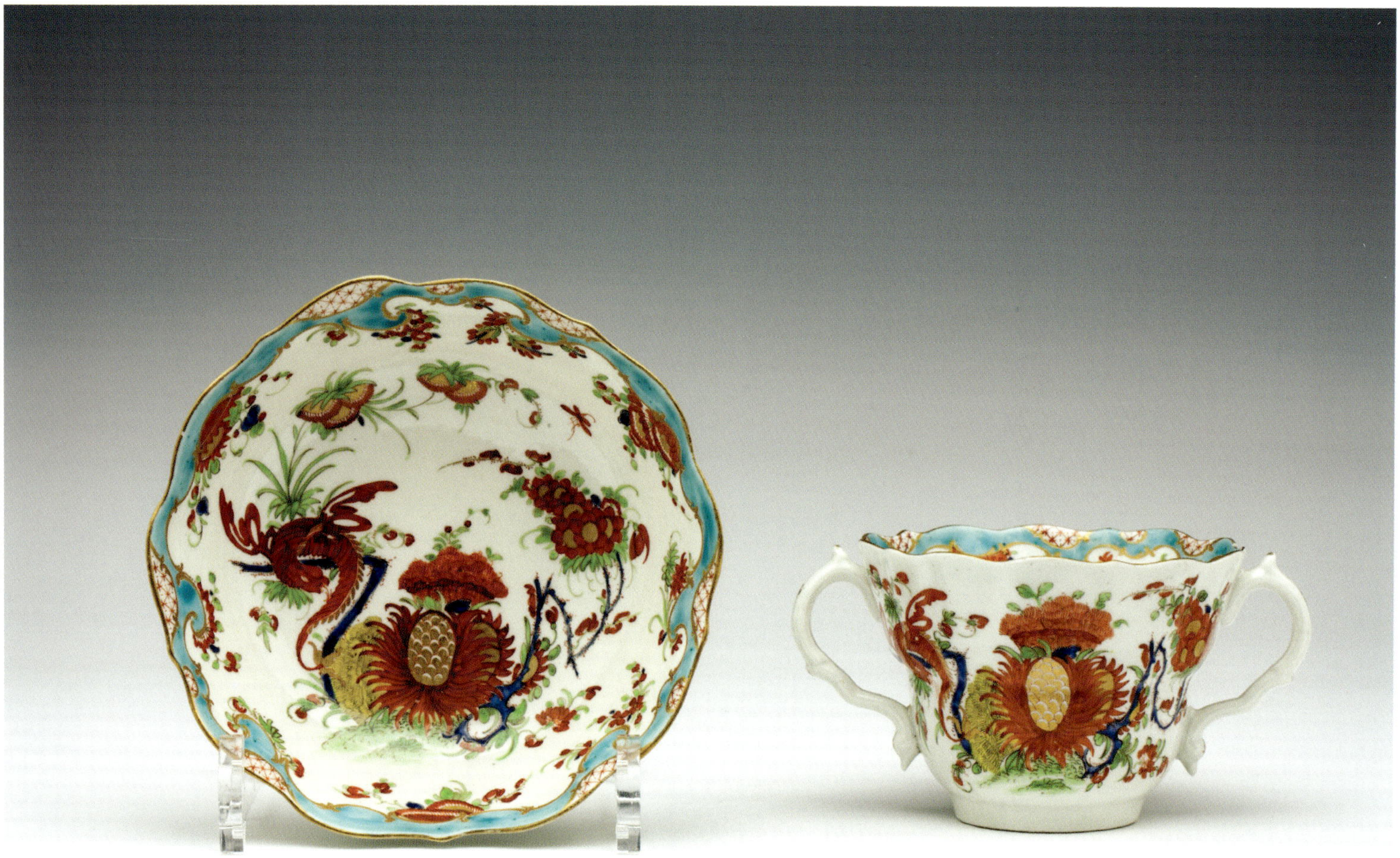

386

386

Caudle cup and saucer

1768–75
Cup ht 7.6 cm, diam. 10.1 cm; saucer diam. 14.8 cm
1957.24.1.344

Fluted with wavy edge, scroll handles; irregular sky-blue border with iron red diapering above, half chrysanthemums below; decorated with the 'Jabberwocky' pattern. The 1769 sale catalogue refers to 'fine old rich dragon pattern, bleu celeste borders'.

387, 388

Pair of vase candlesticks

About 1780
Each ht 21.6 cm
1957.24.1.354 and 357

Ogee body rising from circular base on square plinth; the covers are reversible, one being dome-shaped with an acorn knop like a vase, the other a candle nozzle with leaf moulded surround; decorated with a sky-blue border with iron red diapering and a 'Jabberwocky' with chrysanthemums. Popular in the eighteenth century, mantelpiece vases that also served as candlesticks were sometimes called *cassolettes*. Very few porcelain examples have survived.

PROVENANCE
H.W. Hughes Collection, no. 90; Albert Amor, London, December 1939, £80.

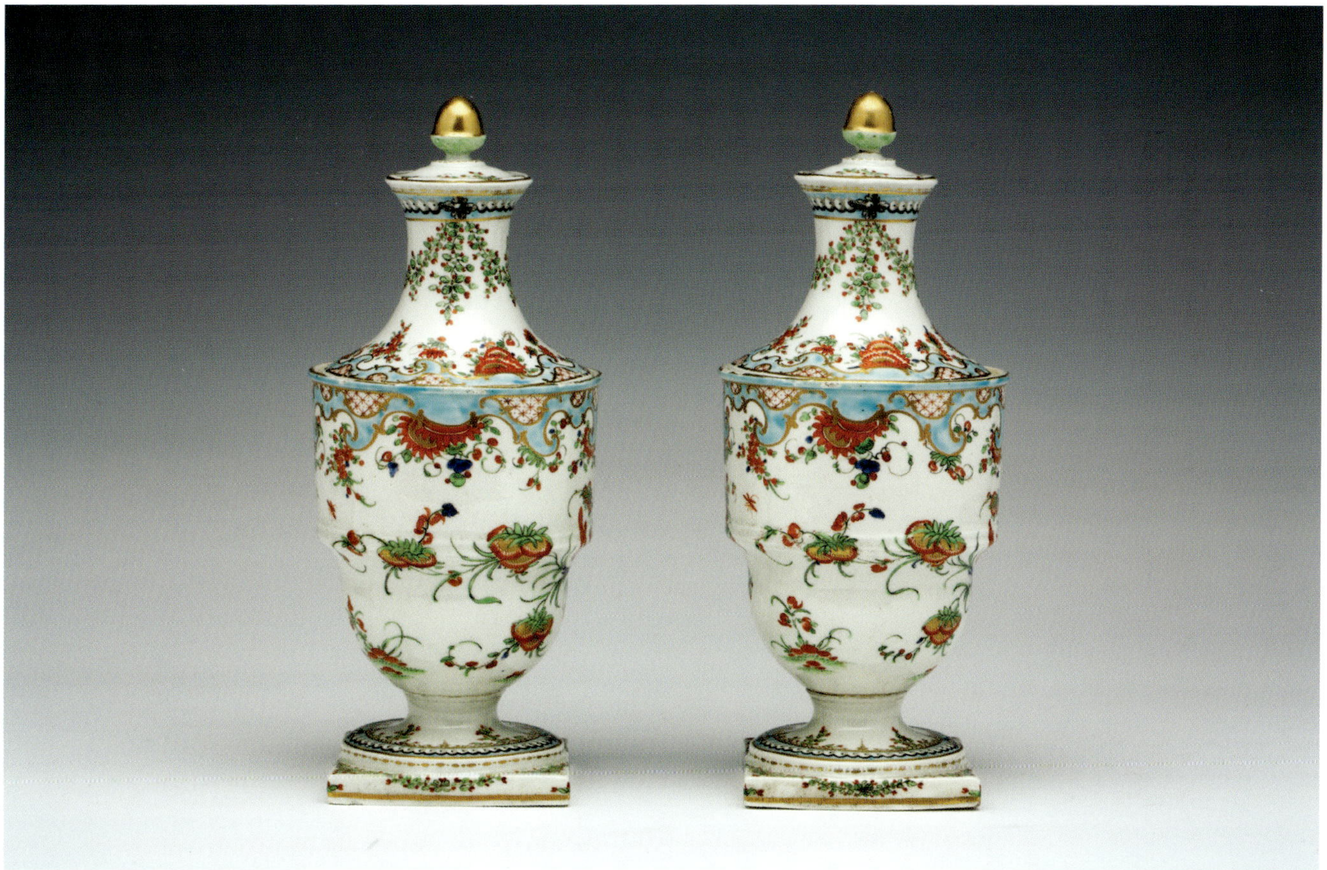

387, 388

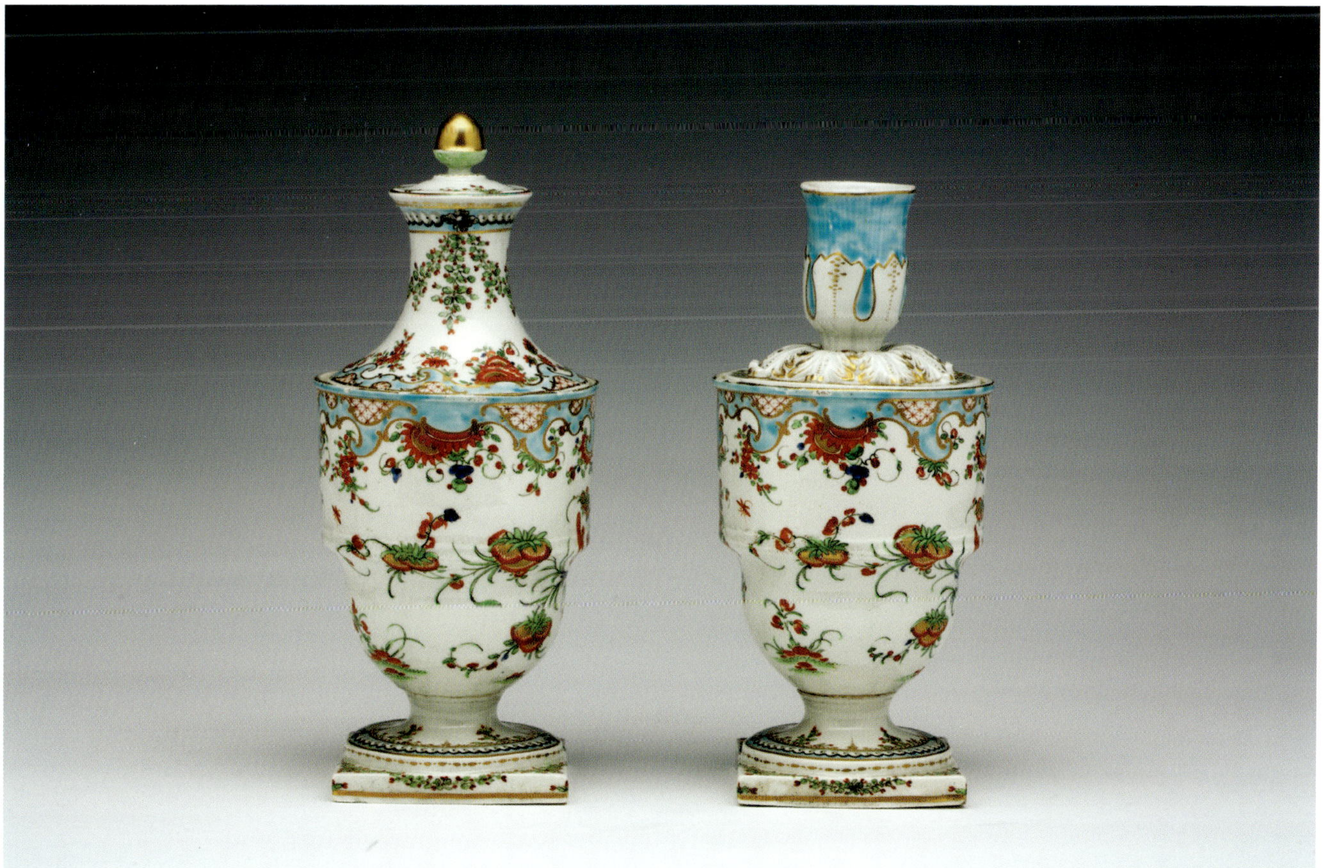

387, 388

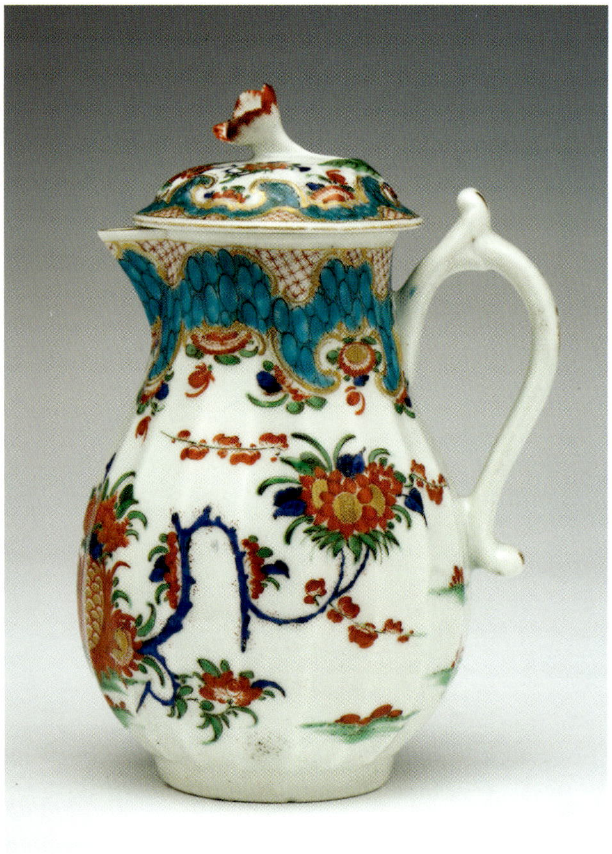

389

389

Covered milk jug

1768–75
Ht 13.7 cm
Mark: fretted square
1957.24.1.374

Ovoid, fluted scroll handle, rosebud knop; irregular sky-blue herring roe pattern border with iron red diapering; decorated with the 'Jabberwocky' pattern.

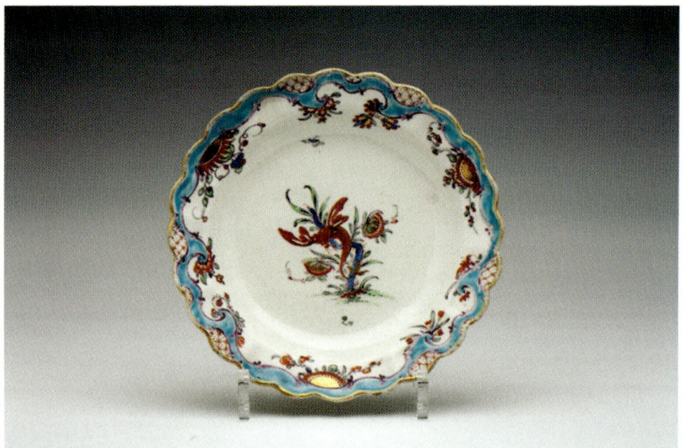

390

390

Plate

About 1785
Diam. 19.4 cm
1957.24.1.382

Scalloped gilt rim; irregular sky-blue border with iron red diaper panels, half chrysanthemums and floral sprays below; in the centre a simplified version of the 'Jabberwocky' pattern.

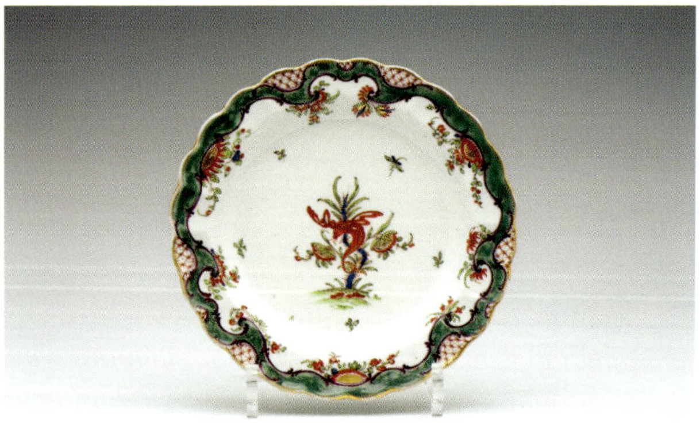

391

391

Plate

About 1785
Diam. 19.4 cm
1957.24.1.725

Similar to no. 390 but with an unusual dark green border, possibly overpainted. A cup with a comparable green border is illustrated in Spero and Sandon 1996, pl. 303.

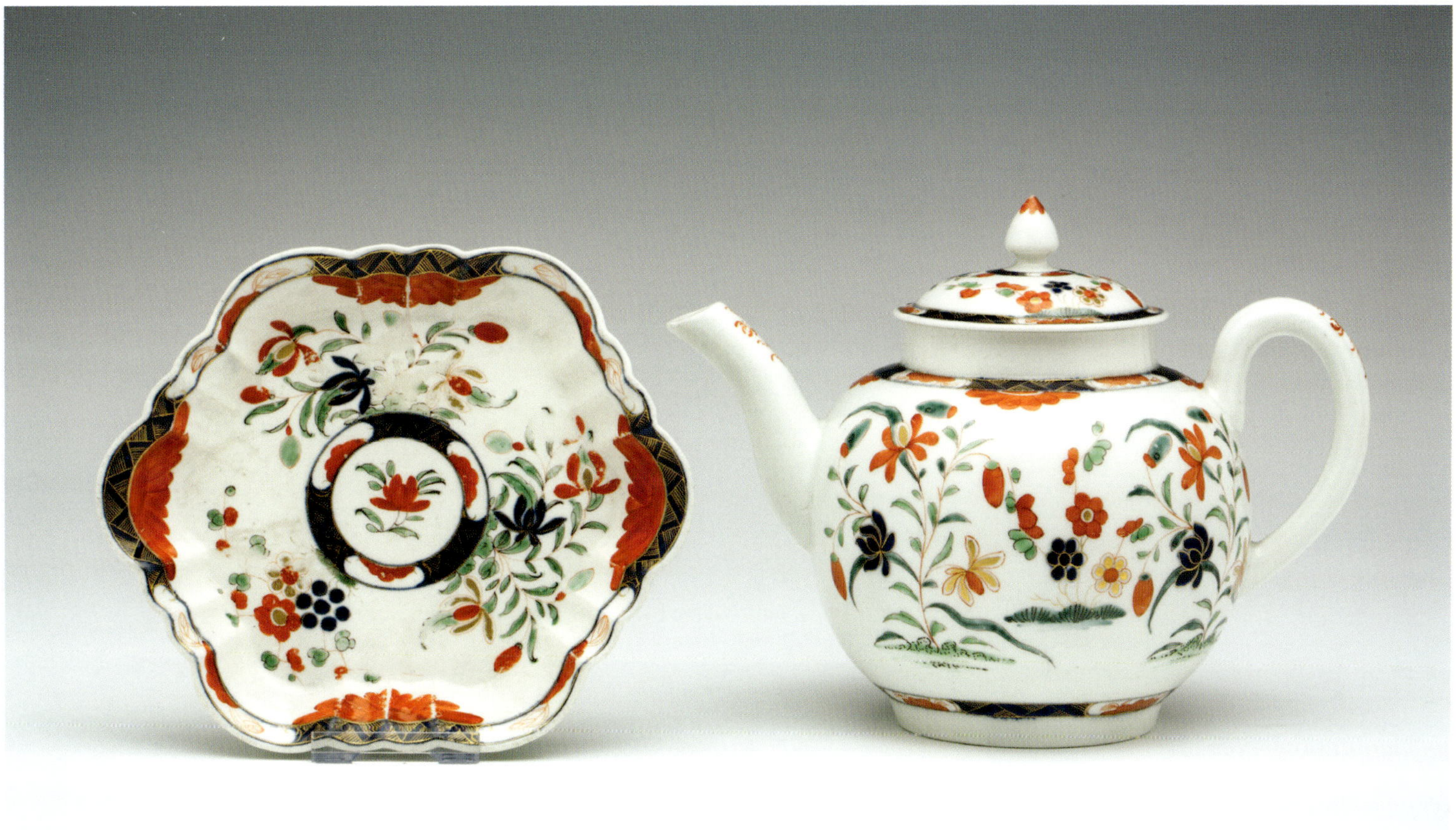

392

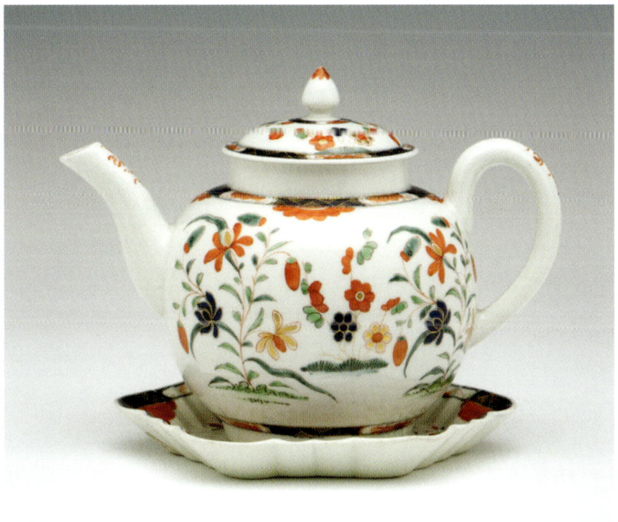

392

392

Teapot and stand

1768–70
Teapot ht 13.8 cm; stand width 14.7 cm
Mark: fretted square on stand
1957.24.1.847

Decorated in Japanese style in red, blue and green with the 'Kempthorne' pattern. The origins of this pattern are discussed in Sandon 1993, p. 213.

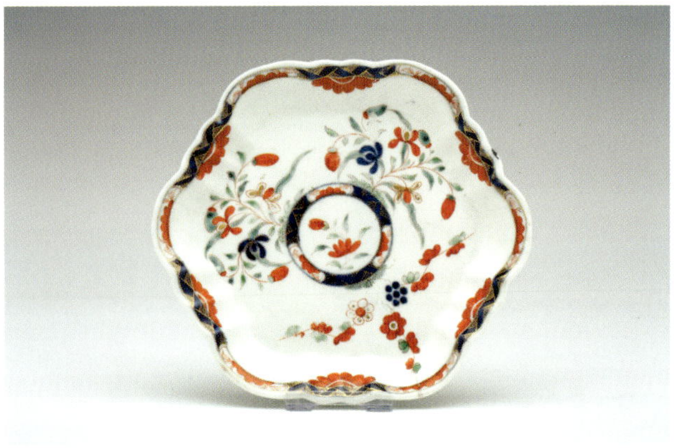

393

393

Teapot stand

1768–70
Width 14.8 cm
Mark: crescent
1957.24.1.741

Decorated in Japanese style with the 'Kempthorne' pattern.

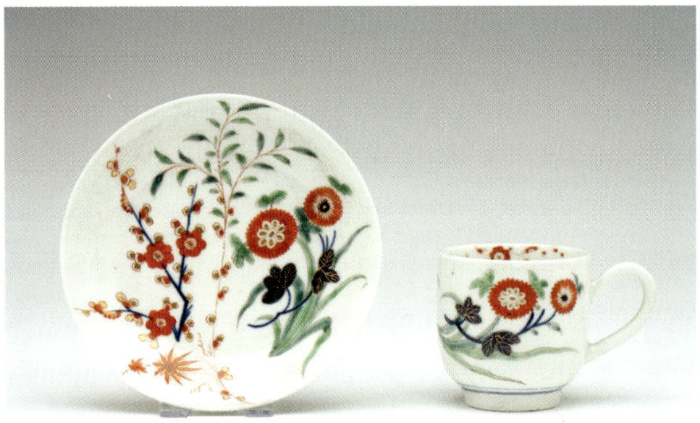

394

394

Coffee cup and saucer

1768–70
Cup ht 5.7 cm, diam. 5.5 cm; saucer diam. 11.7 cm
1957.24.1.964

Ribbed loop handle; decorated with prunus sprays and chrysanthemums in red, blue, green and gold; plain white rim with two sprays inside.

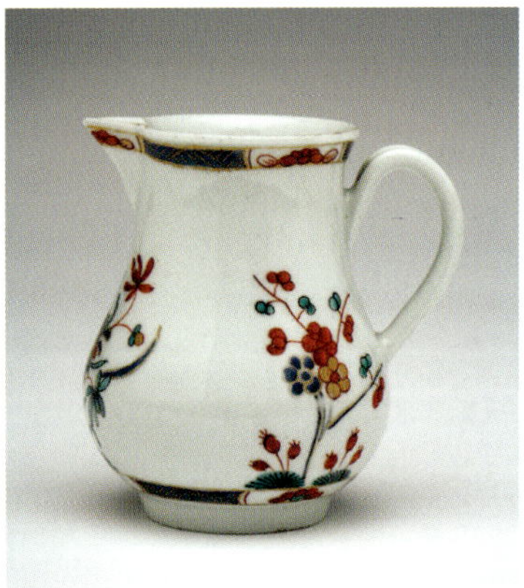

395

395

Cream jug

1765–70
Ht 8 cm
1957.24.1.1049

Bell-shaped, ribbed loop handle; Oriental-style borders on neck and around base; decorated with prunus and floral spray with long green leaves under spout.

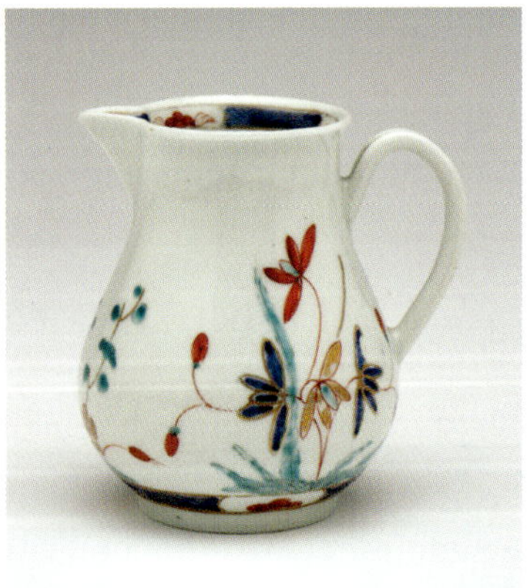

396

396

Cream jug

1765–70
Ht 8.2 cm
1957.24.1.848

Bell-shaped, ribbed loop handle; border of blue and red inside rim, repeated around base; prunus spray below spout, flowers with long petals on either side.

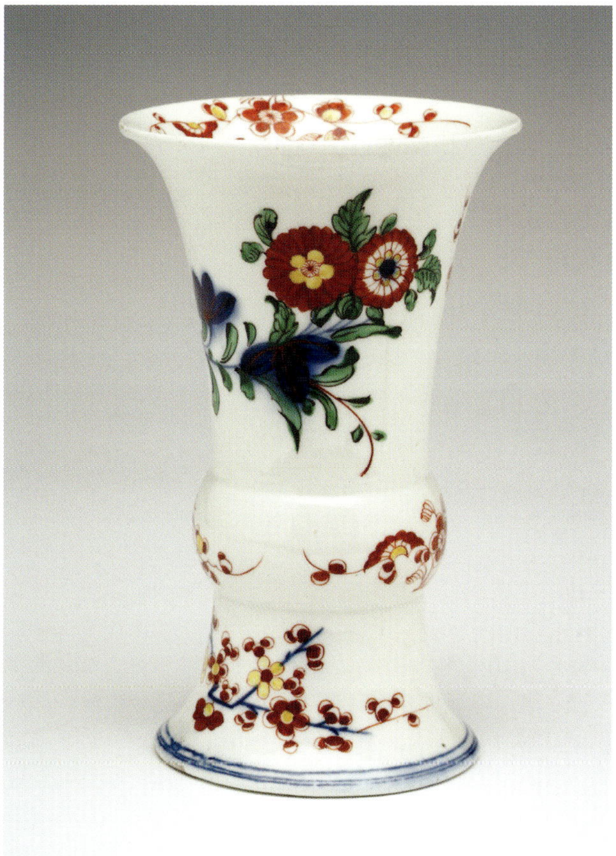

397

397

Vase

1768–70
Ht 14.8 cm
Mark: fretted square
1957.24.1.859

Shape based on Chinese bronze *gu*, a ceremonial vase with flared neck, decorated with prunus and chrysanthemums mainly in red and yellow with green and blue foliage.

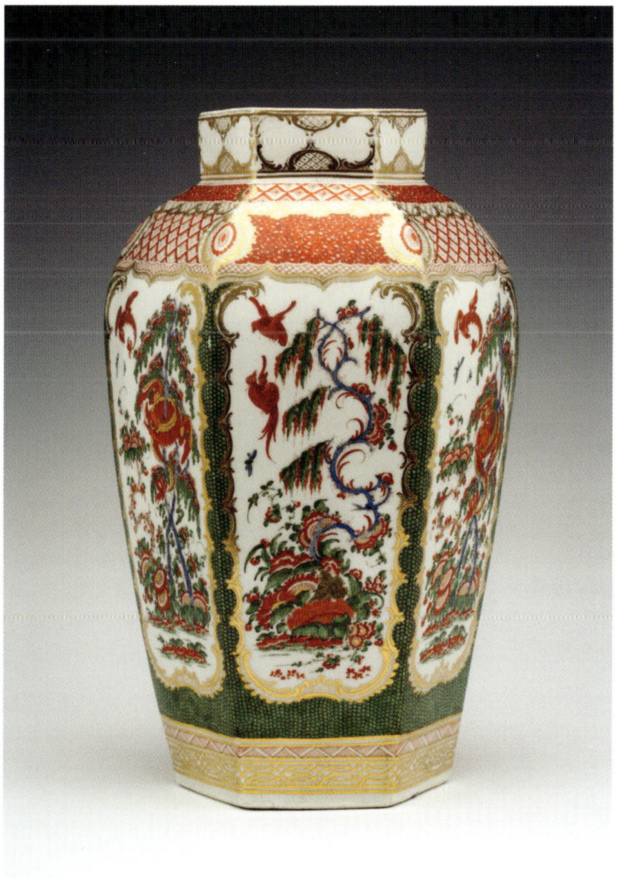

398

398

Vase

1765–8
Ht 29 cm
1957.24.1.279

Hexagonal, cover missing; alternate panels of red diaper and red speckled white around shoulder; green shagreen defined by scroll gilding separates six panels painted with Oriental plants, jabberwockies and ho-ho birds. A similar pair of vases with covers is illustrated in Spero and Sandon 1996, pl. 302.

PROVENANCE
Tilley & Co., London, 1947, £70 (pair).

REFERENCE
Christie's, London, 29 May 1990, lot 506.

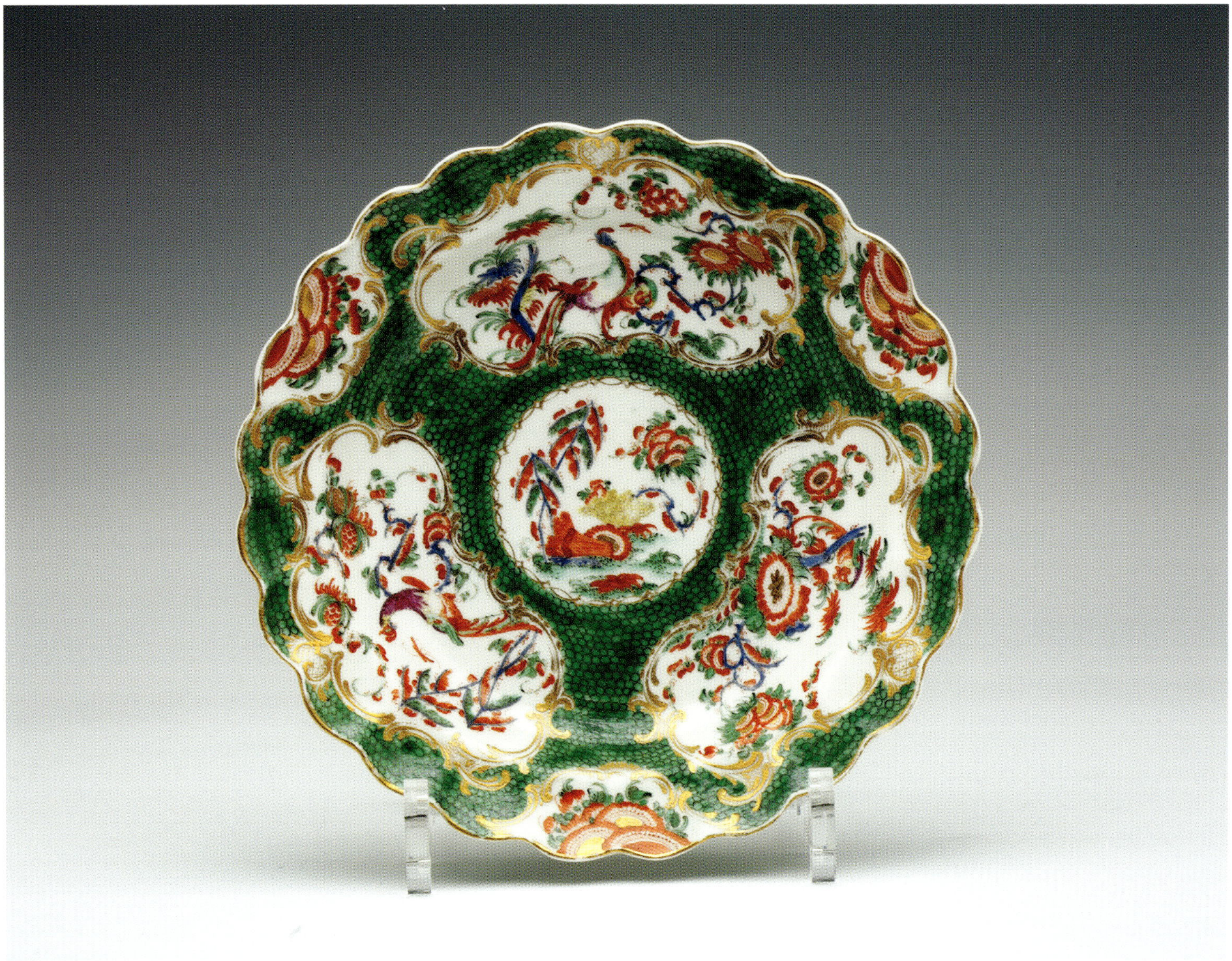

399

399

Plate

About 1770
Diam. 19 cm
1957.24.1.905

Wavy gilt rim; green shagreen ground, three gilded rococo panels decorated with Japanese-style exotic birds, chrysanthemums, wheatsheaves and other motifs grouped around central circular panel; most likely to be from a single service.

PROVENANCE
Albert Amor, London, 21 July 1954, £250 (pair).

REFERENCES
Spero and Sandon 1996, pl. 254; McNair 2007, pl. 238.

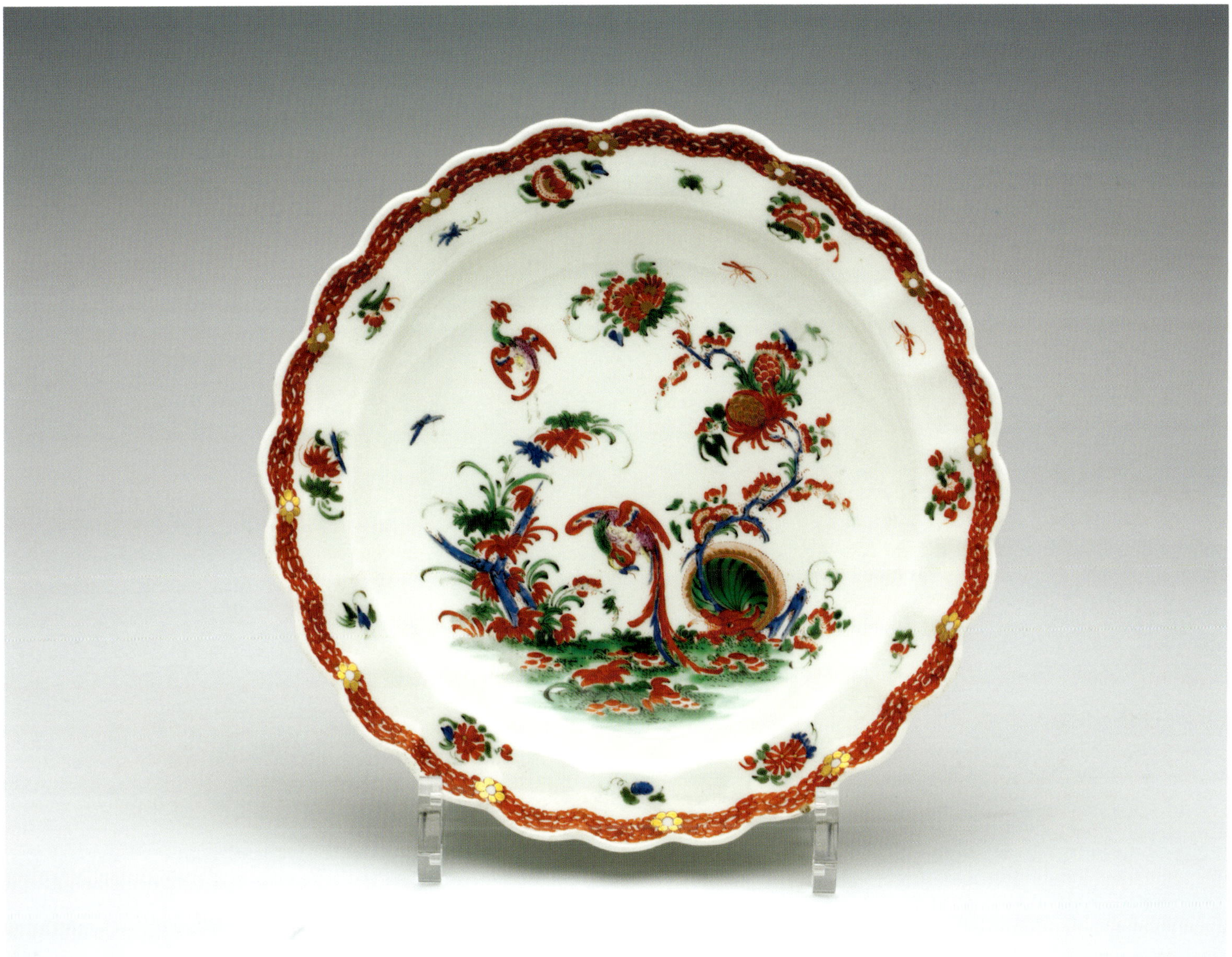

400

400

Plate

About 1770
Diam. 19.5 cm
1957.24.1.200

Wavy rim; *rouge de fer* border, Oriental-style decoration with a phoenix between exotic foliage and a strange dragon with green, gold and fawn body.

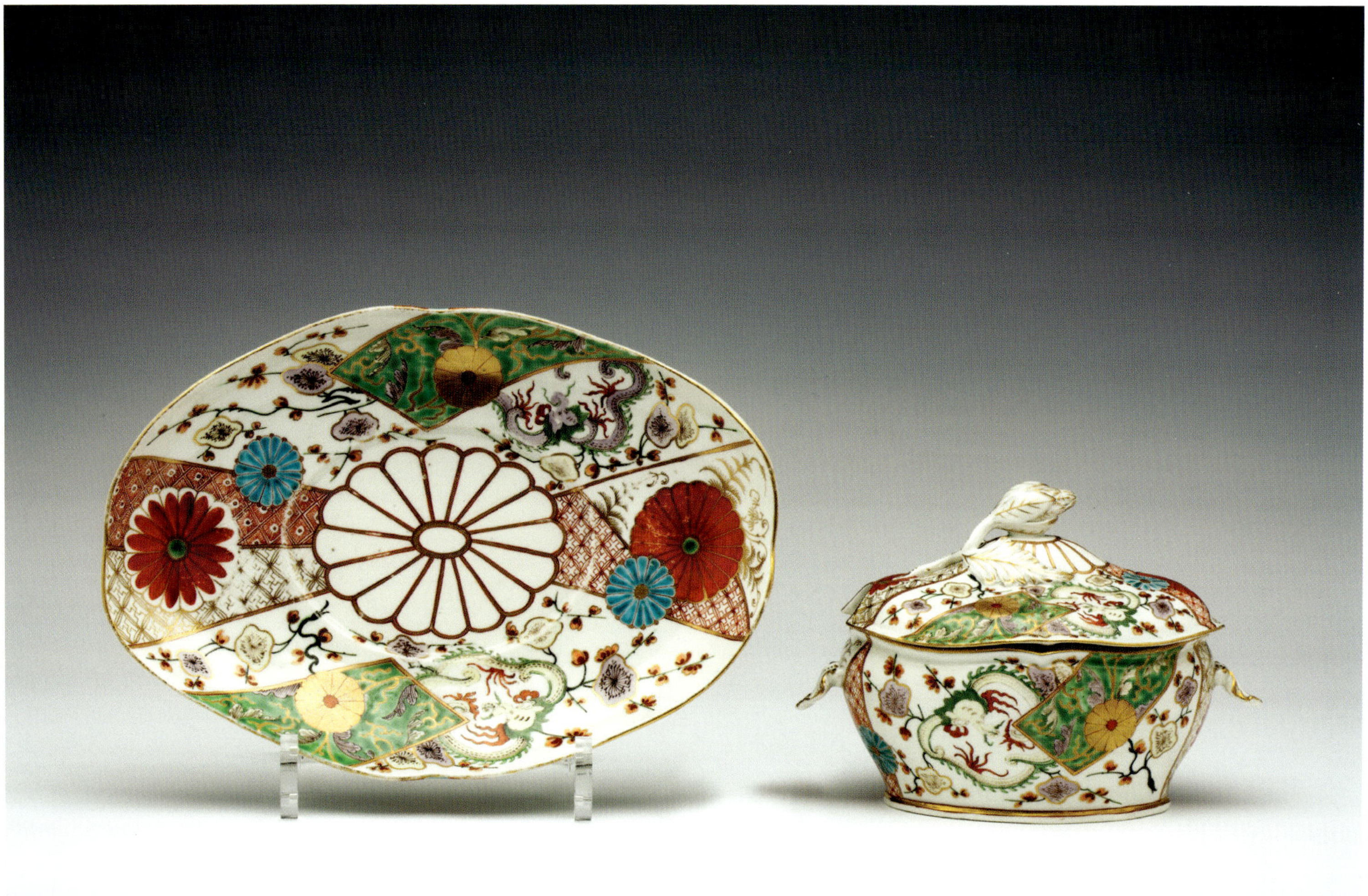

401

401

Tureen, cover and stand

About 1770
Tureen and cover ht 11.7 cm, length 16.8 cm; stand length 23.3 cm, width 16.4 cm
Mark: open gold crescent on tureen and stand
1957.24.1.900

Artichoke knop, shell-shaped handles; decorated in Imari style in green, red, sky blue and mauve with gilding, known as the 'Brocade' pattern; floral spray inside tureen. A shell-shaped dessert dish is illustrated in Spero and Sandon 1996, pl. 273.

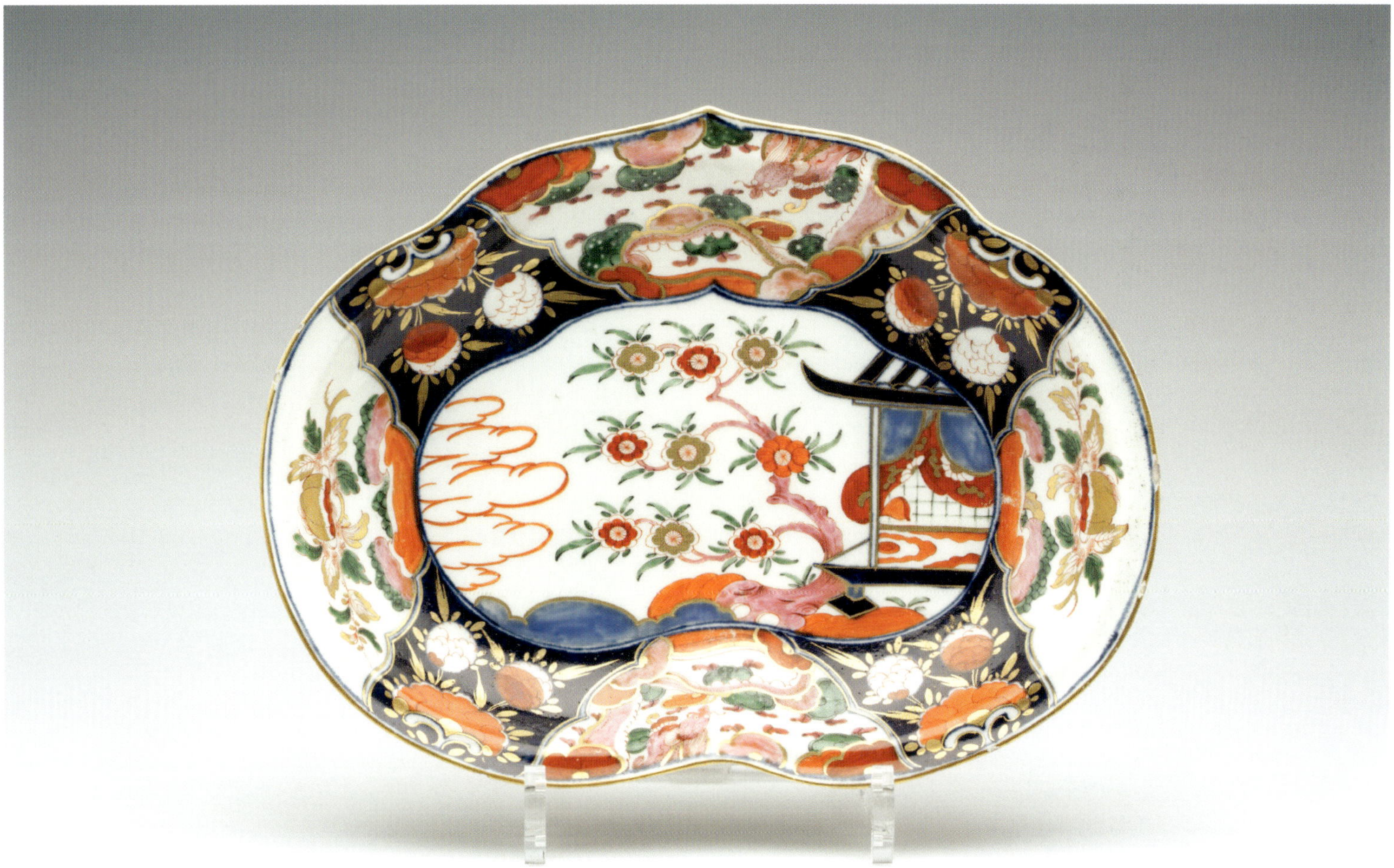

402

402

Heart-shaped dish

1770–72
Length 26.4 cm, width 19.2 cm
1957.24.1.716

Decorated in Japanese Imari style with the 'Pavilion' pattern in underglaze blue and polychrome enamels, with an open-sided pavilion or pagoda beside flowering prunus, stylised clouds on left; flower sprays on reverse. An oval basket with similar pattern is illustrated in Spero and Sandon 1996, pl. 275. A covered tureen and stand are illustrated in Bonhams, London, 7 March 2007, lot 136.

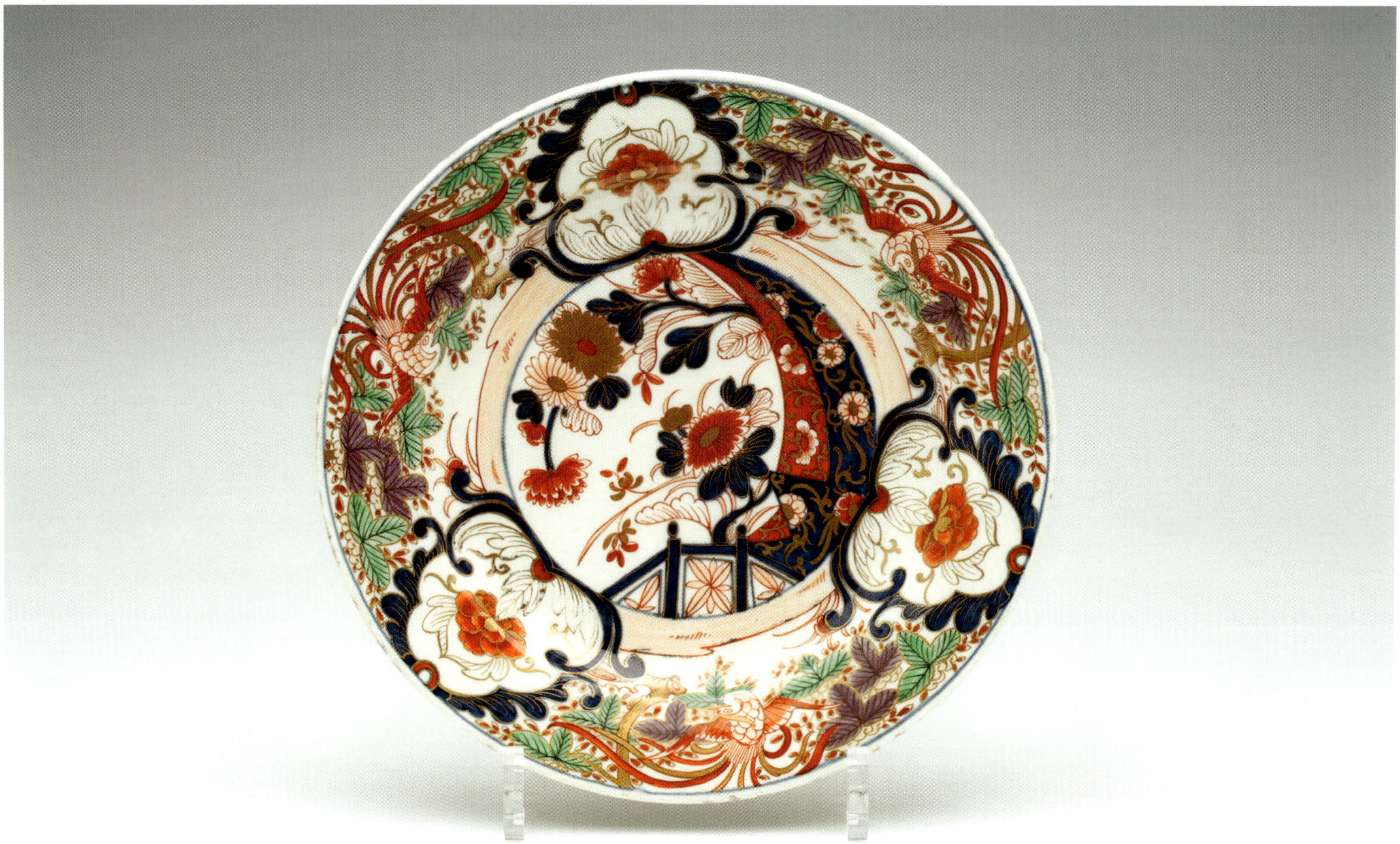

403

403

Plate

1775–80
Diam. 22.3 cm
1957.24.1.1081

Japanese Imari-style decoration with intricate chrysanthemum and brocade pattern; on the rim, three foliate cartouches with peonies separated by phoenixes amongst foliage; possibly a replacement piece for an Oriental service.

404

Vase

About 1775
Ht 28.3 cm
1957.24.1.732

Hexagonal; decorated with Japanese-style flowering plants, three ribs decorated in wet blue and gilt with red scale circles, three narrower ones with stippled green and turquoise chain.

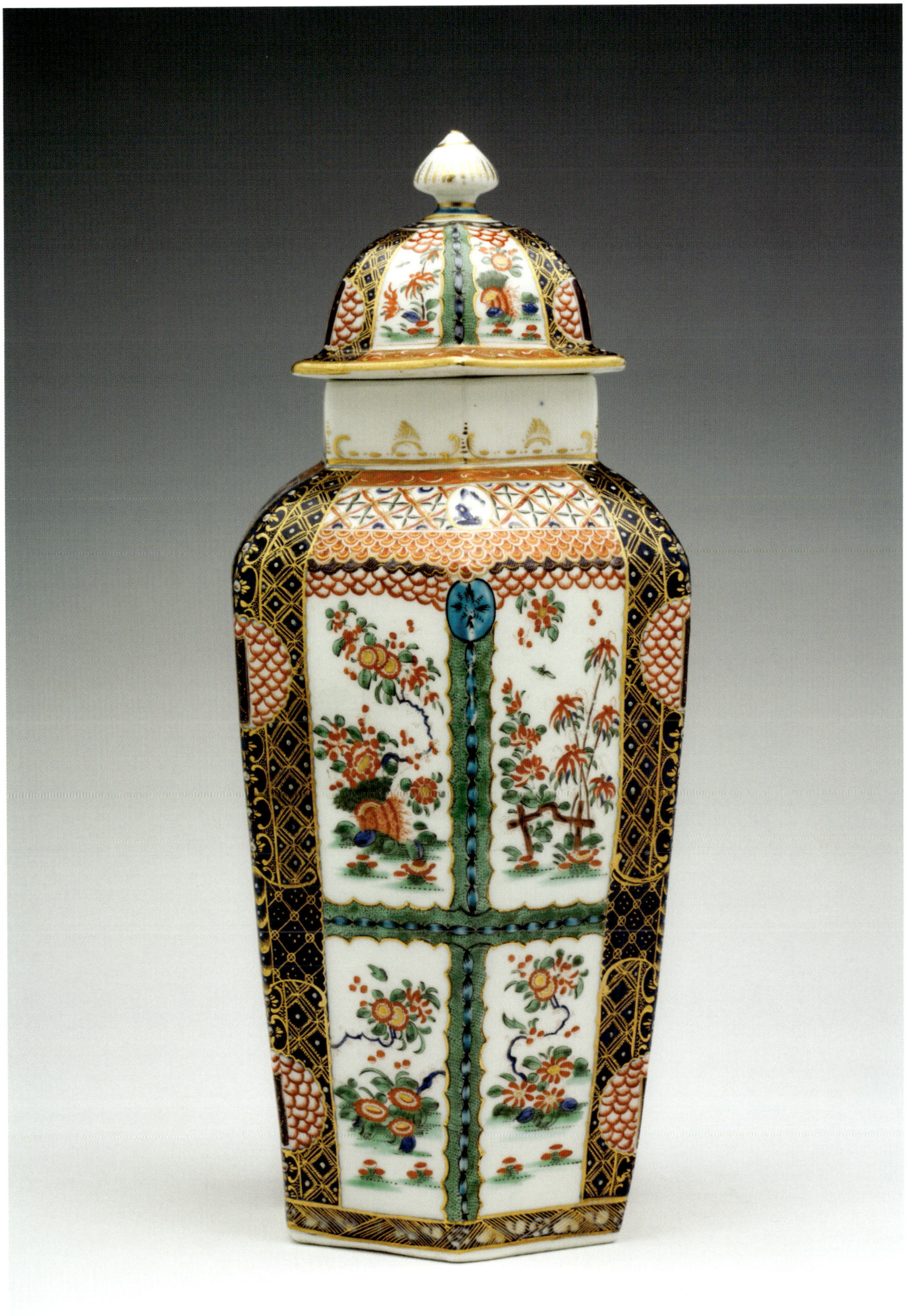

404

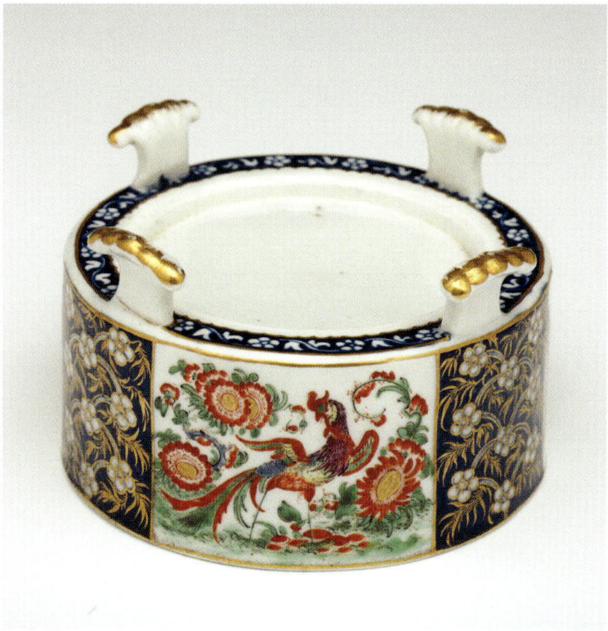

405

405

Standing or master salt

About 1770
Ht 6.5 cm, diam. 10 cm
1957.24.1.722

Circular with four napkin or plate rests on top; decorated in Japanese style with three gilded wet blue panels with white flowers, chrysanthemums and ho-ho birds between.

This may be derived from earlier metal forms such as the Moody Salt, hallmarked London, 1664–5, in the Victoria and Albert Museum (M.347-1912). A similar shape is also found in delftware.

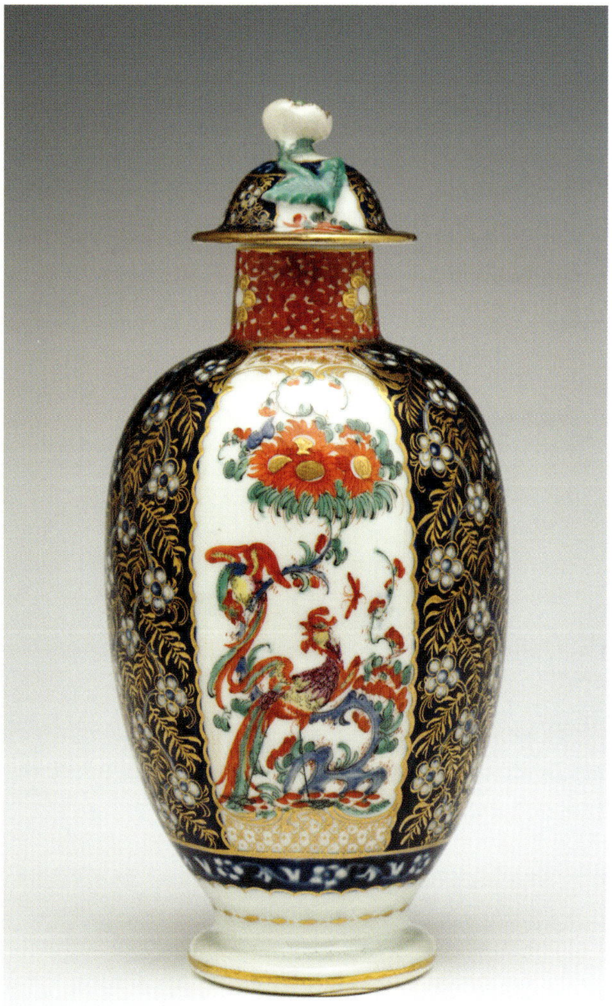

406

406

Tea canister

About 1770
Ht 16.8 cm
Mark: fretted square
1957.24.1.721

Decorated with three gilded wet blue panels with white flowers, and three with Japanese-style decoration with ho-ho birds and chrysanthemums; neck is red with three gold *mons*.

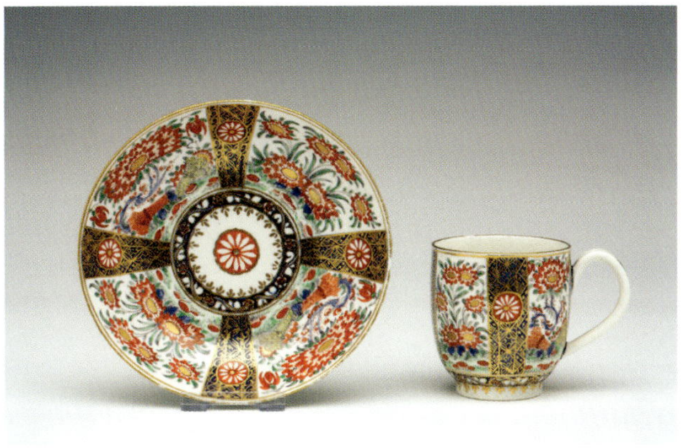

407

407

Coffee cup and saucer

1768–75
Cup ht 6.3 cm, diam. 5.6 cm; saucer diam. 12.4 cm
Mark: fretted square on both
1957.24.1.733

Gilt rim, four underglaze blue diapered bands with *mons* radiate from central circle with white chrysanthemum on red ground; alternating panels of chrysanthemums and wheatsheaves between, all in red, blue, green and gold.

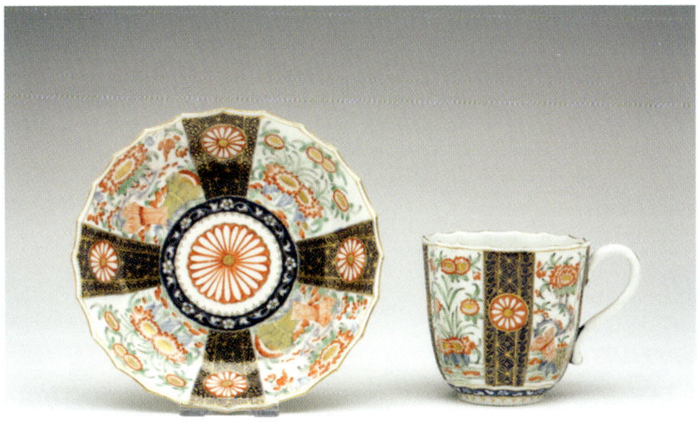

408

408

Coffee cup and saucer

1770–80
Cup ht 7.1 cm, diam. 6.8 cm; saucer diam. 13.2 cm
Mark: fretted square and open red crescent on both
1957.24.1.715

Fluted shape; gilt rim, four underglaze blue bands with red *mons* radiate from central circle with red and white formal chrysanthemum, panels of chrysanthemums and wheatsheaves between.

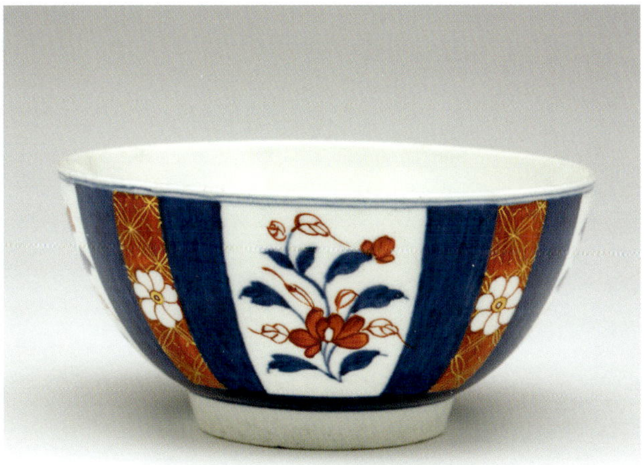

409

409

Bowl

1770–80
Ht 5.8 cm, diam. 12 cm
1957.24.1.719

Imari-style decoration with vertical wet blue and red diapered panels, floral sprays between; probably decorated outside the factory.

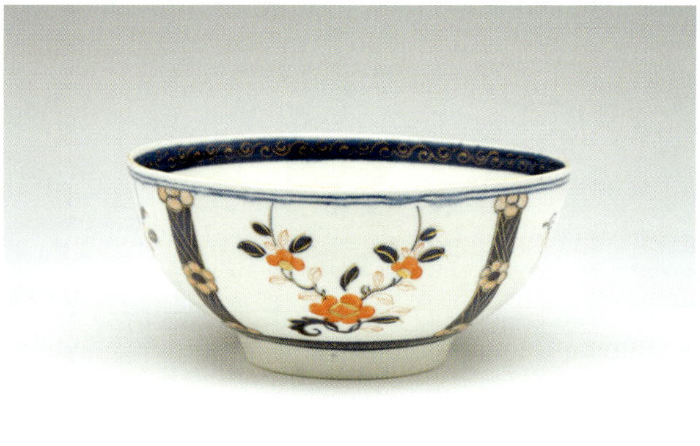

410

410

Bowl

About 1775
Ht 7 cm, diam. 15.3 cm
1957.24.1.724

Four panels of red and blue floral sprays separated by blue uprights with pink formal chrysanthemums, blue border inside rim.

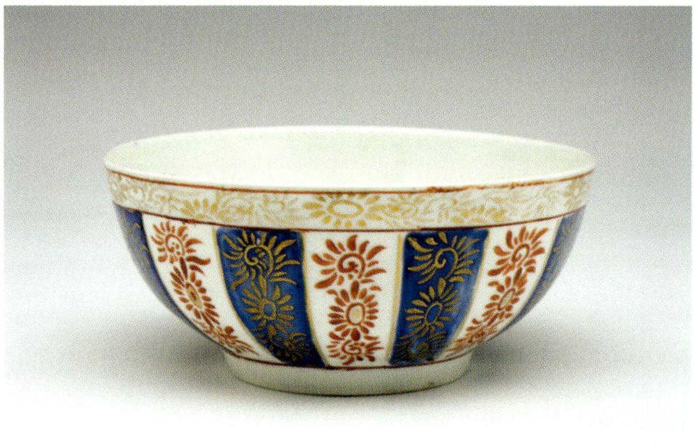

411

411

Bowl

1770–75
Ht 6.7 cm, diam. 15.2 cm
1957.24.1.708

Border of gilt scrolling, sixteen vertical panels below, alternately overglaze blue with gilding and white with formal red foliage, red line around base; decorated outside the factory.

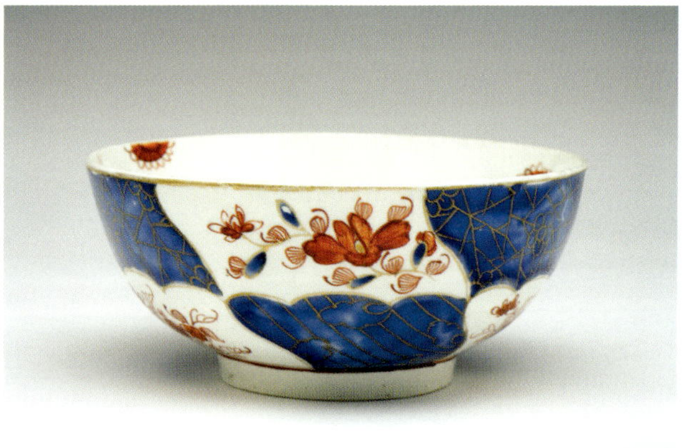

412

412

Bowl

About 1770
Ht 6.9 cm, diam. 15.4 cm
1957.24.1.712

Twelve irregularly shaped panels in 'Queen's' pattern, decorated alternately in overglaze blue with cracked ice gilding and white with red and blue flower sprays; decorated outside the factory.

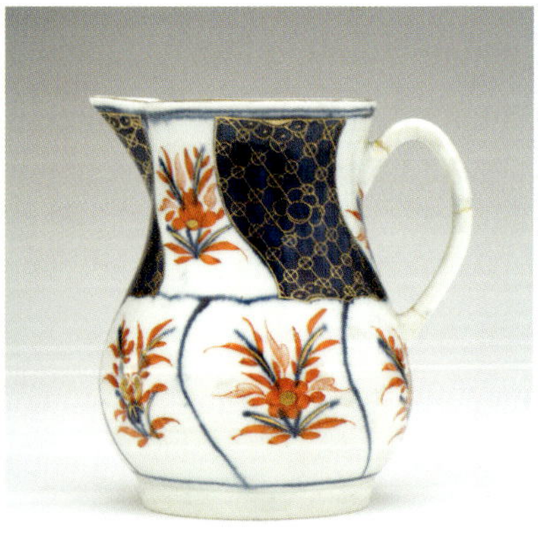

413

413

Cream jug

About 1770
Ht 8.5 cm
1957.24.1.21

Ovoid, ribbed loop handle; six lower panels are decorated with red and blue sprays, three of the upper panels are of wet blue with gilt diaper, the others as below.

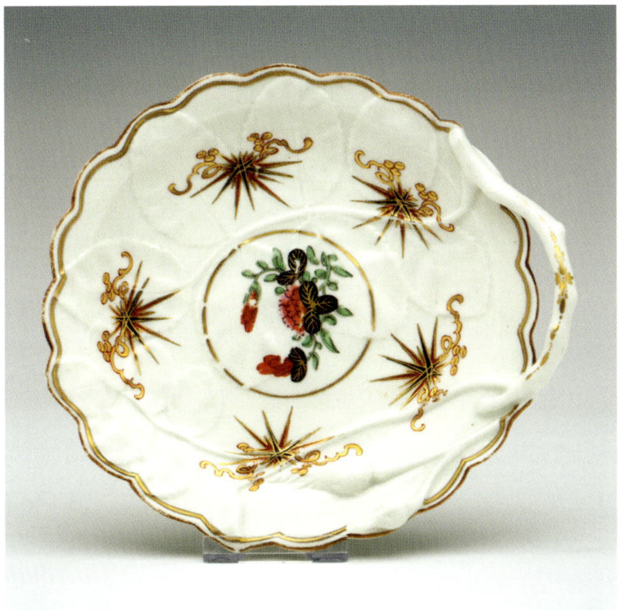

414

414

Sweetmeat dish

About 1775
Length 15 cm
1957.24.1.860

'Blind Earl' moulded shape; painted in Oriental style with five seven-pointed stars in black and red with gilding, floral spray in centre. A coffee pot is illustrated in Spero and Sandon 1996, pl. 293, and a teapot and coffee pot in Bonhams, London, 7 March 2007, lot 74, all with similar decoration.

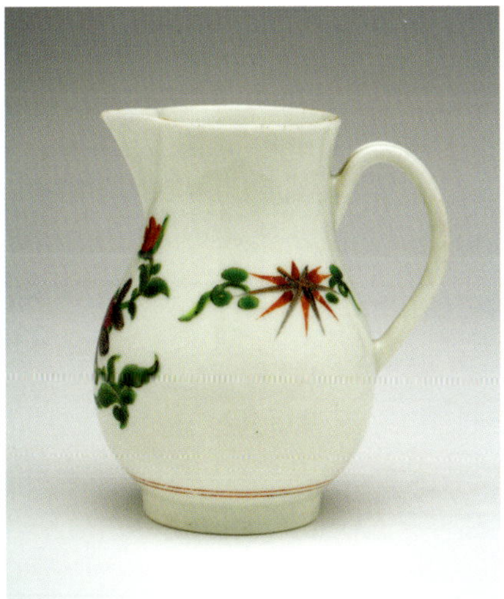

415

415

Cream jug

1770–72
Ht 9.1 cm
1957.24.1.986

Ovoid, ribbed loop handle; decorated on both sides with a ten-pointed star in grey, black and red, floral spray below spout.

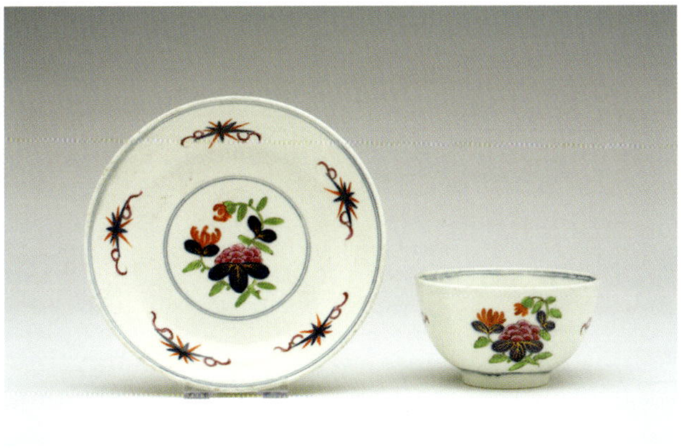

416

416

Teabowl and saucer

About 1770
Bowl ht 4.3 cm, diam. 7.4 cm; saucer diam. 11.8 cm
1957.24.1.1070

Decorated in Oriental style with formalised peony and star symbols in dark blue and red, underglaze blue lines around rim and centre of saucer.

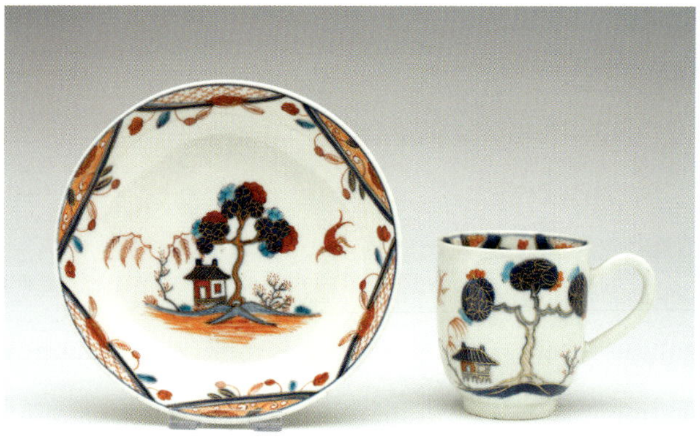

417

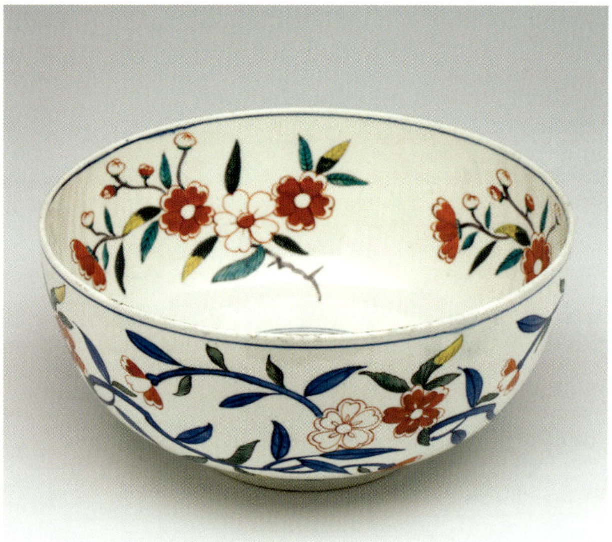

418

417

Coffee cup and saucer

1770–80
Cup ht 6.6 cm, diam. 5.6 cm; saucer diam. 12.7 cm
1957.24.1.224

Some underglaze blue with added polychrome decoration; house beneath a tree in centre; a standard Chinese Imari pattern.

418

Punch bowl

About 1780
Ht 11.1 cm, diam. 23 cm
Mark: red *10* on base
1957.24.1.843

Decorated both inside and out with boldly drawn flowers in blue, red and green in Japanese Imari style; influenced by Chinese decoration.

REFERENCE
Spero and Sandon 1996, pl. 269.

419

Bowl

About 1775
Ht 7 cm, diam. 15.2 cm
1957.24.1.839

Irregularly oval cartouches with formal sprays of Oriental flowers on opposite sides, underglaze blue chrysanthemums and radiating foliage between.

420

Punch bowl

1775–80
Ht 9.9 cm, diam. 23.8 cm
1957.24.1.256

Broad sky-blue pearled band inside rim, outside decorated with Oriental-style large and small orange and blue chrysanthemums on puce line with smaller flowers between.

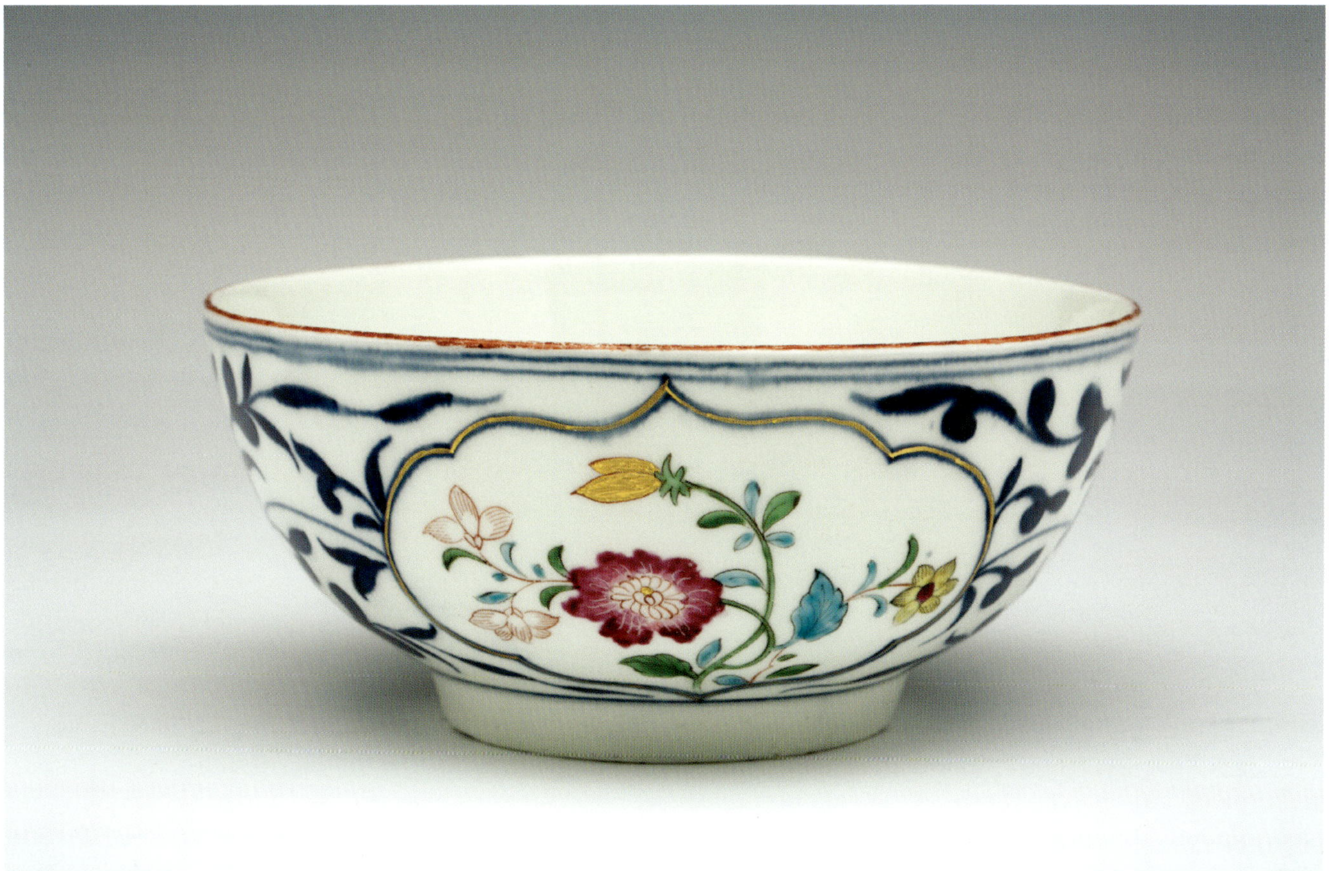

419

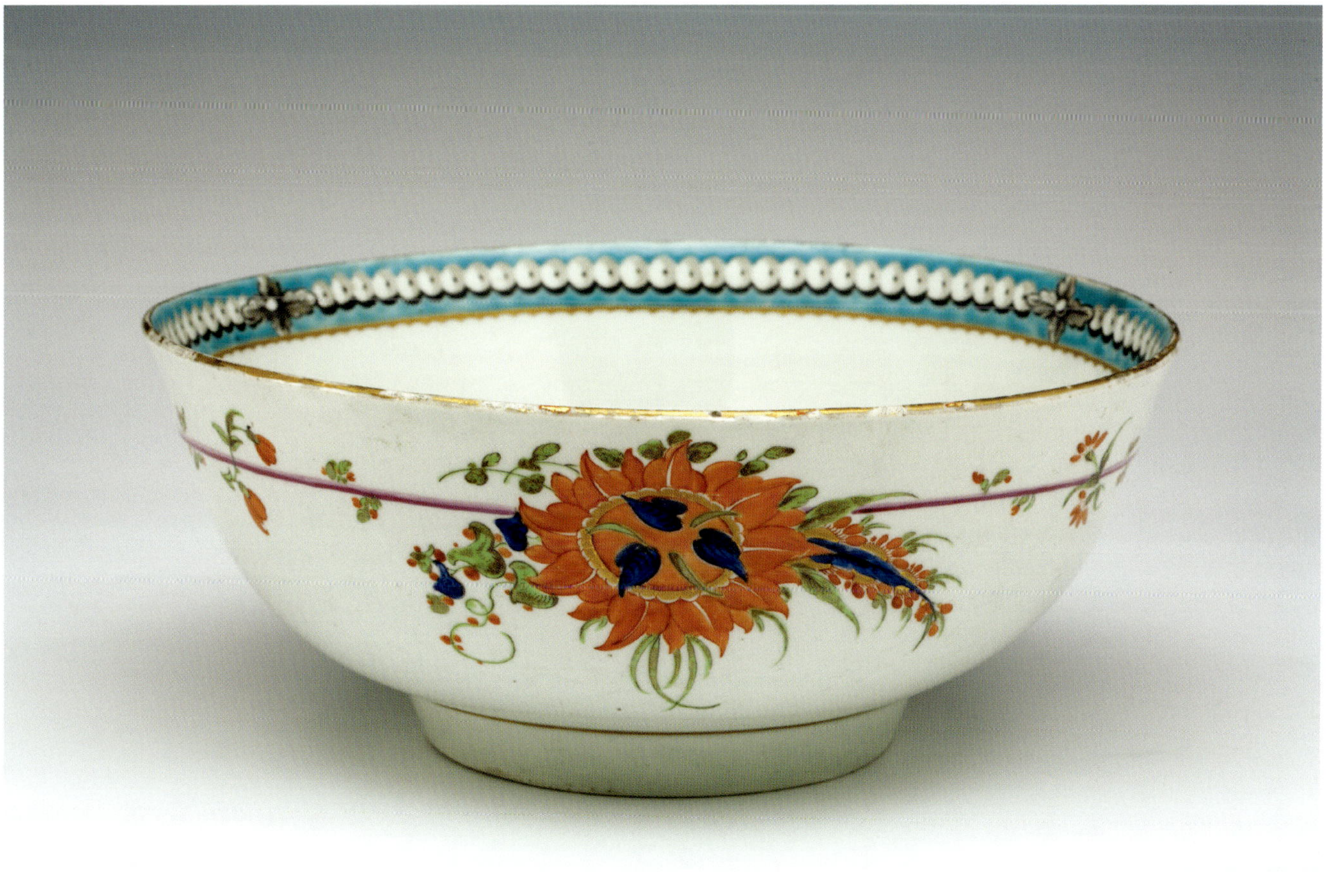

420

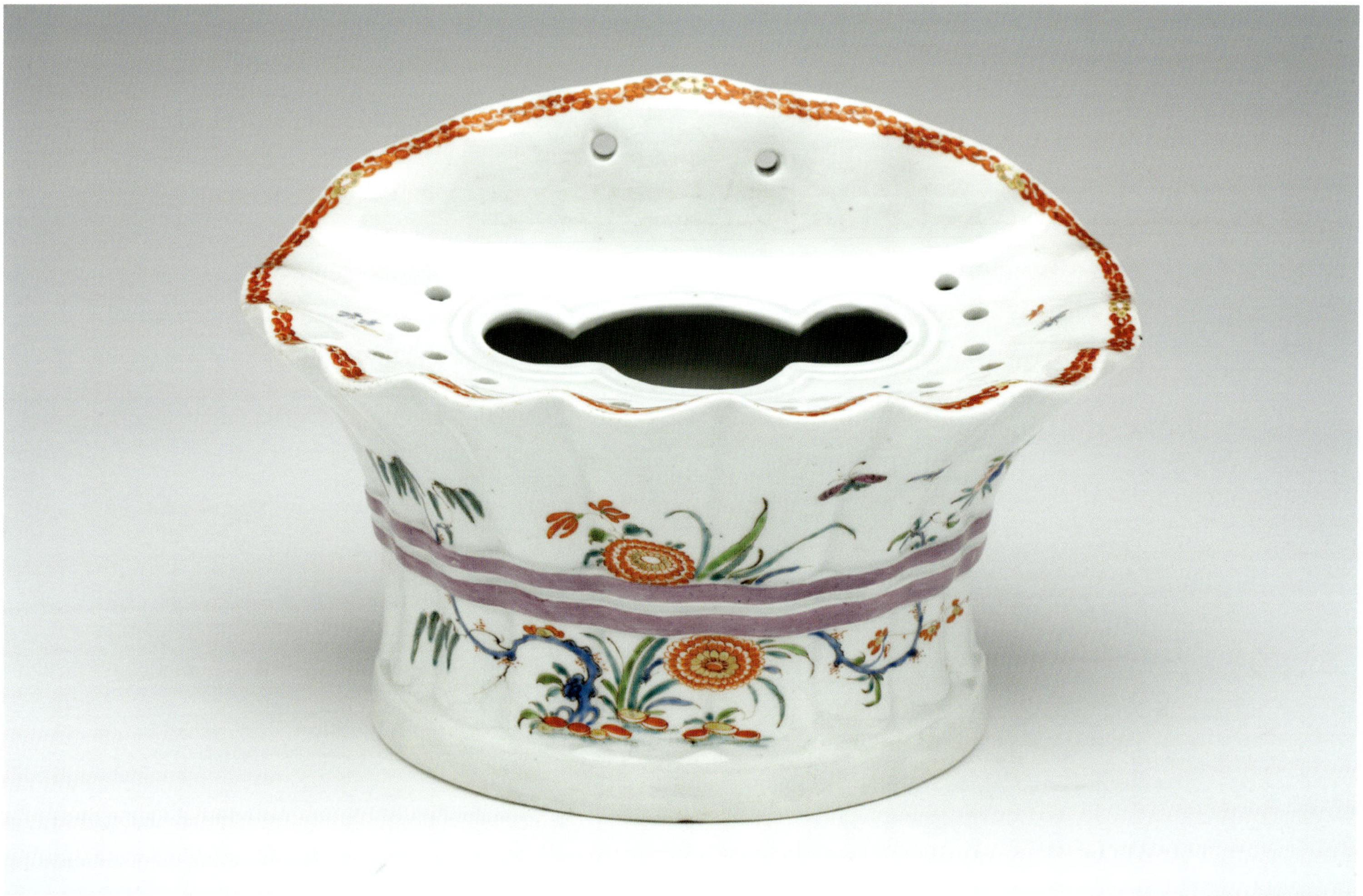

421

421

Bough pot

1768–70
Ht 14.3 cm, length 19.6 cm, width 13.1 cm
1957.24.1.838

Fluted edge with *rouge de fer* border, twenty-five circular holes around irregular-shaped moulded aperture on the top and two further holes on the back; two horizontal moulded bands around the middle picked out in mauve; decorated with Kakiemon-style chrysanthemums, willows and insects. This unusual shape is probably derived from French pottery and is designed to stand or hang on a wall.

PROVENANCE
Sotheby's, London, 16 June 1953, lot 114, £45 (pair).

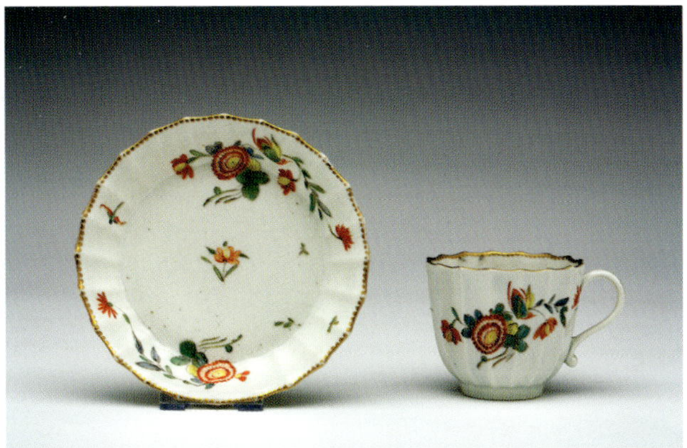

422

422

Coffee cup and saucer

About 1765
Cup ht 5.7 cm, diam. 6.3 cm; saucer diam. 11.8 cm
Mark: fretted square on saucer
1957.24.1.960

Fluted; gilt dentil edge, painted with Oriental flowers in orange, yellow and blue with pale green leaves.

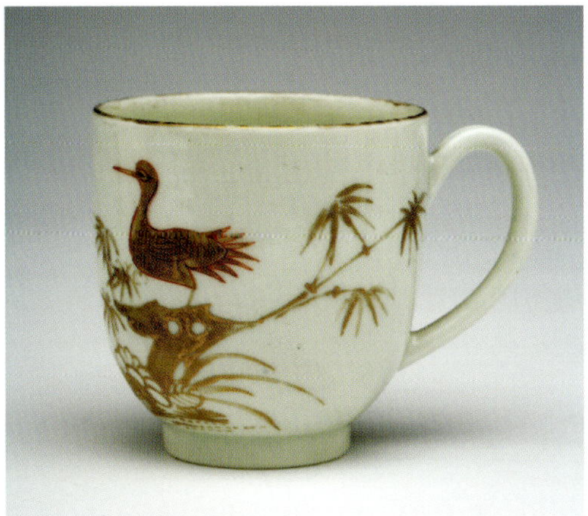

423

423

Coffee cup

1760–65
Ht 6 cm, diam. 5.5 cm
1957.24.1.958

Ribbed loop handle; gilt rim, unusually decorated entirely in red and gold; bird with outspread tail feathers standing on rock near palmate foliage.

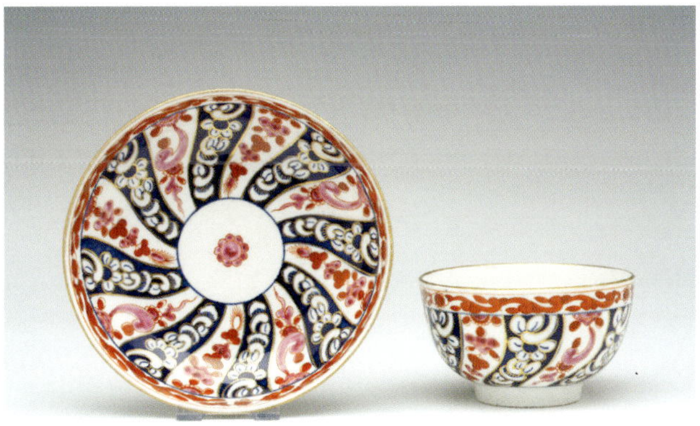

424

424

Teabowl and saucer

1770–80
Bowl ht 5.2 cm, diam. 8.8 cm; saucer diam. 13 cm
1957.24.1.707

Underglaze blue spiral bands alternating with panels in red and pink with gilding. Although Japanese in origin, the inspiration for this design was probably Meissen, where it is found on a spirally moulded body. It was also imitated on Chinese porcelain made for export to the Turkish market. By the mid-nineteenth century this was known as the 'Queen Charlotte' pattern, although there is no evidence that a service in this design was ordered when she visited the factory with George III in 1788. It had previously been called the 'Whorl' or 'Catherine Wheel' pattern, and may be the 'fine old scrole Japan' described on a breakfast service sold in 1769.

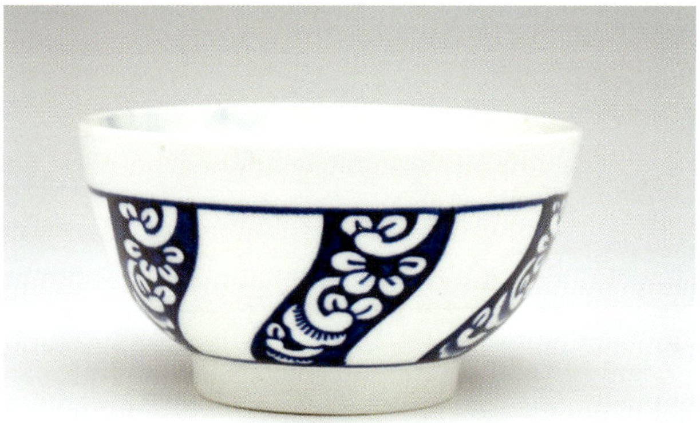

425

425

Bowl

1770–75
Ht 5.8 cm, diam. 10.4 cm
1957.24.1.834

Unfinished; white panels alternating with underglaze blue spiral bands; chrysanthemum pattern left in white.

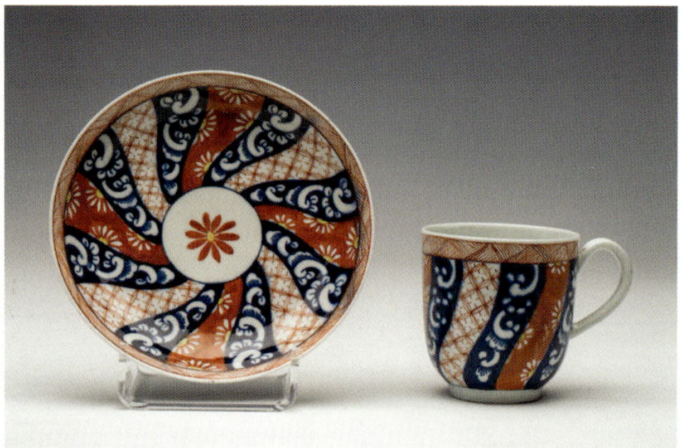

426

426

Coffee cup and saucer

About 1770
Cup ht 7.2 cm, diam. 6.7 cm saucer diam. 13.5 cm
Mark: fretted square
1957.24.1.713

Decorated with panels of underglaze blue and two designs in iron red, radiating from a white circle with flower motif; similar to the 'Queen Charlotte' pattern (see no. 424) but in a different palette, possibly decorated outside the factory.

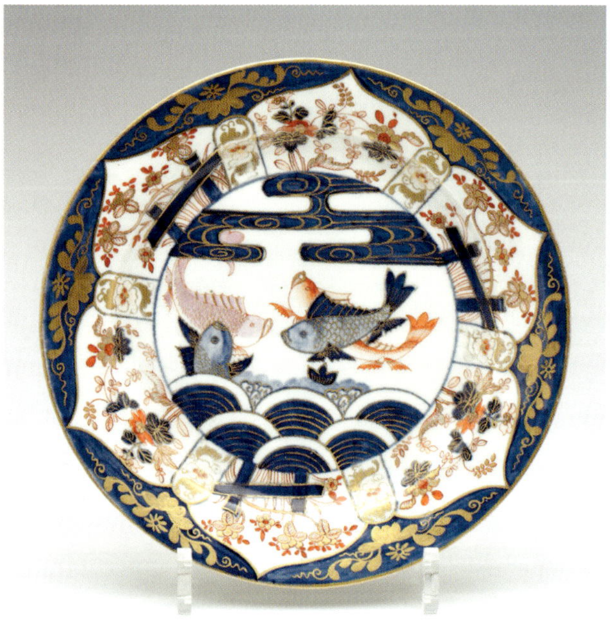

427

427

Plate

1775–8
Diam. 22.3 cm
1957.24.1.727

Dark blue border with gilt edge, six panels with flowers and fencing below, circular panel in centre with carp (a symbol of long life) leaping from waves, horizontal blue thunderclouds above; copied from a Japanese Imari pattern of 1710–20. Hobson (1923) illustrates a Japanese Imari dish from the late seventeenth century alongside a Worcester example.

REFERENCES

Spero and Sandon 1996, p. 472; Dawson 2007, pl. 100.

7
Overglaze Coloured Grounds

OVERGLAZE COLOURED GROUNDS were gradually introduced at the Meissen porcelain factory from the late 1720s and at Vincennes-Sèvres in the early 1750s. Chelsea was the first English factory to use them, in emulation of Sèvres. Here claret and turquoise grounds were particularly successful in the 1760s, although the factory would appear to have had some difficulty with yellow and green.

A pale yellow ground was used at Worcester from the mid-1750s, but the main impetus came after the closure of the Chelsea factory in 1769, when some of its best decorators moved to Worcester. The auction of Worcester porcelain on 4 May 1769 by Mr Burnsall of Berkeley Square included items 'in the beautiful Colours of Mazarine Blue and Gold, Sky-blue, Pea-green, French-green, Sea-green, Purple, Scarlet, and gold and other variety of colours, richly decorated and with chased and burnished Gold'. It is likely that this sale included both factory and Giles decoration. Yellow as a ground colour is not mentioned, perhaps because it had been in use for some time; sky blue is thought to correspond with the Worcester factory's turquoise ground, mazarine blue with underglaze solid blue or *gros bleu*, and scarlet with a deep orange colour. Worcester coloured grounds were aimed at the sophisticated London market previously catered for by the Chelsea factory.

Apple green, introduced at Worcester about 1769–70 and popular in the 1770s, was derived from the *pomme verte* of Sèvres, where it was introduced in 1756. This enamel was thick and opaque, hard to control during kiln firings, and would not take gilding: gilt lines and scrolls outline but never overlap the ground colour. Owing to the technical difficulties, there is considerable controversy over items with green ground colour, many of which are thought to have had decoration added at a later date. 'French green' describes a darker colour, which occurs only as a border design with large triangular dentils, usually found on dessertwares.

Turquoise, or *bleu celeste*, invented by Jean Hellot (1685–1766) at Vincennes in 1753, was introduced at Chelsea in about 1760. It was used initially at Worcester as a border on designs such as 'Jabberwocky' and as a solid ground for a short period in the late 1760s. After 1775 it was again used only as a border.

Worcester was more successful than other English factories in achieving a well-controlled yellow ground; it was not mastered elsewhere in England until Derby in the 1790s. The use of yellow suggests a Meissen influence, although it was used at Vincennes-Sèvres from about 1751. Genuine examples are often associated with puce scrollwork or detailing: the yellow ground needed a lower firing temperature and was always added later.

The Worcester factory is known to have used a scarlet ground colour; this most likely refers to the varying shades of orange-red used in conjunction with Oriental designs. Lot 66 on the second day of the Christie's sale of Worcester porcelain in December 1769 is listed as 'fine old scarlet japan pattern'. The use of overglaze blue and puce monochrome with this ground colour may indicate decoration added outside the factory.

The 'Purple' mentioned in the Burnsall sale catalogue may refer to claret, which is the most controversial ground colour today, as many pieces exhibit signs of redecoration.

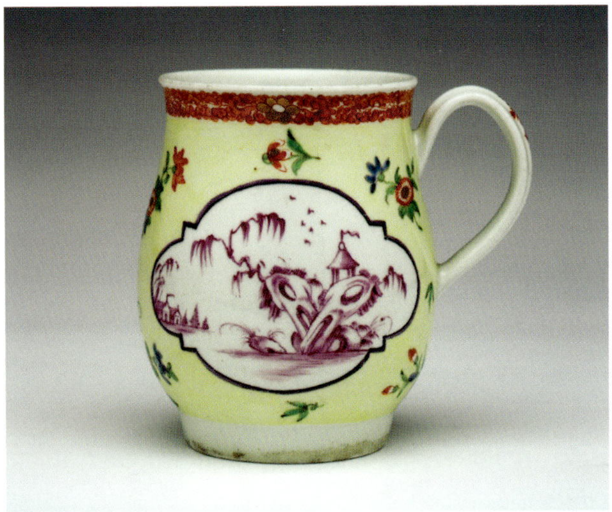

428

428

Mug

1757–60
Ht 11.5 cm, diam. 8 cm
1957.24.1.663

Bell-shaped, ribbed loop handle; light yellow ground with puce Chinese landscape within purple lined cartouche, floral sprays, *rouge de fer* border around rim.

PROVENANCE
Sotheby's, London, 11 April 1950, £36 15s.

REFERENCE
Spero 1984, pl. 27.

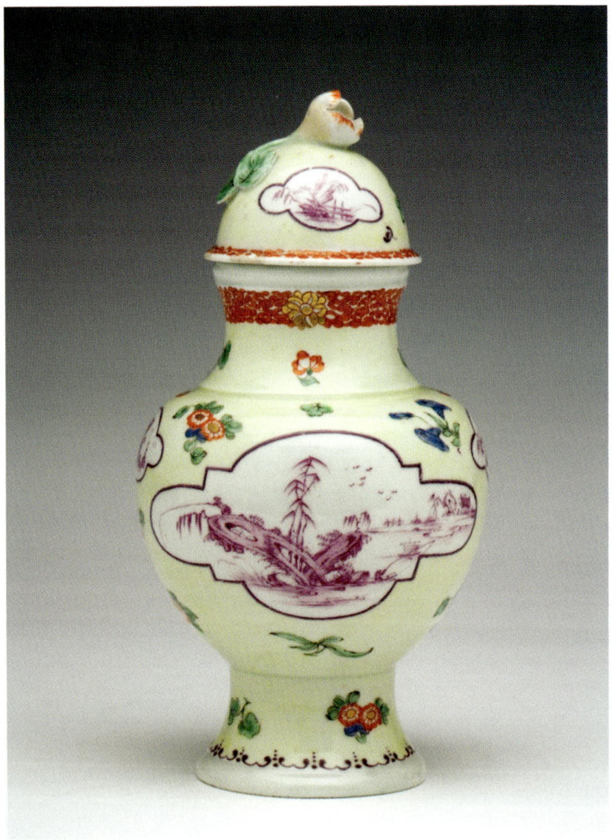

429

429

Vase with cover

1757–60
Ht 17.2 cm
1957.24.1.680

Oviform body on conical spreading foot, concave neck, domed cover with rosebud knop; light yellow ground with scattered flower sprays, purple line defining reserves painted with puce scenes, *rouge de fer* border.

PROVENANCE
Sotheby's, London, 15 July 1952, lot 156, £92.

430

Jug

About 1758
Ht 22.4 cm
1957.24.1.659

Cabbage-leaf moulding, bearded masked spout; light yellow ground with floral sprays, coat of arms of a female member of the Hay family within puce scroll border. Marshall believed that this was made for the Countess of Erroll, who died in 1758, which therefore dated the yellow ground; however, it was pointed out after his death that she would have had a coronet above the lozenge as she was Countess in her own right. It is likely that the jug was made for another female member of the Hay family living nearer to Worcester, and that it was still owned by descendants of the Hays until 1921.

PROVENANCE
Christie's, London, February 1944, £147 18s.

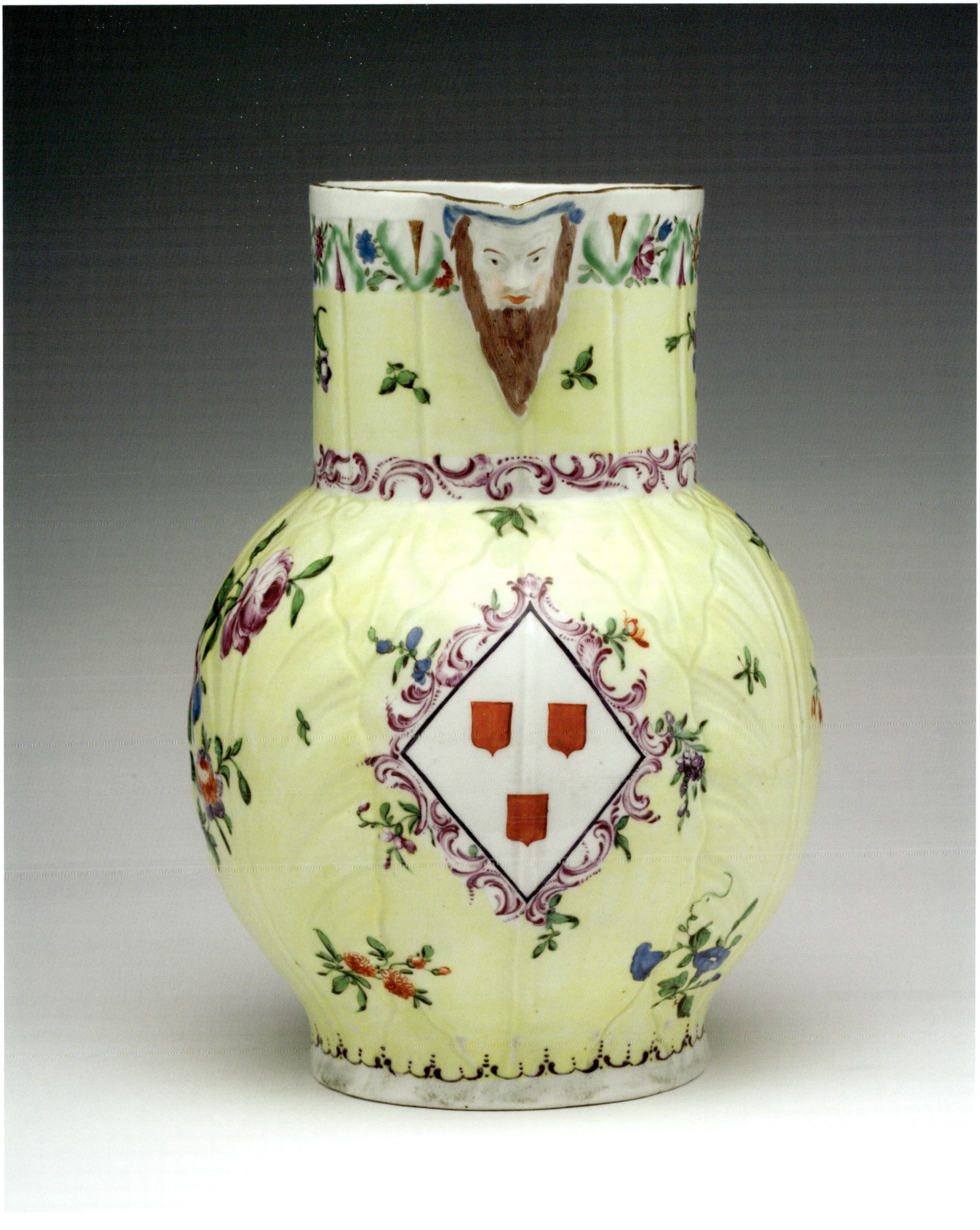

430

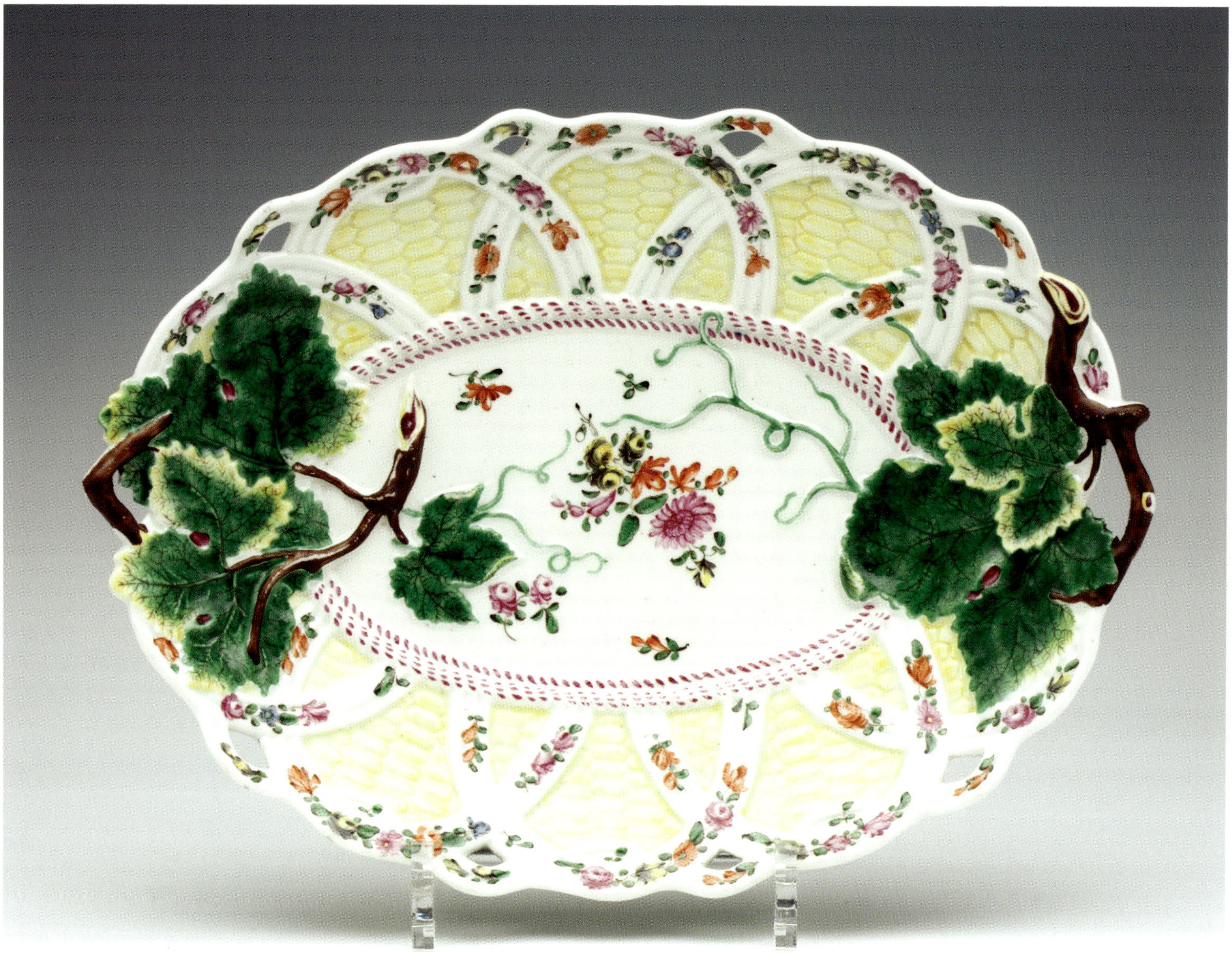

431

431

Dish

About 1765
Length 29.8 cm, width 22.3 cm
1957.24.1.660

Oval, border moulded with overlapping loops; painted with scattered flowers on a yellow ground, brown twig handles with vine leaves, central flower spray within an oval gadrooned border picked out in puce.

REFERENCES
Spero and Sandon 1996, pl. 257; Bonhams, London, 7 March 2007, lot 106.

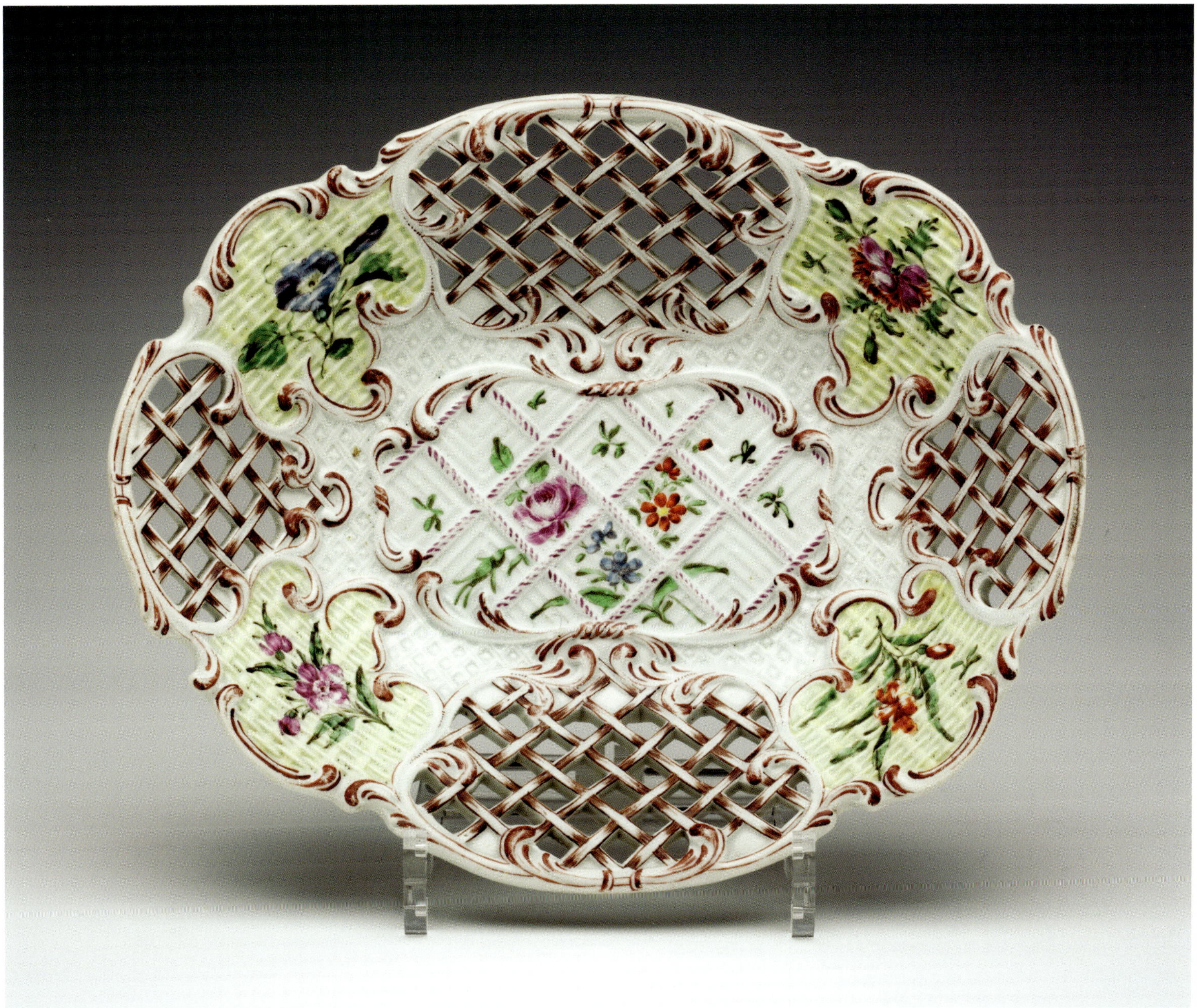

432

432

Dish

About 1760
Length 26.4 cm, width 22.2 cm
1957.24.1.686

Oval; four panels of moulded basketwork coloured pale yellow, alternating with four panels of pierced latticework picked out in rust brown; painted in colours with scattered sprays of European flowers and foliage. Although echoing Staffordshire stoneware, the more likely inspiration for this shape is rococo silver from the 1740s.

REFERENCES
Reynolds 1999, pl. 17; Spero and Sandon 1996, pl. 256.

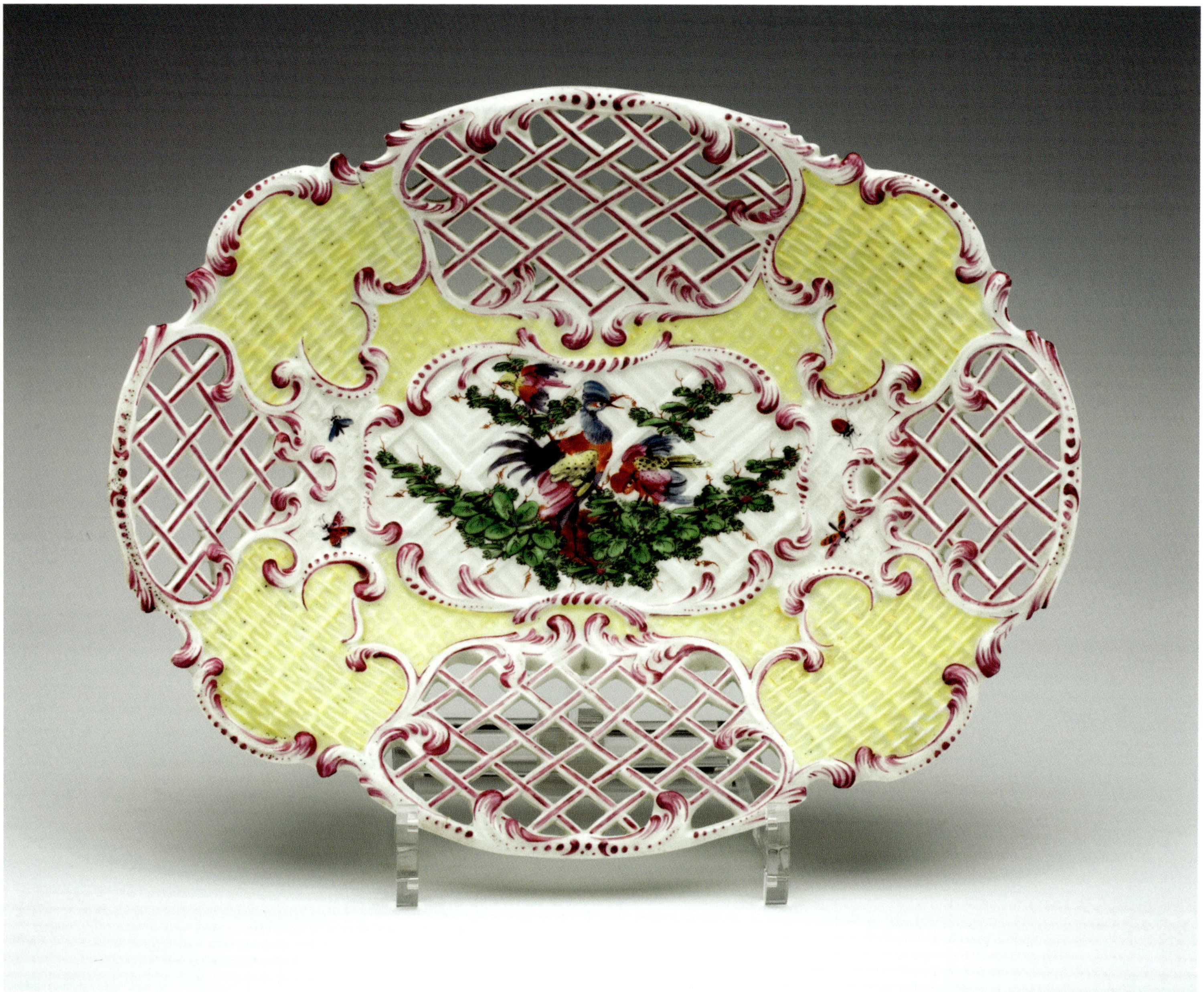

433

433

Dish

1762–5
Length 26.9 cm, width 21.7 cm
1957.24.1.682

Oval; moulded with yellow basketwork and pierced trellis outlined in puce, centre painted with birds on branches.

PROVENANCE
H.W. Hughes Collection, no. 129, £13.

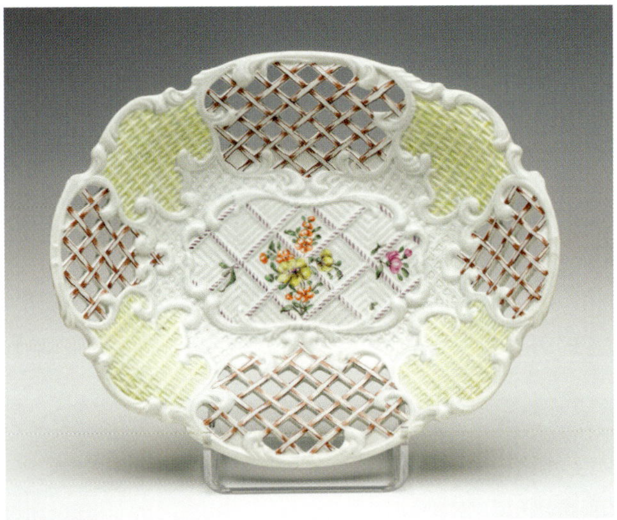

434

434

Dish

1762–5
Length 26.5 cm, width 22.7 cm
1957.24.1.690

Oval; yellow basketwork moulding between open trelliswork panels picked out in brown, central moulded panel with floral decoration.

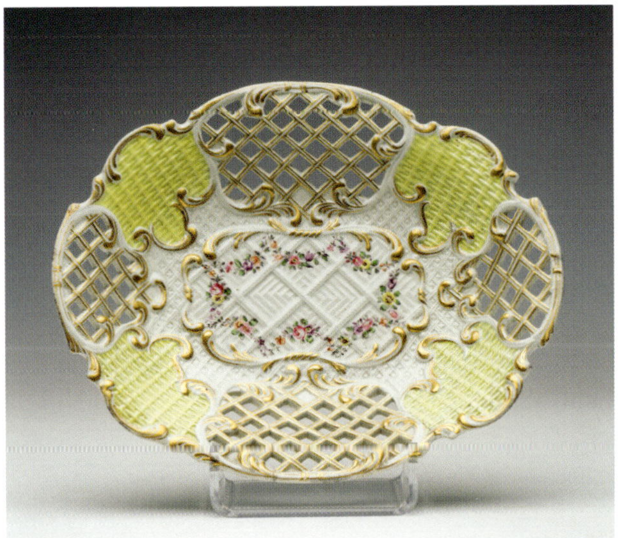

435

435

Dish

1762–5
Length 26.2 cm, width 22.4 cm
1957.24.1.685

Oval; basketwork moulding with pierced trellis, oblong central panel with eight floral wreaths; flowers, gilding and yellow ground added later.

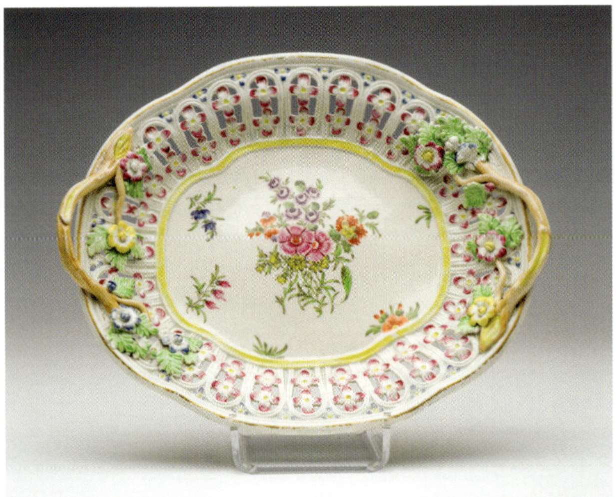

436

436

Basket stand

1768–70
Length 26.3 cm, width 21.9 cm
1957.24.1.770

Quatrefoil form, branch handles, applied flowers; pierced border with pink mayflowers, European flowers in well defined by yellow edge.

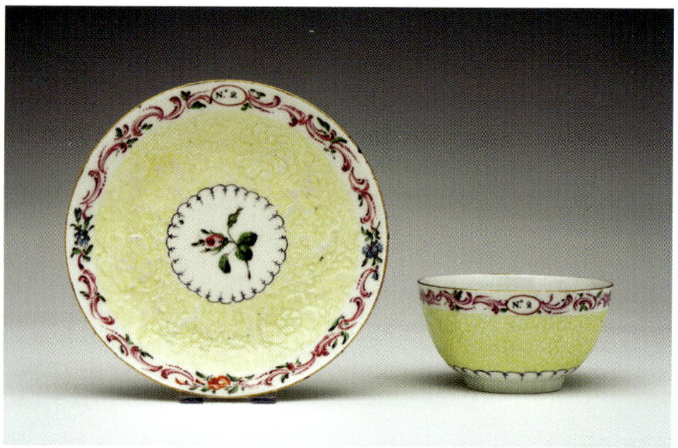

437

437

Teabowl and saucer

About 1765
Bowl ht 4.9 cm; diam. 8.7 cm; saucer diam. 13.8 cm
Mark: small purple crescent on both
1957.24.1.691

Florally moulded yellow ground, gilt edge, puce scroll border with flower sprays at three points, oval cartouche with *No. 2* in black at fourth; centre painted with rose spray within loop bordered circle.

PROVENANCE
Albert Amor, London, 19 February 1952, £105.

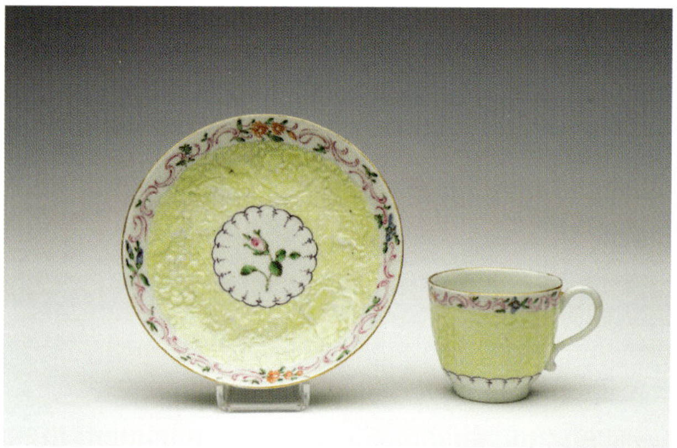

438

438

Coffee cup and saucer

About 1765
Cup ht 5.9 cm, diam. 6.5 cm; saucer diam. 13.5 cm
1957.24.1.662

Florally moulded yellow ground, border with puce scrolls and flowers; reserve on saucer picked out in purple and painted with rose spray.

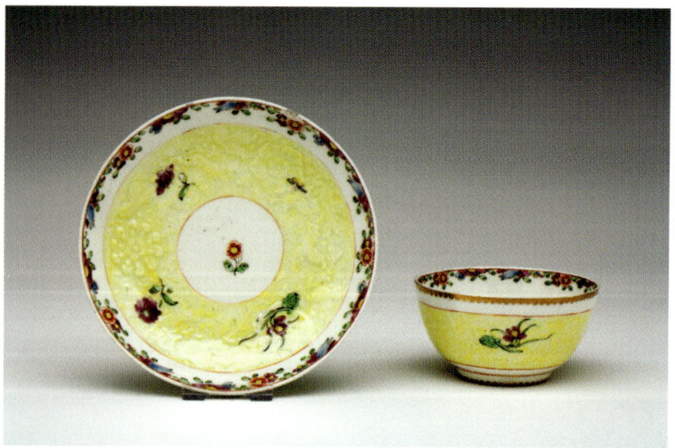

439

439

Teabowl and saucer

1765–70
Bowl ht 4.6 cm, diam. 8.7 cm; saucer diam. 13.5 cm
1957.24.1.694

Florally moulded yellow ground with flower sprays and an insect, formal polychrome floral border around inside of cup and edge of saucer; some decoration possibly added later.

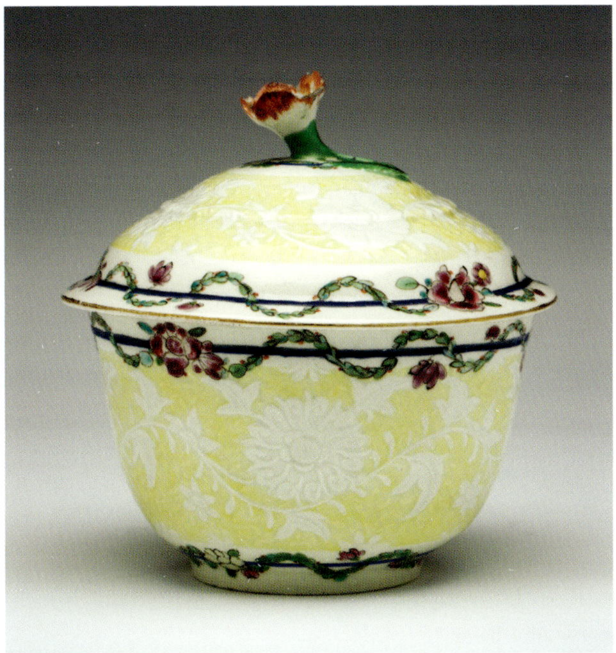

440

440

Sugar bowl and cover

1760–65
Ht 13.1 cm, diam. 10.8 cm
1957.24.1.687

Florally moulded light yellow ground, white borders with blue line entwined with green leaves and flowers, cover with rosebud knop; all decoration added later.

PROVENANCE
Sotheby's, London, 18 October 1955, £125.

441

Spoon tray

About 1765
Length 15.9 cm, width 9.5 cm
1957.24.1.705

Hexagonal oblong, wavy gilt dentil edge; florally moulded yellow ground, border with puce scrolls and flowers, central oblong with two coloured butterflies; yellow ground probably added later.

PROVENANCE
H.W. Hughes Collection, no. 225, £12

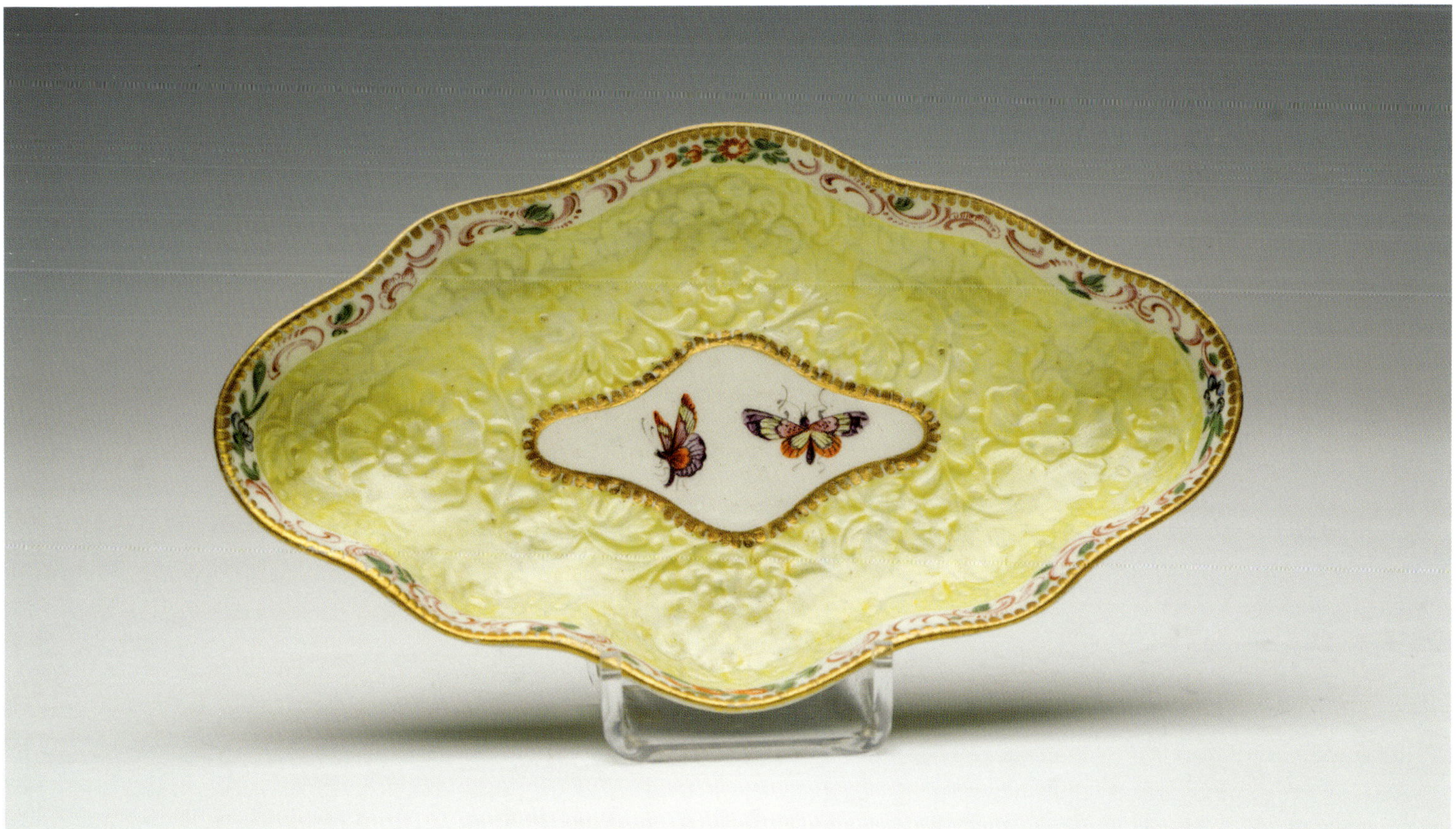

441

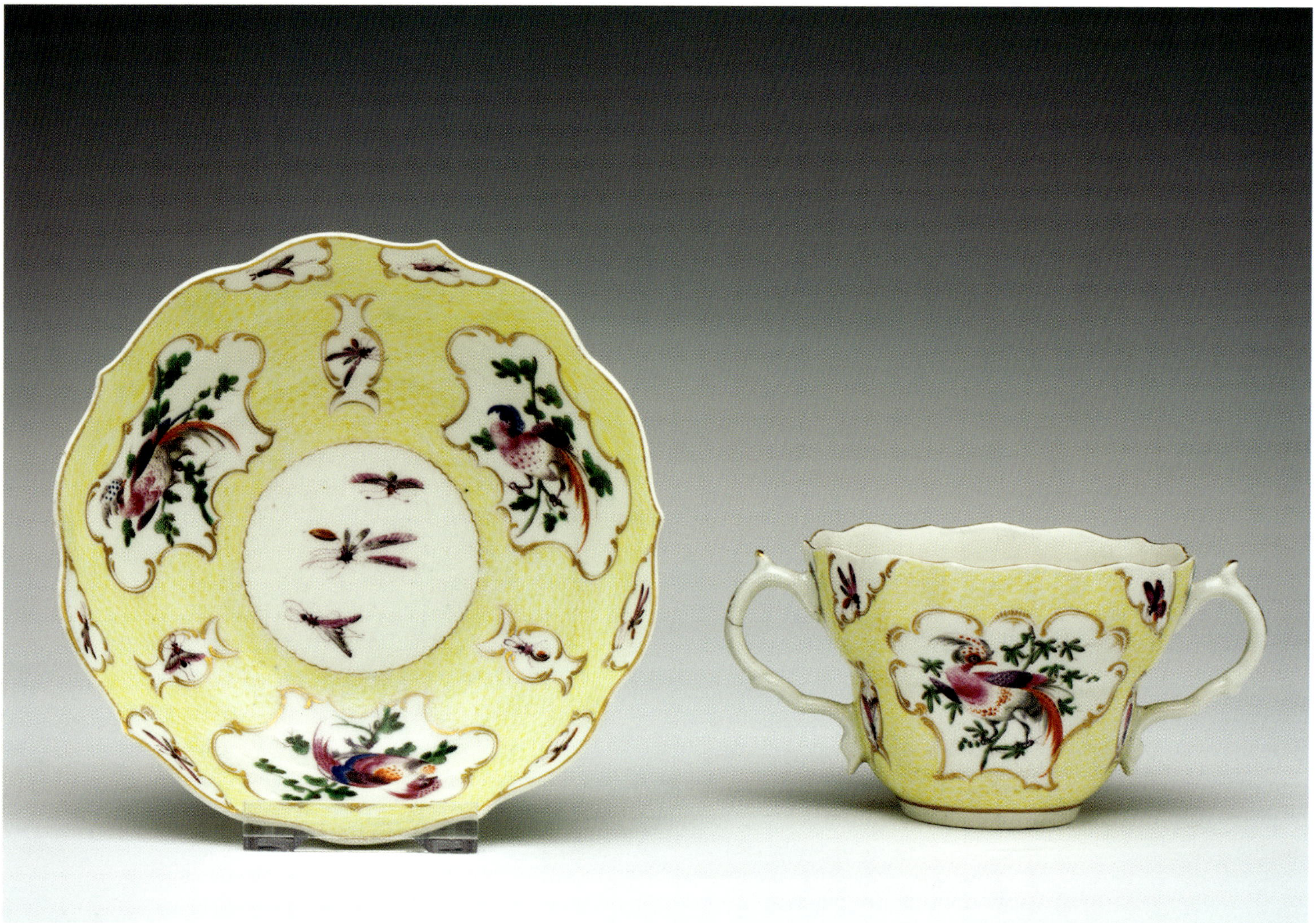

442

442

Caudle cup and saucer

1765–70
Cup ht 6.3 cm, diam. 9.4 cm; saucer diam. 14.6 cm
1957.24.1.684

Ogee shape, solid scroll handles; wavy gilt rim, upward yellow scale ground, three large rococo gilt scroll bordered reserves painted in colours with exotic birds, smaller reserves with insects.

This yellow scale decoration, possibly derived from Meissen, is rarer than the solid yellow ground and only seen with exotic birds. The leaves on the cup are different from those on the saucer, as is also the case with a similar cup and saucer, but with pierced handles, sold by Mr Marshall at Sotheby's, London, in 1953. Similar decoration may be seen on a covered milk jug (Spero 1984, pl. 26); a pair of caudle cups with pierced handles and a tea canister (McNair 2007, pls. 216, 217); a slop bowl, teacup and saucer (McKeown 2006, pl. 54); and a teapot (Gardiner Museum, Toronto, no. G83.1.1149 1-2).

PROVENANCE
H.W. Hughes Collection, no. 273, 12 February 1944, £65.

REFERENCES
Reynolds 1999, pl. 17; Amor 1985.

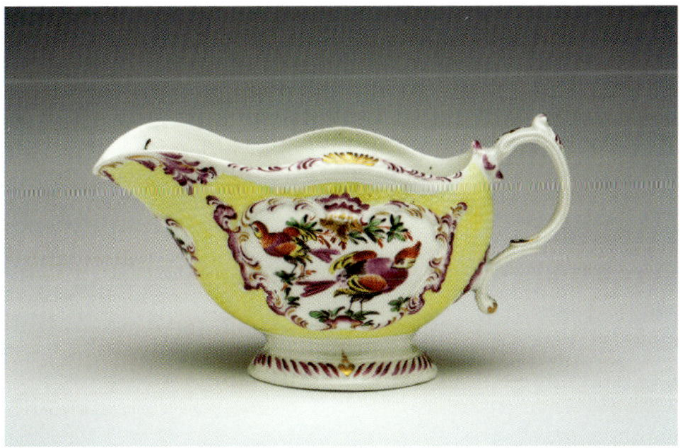

443

443

Sauceboat

1765–68
Length 20 cm
1957.24.1.1072

Yellow basketwork ground, puce outlined rococo panels with dishevelled birds and flowers, oval base with puce gadrooning and gold hearts, interior with two flower sprays. Marshall thought that this was probably decorated outside the Worcester factory.

REFERENCE
Spero and Sandon 1996, pl. 266.

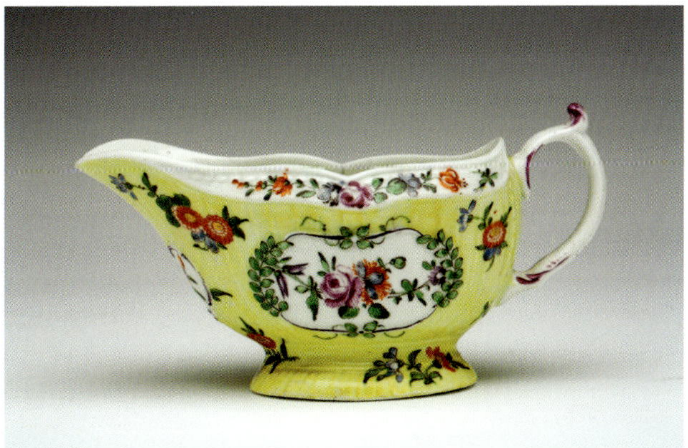

444

444

Sauceboat

1760–65
Length 20 cm
1957.24.1.1071

Yellow ground, fluted with moulded panels of European flower festoons, scattered Oriental flowers, floral sprays on rim and in interior, puce touches on rococo handle.

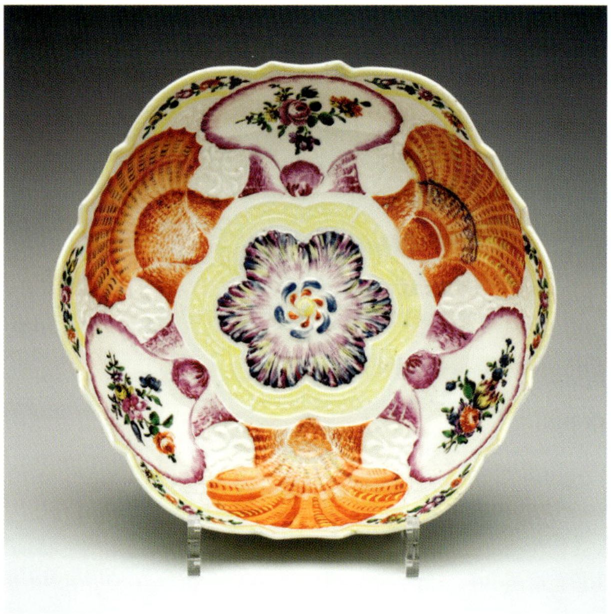

445

445

Junket dish

About 1770
Diam. 24 cm
1957.24.1.255

Moulded with scallop shells, three in orange, three outlined in puce with flowers; large moulded six-petalled flower in centre within yellow border; barbed and arched rim with yellow borders framing garlands of flowers.

PROVENANCE
Drane Collection.

REFERENCE
Sotheby's, London, 13 April 2011, lot 168.

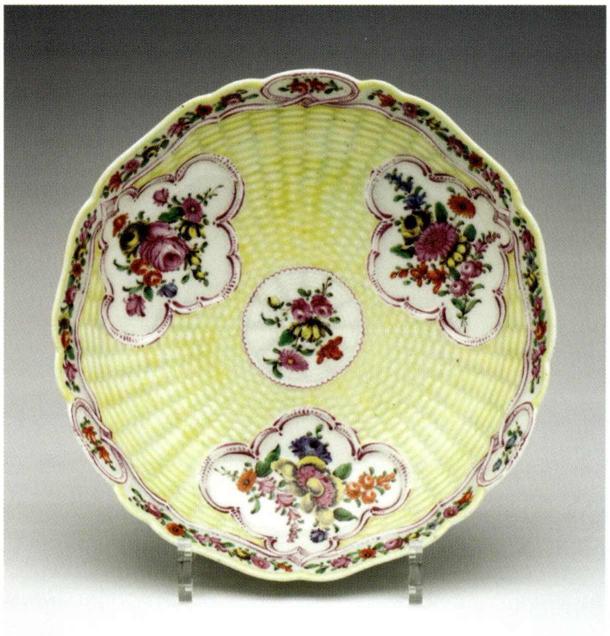

446

446

Junket dish

1762–5
Ht 5.2 cm, diam. 22.7 cm
1957.24.1.679

Moulded yellow basketwork, pink scrolled rococo cartouches with flowers, floral border interrupted with three puce bows, wavy yellow moulded edge.

REFERENCES
McNair 2007, pl. 222; Sandon 2008, pl. 33.

447

Coffee cup and saucer

1770–75
Cup ht 6.3 cm, diam. 6.1 cm; saucer diam. 13.5 cm
1957.24.1.677

Ribbed with gilt scalloped edge; yellow ground, floral panels outlined in mauve, puce double C scroll border with flowers around rim of saucer; later decoration.

PROVENANCE
H.W. Hughes Collection, no. 177, £17.

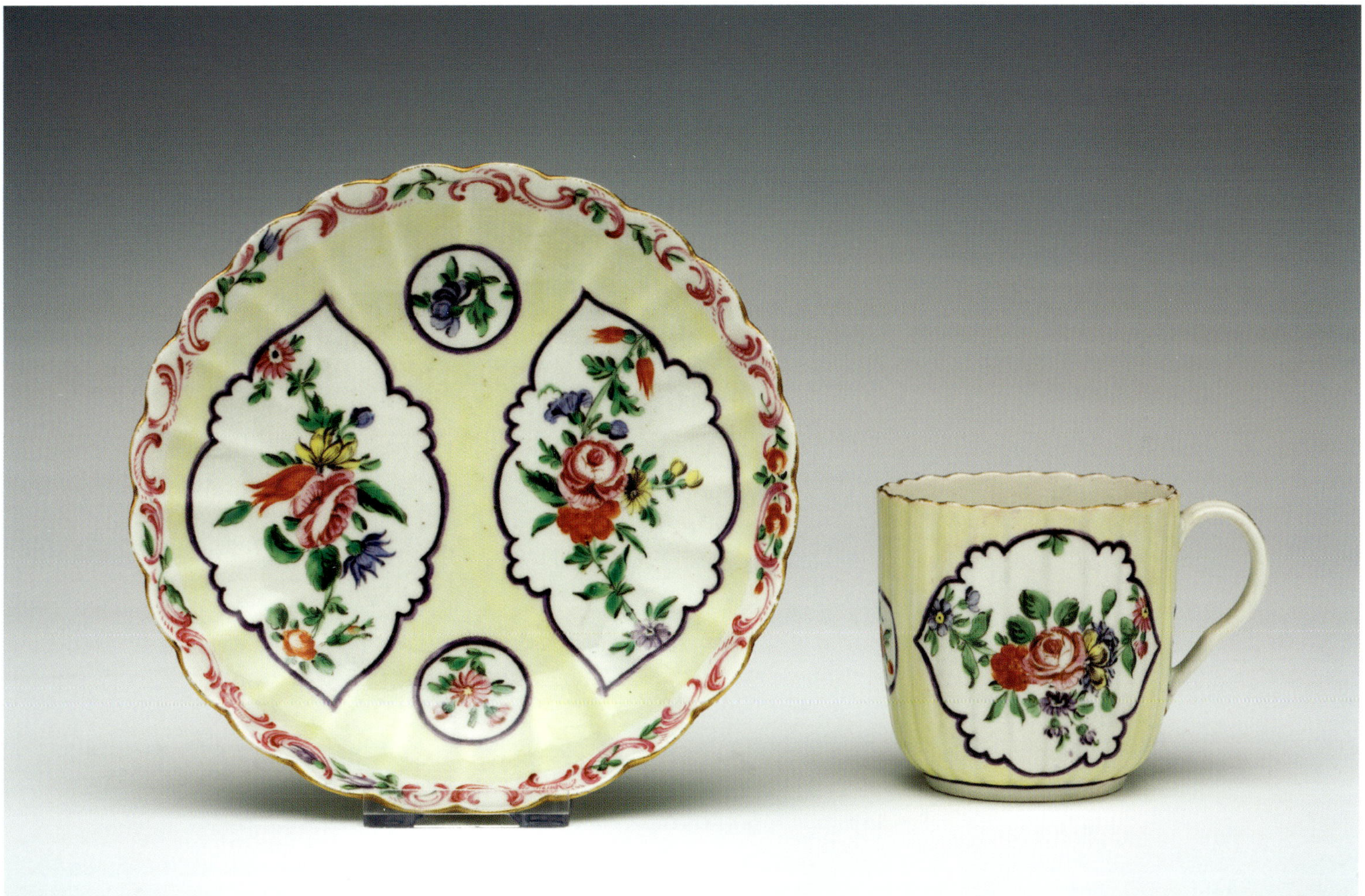

447

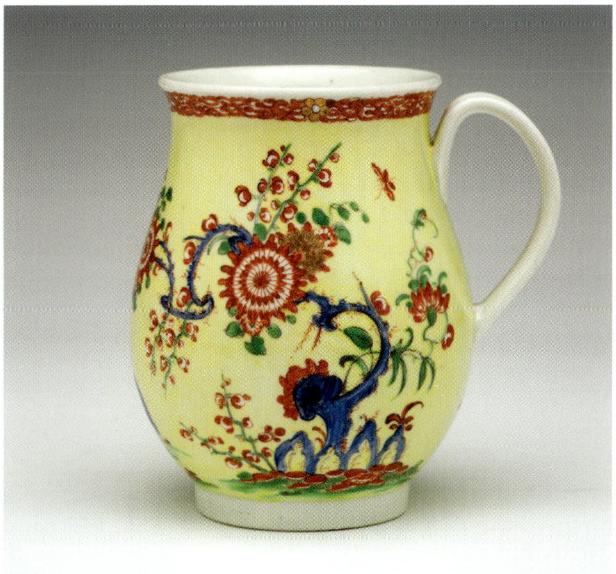

448

448

Mug

1758–60
Ht 12.4 cm
1957.24.1.665

Bell-shaped; iron red border below rim, decorated with the 'Quail' pattern; yellow ground added later.

PROVENANCE
Christie's, London, 7 July 1953, lot 90, £178 10s.

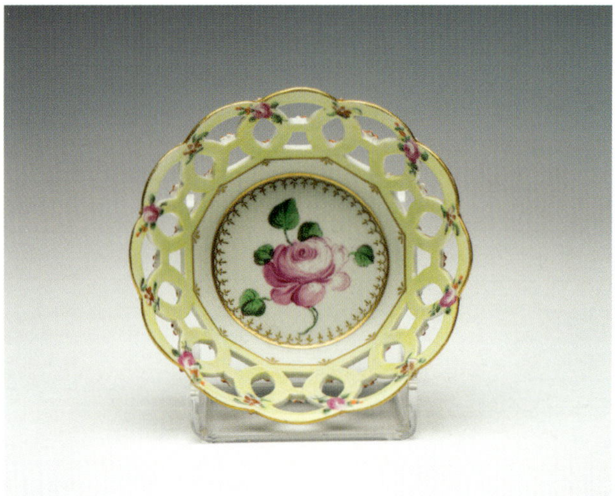

449

449

Basket

About 1765
Ht 5.5 cm, diam. 12.9 cm
1957.24.1.664

Sides formed by twelve intersecting circles with pink applied flowers on exterior, rose spray in base; yellow ground and gilding added later.

450–454

Cabaret service

1770–72
1957.24.1.667–671

Each piece is decorated with dry blue flowers on a sulphur yellow ground. The gilded handles have chevrons diminishing in size, a feature often found on pieces decorated by James Giles. The yellow ground was probably added later. Blue and yellow, as a combination, appeared on early Vincennes porcelain in the 1740s.

It is extremely rare to find a complete cabaret. The name, which is French, refers to a tea or coffee set which has its own porcelain tray. If there is one cup it is a *solitaire* and if two cups a *tête a tête*.

Frank Tilley, a well-known London dealer, is credited with persuading Sotheby's to send this rare service 'into the country for Mr Marshall to see', as he was in a nursing home at the time. He was assured by Mrs Marshall that this method was 'the only means of preventing her husband from leaving his bed and coming to town as soon as he saw the catalogue'.

PROVENANCE
J.G. Gray; Sotheby's, London, 28 October 1952, lot 105, £528.

REFERENCE
Reynolds 1999, pl. 34.

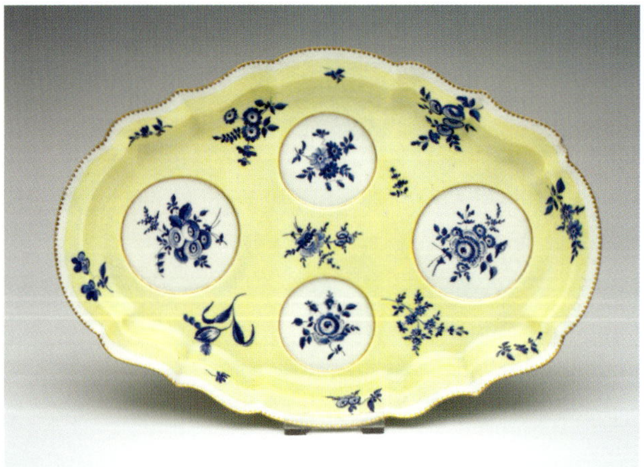

450

450

Tray

Length 30.3 cm, width 21.1 cm
1957.24.1.667

Oval with wavy edge; gilt dentil edge, four circular white reserves with dry blue flowers.

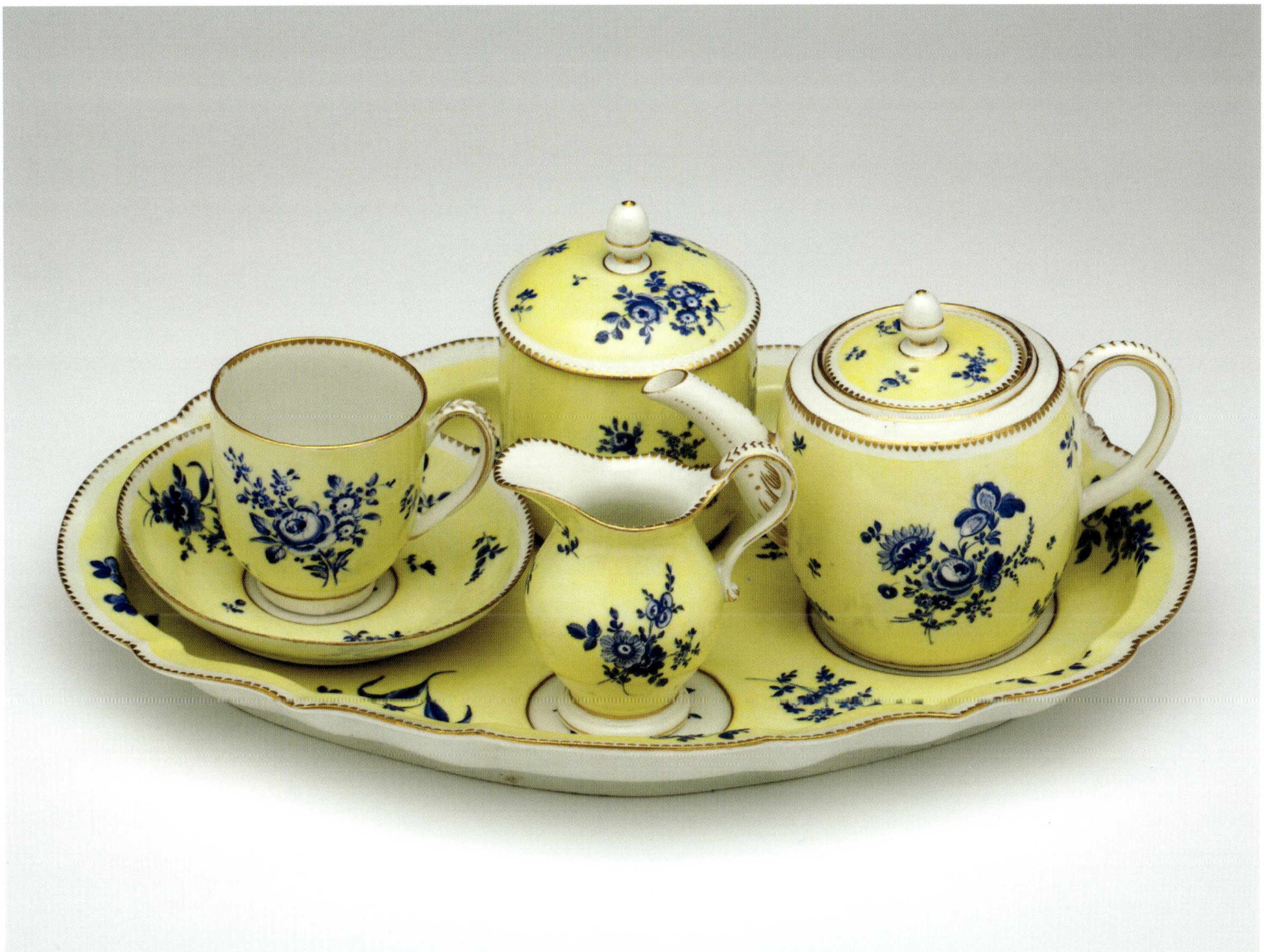

450–454

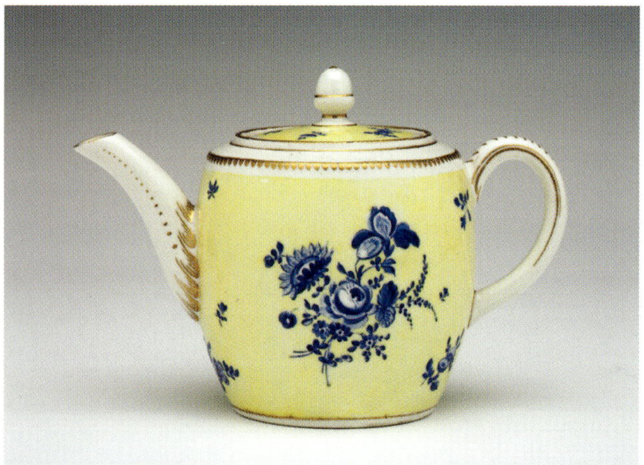

451

451
Teapot
Ht 10.2 cm
1957.24.1.668

Barrel shaped with flush lid and acorn finial.

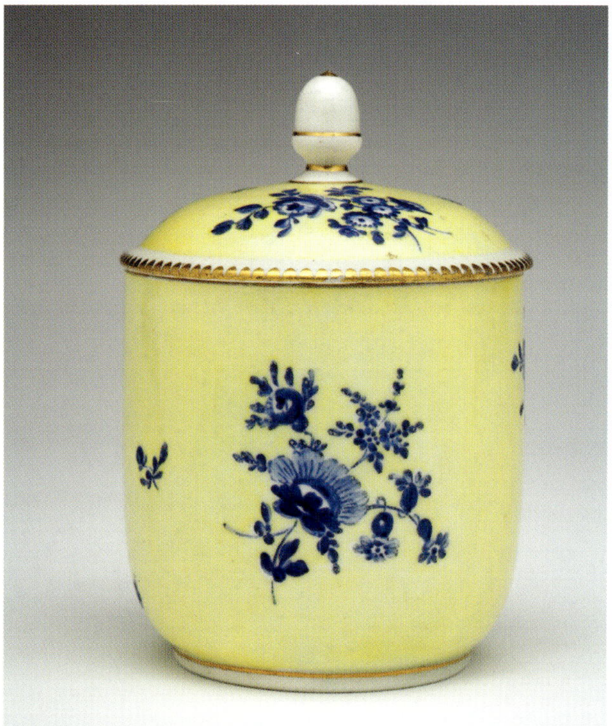

452

452
Sugar bowl
Ht 10.8 cm, diam. 6.8 cm
1957.24.1.669

Cylindrical with low domed cover and acorn finial.

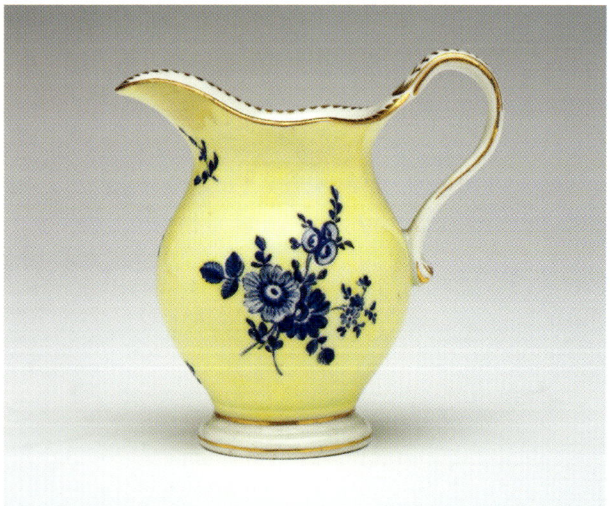

453

453
Jug
Ht 8cm
1957.24.1.670

Ovoid, narrowing at foot and neck with wavy rim, flared mouth.

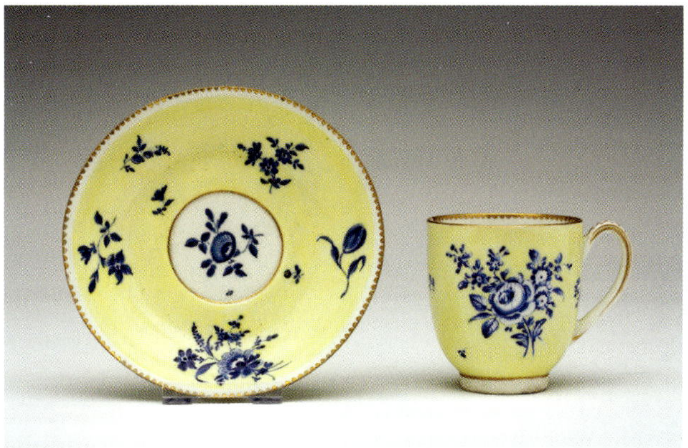

454

454

Coffee cup and saucer

Cup ht 6.1 cm, diam. 5.5 cm; saucer diam. 11.1 cm
1957.24.1.671

Cup with gilt loop handle, saucer with dry blue spray in white well.

REFERENCE
Reynolds 1999, pl. 34.

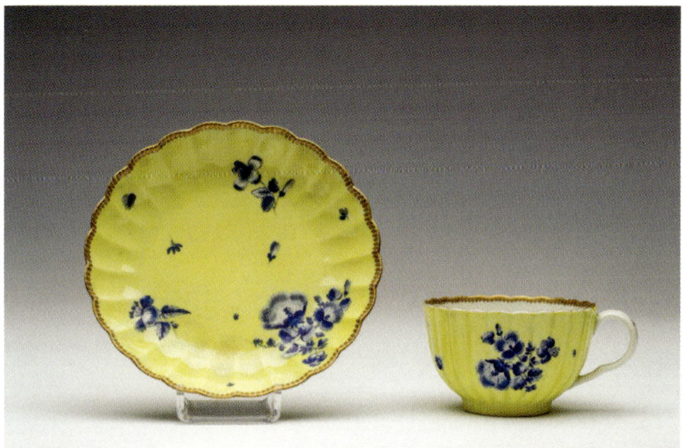

455

455

Teacup and saucer

1770–75
Cup ht 4.9 cm, diam. 7.6 cm; saucer diam. 12.8 cm
1957.24.1.666

Scalloped gilt dentil edge; sprays of dry blue flowers, sulphur yellow ground added later.

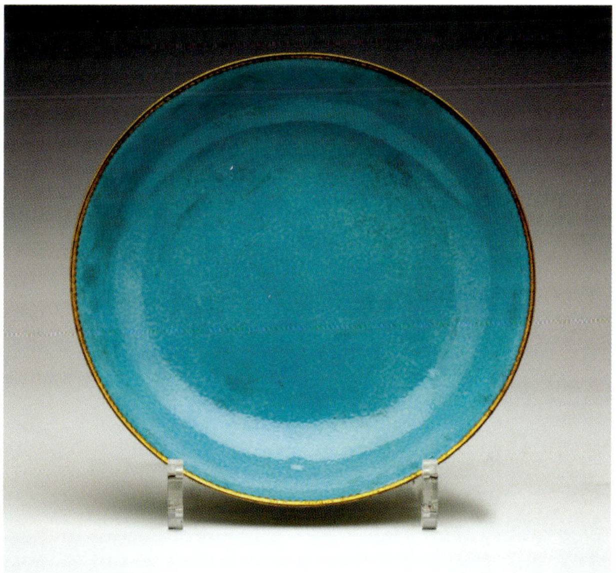

456

456

Cake dish

About 1772
Diam. 19.1 cm
1957.24.1.356

Gilt dentil edge, the entire decoration in sky blue with an uneven 'orange-peel' surface. According to Marshall, it was 'acquired many years ago in the turnstile off Lincoln's Inn Fields for 45s'.

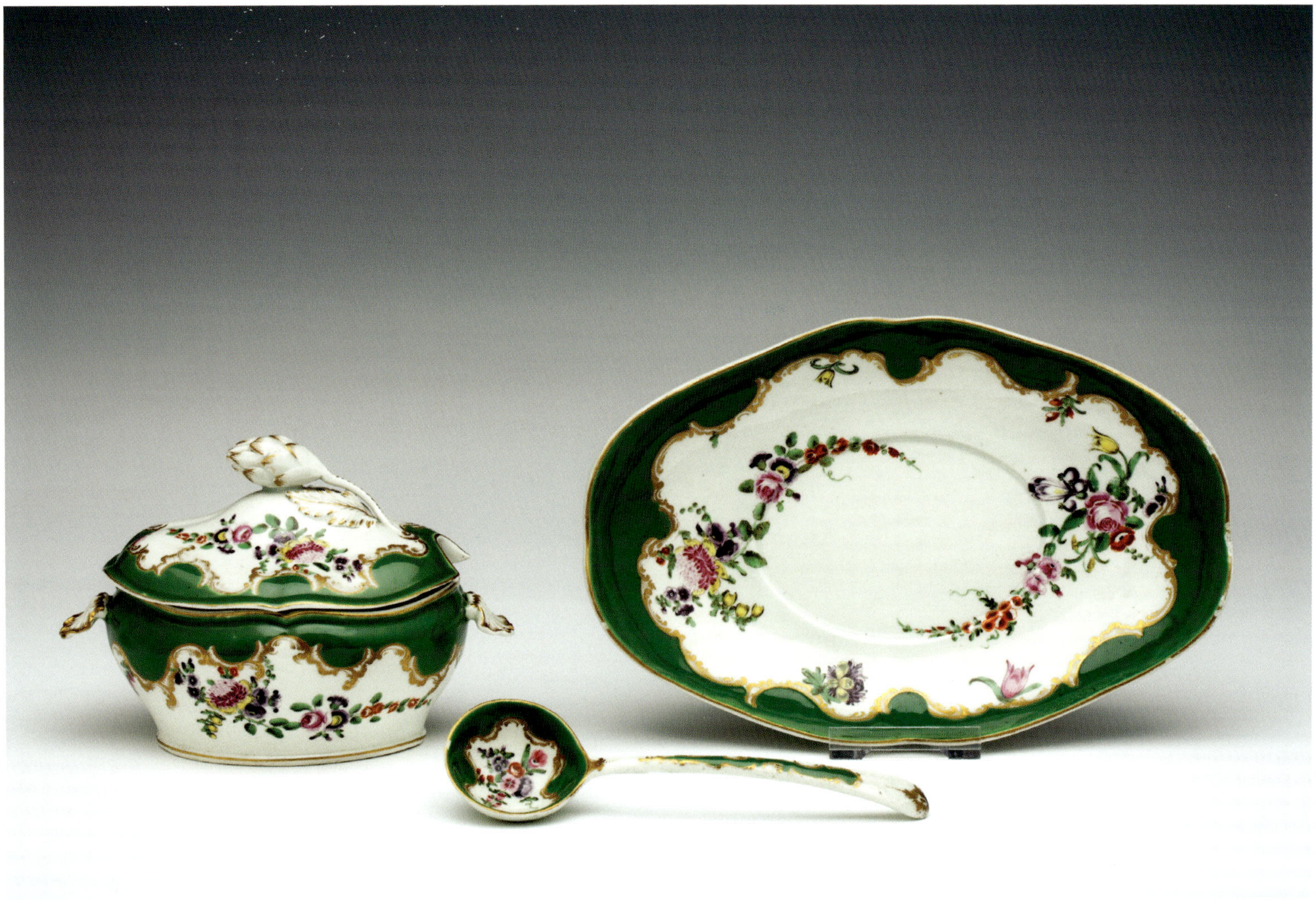

457

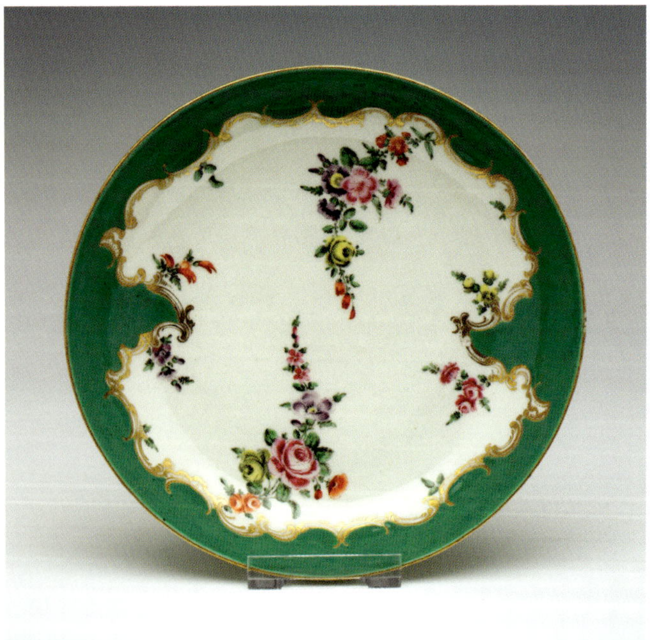

458

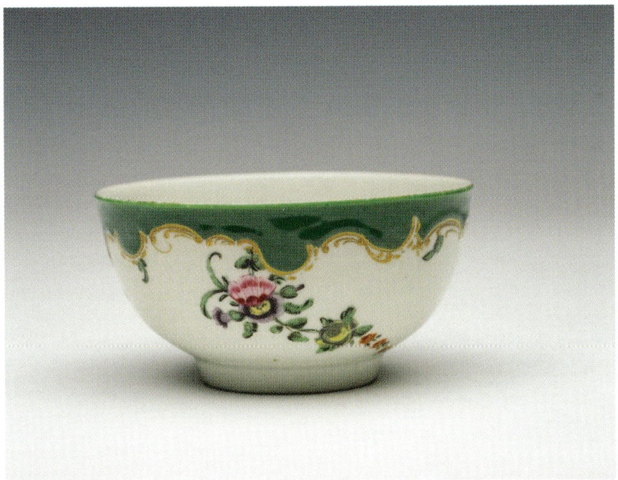

459

457

Tureen with stand and ladle

1769–72
Tureen ht 11.9 cm, length 17.5 cm, width 11cm; stand length 23.8cm, width 15.9 cm; ladle length 17 cm
1957.24.1.433

Oval tureen with moulded shell handles; cover surmounted by artichoke knop with stalk and two leaves; ladle with rounded bowl and curved shank. Each piece has an irregular green border edged with gilt scrolls, from which depend two floral wreaths and flower sprays.

This pattern, the 'Marchioness of Huntly', takes its name from a dessert service in the same pattern sold by the second wife of the 10th Marquess in 1882. A pair of similar tureens is illustrated in McNair 2007, pl. 245.

REFERENCES
Reynolds 1999, pl. 25; Sotheby's, London, 13 April 2011, lot 166.

458

Cake dish

About 1770
Diam. 18.7 cm
1957.24.1.456

Irregular green border with scroll gilding, from which depend wreaths and sprays of flowers; the 'Marchioness of Huntly' pattern.

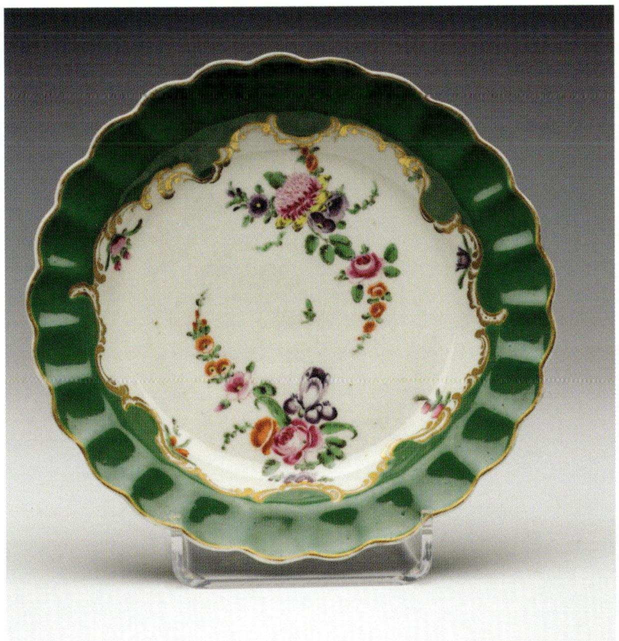

460

459

Bowl

About 1770
Ht 5.1 cm, diam. 10.3 cm
1957.24.1.449

Irregular green border with scroll gilding, two wreaths and floral sprays below; the 'Marchioness of Huntly' pattern.

460

Dish

About 1770
Diam. 15.9 cm
1957.24.1.451

Fluted with scalloped edge; gilt rim, irregular green border with scroll gilding, floral wreaths and sprays depending; the 'Marchioness of Huntly' pattern.

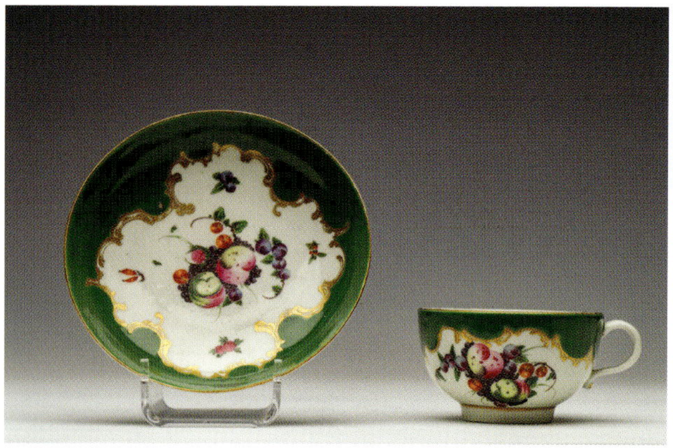

461

461

Teacup and saucer

About 1770
Cup ht 4.8 cm, diam. 7.9 cm, saucer diam. 13 cm
Mark: crossed swords and *9* with a dot.
1957.24.1.457

Irregular green border with gilding; decorated with bunches of spotted fruit and various floral sprays.

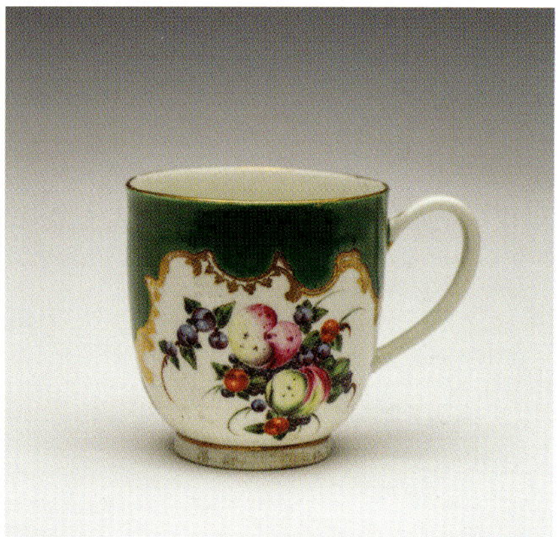

462

462

Coffee cup

About 1770
Ht 6.3 cm, diam. 5.8 cm
1957.24.1.447

Irregular green border edged with gilding; decorated with bunches of spotted fruit and floral sprays.

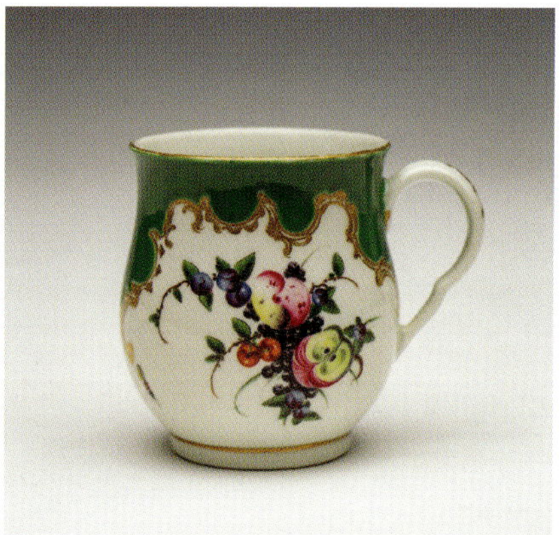

463

463

Custard cup

About 1770
Ht 7 cm, diam. 5.6 cm
1957.24.1.443

Bell-shaped; irregular green border with scroll gilding; decorated on one side with a bunch of fruit and on the other with a spray of blue plums and three butterflies.

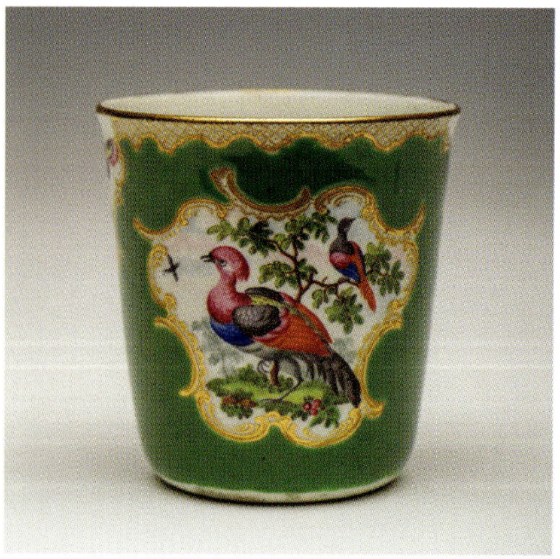

464

464

Beaker

About 1770
Ht 7.4cm, diam. 7 cm
1957.24.1.445

Green ground with gilding, birds and insects in reserves; decorated in the nineteenth century.

PROVENANCE
Darcy Taylor Collection; Sotheby's, London, 10 April 1957, lot 67, £320.

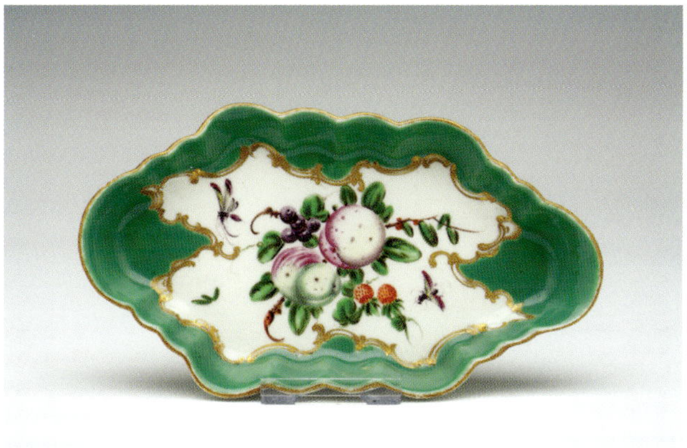

465

465

Spoon tray

About 1770
Length 15.2 cm
1957.24.1.706

Hexagonally fluted with wavy gilt rim; irregular green border defined by gilding, spotted fruit and insect decoration.

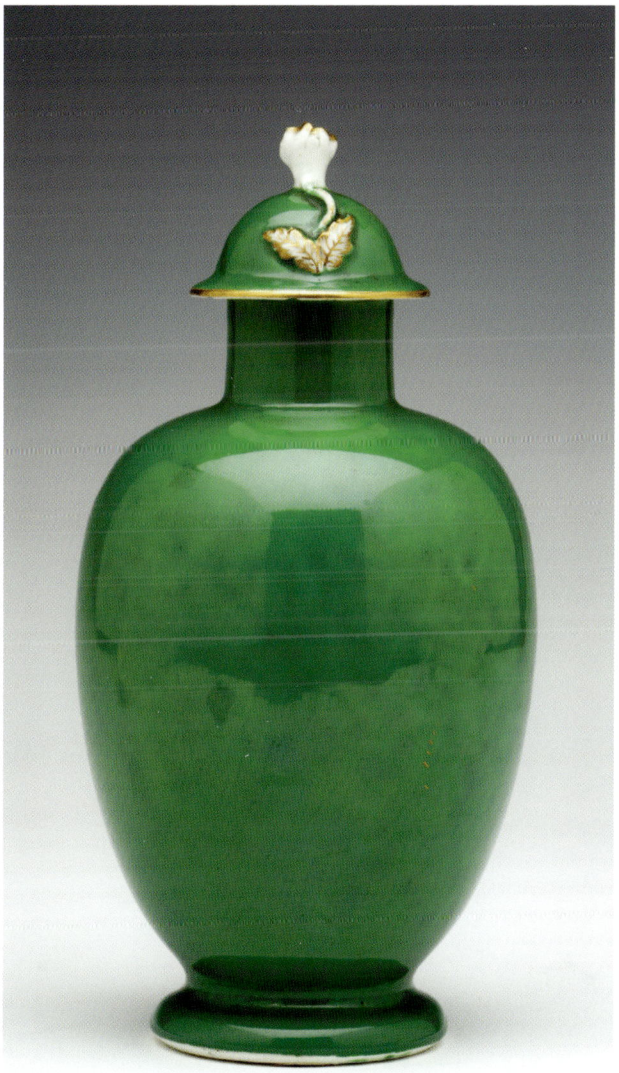

466

466

Tea canister and cover

1770–72
Ht 16.4 cm
1957.24.1.439

Slender, ovoid shape; plain green ground, gilding on white rosebud knop and rim. A coffee cup and saucer with similar decoration are illustrated in Spero and Sandon 1996, pl. 253.

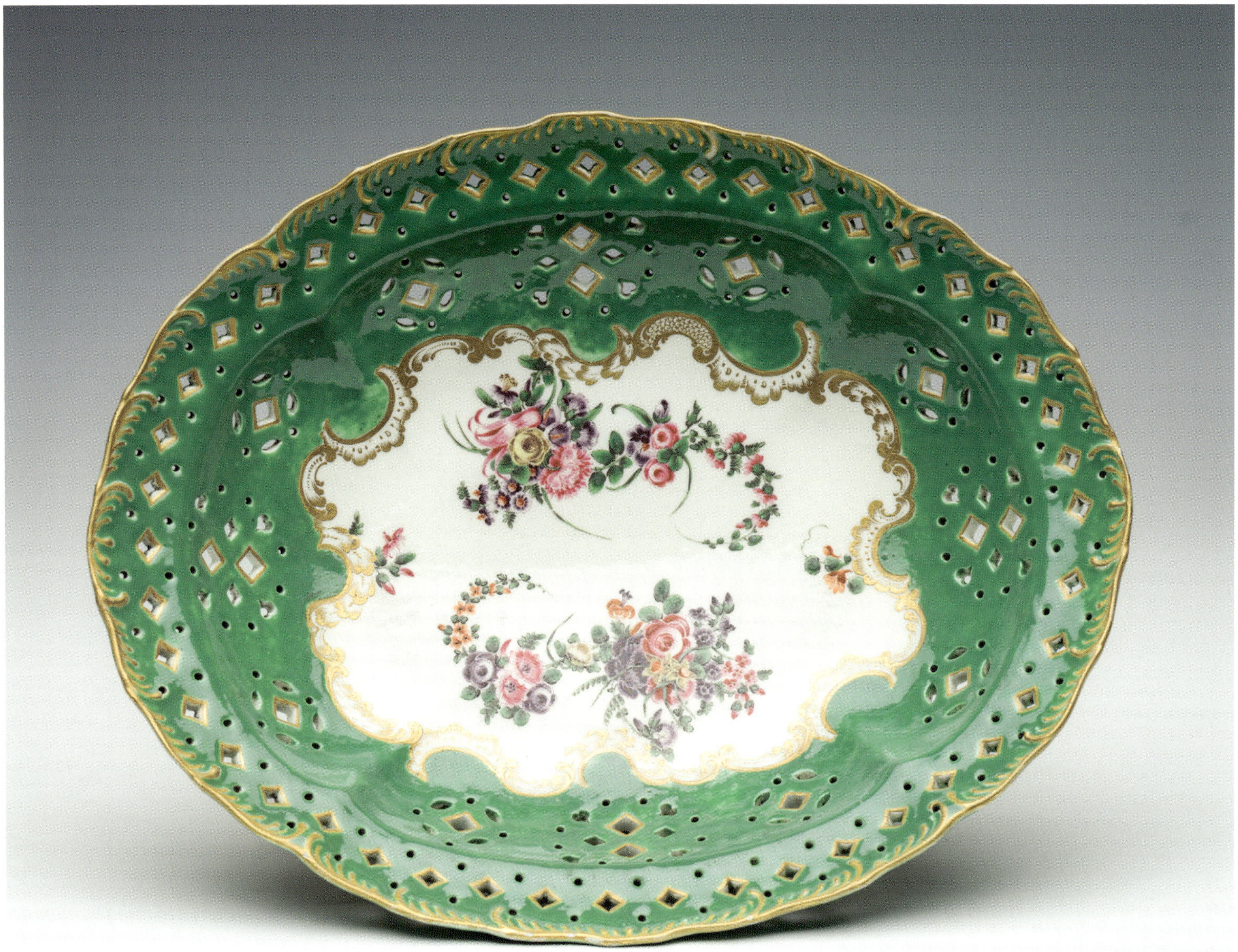

467

467

Dessert dish

About 1770
Ht 8.6 cm, length 29.6 cm, width 24.4 cm
1957.24.1.435

Pedestal dessert dish with feathered gilt edge, pierced sides; wide green border with gilding, floral sprays in central reserve.

PROVENANCE
Christie's, London, 7 July 1953, lot 78, £262 10s.

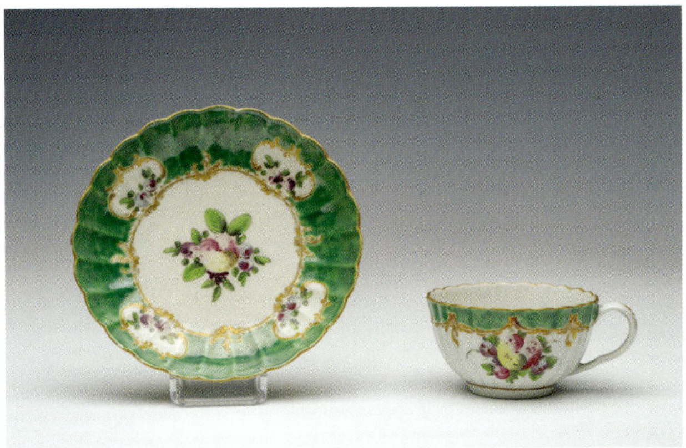

468

468

Teacup and saucer

1775–80
Cup ht 4.7 cm, diam. 7.8 cm; saucer diam. 13.3 cm
1957.24.1.454

Ribbed cup, fluted saucer with scalloped gilt edge; green border with fruit decoration in white reserves. The decoration may all have been added later.

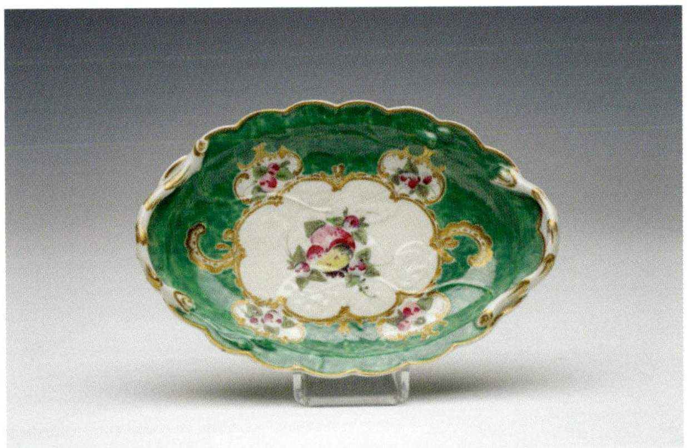

469

469

Sweetmeat dish

About 1775
Length 16.3 cm, width 11.2 cm
1957.24.1.459

Oval shape with 'Blind Earl' moulding, rustic handles; green border with white reserves containing spotted fruit; polychrome decoration added later.

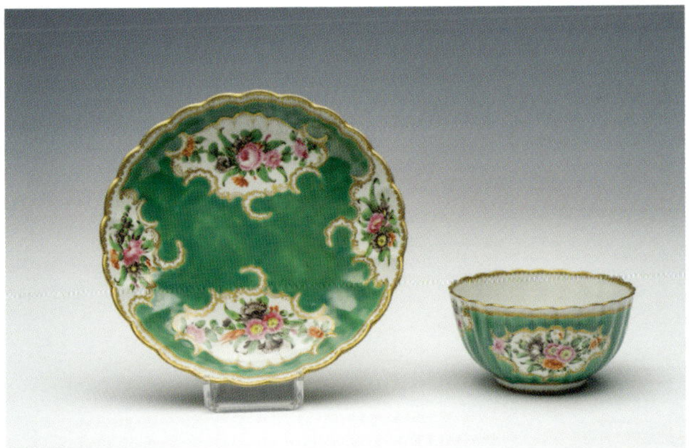

470

470

Teabowl and saucer

1780–85
Bowl ht 4.5 cm, diam. 8.4 cm; saucer diam. 13.7 cm
1957.24.1.450

Scalloped gilt dentil edge; green ground with four irregular reserves with floral bouquets; decoration added later.

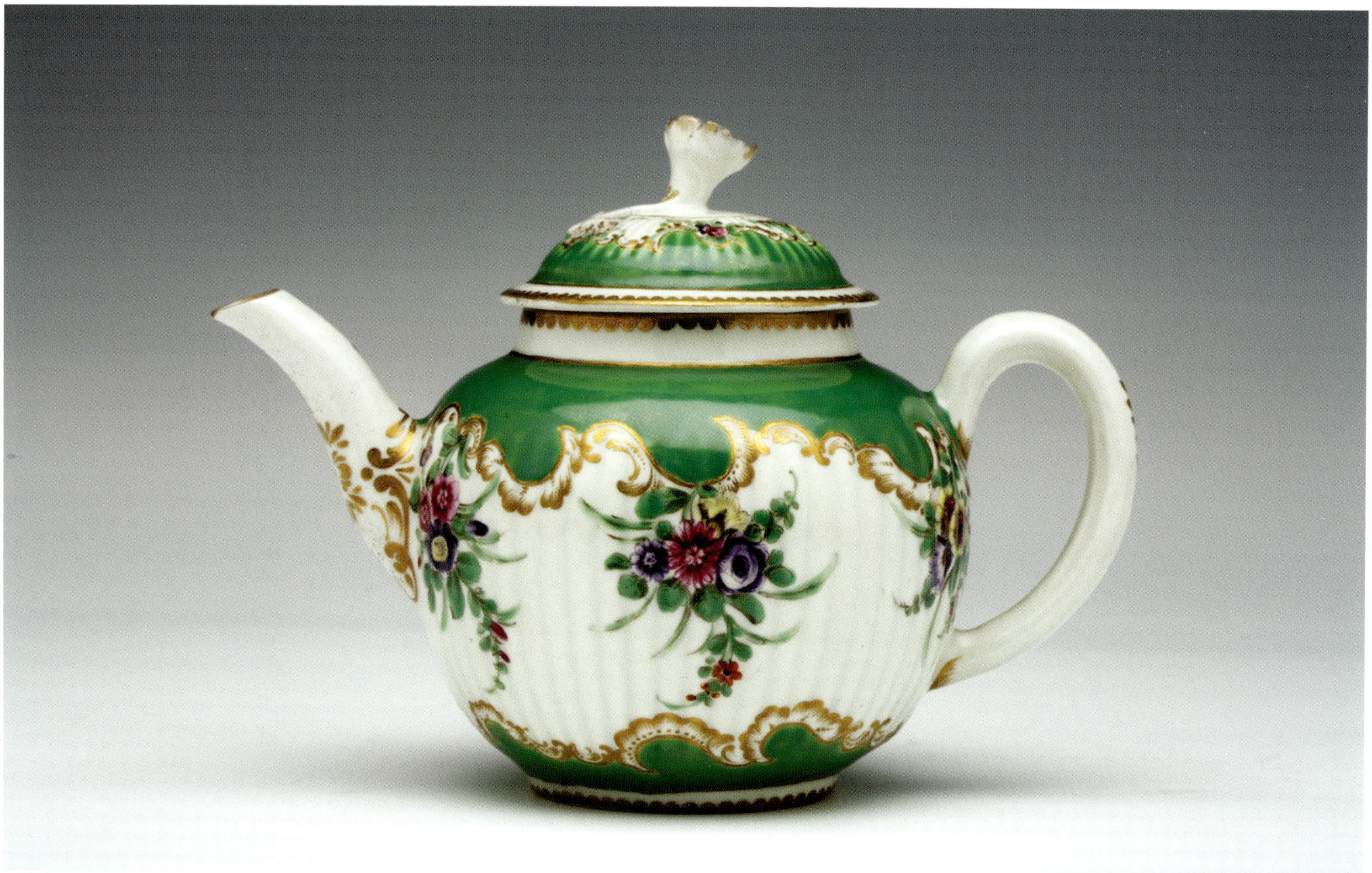

471

471

Teapot and lid

1780–85
Ht 11.8 cm
1957.24.1.441

Globular, closely ribbed body with plain loop handle, rosebud knop; gilt dentil edge, irregular green border with scroll gilding, five bouquets of European flowers; decoration added later.

472

Plate

About 1775
Diam. 19.4 cm
1957.24.1.464

Fluted edge, gilt rim; decorated in the nineteenth century with irregular pale green border and flower sprays.

473

Plate

About 1775
Diam. 19 cm
1957.24.1.460

Scalloped gilt rim, blue-green rococo shaped border with purple floral festoons, central bouquet of flowers.

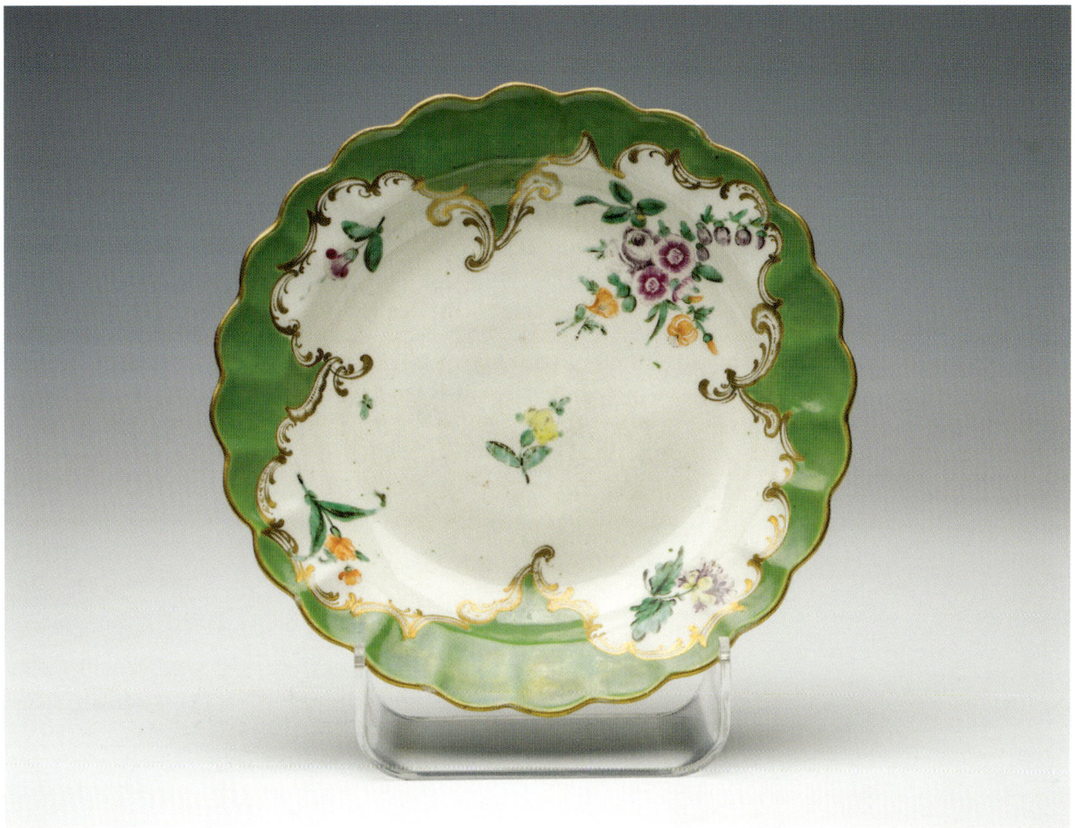

472

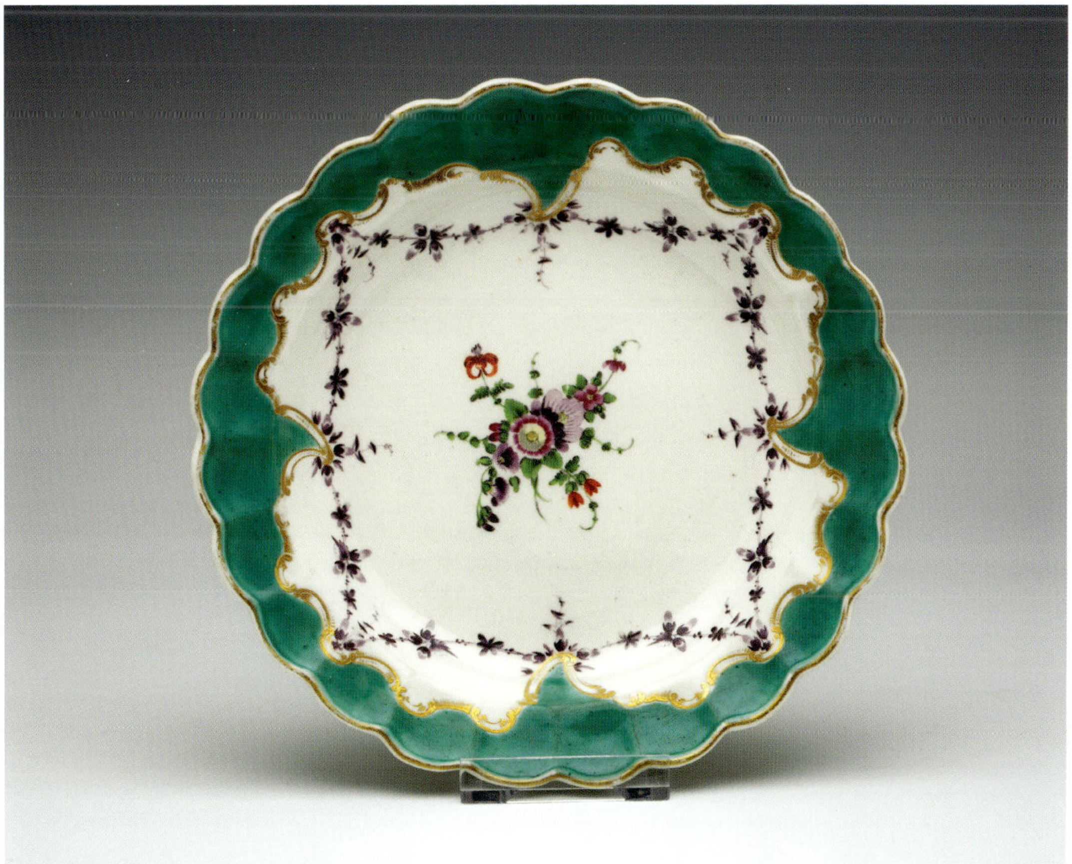

473

474

Vase

1765–70
Ht 41 cm
1957.24.1.271

Slender, octagonal shape with wider raised band in the middle; eight panels decorated with Japanese-style flowers and birds, separated by orange and gilt patterned ribs. The interior has a border of scattered sprays of flowers.

This flared vase or *gu* shape was used for Chinese bronzes from the late Shang period and was copied by Chinese potters. There are two similar vases in the Museum of Royal Worcester Porcelain, together with a taller octagonal case with cover (figs 26–28).

REFERENCE
Reynolds 1999, pl. 21.

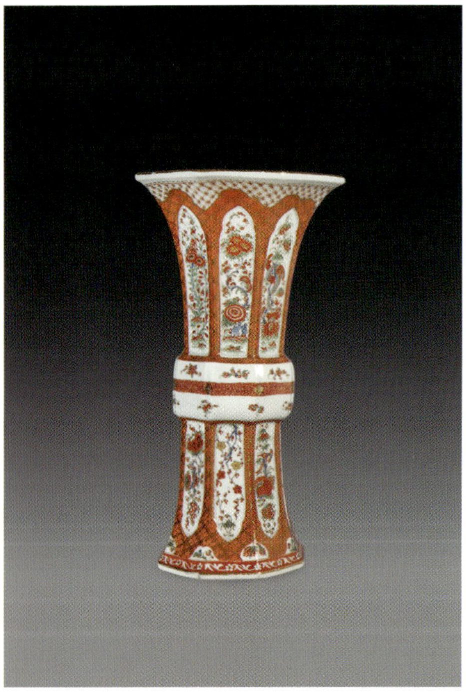
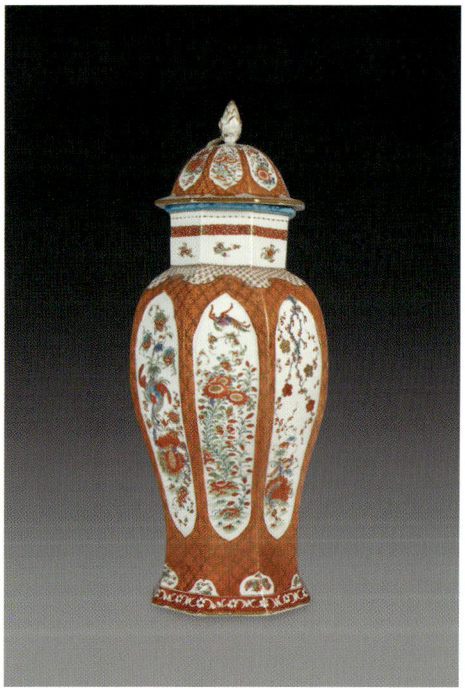
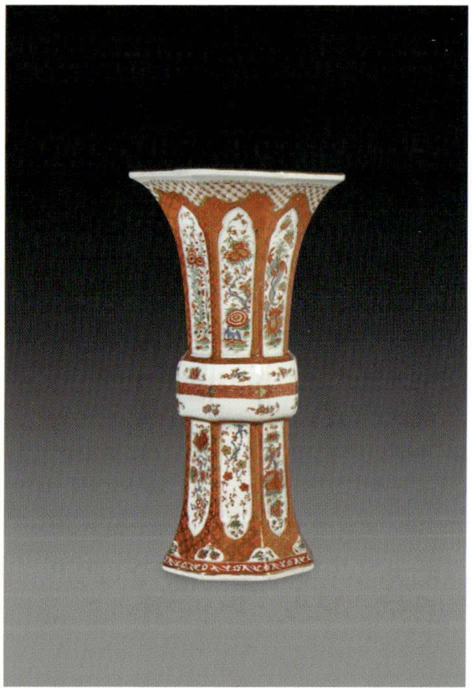

Figs 26–28 Garniture of three similar vases. © Museum of Royal Worcester Porcelain

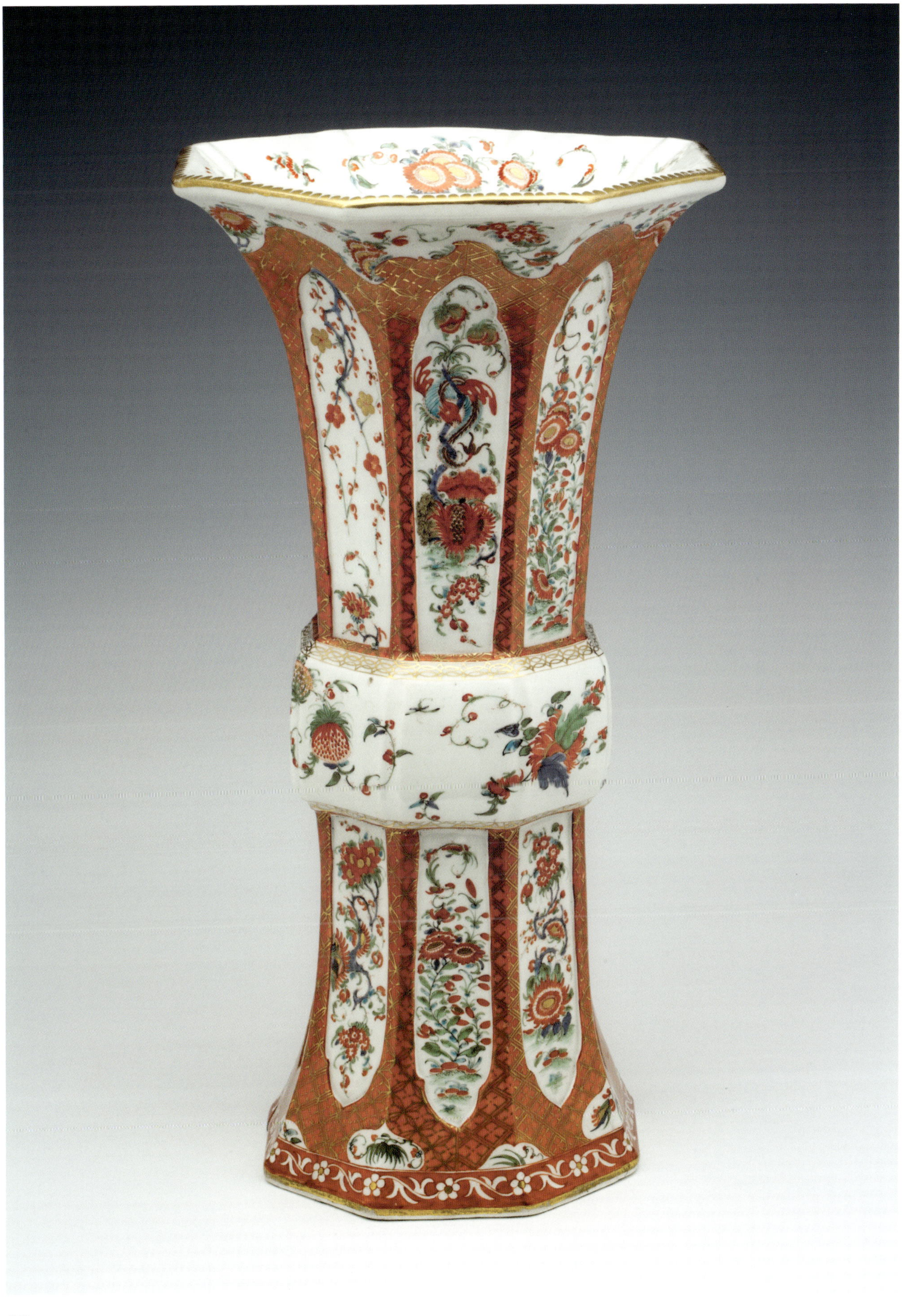

474

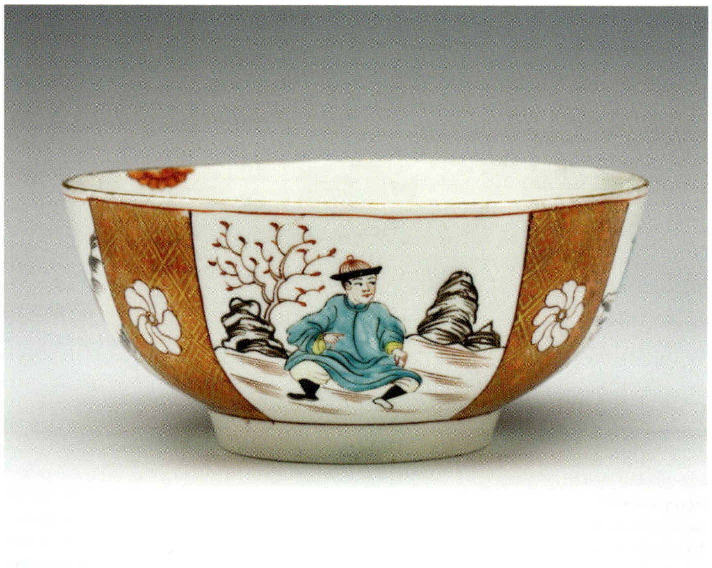

475

475

Bowl

About 1770
Ht 6.9 cm, diam. 15.4 cm
1957.24.1.258

Oriental-style decoration; four gilt diapered orange bands with white *mons* separating white panels, each with a seated Oriental figure.

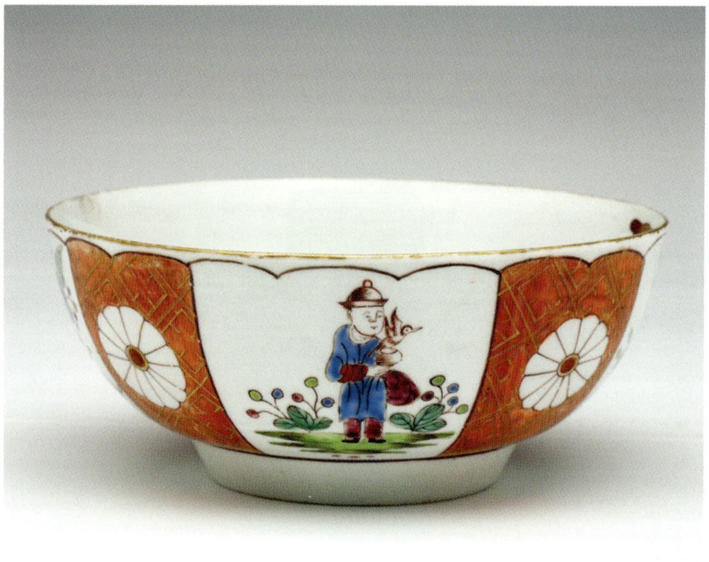

476

476

Bowl

About 1770
Ht 6.5 cm, diam. 15 cm
1957.24.1.262

Oriental-style decoration; four white panels, two of which contain a standing Oriental figure holding a bird and two with formal flower sprays, separated by gilt-diapered orange panels with a white *mons*.

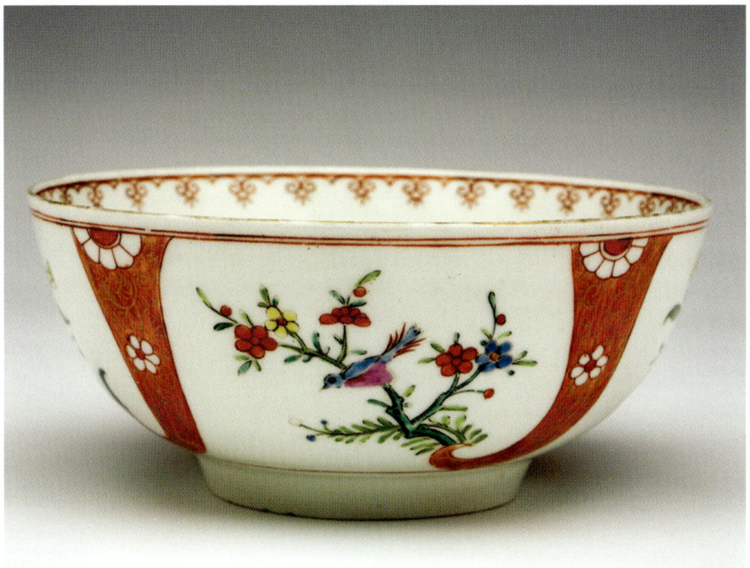

477

477

Bowl

1775–80
Ht 6.9 cm, diam. 14.8 cm
1957.24.1.259

Below a thin double orange line, four panels decorated with Oriental flowers and foliage, two also containing a bird perched on a branch, separated by vertical cornucopia-shaped orange bands, scrolled in gold with white *mons*; orange dagger and loop border inside rim.

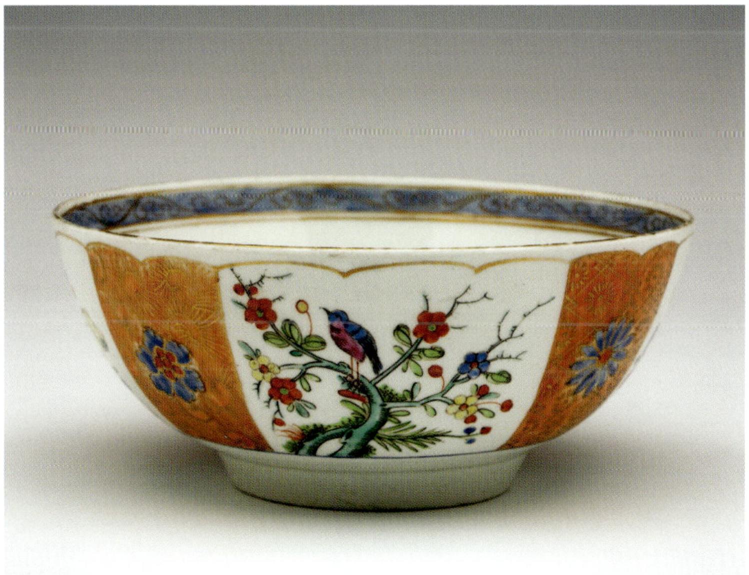

478

478

Bowl

1775–80
Ht 6.6 cm, diam. 14.8 cm
1957.24.1.261

Four panels decorated with Oriental flowers and foliage, two containing a bird perched on a branch, separated by gilt-diapered orange panels with blue formal chrysanthemum; pale blue and gilt border inside rim.

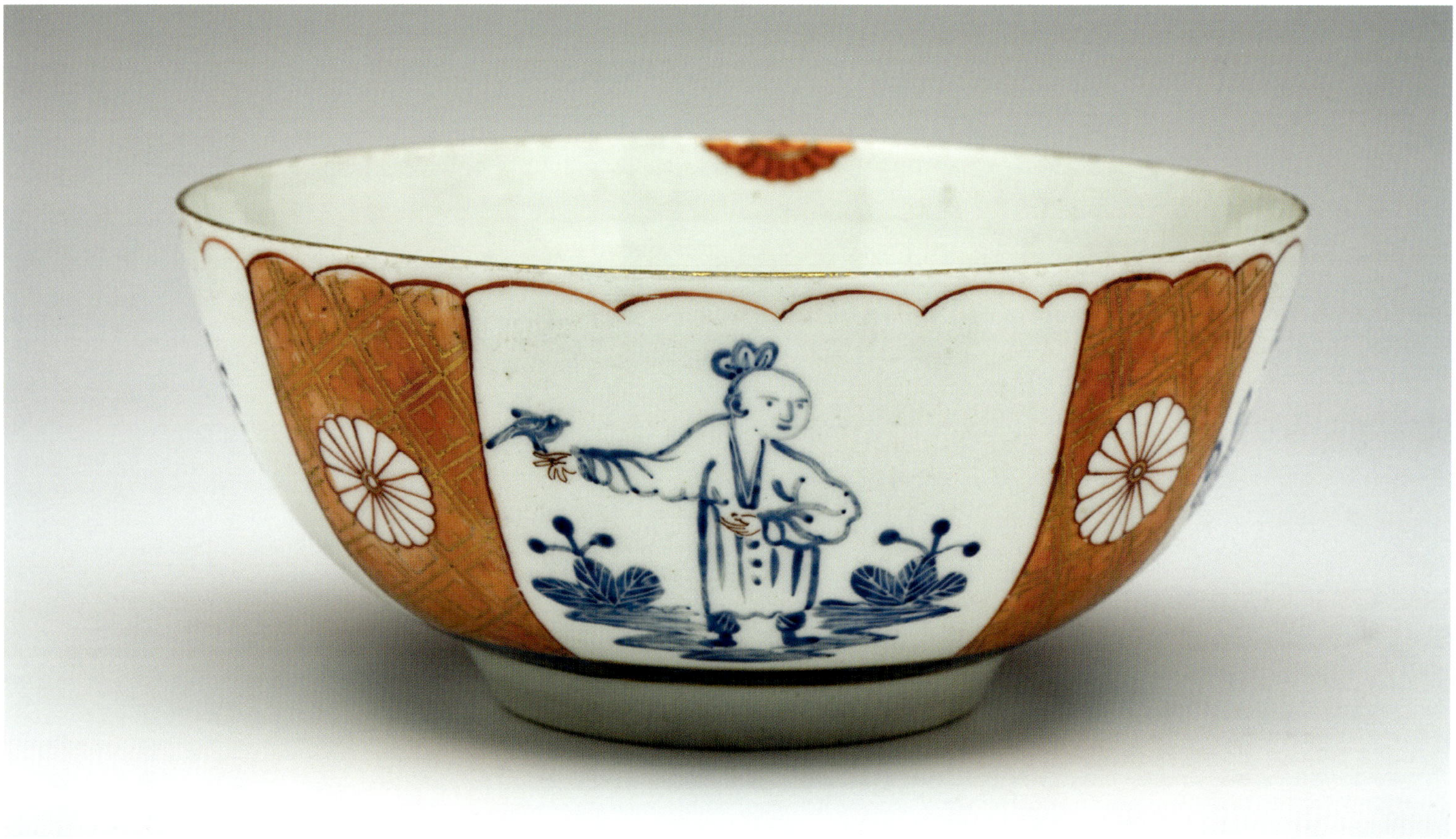

479

479

Bowl

1775–80
Ht 6.8 cm, diam. 14.9 cm
1957.24.1.260

Oriental-style decoration; four white panels decorated in overglaze blue, two with Oriental figures and two with formalised flowers, separated by gilt-diapered orange band with white *mons*.

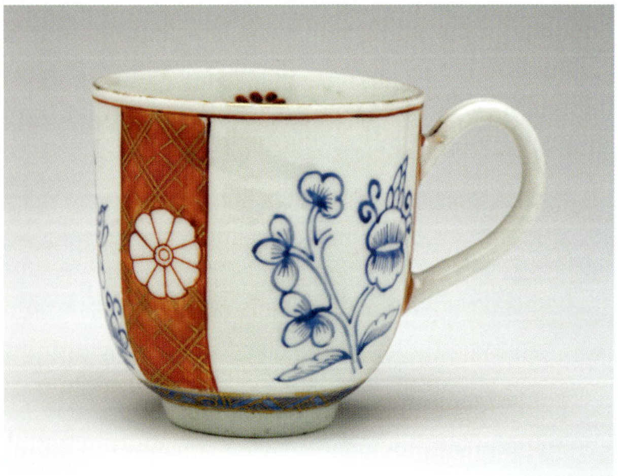

480

480

Coffee cup

1775–80
Ht 6.2 cm, diam. 5.9 cm
1957.24.1. 263

Three gilt-diapered orange bands with white *mons* between panels decorated in overglaze blue, one with a boy holding a bird, the other two with an Oriental flower spray; blue and gold border around base, three formal chrysanthemums inside cup.

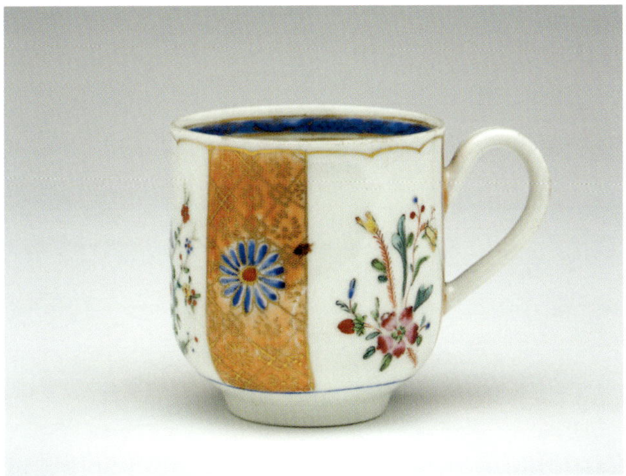

481

481

Coffee cup

1775–80

Ht 6.4 cm, diam. 5.7 cm

1957.24.1.265

Three gilt scrolled orange bands with a formal blue chrysanthemum, separate white panels with Oriental flowers and foliage, one with a bird in centre; blue and gold border inside rim.

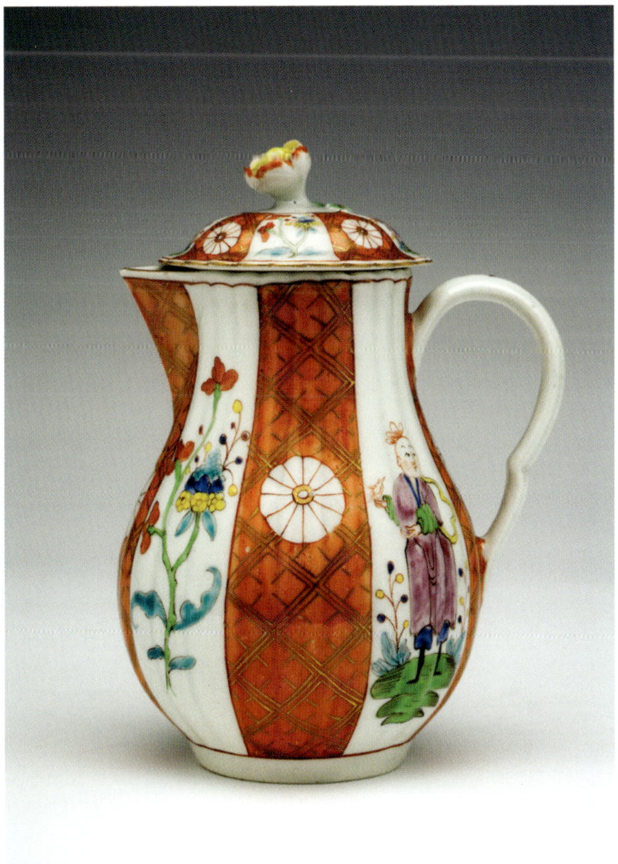

482

482

Covered milk jug

About 1775

Ht 14 cm

1957.24.1.264

Ribbed body, broken loop-shaped handle, rosebud knop; four vertical gilt-diapered orange bands separate four white panels, two with Oriental flower sprays and two with Oriental figures with 'ridiculous stick-like legs', as described by Marshall.

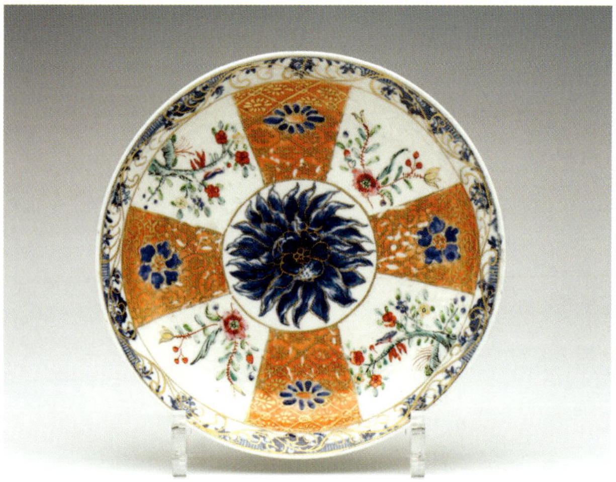

483

483

Plate

About 1770
Diam. 17.7 cm
Mark: crescent
1957.24.1.1086

Florally moulded; underglaze blue border of formalised flowers with chrysanthemum in centre, overdecorated with four orange panels with gilt diaper and scrolls, blue *mons*; four white panels with birds and Oriental-style foliage between.

PROVENANCE
Leonard Crow, Welwyn Garden City, 18 November 1957, £21.

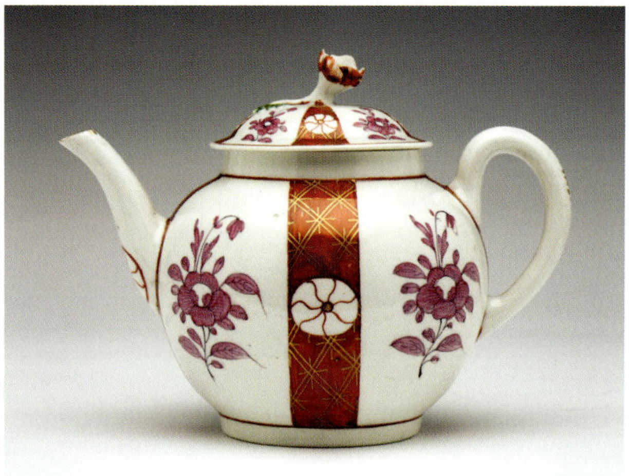

484

484

Teapot

1770–72
Ht 14.1 cm
1957.24.1.276

Globular, loop handle, rosebud knop; four white panels with mauve floral sprays, separated by gilt-diapered orange bands with white chrysanthemum *mons*.

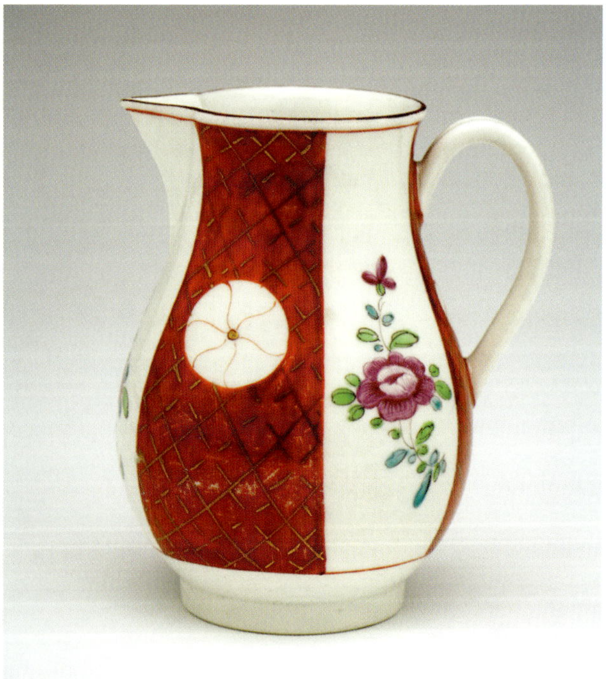

485

485

Milk jug

1768–70
Ht 9.5 cm
1957.24.1.267

Ribbed loop handle; red line around rim and base, three vertical orange bands with white *mons*, intervening panels with simple European flower sprays.

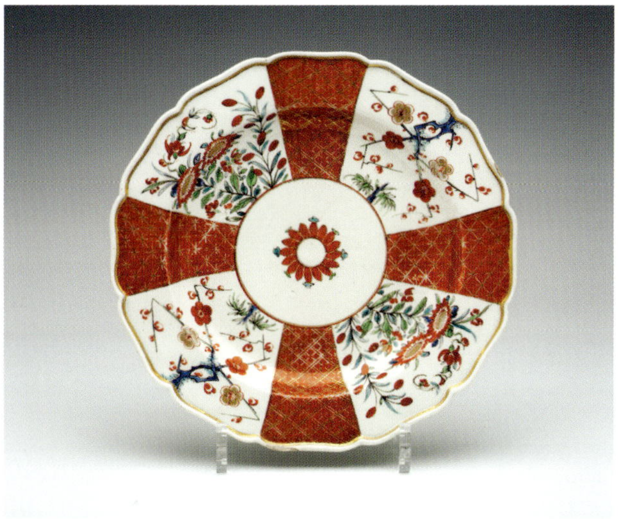

486

486

Plate

1770–72
Diam. 23.1 cm
1957.24.1.280

Wavy edge; four white panels radiate from central circle with orange *mons*, two decorated with prunus sprays and two with chrysanthemums, separated by four orange bands with two different styles of gilt diapering.

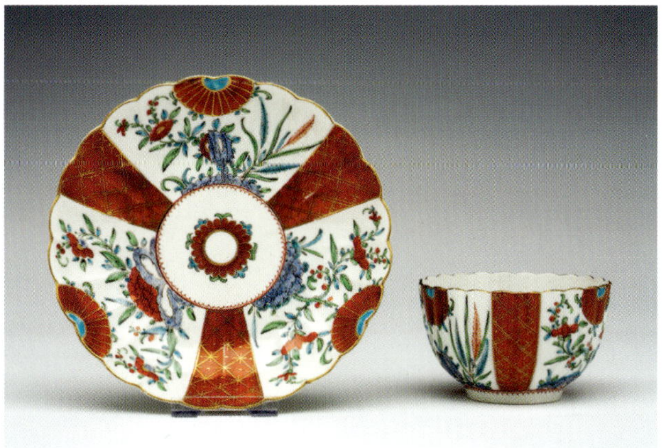

487

487

Teabowl and saucer

1780–85
Bowl ht 4.9 cm, diam. 7.1 cm; saucer diam. 13.4 cm
1957.24.1.277

Scalloped gilt edge; three tomato-red panels, gilt diapered, radiate from white circle with red and green medallion; between these are three panels of formal Oriental flowers with half-chrysanthemum on rim.

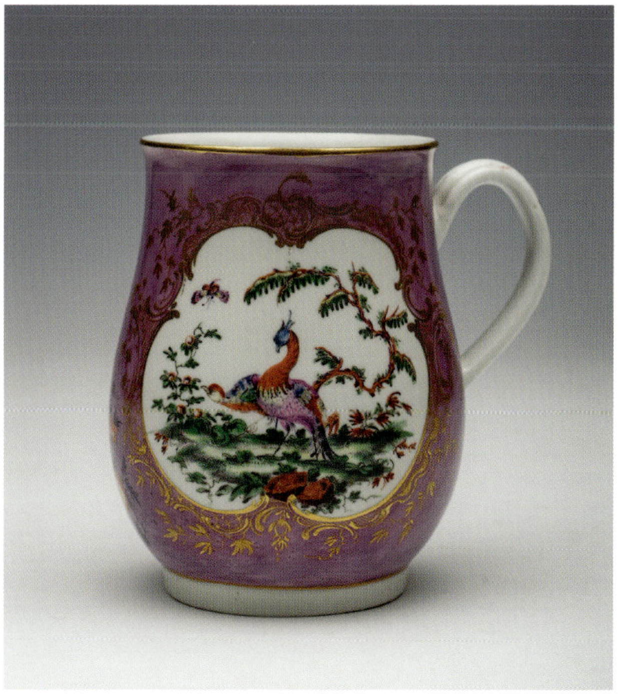

488

488

Mug

1760–65
Ht 12.2 cm
1957.24.1.880

Bell-shaped, ribbed loop handle; the unusual, and probably experimental, lilac pink ground, gilding and decoration are now considered to have been done at the Worcester factory.

PROVENANCE
Albert Amor, London, 10 December 1951, £250.

8
Underglaze Blue Grounds

Worcester porcelain has been long associated with blue grounds. Although the origins of underglaze blue can be traced from late seventeenth-century Chinese porcelain to Meissen and Sèvres, the Worcester factory was driven by a desire to emulate Chelsea and compete in the sophisticated London market.

A powder blue ground was introduced at Worcester in about 1760. This technique was used at Meissen and possibly at Sèvres, and was widely used at Bow, where it was introduced in 1758, and also at Lowestoft, Derby, West Pans, near Edinburgh, and to a lesser extent at Caughley. A Chinese invention, it originated during the Kangxi period of the Qing dynasty (1662–1722). Powdered cobalt blue was blown on to the unglazed or biscuit surface through a tube with one end covered with gauze. Fan-shaped or circular reserved panels were masked and the powder adhered to a thin wash of oil. Initially the panels were painted only in blue with Chinese scenes, but by 1765–8 they were being enamelled with Kakiemon, fancy birds or European flower decoration. The Lord Dudley service (no. 580) is unusual in being decorated with Watteau-type figures.

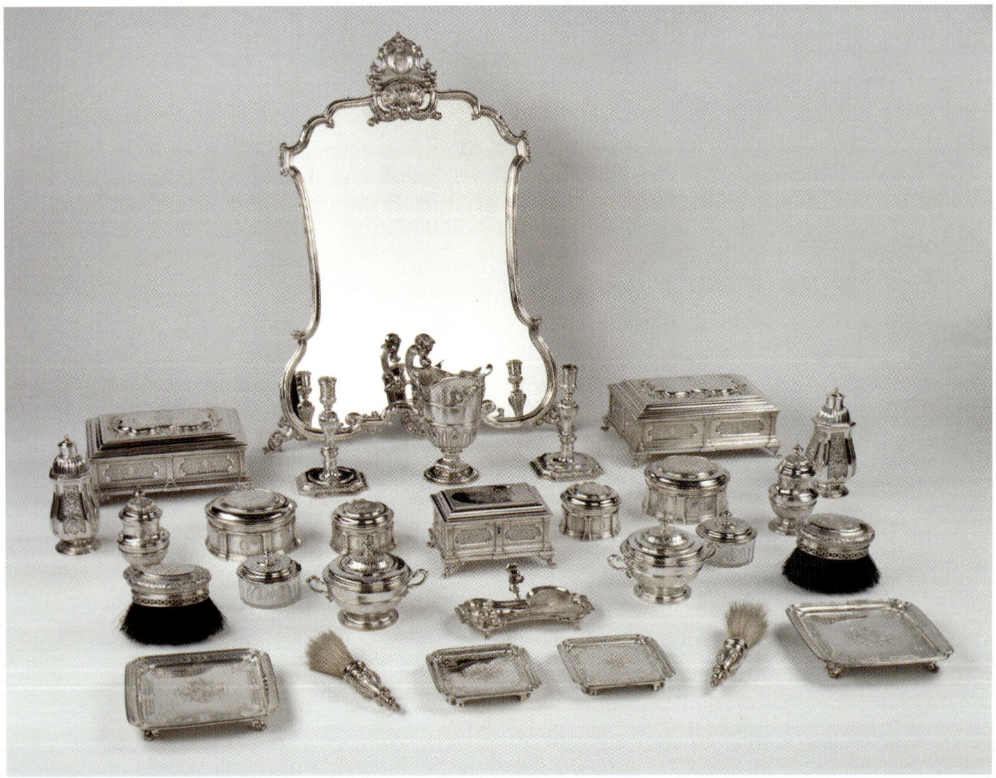

Fig. 29 Paul de Lamerie, mirror from the Treby Toilet Service, silver, 1724–5. © Ashmolean Museum, University of Oxford, WA1946.57

Scale blue grounds were largely a Worcester invention from about 1765. Although some technical improvements had been made, at both Worcester and Chelsea, the blue ground was dark and sometimes ran badly. A solution introduced at Worcester was to break up the solid ground. The most likely influence for this was the finely painted Mosaik patterns in overglaze colours of Meissen and Berlin from about 1760–61, although faint scale patterns can also be found on some Chinese porcelain. Unglazed wasters from the Worcester factory site demonstrate how this effect was achieved. Reserve panels, often reflecting the elaborate shapes of rococo mirrors (fig. 29), were marked out and a light wash of cobalt oxide applied over the ground area. Once dry, scales were carefully painted over the blue wash layer in a less diluted and thus darker solution of cobalt oxide; this work was often carried out by children aged between ten and fourteen. Larger, clearer scales are thought to indicate an earlier date. The scale pattern added variety and animation to the solid blue ground and, although the effect was sometimes partially lost in the process of glazing and firing, this could be offset by gilding. Most blue scale grounds were enamelled at the Worcester factory, although the Giles workshop was responsible for the richest designs, such as the various Lady Mary Wortley Montagu patterns (nos. 858–861).

Solid blue grounds were introduced at Worcester around 1768–70, inspired by the gros bleu of Sèvres and the mazarine blue of Chelsea. The term 'wet blue' was first used by nineteenth-century collectors to describe this coloured ground and it only applies to pieces made before the early 1780s. Worcester was more successful than any other factory in producing an even blue ground colour, but it could still smudge and run. Gilding was an essential part of any design, not only to mask any blurring but also to lighten the effect. This type of ground is often associated with identifiable painters, such as Jefferyes Hammett O'Neale (nos. 559–568 and 572–574) and John Donaldson (nos. 575–578).

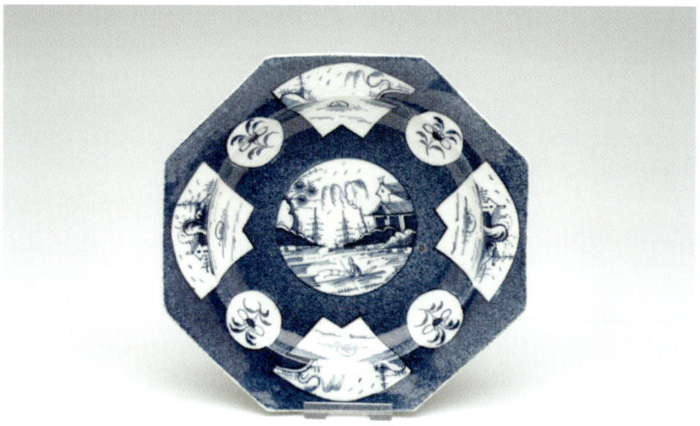

489

489

Plate

1770–72
Diam. 16.9 cm
Mark: simulated Chinese characters including a cursive *W*
1957.24.1.723

Octagonal; powder blue ground, larger fan-shaped reserves painted with a landscape, smaller ones with flowers; three blue sprays on reverse of rim.

REFERENCE
Branyan, French and Sandon 1989, pattern no. I.B 27.

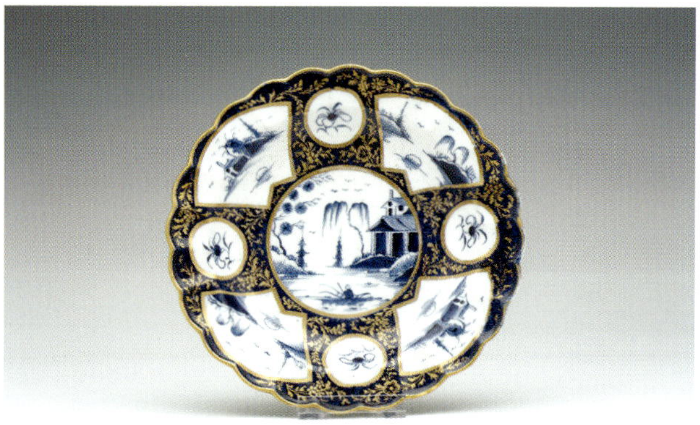

490

490

Plate

1768–70
Diam. 18.5 cm
Mark: simulated Chinese characters
1957.24.1.729

Powder blue ground with floral gilding, reserves decorated in underglaze blue with Chinese landscapes and flowers; three sprays on reverse.

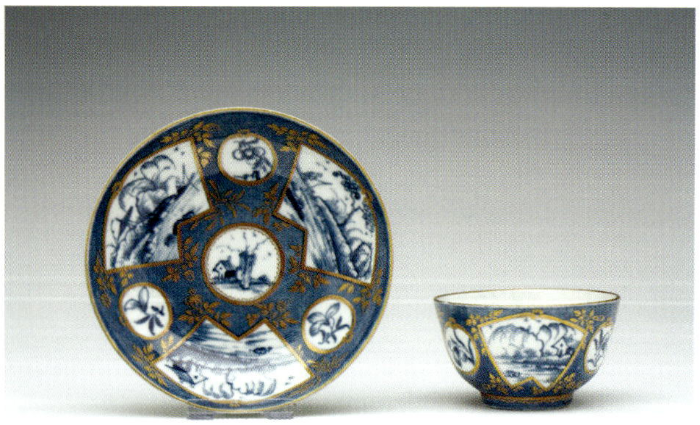

491

491

Teabowl and saucer

1762–5
Bowl ht 4.2 cm, diam. 7.3 cm; saucer diam. 11.9 cm
Mark: crescent and fretted square on both
1957.24.1.734

Powder blue ground with gilding, fan-shaped reserves and central circle painted with Chinese scenes, smaller circular reserves with foliage or flowers.

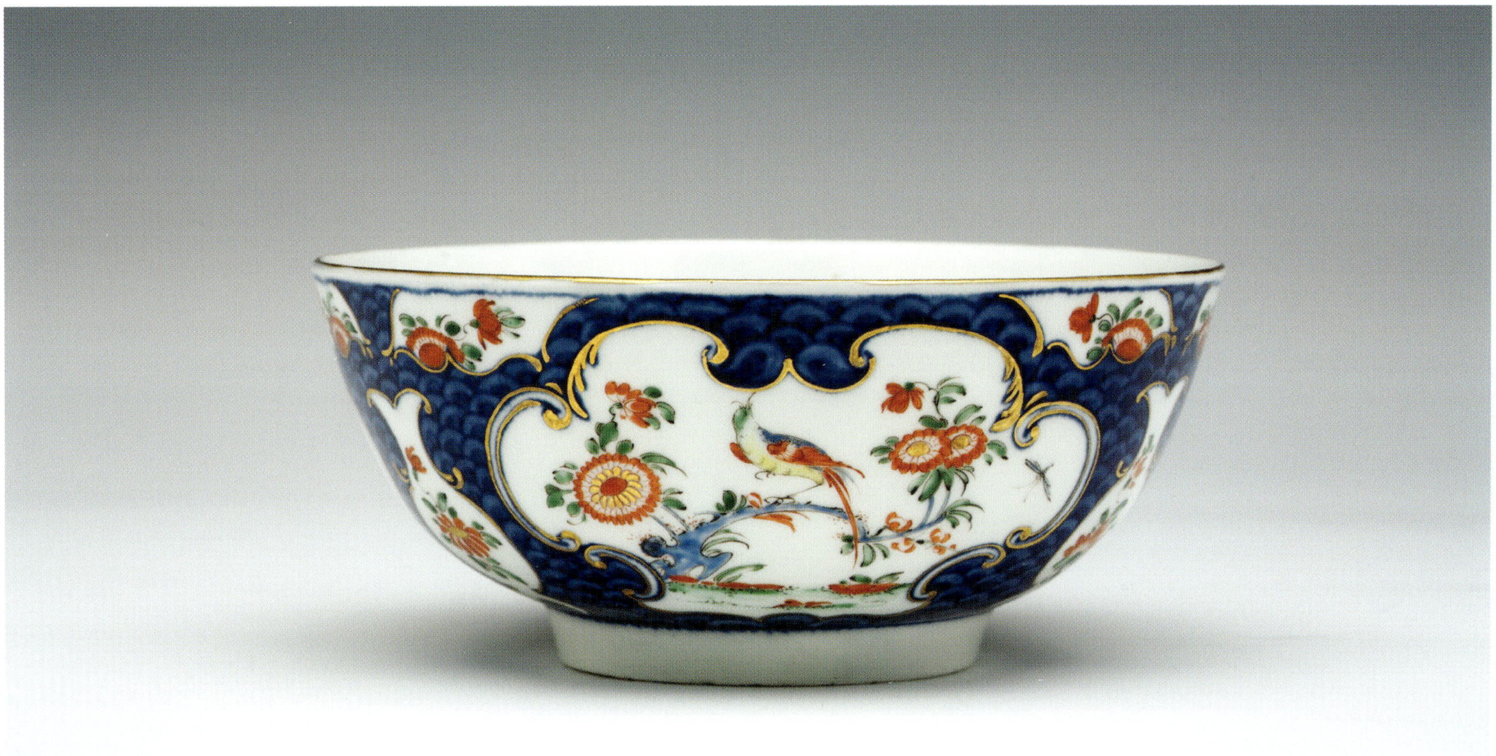

492

492

Bowl

1770–75
Ht 6.7 cm, diam. 14.8 cm
1957.24.1.541

Upward blue scale ground, one mirror-shaped panel painted with a bird on a bough, the others with formal Japanese-style flowers.

PROVENANCE
Tilley & Co., London, 1 October 1950, £27.

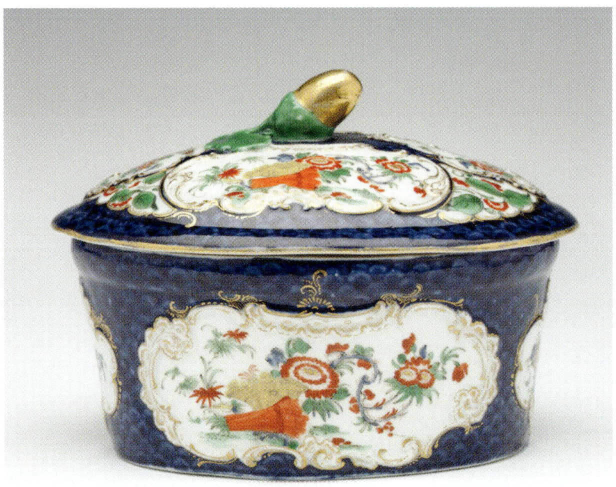

493

493

Potted meat dish and cover

1765–70
Length 12.8 cm, width 10.1 cm, ht 10 cm
Mark: fretted square
1957.24.1.143

Oval, domed cover with gilt acorn knop; blue scale ground, moulded reserves decorated with Oriental flowers and foliage.

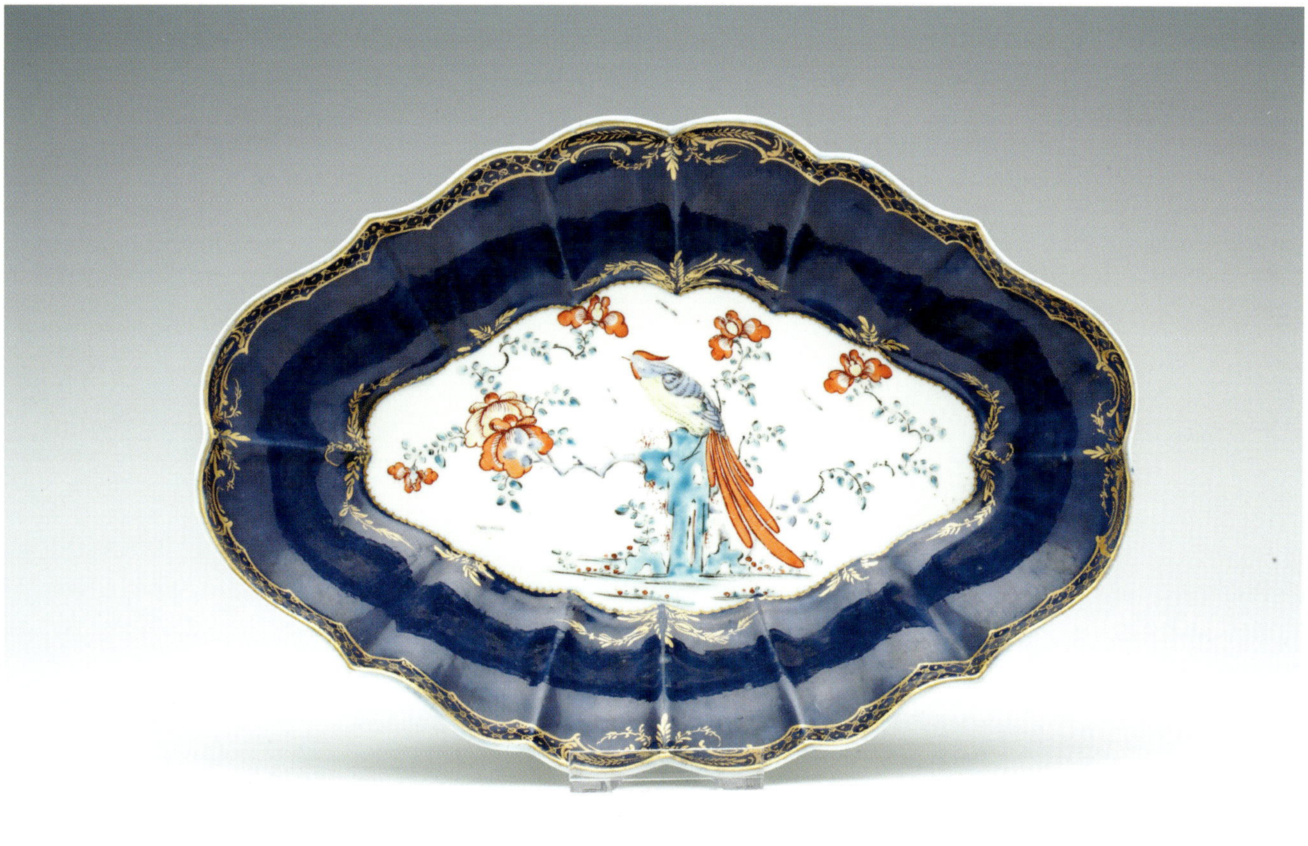

494

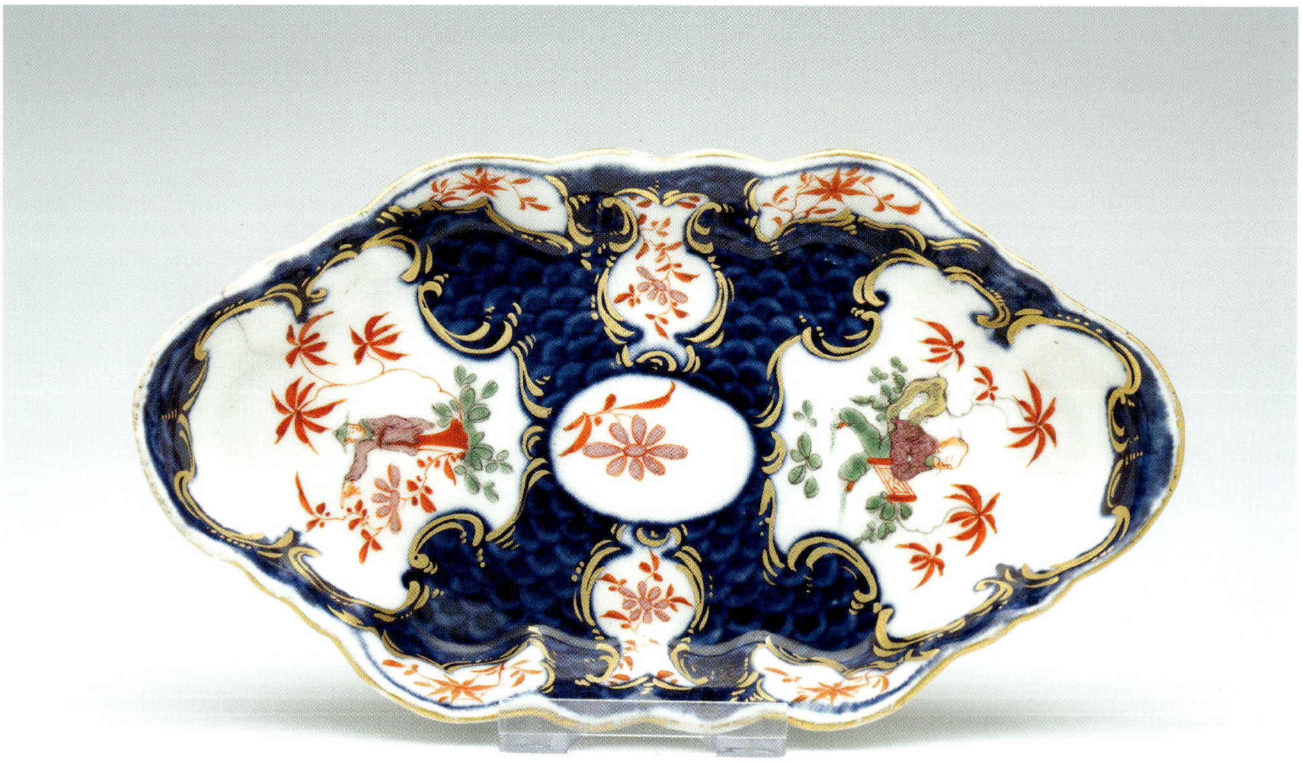

495

494

Dish

1770–75
Length 26.7 cm, width 19.1 cm
Mark: crescent
1957.24.1.566

Lozenge-shaped; wide wet blue border with gilding, central reserve painted with a ho-ho bird perched on a hollow rock; the 'Sir Joshua Reynolds' pattern.

The bird and the flowering foliage are derived from a Japanese version of a Chinese design; this is possibly the 'fine old Japan pheasant pattern' listed in Christie's 1769 sale catalogue.

REFERENCE
Spero 1984, pl. 132.

495

Spoon tray

About 1768
Length 15 cm, width 8.3 cm
1957.24.1.114

Blue scale ground with gilding, Chinese figures and palmate foliage in reserves, from the 'Bodenham' service; possibly decorated outside the Worcester factory. This pattern takes its name from the sale of the Bodenham Collection in 1872, which included a service of this design. A cup and saucer from the same service are illustrated in Spero and Sandon 1996, pl. 456.

PROVENANCE
Albert Amor, London, 17 March 1949, £13 10s.

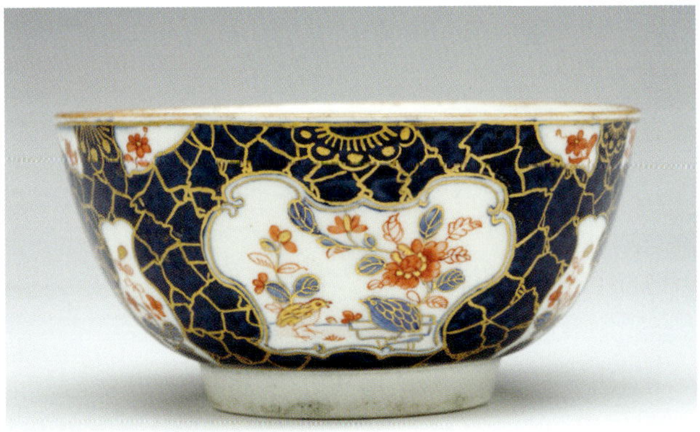

496

496

Bowl

About 1770
Ht 5.2 cm, diam. 10.1 cm
Mark: fretted square
1957.24.1.974

Blue scale ground with cracked ice gilding, fawn rim; decorated with quails, possibly by the Giles workshop.

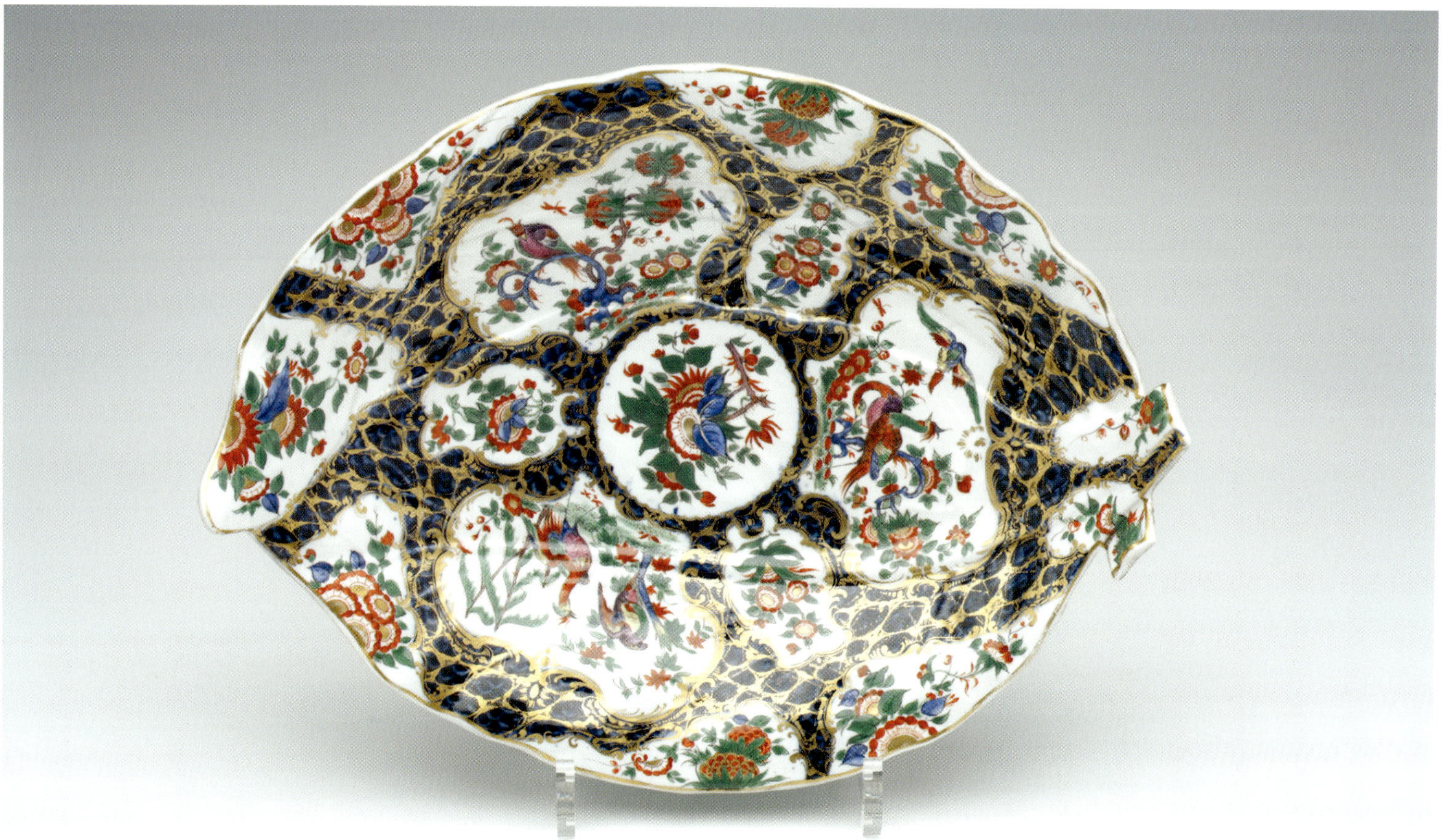

497

497

Dish

About 1770
Length 31.8 cm, width 24.6 cm
Mark: fretted square
1957.24.1.737

Double leaf shape; blue scale ground with cracked ice gilding; three mirror-shaped reserves decorated with birds, the others with Oriental flowers.

498

Pot-pourri vase and cover

About 1770
Ht 26.9 cm
Mark: fretted square
1957.24.1.542

Oviform with spreading foot, pierced domed cover; wet blue ground with gilt reticulation, panels decorated with Japanese Imari-style birds, foliage and flowers; probably once part of a group of three or five.

PROVENANCE
Denis Bert, Hull, 21 February 1947, £225.

REFERENCE
Dawson 2007, pl. 36.

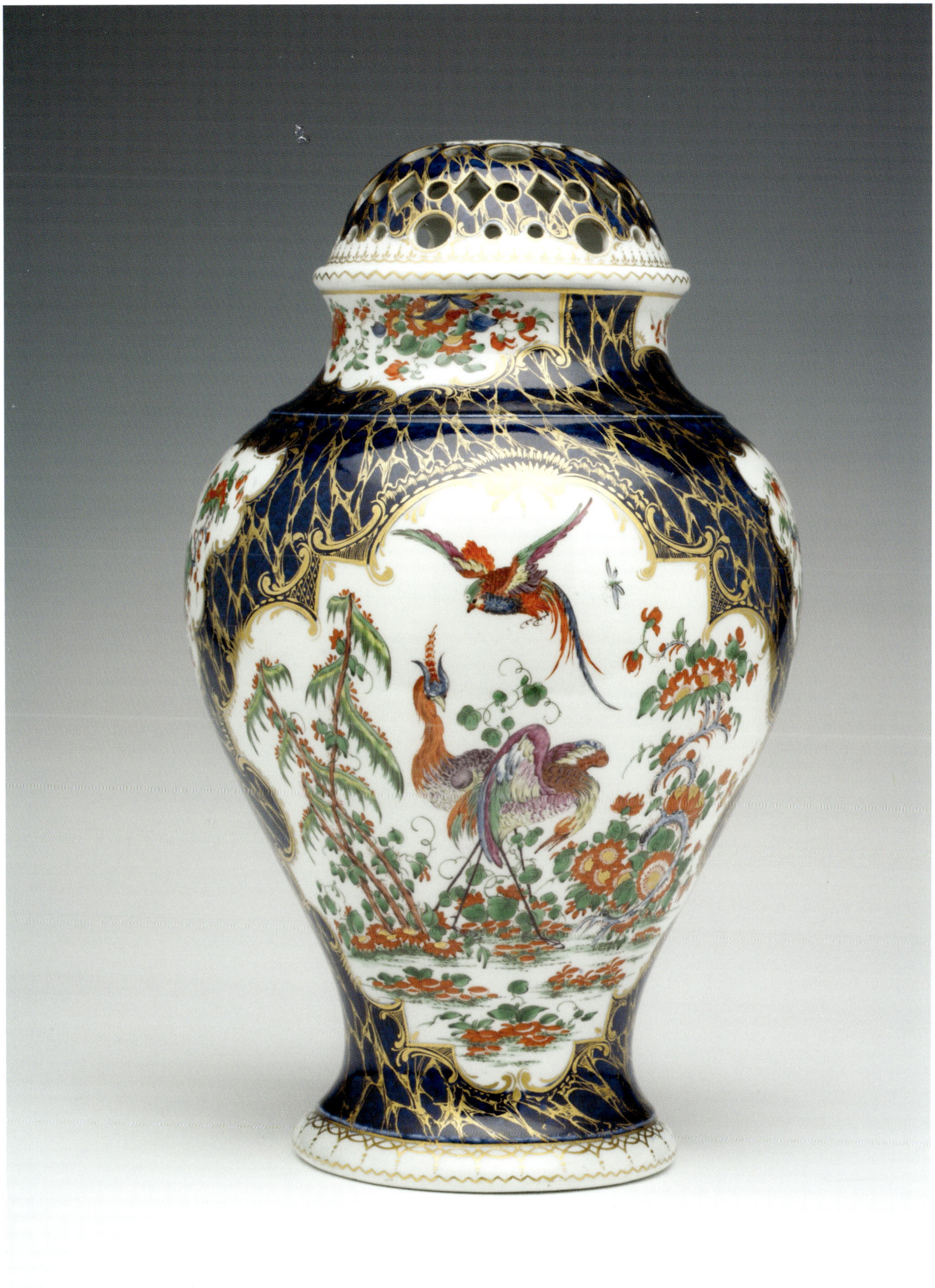

498

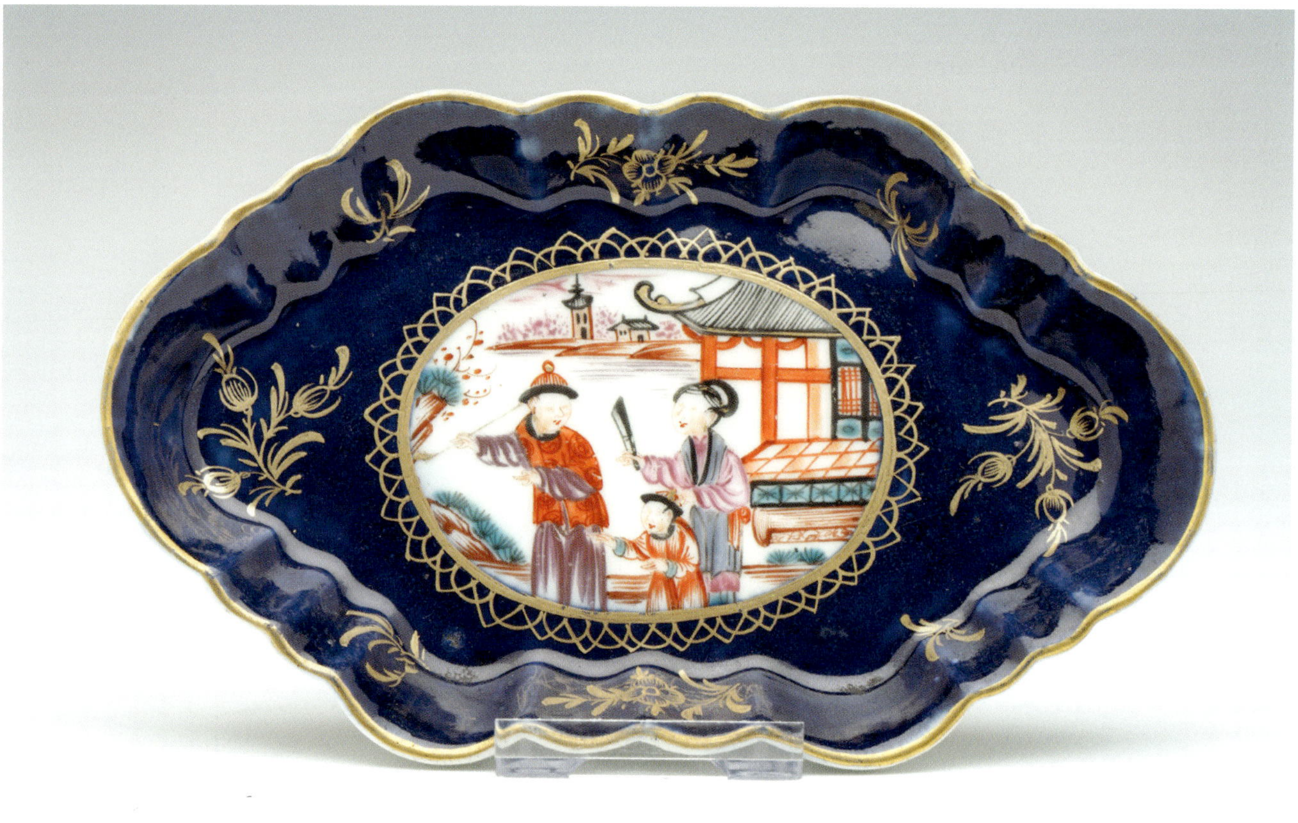

499

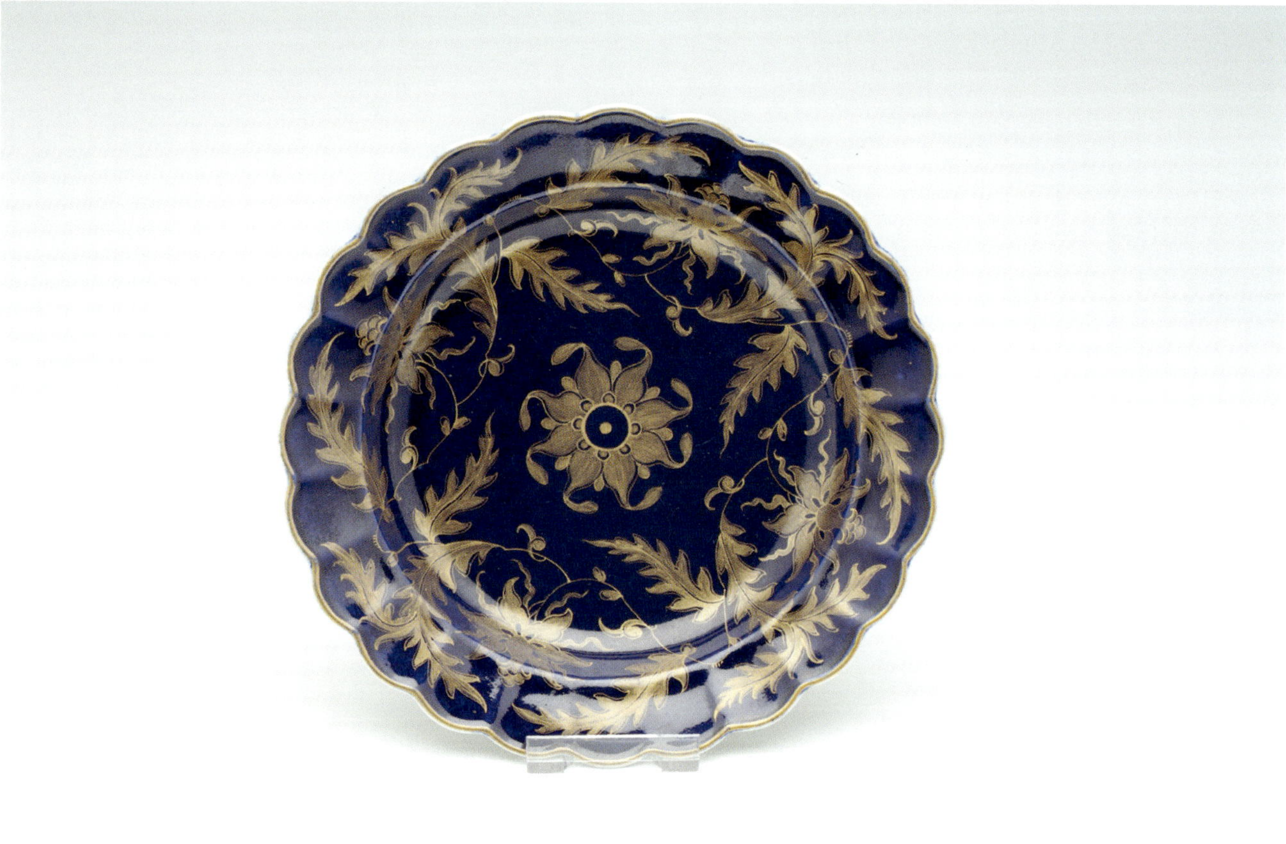

501

499

Spoon tray

1770–72
Length 14.7 cm, width 9.2 cm
Mark: crescent
1957.24.1.703

Wavy gilt edge, wet blue ground with light gold flower sprays, reserve painted with Chinese scene of a man with a pipe accompanied by a lady and child on a terrace.

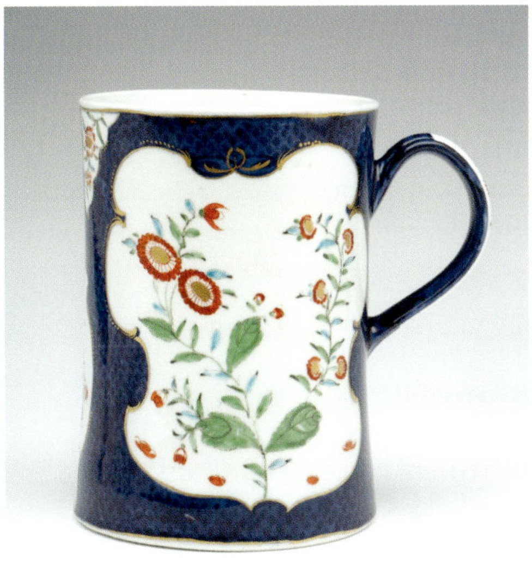

500

500

Tankard

1770–75
Ht 15 cm, diam. 10.6 cm (at base)
Mark: fretted square
1957.24.1.578

Cylindrical; blue scale ground, light gilding defining panels of Oriental flowers and foliage.

501

Plate

1775–80
Diam. 21.2 cm
1957.24.1.563

Scalloped gilt edge, very deep wet blue ground decorated with formal gilded Oriental flowers, serrated leaves and tendrils, a large flower-head in centre. This decoration derives from gilded ornament seen on blue glazed Chinese porcelain from the Kangxi period.

REFERENCE
Bonhams, London, 31 March 2010, lot 288.

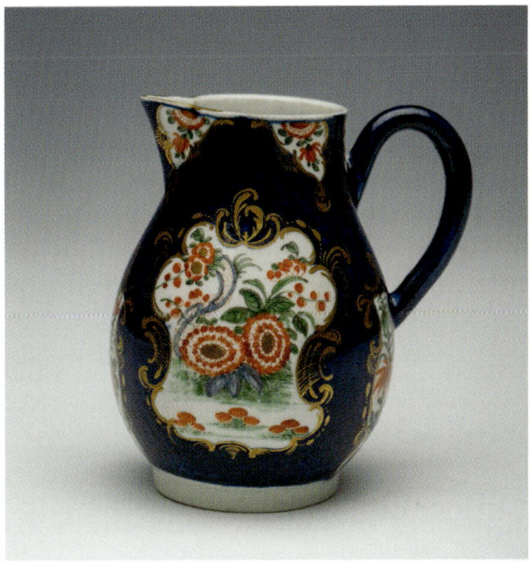

502

502

Milk jug

About 1770
Ht 12 cm
Mark: fretted square
1957.24.1.564

Pear-shaped with V-spout and blue loop handle; blue scale ground, gilt scrolling edges reserves with chrysanthemums, prunus and wheatsheaves; cover missing.

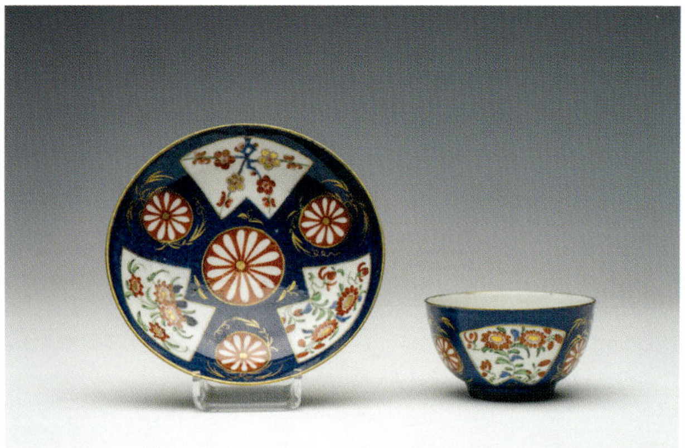

503

503

Teabowl and saucer

1768–70
Bowl ht 4 cm, diam. 7.2 cm; saucer diam. 11.7 cm
1957.24.1.731

Gilt edge, deep powder blue ground; fan-shaped reserves with chrysanthemums or prunus and circular ones with formalised red and white flowers.

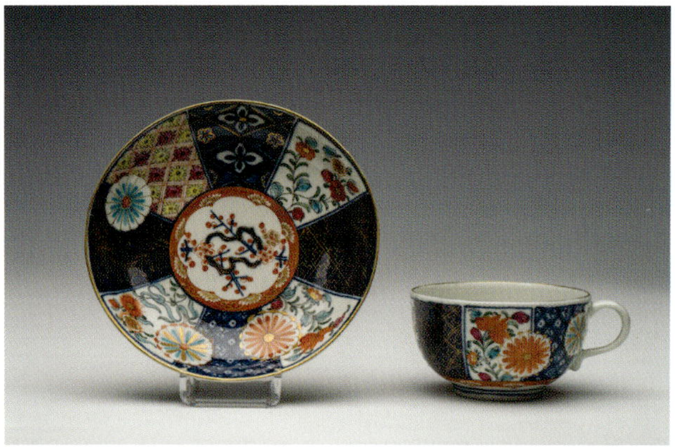

504

504

Teacup and saucer

1768–70
Cup ht 4.6 cm, diam. 8 cm; saucer diam. 13.1 cm
Mark: five mock Chinese characters
1957.24.1.728

Imari-inspired decoration with differing underglaze blue bands separating coloured panels interrupted by three chrysanthemum *mons*; two sprays on back of saucer.

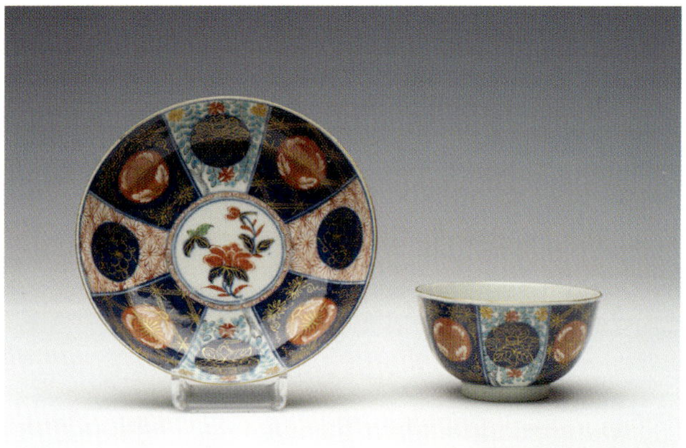

505

505

Teabowl and saucer

About 1770
Bowl ht 4.1 cm, diam. 7.5 cm; saucer diam. 11.7 cm
Mark: crescent on both
1957.24.1.726

Varied panels with *mons*, four in underglaze blue, central floral spray – the 'Old Mosaic Japan' pattern.

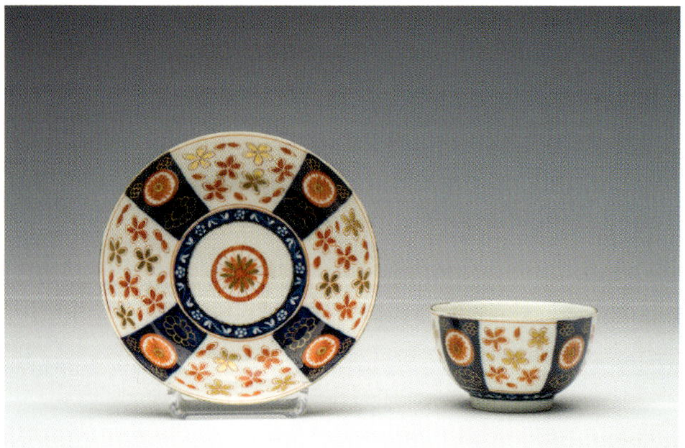

506

506

Teabowl and saucer

About 1770
Bowl ht 4.3 cm, diam. 7.2 cm; saucer diam. 11.9 cm
Mark: fretted square
1957.24.1.730

Four wet blue bands with red *mons* radiating from central circle, scattered red or gold stars or five-petalled flowers; probably the 'Fine Old Japan Star' pattern described by Marshall, from Christie's, London, December 1769 sale.

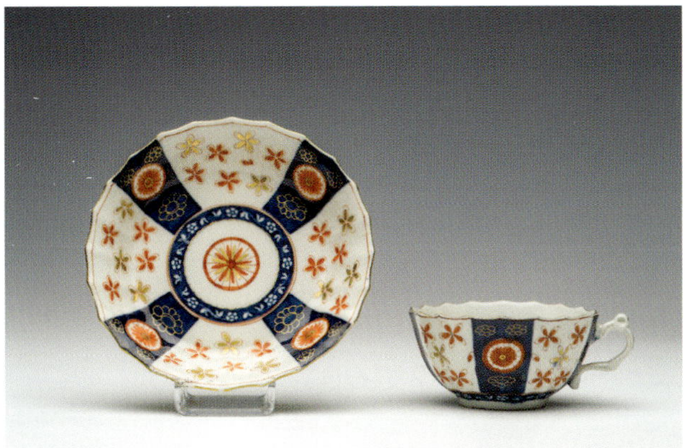

507

507

Teacup and saucer

About 1770
Cup ht 4.5 cm, diam. 8.5 cm; saucer diam. 12.9 cm
Mark: fretted square on both
1957.24.1.50

Fluted with scalloped edge and scroll handle; decorated with four wet blue bands with formal chrysanthemums, scattered red or gold stars or five-petalled flowers between; Marshall's 'Fine Old Japan Star' pattern.

508

Teacup and saucer

1768–72
Cup ht 5 cm, diam. 8.4 cm; saucer diam. 13.1 cm
Mark: crescent on both
1957.24.1.551

Gilt rim, blue scale ground, gilt-edged mirror and claw-shaped reserves painted with exotic birds and insects.

REFERENECE
Sandon 1993, p. 214.

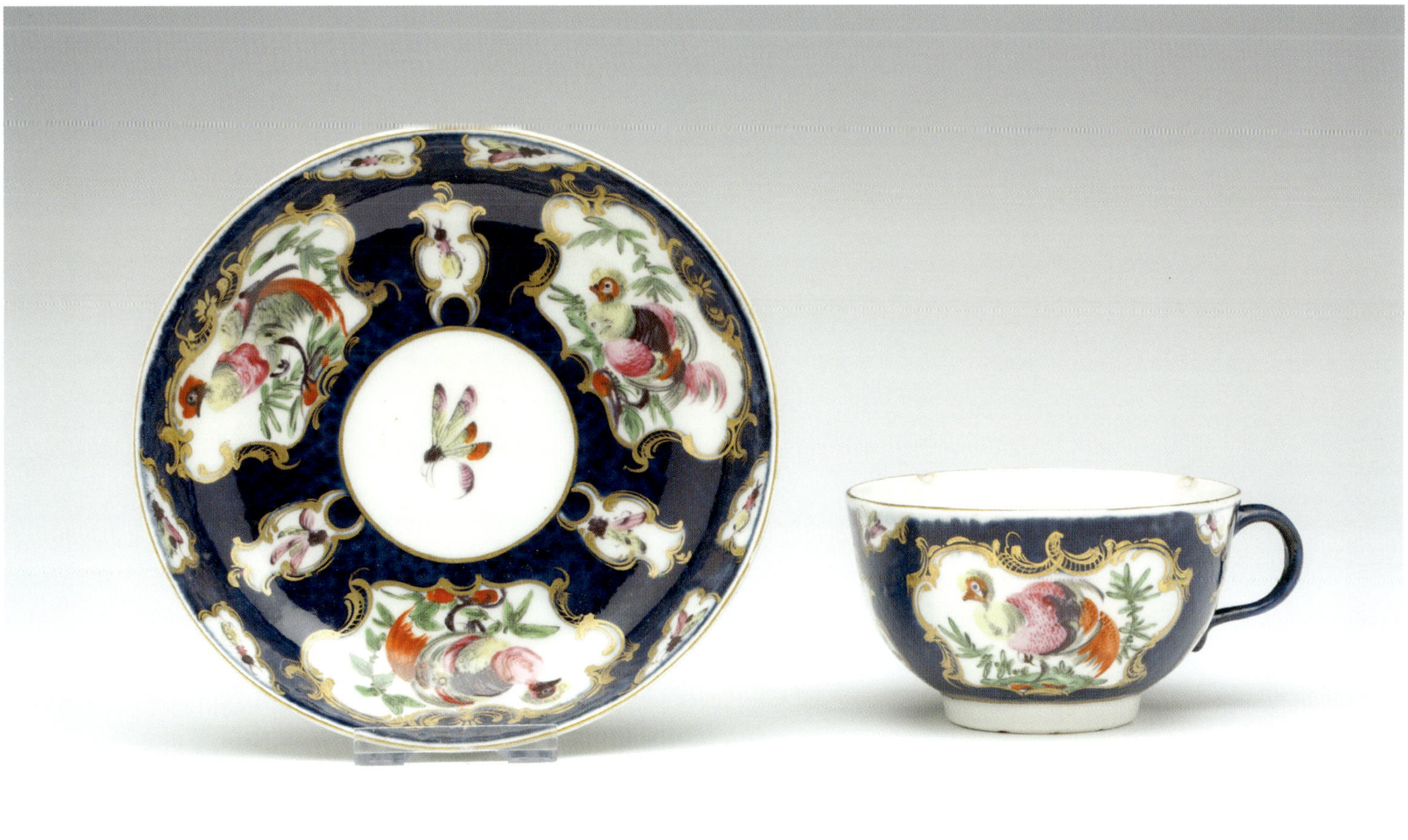

508

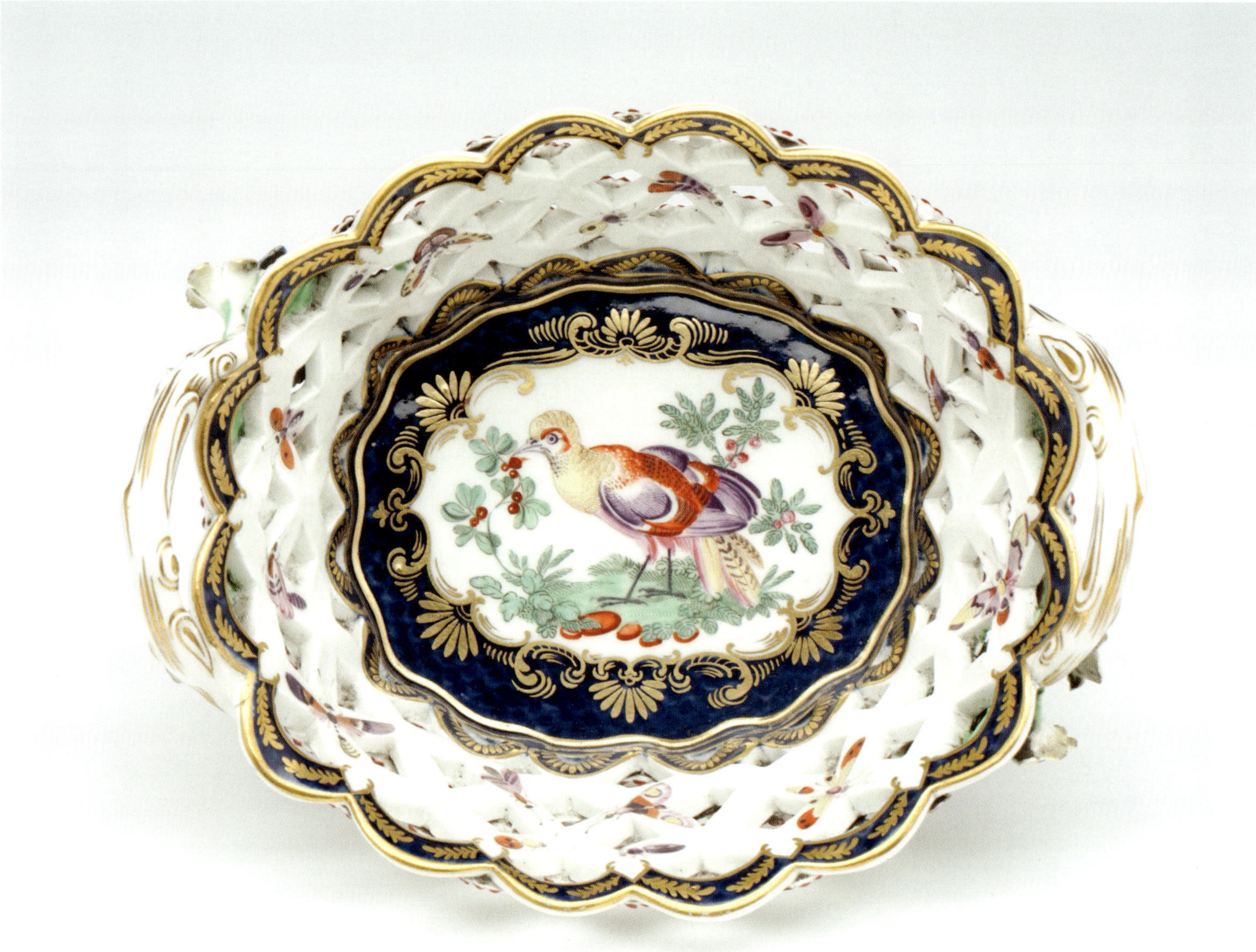

509

509

Oval basket

About 1770
Ht 8.1 cm, length 18.6 cm, width 15.4 cm
1957.24.1.567

White twig handles with applied flowers, pink florettes at intersections of strapwork, gilded blue scale border with exotic bird in well; various insects on pierced sides.

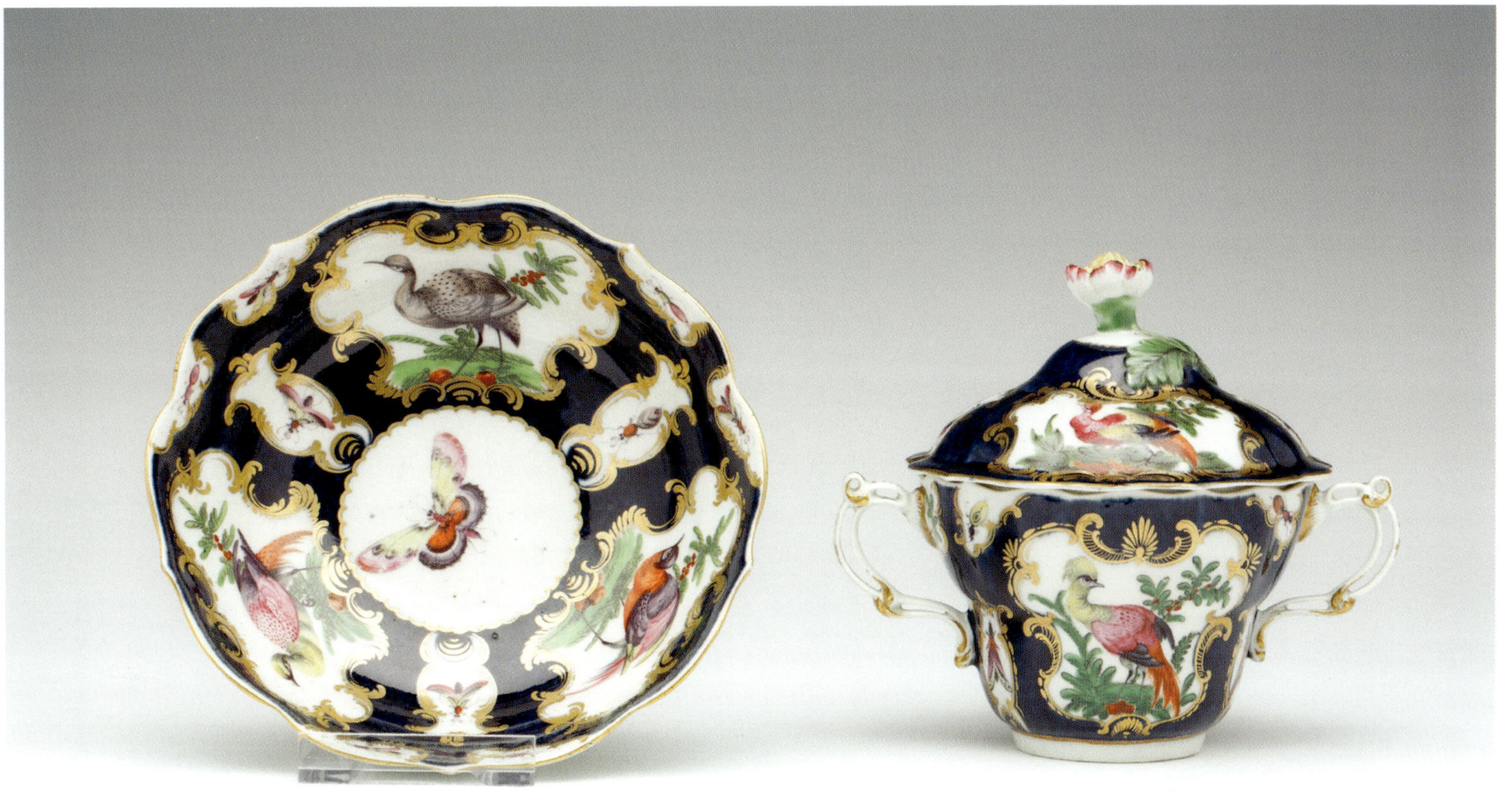

510

510

Caudle cup, cover and saucer

1768–72
Ht 12.7 cm, diam. 9.6 cm; saucer diam. 14.7 cm
Mark: fretted square on saucer
1957.24.1.549

Ogee shape, domed cover with rose knop, pierced handles; blue scale ground with exotic birds in rococo reserves; unusual brown bird on saucer.

PROVENANCE
Christie's, London, 26 May 1949, lot 127, £37 16s.

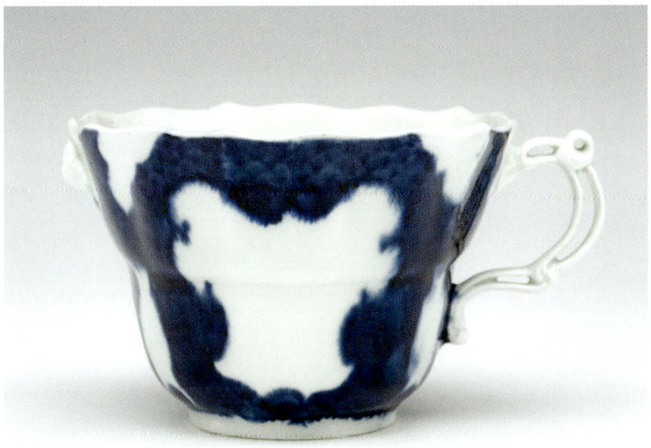

511

511

Caudle cup

About 1770
Ht 6.9 cm, diam. 9.6 cm
Mark: fretted square
1957.24.1.832

Unfinished; ogee shape; decorated in underglaze blue leaving rococo reserves; one handle cut off before glazing.

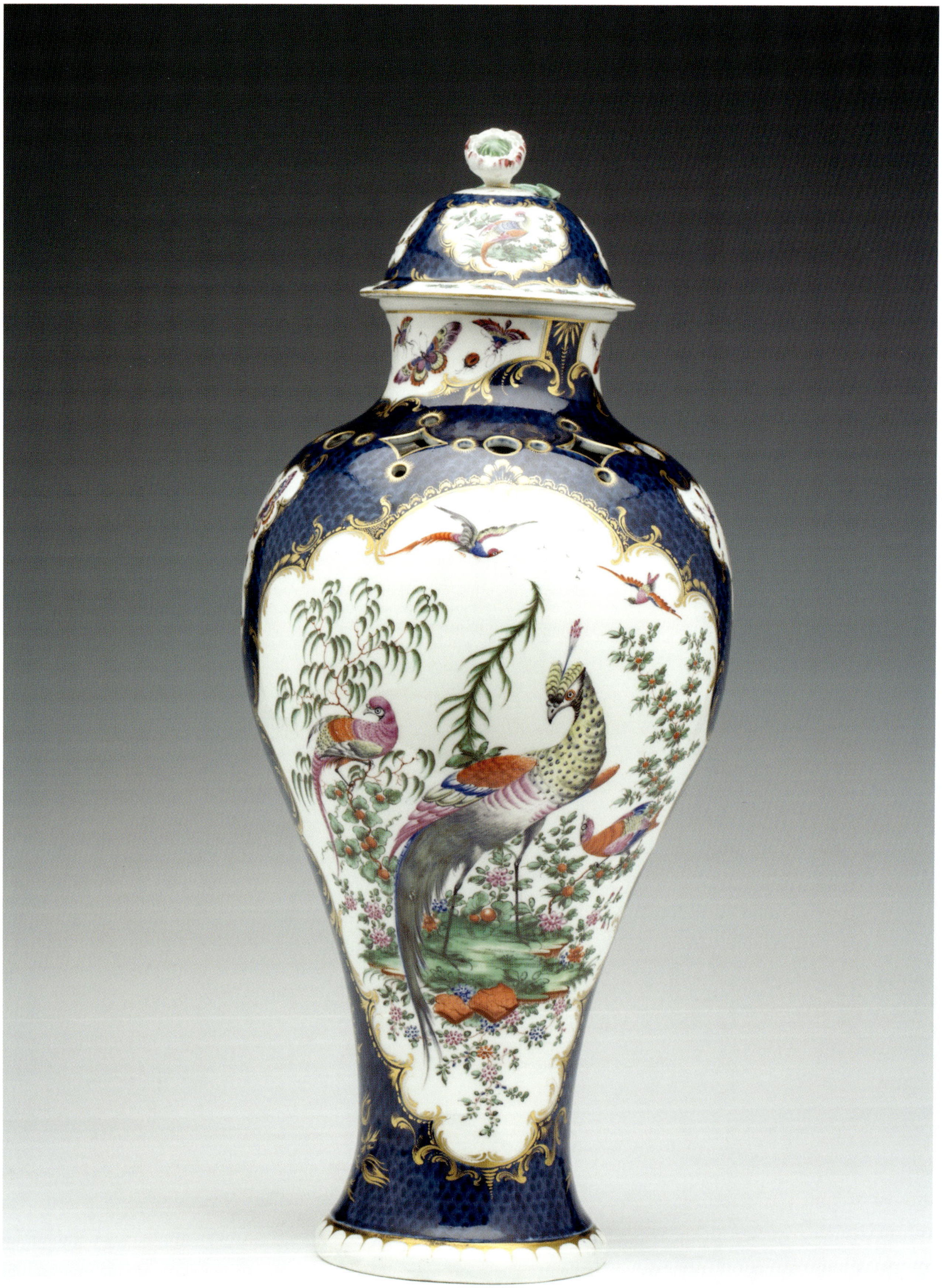

512

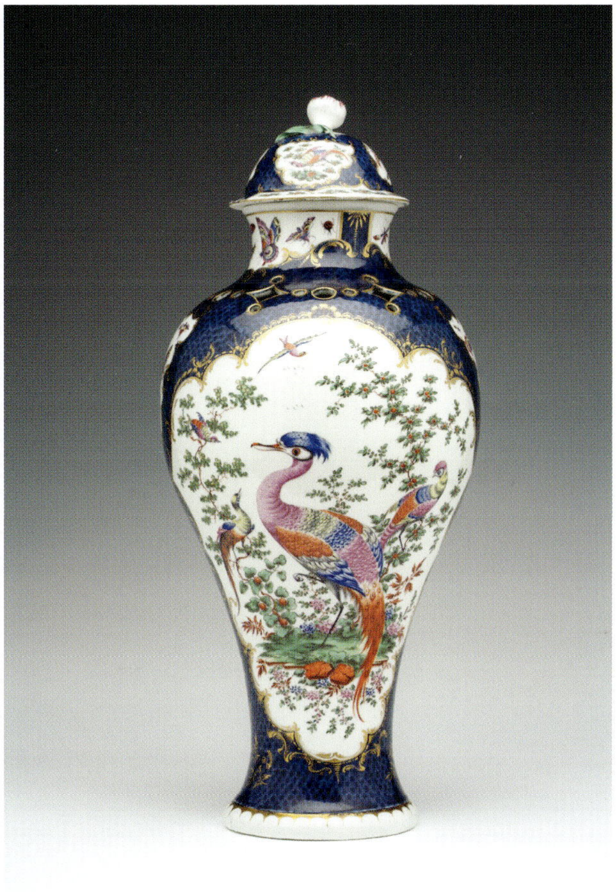

512

512

Vase

About 1770
Ht 40.4 cm
1957.24.1.539

Baluster shape with pierced shoulders, domed cover with rose knop; blue scale ground, gilt edged reserves decorated with exotic birds and insects. A pair of similar pot-pourri vases in the Colonial Williamsburg Collection is illustrated in Clarke 1987, pl. 16.

PROVENANCE
Tilley & Co., London, 1 October 1950, £135.

513

Broth bowl, cover and stand

1768–70
Broth bowl ht 11.4 cm, diam. 9.7 cm; stand diam. 17.6 cm
Mark: fretted square on both
1957.24.1.562

Blue scale ground with exotic birds and insects in rococo reserves; the style of gilding on the stand differs from that on the broth bowl.

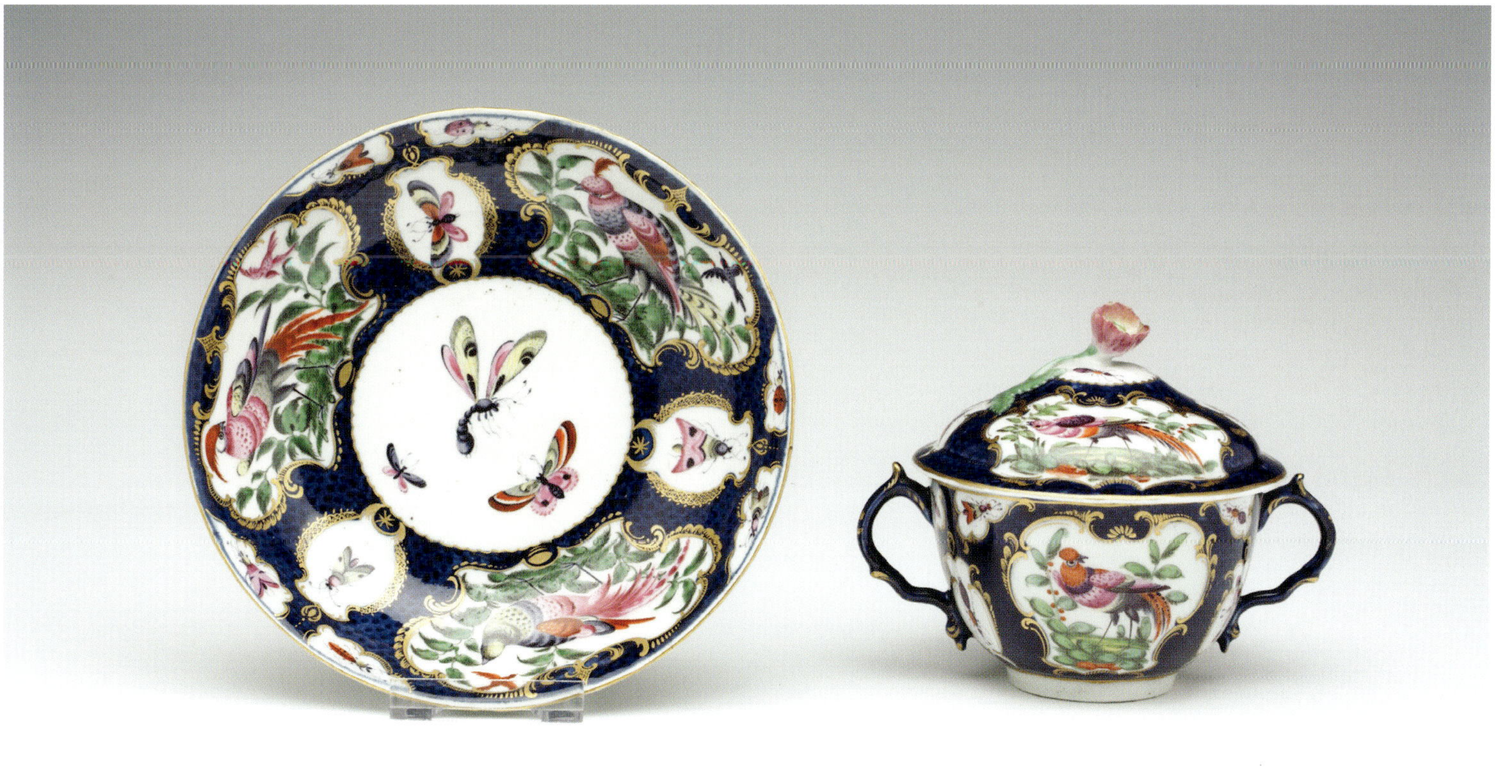

513

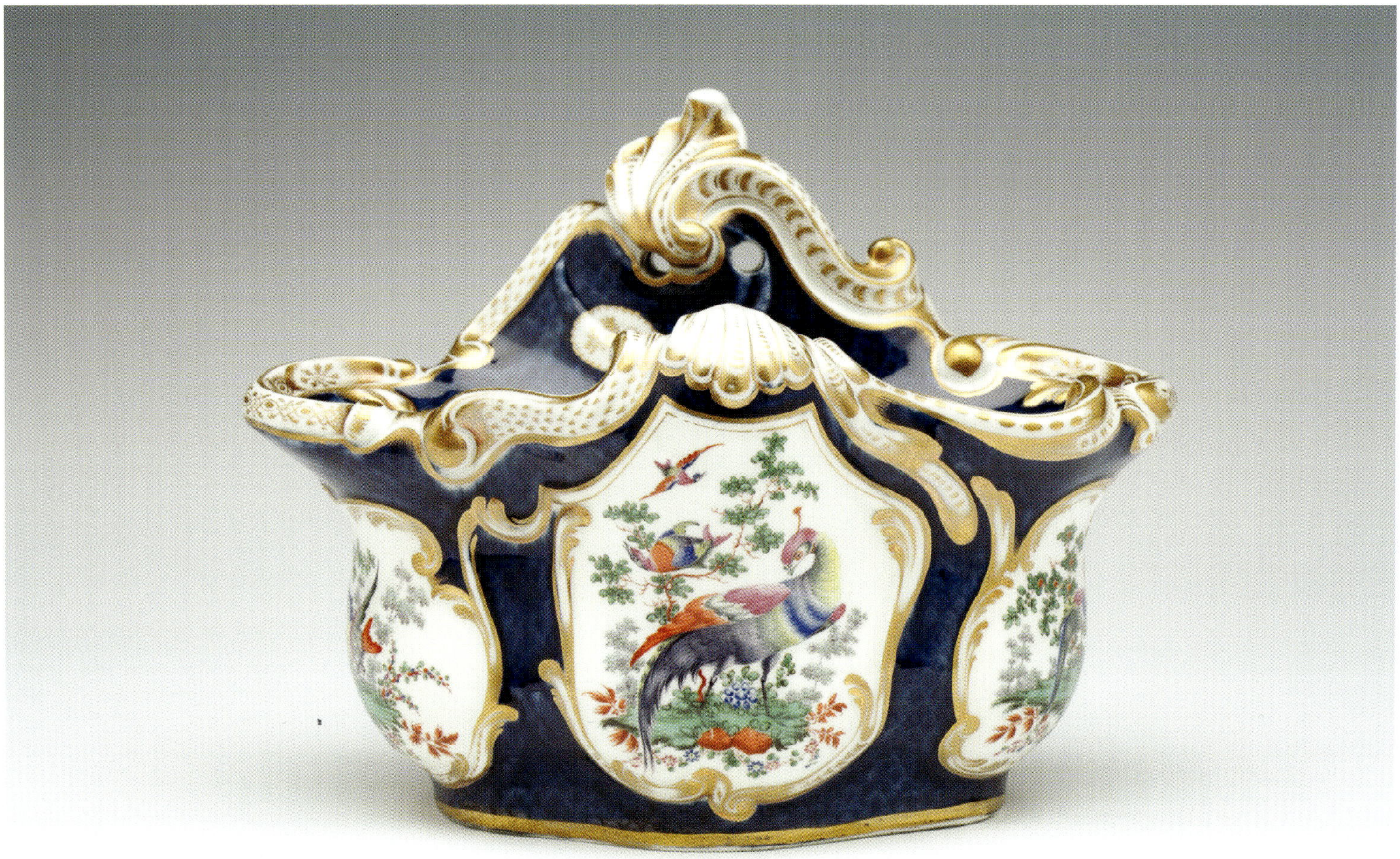

514

514

Bough pot

1768–70

Ht 17.1 cm, length 21.9 cm, width 13.4 cm

Mark: fretted square

1957.24.1.546

Bombé form with shell and rococo moulded edges; blue scale ground, three reserves with exotic birds, foliage and flowers, one on reverse with flying birds and insects.

This rococo shape, not known at any other English porcelain factory, was conceived in pairs, possibly to sit flat on a mantelpiece and intended either for growing flowering bulbs or for cut flowers. The pierced holes also allow for hanging on a wall.

PROVENANCE

Ayer & Co. Ltd., Bath, 24 October 1950, £195 (pair).

REFERENCES

Bonhams, London, 7 March 2007, lot 177; Sothebys's, London, 13 April 2011, lot 182.

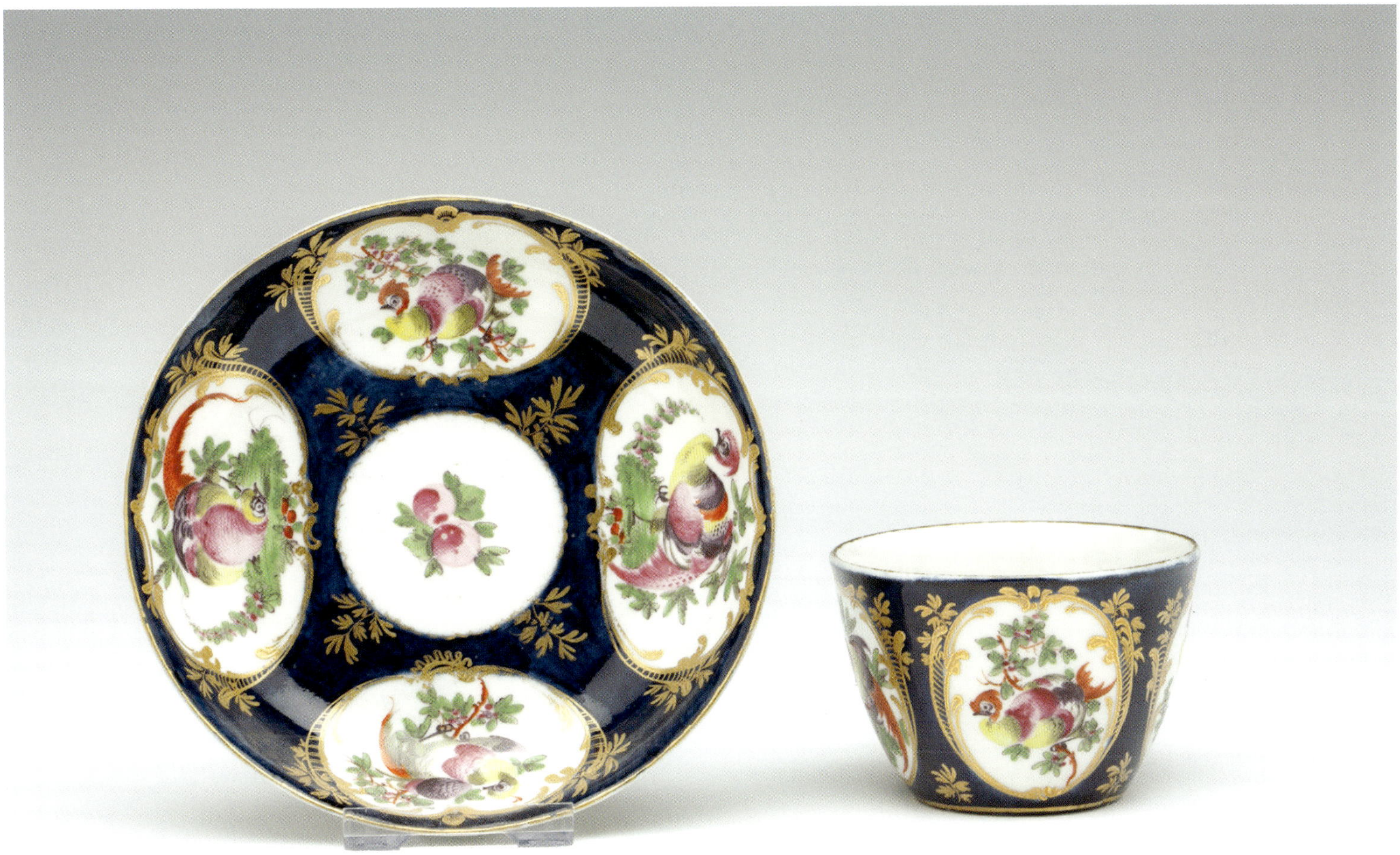

515

515

Teabowl and saucer

1775–80
Cup ht 4.7 cm, diam. 6.9 cm; saucer diam. 11.8 cm
1957.24.1.142

Conical bowl, wet blue ground, gilded oval reserves with exotic birds, plump with incurving tails; plum spray in centre of saucer. From the so-called Duchess of Kent service.

A service of this design is reputed to have belonged to the Duchess of Kent, mother of Queen Victoria. She was born in 1786, too late to have been its original owner, and married the Duke of Kent in 1818.

REFERENCE
Spero and Sandon 1996, pl. 317.

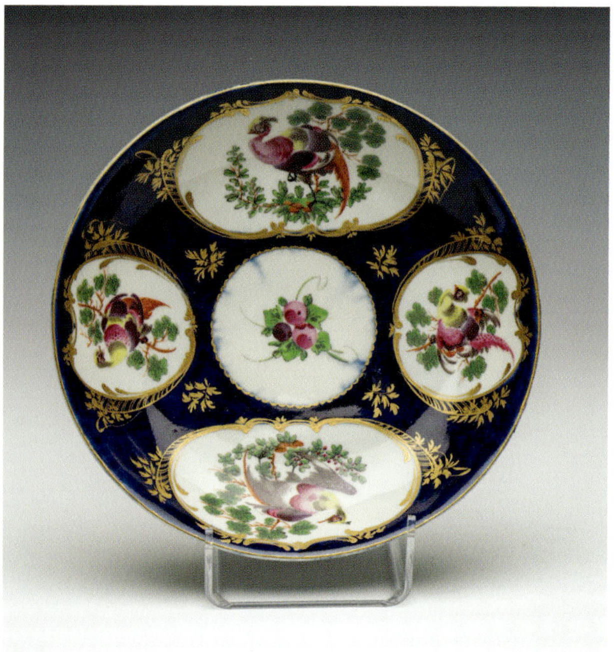

516

516

Cake dish

1775–8
Diam. 18.2 cm
1957.24.1.574

Gilt rim, wet blue ground, four oval panels painted with exotic birds with incurving tails, the central circle with a plum spray. From the Duchess of Kent service.

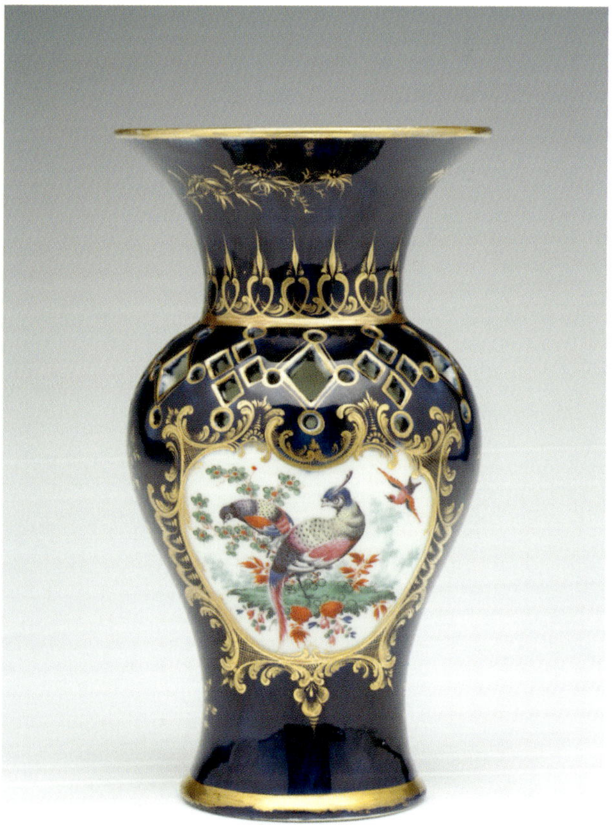

517

517

Pot-pourri vase

1770–75
Ht 16.2 cm
Mark: fretted square
1957.24.1.548

Baluster shape with pierced shoulders; wet blue ground with rich gilding, panels of exotic birds.

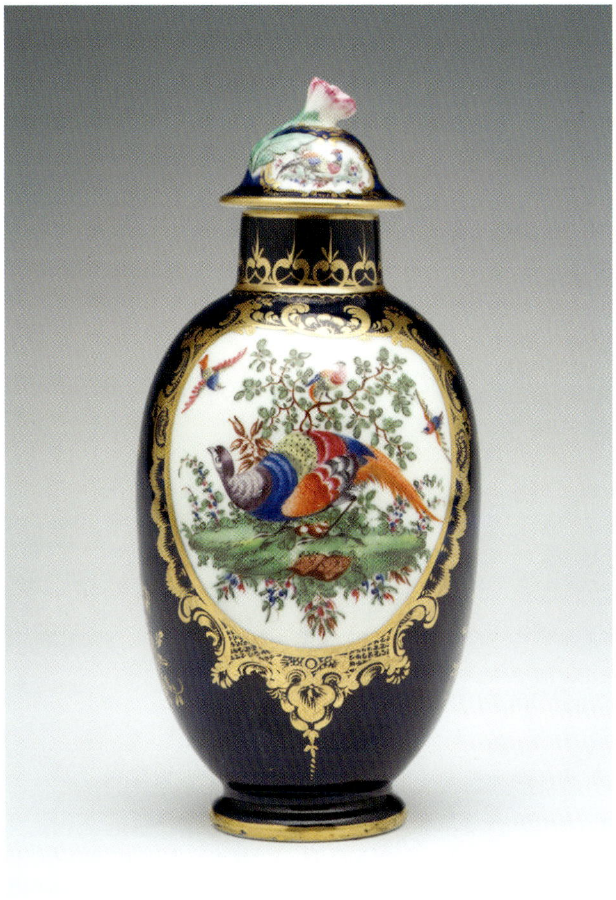

518

518

Tea canister and cover

1775–80
Ht 16.4 cm
1957.24.1.558

Ovoid, domed cover with rosebud knop; wet blue ground, richly gilded, oval reserves painted with exotic birds.

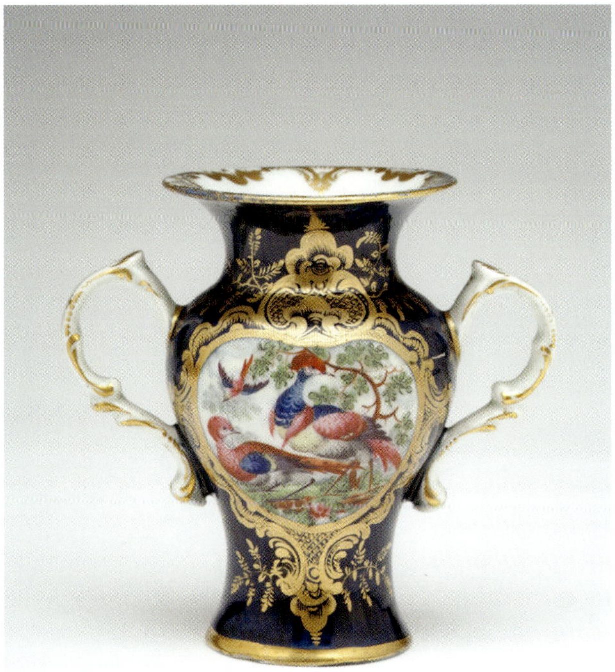

519

519

Vase

1775–80
Ht 9.8 cm
1957.24.1.135

Baluster shape with flared mouth and scroll handles; wet blue ground with heart-shaped panels, outlined with rich gilding, painted with exotic birds.

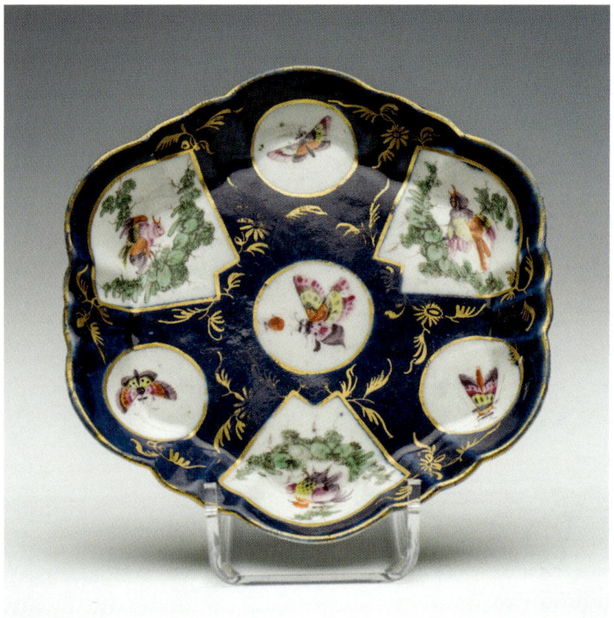

520

520

Teapot stand

1765–8
Width 14.1 cm
1957.24.1.110

Hexagonal; wet blue ground with sparse gilding, three fan-shaped reserves with exotic birds, three circular ones with butterflies; central circular reserve.

521

Coffee cup and saucer

About 1775
Cup ht 6.4 cm, diam. 5.8 cm; saucer diam. 11.9 cm
Mark: crescent on both
1957.24.1.140

Gilt dentil edge, wet blue ground with diaper gilding framing reserves painted with exotic birds. 'Marchioness of Ely' pattern.

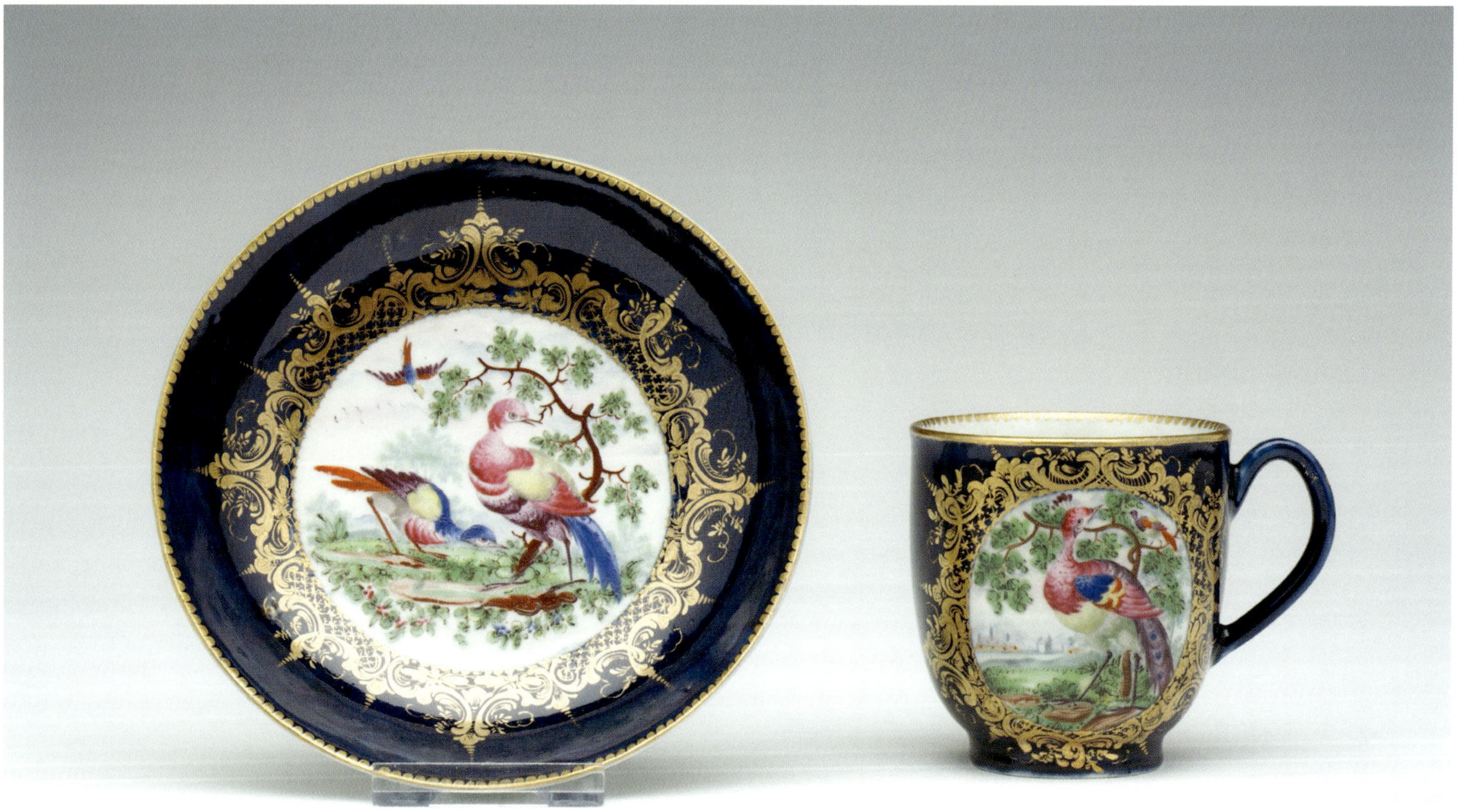

521

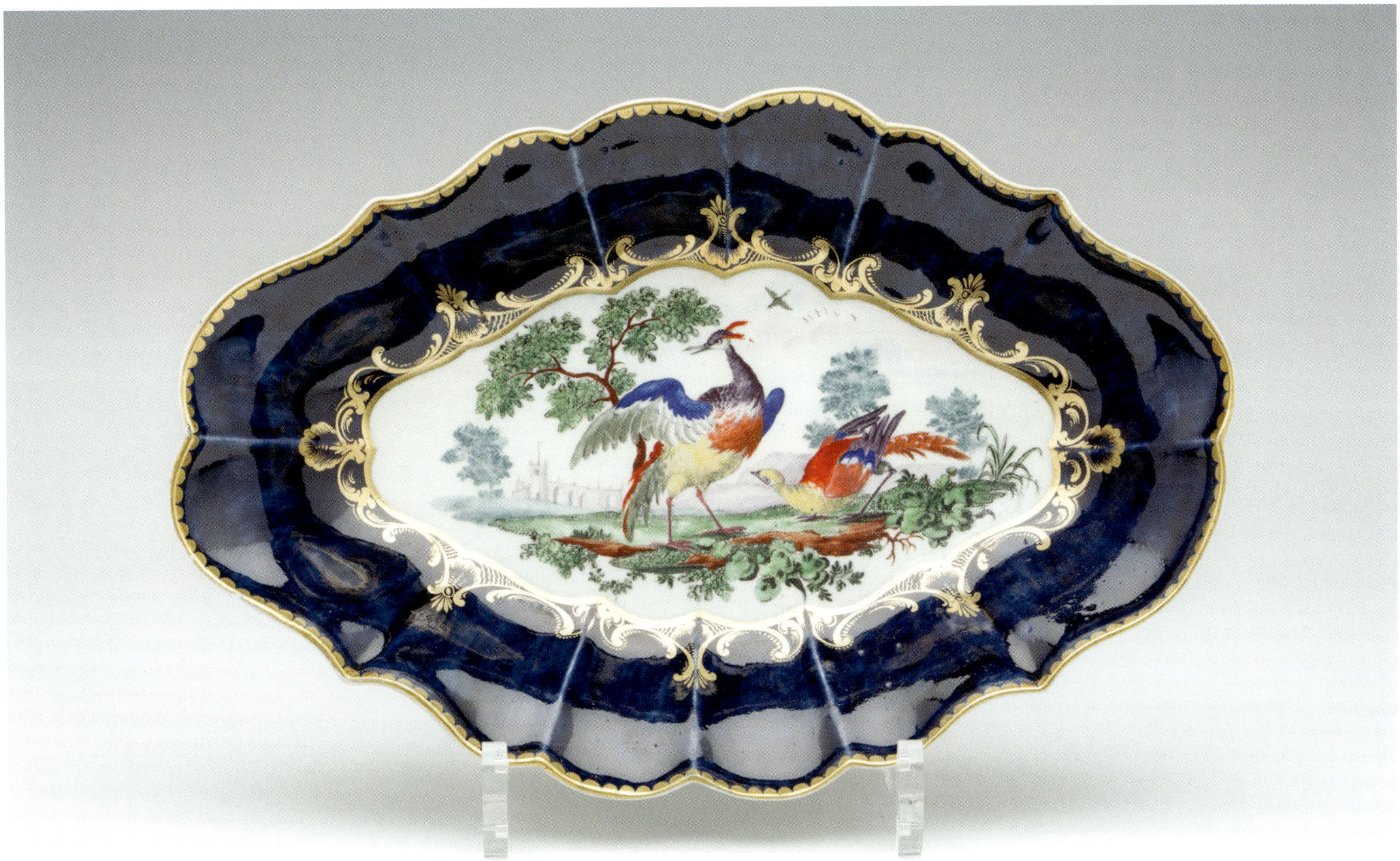

522

522

Dish

1770–72
Length 26.2 cm, width 17.9 cm
Mark: fretted square
1957.24.1.572

Fluted, lozenge shape; wide wet blue border with gilding, central reserve painted with two exotic birds in landscape with distant castle.

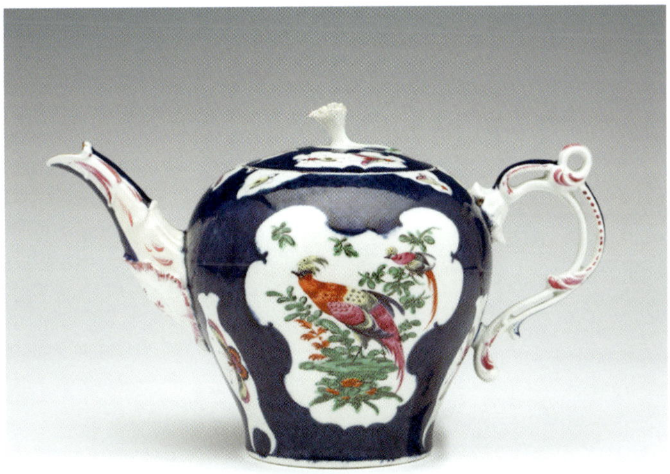

523

523

Teapot

1765–70
Ht 14.2 cm
Mark: fretted square
1957.24.1.553

Inverted pear shape with moulded spout, pierced scroll handle; blue scale ground with exotic birds and insects in reserves; no gilding.

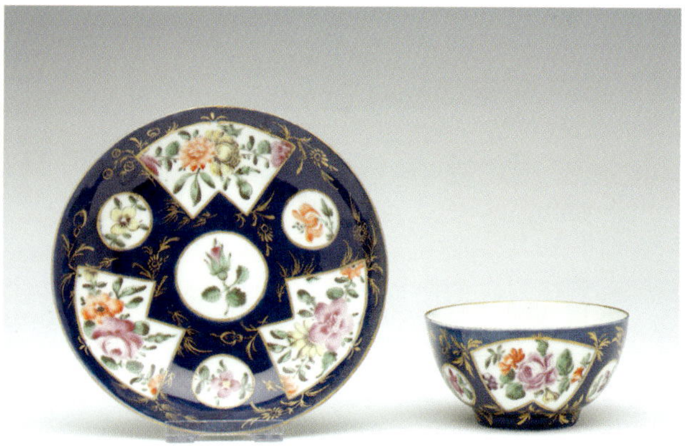

524

524

Teabowl and saucer

1768–70
Cup ht 4 cm, diam. 7.2 cm; saucer diam. 11.9 cm
1957.24.1.138

Gilt edge, wet blue ground with light floral gilding, fan-shaped and circular reserves with European flowers.

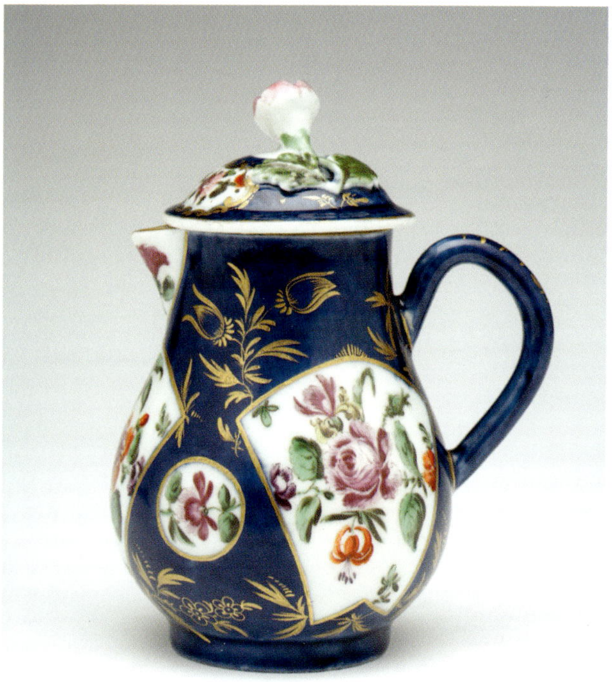

525

525

Milk jug

About 1768
Ht 8.5 cm (without cover)
1957.24.1.552

Pear shaped; wet blue ground, fan-shaped and circular reserves decorated with flowers, sparse gilding between; replacement cover.

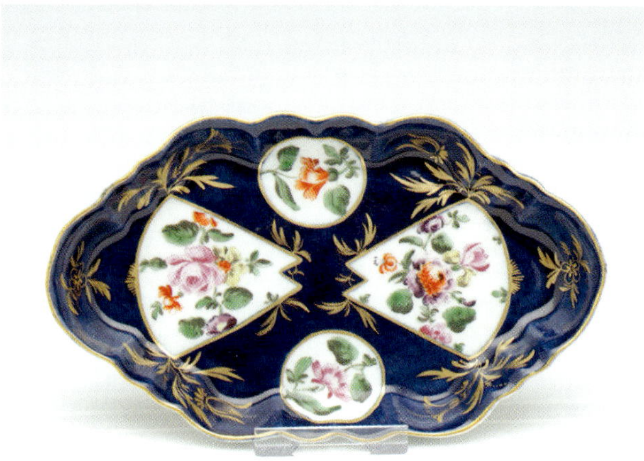

526

526

Spoon tray

1768–70
Length 15 cm, width 8.9 cm
1957.24.1.108

Hexagonal oblong with wavy gilt edge; wet blue ground with lightly gilded flower sprays, fan-shaped and circular reserves decorated with European flowers.

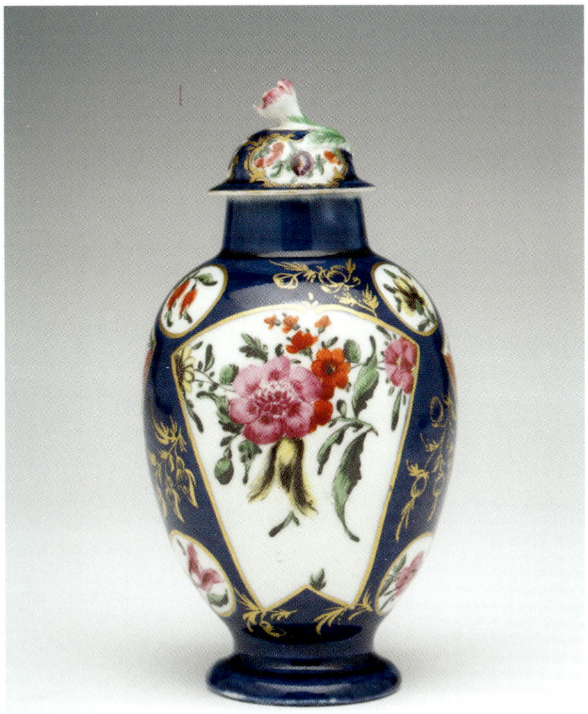

527

527

Tea canister and cover

About 1768
Ht 15 cm
1957.24.1.560

Ovoid, cover domed with rosebud knop; sparsely gilded wet blue ground, fan-shaped and small circular panels decorated with European flowers.

528

Dish

About 1765
Length 25.8 cm, width 19 cm
1957.24.1.581

Double leaf form; wet blue ground with sparse gilding; one circular and three fan-shaped reserves with European flowers, central oval decorated with butterflies.

REFERENCES
Sandon 1993, p. 267; Bonhams, London, 7 March 2007, lot 176.

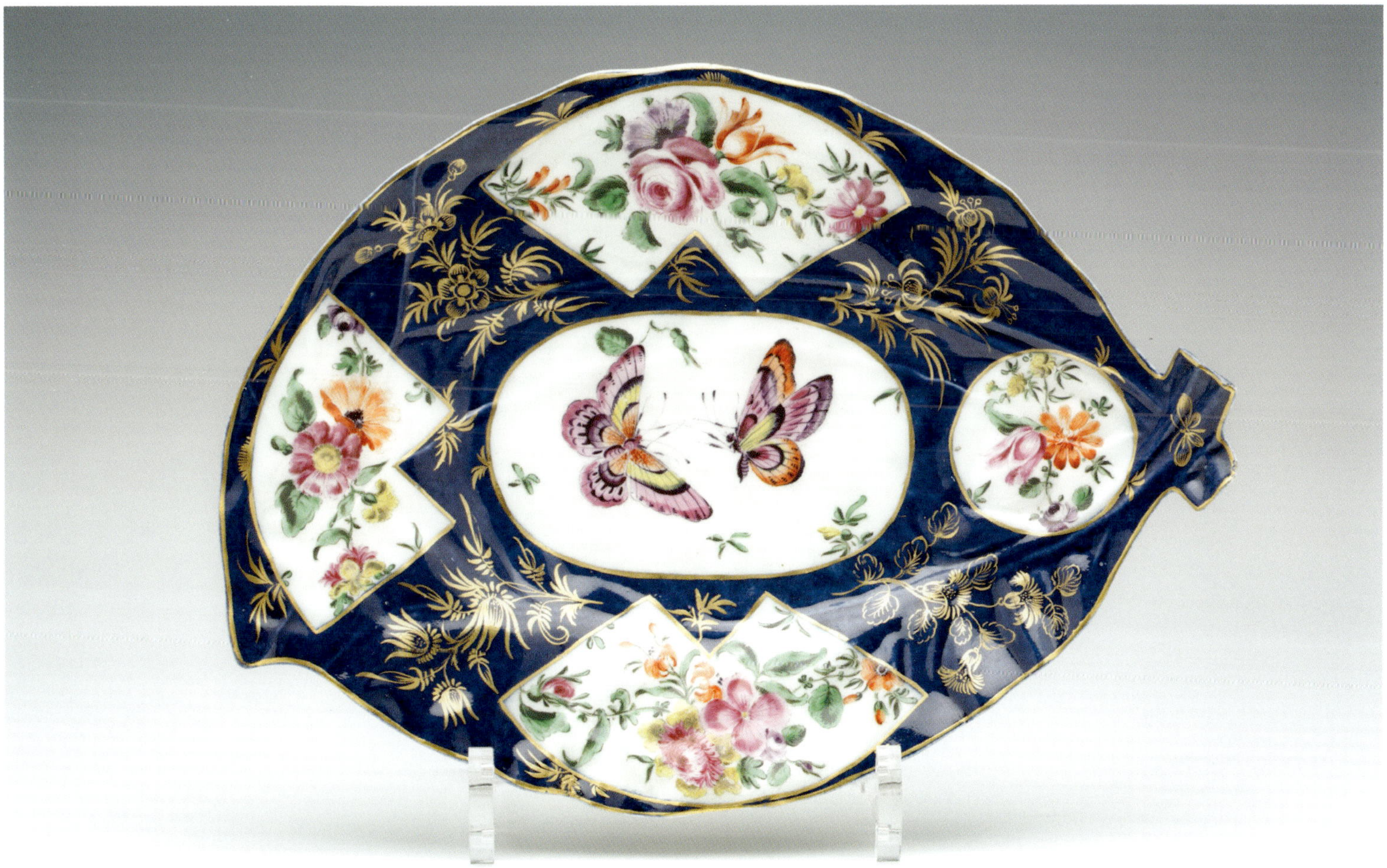

528

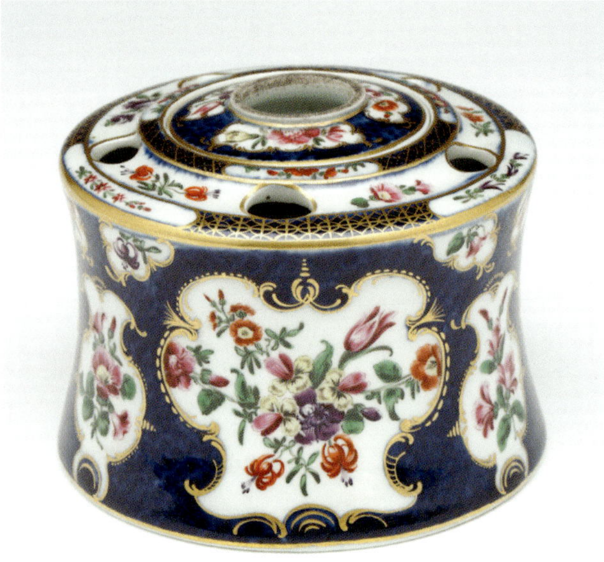

529

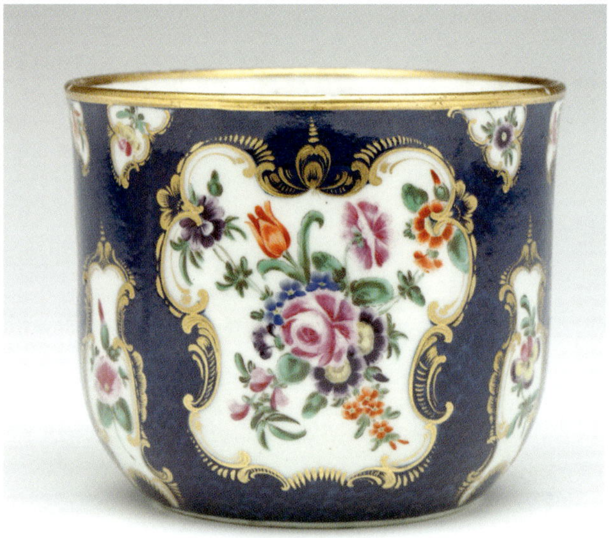

530

529

Inkwell and inkpot

About 1768
Ht 7.8 cm, diam. 10.6 cm
Mark: fretted square
1957.24.1.554

Circular with concave sides and removable central well surrounded by quill holes; blue scale ground, rococo reserves with floral decoration. Inkwells are rare from all eighteenth-century factories.

REFERENCES
Spero and Sandon 1996, pl. 327; Sotheby's, London, 13 April 2011, lot 182.

530

Fingerbowl

About 1770
Ht 8.4 cm, diam. 9.9 cm
Mark: fretted square
1957.24.1.128

Cylindrical; blue scale ground, gilt edge, rococo reserves painted with flowers.

PROVENANCE
H.W. Hughes Collection; Russell, Baldwin & Bright, Worcester, 6 December 1945, £42 (pair).

531

Coffee cup and saucer

About 1770
Cup ht 6.6 cm, diam. 5.8 cm; saucer diam. 12 cm
Mark: fretted square on both
1957.24.1.144

Blue scale ground with rococo, mirror-shaped, claw and triangular reserves decorated with European flowers.

532

Coffee cup and saucer

About 1768
Cup ht 7.5 cm, diam. 6.8 cm; saucer diam. 12.9 cm
Mark: crescent on cup, cursive *W* on saucer
1957.24.1.833

Unfinished; blue scale ground with undecorated reserves.

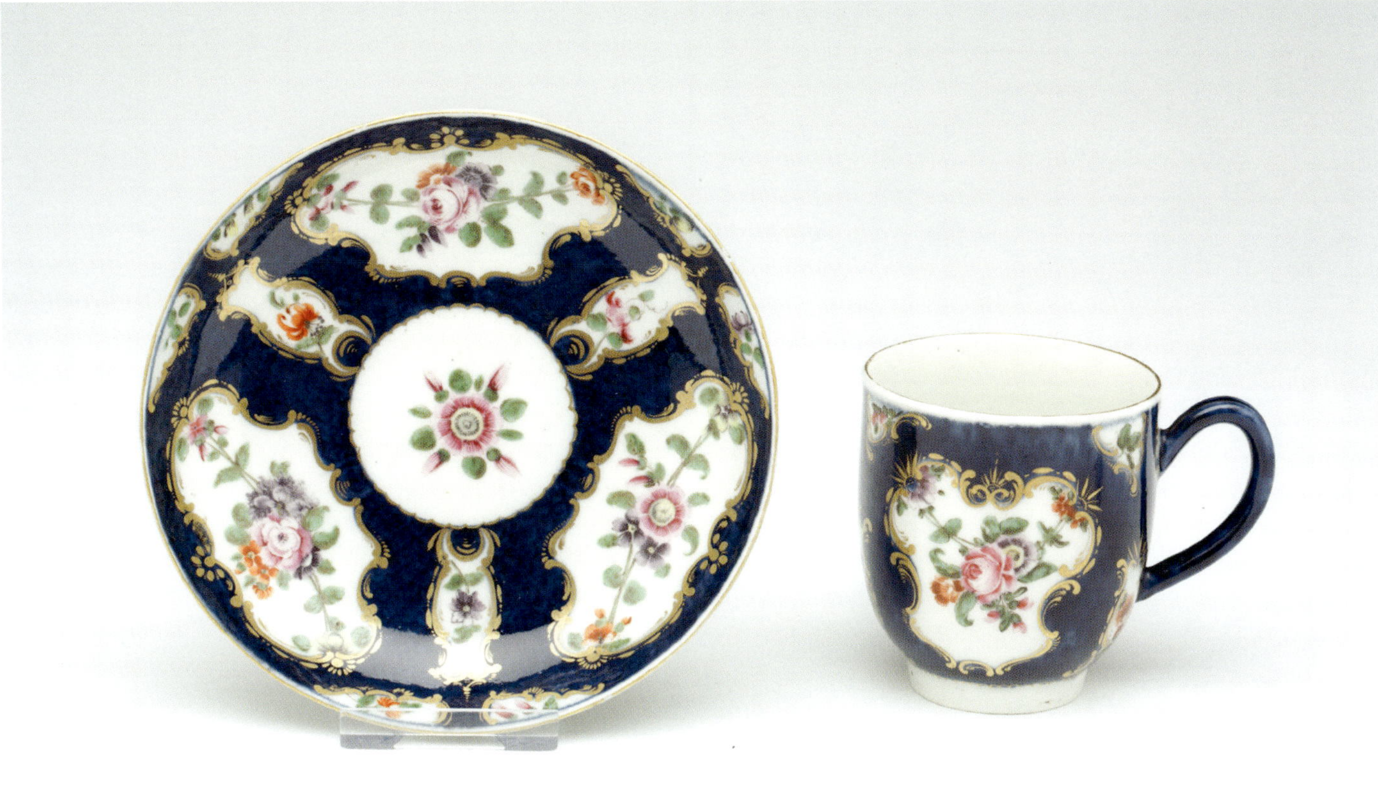

531

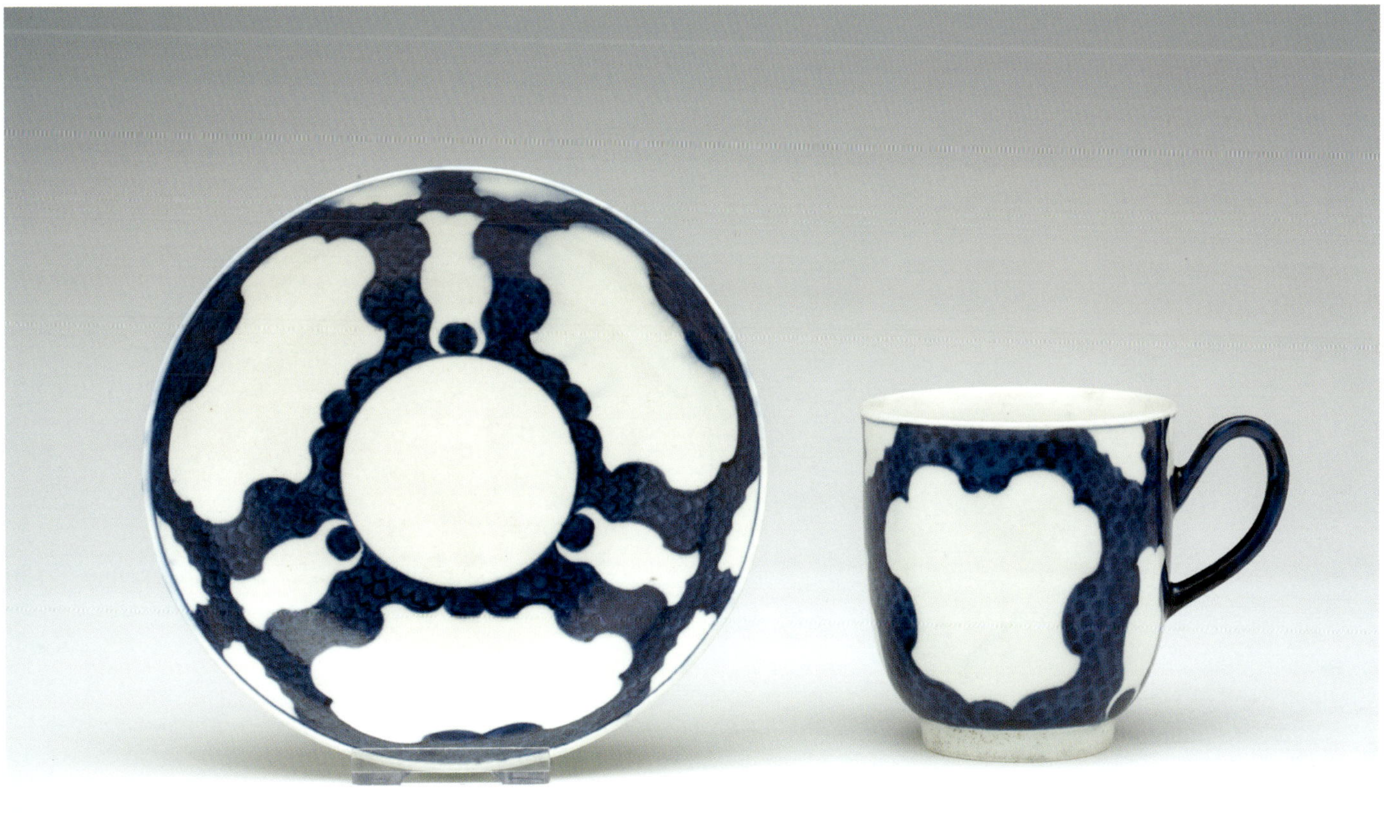

532

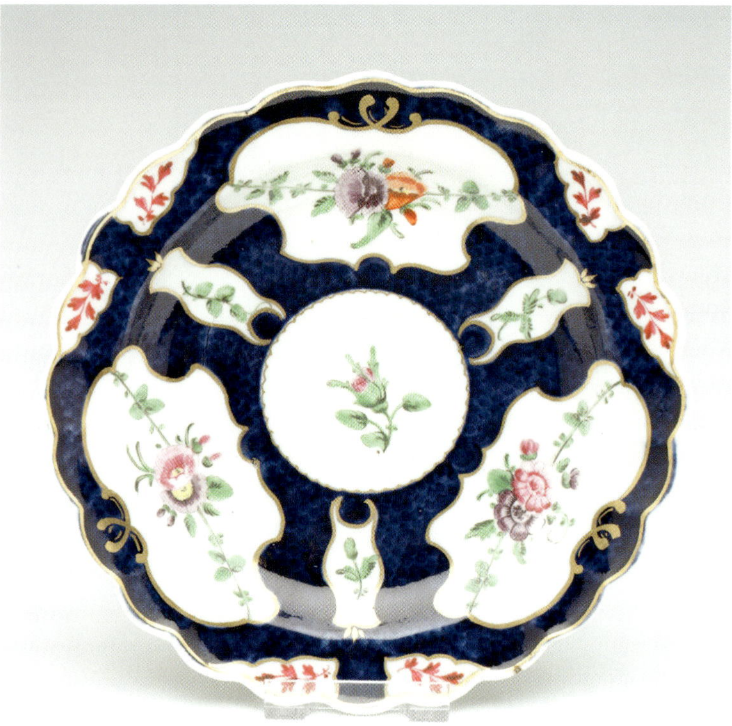

533

533

Plate

1768–70
Diam. 19.3 cm
Mark: cursive *W*
1957.24.1.585

Scalloped rim; blue scale ground, gilt edged reserves with floral decoration, small triangular reserves at edge with puce monochrome leaf sprays.

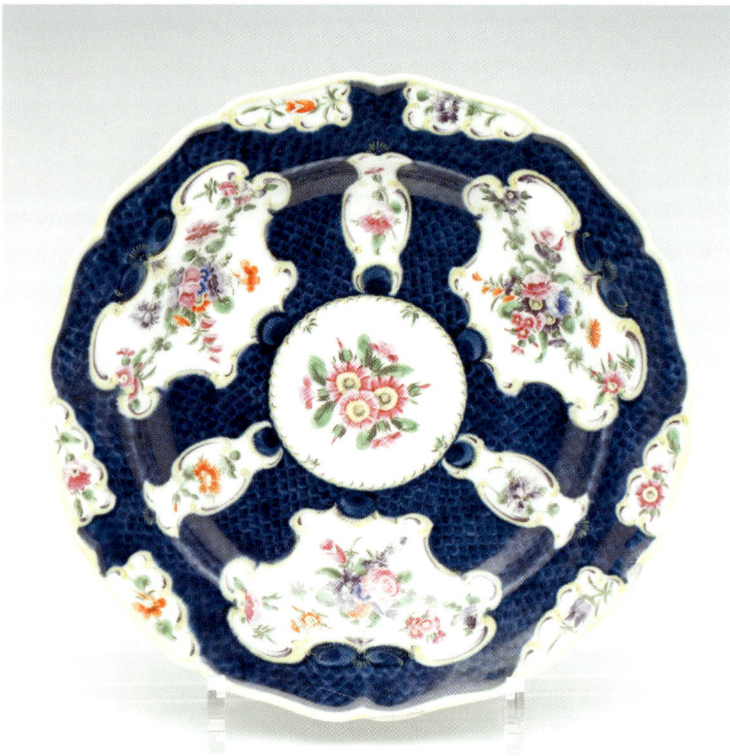

534

534

Plate

About 1770
Diam. 22.5 cm
Mark: fretted square
1957.24.1.580

Blue scale ground, European flowers in reserves, rim and detailing defined in yellow instead of gilding.

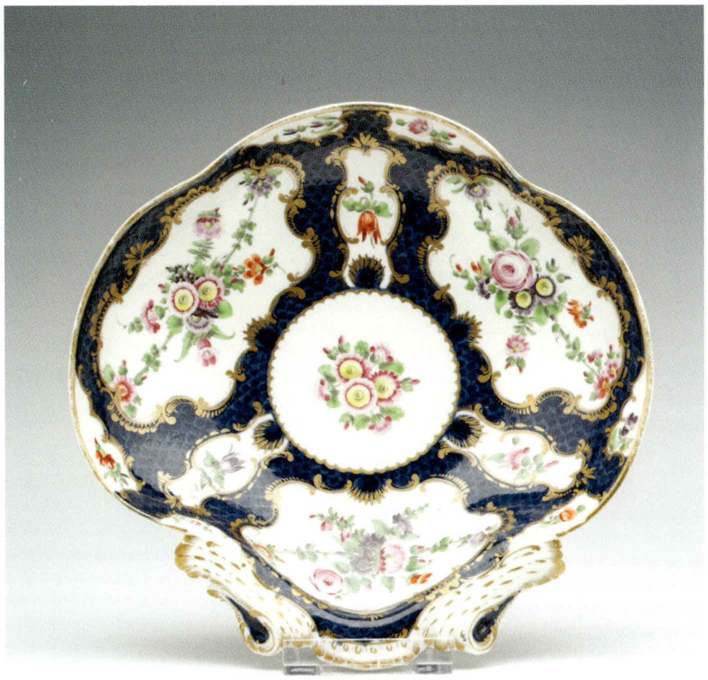

535

535

Shell-shaped dish

1770–75
Width 19.4 cm
Mark: crescent
1957.24.1.109

Moulded handle; blue scale ground, reserves decorated with flowers.

536

Dish or stand

1768–72
Length 20 cm, width 14.5 cm
Mark: fretted square
1957.24.1.113

Oval; blue scale ground with gilt floral sprays, moulded panels defined by gilding, painted with European flowers, large bouquet in centre.

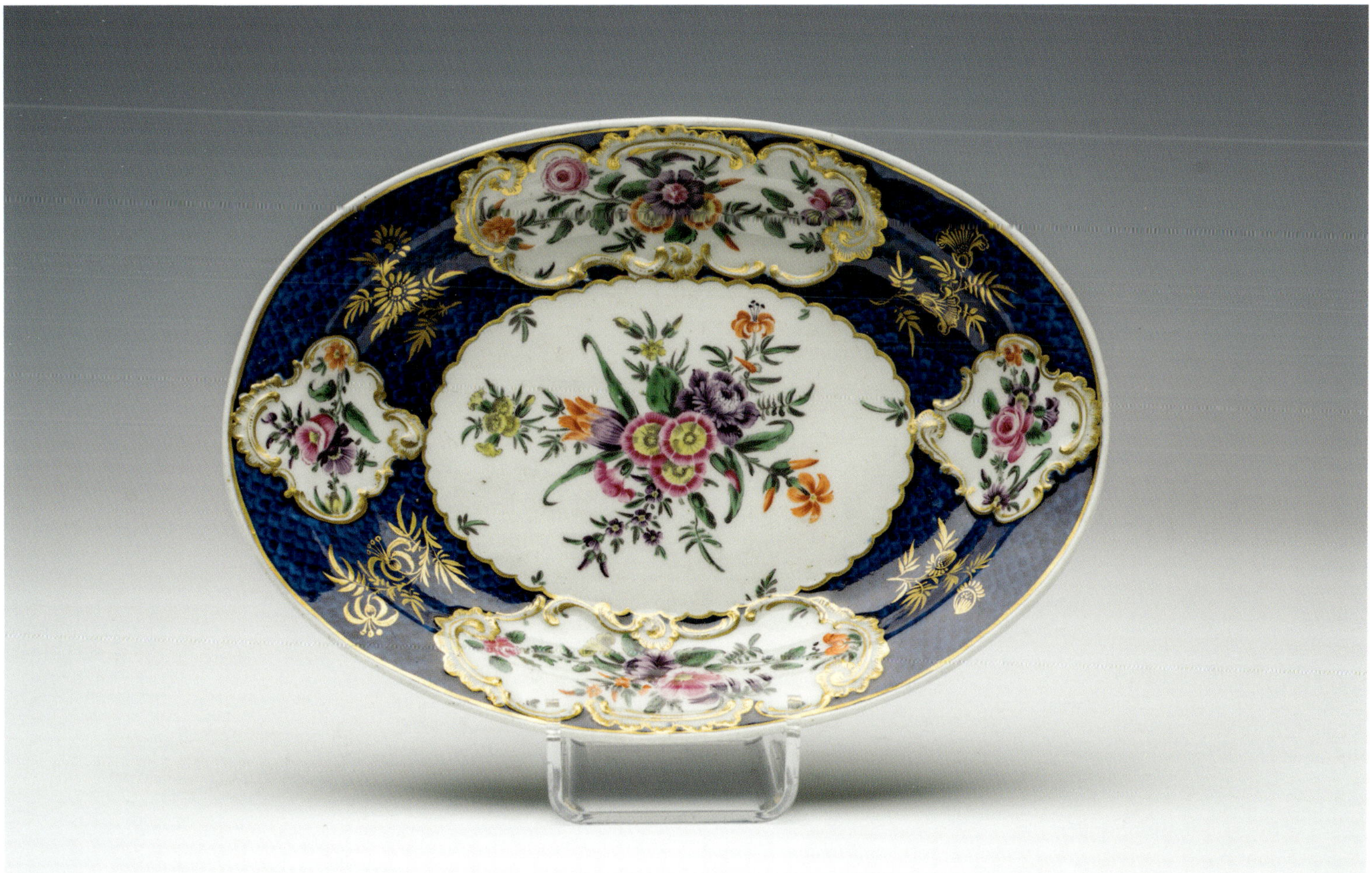

536

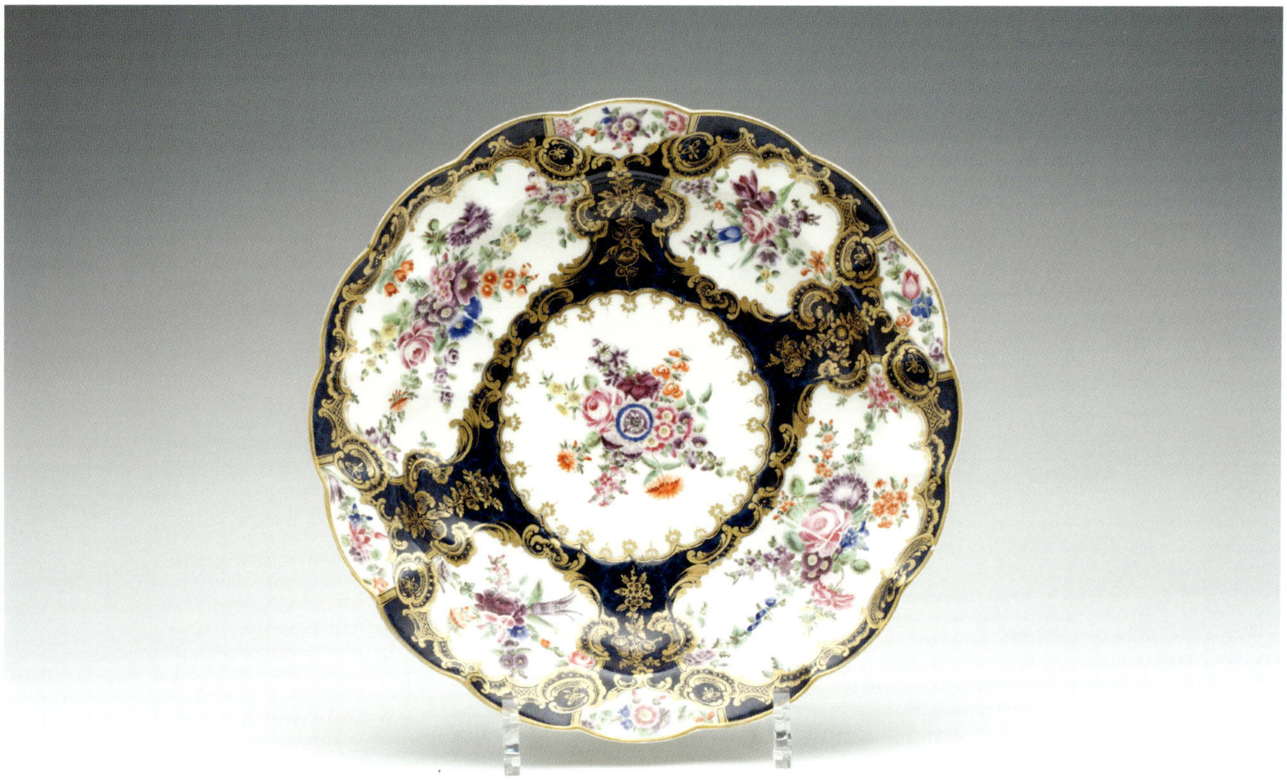

537

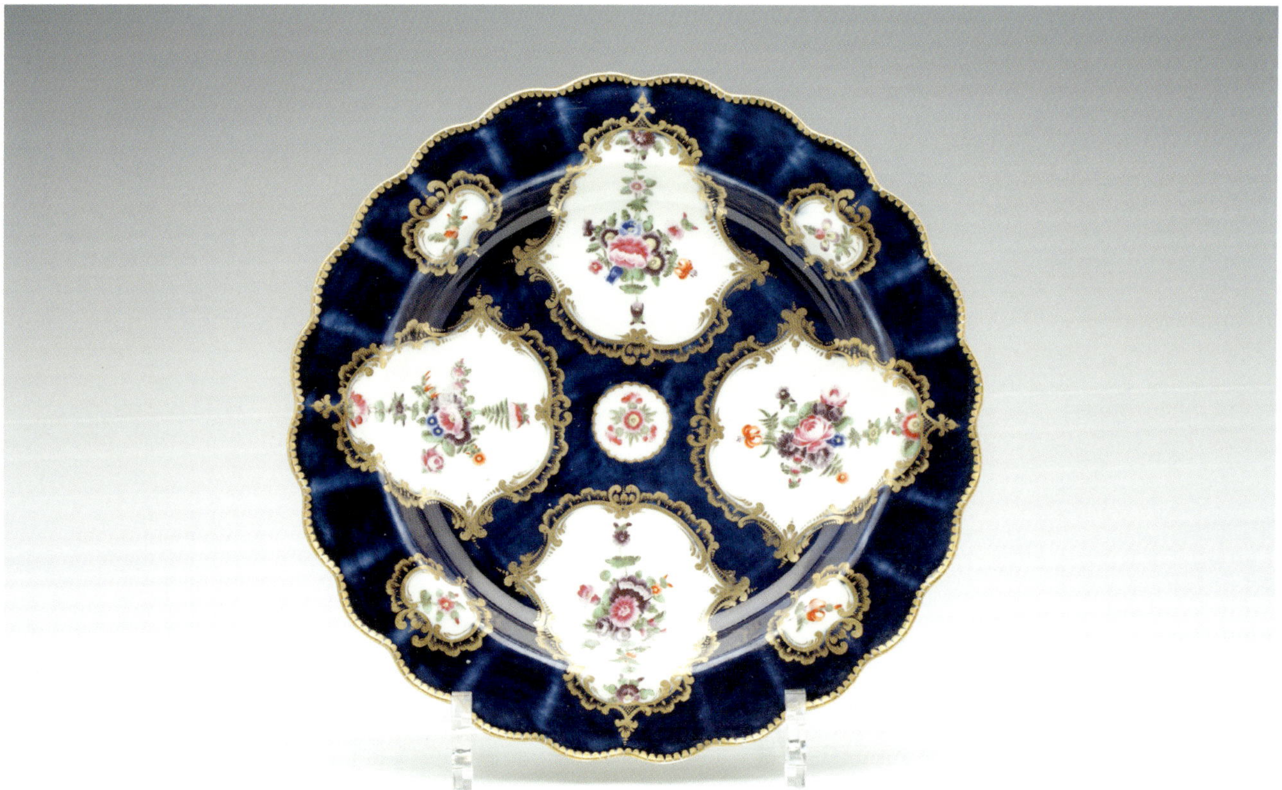

538

537

Dish

1768–72
Diam. 24.9 cm
Mark: fretted square
1957.24.1.538

Scalloped edge; blue scale ground, rich gilt scrolling defining reserves painted with floral bouquets.

538

Plate

About 1770
Diam. 21.6 cm
Mark: fretted square
1957.24.1.561

Scalloped gilt dentil edge; deep wet blue ground, reserves edged with rich feathered gilt scrolling and painted with floral posies. A service with this distinctive decoration belonged to Angela Georgina, Baroness Burdett Coutts (1814–1906), a great philanthropist and the first woman to be created a baroness in her own right.

REFERENCE
Spero 1984, pl. 134.

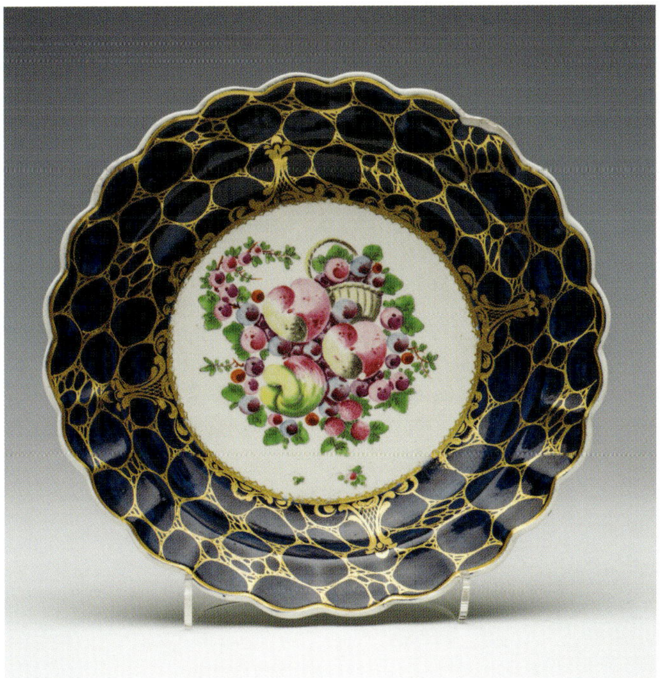

539

539

Cake dish

1775–80
Diam. 19.7 cm
Mark: open crescent
1957.24.1.579

Fluted with wavy rim, wide wet blue border marbled in gold, basket with spotted fruit in centre. This type of gilding is derived from the *caillouté* style of Sèvres, simulating pebbles.

REFERENCE
Spero and Sandon 1996, pl. 319.

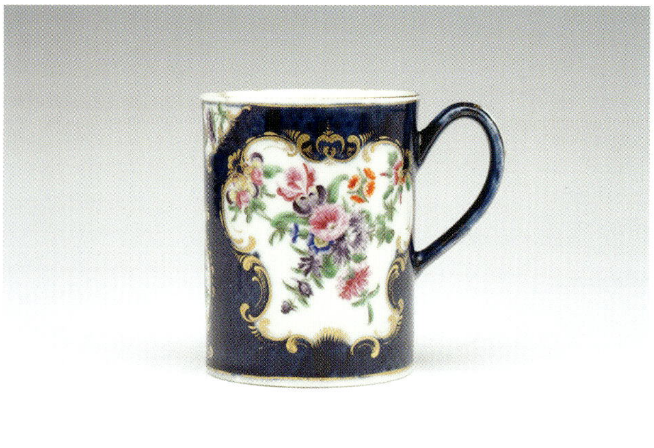

540

540

Mug

1768–72
Ht 9 cm, diam. 6.9 cm
Mark: fretted square
1957.24.1.556

Cylindrical with ribbed loop handle; blue scale ground, gilt rim, rococo reserves painted with bouquets and sprays of flowers.

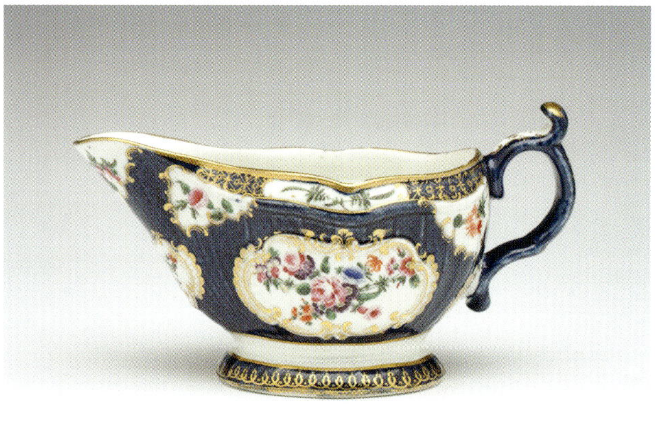

541

541

Sauceboat

About 1770
Ht 10.8 cm, length 18.7 cm
Mark: fretted square
1957.24.1.537

Moulded edge and border; blue scale ground with gilding, flowers in reserves.

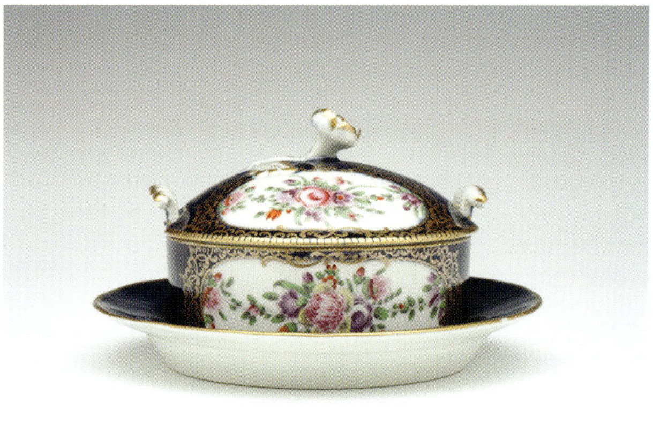

542

542

Butter dish, cover and stand

1770–75
Butter dish ht 8.1 cm, diam. 10.9; stand diam. 16.1 cm
Mark: crescent on stand
1957.24.1.139

Circular, with two lug handles, domed cover with rosebud knop; wet blue ground; European flowers in oval reserves defined by rich scroll and lambrequin gilding; gilt dentil edges on cover and stand.

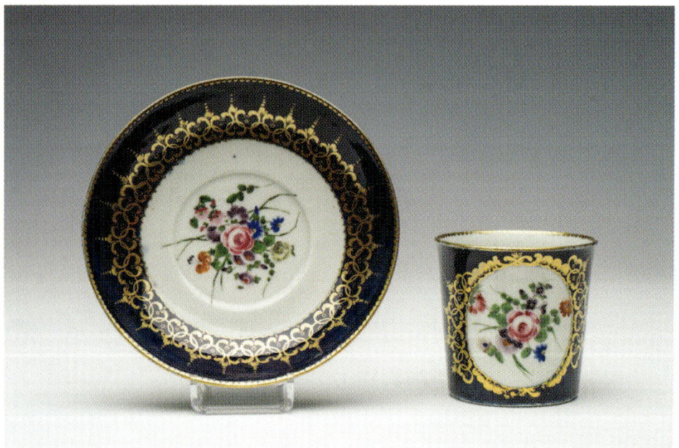

543

543

Tumbler and stand

1775–80
Tumbler ht 7.2 cm, diam. 7.1 cm; stand diam. 13.9 cm
Mark: crescent
1957.24.1.125

Wet blue ground, gilt dentil edges, oval reserves on tumbler with bouquets of European flowers defined by scroll and lambrequin gilding; similar circular reserve on stand, with central depression into which the tumbler fits.

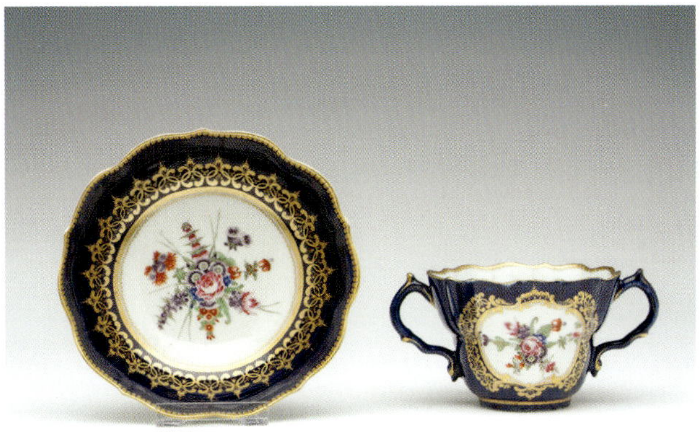

544

544

Caudle cup and saucer

1770–75
Ht 7.1 cm, diam. 9.8 cm; saucer diam. 14.9 cm
Mark: fretted square on both
1957.24.1.545

Wavy gilt dentil rim, double rococo handles; wet blue ground, gilt scrolling defining panels of natural flowers.

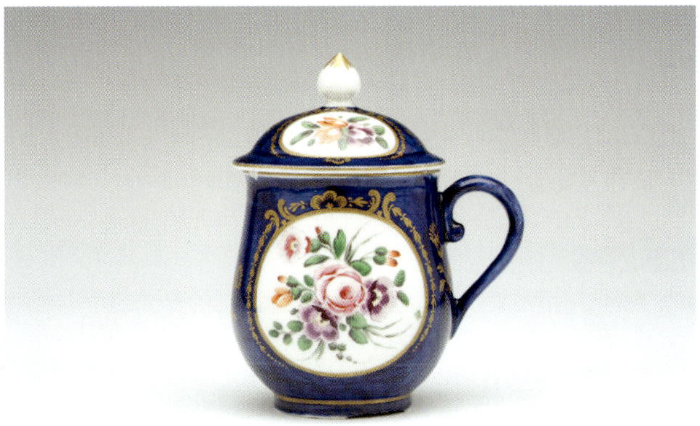

545

545

Custard cup and cover

1775–80
Ht 9.6 cm, diam. 5.3 cm
Mark: crescent
1957.24.1.133

Blue ground, white conical knop; circular panels of flowers defined by a gilt wreath.

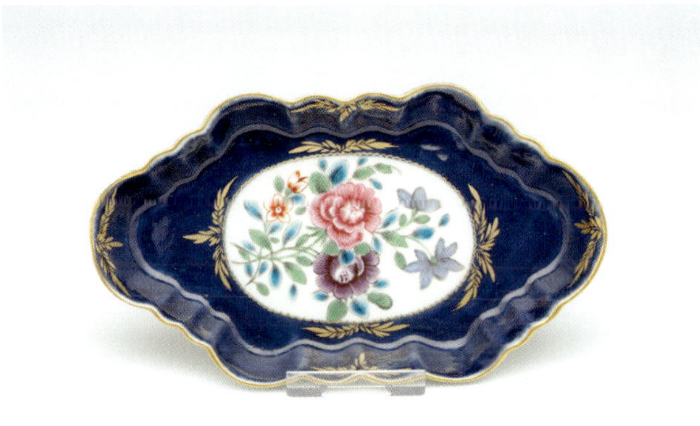

546

546

Spoon tray

1780–85
Length 15.2 cm, width 8.9 cm
Mark: crescent
1957.24.1.702

Gilt edge, sparsely gilded wet blue ground, central oval reserve decorated with flowers.

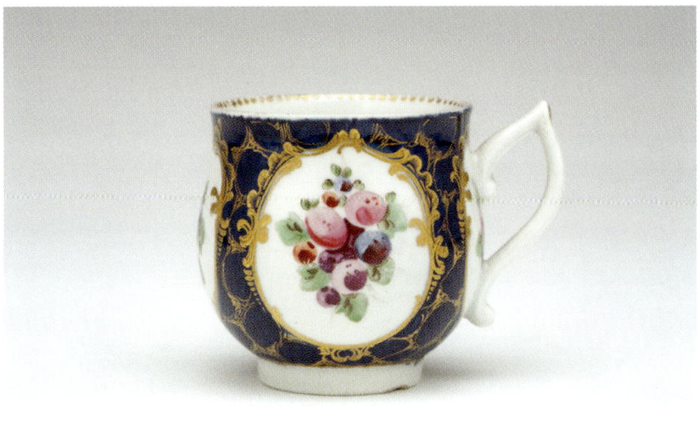

547

547

Coffee cup

1768–72
Ht 6 cm, diam. 5.4 cm
Mark: crescent
1957.24.1.116

Bell-shaped, peaked handle; wet blue ground with cracked ice gilding; four roughly oval reserves, defined by gilding, decorated with fruit and foliage.

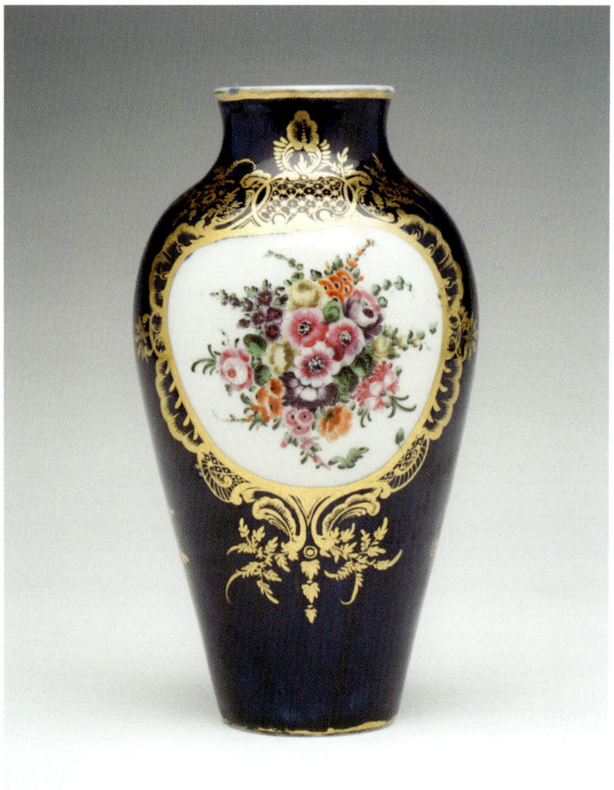

548

548

Vase

1770–75
Ht 17.1 cm
Mark: crescent
1957.24.1.544

Slender, ovoid form; wet blue ground, intricate gilding around reserves with flowers.

549

Plate

1770–75
Diam. 29.1 cm
Mark: fretted square
1957.24.1.540

Scalloped rim with gilt dentil edge, wide wet blue border defined by elaborate lambrequin gilding, floral bouquet in centre.

550

Plate

1770–75
Diam. 22.5 cm
Mark: fretted square
1957.24.1.559

Gilt dentil edge, wide wet blue border, floral bouquet in centre surrounded by gilding.

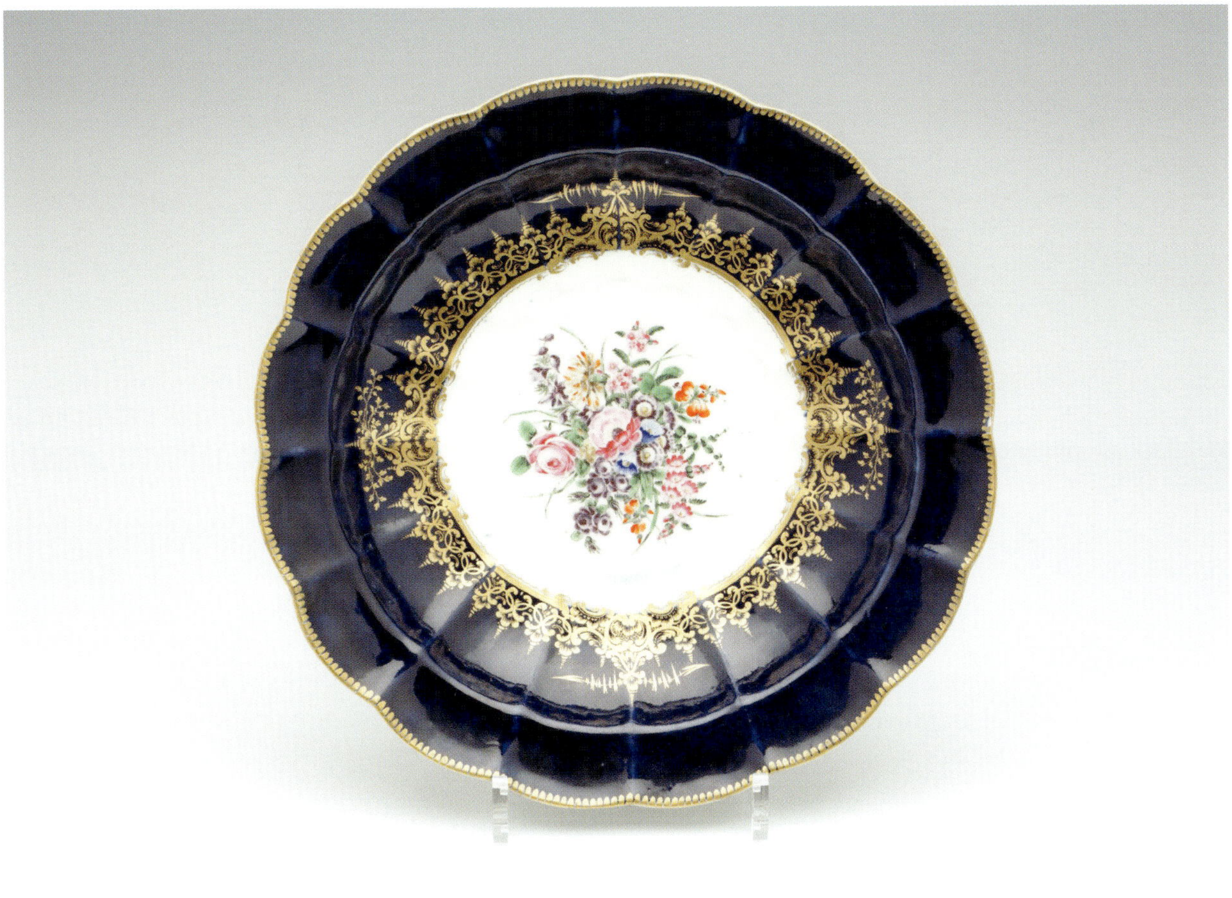

549

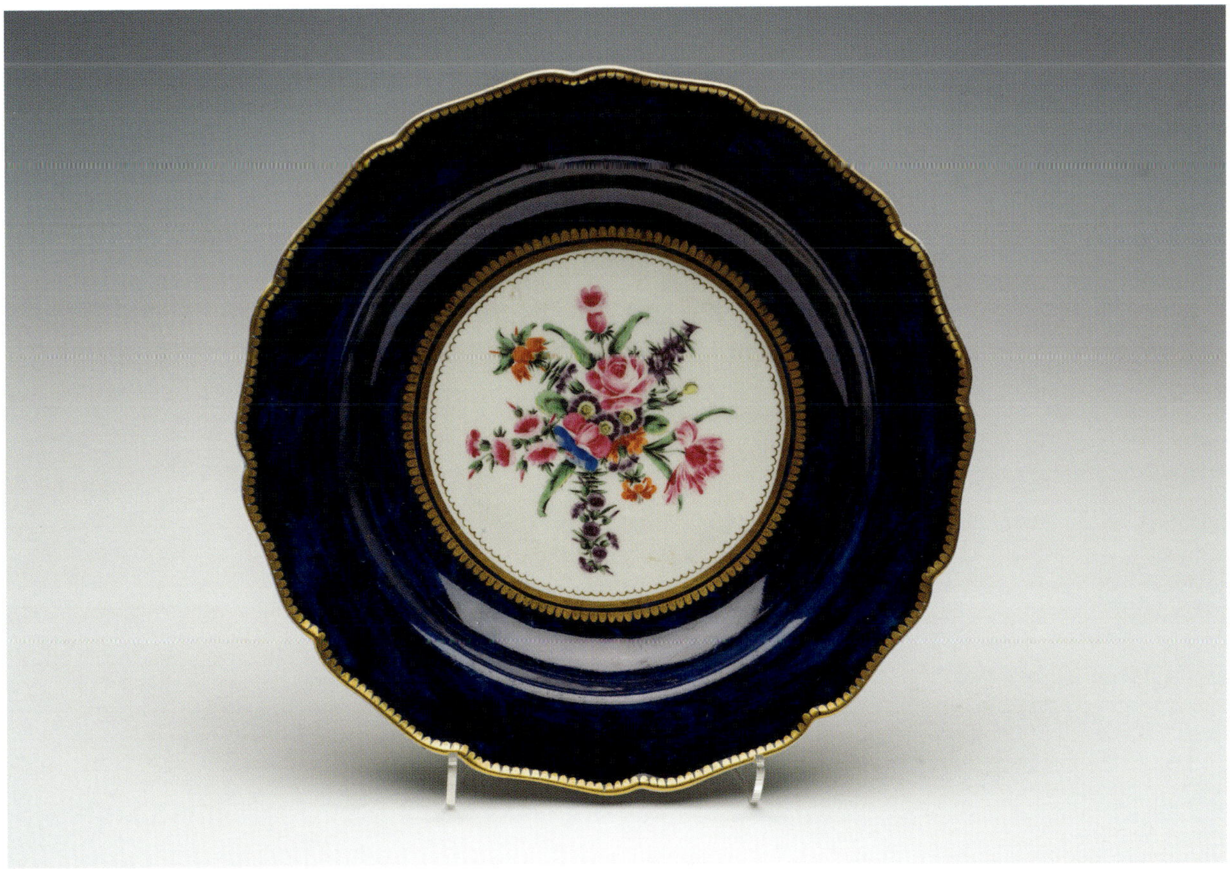

550

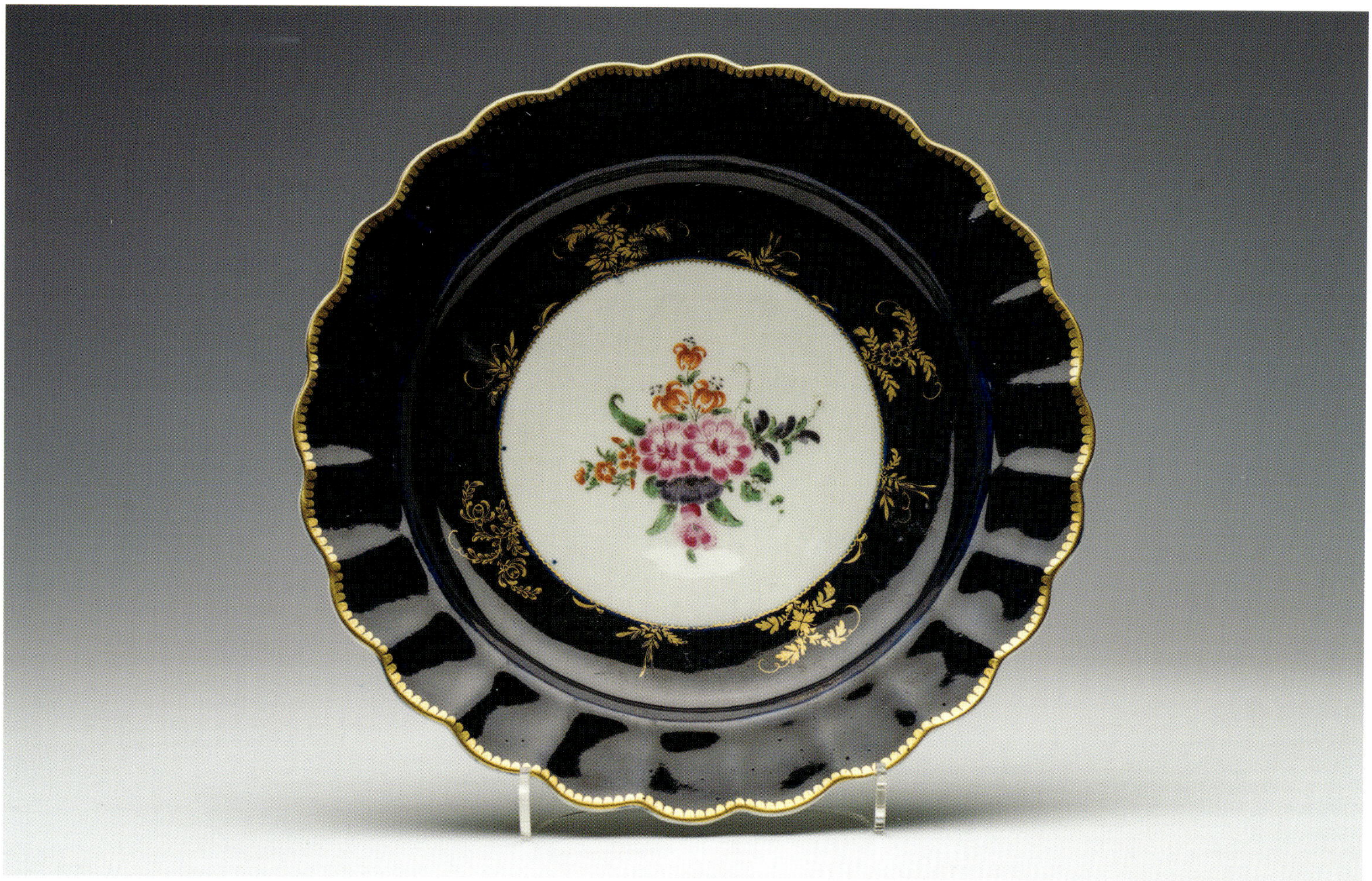

551

551

Plate

1770–75
Diam. 21.7 cm
Mark: fretted square
1957.24.1.565

Scalloped gilt dentil edge, fluted rim; wet blue ground with sparse gilding around central reserve with floral bouquet.

552

Basket moulded dish

1770–72
Length 30.4 cm, width 21.6 cm
Mark: fretted square
1957.24.1.38

Moulded interlacing strapwork picked out in wet blue with gilding, moulded vine leaves, branch handles, basketwork reserves with flowers and insects, butterflies in oval well, edged with gadrooned moulding.

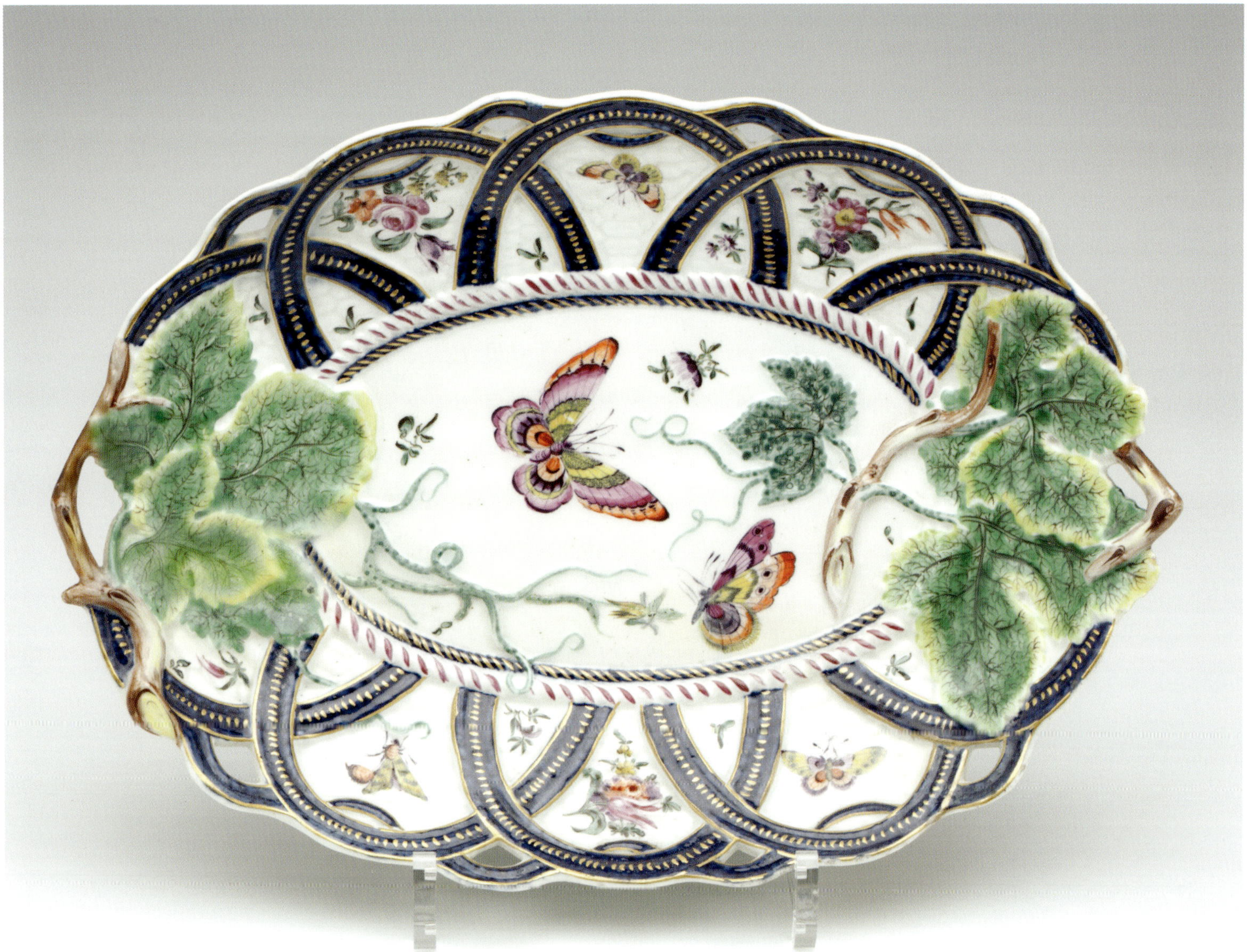

552

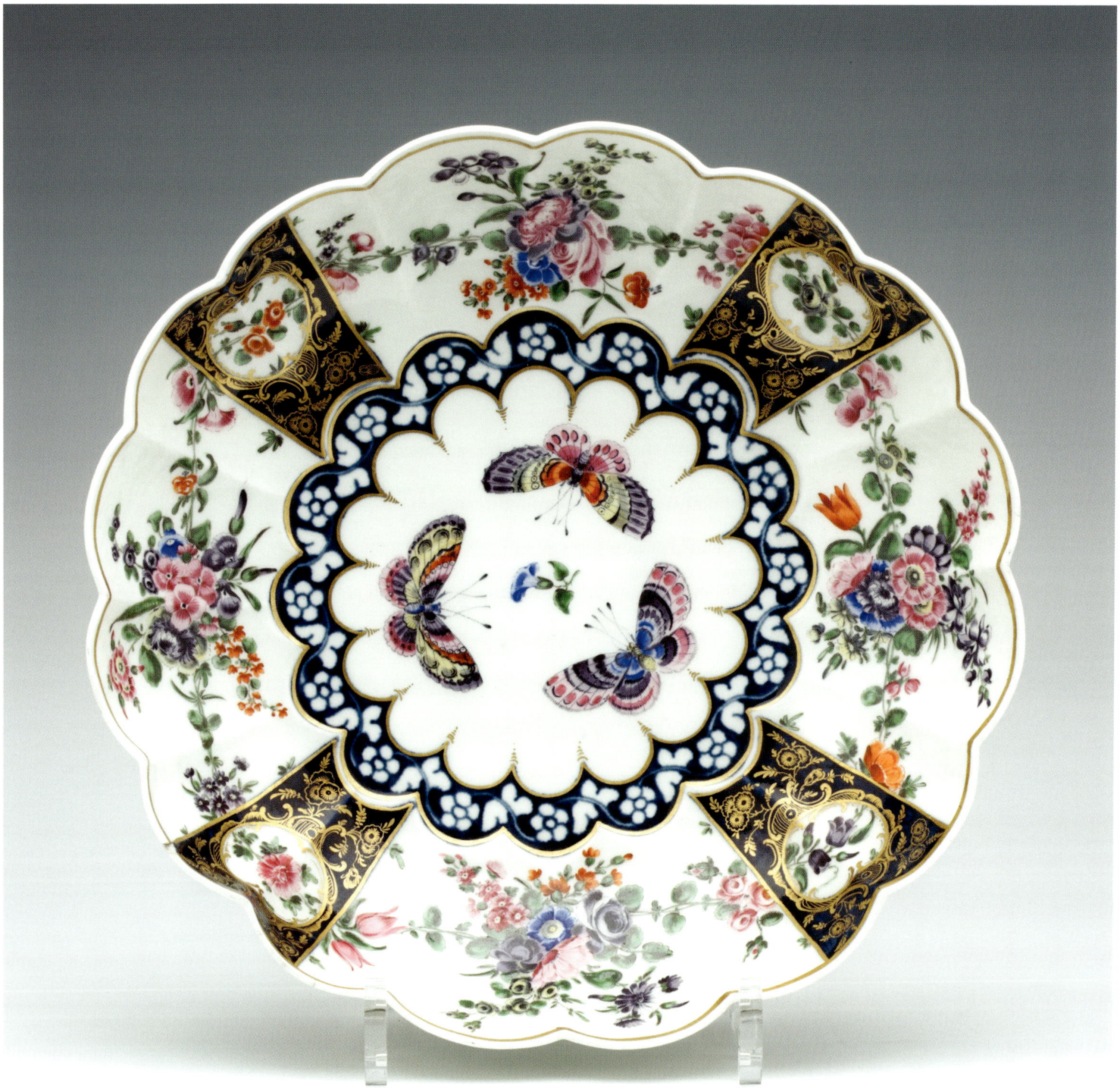

553

553

Junket dish

1768–70
Ht 6.5 cm, diam. 25.6 cm
Mark: fretted square
1957.24.1.3

Fluted; floral decoration separated by wet blue and gilt panels with floral reserves, butterflies in centre within an underglaze blue scalloped border.

REFERENCE
Bonhams, London, 7 March 2007, lot 100.

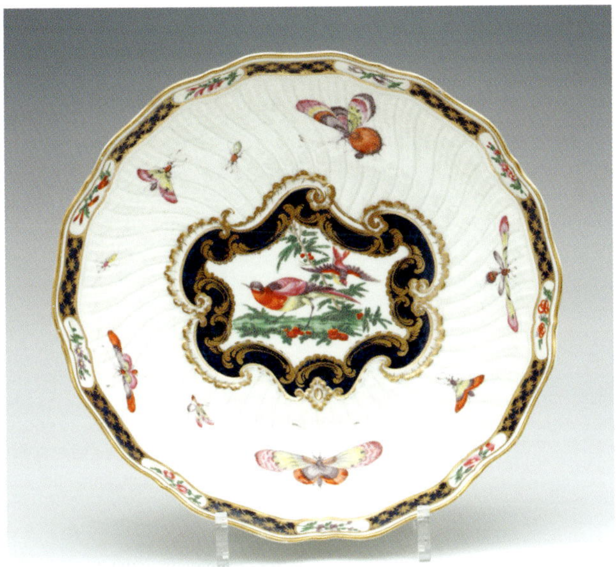

554

554

Junket dish

1770–75
Ht 7 cm, diam. 25.7 cm
Mark: fretted square
1957.24.1.5

Oblique wavy fluting; alternating floral and gilded blue scale panels around edge, central scroll moulded panel edged in blue and gold, painted with two exotic birds surrounded by butterflies and insects. A similar dish was exhibited by Albert Amor, London, October 1993.

REFERENCE
Bonhams, London, 7 March 2007, lot 166.

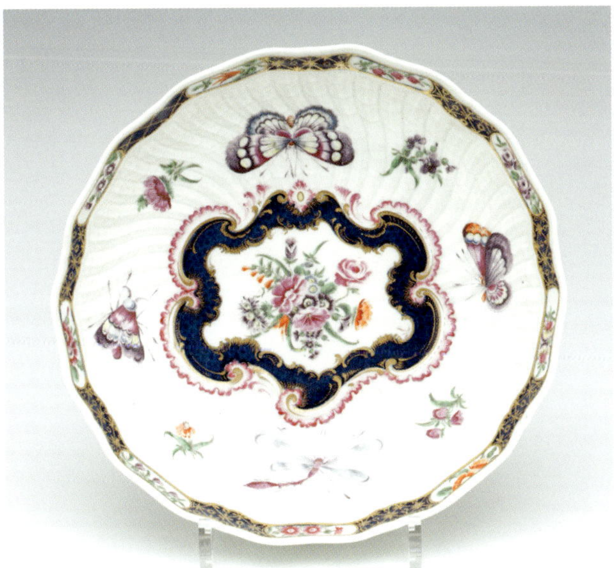

555

555

Junket dish

1770–75
Ht 6.7 cm, diam. 25.2 cm
Mark: fretted square
1957.24.1.1

Oblique wavy fluting radiating from a central reserve of flowers surrounded by a rococo blue scale border, blue scale and gilt panels below rim.

REFERENCES
Sandon 1993, p. 212; Bonhams, London, 7 March 2007, lot 167.

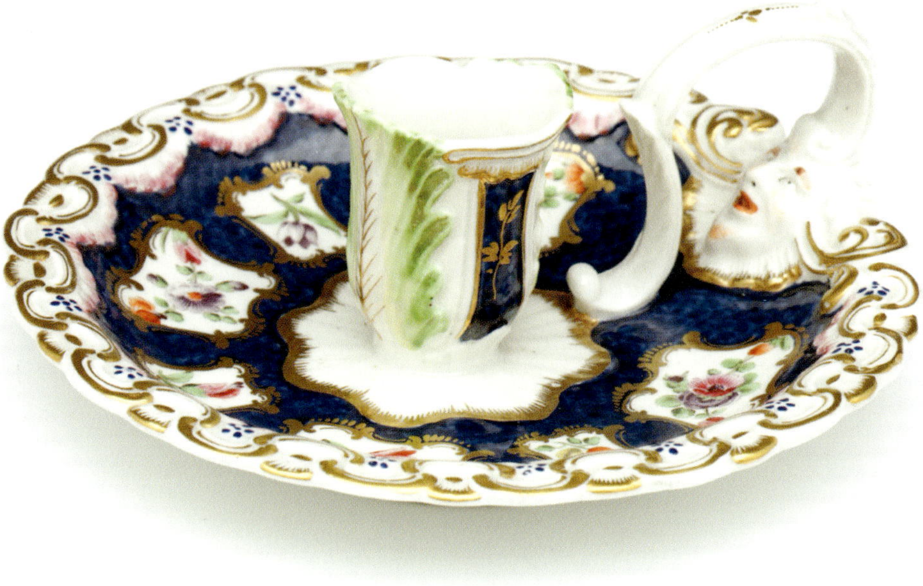

556

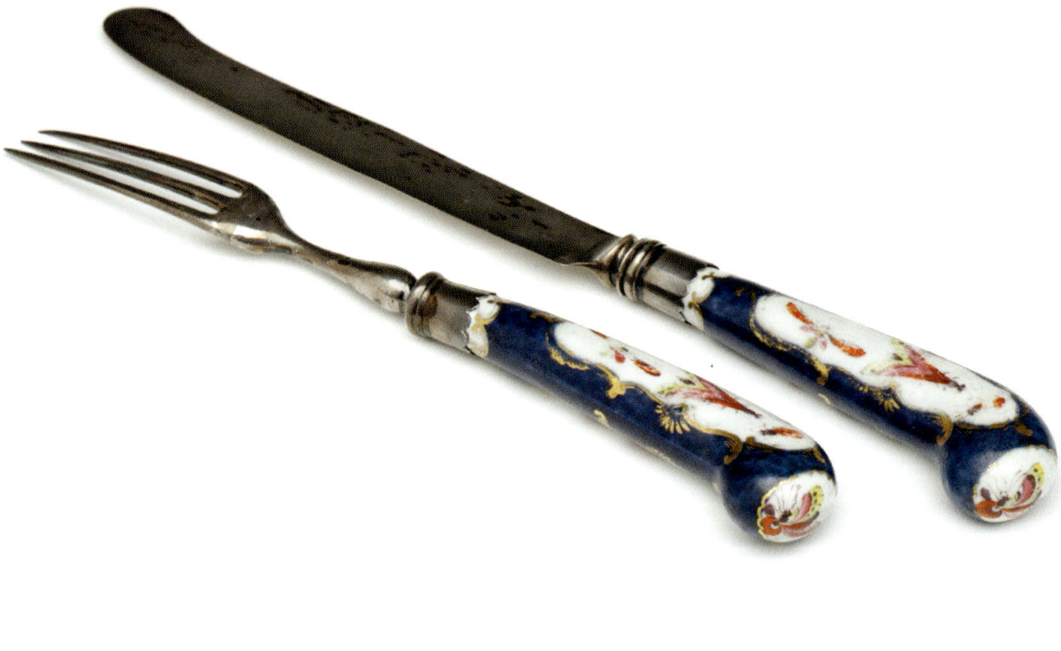

557

556

Chamber candlestick

1770–75
Ht 5.7 cm, diam. 14.4 cm
Mark: open overglaze blue crescent
1957.24.1.569

Moulded solid border picked out with gilding, mask under handle; blue scale ground edged with carmine moulding, painted with European flowers in reserves; nozzle has two leaf panels separated by two blue scale ones.

REFERENCE
Spero and Sandon 1996, pl. 332.

557

Knife and fork handles

1763–5
Knife length 22.4 cm; fork length 18.5 cm
1957.24.1.576

Blue scale ground with gilding, panels decorated with coloured insects. From an extensive service purchased from 1764 by Thomas Cobbe, son of Charles Cobbe, Archbishop of Dublin, for use at Newbridge House, Dublin.

REFERENCES
Dawson 2007, pl. 31; Bonhams, London, 2 November 2011, lot 107.

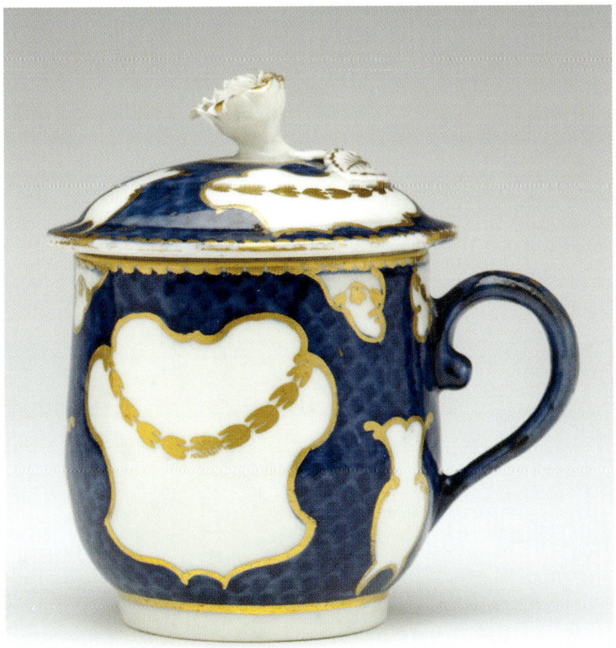

558

558

Custard cup and cover

About 1770
Ht 8.1 cm, diam. 5.5 cm
Mark: crescent
1957.24.1.122

Blue scale ground with gilt edged reserves, white rosebud knop, gold festoons added later.

PROVENANCE
Frank Hurlbutt Collection; Sotheby's, London, 30 July 1946, lot 33.

559

Dish

1768–70
Diam. 29.7 cm
Mark: fretted square
1957.24.1.105

Blue scale ground with variously decorated reserves around the central fable of 'The Ass and the Little Dog', after no. LXXXI from *Aesop's Fables with His Life: in English, French & Latin* (London 1687) illustrated by Francis Barlow (about 1626–1702).

Painted by Jefferyes Hammett O'Neale, the principal fable and myth painter at the Chelsea factory from about 1751 to 1758. He worked at Worcester from 1768 to 1770, returning to London 1771–3. Distinctive O'Neale features that appear on this dish include the brown rocks in the foreground, the blue hill in the distance, the overhanging eave and the spotted cows and other animals in the smaller panels.

In this fable the ass, who is often beaten, sees his master fondling his lapdog and thinks that if he also gets onto his master's lap, he too will be caressed. This dish shows him attempting to do so, leading to another beating.

PROVENANCE

Sotheby's, London, 21 February 1947, £225.

REFERENCES

Reynolds 1999, pl. 18; for further discussion of O'Neale see Sandon 1993, p. 250; Hanscombe 2010; Bonhams, London, 7 March 2007, lot 173.

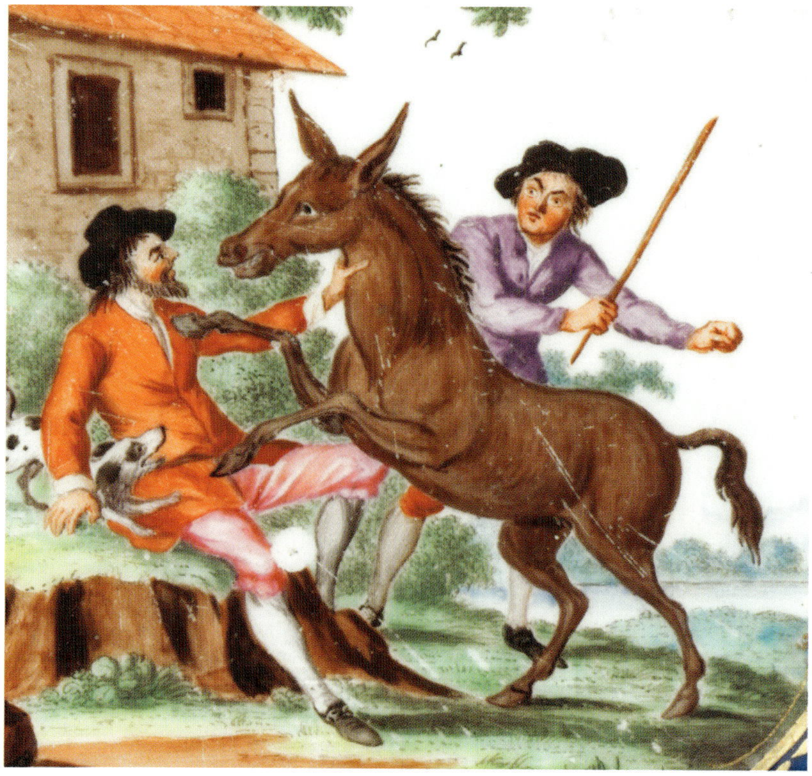

559 (detail)

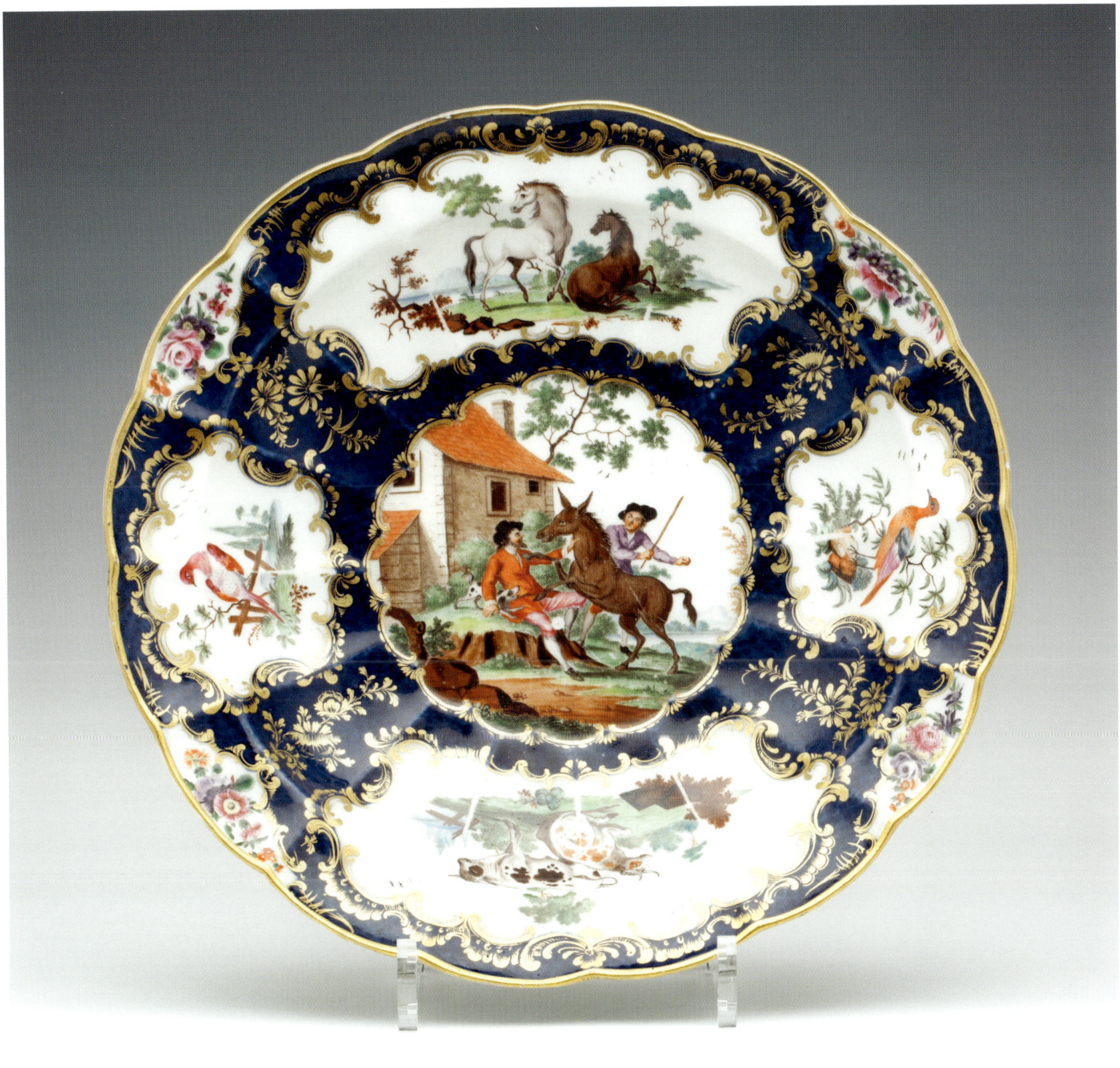

559

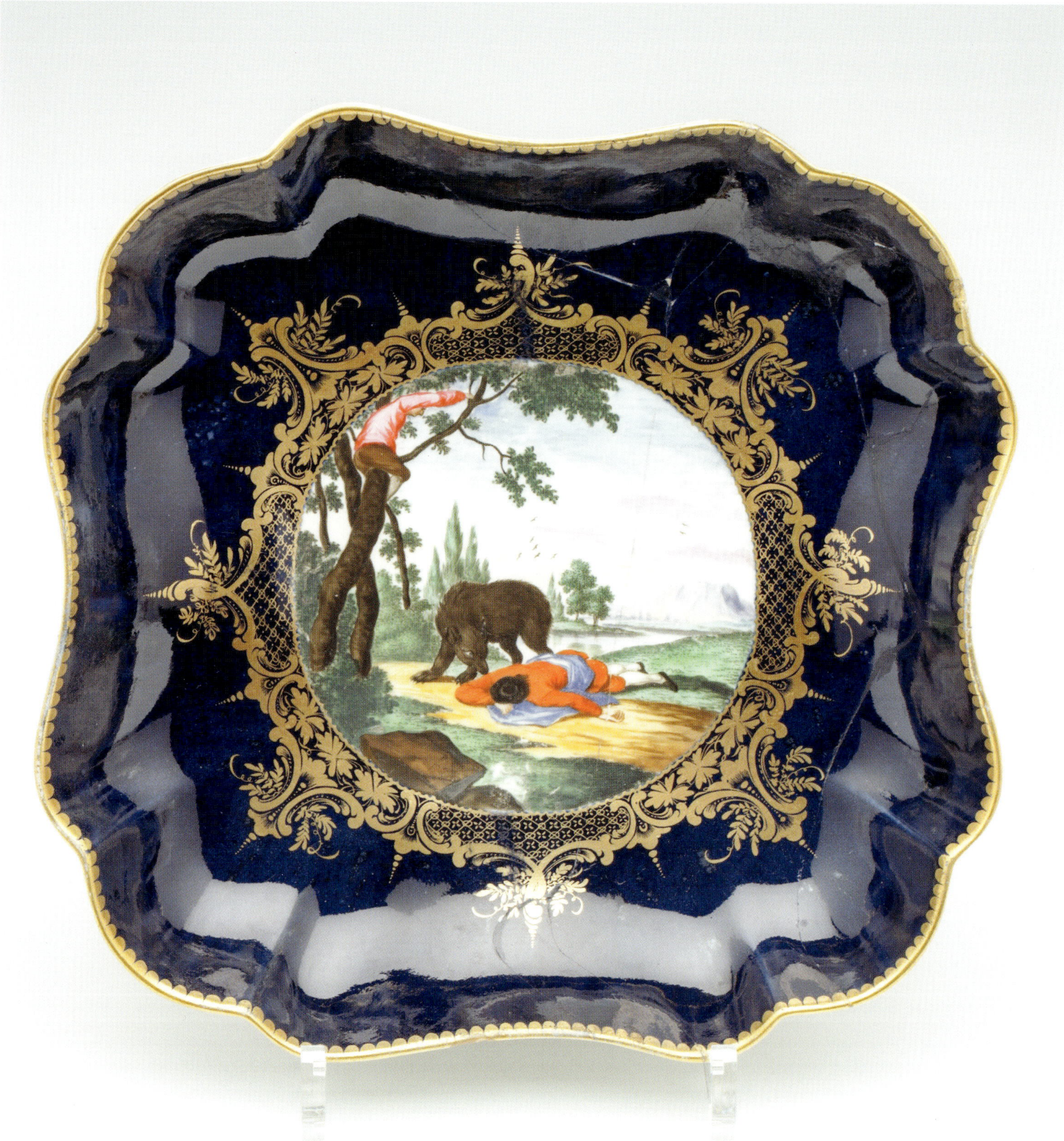

560

560

Dish

About 1770
27 cm square
Mark: fretted square
1957.24.1.145

Fluted square shape; wet blue ground with gilt dentil edge, circular central panel defined by rich diaper and gilt scrolling, painted by Jefferyes Hammett O'Neale with a scene from Aesop's fable of 'The Travellers and The Bear', no. LXXXVII from Barlow's 1687 edition of *Aesop's Fables.*

PROVENANCE
H.W. Hughes Collection; Russell, Baldwin & Bright, Worcester, 6 December 1945, lot 57, £10 10s.

REFERENCES
Marshall 1954, chap. 3; Hanscombe 2010; Crane 2005; Dawson 2007.

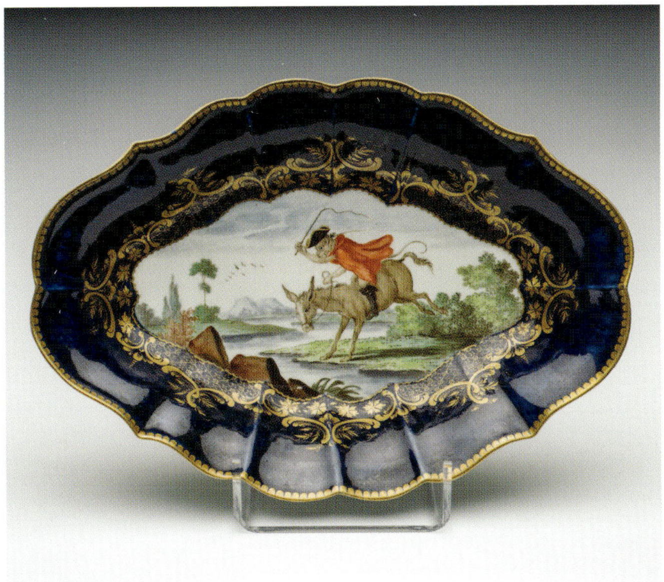

561

561

Dish

About 1768
Length 23.7 cm, width 17 cm
Mark: fretted square
1957.24.1.130

Lozenge shape; fluted wet blue border with gilt dentil edge; centre, defined by rich gilding, decorated by Jefferyes Hammett O'Neale with a scene from the fable of 'The Monkey and the Ass': monkey in a red coat with upraised whip trying to force donkey to cross stream.

PROVENANCE
Mrs V.M. Rayner; Sotheby's, London, 17 March 1950, lot 26, £150 (pair).

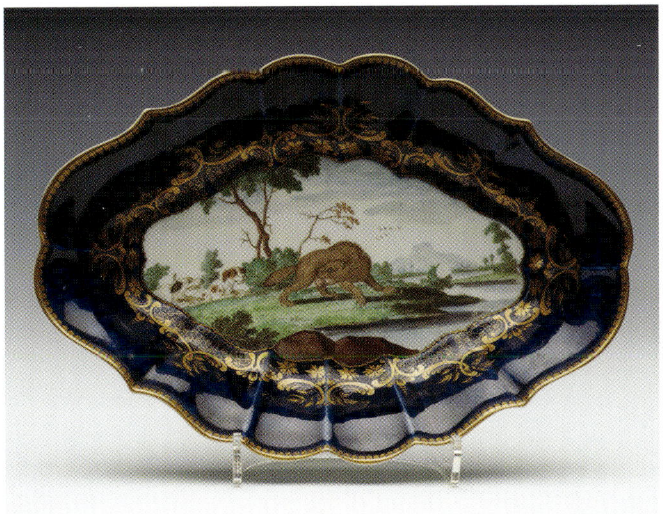

562

562

Dish

About 1768
Length 24 cm, width 16.6 cm
Mark: fretted square
1957.24.1.124

Lozenge shape; fluted wet blue border with gilt dentil edge, centre, defined by rich gilding, painted by Jefferyes Hammett O'Neale with a scene from the fable of 'The Hunted Beaver', no. XIX from Barlow's 1687 edition of *Aesop's Fables.*

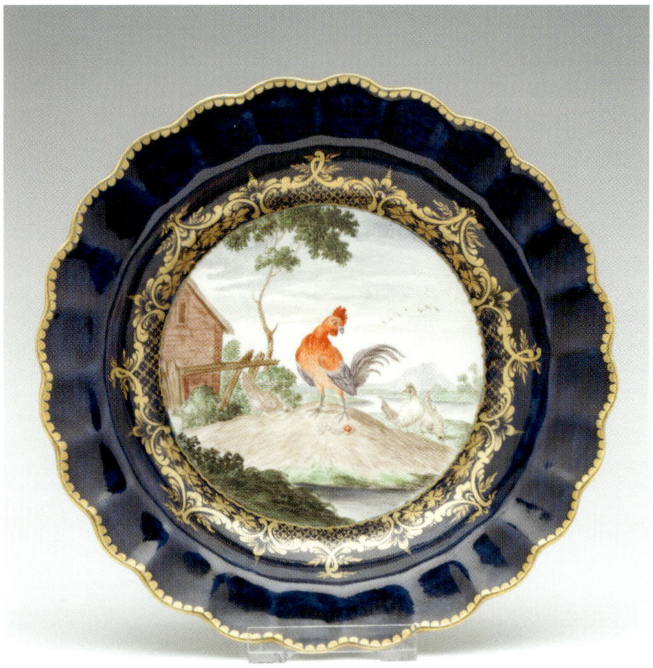

563

563

Plate

About 1768
Diam. 19 cm
Mark: fretted square
1957.24.1.117

Scalloped, gilt dentil edge, wet blue border, central circular reserve surrounded by rich gilding, painted by Jefferyes Hammett O'Neale with a scene from the fable of 'The Cock and the Precious Stone', no. I from Barlow's 1687 edition of *Aesop's Fables*.

PROVENANCE
Christie's, London, 21 April 1953, lot 91 (pair), £189.

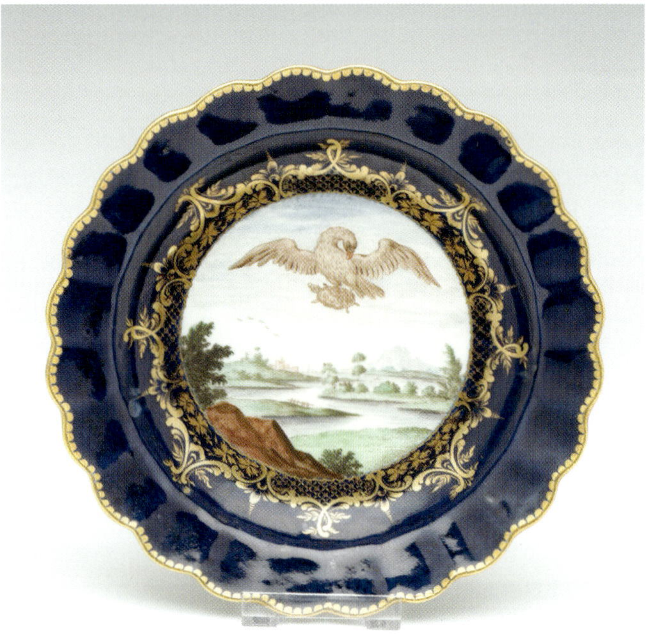

564

564

Plate

About 1768
Diam. 19 cm
Mark: fretted square
1957.24.1.121

A pair with no. 563, painted by Jefferyes Hammett O'Neale with a scene from the fable of 'The Tortoise and the Eagle', CX from Barlow's 1687 edition of *Aesop's Fables*.

PROVENANCE
Christie's, London, 21 April 1953, lot 91 (pair), £189.

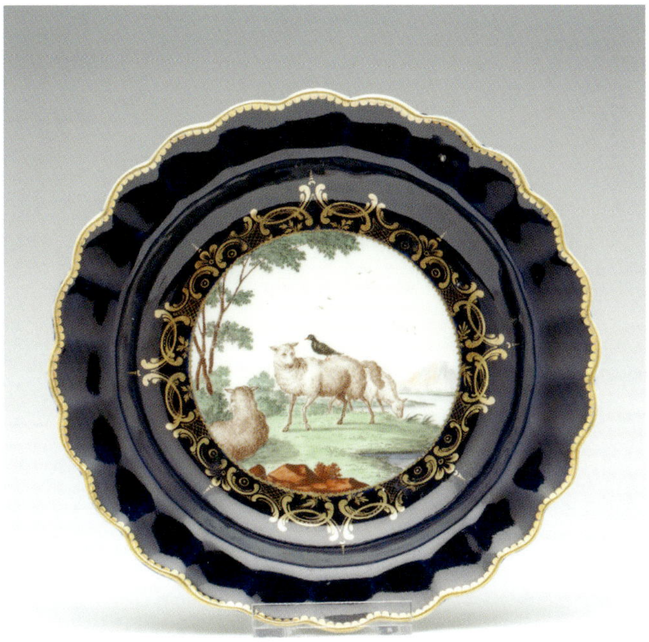

565

565

Plate

About 1768
Diam. 19.1 cm
Mark: fretted square
1957.24.1.136

Fluted wet blue border, gilt dentil edge, rich gilding surrounds central panel painted by Jefferyes Hammett O'Neale with scene of three sheep, one with a black bird with red legs and a beak on its back (source unknown).

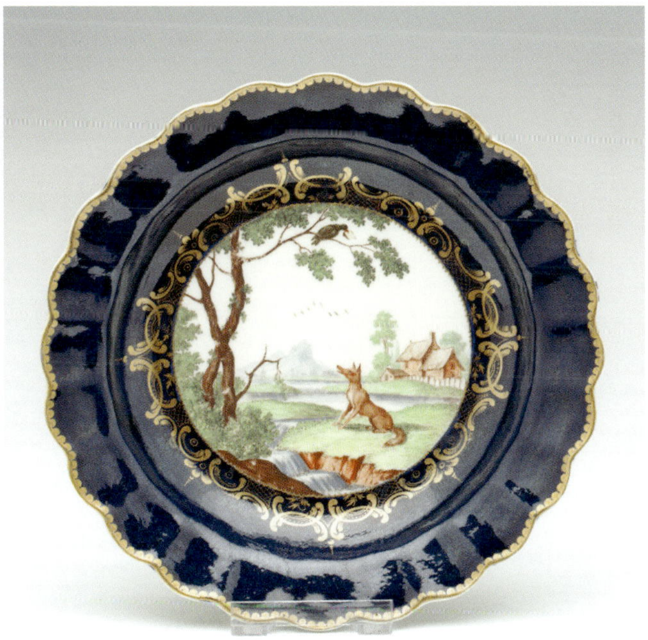

566

566

Plate

About 1768
Diam. 19.2 cm
Mark: fretted square
1957.24.1.132

A pair with no. 565, painted by Jefferyes Hammett O'Neale with a scene from the fable of 'The Fox and the Crow', LXVII from Barlow's 1687 edition of *Aesop's Fables*.

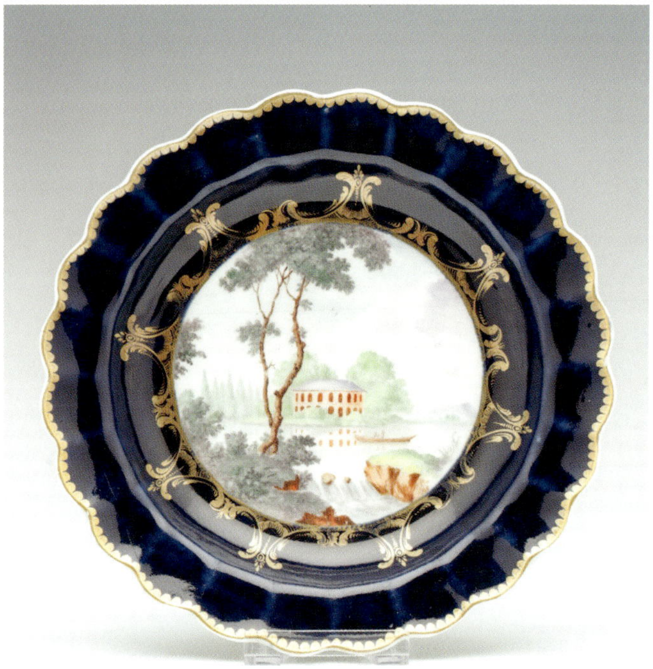

567

567

Plate

About 1770
Diam. 19.2 cm
Mark: fretted square
1957.24.1.131

Scalloped, gilt dentil edge, wet blue border with gilding surrounds central circular panel painted by Jefferyes Hammett O'Neale with a lake scene, including a domed rotunda on an island and a boat with two figures in the foreground. A pair with no. 568.

In addition to his depictions of fables, O'Neale also specialised in landscapes such as this one, some with prominent ruins, which had become fashionable as a result of interest in the Grand Tour. Characteristic features are his treatment of trees and a cascading waterfall. Barret 1958, pl. 80, illustrates a vase with a waterfall, signed *O'Neale inv. & c.*

PROVENANCE
Darcy Taylor; Sotheby's, London, 9 April 1957, lot 38 (pair).

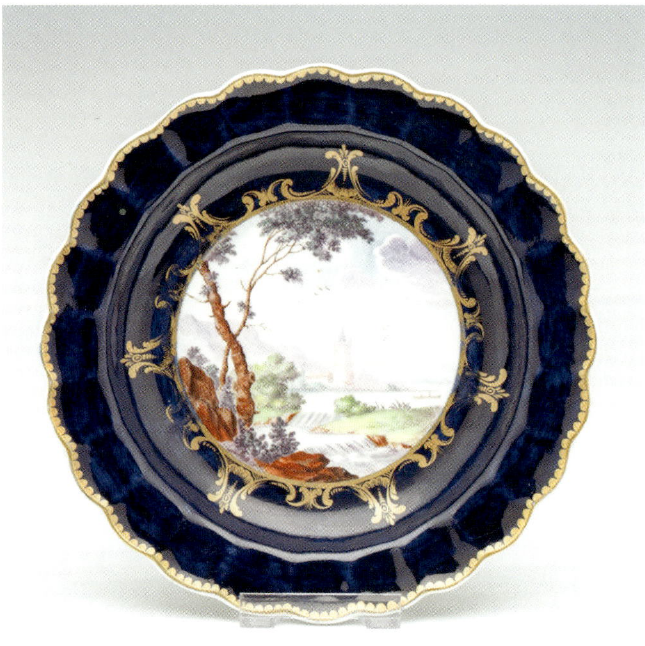

568

568

Plate

About 1770
Diam. 19.1 cm
Mark: fretted square
1957.24.1.137

A pair with no. 567, central panel painted by Jefferyes Hammett O'Neale with a lake scene with castle in the distance, a waterfall and brown rocks in the foreground.

PROVENANCE
Darcy Taylor; Sotheby's, London, 9 April 1957, lot 38 (pair).

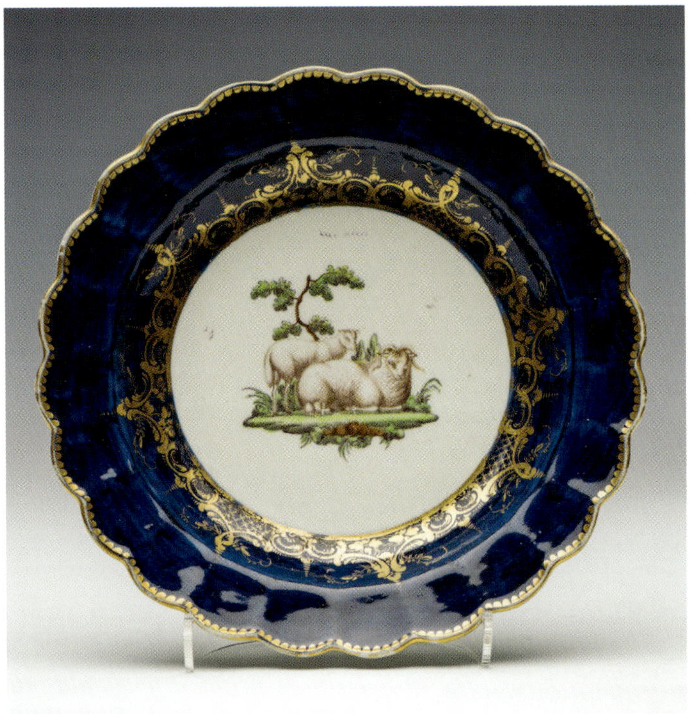

569

569

Plate

1780–85
Diam. 19.6 cm
Mark: crescent
1957.24.1.148

Scalloped, gilt dentil edge, wet blue border with rich gilding surrounding painting of seated ram with standing ewe behind. A pair with no. 570.

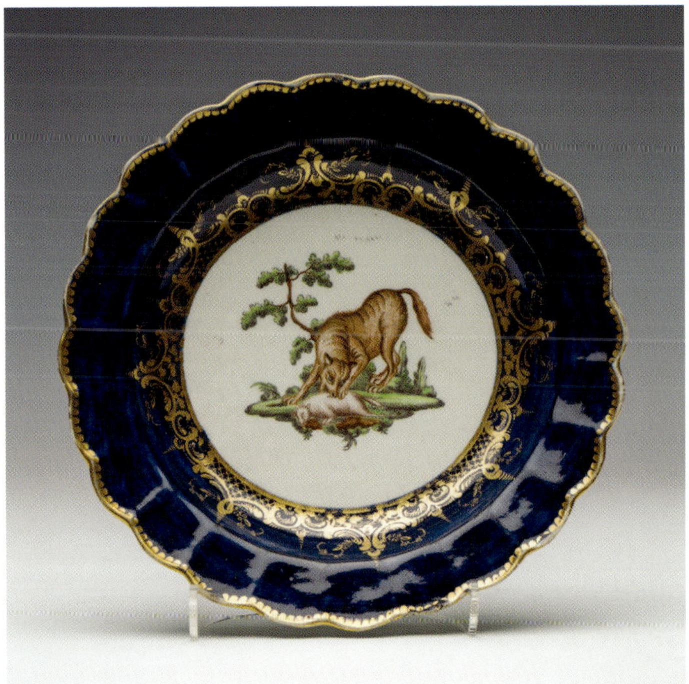

570

570

Plate

1780–85
Diam. 19.9 cm
Mark: crescent
1957.24.1.146

Scalloped, gilt dentil edge, wet blue border with rich gilding surrounding painting of a wolf eating a lamb. A pair with no. 569.

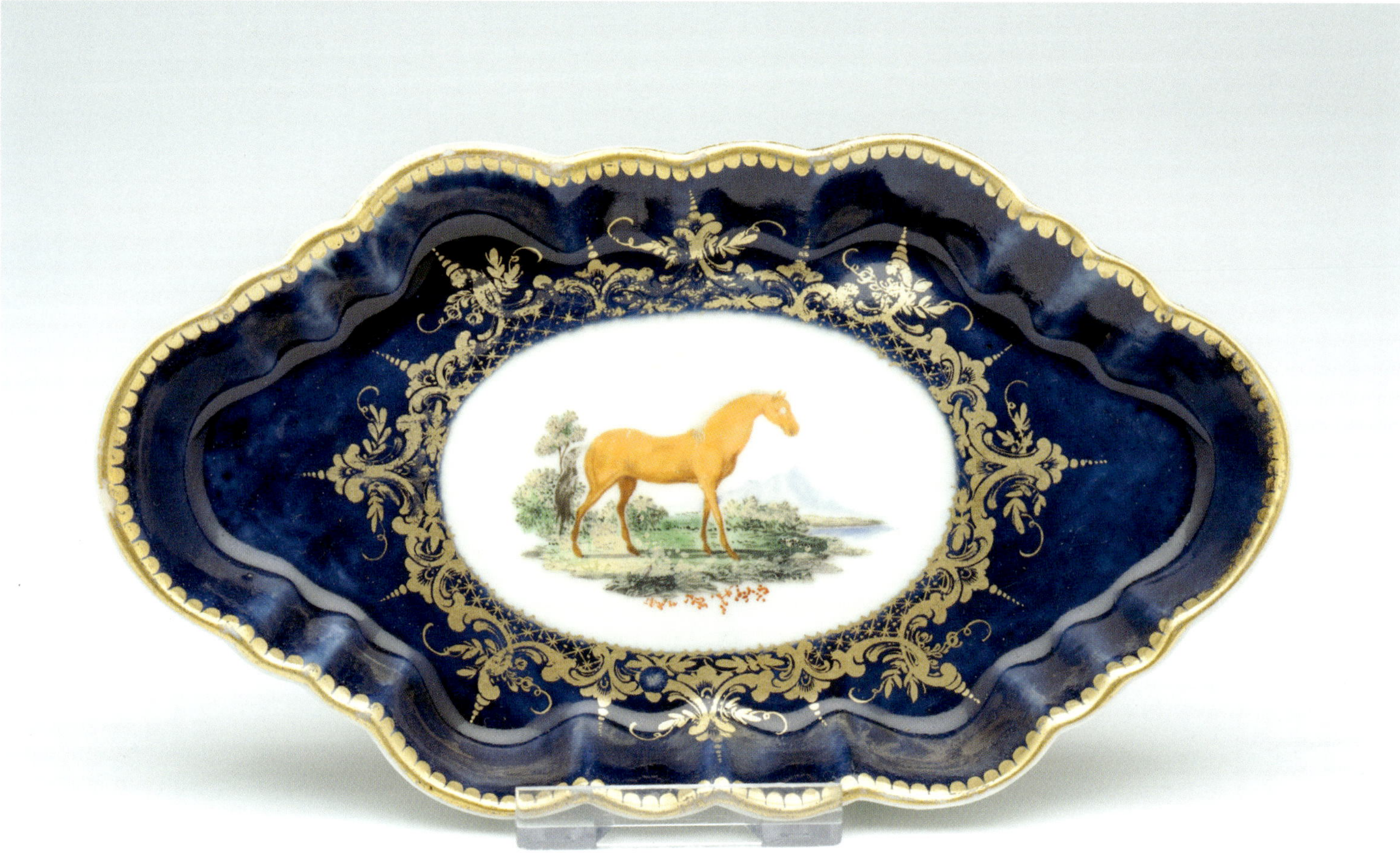

571

571

Spoon tray

1770–72
Length 15.2 cm
Mark: fretted square
1957.24.1.701

Gilt dentil edge; wet blue ground, rich arabesque gilding around oval reserve painted with a chestnut horse. Teawares such as this were possibly painted by Jefferyes Hammett O' Neale, but more likely by a follower. Possibly from the same service are a tea canister illustrated in Spero and Sandon 1996, pl. 323, a coffee cup and saucer in Bonhams, London, 7 March 2007, lot 172 and a teapot and covered milk jug in the Museum of Royal Worcester Porcelain, inv. 1131 (figs 30–33).

PROVENANCE

H.W. Hughes Collection, 12 February 1944, no. 231.

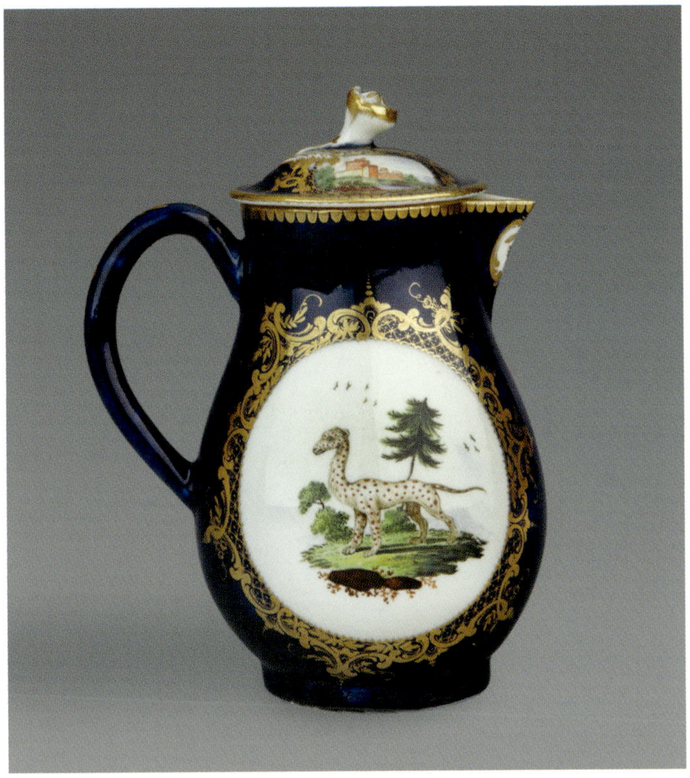

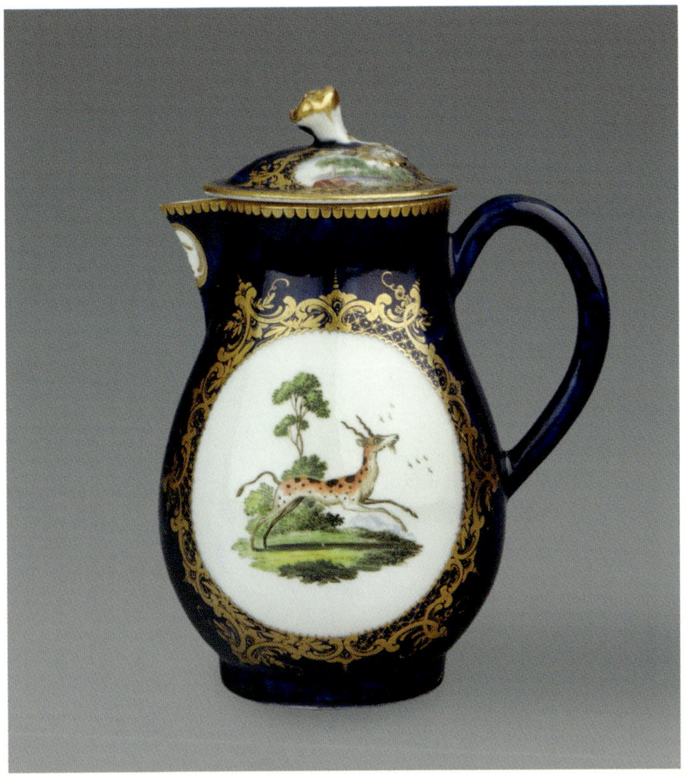

Figs 30–31 Covered milk jug, painted with a cameleopard, possibly by Jefferyes Hammett O'Neale. © Museum of Royal Worcester Porcelain, no. 1131

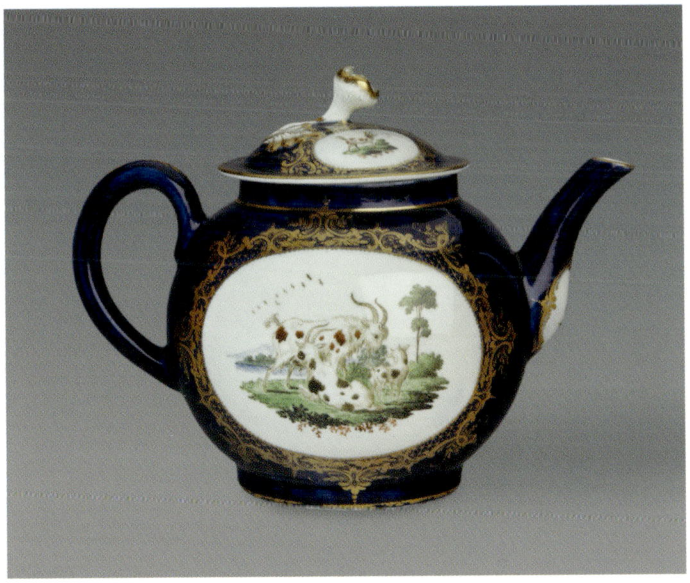

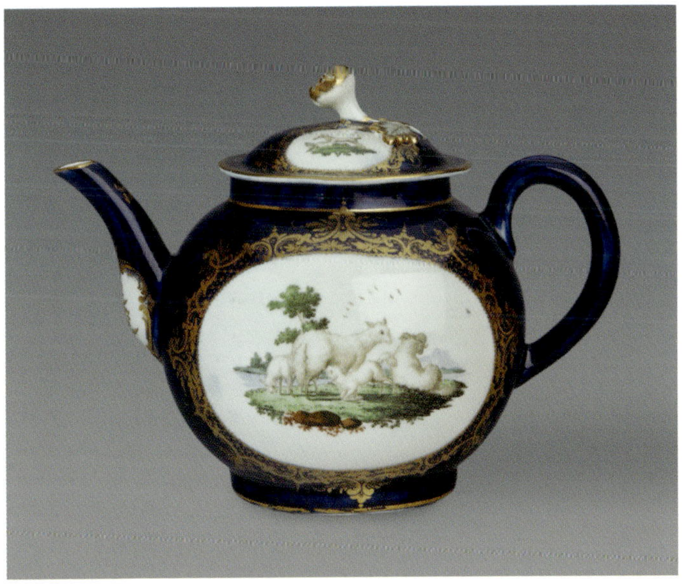

Figs 32–33 Teapot painted with domestic animals, possibly by Jefferyes Hammett O'Neale. © Museum of Royal Worcester Porcelain, no. 1130

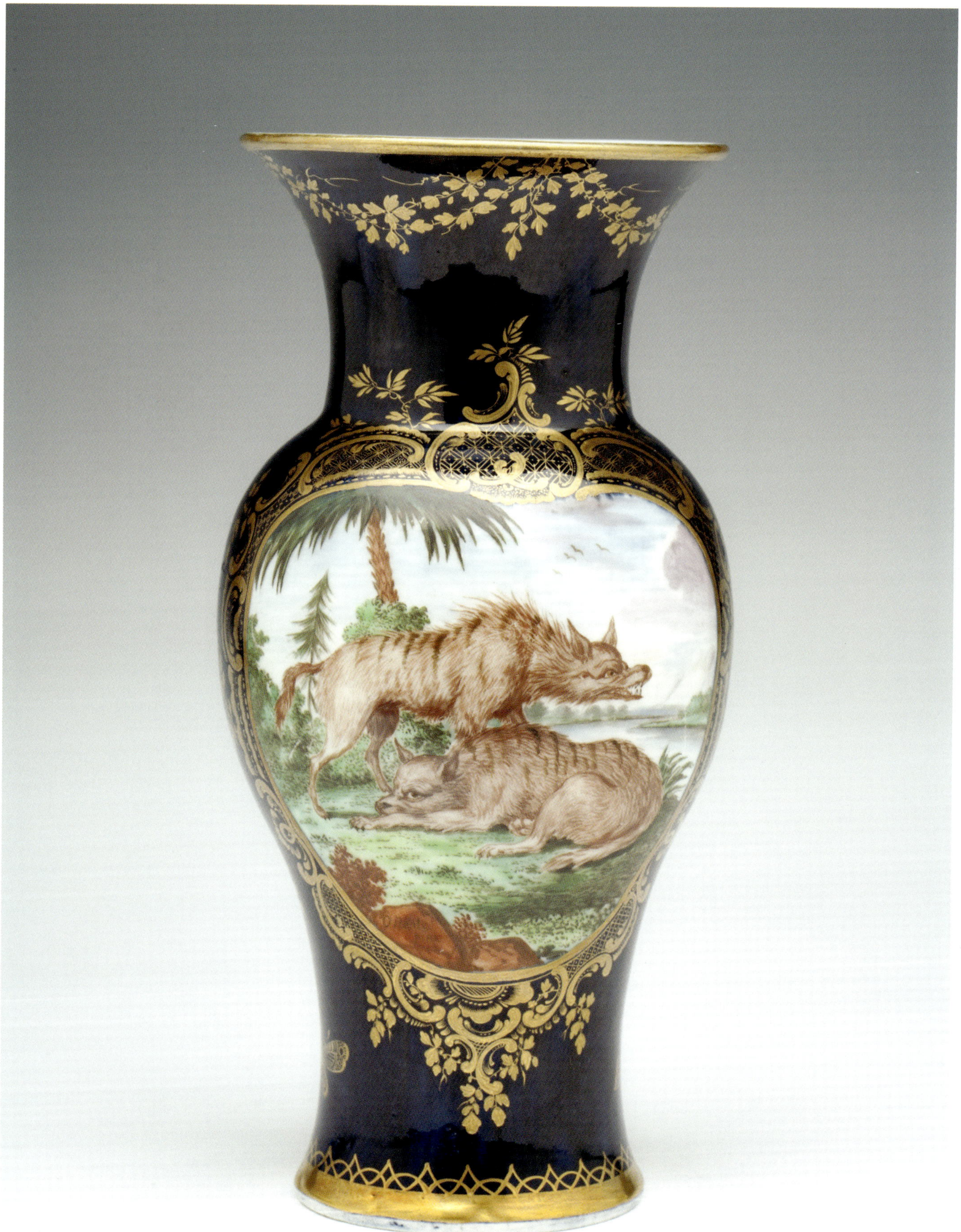

572

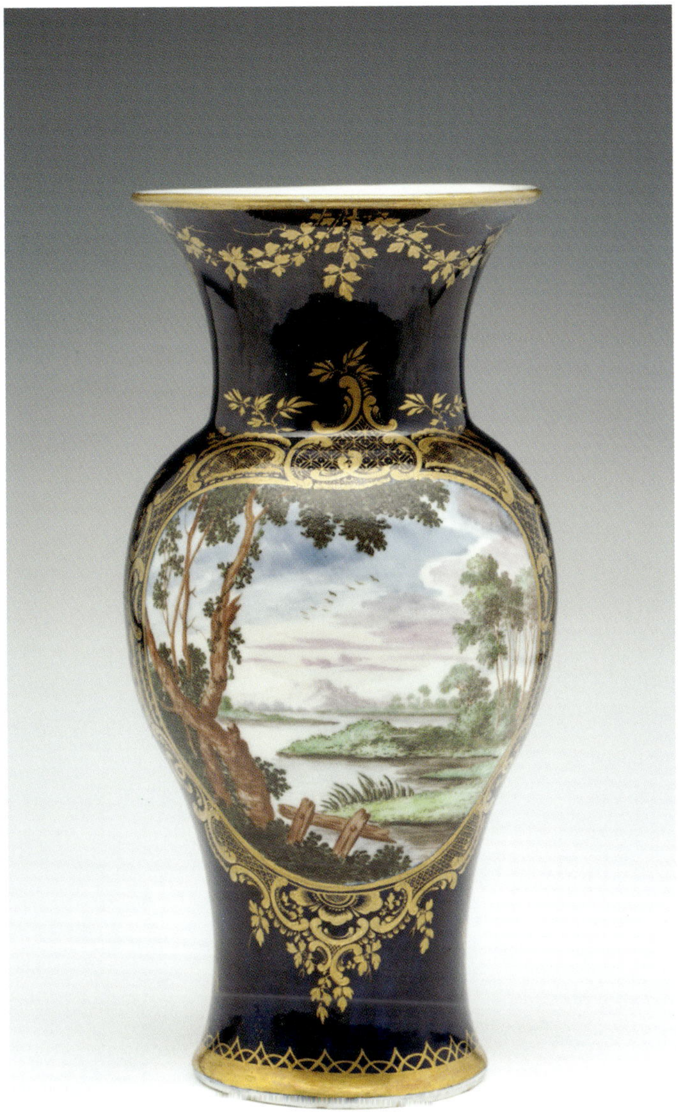

572

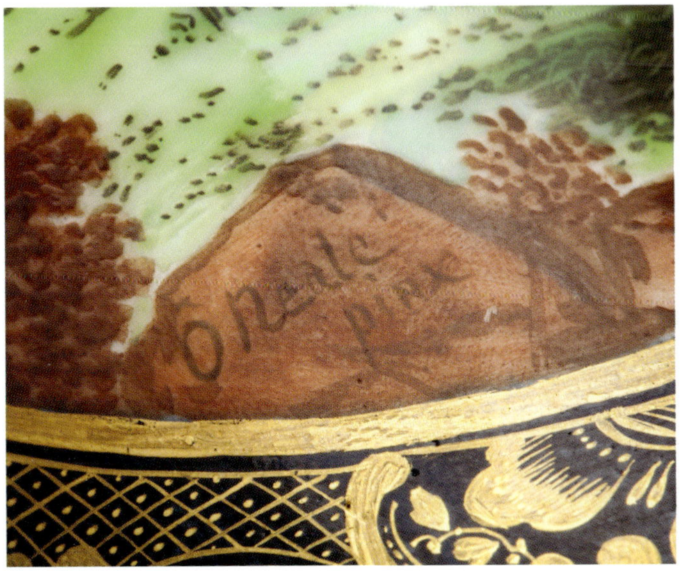

572 (detail showing signature 'O'Neale pinx')

572

Vase

1768–70
Ht 22.3 cm
Mark: fretted square
1957.24.1.104

Baluster shape with flared neck; wet blue ground enriched with gilding; one heart-shaped reserve painted with a watery landscape, distant blue-grey mountains with purple clouds above, the other with two hyenas and the signature *O'Neale pinx* on brown rock on left.

PROVENANCE
J. Rochelle Thomas of Torquay and Sevenoaks, 30 April 1943, £225.

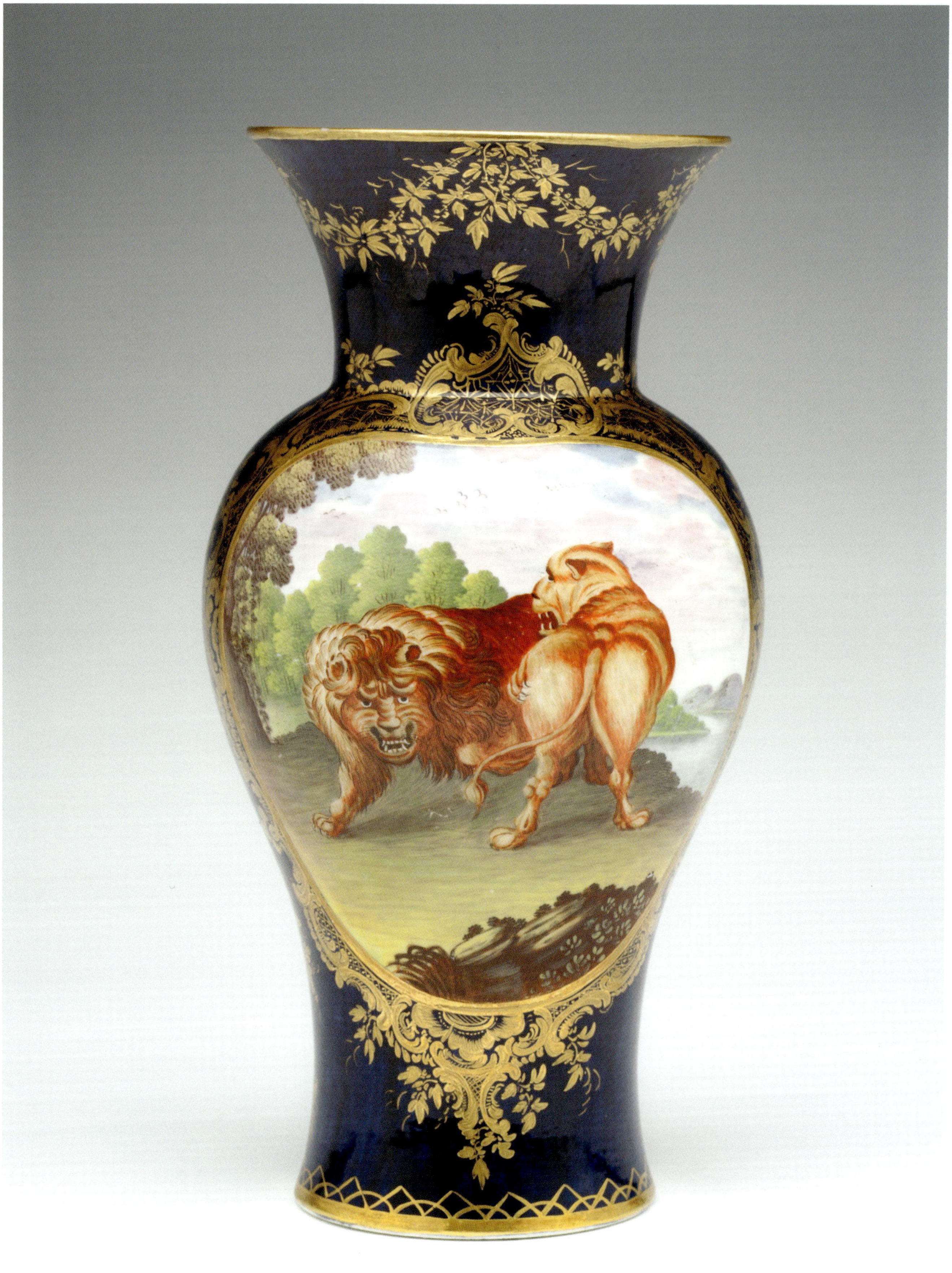

573

573

Vase

1768–70
Ht 20.9 cm
1957.24.1.106

Baluster shape with flared neck; wet blue ground enriched with gilding. Decorated by Jefferyes Hammett O'Neale with, in one reserve, a landscape with water, a distant hill with a tower, purple and white clouds above; in the other, a lion and lioness.

Nos. 572 and 573 were considered by Marshall to be a pair, but the height and gilding differ.

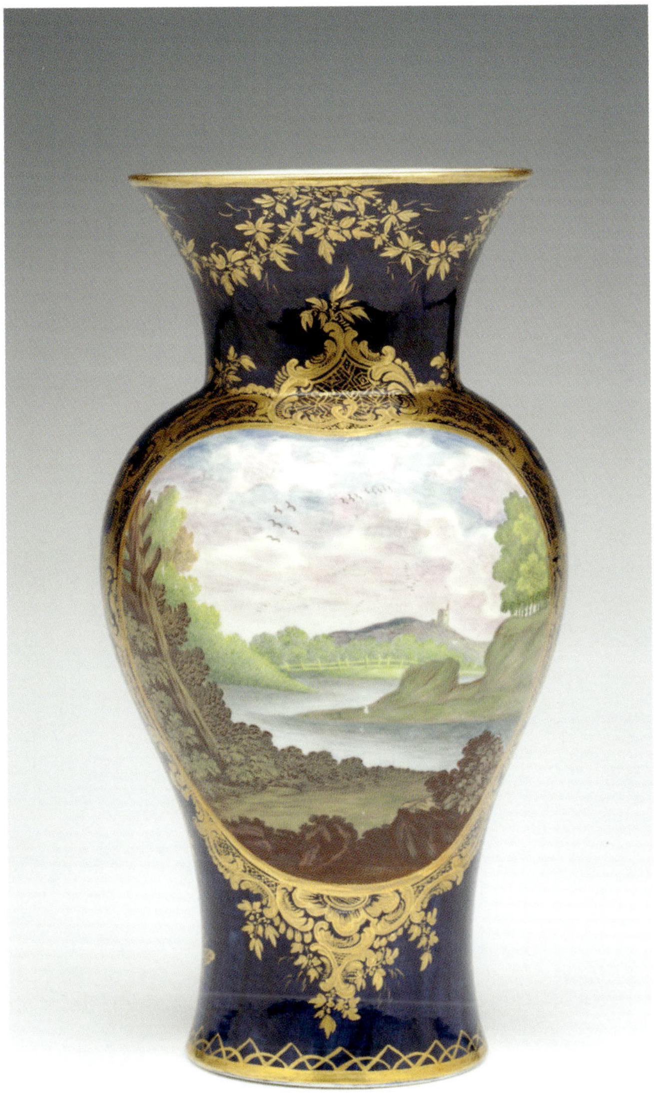

573

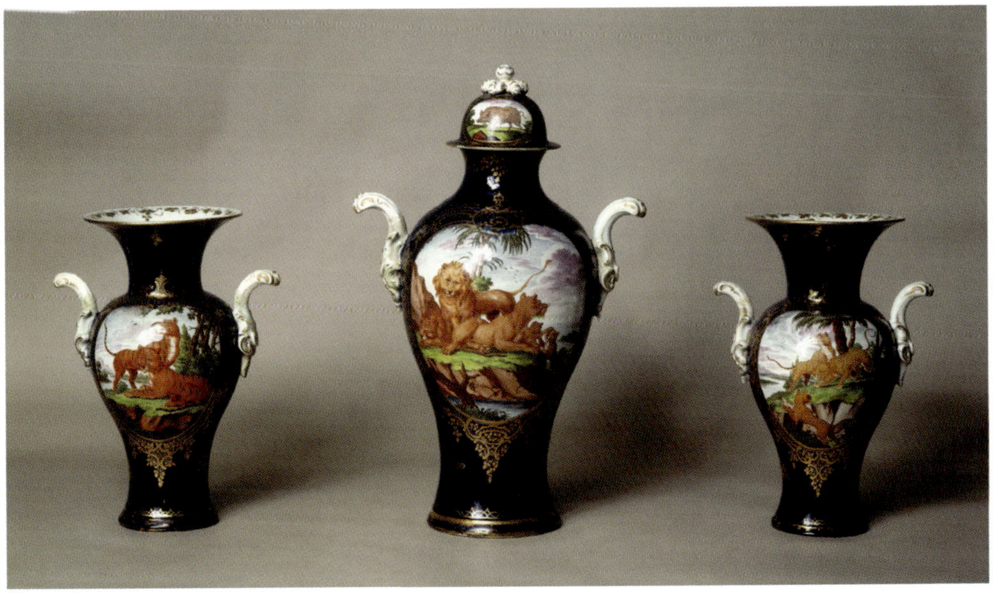

Fig. 34 Garniture of three vases decorated by Jefferyes Hammett O'Neale, *c.*1770. Mount Vernon, USA, W-972/A and B, W-2260. Courtesy of Mount Vernon Ladies' Association

Donated in 1786 by Samuel Vaughan, an English merchant, for George Washington's 'New Room', the large dining room at Mount Vernon, to be placed on the Italian mantelpiece that he had previously given.

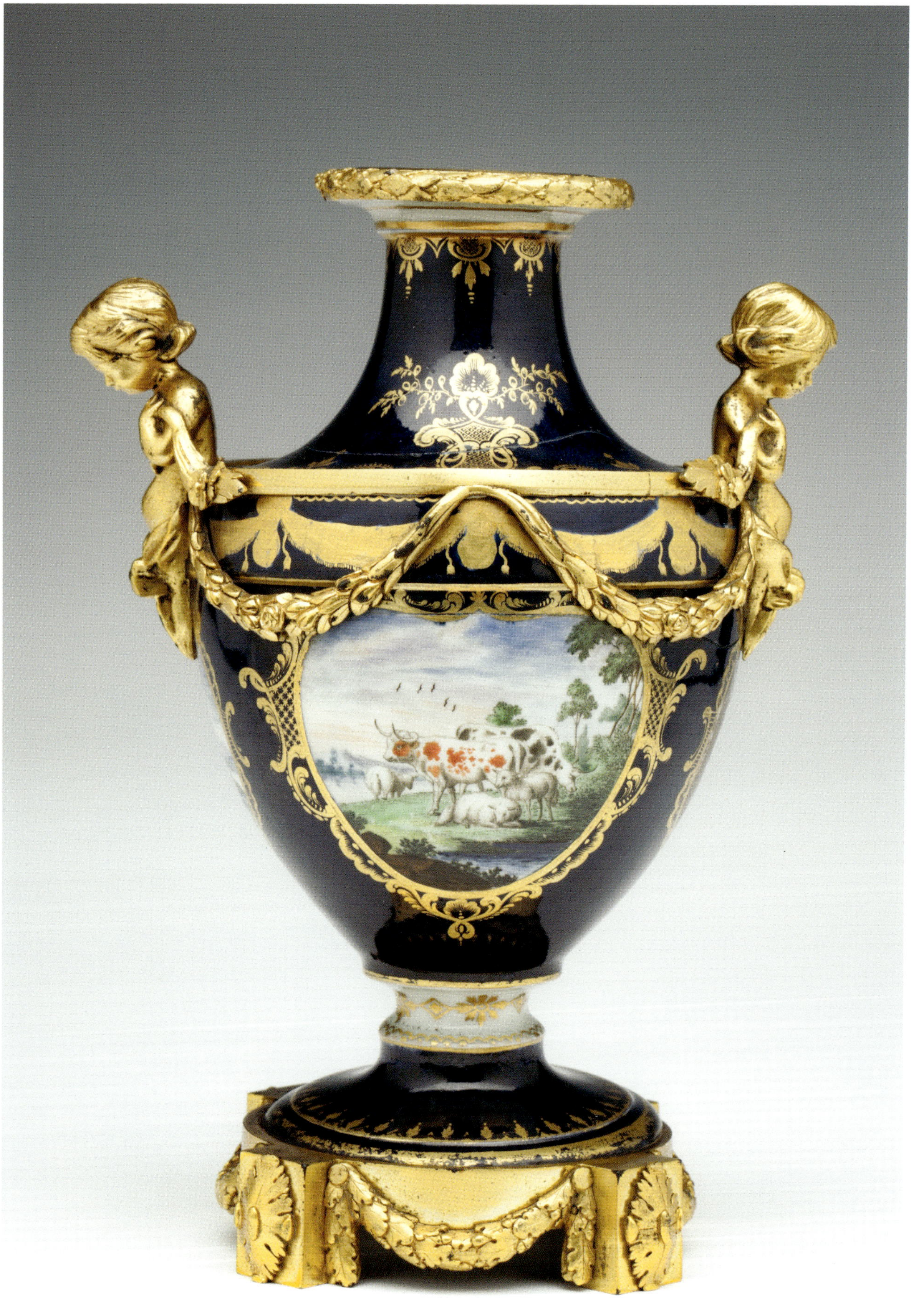

574

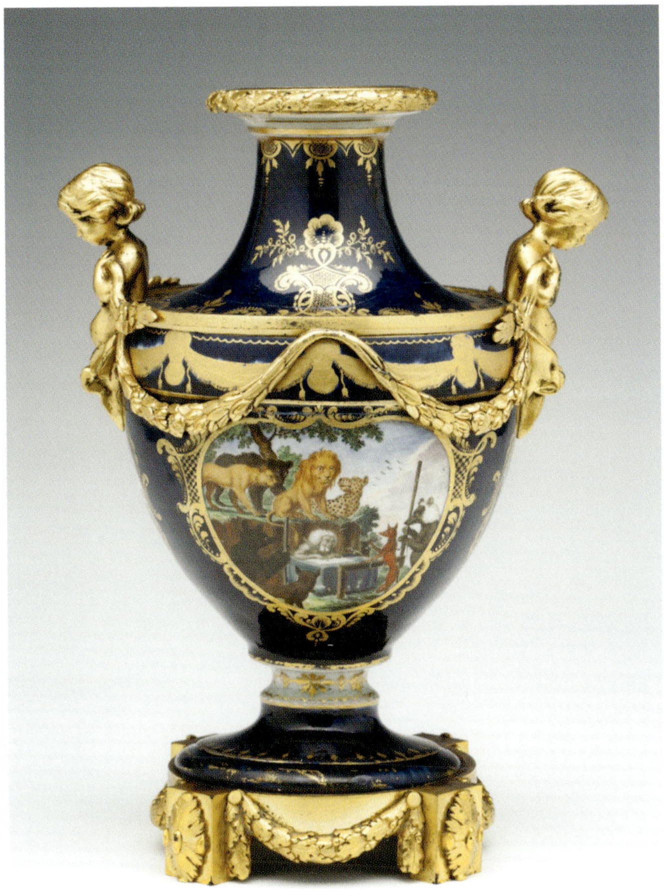

574

Vase

1768–70
Ht 24.5 cm
1957.24.1.107

Neoclassical urn shape decorated by O'Neale; deep wet blue ground with two large heart-shaped panels, one painted with 'The Trial of the Fox' by a monkey judge, the other with spotted cows and sheep; two oval panels under handles, one with an obelisk and the other with a landscape. The ormolu mount was probably added about 1840.

The source of this scene is unknown; a fable of 'The Trial of the Fox' appears as no. V of *Thirteen Moral Fables* by poet Robert Henryson (1425–1500) of Dunfermline, Scotland.

574

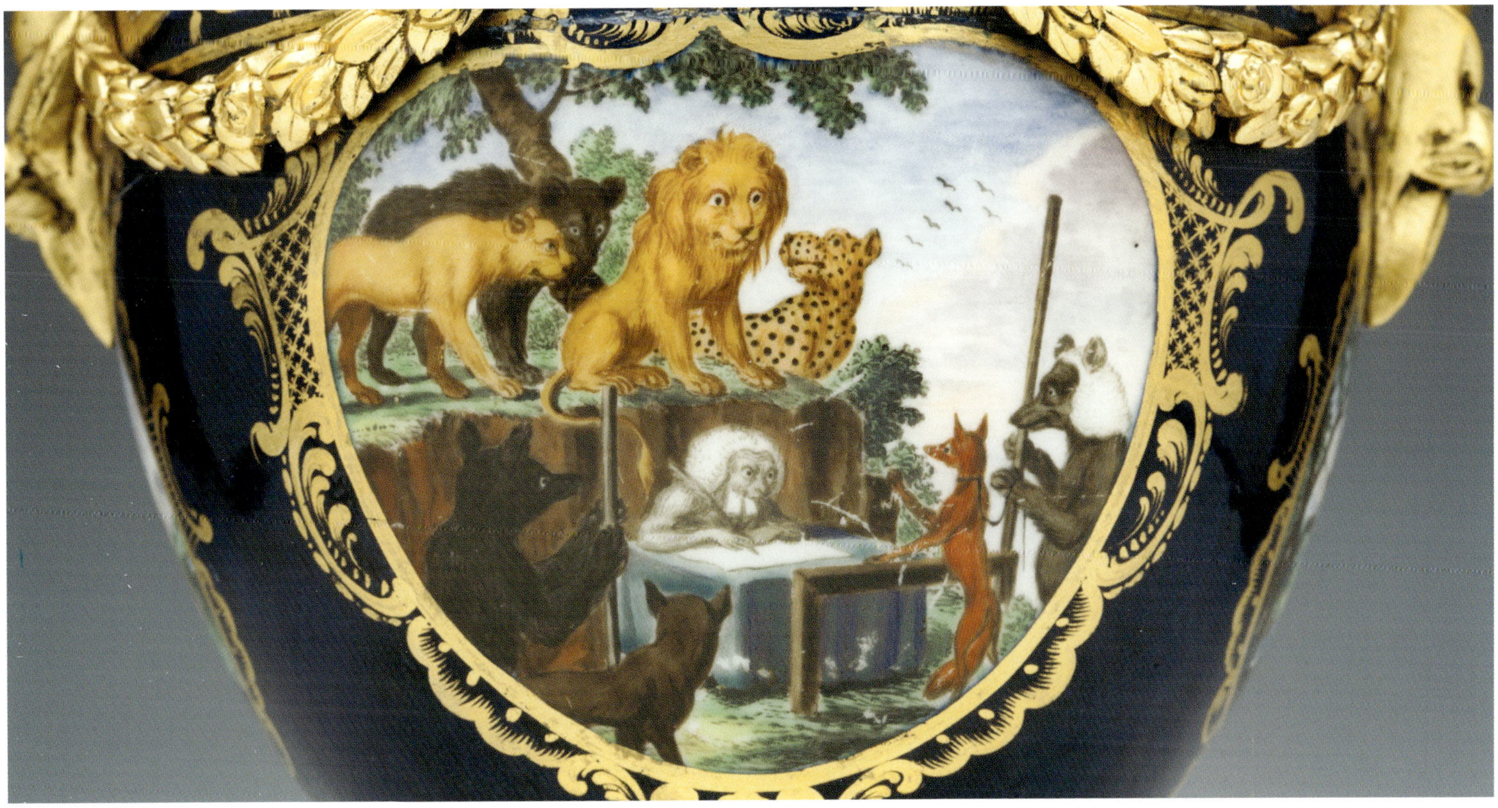

574 (detail)

TRIO OF VASES (575–577)

All painted by John Donaldson with equestrian scenes in the style of Philips Wouwerman of Haarlem (1619–1668). After painting fruit, flowers, landscapes and figures in his home city, Donaldson moved to London in 1760 where he mainly painted portraits and miniatures, and also made etchings. Soon after his arrival he began to decorate Chelsea porcelain and is mentioned in Boswell's London Journal for Friday, 4 March 1763 as 'a kind of speculative being and must forsooth controvert established systems…'. According to Barrett, 'a favourite rich puce, the stippling of the cheeks, well delineated features and lush foliage' are typical of Donaldson's work.

PROVENANCE
Charles J. Dickins Collection sale, 1879; Christies, London, 22 November 1950, lot 4, £1,260.

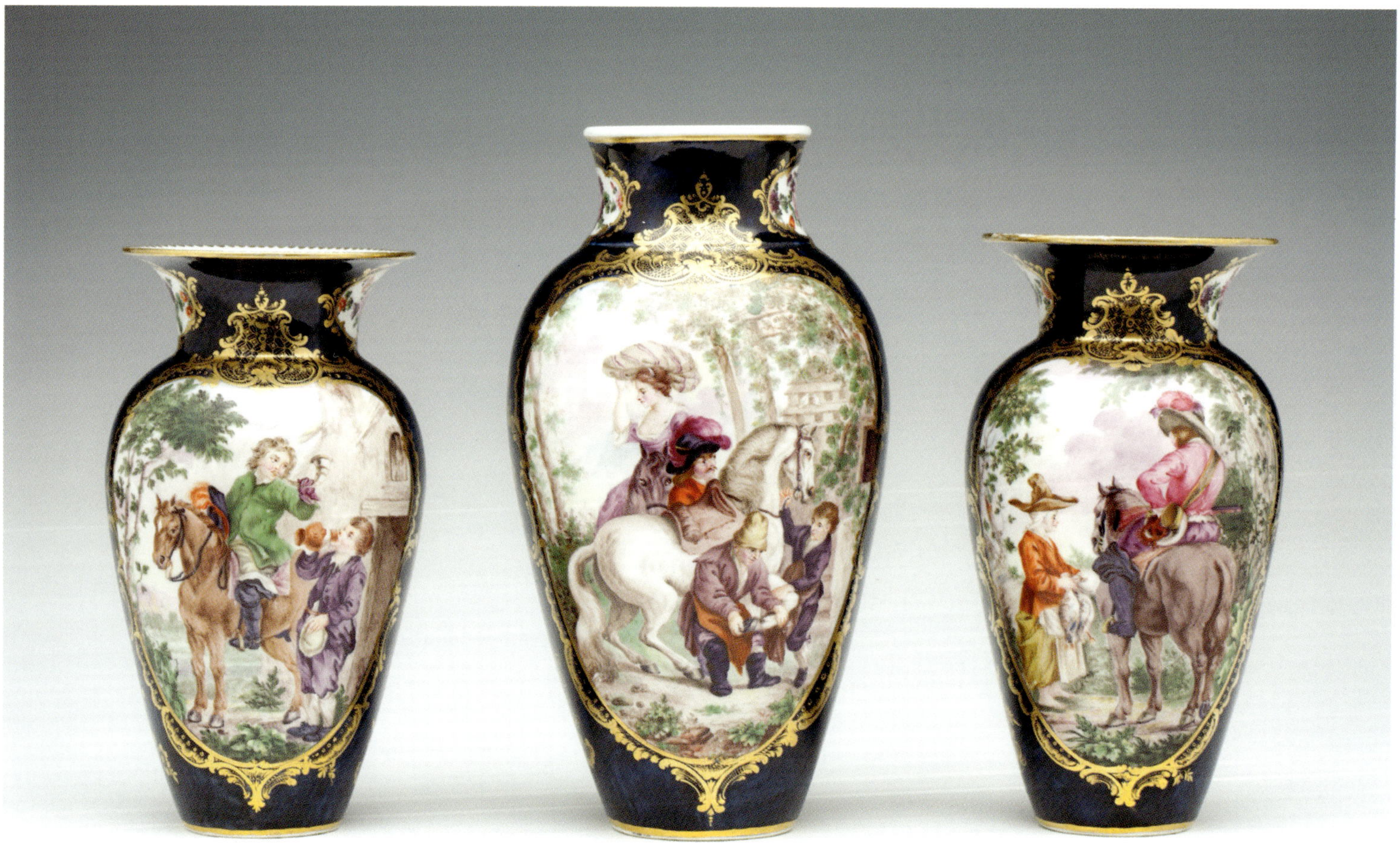

575–577

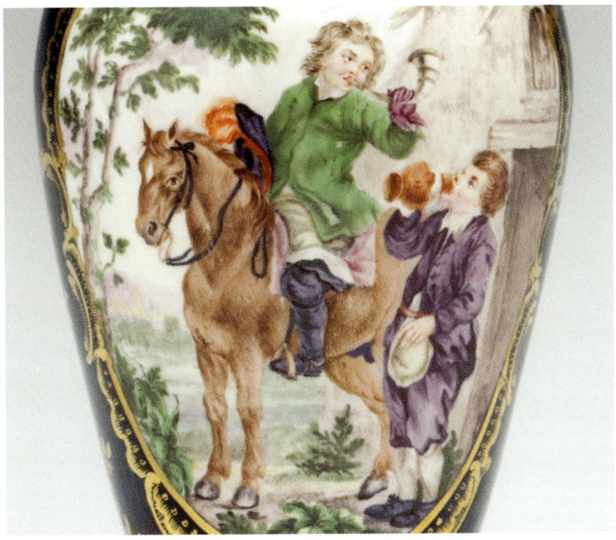

575 (detail)

575

Vase

About 1770
Ht 17.5 cm
Mark: fretted square
1957.24.1.115

Ovoid shape, wet blue ground, gilt dentil rim; oval reserve defined by gilt scrolling with horn player in green doublet on brown horse, boy drinking from mug standing nearby, European flowers on reverse.

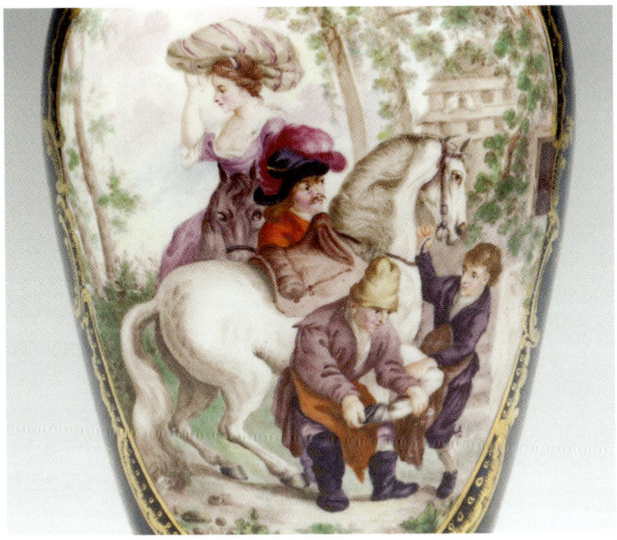

576 (detail)

576

Vase

About 1770
Ht 21.2 cm
Mark: fretted square
1957.24.1.119

Ovoid shape, wet blue ground, gilt dentil rim; oval reserve with white horse held by boy whilst being shod, cavalier and lady stand behind, European flowers on reverse. The rim is plain, indicating a missing cover.

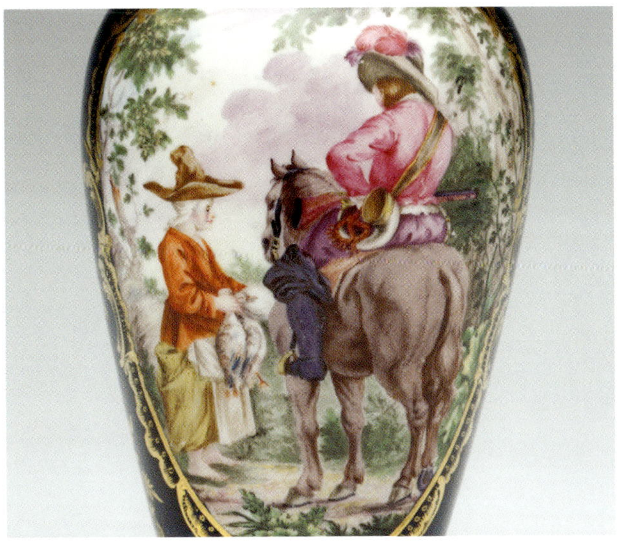

577 (detail)

577

Vase

About 1770
Ht 17.5 cm
Mark: fretted square
1957.24.1.123

Ovoid shape, wet blue ground, gilt dentil rim; oval reserve with mounted horseman talking to woman with ducks, European flowers on reverse.

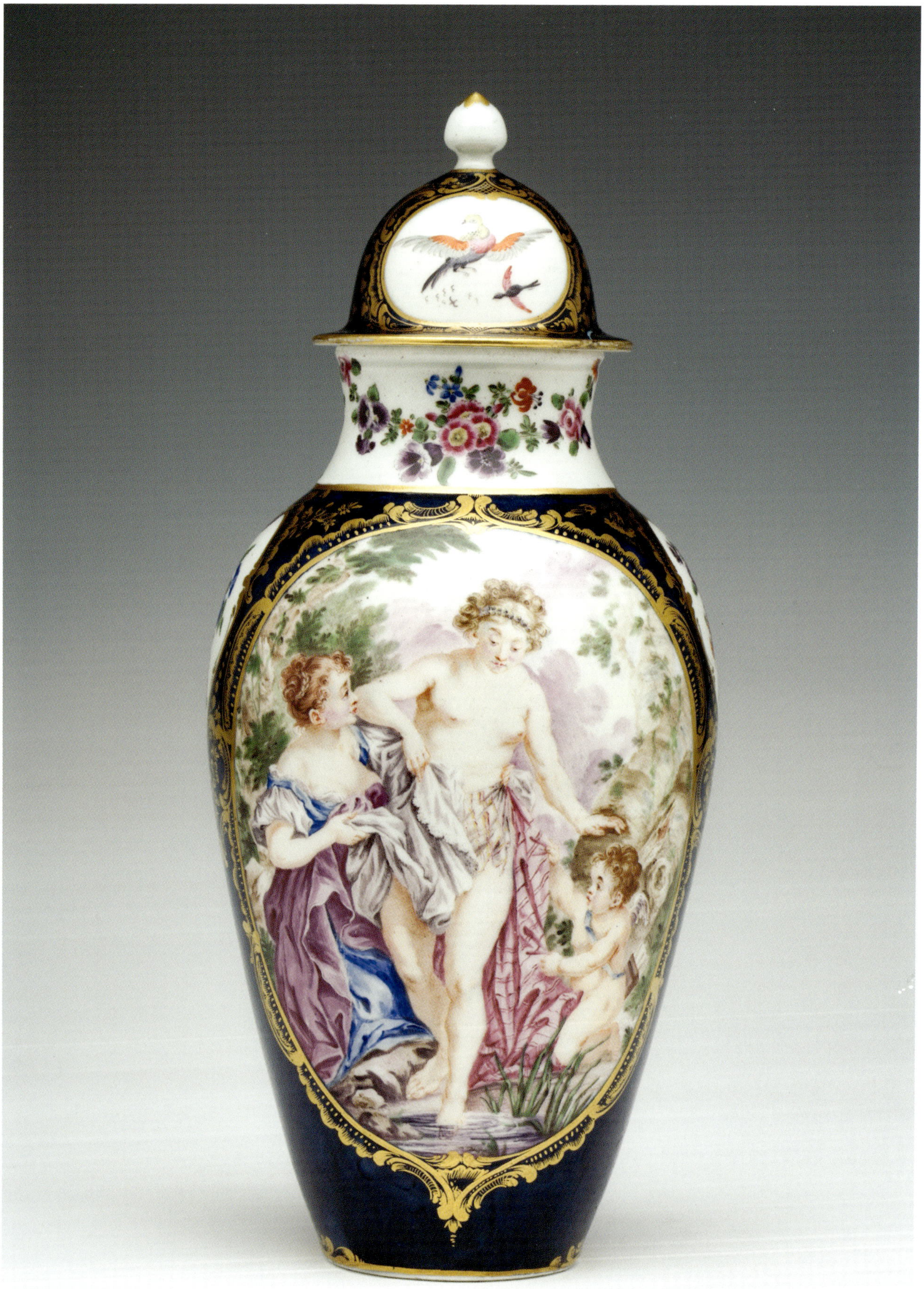

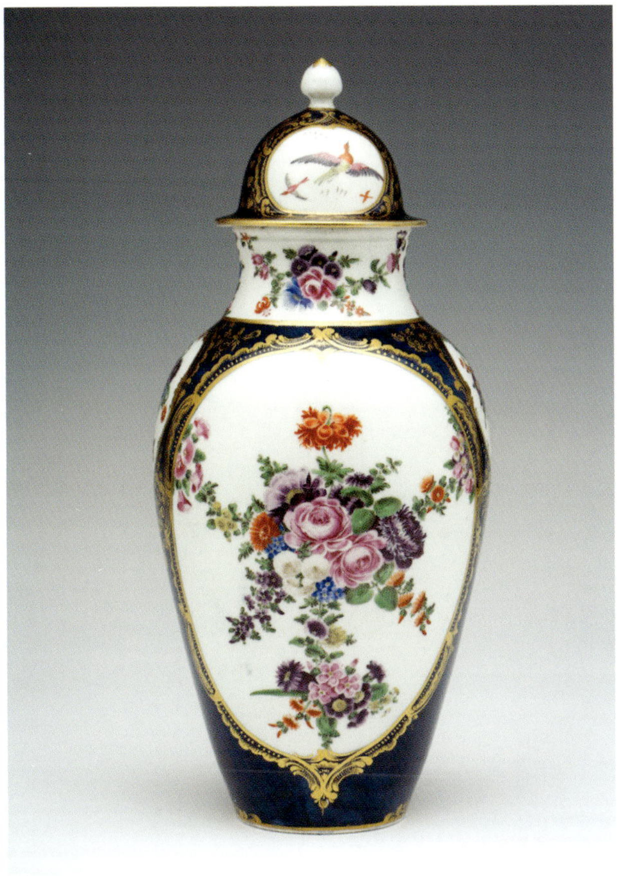

578

578

Vase

1768–70
Ht 26.7 cm (with cover)
Mark: fretted square
1957.24.1.134

Ovoid, white neck with floral wreaths; on shoulders, two small heart-shaped panels; oval panels on either side enclosed by wet blue ground with gilding, painted by John Donaldson, one with a lady bathing based on *The Bather* by François le Moyne (1688–1737), painted in 1724 and now in The Hermitage, Leningrad (fig. 35). Replacement cover.

A garniture of three similar vases signed by Donaldson (fig. 36) is in the Museum of Royal Worcester Porcelain: these are painted with scenes after François Boucher's *Birth of Bacchus*, *Leda and the Swan* and *Europa and the Bull*.

PROVENANCE
H.W. Hughes Collection, 12 February 1944, lot 4, £100.

REFERENCES
Reynolds 1999, pl. 19; Museum of Royal Worcester Porcelain, inv. 1126.

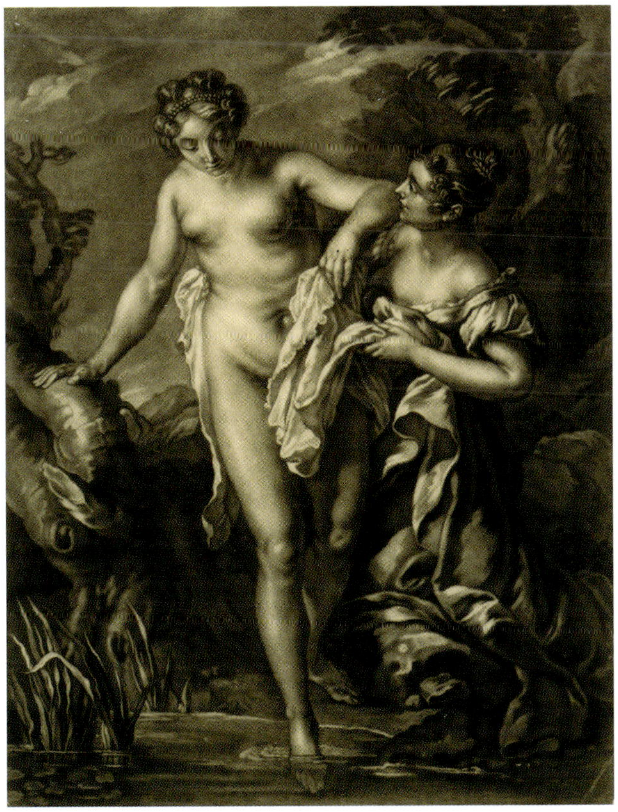

Fig 35 Laurent Cars after François le Moyne, *The Bather* (The Hermitage, Leningrad), mezzotint, 1731, reproduced by J. Johnson. © The Trustees of the British Museum, London, 1881,0611.276

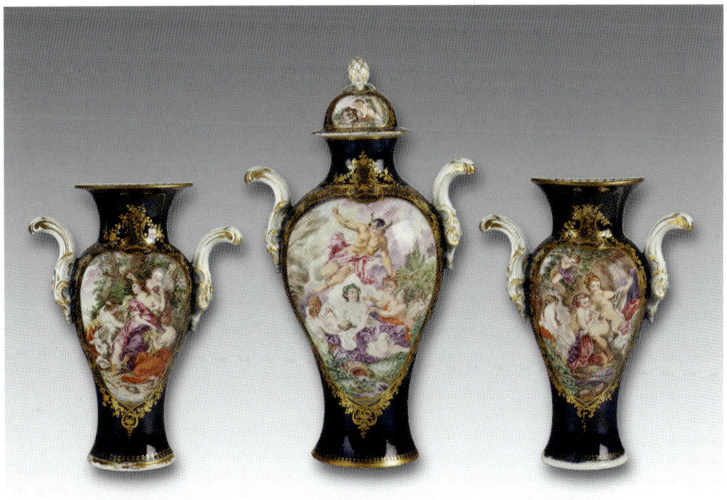

Fig 36 Garniture of three vases decorated by John Donaldson. © Museum of Royal Worcester Porcelain, no. 1126

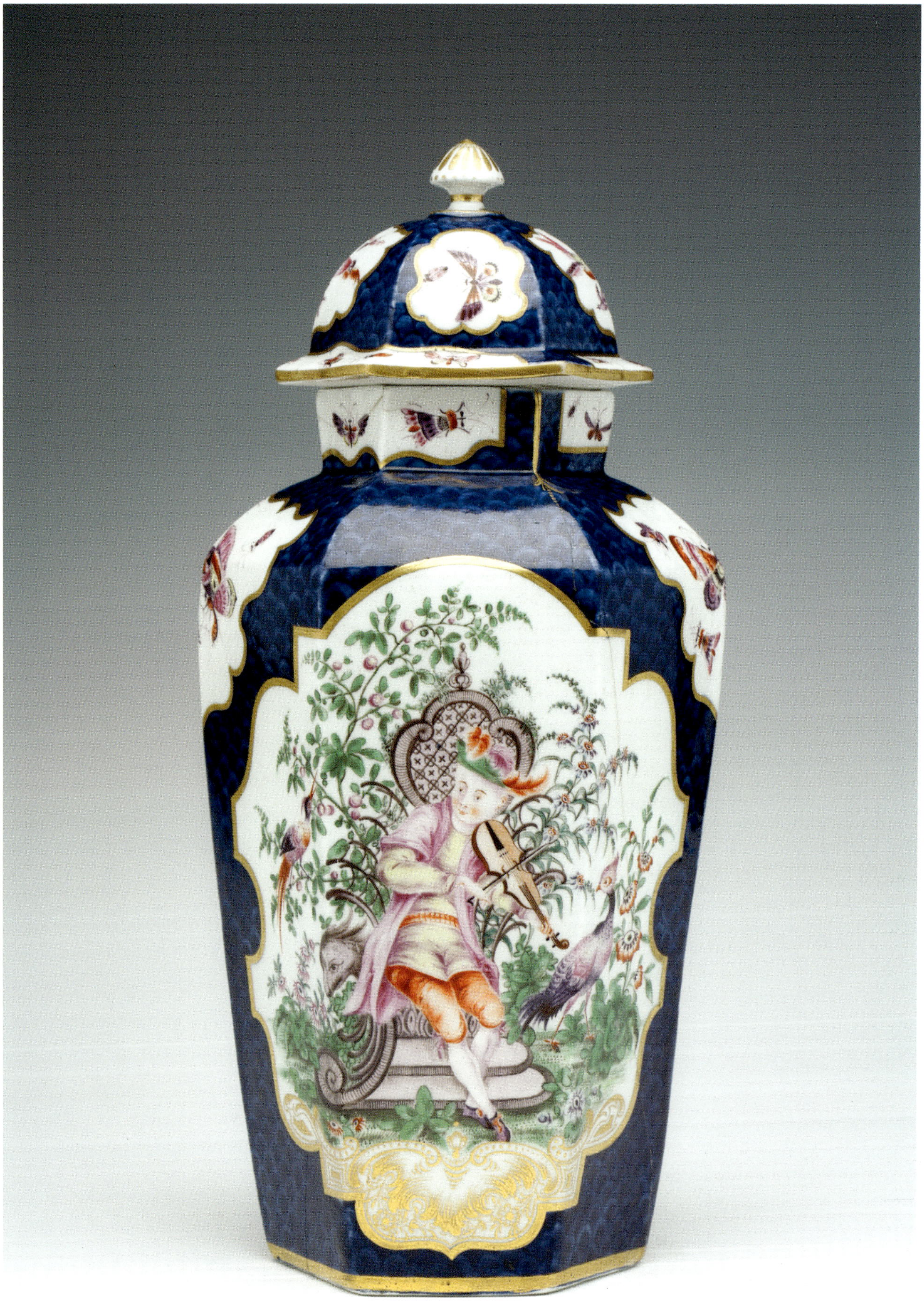

579